MARI NAWI
Aboriginal
Odysseys

Bennelong Point from Dawes Point, c. 1804
Attributed to John Eyre (b. 1771)
Watercolour on card
V1/1810/1
Mitchell Library, Sydney

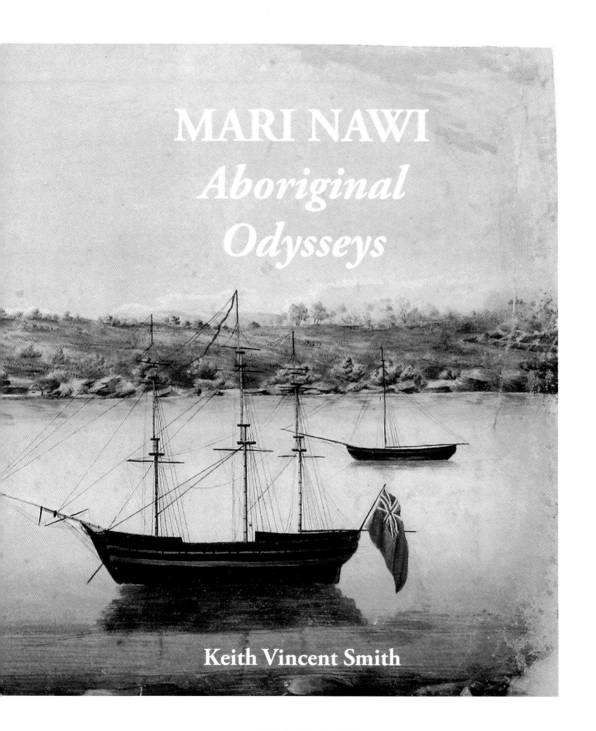

MARI NAWI
Aboriginal

Odysseys

Keith Vincent Smith

ROSENBERG

First published in Australia in 2010
by Rosenberg Publishing Pty Ltd
PO Box 6125, Dural Delivery Centre NSW 2158
Phone: 61 2 9654 1502 Fax: 61 2 9654 1338
Email: rosenbergpub@smartchat.net.au
Web: www.rosenbergpub.com.au
Copyright © Keith Vincent Smith 2010

National Library of Australia Cataloguing-in-Publication entry

Author: Smith, Keith, 1939-

Title: Mari Nawi Aboriginal Odysseys / Keith Vincent Smith.

Edition: 1st ed.

ISBN: 9781921719004 (pbk.)

Notes: Includes index.

Subjects: Aboriginal Australians--History.
Aboriginal Australians--Boats.
Aboriginal Australians--Travel.
Shipping--Australia--History.
Australia--History--1788-1851.

Dewey Number: 994.02

Printed in China by Prolong Press Limited

Cover illustrations
Front
Nouvelle Hollande — Gnoung-a gnoung-a, mour-re-mour-ga (dit Collins)
Barthelmy Roger (1767–1841) after Nicolas-Martin Petit (1777–1804)
Engraving
Plate 21, *Atlas*, François Péron, *Voyage de découvertes aux terres Australes* … Paris 1811,
Mitchell Library, Sydney.
H.M.S. *Daedalus*
John Bayly after Lt Evans
Aquatint, hand-coloured
PAD 6003, National Maritime Museum, Greenwich
Back
Whaleboat showing position of crew
Artist unknown
Watercolour and pencil
A-032-025,
Alexander Turnbull Library, Wellington, New Zealand

CONTENTS

The generous support and assistance of the City of Sydney's
History Program is gratefully acknowledged.

STATE LIBRARY™
NEW SOUTH WALES

The generous assistance of the State Library of New South Wales
in the production of this book is gratefully acknowledged.

DEDICATION

To Irene, as ever

ACKNOWLEDGMENTS

I first visited the Mitchell Library in Sydney in 1954, when a librarian suggested I should seek help for a school essay on the 1808 overthrow of Governor William Bligh from a man nearby wearing a homburg hat. He turned out to be Dr HV Evatt, who had written *Rum Rebellion* in 1938.

Mari Nawi: Aboriginal Odysseys is published to coincide with the exhibition of the same name in the Galleries of the Mitchell Wing of the State Library of New South Wales, Sydney, from 20 September to 12 December 2010, in the library's centenary year.

This book was chiefly researched in the Mitchell, Dixson and State Libraries of New South Wales, whose unique collections provide the majority of the documentary evidence and images reproduced here. I am indebted to Mitchell Librarian Richard Neville, the Exhibition staff, especially Lisa Loader and Martin Wale, and the librarians, particularly Melissa Jackson and Ronald Briggs. I was privileged, with Anthony (Ace) Bourke, to curate the exhibition *Eora: Mapping Aboriginal Sydney, 1770–1850* at the Mitchell Library in 2006.

I would like to thank David Rosenberg, who instigated the publication of *King Bungaree* (1992), *Bennelong* (2001) and this work. My grateful thanks to Dr James Kohen and Terry Widders, who guided me through three degrees in Aboriginal Studies at Macquarie University, Sydney. I acknowledge the generous encouragement from Rachel Perkins, Darren Dale, Timothy McCormick, Jeremy Steele and Lisa Murray.

I have drawn on the original material resources of the National Library of Australia, Canberra; State Records, New South Wales, Sydney; Tasmanian Museum and Art Gallery, Hobart; Public Record Office, London; Botany Library, Natural History Museum, London; British Library, London and Hocken Library, Dunedin.

The following institutions have provided portraits and other images for which they retain the copyright: Mitchell and Dixson Libraries, State Library of New South Wales, Sydney; National Library of Australia, Canberra; Lesueur Collection, Muséum d'Histoire Naturelle, Le Havre; National Maritime Museum, Greenwich; Natural History Museum, London and the Alexander Turnbull Library, Wellington.

A View of Sydney Cove, New South Wales, 1804. Engraved by Francis Jukes (1746–1812) after Edward Dayes (1763–1804). Handcoloured aquatint. Dixson Library, Sydney.

PREFACE

Seachange

They came from the sea.

The First Australians reached this continent some 60 000 years ago, crossing the waters on logs or rafts. Their descendants populated the country, spreading out to inhabit every climatic niche, including the coasts and estuaries, mountains, forests and deserts.

Some Aboriginal people believe their ancestors always lived in Australia. In oral stories others tell of sky heroes who arrived by canoe in the Dreaming.

Many would return to the sea.

From the early eighteenth century, fleets of praus from Makassar and Bugis in South Sulawesi (Indonesia) traded with Aboriginal people in Arnhem Land (Northern Territory) for trepang (sea cucumber) and tortoiseshell. Some Aborigines intermarried and had children, some worked on the praus and a few went to Indonesia with the returning boats.

This sweeping history explains, in part, what happened to the displaced Aboriginal clans following the establishment of the convict colony at Sydney Cove in 1788 and the devastating impact of the smallpox epidemic that killed hundreds in April–May 1789. It is, therefore, also an account of the ongoing cross-cultural contact of our shared history.

Mari Nawi: Aboriginal Odysseys is a journey across time, place and cultures. It describes how, when faced with dispossession by the British colonists, Aboriginal men and women, skilled at using watercraft, adapted to the new reality and remade their lives by voyaging on foreign sailing ships. This book reveals and celebrates the significant role they played in Australia's early maritime history.

The focus is on the experiences and lives of seafarers who sailed on English ships through Port Jackson (Sydney Harbour) to destinations throughout the world in the period 1790–1850. They faced cruel seas, winds and currents in small, leaky ships. Some survived shipwreck or were marooned for months without supplies on isolated islands. With remarkable resilience, they became guides, go-betweens, boatmen, sailors, sealers, steersmen, whalers, pilots and trackers, valued for their skills and knowledge, while some few were exiled as Aboriginal 'convicts'.

Most were young, courageous, adventurous and physically strong, good swimmers and skilled spearmen, uniquely fitted for the hazards of life at sea. They sailed the

Australian coast to sealing and whaling grounds in Bass Strait, the icy sub-Antarctic and New Zealand; to international ports in Timor, Mauritius, Bengal, Britain, Canada, Hawaii, and Tahiti; and to San Francisco and Rio de Janeiro.

They were present at critical events as they followed the expanding geography of exploration and 'rediscovery' and the establishment of settlements like Newcastle, Hobart and Melbourne.

So, Aboriginal seafarers sought and found a place in colonial society, gaining status and confidence in dealing with officers and officials. They crossed conventional social boundaries. Aboard ships all members of the crew worked, ate, talked, slept, smoked and drank together and learned something of each other's language and customs. They spent months away, mixing with European sailors and ex-convicts and Indigenous Pacific Island companions: New Zealand Maoris, Otahetians (Tahitians) Sandwich Islanders from Hawaii and also Indian lascars. There was little or no racism on these ships.

'They strive, by every means in their power, to make themselves appear like the sailors with whom they associate, by copying their customs, and imitating their manners; such as swearing, using a great quantity of tobacco, drinking grog, and other similar habits', wrote David Dickinson Mann in 1811. 'A sailor's life would suit these blacks more than any other, except a gentleman's', wrote Dr Roger Oldfield in the *South Asian Register* (Sydney, 1828).

Theirs was a canoe culture and they called the foreign ships Murray Nowey (*mari nawi*), meaning 'large canoes'. Through pictorial and verbal evidence it can be seen that, 50 years after James Cook visited Botany Bay, Aboriginal people had not relinquished the use of their bark canoes in Port Jackson. This suggests that their relationship with Sydney's waterways might have been as deep as their connection with the land.

This work is based on the PhD thesis *Mari Nawi: Aboriginal voyagers in Australia's maritime history*, submitted to Macquarie University, Sydney, in August 2008. Through painstaking and detailed research, from diverse original sources, including ships' musters, logs, journals, shipping news and newspaper 'claims and demands', dozens of Aboriginal voyagers have been rescued from obscurity to take their place in history. The contemporary portraits by English, French and Russian artists preserve in a moment of time the faces of these individuals and affirm their existence. Some images illustrate the ships on which they sailed and the ports in which they anchored. New research has clarified some historical facts and corrected some long-standing errors.

Because they took positive action in remaking their lives to participate in the dominant settler culture, these Indigenous pioneers can truly be said to have been agents of their own destiny. Here are their stories.

1 Highways in the stream

Even before they could walk, Aboriginal children sat in canoes, clasped between their mothers' knees and crossed ankles as they fished, the way in which, wrote Surgeon John White in July 1788, 'they always carried their infants'.[1] Women and children sang while they fished, and laughed and joked with each other.

Saltwater, as much as the land, was the natural habitat of the Indigenous people of the Sydney coastal area, who called themselves Eora ('people').[2] Theirs was a canoe culture and for countless generations they depended on seafood for their existence.

View of Port Jackson in New Suoth [sic] *Wales*, c. 1790, Artist unknown, Engraving, SSV1/HAR/1790–1792, Mitchell Library, Sydney.

The harbours, rivers, creeks and lagoons, sandy beaches and muddy estuaries were their natural highways and principal sources of fish and shellfish.

Men and women skimmed across the water in their fragile bark canoes. Inland, at the Hawkesbury and Nepean Rivers, canoes 'differed in no wise from those found on the seacoast', wrote Marine Captain Watkin Tench.[3]

Although they burned and maintained pathways through the bush, the waters of the harbour of Port Jackson, Botany Bay to the south, the Parramatta River running west and the Hawkesbury River to the north, were crowded with men, women and children coming and going by canoe. Long after the occupation of their land in 1788, Sydney's Aboriginal clans had not relinquished these waterways, which were their true highways.

Aboriginal couple in canoe, Nicolas-Martin Petit (1777–1804), Pencil, charcoal and ink 20025.1, Muséum d'Histoire Naturelle, Le Havre.

The canoe (*nowey* or *nawi*) was about three to four metres long and about one metre in width, shallow and shaped from a straight sheet of bark bunched at each end and tied with cord or vines. Spacer sticks were jammed across the centre to hold the sides apart in tension. Bark for canoes was taken from the stringybark (*Eucalyptus obliqua*) or from the *goomun* or 'fir tree' (*Casuarina* species).[4]

Royal Navy Lieutenant William Bradley, who saw Aboriginal men making canoes and shields, noted that that they used a stone wedge to prise off the tree bark, with 'a junk of wood for a Mallet or Maul … they cut the bark round to the length they want & enter the wedges leaving it in that state sometime before they take it off altogether'.[5] Using prepared bark shaped over a fire, a canoe could be made in a day. The highest part of the canoe was seldom more than 15 centimetres above the water, yet the Eora skilfully navigated these simple craft.[6] 'They were by far the worst Canoes I ever saw or heard of', wrote Bradley, while admitting that they were paddled through heavy surf without overturning or taking in water.[7] 'Four or five people will go, in the small things, with all their Spears & Emplements for procuring their subsistence', observed John Gardiner of HMS *Gorgon*.[8]

Aboriginal women fished from canoes using handlines with shell lures. 'In general, we observe the canoe occupied by the Women who fish with hook & line, which I never noticed any of the men to use', wrote Bradley in October 1788.[9] Men usually caught fish in shallow water or from the rocks with a *mooting*, a long spear headed with three or four prongs, called a fizgig by the English.[10] The combination of these techniques, together with net fishing, yielded a wide variety of species.

Watching from HMS *Sirius* with his telescope on 9 February 1788, Surgeon George Worgan observed five canoes:

> … when they got near the Rocks, many of the Men got out, and by the help of a Spy-Glass, I could see them very busy in striking the Fish with their Spears, and I saw them take two or three tolerably large ones in this manner; the Women, remained in the Canoes employed in fishing with a Hook & Line, the Fish, they caught, appeared but small, after having caught a good many, they went on shore a little way up in the Wood, lit a Fire, and sat down round about it, in the Afternoon, they got into their Canoes, and returned, passing by the Ship again, they hollowed [*sic*], jabbered & pointed.[11]

Fires burning in the middle of the canoes were used to cook fresh fish or mussels and other shellfish, which the women spat into the water to attract the fish. Women, who sat in the front of the canoe, often had burn marks in the small of the back.[12]

When worn and old, canoes began to leak and take in water, which was baled out by hand with the help of a flat stone or slate.[13] Holes in the bark were patched with strips of paperbark and sealed with the waterproof gum from the grass tree.[14]

Nicolas-Martin Petit's drawing of an Aboriginal couple shows the small fire that burned in the canoe and the paddles used to propel them. *Na-ro-wang* or paddles, about 60 centimetres long, were made of wood or bark and shaped like an English pudding stirrer.[15] 'They have two paddles one in each hand with these they make their Canoes go amazingly swift', wrote midshipman Henry Waterhouse.[16]

Hand fishing lines were spun from long strips of bark, which women rolled on the inside of their thighs, 'so as to twist it together, carefully inserting the ends of each fresh piece into the last made', as Tench explained.[17] These bark lines were soaked in a solution of the sap of the red bloodwood tree (*Eucalyptus gummifera*) to prevent them fraying.[18]

Burra or fishhooks were chipped and ground into a crescent shape from a large shell, usually the wavy turban (*Turbo undulates*), using a long, rounded stone file. The shiny hooks did not have a barb to snag fish, but were used as lures, without bait. 'They nevertheless catch fish with them with great facility', said Collins.[19] The Indigenous people of south-eastern Australia had fished with hooks and handlines for at least two millennia. A shell fishhook found by archaeologists in the Sydney area was found to be 600 years old, while stone files, 2000 years old, used to shape lures were recovered from rock shelters near Curracurrang Cove in the Royal National Park, south of Sydney.[20]

The shafts of the *mooting* were made from lengths of the flowering stem of the grass tree (*Xanthorrhea* species), glued end-to-end using the yellow resin or gum of the same plant. David Collins said some fizgigs were made of wattle (*Acacia* species), about 4.5 to 6 metres in length, with four wooden prongs fastened by gum at the head.[21] The prongs were hardened in the fire and headed with animal bone points, sharp fish bones or teeth, or stingray spines stuck on with gum. The *mooting* was always propelled by hand, without a *womera* or spear-thrower.

Men used canoes mainly to cross from one cove to another, but sometimes as a platform for spearing fish. 'In these canoes they will stand up to strike fish at which they seem expert', wrote Bradley.[22] This technique was used in deep water to take fish like mullet as they leapt from shoals. 'Baneelon [Bennelong] has been seen to kill more than twenty fish by this method in an afternoon', wrote Tench.[23]

On Sunday 17 August 1788, Governor Arthur Phillip sent out four ships' boats to count the number of Aboriginal people and canoes around Port Jackson. The tally from this census was 67 canoes, containing 94 men, 34 women and nine children. This was despite the fact, Phillip wrote, that 'It was the Season in which they make their new Canoes, and large parties were known to be in the woods for that purpose'.[24]

It was a different picture in May 1789, at the height of the smallpox epidemic that swept through the Port Jackson clans. On the return of HMS *Sirius* with rations from the Cape of Good Hope, John Hunter was surprised 'at not having seen a single native on the shore, or a canoe as we came up in the ship; the reason of which I could not comprehend, until I was informed that the small-pox had made its appearance'.[25] As if to signal the end of the epidemic, a group of 20 canoes passed Sydney Cove going down the harbour on 20 June 1789. 'This was the first time any number of them had been seen together since the Small Pox having been among them', Bradley noted.[26]

A canoe might also act as a coffin for respected Aboriginal men. A young man from the Burramattagal (Parramatta clan) named Ballooderry was buried in Governor Phillip's garden (present Circular Quay precinct) near Bennelong Point on 17 December 1791 in a funeral organised by Bennelong. Ballooderry's body was wrapped in his English jacket and blanket and then laid in his canoe with a spear, throwing-stick, pronged fishing spear and his initiation waistband.[27] Watkin Tench mentioned the discovery of the grave of a Gweagal (Botany Bay clan) warrior whose body was also placed in a bark canoe.[28]

Aboriginal men and women often used their canoes to visit sailing ships moored in Port Jackson. Early in 1788, some 'young gentlemen' from HMS *Sirius* met an elderly Aboriginal man in the bush and one of the sailors used a knife to trim the man's long beard. A few days later, the same man came alongside *Sirius* and pointed to his beard. 'Various arts were ineffectually tried to induce him to enter the ship; but as he continued to decline the invitation, a barber was sent down into the boat along-side the canoe, from whence … he complied with the wish of the old beau, to his infinite satisfaction', wrote Tench.[29] In October 1791, a sailor from a convict transport ship deliberately scuttled a canoe belonging to an Aboriginal man paddling around the ship. The seaman was confined to his ship and ordered to give the man a complete set of clothing in the hope that he would not seek revenge.[30]

Two women passengers on English ships moored in Sydney Cove reported happier meetings. 'The natives very frequently surrounded our vessel with their canoes', wrote Mary Ann Parker, wife of Captain John Parker of the storeship HMS *Gorgon* in 1791. 'The women often held up their little ones, as if anxious to have them noticed by us. Sometimes, for the sake of amusement, I have thrown them ribbands and other trifles, which they would as frequently tye round their toes as any other part of their person', she wrote.[31]

'I had often seen the natives at a distance paddling their little canoes down the cove', wrote Mary Anne Reid, wife of Captain Hugh Reid of the convict transport ship *Friendship*. One morning in February 1800, she was 'rather surprised at hearing a strange humming noise under the cabin window'. Looking out, she saw a bark canoe tied to the ship's rudder chains, with an Aboriginal woman and a baby in her lap. She continued:

> The embers of some half-burnt wood were smoking before her as she sat cross-legged at her employment; she had a fishing-line in each hand over the side of her little boat, and was humming her wild notes, either to entice the fish or to quiet the infant. I saw her draw up a small fish with one of the lines; she immediately applied her teeth to the neck of it, which instantly ceased struggling. Taking it off the hook, she put it upon the embers, and blew them into a flame; before it was warm through she began to eat it, apparently with great relish; after which she gave her child the breast, and continued her labours.

Mary Anne Reid threw the woman a biscuit, which she ate, and some linen, which she put aside. She was about 28 years of age, with matted, dirty hair, and her child about three months old. The woman became a frequent visitor to the ship and 'never went away empty-handed', but could not be persuaded to climb on board. She managed her light canoe with great dexterity. 'With a paddle in each hand, about eighteen inches long, she could turn it in all directions, and make it go as fast as our boats with two men rowing in them.'[32]

Arriving in Sydney on the ship *Porpoise* in November 1800, nurseryman George Suttor was impressed by the 'novel sight' in the harbour of 'several bark canoes of the natives, generally with one or two native women fishing'.[33]

In 1803, the first Tahitians to visit Port Jackson were pleased to see Aborigines bringing fish to their ship (a familiar sight in their own culture), but were surprised when the Aborigines at first refused to share the fish with them. 'After some pause, however, the natives gave them a few of their fish', wrote John Turnbull, 'and made a repast of them after their own manner'.[34]

In 1811, Jane Brooks observed 'very tiny canoes with a gin [woman] fishing in them, quite alone, sometimes with a streak of smoke from it, and we supposed she was cooking'.[35]

In August 1814, Aleksey Rossiyski, a *sturman* (steersman or navigator) on the Russian-American Company cargo ship *Suvorov* persuaded a group of Aborigines who had been feasting on mussels at Bennelong Point to barter their shields and 'bludgeons' — tapered wooden clubs or waddies. 'That same afternoon, at about 3 p.m. we were visited by two little craft containing four natives, amongst them two men whom I had not seen before, and they brought me their weapons', Rossiyski wrote. He chose three spears, a shield, two 'bludgeons' and a large club, giving in return 'some threadbare clothing, a small mirror, some beads, and a bottle of rum, but the Aborigines gave back the clothing and asked for another bottle of rum'.[36]

There is even later evidence for the continuing presence of Aboriginal canoes on the harbour. In 1822, Governor Lachlan Macquarie established an Aboriginal settlement for the Sydney 'Tribe' at Elizabeth Bay. Obed West recalled the scene in his 'Reminiscences' in the *Sydney Morning Herald* (1882):

> The blacks managed to provide in a measure for their wants by fishing, and the scene in and about the bay was rendered peculiar by seeing the blacks in their frail canoes as they floated about, engaged in this work.[37]

At times the fragile vessels were paddled through the surf and the ocean. 'Each Tribe', observed Surgeon Worgan, 'according [to] the number, have 6, 8, or 10 Canoes, in these contemptible Skiffs (which display very little art or Ingenuity) they paddle (with two things like Pudding stirrers) from one Cove to another even up and down the Coast, keeping as close to the Rocks as possible'.[38] The author of *An Authentic and Interesting Narrative of the Late Expedition to Botany Bay …* (1789), admired the Eora's 'dexterous management' of their canoes, their swift paddling 'and the boldness that leads them several miles in the open sea'.[39]

Mari nawi: 'Big canoes'

The first sailing ships that entered the world of the Indigenous people of Botany Bay and Port Jackson caused fear and wonder. They thought they were giant birds, monsters or floating islands and that the figures climbing the masts were devils or possums.

After a voyage of eight months from Portsmouth in England, HMS *Sirius*, the storeship *Supply* and 10 convict transport ships anchored in Botany Bay on 19–20 January 1788. In a report printed in London in 1789, an anonymous officer wrote:

> The natives alarmed, ran along the beach in seeming great terror, and made much confused noise; they seemed very frightened, so much that they took their canoes out of the water upon their backs and ran off with them into the country, together with their fishing tackle and children.[40]

When she met the artist George French Angas at Camp Cove, near South Head, in 1845, Cora Gooseberry Bungaree spoke of her father's reaction to the First Fleet ships at Botany Bay in 1788. Baringan Caroo, as she was first named, was the daughter of Moorooboora of the Murro-ore-dial clan at today's Maroubra. Her story tends to authenticate the officer's description:

> On the approach of the vessels, the natives, who had never seen a ship before, imagining them to be huge sea-monsters, were so terrified that they ran into the bush, and did not stop to look back until they reached a place now called Liverpool, distant about twenty miles, where they hid themselves in trees.[41]

Stories were told about the visit years before of a solitary vessel that lingered for one week at Kamay (Botany Bay) before returning to the sea. This was the English discovery ship HM Bark *Endeavour*, commanded by Lieutenant James Cook. 'They thought they was [*sic*] the devil when they landed first, they did not know what to make of them. When they saw them going up the masts they thought they was [*sic*] opossums', Maroot, an Aboriginal elder of the Kameygal on the north shore of Botany Bay, told his son Boatswain Maroot.[42]

Finding Botany Bay unsuitable, Governor Arthur Phillip decided to establish a permanent settlement in a small sheltered cove in a harbour to the north that James Cook, passing by in 1770, had named Port Jackson. The people on these ships had come to stay. On 26 January 1788, the white-sailed vessels came to anchor in Warrane or Warang (Sydney Cove).[43] From them some 1000 men, women and children — transported prisoners and marines — came ashore to establish the convict colony of New South Wales.

'We have Never been able to Persuade them to come in to the Camp or on board the Ships tho they frequently Pass & once three Canoes came alongside the

Murray Nowey
Philip Gidley King (1758–1808)
Journal … on HMS Supply, April 1790
C115, Mitchell Library, Sydney

Supply but would not come in', David Blackburn, master of HMS *Supply*, wrote in a letter to his sister Margaret in July 1788.[44]

However, the Eora soon grasped the relationship between their canoes and the First Fleet ships. They named the largest vessel, the 20-gun HMS *Sirius* (540 tons), Murray nowey (*mari nawi*) or 'large canoe' and the smallest, the eight-gun brig HMS *Supply* (168 tons), Narrong Nowey (*narang nawi*) or 'small canoe'. Early in 1791, after Bennelong and the Eora 'came in' peacefully to the Sydney settlement, Blackburn noted: 'they [Natives] often Come on board our ship, which they call an Island & are very troublesome for Bread, which they are extremely fond of'.[45]

Cruwee (Crewey), who claimed to be at Kundal (Kurnell) when the *Endeavour* entered the bay on 29 April 1770, told Obed West: 'they thought the vessels were floating islands'. West wrote: 'I have often conversed with Cruwee, who was an intelligent fellow … It was very amusing to hear him describe the first impression the blacks had of the vessels, and although very fearful, they were curious and would, with fear and trembling, get behind some tree and peep out at the monsters which had invaded their shores'.[46] Judge Advocate Collins, who recorded 'Boo-roo-wang --- An island' in his 'New South Wales' Vocabulary, added in a footnote: 'This word they applied to our ships'.[47]

Frustrated by his inability to communicate with the Indigenous people, who had not ventured into the English camp at Sydney since February 1788, Governor Phillip gave orders to capture one or more by force. A well-built man was abducted from Manly Cove on 30 December 1788 and taken to Phillip's canvas house near the Tank Stream. He was washed, his hair was cut and combed and his beard shaved off, then he was dressed in a shirt, jacket and pair of 'trowsers'. In February 1789, Phillip took this man, Arabanoo, on the *Supply*, which was leaving for Norfolk Island. He stepped aboard with distrust and reluctance and jumped overboard at the first opportunity. Arabanoo found he could not dive under the water because his English clothes kept him afloat. He looked sullen when brought back to the ship but cheered up when Phillip called him to get into the boat to go ashore.[48]

Captain John Hunter met Arabanoo on 2 May 1789 when HMS *Sirius* returned to Sydney with urgently needed food supplies from the Cape of Good Hope. Despite his first experience, Arabanoo 'expressed a great desire to come on board my *nowee*; which is their expression for a boat or other vessel upon the water', and dined on the ship with Governor Phillip the following day.[49] Arabanoo died from smallpox two week later, on 18 May 1789.

Six months later, Bennelong and Colebee were captured at Manly Cove on 25 November 1789. In contrast to Arabanoo, Bennelong displayed a lively interest when taken on a tour of HMS *Sirius* less than three weeks later. 'He came on board the Sirius without the smallest apprehensions for his safety', wrote William Bradley. 'He looked with attention at every part of the Ship & expressed much astonishment particularly at the Cables.'[50]

In 1802 a group of Sydney Aborigines placed sufficient trust in the French sailors of the ship *Géographe*, moored in Port Jackson, to perform a corroboree on deck, according to the geographer Charles Pierre Boullanger.[51]

The missionaries Daniel Tyerman and George Bennett, who visited Australia in 1824, recorded a fragment of an Aboriginal story that they related to the Biblical deluge. They wrote:

> They are said to have a tradition of the deluge, when the waters overtopped the Blue Mountains, and two men only escaped the devastation, in a *Kobon noe*, or large ship.[52]

2 A passage to Norfolk Island

The first Aboriginal Australian to sail out of Port Jackson through the Sydney Heads on an English ship was a 10-year-old orphan whose father had been killed in battle and whose mother was bitten in half by a shark. In 1791, this 'little native boy, named *Bon-del*' boarded the storeship HMS *Supply*, bound for the isolated Pacific Ocean settlement at Norfolk Island.

Bondel had attached himself to Captain William Hill of the New South Wales Corps and went to live in Hill's thatched hut by the Tank Stream in Sydney Town.[1] When Hill was ordered to Norfolk Island, Bondel, wrote Watkin Tench, embarked with him 'at his own earnest request'.[2] In his journal, Lieutenant William Bradley said Bondel 'was much pleas'd at the Idea of a Voyage, he is the first who has had confidence & Courage enough to go to Sea'.[3]

A View of Sydney on Norfolk Island, c. 1805, John Eyre (b. 1771), Watercolour, Original: V8/Norf Is/1 Mitchell Library, Sydney.

The *Supply* left Port Jackson on 22 March and arrived at Norfolk Island on 6 April 1791. In the ship's muster, Hill is included with 'Supernumeraries Borne for Victuals Only', but Bondel is not listed.[4]

When the *Supply* returned to Sydney on 30 May without Bondel, his friends 'inquired eagerly for him', wrote Tench.[5] Many of them wanted to go to Norfolk Island, where, they were told, there was plenty of birds and other game. 'Perroquets, parrots, Doves, & other birds we saw in great quantitys & so very tame that they might have been knocked down with sticks', wrote the island's commandant Philip Gidley King in his journal.[6] The 'other birds' that were so easy to catch as they nested in their burrows were at first called Providence petrels or Mount Pitt birds (*Pterodroma solandri*) and later mutton-birds.

Bondel came home on 8 September 1791 aboard the 298-ton convict transport *Mary Ann*, whose master and part owner Mark Monroe (or Munro) usually hunted for whales off Greenland. Monroe told David Collins that Bondel had left the island reluctantly and during his five-month stay 'seemed to have gained some smattering of our language, certain words of which he occasionally blended with his own'.[7]

It was perhaps through Monroe's influence that Bondel (later called Bundle or Bundell) became a sealer and sailor. By the time he signed on the survey ship HMS *Bathurst* with Phillip Parker King at the age of 30 in 1821, he had lost an eye. Two years later it was 'Old Bundell' who held Bennelong's son Dicky (christened Thomas Walker Coke) in his arms as he died at Parramatta.[8]

Captain James Cook had sighted and named Norfolk Island on 10 October 1774 during his second voyage around the world on HMS *Resolution*. The small volcanic island's birds, tall cabbage trees, abundant stands of flax and other plants resembled those he had seen in New Zealand and the whole island was densely covered with giant Norfolk Island pines (*Araucaria heterophylla*). Flax (*Phorium tenax*) was valued for making sailcloth and ropes, while at first sight the tall spruce pines seemed ideal for ships' masts. Cook's landing parties saw no inhabitants.

On 27 November 1791, William Dawes's principal language informant, a girl about 15 years of age named Patyegarang (Grey Kangaroo), told Dawes that a white man had beaten her and her two male friends, Poondah (Boneda) and Pundal (Bondel).[9] HMS *Supply* had left Sydney Cove the previous day, bound for England.[10] Lieutenant Henry Lidgbird Ball, the ship's commander, took a live kangaroo, intended as a present for King George III, but did not mention any New South Wales Aborigine on board.[11] When the ship docked at Plymouth in April 1792, the *British Journal* reported: 'The Supply has brought home several large Congaroos [kangaroos], a native that has been civilised, and a very singular plant, of a lively green'.[12] The English surgeons sometimes took Aboriginal men injured in ritual revenge battles aboard their ships for treatment. If Bondel left Port Jackson on *Supply*, he might have been this unidentified voyager and therefore the first

Indigenous Australian to reach England, preceding Bennelong and Yemmerrawanne by one year.

Bondel's guardian William Hill left Norfolk Island on the whaling ship *Chesterfield* bound for India on 27 May 1793 but was killed in an ambush when he went ashore at Tate's Island near Timor.[13]

Bennelong wanted to go to Norfolk Island in Bondel's wake. On the morning of 16 October 1791, he came into Sydney Town, carrying a bundle of spears, a fishing spear, bones to make spear points, a *mogo* or stone hatchet and his basket, ready to be packed up. In a letter written that day to his mother in England, William Neate Chapman (soon to be storeman at Norfolk Island) said Bennelong 'has taken a fancy to go with us to Norfolk Island. The Governor is to give him two Nankeen Dresses, 6 white shirts & a Trunk to keep them in, which pleased him very much'. Nankeen was a Chinese cotton cloth dyed buff yellow. That night Bennelong, who Chapman described as 'a very well behaved man', drank tea and ate supper with Governor Phillip and his officers.[14]

'The Natives are now on the most sociable terms with us, and Bannelong the native who was so long in the Governors Family goes with me to Norfolk', King advised Sir Joseph Banks on 25 October 1791, adding, 'as it is a voluntary offer of his own I hope we will be able to instruct him in English'.[15] On 26 October, King, newly appointed lieutenant commandant of Norfolk Island, his wife, Captain William Paterson, his wife, the Reverend Richard Johnson and Surgeon William Balmain, sailed to the island aboard HMS *Atlantic*.[16]

Bennelong might have gone to Norfolk Island, although he is not mentioned in King's journal or in the official victualling list. Bennelong's wife, Barangarro, was ill at this time, which is one reason he might have postponed the voyage. If he did go, Bennelong's stay was brief, because he was back in Sydney by 14 December 1791, when his friend Ballooderry became ill. He could have returned on the convict transport *Queen*, which reached Sydney from Norfolk Island on 5 December. The voyage from Sydney to Norfolk Island usually took about 10 days each way and Chaplain Johnson had notified a friend to expect him back in Sydney 'about Christmas'.[17]

Bennelong is more likely to have visited the island in August 1792, when David Collins noted that 'The Atlantic sailed on the 19th for Norfolk Island, having also on board two settlers from the marine department, twenty-two male convicts, an incorrigible lad who had been drummed out of the New South Wales Corps, three natives and a free woman, wife to one of the convicts'.[18] *Atlantic* returned to Sydney on 30 September 1792. Bennelong and Yemmerrawanne were definitely on board the storeship when it left Sydney for England on 11 December 1792. The voyaging 'natives' might have been Bennelong and Yemmerrawanne on a shakedown cruise, perhaps accompanied by Nanbarry or one of the men's wives.

The Pitt off Dover 1787 [Detail], John William Edy (c. 1760–1805), Aquatint and etching, 20 July 1789
PA15921, National Maritime Museum, Greenwich.

Aboriginal women at sea

Not only Aboriginal men went on board foreign ships. Some adventurous women from the Sydney coastal area chose — or were perhaps forced — to sail into the unknown oceans.

The idea that five Eora women stowed away on the 775-ton East India Company ship *Pitt*, which sailed from Sydney Cove on 11 April 1792 to the Bengali port of Calcutta (Kolkatta), on the Hoogly River, is astonishing. It raises questions about their fate: they might have disembarked at Calcutta, sailed on to England in the *Pitt*, or somehow found a way to return home. The following item appeared in the *Calcutta Gazette* on 18 October 1792:

> We learn that the Captain of the Pitt has brought from Botany Bay a curious beast called a "Congaree." He is about the size of a large monkey. Five female natives of Botany Bay are likewise on board the Pitt as they are entirely a different race of people, they will no doubt excite the observation of the curious.

'Several girls, who were protected in the settlement, had not any objection to passing the night on board of ships', wrote Judge Advocate David Collins. In return they might receive 'a loaf of bread, a blanket, or a shirt … when either was offered by a white man, and many white men were found who held out the temptation'. Perhaps the women had gone on the ship for the night, but remained or were locked in a cabin by some of the crew. The *Pitt* sailed from Sydney to Norfolk Island on 7 April 1792 and left for Bengal via Batavia (Jakarta) one month later. The ship went on to England and would make further voyages to New South Wales.

In September 1794, one of Bennelong's sisters and another woman, the wife of his young kinsman Yemmerrawanne, left Sydney, bound for Norfolk Island aboard the storeship HMS *Daedalus*. Almost two years had passed since the two men had sailed to England. The women could not know that Yemmerrawanne had died from a lung ailment four months earlier (in May 1794) or that Bennelong would not come back to Sydney for a further year. David Collins indicated that the Aboriginal women were victims of harassment, who wanted to 'withdraw from the cruelty which they, with others of their sex, experienced from their countrymen'. They were to be cared for by the island's Lieutenant Governor, Philip Gidley King. Warreweer, one of Bennelong's sisters, might have been one of these voyagers. She had recently lost a child and her husband Gnung-a Gnung-a Murremurgan had fought over her with a man called Wyatt when he returned to Sydney in April 1794 from a long sea voyage on the storeship HMS *Daedalus*.

Tom Rowley in India and New Ireland

Tom Rowley, a young Aboriginal man 'well known in the settlement at Sydney', who took his name from Lieutenant Thomas Rowley of the New South Wales Corps, left Sydney Cove on the whaler *Britannia* in June 1795. The ship loaded provisions in Calcutta (Kolkatta) and Madras (Chennai), and stopped for wood and water at Gower's Harbour, New Ireland, while returning, anchoring in Sydney in May 1796.[19]

Tom Rowley was shot and killed on the north shore of Port Jackson in October 1797. William Miller, who was charged with his murder, was acquitted on the grounds he had shot Tom accidentally.[20]

Nanbarry becomes a sailor

At the age of nine, Nanbarry or Nanbree was brought into the Sydney settlement on 15 April 1789, seriously ill from smallpox, which had killed his parents. He recovered after treatment by Surgeon John White, who adopted him.[21] After his initiation in the *Yoo-long Erah-ba-diang* ceremony at Woccanmagully (Farm Cove) early in 1795, Nanbarry, nephew of the Cadigal leader Colebee (Sea Eagle), became a seaman on HMS *Reliance*, which made regular trips to and from Norfolk Island. The muster confirms that Nanbarry went on at least two such voyages, but he is not listed on the ship's longer journeys to England.

Nanberry, a Native Boy of Port Jackson, living with
M`<sup>r</sup>`. White — the Surg`<sup>n</sup>` Gen`<sup>l</sup>`
George Raper (1769–1797)
Ink and watercolour
Raper Drawing — No. 3,
Natural History Museum, London

HMS *Reliance*, commanded by Henry Waterhouse, left Sydney Cove on 29 May 1798 with provisions for Norfolk Island, accompanied by the colonial schooner *Francis*. The muster book listed 'Nanberry, Wingal and Bongary Port Jackson for a Passage to Norfolk Island'. This was the first known sea voyage of Bungaree (Bongary), the Broken Bay leader who later sailed with Matthew Flinders. The three Aboriginal crewmen were discharged from the ship in Port Jackson on 27 July 1798. Wingal came from Port Stephens to the north of Sydney.[22]

In 1799, eight years after his first voyage, Bondel, now usually called Bundle, sailed with 'Nanberry' in *Reliance* from Sydney to Norfolk Island on 2 November. They were discharged in Sydney on 26 December. Governor John Hunter ordered the *Reliance*, 'worn out and no longer capable of rendering any service to the settlement', to be repaired and fitted for sea. She sailed for England on 3 March, arriving at Plymouth on 26 August 1800.[23]

In *The Present Picture of New South Wales* (London, 1811), David Dickinson Mann named 'Bundell' among Aboriginal men who had 'made themselves extremely useful on board colonial vessels employed in the fishing and sealing trade, for which they are in regular receipt of wages'. Mann, an emancipated convict and sometime clerk to Governor Philip Gidley King, was referring to the period before March 1809 when he left New South Wales.[24]

Bundle might have been one of 'Two Natives' who sailed with 13 other crew on the colonial schooner *Brothers*, which left Sydney on a sealing voyage to Bass Strait on 29 December 1812.[25] This was the first command of James Kelly, who kept a log of the voyage, bound with the log of his next voyage on the *Mary and Sally*, now in the Crowther Collection of the Public Library of Tasmania in Hobart. Unfortunately, the front section of Kelly's leather-bound manuscript has been torn off and lost. The first surviving entries refer to the *Mary and Sally*, which took on wood and water at Twofold Bay. The first reference Kelly made to the crew was in March 1813, when the ship was anchored at Elephant Bay, off King Island, in Bass Strait:

CLAIMS AND DEMANDS.

THE following Persons being about to depart the Colony, request all Claims and Demands against them to be presented for Payment to themselves immediately :

In the Perseverance,

Mr. David Smith	Robert Brown
Wm. Needham	Jackey Mytye
Wm. Mansell	Wm. Humphries
James Brownie	Simon Pugh
John Gilbertson	Joseph Halfpenny
John Newton	Dick, a New Zealander
—— Cooper	James Wise
Thomas Weston	Joseph Thorn.

In the Brothers.

Thomas Cubit	Thomas Brady
Thomas Heff	John Griffiths
William Williams	Patrick Masterman
William Hughes	William Nelson
John Harket	John Read.
Henry Shaffery	Charles Ferrer
James White	Two Natives.

In the Minstrel—J. Lyon.

In the Brothers … Two Natives
Claims and Demands,
Sydney Gazette, 5 December 1812

Friday 26th
Squalls of rain sent the Boat on shore and got a Load of fire Wood … This day Discharged Bundle by his own Request, and shipped on Board Charles Peterson and Christian [sealers on King Island].[26]

The *Brothers* returned to Sydney on 31 May 1813, with 7070 sealskins.[27] It is not known how Bundle found his way back to Sydney from King Island, but ships regularly supplied provisions to the sealing gangs there.

In 1816 Bundle was sealing at Kangaroo Island from the 92-ton brig *Rosetta*, built at Richmond on the Hawkesbury River by James Kelly's brother-in-law Jonathan Griffiths. The master, William Rook, brought the brig to Port Jackson on 4 December 1815. 'Bundell, a native' appeared in a Claims and Demands notice in the *Sydney Gazette* (9 December 1815).[28] He sailed aboard *Rosetta* from Richmond on the Hawkesbury River for Kangaroo Island on 1 January 1816. The brig returned to Sydney on 24 July with 2000 sealskins and 50 tons of salt.[29] Kangaroo Island lies about 113 kilometres south of Adelaide, the present capital of South Australia.

3 Bennelong's voyages

On the orders of Governor Arthur Phillip, two Aboriginal men were captured at Manly Cove on the north shore of Port Jackson on 25 November 1789. Colebee, a Cadigal, soon escaped, but the other man, Wollarawarre Bennelong, a Wangal from the south shore of the Parramatta River, was detained in Sydney Cove as the governor's 'guest' until May 1790, when he jumped the paling fence to freedom. After negotiations with Phillip, Bennelong returned peacefully to the Sydney settlement in September 1790. At his request the governor built Bennelong a brick hut at Bennelong Point, where the Sydney Opera House now stands.[1]

Bennelong (c. 1764–1813) formed an unlikely friendship with Phillip, who later took him to England. 'I think my old acquaintance Bennillon will accompany me when ever I return to England, & from him when he understands English, much information may be attained, for he is a very intelligent', Phillip wrote in a letter to Sir Joseph Banks in London in December 1791.[2] Phillip's statement is the only indication of his reasons for taking Bennelong and Yemmerrawanne to England with him one year later.

It was to be an epic journey. Bennelong and his young kinsman Yemmerrawanne were the first Australian Aborigines to cross 10 000 miles of ocean to the other side of the world. The ship took six months to reach England, sailing via Cape Horn and stopping at Rio de Janeiro in Brazil. Bennelong was about 29 years of age, some 10 years older than his companion, who had been initiated just two years before. Both men suffered from the cold, damp English climate and became ill. Yemmerrawanne died of a lung infection in May 1794 and was buried at Eltham, now a suburb of London.

When he returned to Sydney on HMS *Reliance* in September 1795, Bennelong had been away for two years and 10 months, 18 months of which he spent on board ships, either at sea or on in the docks.

On 10 December 1792, the two Aboriginal men boarded the 422-ton capacity storeship HMS *Atlantic*, moored at the Governor's Wharf on the eastern side of Sydney Cove. David Collins described the scene:

With the governor there embarked, voluntarily and cheerfully, two natives of this country, Bennillong and Yem-mer-ra-wan-nie, two men who were much attached to his person; and who withstood at the moment of their departure the united distress of their wives, and the dismal lamentations of their friends, to accompany him to England, a place they well knew was at a great distance from them.'[3]

Two weeks out from Sydney the passengers on the *Atlantic* celebrated the festive season. 'Tuesday Decbr 25 this being Christmas day, His Excellency the Govr gave Evry mess in the Ship a joint of fresh pork and some punkin [pumpkin] and $1/2$ pint of Rum to Each man', wrote marine private John Easty in his journal. In one month the ship ran 4500 miles, coasting 'Terry dele fugo' (Tierra del Fuego) at the southern extremity of South America and rounding the treacherous Cape Horn into the Atlantic Ocean. *Atlantic* anchored on 7 February 1794 in the vast harbour of Rio de Janeiro, where the two men were probably allowed to go ashore. Hearing of renewed trouble between England and France, Governor Phillip purchased some guns to strengthen the ship's defences.[4] The passengers were back on board on 4 March and the *Atlantic* put out from Rio three days later.

While they might have been spared the indignity of taking part, Bennelong and Yemmerrawanne witnessed the Crossing of the Line ceremony when the ship passed the Equator on 3 April, a cloudy day. In this grotesque ritual, inexperienced young sailors were ducked in the ocean by drunken old tars decked out as mermaids in seaweed petticoats. Officers and gentlemen usually avoided the ordeal by paying a ransom in cash or liquor. In Easty's opinion, 'the 2 Natives' thought the figure of Neptune really was 'a man who Lived in the Sea'.

Englánd-a (In England)[5]

After six months at sea, HMS *Atlantic*, shadowed through the English Channel for two days by an armed French privateer, made landfall at six o'clock on Sunday evening, 19 May 1793. They had reached the safe haven of Falmouth Harbour, protected by the massive Pendennis Castle, built high on a Cornish cliff in 1544 by Henry VIII to face an earlier French threat. At 7 o'clock next morning, wrote Easty, 'His Excellency Arthur Phillip went on shore and the 2 Natives and Mr Alley to Proceed on thare way to London.'[6]

Bennelong and Yemmerrawanne only briefly felt solid earth underfoot before mounting the horse-drawn carriage that would take them to London. Eventually, they reached the outskirts of the city, capital of the far-reaching British Empire, where the fields gave way to smoky chimneys. William Waterhouse, father of Midshipman Henry Waterhouse, was responsible for Bennelong and Yemmerrawanne's welfare in London. They lodged at his house in 125 Mount Street, Mayfair, near Berkeley Square. No expense was spared to provide the 'natives of New Holland' with food, suitable clothing, entertainment and board and lodging. They had servants to attend

Banalong, c. 1793
WW [William Waterhouse]
Pen and ink wash
DGB 10 f. 13
Dixson Library, Sydney

Ben-nil-long
James Neagle (1760–1822)
Engraving from David Collins, *An Account of the English Colony in New South Wales …* London, 1798
Mitchell Library, Sydney

them, wash and mend their clothes and repair their shoes, while coaches were hired to take them sightseeing, swimming and to the theatre. The daily activities of Bennelong and Yemmerrawanne can be unravelled from pages of inked figures in British pounds, shillings and pence in the accounts of Treasury Board Papers now held in the Public Records Office, London. These documents provide a kind of 'biography in bills' for their upkeep. William Waterhouse sent the itemised accounts to Phillip, who claimed them from the Treasury in Whitehall.[7]

On the day of their arrival, 21 May 1793, Bennelong and Yemmerrawanne were fitted out at the London tailors, Knox & Wilson, with long frock coats of superfine green cloth with plated buttons, breeches, striped waistbands, underwear and spotted 'pepper and salt' waistcoats at a cost of £15.00 each.[8] Phillip paid their accounts promptly and received receipts for them. Bennelong is wearing his spotted waistcoat in the sketch by 'WW', which must have been drawn at this time and became the model for later portraits.

The *Times* of 22 May 1793 recorded the arrival of *Atlantic*, commanded by Lieutenant Richard Bowen, at Falmouth, adding 'Governor PHILLIPS [*sic*] is come home in this ship'.[9]

Bennelong and Yemmerrawanne aroused some interest in the British newspapers. On 28 May both the *General Evening Post* and the *London Packet* reported: 'Governor Phillip has brought home with him two of the natives of New Holland, a man and a boy, and brought them to town.' With a mixture of ignorance, racial intolerance and the popular quasi-science that predated Social Darwinism by almost a century, the writers concluded that the two Australians represented 'a lower order of the human race'.

'Governor PHILLIPS on his arrival from Botany Bay' was among several gentlemen presented to King George at St James's Palace on 24 May 1793, according to the *Times*.[10] There is no reliable evidence to substantiate Isadore Brodsky's claim in *Bennelong Profile* (1973) that 'on May 24, Governor Phillip was presented at court together with Bennelong and Yemmerrawannie'. Brodsky, in fact, reproduces a letter from Windsor Castle stating that 'there was no information about him [Bennelong] in the Royal Archives'.[11] John Turnbull, author of *A Voyage Around the World*, published in London in 1805, who visited Sydney in 1801, merely says that when Bennelong was in England 'he was presented to many of the principal nobility and the first families of the kingdom'. Turnbull makes no mention of Bennelong being received by the king.[12]

On 1 June 1793, according to the *London Packet*, the 'Natives of New South Wales brought to England by Governor Phillip' were taken to the window of a building in St James's Street from which they could 'see the company going to St James's'. The writer observed 'What their ideas were, we will not attempt to guess'.[13] In the light of this report, it is doubtful that Bennelong and Yemmerrawanne were at St James's

Court in the previous week. It is possible that they watched the comings and goings at the Palace from Chatham House at No. 10 St James's Street, home of the Prime Minister William Pitt the Younger. 'On the following day [2 June] Governor Phillip was presented to the Queen.'[14] There was no mention, said Brodsky, 'of whether Bennelong and the boy were there'.[15]

Phillip took Bennelong and Yemmerrawanne to the King's Theatre at the Haymarket on the night of Saturday 8 June, where they watched the Opera from a private box. According to the *Morning Post* they 'remained in a state of stupidity during the singing, but … were much charmed with the dancing and scenery'. They might also have been charmed by the parade of society women in their 'lilack and yellow' dresses.[16] Later in June they were taken on a tour of 'Country Seats of the Nobility' at which they demonstrated 'their manner of throwing the spear, dancing, &c.'[17]

Arthur Phillip wrote to Home Secretary Henry Dundas in late July 1793 to resign his post as Governor of New South Wales, saying he had been advised that his illness, 'the complaint I labour under', might require assistance not available in such 'a distant part of the world'. Phillip had already been to Bath, seeking a cure in the famous medicinal spa waters. He asked Dundas for the 'liberty to leave town, for, although I had given up all hope of the Bath waters being of any service in my complaint, they may in other respects be beneficial'.[18]

About six weeks after his arrival in England, Bennelong fell ill, possibly from a cold or influenza, which lingered for a further month. He was treated on 12 July 1793 with a mixture prescribed by Dr Blane and made up by an apothecary, Mr GG Vivers. Gilbert Blane (1749–1834), a Scot, was a Royal Navy surgeon to the West Indies Fleet under Admiral Rodney. In 1794–95 he introduced the use of lemon juice in Royal Navy ships to fight scurvy. Later, limes were issued, which gave rise to the slang term 'limey' for an English sailor. Bennelong was again given Dr Blane's medication two days later.[19]

Bennelong was well enough to see the Tower of London, St Paul's Cathedral and other London sights with Yemmerrawanne on 15 July 1793.[20] They must have gasped with surprise at the exotic animals caged in the Tower Zoo. There was a 'monstracious lion' with huge teeth called Old Nero as well as elephants, bears, monkeys, leopards, tigers and wolves.[21] Two weeks later Bennelong was again dosed with Dr Blane's mixture. Despite his lingering illness, the 'Two Natives of Botany Bay' went on further outings and went swimming in the warmer weather. They inspected some military camps, for the purpose, observed the Duke of Richmond, 'of impressing them with a just idea of the *military genius of the country!*'[22] On 2 August the two men went by coach to Sadler's Wells at Islington on the northern outskirts of the city.[23] In the eighteenth century, Sadler's Wells, built on the site of a Roman mineral springs, was the home of a 'Musick House', which featured pantomimes, tightrope walkers and dancers. The seat backs were fitted with ledges to hold wine bottles and glasses and cold meat and cakes served during the performances. Perhaps the swimming or the feasting caused a relapse, because Bennelong was once again dosed with Dr Blane's medicine on 13 August.[24] He seems to have recovered his health fully after that date.

Both men were in good health for the first four months, but then became frail, sick and dispirited:

> The two natives of New South Wales at present in this metropolis, are in appearance scarcely human; they continue to reside in Mount Street, Berkley-square, in the neighbourhood of which they are to be seen daily; they cannot walk without the support of sticks, and appear to have lost all that agility they are said formerly to have possessed; one of them appears much emaciated; notwithstanding they are indulged in every inclination, they seem constantly dejected, and every effort to make them laugh has for many months past been ineffectual.[25]

It was Yemmerrawanne who appeared 'much emaciated'. His illness grew more severe in early October 1793 and he injured his leg about the same time.[26] On 15 October a coach took Yemmerrawanne and Bennelong from Mount Street to Charing Cross, where they caught a stagecoach that took them to the village of Eltham, three miles south of Greenwich. At Eltham they lodged at the home of Edward Kent, who is likely to have been employed by Viscount Sydney (Thomas Townshend, 1733–1800).

Leaving Yemmerrawanne in his sickbed at Eltham, Bennelong went to London by coach to Mount Street in November 1793. Meanwhile, Dr Blane was called to visit Yemmerrawanne at Eltham. A claim for £1.3.1 at the end of the account reads: 'Two Beds, coverings and furniture (all rendered totally useless) and extra attendance Fires and lights during Yemmerawanya's sickness'.[27]

Again Yemmerrawanne rallied, but the cold English winter weather might have aggravated his condition. Early in December 1793, gloves and nightcaps were added to Bennelong and Yemmerrawanne's wardrobe. Exercise was also encouraged (or prescribed). On 30 January 1794 William Waterhouse bought Yemmerrawanne a warm blue greatcoat from Mr J West at a cost of £1.5.0,[28] while Bennelong was also given a winter jacket.[29]

On 23 December, 'Bannellong went to a play at Covent Garden theatre'.[30] He returned to Eltham on Christmas Eve, then went back to Mayfair after the New Year on 5 January 1794.

For six months Yemmerrawanne lay grievously ill, but somehow managed to regain his strength. On Wednesday 16 April 1794, the two men, described by *The Oracle and Public Advertiser* as two '*sooty natives* of New South Wales, brought over by Governor Phillips', visited the Houses of Parliament at Westminster, where they were 'introduced to several persons of consequence'. The journal's reporter was impressed by the bearing, wit, intelligence and good grasp of English of the two, who exhibited 'nothing of the character of savages':

> They do not, by any means, correspond with the description we at first received of our Antipodes; for, instead of that vacuity of intellect, and barrenness of observation, which we were led to expect of them, one, in particular, displays much shrewdness and curiosity.

Bennelong embroidered a droll story about his *Bulla Muree Deein* ('Two big women') that had been well received in Sydney in 1790, by adding an extra wife. The *Oracle* continued 'One of them, a very merry fellow, says, he regrets nothing so much as the inconvenience he finds in the absence of his three wives, for whom he had not yet been able to find a substitute in this country.'[31]

Their appearance in the House of Commons 'excited much curiosity' according to *The World*.[32] They were 'highly pleased' to meet the Speaker, Henry Addington, (Viscount Sidmouth) and 'answered acutely several questions'.[33] The cost of their excursion, entered as 'Expenses to Mr Hastings Trial', was two shillings.[34] Warren Hastings (1732–1818), first Governor General of India, had been impeached by Edmund Burke (1729–97) in the House of Lords in 1788, the year Bennelong and Yemmerrawanne first saw English ships in Sydney Cove. The trial dragged on until 1795 when Hastings was acquitted, but ruined by the costs of the trial, having reputedly spent £100 000 on his defence.

Yemmerrawanne, who was now being treated with Dr Fothergill's Pills, might not have been able to share in the ribaldry. The Quaker physician and amateur naturalist John Fothergill (1742–1780) had been a member of the Royal Society and an acquaintance of Sir Joseph Banks.[35] Although Fothergill had died 14 years earlier, the popularity of his prescriptions continued for generations. There is a suspicion that the pills contained the corrosive poison mercuric chloride, which Fothergill had prescribed in other cases and which would certainly have hastened the inevitable.

One year after his return to Port Jackson, in August 1796, Bennelong dictated a warm letter to Lord Sydney's steward, Mr Phillips, who seems to have been responsible for the two New South Wales natives while at Eltham. Bennelong included a special message: 'Sir, you give my duty to Ld Sydney, Thank you very good my Lord. very good: hope very well all family'. The scribe signed 'Bannolong' at the foot of the page.[36]

A year later, in August 1797, Henry Waterhouse wrote to Lord Sydney: 'He [Bennelong] 'still remembers his English benefactors with gratitude & constantly desires me to say something that englishmen would say for him, & never misses enquiring what is become of your Lordships family'.[37]

Yemmerrawanne died from a lung ailment about one year after his arrival in England. He was buried in the churchyard of St John's Church, Eltham, where

Yuremany [Yemmerrawanne], *one of the first natives brought from New South Wales by Govr. Hunter and Captn. Waterhouse*
Artist unknown
Silhouette
DGB 10 f.14,
Dixson Library, Sydney

Entry in the Eltham Parish Register by the Reverend J. J. Shaw-Brooke, 21 May 1794
Yemmurrvonyea Kebarrah, a Native of New South Wales, died May 18th 1794, supposed to be aged 19 years, at the house of Mr Edward Kent.
Photograph courtesy of Jeremy Steele.

a granite tombstone was erected at a cost of £6.16.00. The inscription reads: 'In Memory of YEMMERRAWANYEA a Native of NEW SOUTH WALES who died the 18th of May 1794 In the 19th Year of his AGE'. Only two people in England, Bennelong and Phillip, would know that Yemmerrawanne could use the name Kebarrah (*kebbara*), given only to an initiated man whose tooth had been knocked out by a *kebba* (stone or rock). Yemmerrawanne's gravestone has been restored and well cared for in the intervening years, but it has separated from his burial place and now rests against the churchyard wall.

The London newspapers briefly noted Yemmerrawanne's death, adding poignantly, 'His companion pines much for his loss'.[38]

Bennelong resumed his usual social activities soon afterwards. On 3 July 1794 he went from Eltham to London by stage coach to see the show at the Drury Lane Theatre, famed for its pantomimes (often featuring Harlequin and Columbine), its stage machinery, painted scenery and spectacles involving, for example, real horses storming a mock castle.

The long return

Major Francis Grose, comm-andant of the New South Wales Corps, now administered New South Wales. The *London Packet* reported on 16 July 1794:

On Tuesday orders were received from the Admiralty for the Reliance, Portlock; and the Supply, Kent; two of his Majesty's store ships, lying off Deptford, immediately to drop down the river on the passage for New South Wales. Captain Hunter, the newly appointed Governor of the Colony … and Bennelong, the only surviving native of Botany Bay, now in England, are going passengers.[39]

In saying that Bennelong was 'the only surviving native of Botany Bay, now in England', the *London Packet* acknowledged the death of Yemmerrawanne. It also projected an early departure date for Captain John Hunter's voyage to Sydney, which certainly did not occur 'immediately'. HMS *Reliance*, 304 tons burden, built at South Shields and classed as a storeship, carried 10 guns and a crew of 59 men. In December 1793, after the hull had been covered with copper sheeting, the ship moored at Deptford Royal Dockyards on the Thames near London for fitting out and loading provisions. John Hunter, newly appointed as Governor of New South Wales, was Captain of the First Fleet flagship HMS *Sirius* in March 1790, when it was wrecked on a reef at Norfolk Island. Back in England, a court-martial had cleared Hunter of any responsibility for the loss of the ship.

On 22 July 1794 Bennelong went by coach from Eltham to the Royal Naval Dockyard at Chatham on the River Medway and returned by a local coach to Mr Waterhouse's in Mount Street. He boarded HMS *Reliance* at Chatham on 30 July 1794, the date shown on a bill of one guinea for the 'Post Chaise to take Mr Benalong on board the Reliance'.[40] Weakened once more by illness, he was forced to endure a prolonged delay before the ship left port. 'Banalong I have embark'd on board the Reliance', wrote Hunter in August.[41] Clothing for Bennelong to take back to Sydney

Supernumeraries borne for Victuals only—
James Williamson
Bannelong
Danl Paine
Signed by Captain John Hunter
Muster of HMS *Reliance*
PRO 7006 ADM 36/10981, Public
Record Office, London

and the chest to stow them away had been purchased before Yemmerrawanne's death. The cost was summarised in a bill dated 1 May 1794:

8 bonnets compleat for the Native Women	£3 - - -
2 Hats for Mr Benalong	1 16 -
2 half Pieces of Ribbon	16 3
a packing box for Gowns Bonnets	8 -
a Chest for Mr Benalong	18 - [42]

Bennelong's bedding for the sea voyage cost £2.11.0.[43] Stored somewhere below deck were 24 iron hatchets that Bennelong had purchased to exchange with his friends and allies in Sydney.

Many of the crew of HMS *Reliance* would distinguish themselves in later years. Henry Waterhouse, third lieutenant on HMS *Sirius*, whose father had been responsible for Bennelong's welfare in London, was now second captain under Hunter's command. The ship's officers included Lieutenant John Shortland, Surgeon George Bass, Master's Mate Matthew Flinders and his brother Midshipman Samuel Flinders. Bass took his boy servant William Martin. A plant cabin was built on *Reliance* to take nursery trees to New South Wales and to bring back plant specimens for Sir Joseph Banks on the return voyage. The ship's cargo included clothing for the convicts, parts of a grain-grinding windmill, a peal of bells and a town clock for the growing Sydney settlement. On the deck, Bass secured a small Thames riverboat with an 8-foot keel and a 5-foot beam, which was named *Tom Thumb*.

Bennelong, James Williamson, a future commissary at Sydney, and Daniel Paine, a master shipbuilder, were entered on the books of *Reliance* as supernumeraries on 15 September 1794. On 25 January 1795, after six months of enforced confinement aboard ship, Governor Hunter was so worried about Bennelong's physical and mental health that he told Under Secretary John King at the Home Office that he feared he might die:

> The Surviving Man (Banilong) is with me, but I think in a precarious state of health, he has for the Past Twelve Months been flattered with the hope of seeing again his Native Country, a happiness which he has fondly looked forward to, but so long a disappointment has much broken his Spirit, & the Coldness of the Weather here has so frequently laid him up, that I am apprehensive his lungs are affected, that was the Cause of the others death, I do all I can to keep him up, but am still doubtful of his living.

In the same letter, but on the following day, 26 January 1795 (seven years since the arrival of the First Fleet at Sydney Cove), Hunter wrote: 'I can form no judgement of the present juncture when we may depart'.[44] This, suggested historian MH Ellis, was 'A matter of just as much anxiety, to his native passenger, that shivering Australian, Bennelong'.[45]

HMS *Reliance* first put to sea on 15 February, but returned to port not long after. The voyage proper did not begin until 2 March 1795, when Captain Waterhouse took the jolly boat to visit the escort HMS *Iris*. She reached Teneriffe on 6 March and *Iris* left with the convoy the following day. *Reliance* with the 382-ton HMS *Supply*, commanded by Captain Henry Lidgbird Ball, sailed on together.

Bennelong was treated by Surgeon George Bass on the *Reliance*. 'Under Bass's care the native made a good recovery and he proved of some use to him on the voyage', wrote Bass's biographer Keith Bowden: 'From him, Bass learnt what he could of the native language spoken about Port Jackson'.[46] While in London during 1800, Bass sent a brief wordlist of the Sydney Language to the linguist William Marsden at the Admiralty.[47] Bass disappeared in 1803 on a voyage from Sydney to South America on the brig *Venus*.

While on HMS *Reliance*, Daniel Paine obtained a 78-word 'Vocabulary of part of the Language of New South Wales' from Bennelong, now in the National Maritime Museum at Greenwich, London.[48]

To ensure the good health of the ship's crew, Bass ordered 'portable soup', lime juice, molasses and fever powders to supplement the normal food ration. In a letter dated 22 July 1797, Mrs Sarah Bass wrote from Lincoln to her son in Sydney, inquiring how he fared with Governor Hunter and Captain Waterhouse. She also asked 'how your patient Banlong does whether his wife and him yet live together'.[49]

In his journal, Daniel Paine recorded the 'accustomed Ceremony of ducking those Persons who had not crossed the Equinoctial line … performed to the no small diversion of both Officers and Men the whole of whom in the end got a complete wetting'. Bennelong, who had already crossed the equator on HMS *Atlantic*, should have been able to avoid this ordeal.

The English ships anchored at Rio de Janeiro in Brazil on 5 April 1795, where Bennelong could marvel once more at the spectacular Sugarloaf Peak and the stone aqueducts, forts, batteries and churches lining the spacious harbour.[50] Fearing that the French had captured the Dutch colony at the Cape of Good Hope, Hunter directed Henry Waterhouse to sail directly to Port Jackson. They left Rio on 2 June. Lightning, gales and squalls of rain dogged the leaky *Reliance*, which shipped 'much water' during the stormy passage south of Van Diemen's Land.[51]

Six more months elapsed before HMS *Reliance* passed through the Heads at Port Jackson and dropped anchor in Sydney Cove on 7 September 1795.[52] It was five years to the day since the payback spearing that Bennelong had arranged against Governor Phillip at the Manly Cove whale feast.

Bennelong immediately asked about his young wife Kurubarabulu (Two Firesticks), who had taken up with a young Cadigal called Caruey (White Cockatoo). She left

Caruey for Bennelong, who gave her a 'very fashionable rose-coloured petticoat and jacket made of coarse stuff, accompanied with a gypsy bonnet of the same colour', purchased in London. Within a few days, to everyone's surprise, wrote David Collins, 'we saw the lady walking unencumbered with clothing of any kind, and Bennillong was missing'. Caruey told Collins he had been severely beaten by Bennelong at Rose Bay and Collins commented that Bennelong 'retains so much of our customs that he made use of his fists instead of the weapons of his country, to the great annoyance of Caruey'.[53] In 1794 the *Morning Post* had mentioned in passing 'the fights & c.' that Bennelong and Yemmerrawanne had seen in London.

After one month, Bennelong left Governor Hunter's house and removed his fine English clothes to wander naked in the bush. 'I must just inform you that Banelong the New Holland Native absconded from the Governor about a week ago in the sulks', Lieutenant Shortland wrote to Lord Sydney. Shortland said Bennelong had sent word that he was at a farm not far from the settlement, but his message had been ignored. 'Mr Banelong was thought much of among his acquaintances & friends on our first arrival here, but that attention is now wearing off fast.' Shortland predicted that in the summer Bennelong would 'run in the Wood's as he did formerly'.[54]

In a letter to his father in London from HMS *Reliance*, Henry Waterhouse wrote: 'The Governor is well. Benelong is turning as great a Savage as ever, all the officers have farms … the Governor Capt. Collins, Benelong &c. &c. desire their particular remembrances'.[55] Waterhouse also wrote to Arthur Phillip, who had entrusted him with money for Bennelong, promising to give it to him 'whenever I can see any opportunity of it rendering any service'. Waterhouse told Phillip:

> He already goes away with the Nativs for days together, has got his old Wife &c., however he shall never want any friendship I can shew him as well on his own account as yours … Benalong desires me to send his best wishes to yourself & Mrs. Phillip.[56]

In November 1795 Bennelong's brick hut was demolished. 'The little hut built formerly for Bennillong, being altogether forsaken by the natives, and tumbling down, the bricks of it were removed to the South Head', wrote Collins. The bricks were used to repair the column at the Look Out, which was plastered and whitewashed so that it could be clearly seen by ships at sea.[57]

In December, the Chaplain's wife Mary Johnson complained that 'the native girl that we had [Boorong] is gone into the Woods as Great a Savage as ever … she pays us a visit now and then quite naked', while 'the native Man that went to England with Governor phillip [Bennelong], is very near as Bad … he has been in the Woods several times and will I have no doubt go quite off soon … theay seem to prefer their own way of Life'.[58] David Collins had known Bennelong since his capture in November 1789 and, like Hunter, was well aware of his long-standing custom of coming and going between the English settlements and the bush. Writing in March 1796, Collins said Bennilong occasionally 'shook off the habits of civilized life, and went for a few days in the woods with his sisters and other friends'.[59]

'I have not my wife: another black man took her away', Bennelong confessed in the letter he dictated and asked to be sent to Lord Sydney's steward Mr Phillips in August 1796. 'We have had murray [big] doings: he speared me in the back … but I am better now: his name is now Carroway [Caruey]'. Soon after Bennelong sailed for England, his young wife Kurubarabulu became involved with Caruey, a Cadigal related to Colebee and Nanbarry. Under traditional marriage laws, Caruey would have been forbidden to live with any woman until he had been initiated. These customs were obviously breaking down and the couple had become partners before Caruey was initiated at Farm Cove in February 1795. At that time Kurubarabulu was about 21 years old, while in Collins's opinion, Caruey was only 16 or 17 years of age. 'To him [Caruey] she became so enamoured', wrote Collins, 'that neither the entreaties, the menaces, nor the presents of her husband at his return, could induce her to leave him. From that time on, she was considered by every one, Bennillong excepted, as the wife of Ca-ru-ay.' Bennelong tried to regain Kurubarabulu's affections by ambushing her, but wrote Collins, 'her screams generally bringing her lover or a friend to her assistance, he was not often successful'. During one such attempt, in February 1798, Bennelong was badly gashed on the head, while Kurubarabulu and Caruey laughed at his rage at being wounded.[60]

Unable to attract a female companion, Bennelong ambushed Colebee's favourite Boorea, a woman from the north shore Cannalgal. Bennelong sent a message to Governor Hunter saying he had been severely hurt in a fight with 'his bosom friend Cole-be' and would not be able to return to eat at the governor's table until his wounds were healed. He asked Hunter to send him some clothes and food 'of which he was much in want'. Bennelong's face was badly disfigured. 'On his coming among us again, he appeared with a wound in his mouth, which had divided the upper lip and broke two of the teeth of that jaw', wrote David Collins. 'His features, never very pleasing now seemed out of all proportion, and his pronunciation was much altered.' For a time, Bennelong's long friendship with Colebee turned to bitterness and rivalry.

Return to Norfolk Island

A few weeks after his fight with Colebee, Bennelong sailed to Norfolk Island, but stayed for only five days. From 3 to 8 April 1796 his name appears in the island's *Victualling Book*, kept by Philip Gidley King, in which he is described as a 'New Hollander'.[61]

HMS *Supply* sailed from Port Jackson for Norfolk Island on 24 March and returned on the evening of 18 April. *Supply* made the round trip in three weeks and four days, 'the quickest passage that had yet been made to and from that island'.[62] There is no account of Bennelong's last known sea voyage.

Bennelong claimed the protection of his 'old friend and fellow voyager' Governor John Hunter in November 1796 when he was suspected of killing an Aboriginal man near Botany Bay and was threatened with death by 'a considerable body' of warriors gathered near the Brickfields (present Chippendale). Bennelong denied killing the man:

> … the governor dispatched him to the place, guarded by some of the military, where he explained to his countrymen that he had not killed the man in question, or any man; and that the soldiers were sent with him, to convince them that the governor would not suffer him, his old friend and fellow voyager (it must be remembered that Bennillong returned from England with the governor in His Majesty's ship *Reliance*), to be ill treated by them on any false pretence; and that he was determined to drive every native away from Sydney who should attempt it. This threat had good effect.

Bennelong's antagonists, said David Collins, were alarmed at the prospect of being driven away from the Brickfields, from which 'they derived so many comforts, and so much shelter in bad weather'.[63] He escaped punishment.

Philip Gidley King, irritable and plagued by gout, returned to Sydney from England in 1800 as Governor of New South Wales, to replace Captain John Hunter, who had been recalled. At this time Bennelong was often away in the bush, but he continued to come into the settlements at Sydney and Parramatta. During King's six-year term as governor of New South Wales, however, Bennelong found himself demoted from the dining room, where he used to take his meals with Governor Phillip, to the kitchen of the expanded Government House, where he had to eat with the servants.

No better country …

Bennelong made himself known to members of the French expedition led by Captain Nicolas Baudin, which spent five months in Port Jackson during 1802 refitting the ships *Géographe* and *Naturaliste*. The French scientists set up their camp, observatory tent and workshops near Bennelong Point. The expedition's naturalist François Péron mistakenly named the Indigenous people living around Port Jackson as Gweagal, who, he wrote, 'acknowledge Benni-long for their chief'.[64] The Gweagal occupied the south shore of Botany Bay. Like many visitors, the French officers assumed that the placename 'Botany Bay' also meant the convict settlement based at Sydney Cove. In a portrait by Nicolas-Martin Petit 'Bedgi-Bedgi' (Bidgee Bidgee) from the Burramattagal (Parramatta clan) and later 'Chief of Kissing Point' (Ryde) was also wrongly said to be from 'la Tribu des Gwea-Gal'.[65]

As the most prominent Aboriginal leader in Port Jackson, Bennelong greeted visiting strangers in the manner adopted in later years by the Broken Bay leader Bungaree, who was then preparing to sail once more with Matthew Flinders.[66] Bennelong often went to visit Pierre Bernard Milius, a young officer who was put ashore sick from *Naturaliste* and was appointed commander of *Géographe* when he recovered. As a concession to European conventions, said Milius, Bennelong covered his naked body with 'a kind of napkin', which he took off when leaving.

In his journal, Milius, who wrote the name as 'Benadou', recounted the story of Bennelong's visit to England, where he had been 'showered with honours and gifts'. However, nothing could make Bennelong forget his native land and he 'constantly testified to his desire to return there'. At the sight of the coast of New Holland, wrote Milius, Bennelong was delirious with joy. 'As soon as he had his feet on dry land, he threw off his clothes and returned to his dear compatriots, the savages.' In 1802 Bennelong had no desire to return to Europe. When Milius invited him to go to France with him, Bennelong replied that there was 'no better country than his own and that he did not want to leave it'. Milius noted Bennelong's craving for alcohol:

> He came to see me several times to ask for a glass of liquor, of which he was very fond. I took advantage of his visits by asking him many questions, which he answered in quite good English. He seemed to have retained a memory of many of the people he had known in England. He drank the health of Lady Dundas and would have willingly drunk to the health of all the English ladies, if I had been disposed to pour out a glass for him.[67]

King of the natives

A body of evidence places Bennelong as the leader of an Aboriginal clan observed on the north side of the Parramatta River, between Kissing Point and Parramatta, in the early years of the nineteenth century.

The French scientist François Péron, who tested Bennelong's strength with his Dynamometer in Sydney in 1802, estimated his age as 35–36 and noted: 'The chief; pleasing figure but somewhat thin'.[68]

'General' Joseph Holt, who arrived in New South Wales in 1800 as a political exile, managed the farms of Captain William Cox, paymaster to the New South Wales Corps. In his *Memoirs* (1838), Holt noted aspects of Aboriginal life and culture around Parramatta at the turn of the nineteenth century under governors John Hunter and Philip Gidley King. According to Holt, while fighting and hostility continued between settlers and natives at the Northern Boundary (north of Parramatta), Hawkesbury River and Georges River settlements, some 50 Aborigines were camped peacefully about the Parramatta River near Clay Cliff Creek. He described Bennelong and his clan visiting Cox's farm. 'The king of the natives his name is Bennelong, that is to say "been long" deemed their king', wrote Holt, who bragged that he had had 'one hundred of both male and female in my yard together'. He sometimes brought the chief and his *gin* (wife) into his house for breakfast and a glass of grog.[69]

Bennelong, wrote George Howe in the *New South Wales Pocket Almanac* (1818), was 'hospitably protected' by Governor King. 'The Governor frequently clothed him and he dined at the servants' table in the kitchen, at which presided Mrs. [Jane] Dundas, the housekeeper, a worthy woman, and the butler, as worthy a young man.' Howe said Bennelong had dressed well and lived well in London, 'yet upon his return to the Colony he fell off spontaneously into his early habits, and in spite of every thing that could be done to him in the order of civilization, he took to the bush, and only occasionally visited Government House'.[70]

Early in January 1805 the Sydney settlers were told that Bennelong was to face a 'torrent of revenge' in a ritual revenge ordeal. 'A number of persons of the first respectability' gathered to witness this event, which turned into an epic combat. Under the heading 'Native amusements', the *Sydney Gazette* published a sarcastic account, couched as a mock Homeric commentary on some ancient 'Plutonic' games. At this period the government newspaper was the only source of information about these clashes. Bennelong successfully faced a steady onslaught, generally of three flights of spears at once, warding off a total of some 100 spears with great

Squire's Brewery, Kissing Point, Unknown artist, V1A/Ryde/5, Presented by Tooth's Brewery, Feb 1957 Mitchell Library, Sydney.

agility, although a few went through his thin parrying shield.[71]

On 14 March 1805 Bennelong took part in a ritual battle in which Cogy (Cogai, Cogie, Cogue, Gogy or Goguey), from the Cow Pastures (Camden) area, was punished for killing a man. Cogy stood his ground armed only with a shield, while Bennelong, Nanbarry and a third man hurled barbed spears at him. This conflict took place on the road between Parramatta and Prospect. Bennelong threw a spear from about four metres that pierced Cogy's hip and passed through his side, while another spear thrown by Nanbarry entered Cogy's back below the loins. Two English bystanders were unable to remove the spear and for the next three weeks Cogy walked about with the shaft sticking out of his body.[72] By 7 April Nanbarry's spear had been extracted and Cogy was well enough to take part in a punishment trial at the Hawkesbury River. Despite his wound, wrote the *Sydney Gazette*, Cogy 'marshalled forth with stoic composure'.[73]

The Reverend William Pascoe Crook, a Congregational parson and missionary who ran a school at Parramatta, stated his opinion of the Aboriginal people in a letter written on 5 May 1805:

> The Natives of this country are more & more Savage though Some of them have been quite Civilized they prefer wandering stark naked in the bush living on worms insects &c this is the case with Bennelong who was in England. He visits the settlements now and then, is very polite, begs a loaf and departs.[74]

Crook's use of the plural 'settlements' implies that Bennelong visited Parramatta as well as Sydney.

Bennelong was enraged in July 1805 when Colebee carried off 'the widow of the deceased Carraway [Caruey]', his former wife Kurubarabulu. He met Colebee in a duel at Farm Cove, but friends of the two men called off the combat after half a dozen spears missed their mark.[75] Caruey, who had been wrongly reported as being killed in an earlier payback, was still alive, so Kurubarabulu was not yet a widow. Caruey died several months later 'in consequence of a spear wound above the knee which brought on a mortification'. His body was wrapped 'in a shell composed of strips of bark' and taken to the Brickfields on Tuesday 17 December 1805 and buried there the following day. 'He was a docile and intelligent fellow [and] a faithful guide to our *bush sportsmen* in search of the pheasant [lyre bird]', said the *Sydney Gazette*.[76]

Bennelong's death and burial

Bennelong died on 2 January 1813 at James Squire's orchard at Kissing Point on the north shore of the Parramatta River.

His obituary in the *Sydney Gazette* was both scathing and belittling, ignoring his previous helpfulness and cooperation with Phillip:

Bennelong died on Sunday morning last at Kissing Point. Of this veteran champion of the native tribe little favourable can be said. His voyage to and benevolent treatment in Great Britain produced no change whatever in his manners and inclinations, which were naturally barbarous and ferocious. The principal officers of Government had for many years endeavoured, by the kindest of usage, to wean him from his original habits and draw him into a relish for civilised life; but every effort was in vain exerted and for the last few years he has been but little noticed. His propensity for drunkenness was inordinate; and when in that state he was insolent, menacing and overbearing. In fact, he was a thorough savage, not to be warped from the form and character that nature gave him by all the efforts that mankind could use.[77]

The one dependable explanation of the reason for Bennelong's death was given in 1815 by Old Philip, brother of both Gnunga-Gnunga Murremurgan ('Collins') and the exiled Musquito, to ship's surgeon Joseph Arnold, who wrote in his journal: 'old Bennelong is dead, Philip told me he died after a short illness about two years ago, & that they buried him & his wife at Kissing point'.[78] Gnung-a Gnung-a or Anganangan had married Bennelong's sister Warreweer, so Philip was also Bennelong's brother-in-law.

Lieutenant William Lawson, in his *Account of the Aborigines* (1838), said:

Bennelong was sent to England in the early part of the Colony ... after being there some time and great pains taken with him on his return to this Country he again took to the bush he could not leave off his wild habits and at length died in the bush with his tribe at Kissing point, which are all now I believe nearly extinct.[79]

While Bennelong's illness might have originated in the many wounds he suffered over the years in the relentless cycle of payback battles, it must also have been aggravated by his 'propensity to drunkenness'. According to 'Atticus', a contributor to the *Sydney Gazette* in March 1817, Bennelong had been 'much addicted to spirit drinking, and for the last five months of his life was seldom sober'.[80]

Writing in 1883, navy lieutenant Richard Sadleir alleged that three natives had been killed in a battle and several wounded, including Bennelong, who was 'dangerously wounded and probably died'. Sadleir did not come to Australia until 1826 and relied on hearsay, as there is no extant report of a payback fight during 1813. 'Thus perished Bennillong, as a drunken savage, after all the advantages he had had of visiting England, and living at the Governor's House', concluded Sadleir.[81] Generations of historians have repeated this notion. The *Australian Encyclopaedia* entry reads:

Bennelong, alienated from his people, became quarrelsome and drunken. He was killed in a fight with other Aborigines in January 1813.[82]

Bennelong was buried, with one of his wives, in James Squire's orchard at Kissing

Point beside the Parramatta River that separated the Wallamattagal territory from that of the Wangal, his birth country. It was just 25 years — half his lifetime — since Bennelong first saw a white man. Unlike Yemmerrawanne, who died in England 19 years earlier, Bennelong was buried in his native land.

When Colebee's nephew Nanbarry, a Cadigal from the eastern shore of Port Jackson, died at Kissing Point on 12 January 1821, he was buried at his request in the same grave as Bennelong. There could be no greater mark of respect. An obituary in the *Sydney Gazette* said Nanbarry had taken to the woods, from which 'he only occasionally emerged for a number of years in order to return with renewed avidity and satisfaction. Mr. Squire we have every reason to believe treated him with particular tenderness.'

Writing in the *Australian Quarterly Journal* (1828), the Reverend Charles Wilton, minister of the Parish of the Field of Mars, said: 'He [Bennelong] lies between his wife and another Chief amidst the orange trees of the garden. Bidgee Bidgee, the present representative of the Kissing Point Tribe, is a frequent visitor to these premises [Squire's orchard] and expresses a wish to be buried by the side of his friend Bennelong.'[83] Bidgee Bidgee, the Kissing Point clan head, told the French voyager Jules Dumont d'Urville that he was the uncle of Bennelong's son 'Dicky', baptised as Thomas Walter Coke.[84] After an illness in which he was nursed by Bundle (Bundell), the boy died at the age of 19 in 1823, after a brief but childless marriage to an Aboriginal girl named Maria (later Maria Lock).[85] If Bidgee Bidgee was Dicky's uncle, Dicky's mother was Bidgee Bidgee's sister Boorong, who would have been Bennelong's last wife and the woman buried in his grave.

The traditional ritual revenge combat or payback fought in Sydney not long after Bennelong's death at Kissing Point was not reported in the Sydney newspapers. It was, though, witnessed by 'a free merchant of India', a passenger on the schooner *Henrietta*, who wrote a letter dated 'off Bass's Straits, 17th April, 1813' that was printed in the *Caledonian Mercury* in Edinburgh more than one year later, on 26 May 1814. The writer described the ritual, in which 'the nearest relative is obliged to stand punishment … he stands at a distance with a shield of hard wood, and the rest throw spears with great dexterity at him, while he defends himself, till wounded, or perhaps killed; and there the affair ends'. He continued:

Lately, in the vicinity of the town ['Sidney'], a battle took place, where about 200 were engaged, I believe in consequence of the death of the celebrated Bennelong, who visited England some years ago, and was taken great notice of. The spears flew very thick, and about thirty men were wounded.[86]

4 Indigenous pioneers

While the start of the nineteenth century signalled revolution in Europe, it brought a period of expansion to the colony of New South Wales. During six years as governor, from 1800 to 1806, Philip Gidley King (1758–1808) encouraged coastal exploration and established new settlements at the Hunter River (Newcastle), the Derwent River (Hobart Town) and the Tamar River at Port Dalrymple and Launceston in Van Diemen's Land.

These initiatives were based on King's knowledge as a navigator and seaman, his practical experience commanding a penal colony on the remote Norfolk Island, and a degree of political expediency. A vital consideration was the fear that the French would lay claim to part of the Australian continent. In 1770, at the age of 12, King went to the East Indies on board the naval frigate HMS *Swallow*. From his association with Australia's first governor, Arthur Phillip, with whom he served as lieutenant from 1792 on HMS *Ariadne* and HMS *Europe*, King had learned to respect and encourage the cooperation of 'civilised' Aborigines like Bennelong as go-betweens to avoid conflict when probing new frontiers.[1]

A few Aboriginal men from the Sydney area accompanied the first ships taking colonists to establish these early settlements. Their skill at bushcraft, finding water, hunting kangaroos and small game and tracking escaped convicts was invaluable. Their knowledge of Aboriginal protocol and their advice and assistance as guides and go-betweens often saved lives. In his introduction to *With the White People* (1990), historian Henry Reynolds called such people 'black pioneers'.[2]

Bungaree at the Hunter River

In 1801 Governor King called on the Broken Bay leader Bungaree to play a minor role in the establishment of a convict settlement at the mouth of the Hunter River, 160 kilometres north of Sydney. He was aware of Bungaree's services two years earlier when he sailed to Moreton Bay with Matthew Flinders aboard the brig *Norfolk*. King sent HMS *Lady Nelson*, commanded by Lieutenant James Grant, a 28-year-old Scot, to examine and survey the entrance to the Hunter River. The expedition was led by Lieutenant-Colonel William Paterson, a keen botanist, who was accompanied by Surgeon

John Harris of the New South Wales Corps, surveyor Francis Barrallier, a French-born Ensign in the Corps, botanist George Caley and artist and naturalist John William Lewin. 'With us likewise,' Grant noted, 'went one of the Natives, named Bangaree'.[3]

Lady Nelson, 52 feet long, with a capacity of 60 tons and a crew of 15 men, was built at Deptford on the Thames in London in 1799. This unusual craft, intended for surveying inshore waters, was fitted with four sliding keels or centreboards, the invention of Captain John Schank, a former commissioner of the Transport Board. When the keels were raised the ship could enter water as shallow as six feet.[4]

Lady Nelson set sail from Port Jackson for the Hunter River on 10 June 1801, accompanied by the 44-ton HM colonial schooner *Francis*, which was to pick up a load of coal. At noon the next day they passed Broken Bay.

On 12 June *Lady Nelson's* pilot repeated the error made by Captain William Reid of the *Martha*, who had mistaken the entrance of Lake Macquarie for the Hunter River. The channel was named Reid's Mistake. Surgeon Harris went ashore to reconnoitre, but could not find any river. He returned with an Aboriginal man who ran to his boat shouting 'Whale Boat!' and 'Budgerie Dick!' — *budgeree* or *budyiri* meaning 'good'. Sailors pursuing the convicts who had seized the *Norfolk* in Broken Bay in October 1800 had probably given him the nickname. 'This man had some fish with him, which he threw into the boat and then jumped into it himself, without the least hesitation', wrote Grant. Budgerie Dick went to the Hunter River on the ship. Grant hoisted a flag on the island (now Nobby's Head) to indicate the entrance of the river. The next day Dick left as the party explored the bush. Two days later, wrote Grant, Dick reappeared with two companions. One of them had visited Sydney and was known to Colonel Paterson, so 'a kind of conversation was kept up'.[5] After landing, Bungaree ran off and was sorely missed. Paterson noted his absence in a letter to Governor King in Sydney on 25 June 1801:

> The Natives here are remarkably shy. I am afraid they have been badly used by the White people Here some time since —
> We have notwithstanding caught two of them in the Woods, treated them kindly and let them go About their business. I hope it may have a good effect. The Native which we brought … with us, Bonjary ran off after we reached the River and has not since returned —[6]

The *Francis* returned to Sydney with 75 tons of coal which was exchanged with the master of the Calcutta-built ship *Marquis Cornwallis* for nails and iron, 'articles that were much wanted', wrote John Hunter, 'thus, for the first time, making the natural produce of the country contribute to its wants'.[7] The coal sold in Bengal.

Bungaree also sailed with the 'Second Fleet' of ships to Newcastle in 1804.

View of Hunters River, near Newcastle New South Wales with a distant view of Port Stephen [Port Stephens], Drawn by R Browne, engraved by W Preston, *Views in New South Wales 1813–14,* a147401 1u.tif, Mitchell Library, Sydney.

Following a short-lived uprising by 250 convicts at Castle Hill, north of Parramatta, in March 1804, nine rebels were killed in the 'Battle of Vinegar Hill' near today's Rouse Hill. Governor King, a Protestant loyalist, came down hard on the Irish convicts. Five were hanged, nine others were flogged and 37 men involved in the uprising were sentenced to hard labour in the coal mines.[8]

King ordered the reopening of the abandoned penal settlement at the Hunter River to accommodate the captured convicts. Three ships, *Lady Nelson*, the cutter *Resource* and the sloop *James*, left Port Jackson on 28 March 1804. At the governor's request, marine lieutenant Charles Menzies disembarked from HMS *Calcutta* to take up the post of commandant at King's Town, later Newcastle.[9] It is likely that Bungaree accompanied the soldiers and convicts. *Lady Nelson* and *Resource* returned to Sydney laden with coal and cedar, but *James*, owned by Thomas Reibey, was dashed to pieces on a beach on the northern side of Broken Bay.[10]

Some Aboriginal men from the Hunter River area had come to Sydney. Governor King sent Bungaree in *Resource* to escort them back to their home country. On 24 May 1804, Governor King wrote to Menzies: 'Six Natives of your neighbourhood having come here soon after you Settled, they now return with Bongaru [Bungaree] in the Resource'. Each man was given rations for six days, a jacket, cap, blanket and four pounds of tobacco.[11] Writing to the governor from King's Town on 1 July 1804, Menzies, then aged 21, praised Bungaree's worth as an intermediary between blacks and whites, put him on the rations and gave him a glowing character reference:

We have always been and still continue on the most friendly terms with the numerous Natives here, to preserve which I have directed the Storekeeper to victual Boungaree. He is the most intelligent of that race I have as yet Seen and Should a misunderstanding unfortunately take place he will be Sure to reconcile them …[12]

Menzies, later Sir Charles Menzies (1783–1866), served with distinction in the Napoleonic Wars and became Queen Victoria's aide-de-camp in 1852 and a general in 1857.

The *Francis* brought news to Port Jackson on 5 September that 'the Native Bungary' had been sent to track a runaway convict cedar-getter who escaped into the bush soon after landing. The *Sydney Gazette* was confident that Bungaree 'would doubtless overtake him before he could proceed to any very considerable distance'. The prisoner was caught soon after.[13] Menzies told King on 5 October 1804 that three runaway convicts on their way to Sydney had killed Bungaree's father (whose name is not known) 'in the most brutal manner' while he was trying to persuade them to return to Newcastle.[14] On 17 October, Menzies wrote again to King, saying he did not think there was sufficient proof to successfully convict the runaways before a criminal court 'for the murder of a Native'.[15]

Bungaree probably returned to Sydney once again on *Resource*. He took part in a ritual revenge combat at Farm Cove on 16 December 1804, which was described by the *Sydney Gazette* as 'the most malignant that has been witnessed'. This battle was to punish 'the heroic Willamannan', from Port Hacking, who avoided 'an immense number of spears' but was wounded in the hand by a spear that passed through his shield. In the melee that followed, Bungaree was seen throwing a returning boomerang, the first reported in the Port Jackson area:

… the white spectators were justly astonished at the dexterity and incredible force with which a bent, edged waddy resembling slightly a Turkish scymetar [scimitar] was thrown by Bungary, a native distinguished by his remarkable courtesy. The weapon, thrown at 20 or 30 yards distance, twirled round in the air with astonishing velocity, and alighting on the right arm of one of his opponents, actually rebounded to a distance not less than 70 or 80 yards, leaving a horrible contusion behind, and exciting universal admiration.[16]

Salamander at Sullivans Cove

The name 'John Salamander' appears in a list of 'Persons Victualled on Full Allowance' from 25 January 1804 at Sullivan Bay, Port Phillip (Victoria). Salamander, an Aboriginal man from the Sydney area, had taken his name from the 'Third Fleet' convict transport *Salamander*, commanded by John Nicol, which dropped anchor in Sydney Cove on 21 August 1791. After unloading her cargo of 101 male convicts, the 312-ton *Salamander* went to sea as a whaling ship.[17]

View of Sullivan Cove 1804, [Sullivans Cove, Van Diemen's Land, with *Ocean* at left], Attributed to George Prideaux Robert Harris (1775–1810), Watercolour, Original SV6B/Sull C/1, Mitchell Library, Sydney.

Fearing the prospect of a French settlement on the north side of Bass Strait, Governor King suggested in 1802 that a strategic British outpost should be established at Port Phillip. King was right to be suspicious of the French. In 1800, a scientific expedition sanctioned by Napoleon Bonaparte, then First Consul of the French Republic, sailed from Le Havre to explore and chart New Holland. While in Port Jackson, François Péron (1775–1810), a naturalist and zoologist aboard *Géographe*, found time to spy out Sydney's defences. In his report to the French Admiralty, Péron recommended an invasion, but concluded that Sydney Cove was too difficult to attack directly, suggesting a landing instead at Broken Bay.[18]

Robert, Lord Hobart, Secretary of State at the Colonial Office in London, appointed David Collins (1756–1810), aged 47, who had served as Judge Advocate for eight years in New South Wales to found this new penal colony. Collins would command a marine detachment, 300 male convicts and some free settlers. On 24 April 1803, they sailed from Portsmouth in HMS *Calcutta*, 1200 tons, a former East Indiaman built of teak and refitted as a Royal Navy warship with 50 guns. This was the largest vessel yet sent to Australia. The ship, commanded by Captain Daniel Woodriff, arrived at Port Phillip Bay on Sunday 9 October 1803. Woodriff found *Ocean*, a chartered trading ship of 401 tons commanded by Captain John Mertho, already moored in the bay.[19] Convicts were landed to set up a camp at Sullivan Bay at the edge of the present Sorrento.[20]

According to George Augustus Robinson, Aboriginal Protector at Port

Phillip (1839), this was the territory of the Bonurong (Boonoorong), who claimed 'the country from Port Phillip to Westernport, along the sea-coast'.[21] The Bonurong regularly visited Sullivan Bay to gather shellfish.[22]

Collins found there was not enough drinking water in Port Phillip Bay to support a settlement and sought Governor King's permission to abandon the settlement and move across Bass Strait to Van Diemen's Land. King chartered *Ocean* to return to Port Phillip with the sloop *Lady Nelson* to assist in moving the convicts to Van Diemen's Land.

Henry Hacking, previously quartermaster on the First Fleet flagship HMS *Sirius*, sailed to Port Phillip aboard *Lady Nelson*, accompanied by Salamander, a 'Sydney native'. *Lady Nelson* left Sydney on Monday 25 December 1803 for Port Phillip and *Ocean* followed the next day.[23] *Lady Nelson* put in to refit in the Kent Group of islands in Bass Strait and left for Port Dalrymple on 30 December 1803.[24] *Ocean* had brought official news that Britain and France were again at war. After landing the convicts, Woodriff sailed for England.

Persons Victualled on Full Allowance 1803–4
25 Janry. 1804
Sullivan Bay, Port Phillip
‡ Supernumaries
‡ John Salamander, Native
Departed 17 Mar, 1804 to Sydney
Supernumaries
26 Feby. 1804
Victualled at Sullivans Cove, Derwent River VDL (Hobart)

‡ Mr. Brown, Botanist; Henry Hacking; Salamander,
A Port Jackson Native

Persons victualled on full allowance
Enclosure No. 2,
Lieutenant-Governor David Collins to Governor PG King,
Sullivan Cove, Van Diemen's Land, 29 February 1804
Historical Records of Australia, Series III, vol. I, 1921:108; 107–227

A few convicts escaped into the bush at Port Phillip. William Buckley, a former soldier transported on the Calcutta, got away on 27 December 1803. 'Among the bolters from the camp at various times, one only lived to see the white man's return thirty years after; this was Buckley', wrote James Bonwick.[25] Buckley, who had lived for 32 years among the Wathaurong, told his biographer John Morgan: 'The natives call that place [Sullivans Bay] Koonan, which means eel, that fish [*sic*] being in great abundance in almost all the streams running into Port Phillip.'[26]

Collins decided to establish his settlement on the Derwent River. Colonists, convicts and marines crowded on board *Lady Nelson* and *Ocean*, which sailed from Port Phillip on 30 January 1804. Because of high seas, strong winds and bad weather they took 16 days to cross Bass Strait. On Thursday 15 February 1804, *Ocean* anchored in the river near the *Lady Nelson*.

Collins chose a new site for the settlement, which he also named Sullivan Cove but later called Hobart Town.[27] Woorrady, an Aboriginal Tasmanian from Bruny Island, told George Augustus Robinson in 1831 that 'the country at Hobart Town is called Nib-ber-loon-ner … and it was inhabited by the Mou-he-neen-ner nation. At Little Sandy Bay, called Kree-wer, there was a large native village'.[28] In *View of Sullivan Cove 1804*, the *Ocean* is moored in the Derwent River at the future site of Hobart.

Salamander, Hacking and the botanist Robert Brown received rations from 26 February 1804. Hacking and Salamander went hunting two days later and shot a kangaroo, which, wrote the Reverend Robert Knopwood in his journal, was 'the first Kangaroo killed in the colony'. Hacking's version of his tussle with Van Diemen's Land Aborigines was printed in the *Sydney Gazette* of 18 March 1804:

> During the Lady Nelson's stay, a large Kangaroo was taken in the Woods by Henry Hacking attended by a Sydney native; but being intercepted by a tribe of the sooty inhabitants, of that neighbourhood, the Kangaroo, between 50 and 60 lbs weight, was for a moment considered as lost. The blacks made use of every policy to wheedle Hacking out of his bounty, but as they did not offer or threaten violence he with counteracting policy preserved it. Although they treated him with much affability and POLITENESS, yet they regarded his companion with jealousy and indignation; and the poor fellow, sensible of his critical and precarious situation, appeared very thankful when safely delivered from their unwelcome presence.

Salamander remained on the rations list until 17 March 1804, although he probably returned to Sydney with Hacking aboard *Lady Nelson*, which arrived in Port Jackson on 14 March 1804.

Henry Hacking (c. 1753–1831) had been first mate on the sloop *Lady Nelson*. A violent man and a heavy drinker, Hacking was transported to Norfolk Island in October 1799 for perjury at a trial involving his convict mistress Ann Holmes. He received a pardon soon after from Governor John Hunter, the former commander of HMS *Sirius*. In 1803 Hacking was sentenced to death for shooting and wounding Holmes in Sydney. He received the death sentence once again in 1804 for stealing naval stores from the hulk of HMS *Investigator* in Port Jackson. In both cases, Governor King pardoned his old shipmate. Hacking was transported to Van Diemen's Land for seven years, but was able to come and go freely from Hobart to Sydney and in June 1804 was appointed coxswain by Lieutenant Governor David Collins, another old acquaintance.

There was a reason for this lenient treatment. Evidence points to Henry Hacking as the man who shot and killed the feared Bidjigal resistance leader Pemulwuy on 2 June

1802. In his journal for 20 July 1802, Samuel Smith, a seaman on Matthew Flinders's HMS *Investigator*, wrote about 'Bumblewoy, a Severe Enemy to White people, as he had Kill'd several'. Bumblewoy is one of many ways of spelling Pemulwuy. Smith continued: 'At length, he was Shot by the Master of the Nelson Brig, that was Shooting in the Woods, his head being brought Tranquillity was again restor'd'.[29] The crew of the *Lady Nelson* did not include a master, but at the time its first mate was Henry Hacking, the former quartermaster and game shooter of HMS *Sirius*.

In October 1802 Governor King informed Lord Hobart in London that two settlers had shot 'Pemulwuye'. However, the governor's clerk, David Dickinson Mann, supported the notion of a single killer. Mann said Governor King had offered a reward 'to any person who should kill him [Pemulwuy] and bring in his head. This was soon accomplished by artifice, the man received the reward, and the head was sent to England in spirits by the Speedy.'[30] Pemulwuy was decapitated and his preserved head sent to Sir Joseph Banks in London. Its whereabouts are unknown.

Mongoul at Twofold Bay

Stephen Tadd, carpenter on the ship *Barwell*, was given a contract to build a boat for the Hawkesbury River wheat trade. Tadd laid the 38 feet long keel in 1798, but could not find any skilled assistants and was paid 7/6d (seven shillings and sixpence) per day for his work. The sloop, renamed the *Contest*, with a capacity of 44 tons, was finally launched at Underwood's Shipyards near the Tank Stream in Sydney Town in May 1804.[31] The *Contest*, owned by Kable & Underwood, left Port Jackson in company with the Colonial cutter *Integrity* on 10 June 1804, bound for Port Dalrymple with a military detachment commanded by Lieutenant Governor William Paterson.[32]

Returning from Van Diemen's Land, the master of the *Contest*, Cadwallader Driffin, went ashore at Twofold Bay with '*Mongoul*, a native of Sydney'. Mongoul, who was, in fact, from Port Stephens near Newcastle, was left on shore with two soldiers and camped near the beach with the Twofold Bay Aborigines. Shortly after, 'owing to some sudden misunderstanding, three spears were darted at *Mongoul*, but were dexterously avoided'. The attackers retreated when the soldiers fired over their heads. Next morning, the Aborigines appeared friendly, until one man seized a knapsack and its contents and they all ran off. The pursuing soldiers found them some 12 to 14 miles inland, 'dressed in the cloathing taken from the knapsack, and dancing'.

> They were instantly closed with, but taking to their spears and other offensive weapons, rendered it necessary to fire upon them. — one was killed, the others followed the party back to their boat, annoying them with spears at every opportunity, which they continued to do until the whole were embarked.[33]

There are no records of Bungaree's activities from 1804 until November 1808, when he was mentioned by the *Sydney Gazette* in a murder report, which points to the possibility that after his father's death, he continued to live in his mother's country around the Hunter's River settlement, then known as 'King's Town'. The murderer concerned was an Aborigine named as 'Port Stevens Robert', also called Mongoul and later Robert or Bob Barratt. Two sailors from the colonial ship *Halcyon* went by boat with a European boy to see the ship *Dundee*, wrecked opposite King's Town. While they were walking on the beach with 'Robert', he suddenly turned and speared John Bosch, one of the sailors. Although wounded, Bosch escaped by diving into the water and swimming out to sea. 'Robert' clubbed and killed the other man, John Spillers, with a *nulla nulla* (club) and mutilated his body. When the boy's corpse was found his head had been scalped. Describing Robert, the newspaper said: 'His visage is rendered remarkable, by a cut which he received from Bungary that has occasioned an indentation nearly in the centre of his forehead'.[34]

Charcoal (Nunberri) at the Shoalhaven

'Charcoal was my regular boatman,' wrote Alexander Berry (1781–1873), a former East India Company ship's surgeon turned captain and successful Sydney merchant in partnership with Edward Wollstonecraft. In June 1822, Berry asked the young Aboriginal man, lame in one leg after a cartwheel accident, to sail with him to the Shoalhaven River, where he planned to establish a farm. 'Next morning he was rugged out in sailors cloathes and appointed *pro forma* Mate of the cutter Blanch', Berry wrote in 'Recollections of the Aborigines' (1838).

Nunberri or Nambre (c. 1803–1840), from Numba on the south side of the Shoalhaven River, was also called Jem, Jemmy, Jeremy, James or Jim Charcoal. He was given a metal breastplate engraved with the title 'Nunberri Chief of the Nunnerahs'. Nunberri was one of several Aboriginal people from the far south coast of New South Wales who visited Sydney and camped in the Domain during 1834. Drawings of some of these men and women by the German-born artist Charles Rodius appeared that year as lithographic prints in his *Natives of New South Wales*.

Broughton (Broten), another Shoalhaven Aborigine, 'who had accompanied the late Mr. Throsby on several journeys into the bush', also sailed to the Shoalhaven with Berry in the tiny 15-ton vessel. Berry gave Broughton, born at Boon-ga-ree or Broughton Creek (near Berry), a rectangular breastplate inscribed 'Broughton Native Constable Shoal Haven, 1822'.

After losing two of his sailors, who drowned in the Shoalhaven, Berry returned to Sydney in the *Blanch* with a motley crew, consisting of the young explorer Hamilton Hume, Wajin, chief of Shoalhaven, Yager, chief of Jervis Bay, and Charcoal. 'I got safe to Sydney with my singular crew after a tedious passage occasioned by fowl [foul] winds', wrote Berry.[35]

NUNBERRI. CHIEF of the NUNNERAHS N. S. WALES, 1834
Charles Rodius (1802–1806)
Lithograph
No. 16, Original PXA615,
Mitchell Library, Sydney

Trackers at Port Macquarie

In 1821, Captain Francis Allman of the 48th Regiment, took Bob Barratt (Mongoul or 'Port Stevens Robert'), Johnny McGill (Biraban) and Boardman (also called Boatman and Jemmy Jackass) to a new penal settlement at Port Macquarie on the north coast of New South Wales. As 'bush constables' their task was to track and capture escaped convicts.[36]

They probably accompanied Allman and his family, who sailed from Sydney Cove aboard the colonial schooner *Prince Regent* on 17 March 1821, with the brig *Lady Nelson* and the schooner *Mermaid*. The little fleet, carrying convicts and soldiers, had a rough passage. The ships were forced into Port Stephens on 22 March, where they sheltered from storms for two weeks and were forced to take refuge once more at Trial Bay, finally anchoring at Port Macquarie on 17 April 1821.

Lady Nelson ran aground on the harbour sandbar on 2 May and was still a wreck in November 1821, when Governor Lachlan Macquarie sailed to Port Macquarie in the government brig *Elizabeth Henrietta*.

Biraban or M'gill (c. 1800–1846) is best known as the informant and helper of the Reverend Lancelot Threlkeld, a Congregational minister and linguist, who

Portrait of McGill
Alfred T. Agate (1812–1846)
Caption — 'done by Mr. Agate at Threlkeld's residence at Lake Macquarie'
Engraving
From Charles Wilkes, *Narrative of the United States Exploring Expedition*, 1838–1842, Washington, vol. 2:253
Mitchell Library, Sydney

in 1824 established a mission for Aborigines at 'Ebenezer' (now Toronto, NSW). Threlkeld, first based at Ba-ta-ba (Bahtahbah or Belmont) on Lake Macquarie, spoke of 'M'gill and his tribe' as belonging to the language group centred on Newcastle and Lake Macquarie.[37] Threlkeld said the boy acquired his name from an army officer, 'Captain M'Gill', who brought him up at the Military Barracks in Sydney, where he learned to speak English. It is likely that he had taken his name from Captain John Mander Gill (that is John M Gill) of the 46th Regiment, who was acting principal engineer on Governor Macquarie's staff until he left New South Wales on the ship *Harriet* on 22 December 1817.[38]

Biriban was in Newcastle in 1819, when he was caricatured as 'Magill', with his body 'painted-up' for a ceremony, in a watercolour portrait by the convict artist Richard Browne.[39] He probably acquired his totem name Biraban ('Eaglehawk') when he completed his initiation rites at the age of about 26 in 1826.[40]

For a few months during 1827, Biriban shot birds and small game for Lieutenant William Sacheverall Coke of the 39th Regiment, second in command of the Newcastle penal colony. Extracts from Coke's notebook show that 'Magill' became Coke's game shooter for a short period after Desmond 'was run through the thigh with a spear and wounded on the leg with a Bomebring [boomerang]'. The travelling artist Augustus Earle, who painted his portrait at the Hunter River in 1826, described Desmond as 'a N.S. Wales Chief'.[41]

On Thursday 10 May 1827, Coke wrote: 'Numbers of Blacks in New Castle coming for clothes all naked. Magill brought me three black Duck. Grand Corroberry'. On Monday 14 May, he recorded: 'About 200 blacks had clothing issued out, before this they were all naked'. Captain Allman, who had taken Biriban to Port Macquarie in 1824, visited Newcastle on 14 May. That evening, wrote Coke, 'Magill brought me five Wild Duck'. On 6 June, Coke stuffed a specimen of a 'Regent Bird' (Regent bower bird) shot by Biriban and on 13 June he brought Coke a 'Saturn Bird' (Satin bower bird).

Cynthia Hunter, who edited Coke's notebook and letters, refers to the wide range of skills used by Aborigines to assist the colonists: 'Coke portrays Aboriginal men and women cooperating with the military as boatmen or pilots, as guides for hunting expeditions and as teachers of food-gathering skills on land and sea'.[42] Lieutenant Coke left Newcastle and sailed to Sydney on 21 September 1827, noting in his journal: 'Savage life undoubtedly preferable to civilized'.[43]

In 1830, Governor Sir Ralph Darling presented Biraban with a brass gorget, engraved with the inscription: 'Barabahn, or Mac.Gill, Chief of the Tribe of Bartabah, on Lake Macquarie; a Reward for his assistance in reducing his Native Tongue to a written Language'.[44]

According to Lancelot Threlkeld, Biraban was a clever artist:

When the first steamboat arrived in the colony, the "Sophia Jane," I requested him to give me a description of it. This he did verbally, and when I required of him a representation, he drew with a pencil on a sheet of paper an excellent sketch of the vessel.

Threlkeld sent Biraban's drawing to the Bishop of Sydney, Reverend WG Broughton, who forwarded it to 'one of the [religious] societies in London'. Biraban's picture has unfortunately not been located. The 250-ton *Sophia Jane*, a sea-going paddle-wheel steamship rigged with sails as a schooner, arrived in Sydney on 15 May 1831 and went into service as a passenger ship between Sydney, Newcastle and Morpeth on the Hunter River. Biriban probably went to see the steamer when it arrived at Newcastle in June that year.[45]

Threlkeld indicated that Biriban also drew other subjects, when he remarked that 'M'Gill ... could take a very good drawing of vessels especially'.[46]

Biraban and Boardman guided the visiting Society of Friends (Quaker) missionaries James Backhouse and George Washington Walker through the bush from Newcastle to Lake Macquarie in April 1836. Backhouse said Biriban, 'a tall, intelligent man', wore a 'red-striped shirt, not very clean, a pair of ragged trowsers, and an old hat. Suspended from his neck, by a brass chain, he had a half-moon shaped, brass breastplate, with his native and English name, and a declaration of his kingly dignity; engraven upon it.' Backhouse described Boardman as 'an interesting looking young man in appearance about 18 years of age and wore a ragged blue jacket and a pair of trowsers'.

On 8 May 1836, 'M'Gill' saw Backhouse and Walker in Sydney while acting as an interpreter with Threlkeld in a Supreme Court trial involving Broken Bay Aborigines. 'We gave them some articles of clothing, with which they were most pleased. — These poor creatures called upon us several times afterwards, during their stay in Sydney. They were mostly in a state of excitement, from strong drink; which they are easily persuaded to take', Backhouse wrote.[47] 'Beerabahr' or McGill, 'Chief of the Lake Macquarie Tribes' was issued with blankets in Sydney during 1836.[48]

According to Threlkeld, Boardman was speared and wounded in a fight in Sydney. He lingered, but died of his wounds and was buried at Irriring (Eraring), near Dora Creek on Lake Macquarie, in December 1839. An Aboriginal man named Ogilore (probably Cobon Gillory), was convicted of his murder and hanged in Sydney in 1841.[49]

Bob Barratt had escaped punishment after murdering two European men at Newcastle in 1808. On 9 December 1827, Barratt and six other Aborigines dived into the surf to rescue seven convicts from a boat swamped on the harbour bar at Port Macquarie.[50] They were rewarded with metal gorgets, one of which was found on the beach at Port Macquarie in 1923.[51]

In 1829, 'Monuggal' (Mongoul), alias Barratt, struck and killed a Brisbane Water Aborigine named Boorondire (Borondo), nicknamed 'Dirty Dick', in the

Boardman, Lake Macquarie Tribe 1836, William Henry Fernyhough (1809–1849), Lithograph signed 'WHF del', *Sketches of the Aborigines of New South Wales,* Published & sold by JG Austin & Co., Nº 12 Bridge Street, Sydney, 1836, Original DL PX47, Dixson Library, Sydney.

Sydney Domain near Bennelong Point. At the time of the killing, Barratt carried a waddy and was conspicuously dressed, like Bungaree, in a white frilled shirt, military jacket and cocked hat with a red feather. Surgeon William Bland told the Coroner's Inquest, held at Cummings Hotel, that Boorondire had died instantly from wounds inflicted by a waddy. Barratt was caught hiding aboard a colonial ship in Sydney Harbour and brought to the hearing. The Coroner returned his verdict: 'That the deceased was wilfully murdered by a native called Monuggal, *alias* Bob Barrett, aided and assisted in the horrid deed by three other individuals, natives, not yet in custody'.[52]

Biriban, who had been sleeping by a fire in the Domain near Bungaree, told Threlkeld that an Englishman swimming at Woolloomooloo discovered Boorondire's body floating in the water the next morning. He said Bungaree and his people immediately steered their boat to the North Shore, where they remained for two days. Threlkeld passed on this information in a letter to the Attorney General on 2 March 1829, in which he stressed that the killing of Boorondire was not a ritual revenge combat, but rather 'a deliberate cruel murder'.[53] Barratt again escaped punishment for his crime. He was sentenced to be transported to Van Diemen's Land, but was discharged from custody.[54]

In 1830, Port Macquarie commandant Henry Smyth appointed the trusted 'Captain Robert Barratt' to command a detachment of 12 Aboriginal men and five women 'to attack the natives of Van Diemen's Land'.[55] This was at the time of Governor George Arthur's 'Black Line' attempt to round up the Palawa (Tasmanian

Aborigines). The Aboriginal volunteers were sent to Sydney, but, in the words of Major Macdonald, commissariat at Port Macquarie, 'the intention was afterwards abandoned'.[56]

Pigeon at King George Sound

The 380-ton French corvette *Astrolabe* entered the vast harbour of King George the Third Sound (now Albany), on the south-west coast of the Australian continent, in October 1826. Jules Sébastien-César Dumont d'Urville (1790–1842), a frigate captain, was the commander of a scientific expedition sent to the South Seas by the French King Charles X. Dumont d'Urville had visited Australia two years earlier on the same ship, then called *La Coquille*, which he renamed to commemorate one of La Pérouse's ships, missing since leaving Botany Bay in 1788.

On 12 October 1826 the French sailors sighted two whaleboats manned by sealers between Observatory and Seal Islands in Oyster Harbour. Left at King George Sound by the Hobart-based schooner *Hunter*, 61 tons, these men had lived and fished at Break-Sea Island for seven months with two Aboriginal women they had captured.

A week later the whaleboats returned, bringing fish, oysters, petrels (mutton-birds), a female seal and some penguins to the French ship. One member of the sealing gang was William Hook, a Maori from Kerikeri on the North Island of New Zealand. 'I learned that the second boat was manned by five Englishmen and an Australian aborigine from Port Jackson, all coming from the schooner *Hunter*', wrote Dumont d'Urville.[57] The man from Port Jackson was Warroba, known as Pigeon, who, because he was on the spot, would soon be acting as a mediator between the Nyungar-speaking Aborigines of King George the Third Sound and the first English settlers in 'West New Holland'.

The *Astrolabe* left King George Sound on 25 October 1826, sailing east to Western Port (Westernport, Victoria), where the crew met more sealers, and to

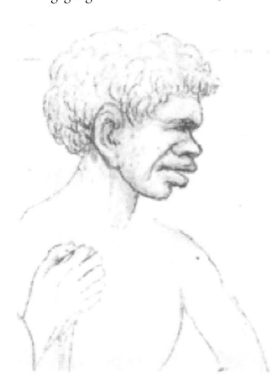

Pigeon [Warroba], 1833
John Glover (1790–1868)
Pencil
Sketchbook 97,
Tasmanian Museum and Art Gallery, Hobart

Jervis Bay, south of Sydney. On 2 December 1826 *Astrolabe* reached Port Jackson, where Governor Sir Ralph Darling warily received Dumont d'Urville. The French mariners had surveyed Oyster Harbour and it was rumoured that they planned to establish a colony there.

Darling hurriedly sent a group of convicts and a detachment of the 39th Regiment under Major Edmund Lockyer of the 57th Regiment in the brig *Amity* to establish a military outpost at King George Sound, where they anchored in Princess Royal Harbour on Christmas Day 1826. Lockyer chose the site for a settlement, which he called Frederickstown. The 142-ton *Amity* had been built in Canada in 1816 of black birch and native timbers. She sailed from Scotland in 1823, bringing migrants to Sydney and was sold to Governor Brisbane in 1824 for use in colonial trade.

The area around King George Sound was inhabited by the Minang (Mineng), who belonged to the widespread Nyungar language group of south-west Australia. Their leaders were Mokaré (c. 1800–1831), his older brother Nakina, and a *mulgarradock* (clever man or doctor) named Coolbun.[58]

Lockyer found that the sealers had killed one Aboriginal man on Green Island in Oyster Harbour. On the afternoon of 10 January 1827, a party of eight sealers came to the *Amity* seeking provisions. Lockyer wrote in his journal: 'Sent for the sealers from the Brig and, on questioning them, ascertained that the native we found dead on Green Island had been murdered by a party of these Sealers'. The following day, Pigeon offered to assist Lockyer to smooth relations between the settlers and the Nyungar. 'Pidgeon the Sydney native conceiving I might find him extremely useful in bringing about a communication and reconciliation with the Natives, and as he appeared an intelligent fellow and was willing to be employed — I have ordered him to be rationed', wrote Lockyer.

Lockyer freed a Nyungar woman who had been abducted by a sealer named Samuel Bailey and also an Aboriginal girl taken from the Recherche Archipelago on the mainland. 'The natives looked on the little Girl and shook their heads, meaning she did not belong to them, and then pointed to Pidgeon and then to the Girl meaning that he must take care of her', wrote Lockyer. He sent the girl, Fanny, about seven years of age, to Sydney for the governor to decide her future. In Sydney the Clergy and Schools Committee decided that 'Fanny Bailey', thought to be nine years old, should be admitted to the Native School at Black Town, west of Sydney She became the fifteenth student at the school and was placed on the rations on 10 March 1827.[35]

Plumes of smoke billowed from twelve fires arranged in a semi-circle behind the English camp in King George Sound. Lockyer reasoned that 'from so many fires there must be assembled a number of the natives'. On 20 January he noticed some strange faces among the Aboriginal visitors and observed: 'The Sydney Native Pidgeon extremely useful in communicating with them, though he cannot understand a word of their Language'. Two days later, while Lockyer was exploring, a convict came running to tell him that some Nyungar had attacked the watering party near the ship. He found the blacksmith, Dennis Dinneen, 'standing in the water with three spears sticking in him'.

On 26 January, Pigeon and Lockyer recovered spears and spear throwers dropped at Mount Melville by the attackers. 'Pigeon tracked them upwards of Three Miles and brought Capt. Wakefield on three of Them within 15 yards.' The Nyungar 'set up a hideous scream and scampered off'. Lockyer found they were from 'one Tribe who live in the neighbourhood of the Lakes to the Westward of Mount Melville'. Six Oyster Harbour men came to the camp as usual 'and on the matter being explained to them they pointed to the Lakes and shook their heads and disclaimed all knowledge of the Fact'.

In February, Pigeon and others were employed to bring in shells to burn for lime to use in building. Lockyer wrote 'the Natives again are constant Visitors'. When a ship was reported outside the harbour on 6 March 1827, Lockyer sent Pigeon 'to the Hill, but he returned without seeing anything'.[60] On 3 April 1827, Edmund Lockyer left King Georges Sound aboard HMS *Success*, which was returning to Sydney from the first settlement on the Swan River (now Perth), leaving Captain Joseph Wakefield in charge.

5 Musquito and Bulldog

Autocratic governors of the colony of New South Wales used their power to exile rebellious Aboriginal people without bringing any legal charge or conviction against them.

Bulldog and Musquito, who were sent by Governor Philip Gidley King to Norfolk Island in 1805, were again transported in 1813 to Van Diemen's Land. Richard Atkins, who succeeded David Collins as Judge Advocate, gave the governor his 'Opinion on the Treatment to be Adopted Towards the Natives', stating that 'the evidence of persons not bound by any moral or religious tye [tie] can never be considered or construed as legal evidence'. In Atkins's opinion Aboriginal people were 'incapable of being brought before a criminal court — and that the only mode at present when they deserve it, is to pursue them and inflict such punishment as they merit'.[1]

In her thesis (2008) Kristyn Harman suggested the term 'Aboriginal convicts' to refer to men like Bulldog, Musquito and Dual (Chapter 6) who were 'sentenced to transportation or whose death sentences were commuted to transportation'.[2]

The Reverend Samuel Marsden said Musquito was a leader of the resistance against white settlement 'on the banks of the Hawkesbury River', north of Sydney.[3] He was probably a member of the Broken Bay clan, as suggested by Tasmanian historian NJB Plomley.[4] Musquito's brother Phillip (Old Phillip) and his wife settled with the Broken Bay leader Bungaree at Georges Head. Visiting Bungaree's farm in November 1816, Governor Lachlan Macquarie and his wife Elizabeth gave 'a Suit of Clothes to Bungaree's wife and daughter and also to Phillip's wife'.[5]

The chain of events leading to the capture, imprisonment and exile of Musquito and Bulldog is complex and difficult to unravel from official accounts because it involved Aboriginal politics that the colonial authorities sought to use to their own advantage. This story is mainly told from articles and government orders published in the official *Sydney Gazette*.

An uprising by Hawkesbury River Aborigines made 1805 a year of violent attacks against settlers along the river. In April, John Llewellyn, a former soldier, was sharing his food with Branch Jack, when the Aborigine seized his musket and called in

20 others. Llewellyn died of spear wounds and Feen Adlam and his servant were killed at a nearby farm.[6] On 21 April Aborigines used tomahawks to kill two stockmen at John Macarthur's farm at Camden. A party of armed settlers pursued an Aboriginal force estimated at more than 300 men.[7]

Governor King issued a General Order on 27 April 1805 that 'required and ordered, that no Natives be suffered to approach the grounds of dwellings of any Settler until the Murderers are given up'. Any settler harbouring 'natives' would be prosecuted.[8]

Musquito was first noted, as 'Bush Muschetta', in May 1805 when he threatened an armed party of settlers at Pendant Hills (Pennant Hills) near Parramatta. This followed the capture of Tedbury, who almost escaped by slipping off his jacket as he was taken over the bridge into Parramatta. Tedbury was the son of the Aboriginal warrior Pemulwuy, who had been killed and decapitated in June 1802. After questioning by Major George Johnston and Marsden, Tedbury was 'brought over' and agreed to cooperate. Tedbury took a group of settlers to a cave at North Rocks, where they found property stolen from the dead stockmen and a tomahawk that might have been used to kill one of them. 'This party fell in with a small cluster, one of whom, called Bush Muschetta [Musquito], saluted them in good English, and declaring a determination to continue their rapacities, made off.' A cache of 40 bushels of corn was recovered from another cave at nearby Jerusalem Rocks from robberies in which Tedbury confessed he had taken part.[9]

In June 1805, nine Aboriginal men described as 'obstinate people' were arrested and jailed in Parramatta soon after fire destroyed a barn and haystacks belonging to Abraham Yeouler at Portland Head on the Hawkesbury River. Two of these prisoners were released when they volunteered 'to go in search of Musquetta [Musquito], who with Branch Jack and one or two more of his associates, still keeps the flames alive'.[10]

In his role as magistrate, Marsden released the remaining seven suspects 'on a promise to use their utmost endeavours to apprehend the native MUSQUITO', who, it was claimed, had led the recent attacks. Musquito was surrendered to the authorities on 6 July 1805. 'We are happy to add, that they fulfilled their promise, and the above Culprit, was last night lodged in Parramatta Gaol,' the *Sydney Gazette* reported.[11] The released men were allies of Tedbury, who was set free on 20 July 'at the earnest intreaty of the friendly natives who assisted in the capture of Musquito, each having pledged himself to bear every severity that any future mischiefs on the part of Tedbury should expose them to'.[12] Bulldog, a youth about 18 years of age, was arrested at the same time as Musquito.

Governor King responded to an approach from the 'friendly' Aborigines, who wished to return to the settlements. A General Order appeared in the *Sydney Gazette* on 7 July:

The NATIVES, after giving up the Principal in the late Outrages, having generally expressed a Desire to COME IN and many being on the Road from Hawkesbury and other Quarters to meet the Governor at Parramatta, NO MOLESTATION whatever is to be offered them in ANY part of the Colony—unless any of them should renew their late Acts, which is not probable, a RECONCILIATION will take place with the Natives generally.[13]

It was discovered that a 13-year-old Aboriginal girl had started the farmhouse fires at the Hawkesbury. She had been raised in the family of Henry Lamb, whose house she had burned down in late May. The girl was caught as she tried to set fire to the farm of Thomas Chaseland, where the Lamb family had taken refuge.[14] In September, Branch Jack was shot and wounded while making his escape after an attack on a boat on the Hawkesbury.[15]

In a report to Lord Camden in London, written the day Tedbury was released, Governor King stated: 'That the natives now confined were principally implicated in the murder of the two settlers and stockmen there can be no doubt on the most circumstantial and conclusive proof'. King admitted that coercive action had been taken and that 'six of the natives — and those the most guilty were shot in a pursuit by the settlers.' In other words, the governor was aware that neither Musquito nor Bulldog was among the ringleaders. King forwarded reports from punitive groups sent against the Aboriginal people. A letter from Major George Johnston said 'Talloon, one of those who murdered Mrs. McArthur's Stockmen', had been shot by a punitive party. 'Talboon' had been described as a 'Mountain native'. A trusted ex-convict named Andrew Thompson said 'a considerable number of them was killed by his party' and Obediah Ikin, an ex-soldier settler, stated that his party 'destroyed many of them'.

Because two more Aborigines than settlers had been shot, wrote King, he would forgo further retaliation. 'I should try the expedient of sending them to another settlement to labour, which has been much approved of by the rest.'[16] Tedbury and his allies had convinced the authorities that the expulsion of Musquito and Bulldog would put an end to further hostilities.

Musquito and Bulldog were imprisoned in Parramatta Gaol. On the night of Monday 5 August, they threatened to set fire to the gaol and to 'destroy every white man within it' and attempted to escape by using a nail to loosen the stonework. The escape was foiled when a white prisoner informed a gaoler.[17]

In *When the Sky Fell Down* (1979), historian Keith Willey questioned whether Musquito and Bulldog had led the Hawkesbury uprising. 'Possibly the true reason why Mosquito and Bulldog were chosen as scapegoats may lie in allegations that they had raped and murdered one or more Aboriginal women — acts which demanded vengeance under the tribe's own laws.'[18] The organiser was more likely to have been Tedbury, who had seized the opportunity to settle some old scores with Musquito on behalf of his father Pemulwuy. The enmity between the two men dated back

10 years, to January 1795, when two Aboriginal women were raped and killed at night not far from Sydney Town. David Collins said that 'another victim, a female of Pe-mul-wy's party … having been secured by the males of a tribe inimical to Pe-mul-wy, dragged her into the woods, where they fatigued themselves with exercising acts of cruelty and lust upon her'.[19]

HMS Buffalo, Ship's Muster Book 1805
Supernumaries at 2/3 allowance no Spirits
Aug 14
Bulldog { D 16th Sept 1805 Norfolk Island
Musquito { D   Natives
Daniel   { D 13th Novr 1805 Derwent
Philip   {   Natives
[D = discharged]

ADM 36, Reel 7018 36/17313, p. 91, Public Record Office, London

On 10 August 1805, Governor King advised Captain John Piper, commandant at Norfolk Island:

The Two Natives Bull Dog and Musquito having been given up by the other Natives as principals in their late Outrages are sent to Norfolk Island where they are to be kept, and if they can be brought to Labour will earn their Food — but as they must not be let to starve for want of Subsistence-they are to be victualled from the Stores —

The storeship HMS *Buffalo* sailed from Sydney Cove on Thursday 22 August 1805, bound for Norfolk Island and Port Dalrymple in Van Diemens Land.[20] Built in the Deptford shipyards on the Thames in London in 1797, *Buffalo* was the first Royal Navy vessel bearing the figurehead of a kangaroo. This novel sight, said Governor John Hunter, 'very much amused the natives, who could have no idea of seeing the animals of their country represented in wood'.[21] Aboard the *Buffalo* were Musquito and Bulldog, being sent as prisoners to Norfolk Island. They were recorded in the ship's muster book as supernumeraries, or passengers surplus to the crew. HMS *Buffalo* reached Norfolk Island on 5 September and Musquito and Bulldog were discharged from the ship on 16 September.

Daniel (Daniel Moowattin), another supernumerary, was a young Aboriginal collector for botanist George Caley, who took him to Van Diemen's Land. *Buffalo* sailed from Norfolk Island on 16 October and reached Hobart Town on 6 November 1805.[22] Daniel was discharged there on 13 November. It is difficult to explain, however, how or why Musquito's brother Philip was given permission to travel on the ship, not as a prisoner but as a free passenger.

Governor King advised Viscount Castlereagh in July 1806 of the 'peaceable demeanour of the Natives of this Country'. Their general good conduct, he wrote, 'will induce me to recall the two who were sent from here to Norfolk Island where they have behaved very quiet and orderly'.[23] Unluckily for Bulldog and Musquito, King did not issue orders for their release before Governor William Bligh succeeded him on 14 August 1806. King referred to the two exiles in a letter advising Bligh on how to handle the Aborigines, whom he acknowledged as 'the real Proprietors of the Soil':

> Much has been said about the propriety of their being compelled to work as Slaves, but as I have ever considered them the real Proprietors of the Soil, I have never suffered any restraint whatever on these lines, or suffered any injury to be done to their person or property — And I should apprehend the best mode of punishment that could be inflicted on them would be expatriating them to some of the other settlements where they might be made to labour as in the case of the two sent to Norfolk in 1804 [sic].[24]

'Bull dog' and 'Muskitoe', described as 'Port Jackson Natives sent to Norfolk by order of Gov[r]. King', were included in the Norfolk Island Annual Return of Inhabitants on 6 August 1812.[25] They remained as prisoners on the island, working as charcoal burners, until 1813, when they were sent to Van Diemen's Land.

Mousquéda ou Mousquita, 1802
Nicolas-Martin Petit (1777–1804)
Pastel, charcoal, pencil and ink
20039.1, Muséum d'Histoire Naturelle,
Le Havre, France

While in Sydney in 1802, Nicolas-Martin Petit (1777–1804), a young artist with the French scientific expedition commanded by Captain Nicolas Baudin, sketched portraits of several Aboriginal men. They included Mousquéda

Detail of Petit's caption

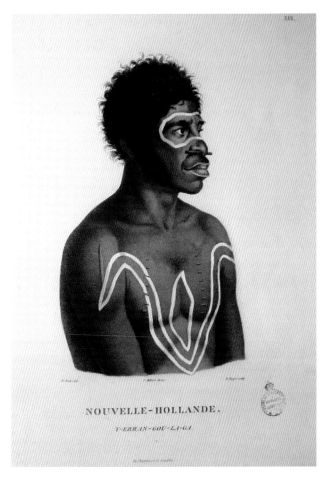

NOUVELLE-HOLLANDE.
Y-ERRAN-GOU-LA-GA.

Nouvelle-Hollande — Y-Erran-Gou-La-Ga, sauvage des environs du port Jackson
[New Holland — Y-Erran-Gou-La-Ga, savage of the Port Jackson area]
Barthelemy Roger (1767–1841) after
Nicolas-Martin Petit (1777–1804)
Engraving
Plate 24, Atlas, *Voyage de découvertes aux terres Australes*, Paris 1811
Mitchell Library, Sydney

or Mousquita, 'painted up' with white circles around his eyes and pipeclay designs on his chest, and a younger man named Toulgra or Bouldogue (Bulldog).

Historian Naomi Parry in the *Australian Dictionary of Biography*[26] and Kristyn Harman in her thesis[27] have confused Petit's Mousquéda with another Aborigine, also called Musquito or Musquetto, who can be identified as a Kameygal, from the north shore of Botany Bay. However, it is more logical that Petit's various portraits of Mousqueda depict the Broken Bay Musquito who was exiled to Norfolk Island and Van Diemen's Land. Petit usually made only one field sketch for a final watercolour portrait of each subject. He spent enough time with one particular group to complete two preliminary sketches each of Mousqueda (Musquito), Toulgra Bouldogue (Bulldog), Musquito's brother Gnoung-a gnoung-a, mour-re-mour-ga (Gnung-a Gnung-a Murremurgan) and Bedgi-Bedgi (Bidgee Bidgee). This was a kinship group, all related by marriage to Bennelong, at that time headman of a clan living near Parramatta. Petit and other members of the French expedition visited Parramatta.

In 1798 the Botany Bay 'Musketer' then aged about 15, guided Benjamin Bowen Carter, surgeon of the American merchant ship *Ann and Hope*, from the 'watering place' (Boora or Long Bay), north of Botany Bay, to 'Frenchmans Garden' or La Perouse. He was rewarded with 'a red waistcoat and some biscuit with which he was highly pleased'.[28]

'Musqueto' took part in a ritual revenge battle in Pitt's Row (Pitt Street) in 1803, when he fended off 64 spears thrown at him 'with rancour and malignancy', of which 17 pierced his shield. 'The 65th and last … entered the calf of his right leg' and the shaft was cut off and extracted.[29] In a 'fit of intoxication' the Kameygal 'Musquito' badly wounded Pigeon (Warroba), a youth from the Shoalhaven, later employed in Tasmania as John Batman's principal tracker. Accordingly, Musquito met Boatswain Maroot (Mirout) early in January 1806 in a combat with clubs outside the Military Barracks in George Street. Musquito knocked down Maroot and split his head open with a crushing blow. That night an ally of Pigeon ambushed Musquito outside the General Hospital at the Rocks and speared him in the chest. The Principal Surgeon Thomas Jamison (or Jamieson) gave orders for him to be taken into the hospital for treatment. Jamison (c. 1753–1811) had been surgeon's first mate aboard HMS *Sirius*.

Musquito lingered for a few days, but before he died named his attacker as Ploge, a Gweagal from the south shore of Botany Bay, also known as Blueit or Blewitt.[30] His body was wrapped in bark and buried in a wooden coffin in Jamison's yard, near the present Jamison Street, Sydney.[31] Jamison left Sydney for England in 1809 and died in 1811. The surgeon's son, Sir John Jamieson, occupied Jamison House when he arrived in Sydney in 1814. It is therefore possible that 'the skeleton of a young man, a native of New South Wales' that Dr Jamieson Junior sent some years later to the Scots anatomist Alexander Monro in Edinburgh was the remains of the Kameygal Musquito.[32]

Bennelong was never an ally of the Botany Bay Musquito, but was related by kinship to his Broken Bay namesake, whose brother Gnung-a Gnung-a Murremurgan had married Bennelong's sister Warreeweer. Bulldog was Bennelong's nephew.

In January 1806, Musquito and Bulldog were prisoners on Norfolk Island.

François Péron (1775–1810), a scientist with Baudin's expedition, studied the Aboriginal people from a physical and anthropological viewpoint. Blind in one eye, Péron had served in the French revolutionary army and studied medicine in Paris. Armed with a portable instrument used to measure human strength, he set out to challenge the notion of the Noble Savage popularised by the philosopher Jean-Jacques Rousseau. The device, called a Dynamomètre or Dynamometer, had been invented in 1798

Nouvelle-Hollande – Toulgra (Bouldogue), 1802
Nicolas-Martin Petit (1777–1804)
Pastel, charcoal, pencil and ink
20043.3
Muséum d'Histoire Naturelle, Le Havre, France

Nouvelle-Hollande, Nlle. Galles du Sud, Ourou-mare, dit Bull-dog par les Anglais, jeune guerrier de la tribu des Gwea-Gal
[New Holland, New South Wales, Ourou-mare, called Bull-dog by the English, young warrior of the Gweagal tribe]
Barthelemy Roger (1767–1841) after Nicolas-Martin Petit (1777–1804)
Engraving
Plate XX, Atlas, Voyage de découvertes aux terres Australes, Paris 1811
Mitchell Library, Sydney

(BELOW) Regnier's Dynamomètre
[Device used by François Péron to measure the strength of Australian Aborigines]
Invented by Edmé Regnier (1751–1823)
From Edmé Regnier, Description et usage du dynamomètre, Paris, 1798:179

by Edmé Regnier (1751–1823). It weighed one kilogram and consisted of an oval steel plate marked with a scale. Pressure was applied by gripping a double steel spring, causing a needle to show a reading on the dial.

AUX TERRES AUSTRALES.   477

TABLE II.

SAUVAGES DE LA NOUVELLE-HOLLANDE.

NUMÉROS des Expériences.	NOMS des INDIVIDUS.	ÂGE.	FORCE des Mains.	FORCE des Reins.	DÉTAILS PARTICULIERS.
		ans.	kilogr.	myriagr.	
1.	COU-DÉ-COU-DÉL.....	10 à 12.	30,0.	10,0.	Joli petit enfant d'une constitution foible.
2.	TOUL-GRA, *dit* BOULDOG	14 15.	31,0.	16,0.	Assez bien conformé, très-vif, très-spirituel, excellent mime.
3.	MO-RO-RÉ...........	16 18.	43,0.	16,0.	Petit, mais assez bien constitué.
4.	CA-POU-ER-RÉ.......	16 18.	45,0.	14,0.	Habitude générale du corps assez forte poar le pays.
5.	EUTÉLOR...........	18 20.	56,0.	15,0.	Brave, audacieux, l'un des plus robustes de sa nation.
6.	OU-ROU-MA-RÉ-GA-LA..	18 20.	47,0.	13,0.	Constitution peu forte; figure sauvage.
7.	OU-ROU-MARÉ........	19 21.	55,0.	19,0.	Bien fait, autant que le type général de la nation peut le permetrre.
8.	ACA-RA-DA PA-RA....	25 28.	44,0.	13,0.	Constitution très-foible; physionomie dure et farouche.
9.	OUI-ROUÉ...........	27 30.	52,0.	16,0.	Torse bien développé; membres grêles; figure fausse et féroce.
10.	OUCA-LA-GA.........	27 30.	58,0.	14,0.	Assez bien fait; physionomie sombre, yeux hagards.
11.	BOURRA-BOURRA......	27 30.	50,0.	13,0.	Court, trapu, beaucoup de poils sur le corps; homme féroce.
12.	PA-RA-MA-RA	30 33.	60,0.	18,0.	Constitution vigoureuse, membres très-alongés; regard cruel.
13.	MOU-GUÉAN.........	30 33.	32,0.	13,0.	Assez bien pris dans sa taille; velu sur tout le corps.
14.	COURÉ-OURÉ-OULOU..	33 35.	55,0.	13,0.	Habitude grêle; membres foibles, ventre saillant.
15.	DAL-RÉ.............	33 35.	46,0.	14,0.	Court, trapn, couleur du corps d'un brun très-foncé.
16.	BÉNIL-LON..........	35 36.	57,0.	16,0.	*Chef;* constitution assez belle, mais un peu grêle.
17.	MA-RA-ORA..........	38 40.	62,0.	15,0.	Barbe très-épaisse; membres très-longs et très-grêles.

Termes moyens des 13 derniers n.ᵒˢ..... { Mains..... .... 51,8 kilogram.
{ Reins................. 14,8 myriagr.

Petit's original pencilled captions to his 1802 field sketches reveal that some of his Aboriginal subjects were wrongly named in the engravings that were subsequently published in Paris in the Atlas of the expedition in 1811 and in a second edition of 1824. These mistakes, never queried by art historians, may be corrected by comparison with Peron's list, published in 1807, recording the names, ages, and physical appearance of 17 men from the Sydney area tested on the Dynamometer.

Peron's list of natives of New Holland

No	Name	Age	Strength of		Particulars
			Hands	Back	
1.	Cou-dé-Cou-dél	10–12	30.0	10.0	Pretty little child of weak constitution
2.	Toul-gra, called Bouldog	14–15	31.0	16.0	Quite well built, very lively, very spiritual; excellent mimic.
3.	Mo-ro-ré	16–18	43.0	16.0	Small, but quite well built.
4.	Ca-pou-er-ré	16–18	45.0	14.0	In general fairly strong for this country.
5.	Eutélor	18–20	56.0	15.0	Confident, bold; one of the sturdiest of his nation.
6.	Ou-rou-Ma-ré-Ga-La	18–20	47.0	13.0	Weak and wild looking.
7.	Ou-rou-Maré	19–21	55.0	19.0	As well built as his nation generally allows.
8.	Aca-ra-da-Pa-ra	25–28	44.0	13.0	Particularly weak stature; hard and wild looking.
9.	Oui-roué	27–30	52.0	16.0	Well-developed torso; thin legs, ferocious and untrustworthy aspect.
10.	Ouca-la-ga	17–30	58.0	14.0	Quite well built; sombre look with haggard eyes.
11.	Bourra-Bourra	27–30	50.0	13.0	Short, stocky, hairy; a ferocious man.
12.	Pa-ra-ma-ra	30–33	60.0	18.0	Athletic appearance, long limbs; merciless look in the eye.
13.	Mou-Guéan	30–33	32.0	13.0	Lean, hairy all over.
14.	Couré-Ouré-Oulou	33–35	55.0	13.0	Thin body, with weak limbs and protruding belly.
15.	Dal-ré	33–35	46.0	14.0	Short, stocky, with deep brown skin colour.
16.	Bénil-lon	35–36	57.0	16.0	The chief; pleasing figure but somewhat thin.
17.	Ma-ra-ora	38–40	62.0	15.0	Heavily bearded with very long and thin limbs.

(OPPOSITE) Aux Terres Australes — Sauvages de la Nouvelle-Hollande Table II from François Péron, *Voyage de découvertes aux terres australes …* Vol. 1, Paris: Chez Arthur Bertrand, 1807:477 Mitchell Library, Sydney.

No. 2 is 'Toul-gra, called Bouldog, age 14–15 … Quite well built, very lively, very spiritual [sic]; excellent mimic'. An engraving of the same person, published in 1811, was captioned 'Ourou-Mare, dit Bull-Dog par les Anglais'. Péron's Table clearly shows that No. 7 'Ou-rou-Maré' is a different person from No 2 'Toul-gra, dit Bouldog'. The error probably occurred because the engraver, Barthelemy Roger, had never visited Australia. By the time of publication, the principal French visitors to Port Jackson in 1802 had died: Baudin at the Ile France (Mauritius) in 1803 and Petit after a fall in 1804. Péron died in 1810.

Barthelemy Roger's engraving in Péron's 1811 Atlas also identified the portrait of Mousquéda or Mosquita as *Y-Erran-Gou-La-Ga*. He might be 'No. 10. 'Ouca-la-ga, age 17–30', described by Péron in his Dynamometer list as 'Quite well built; sombre look with haggard eyes', a description that could apply to Musquito.

Nicolas-Martin Petit had studied in Paris with the famous French classical master Jacques Louis David. In his essay 'Images of Natural Man' (1988), anthropologist Rhys Jones remarked: 'The portraits are beautiful drawings, with individual personalities sensitively depicted. They were obviously posed, under conditions that allowed the artist scope for his skill, and they represent one of the best series of portraits ever done of Australian Aboriginal people.'[33]

Petit added the words '*Toulgra (mère)*' to his drawing of an Aboriginal woman titled *Oui-ré-kine*, indicating that she was the mother of Toulgra Bulldog.[34] William Dawes recorded Oui-ré-kine or Worogan (Crow) as a sister or half-sister of Bennelong.[35] She was the wife of Yeranabie Goruey, son of Maugoran, a leader of the Burramatta (Parramatta clan) who is recorded in Péron's list as 'No. 13 Mou-Guéan, age 30–33 … Lean, hairy all over'.

Petit probably drew some of the men when Péron was testing their strength on the Dynamometer. One man with his long hair wrapped in paperbark strips is captioned Mororé. This corresponds with Péron's 'No. 3. Mo-ro-ré', although the engraving of this subject appears in the *Atlas* as *Cour-Rou-Bari-Gal*.

Van Diemen's Land

'Mosquetto (Port Jackson Native)' was listed as a passenger on the ship Minstrel, 315 tons, which left Norfolk Island on 13 February 1813 and arrived at Port Dalrymple on the Tamar River in Van Diemen's Land on 4 March 1813.[36] *Minstrel* and *Lady Nelson* transported the last settlers and soldiers to leave the island.[37]

Phillip must have heard of Musquito's transfer to Van Diemen's Land, because in May 1813, he attempted to make contact with his brother by enlisting on a whaling voyage to Van Diemen's Land aboard the 110-ton brig *Active*, which twice called at Hobart Town.[38] The ship put out from Hobart to seek black whales in Frederick

Henry Bay, Oyster Bay and other inlets during the spawning season. Thirteen-year-old Joseph Barsden, employed on board as a 'boy', wrote in his journal: 'We procured 80 Tons of oil by Sept. when we ran into Hobart Town to refit and lay in stores for Sydney, w[h]ere we arrived on the 27th of that month'.[39] 'Old Phillip' had faced spears in a punishment ritual after another brother, Gnung-a Gnung-a Murremurgan, was found dead near the Dry Store (present Macquarie Park near Bridge Street, Sydney) in 1809.[40]

Musquito was sent to work as a stock keeper for the wealthy settler and merchant Edward Lord (1781–1859), who came to Van Diemen's Land as a marine lieutenant in February 1804.

In 1814, Phillip and others attempted to secure Musquito's release through official channels. They succeeded in obtaining permission from Governor Lachlan Macquarie to free Musquito and allow him to return to Sydney. The governor's secretary, Thomas Campbell, wrote to Lieutenant Governor Thomas Davey in Hobart:

Secretary's Office, Sydney
17th August 1814

Sir,
Application having been made by some of the Natives of this District on behalf of a Native formerly banished from this by the late Governor King to Norfolk Island and who lately removed from there to Port Dalrymple on the first evacuation of that Island, soliciting that He might be returned to his Native Place, His Excellency has been pleased to Accede to said Solicitation and I have it now in Command to request that you will give Orders for the said Native being embarked for this by the earliest opportunity. — He is called Mosquito, and a Native called Phillip proceeds by this occasion (the Kangaroo) who says he is brother to Mosquito and who is very Solicitous for the return of his Brother, will probably wait upon you, on behalf of Mosquito. —

Thos. Campbell [41]

It is not known if Phillip sailed on the colonial brig *Kangaroo*, which left Sydney in October 1814 and moored in the Tamar in Van Diemen's Land on 5 November. After leaving on 4 January 1815, the *Kangaroo* was forced back into port and sailed again on 26 January 1815, anchoring in Sydney Cove in February.[42] Early in 1815, Phillip was one of the Aboriginal 'settlers' at Bungaree's farm at Georges Head. On 18 July 1815 Old Phillip told Dr Joseph Arnold in Sydney about Bennelong's illness and death.[43]

In October 1817, Lieutenant Governor Sorell sent a further request to Governor Macquarie to repatriate Musquito:

Musquito, a native of Port Jackson, who has been some years in this Settlement and who has also served constantly as a guide with one of the parties, and had been extremely useful and well conducted, also at his own desire goes to Sydney. I beg leave further to solicit Your Excellency's humane consideration of him on account of his useful Services.[44]

However, Musquito remained in Van Diemen's Land and continued to be employed by Lord. The ship *Frederick*, owned or leased by Lord, and commanded by Captain Williams, left Port Jackson on 31 January 1818, for Hobart.[45] A Claims and Demands notice appeared in the *Hobart Town Gazette* on 14 February:

> It being the intention of Mr EDWARD LORD to leave the Colony on the Departure of the ship Frederick, he requests all claims against himself be forthwith furnished — ALSO, his two Servants MUSKITO and JAMES BROWN (natives of these Colonies).

This was disastrous voyage. A report on the same page of the Hobart newspaper said the *Frederick* 'ran out of the river early yesterday morning [Friday 13 February], without a Port Clearance', but was still in sight and was expected to return.[46] The *Frederick* came back to Hobart on Sunday (15 February) and sailed again on Wednesday (18 February) for the Isle of France (Mauritius), with a cargo of 61 head of cattle.[47] After an absence of eight weeks, 'due to the wildness of the weather', the ship returned to Hobart again early in April.[48] It is not known if Musquito and James Brown were still on board. If they were, they must have been anxious to go ashore at Hobart.

Once more en route to Mauritius, the ill-fated *Frederick* ran aground and broke in two on Cape Flinders near Stanley Island in Torres Strait on 1 August 1818. Of the crew of 27 men, 22 had launched a longboat, but were never heard of again. Captain Phillip Parker King and his crew on HMS *Mermaid* sighted the wreck of the *Frederick* in July 1819, but found no trace of survivors.[49]

There is conclusive proof that Musquito was not on the wrecked ship in Torres Strait, because on 10 September 1818, Musquito and John McGill tracked and came close to capturing the notorious bushranger Michael Howe thousands of kilometres away in Van Diemen's Land. In sworn testimony to the Reverend Robert Knopwood in Hobart, McGill said that, while he was out hunting kangaroos at the Fat Doe River (now the Clyde River, near Bothwell), Howe came to his hut, smashed his musket and left with his three blankets, two shirts and other articles. McGill stated:

> As soon as we saw him I and Muskato [Musquito] rushed up, Howe picked up his fowling piece and was away, leaving behind his knapsack and several other articles. Muskato fired at him. I tried but my piece missed fire. He then made his escape across the river. He called his dogs. We saw no more of him. We then returned to where Michael Howe's fire was and took up his knapsack, pistols, tin kettle, three dogs and several other articles — everything but two blankets.[50]

Howe was captured and killed one month later, on 21 October 1818. Sorell reported to Governor Lachlan Macquarie in Sydney on 18 November 1818:

> [Item 8] … the Chief and only remaining Bush-ranger of the old Gang Michael Howe, was killed

on the 21st ult. — He had lately robbed several Stock-Men's Huts, and his Dogs, pistols, knapsack etc. were taken from him about a Month before by McGill … accompanied by Musquito, a Native of Port Jackson.[51]

Musquito was never rewarded with a passage home to New South Wales, 'a promise, unhappily forgotten', as John West wrote in his *History of Tasmania*.[52] He joined the Tame Mob, a group of Palawa (Aboriginal Tasmanians) associated with the Oyster Bay tribe. The Reverend William Horton, who met Musquito at Pitt Water in June 1823, said the Palawa were 'governed by a Native of Port Jackson named Muskitoo', who had been made a leader because of his 'superior skill and muscular strength'.[53]

According to the *Hobart Town Gazette*, 200 Aborigines appeared towards the end of October 1824 at the property of James Hobbs, near York Plains, where they killed a stock keeper named James Doyle. The report continued:

> Since writing the above, we have if in our power to state, that another poor fellow has been speared by Musquito at Pitt Water. — The man it seems was enticed from his house by Musquito cooying [crying cooee] till he brought him within his reach, when he drove the spear into his back, while returning to get him some bread.[54]

George Arthur, who replaced William Sorell as lieutenant governor of Van Diemen's Land on 14 May 1824, offered a reward for the capture of Musquito. West wrote:

> Teague, an aboriginal boy, brought up by Dr. Luttrell, was dispatched with two constables. They overtook Musquito at Oyster Bay: he resisted, but was shot in the groin, and being unarmed was captured, with two women, and conveyed to Hobart Town.[55]

In November 1824, Mosquito was convicted of the murder of William Hollyoak at Grindstone Bay and charged with abetting the murder of a Tahitian servant named Mammora, whose body was found in a creek. He was sentenced to death. Mosquito, with a Tasmanian Aborigine called Black Jack who had been convicted of murder, and six bushrangers were hanged in Hobart Town on 25 February 1825.[56]

After his sentence, Mosquito, in conversation with his gaoler, Mr Bisdee, was reported to have said:

> 'Hanging no good for black fellow.'
> Mr. Bisdee. 'Why not as good for black fellow as for white fellow, if he kills a man?'
> 'Very good for white fellow, for he used to it.'[57]

6 Dual: sentenced and reprieved

In 1814 a young Aboriginal man named Doual (Dual) accompanied Hamilton Hume and his brother John on an overland trip across the Razorback Range and through the rugged Bargo Brush to country near Berrima and Bong Bong, New South Wales. The redheaded Hamilton, born at Parramatta was just 17 years of age.[1] The Reverend William Ross of Goulburn later described Dual as 'a black boy, a native of Appin'.[2]

Two years later, in April 1816, Dual, from the Cowpastures area near Camden, was captured by soldiers at Appin and banished to Van Diemen's Land for seven years by Governor Lachlan Macquarie. His early arrest might well have saved Dual's life.

'Dewall' (Dual) and his brother Yellaman or Yellowman were included in a list of 'Names of Hostile bad Natives! — as per Mr. McArthur', written in April 1816 by Governor Macquarie, who had sent troops to put down an Aboriginal uprising at the frontiers of settlement. John Macarthur, the influential army officer and pastoralist, was in England at this time and could not have been the author of the list. Three stockkeepers employed by his wife Elizabeth Macarthur had been killed by Aborigines and she is more likely to have provided the names. John Macarthur returned to Sydney in September 1817 after an absence of more than eight years.

Names of Hostile bad Natives!
    As per Mr. McArthur
    1 – Murrah — very bad — X
    2 – Wâllâh — do.
    3 – Yellaman — do.
    4 – Dewall —
    5 – Battagallie.
    6   Daniel — }
    7   Coggie — } All inspected
    8   Mary-Mary}

    X This is the same Man who speared Mr. McArthur's Overseer, and who threw Spears at the Soldiers at Cox's River some time since.[3]

Dual and Yellaman were prominent men of the Murringong clan, which occupied the Cowpastures Plains southwest of Sydney.[4] In the Sydney coastal language *Doo-ul* meant 'a short spear'.[5]

In 1816, after two years of drought, the Gundungurra mountain warriors, hungry for ripe corn, attacked settlers in the outlying Cowpastures district, burned their houses and sheds, speared their cattle and plundered their crops, forcing some to abandon their farms. They killed four of George Thomas Palmer's men on the Nepean River as well as the three men who worked for Mrs Macarthur at Camden. A militia of 40 settlers armed with muskets, pistols, pitchforks and pikes clashed with an Aboriginal war party at Upper Camden and retreated under a shower of spears and stones.[6]

The Appin Massacre

While satisfied with his efforts at 'civilising' the friendly Aborigines around Port Jackson, Governor Macquarie determined on a tough stand against those waging war against the settlers. Macquarie told Earl Bathurst in a dispatch to London dated 8 March 1816: 'It is my Intention, as soon as I shall have Ascertained What Tribes Committed the late Murders and Depredations, to send a Strong Detachment of Troops to drive them to a Distance from the Settlements of the White Men'.[7] Hearing of the punitive expedition, Doctor Charles Throsby of Glenfield Farm near Liverpool, wrote a personal letter, dated 5 April 1816, to chief police magistrate D'arcy Wentworth, defending three of the alleged Aboriginal ring-leaders, Bitugally, Duel (Dual) and Yelloming (Yellaman). Throsby said steps should be taken to prevent friendly natives being injured. He told Wentworth that the previous day John Warby and Bush Jackson had taken Boodburry [Budbury], another Cowpastures man, from his farm. 'Boodburry and the others returned shortly afterwards, apparently under a considerable impression of fear, which I have as much as possible endeavoured to dissipate …'[8]

In a document dated 9 April 1816, Macquarie included Warby, Bundle and Budbury among 'White and Black Guides' in Captain James Wallis's detachment, which marched from Sydney to the Airds and Appin districts on 10 April 1816. This Bundle, like Dual, was from the Cowpastures and not the seafaring Aboriginal man also called Bondel or Bundle. Other Aboriginal guides were Bidgee Bidgee and Harry, who joined William Pawson [Parsons] in Captain Schaw's detachment, ordered to Parramatta, Windsor and the Kurry Jong [Kurrajong] Brush, the Grose River and the Nepean. Nurragingy (Creek Jemmy) and Colebee joined Schaw at Windsor, while Tindall and Bush Jackson were assigned to Lieutenant Charles Dawe's detachment bound for the Cowpastures.[9]

Governor Macquarie's orders were clear. The three military detachments were to 'proceed to those Districts most infested and Annoyed by them on the banks and Neighbourhoods of the rivers Nepean, Hawkesbury and Grose'. They were to take as many Aboriginal prisoners as possible. Those who resisted or fled were to be shot and their bodies hung 'on the highest trees and in the clearest parts of the forest'.[10] In his journal that day, Macquarie wrote that he felt compelled, though unwillingly, to chasten the tribes and to 'inflict terrible and exemplary punishments upon them'.[11]

Bundle and Budbury were reluctant to track their own people and John Warby said he would take no responsibility for them. Wallis said Warby 'winked' when they both absconded on the night of 11 April. 'I was exceedingly annoyed', wrote Wallis. Warby disappeared on 13 April and returned the following day, but refused to cooperate further.[12] As usual the Aboriginal warriors were elusive, disappearing into the bush as the military force approached. However, Lieutenant Dawes's troops, guided by Tindall from the Cowpastures, killed an unknown number of Aborigines and captured a 14-year-old boy.

In 1814, as Hume's guide, Dual had been regarded as a 'friendly' Aborigine. In the conflict of 1816, he was considered to be 'hostile' and sought refuge at the farm of Hume's uncle, John Kennedy, who had settled at Appin. Lieutenant Adamson George Parker, who commanded a detachment of the 46th Regiment, captured Dual, Yellaman and Battany Quick at the farm. Parker filed his report of the incident on 9 May 1816:

> I marched to Mr. Woodhouses on the Morning of the 2[n]d of April and received the same Evening Duale and Quick [Battany Quick] two Hostile Natives who had been taken on Mr. Kennedy's Farm in the Morning. On the following day I sent Duale to Liverpool in charge of McCudden the Constable and detained Quick, who had volunteer'd to show me that Body of Natives to which he belong'd …
>   On the 5th I arrived in Sydney and lodg'd my Prisoners in the Gaol immediately.[13]

In his report, Captain Wallis graphically described how his detachment had stumbled upon a sleeping Aboriginal camp in the moonlight on 17 April 1816 and the massacre that followed:

> A little after one o'clock we marched. A few of my men who wandered on heard a child cry. I formed line ranks, entered and pushed up through a thick brush towards the precipitous banks of a deep rocky creek. The dogs gave the alarm and the natives fled over the cliffs. A smart firing now ensued. It was moonlight. The grey dawn of the moon appearing so dark as to be able to discover their figures bounding from rock to rock. I regret to say some had been shot and others met their fate while rushing in despair over the precipice. Twas a melancholy but necessary duty I was employed upon.
>   Fourteen dead bodies were counted in different directions, the bodies of Durelle and Kanabygal I had difficulty getting up the precipice. I regretted the death of an old native Balyin and the unfortunate women and children from the rocky place they fell in. I found it would be almost impossible to bury those.[14]

Two women and children were captured. Following Macquarie's orders, the bodies of the dead men were hung up in the trees 'to strike the survivors with the greatest Terror'.

Evidently acting without orders, Lieutenant Parker severed the heads of Kanabaygal and Durelle. This fact was hidden until January 2002, when the skull of an Aboriginal man recorded as Canimbeiglei (Kanabaygal) was returned from Scotland to the National Museum of Australia. Documentation reveals that Lieutenant Parker passed Kanabaygal's skull to Mr Patrick Hill, a Royal Navy surgeon. Hill, superintendent of convicts on the transport ship *Atlas*, left New South Wales on 28 October 1816 aboard the ship *Willerby*. In England, Hill gave Kanabaygal's skull to Sir George Mackenzie (1780–1848), author of *Illustrations on Phrenology* (Edinburgh, 1820), who deposited it in the University of Edinburgh. The skull of an unidentified person with a similar history, probably that of Durelle, was also returned.[15]

Royal Navy Lieutenant Richard Sadleir mentioned that Hill had supplied an Aboriginal skull to Mackenzie in written evidence to the Legislative Council 'Committee on the Aborigines Question' in Sydney in 1833. Sadleir stated that Aborigines were 'capable of intellectual improvement', adding that 'Sir George McKenzie [*sic*], a celebrated phrenologist, having received a skull from Patrick Hill, Esq., speaks of their intellectual abilities as by no means despicable …'[16] According to the *Edinburgh Review*, Mackenzie published an illustration 'drawn from the skull of Carnimbeigle, a chief of New South Wales, who was killed by a party of the 46th Regiment in 1816'.[17]

William Byrne, whose widowed mother married William Sykes of Appin, was a child aged eight in 1816. The Sykes's property 'Mount Briton' adjoined the farms of William Broughton and Byrne's brother-in-law John Kennedy. Many years later, Byrne remembered three Aboriginal rebels being beheaded. He said that soldiers 'ran a portion of the tribe into a drive, shot sixteen of them, and hanged three on McGee's Hill. They afterwards cut off the heads and brought them to Sydney, where the Government paid them 30s [shillings] and a gallon of rum each for them.'[18] The *Sydney Gazette* confirmed the Aboriginal deaths in what is now called the 'Appin Massacre':

> Durelle and Canibigal were among 14 Aborigines killed on 17 April 1816 by Captain Wallis's party on Broughton's Farm. Two women and children were taken prisoner.[19]

In honour of the King's Birthday on 4 June 1816, Governor Macquarie released 15 Aboriginal men and women suspected of taking part in the hostilities 'with the exception of D̲ual who is still retained in prison'.[20] On 30 July 1816 Macquarie issued a Public Notice and Order officially banishing 'a Native Black Man of this Colony, called and known by the Name of Dewal or Dual'. Macquarie waived the

HOBART TOWN IN 1817.

Hobart Town in 1817 Kangaroo Govt. Schooner, Charles Jeffreys (1782–1826), Lithograph, SSV6/1817/1, Mitchell Library, Sydney.

death sentence, which he commuted to 'Banishment from this Part of His Majesty's Territory of New South Wales to Dalrymple, in Van Diemen's Land, for the full Term of Seven years'.[21]

Macquarie also informed Major James Stewart, commandant at Port Dalrymple, of Dual's sentence. 'You will accordingly order the said Native Convict (Dewall) to be kept at Hard Labour and to be fed in the same manner as the other Convicts.'[22] Dual was sent to the Port Dalrymple settlement aboard the armed colonial brig *Kangaroo*, commanded by Lieutenant Charles Jeffreys, which left Sydney on 5 August 1816.[23] There are no records of his activities in Van Diemen's Land, but it is likely that Dual was called on to track escaped convicts and bushrangers.

Two years later, on 1 December 1818, Governor Macquarie's secretary John Thomas Campbell wrote from Sydney to William Sorell, Lieutenant Governor of Van Diemen's Land, requesting that Dual be 'sent hither by the earliest opportunity'.[24] Sorell replied on 2 January 1819:

> The Man Dual also requested to be sent up, having been resident at Port Dalrymple; I gave directions to Major Cimetiere [Cimitiere] to send him up by the first conveyance from thence, and I hope he will have arrived.[25]

Dual left Port Dalrymple on 1 August 1818 aboard the schooner *Sindbad* commanded by Captain John Payne, which anchored in Sydney on 25 August.[26] On 30 January 1819 Campbell informed Major Gilbert Cimitiere, the new commander at Port Dalrymple, that Dual had arrived in Sydney 'a few days ago'.[27] He was reunited with his brother Yellaman, who had been outlawed by Governor Macquarie in 1816 after the frontier troubles.[28]

Less than three months later, on 25 April 1819, Dual joined two Gundungurra men who accompanied Charles Throsby (1771–1828) and his party on a journey of exploration from Camden to the Campbell River near Bathurst.[29] It is likely that Throsby, who had defended Dual and Yellaman in 1816, used his influence to persuade Governor Macquarie to bring Dual back from Van Diemen's Land. In a letter to Macquarie, Throsby said he was accompanied by 'Coocooyong, Duel [Dual] and Bian, Natives, the former as Guide, the two others as Interpreters'. Throsby's party passed Lake Burra Burra, 10 kilometres north of the present Taralga on 4 May 1819.[30] According to Macquarie, Coocooyong (Cookoogung) and Bian (Byan or Bhoohan) were the sons of Nagaray of the Burra-Burra clan of the Gundungurra, who was aged about 70 in 1820. The governor described Bian as 'a very fine intelligent lad'.[31]

Cookoogung's totem was probably the bronze cuckoo (*Chalcites* species), recorded as *cookooeang* in the Gundungurra Vocabulary compiled by surveyor Thomas Mitchell.[32]

Three years after his exile to Van Diemen's Land, Dual was thoroughly rehabilitated. Governor Macquarie named Cookoogong chief of the Burra Burra and rewarded Dual and Bian with metal breastplates, clothing and bedding.[33] A report in *The Times*, London, on 1 November 1819, mentioned the part played by the 'two native guides, Cookoogonn [*sic*], chief of the Burrah-burrah tribe, and Dual' in Throsby's expedition.[34]

According to William Macarthur, Dual's brother Yellaman died of influenza in 1820.[35] Dual and another brother, Cowpasture Jack (Nullanan), guided John Kennedy and Hamilton Hume, who set out from Appin to select land at the Shoalhaven in June 1822. At Berkeley, near Wollongong, they were joined by Udaa-Duck, employed by landowner Robert Jenkins, who went to Lake Bathurst with them.[36]

James Atkinson (1795–1834), formerly principal clerk at the Colonial Secretary's Office in Sydney, was the author of *An Account of the State of Agriculture & Grazing in New South Wales*, published in London in 1826. It is possible that Dual was one of three Aboriginal guides depicted in an illustration in Atkinson's book. Atkinson referred to the valuable services of 'black Natives … as guides, they having the most intimate knowledge of the localities of the country'. He added: 'I have performed many long journeys in this manner myself, without any other attendants than two black Natives, on whose fidelity I could rely.'[37] Atkinson knew Hamilton Hume and Captain William Hovell, who stopped to have breakfast with him at 'Oldbury',

An Exploring Party in New South Wales, 1826, Artist unknown (possibly Richard Read Senior), Hand-coloured aquatint, Plate 1 in James Atkinson, *An Account of the State of Agriculture & Grazing in New South Wales*, London: J. Cross, 1826:137, Original SSV*Expl/1, Mitchell Library, Sydney.

his property near Bong Bong, on 7 October 1824, at the start of their overland expedition to Westernport in Port Phillip.

Jules Dumont d'Urville (1790–1842), commander of the French corvette *Coquille*, met 'Douel' in 1824 at a 'great gathering' of Aboriginal clans assembled near the present Central Railway in Sydney for a ritual payback combat over the death of Bennelong's son Dicky one year earlier. Those taking part included clans from the Hunter River, Emu Plains, Broken Bay and Illawarra. D'Urville described Dual as 'one of those robust savages, whose vigorous physique had already surprised me'. He gave him a shilling for answering 'questions put to him in English':

> So I learned he was called Douel, and that he was chief of the bellicose Mericon [Murringong] tribe that lives on the Cowpastures Plains; he commanded sixteen warriors, all as strong as he was.

Dual, who did not take part in the combat, told d'Urville that his people did not eat human flesh, 'but the mountain tribes have no scruples about it'.[38]

Dual and 'Blang' (Bian) were among the 'chiefs' who attended the annual Native Conference at Parramatta in January 1826, seated at the head of their individual clans.[39] In 1833, Dual, said to be aged 40 and from Camden, collected blankets at Stonequarry (Picton).[40]

In his undated *Memorandum*, William Macarthur said:

Dual was killed by some natives from Illawarra 5 Islands [Wollongong area] in a fight between the tribes and the Nonaguray [Norongeragal] Natives — a man of the latter tribe had put a five islander to death they came up to avenge it, & falling in with Dual killed him.[41]

Writing in 1892, Richard Hill said the Norongeragal were located at Bottle Forest (present Heathcote), near the Royal National Park, south of Sydney.[42]

7 Tristan: a runaway in Rio

Tristan, an Aboriginal boy aged five, sailed for Norfolk Island in 1795 with his guardian, the Reverend Samuel Marsden (1764–1838). This was Tristan's first sea voyage, but not his last.

Samuel Marsden and his wife Elizabeth, who arrived in Sydney in March 1794, took Tristan into their home shortly afterwards. They usually referred to him in correspondence as their 'native boy'. Marsden, the second chaplain of the colony of New South Wales, moved from Sydney Town to Parramatta on 13 July 1794.[1] Memorably described by Robert Hughes in *The Fatal Shore* (1987) as 'a grasping Evangelical missionary with heavy shoulders and the face of a petulant ox', Marsden became known as 'The Flogging Parson' for the harsh punishments he ordered as a magistrate.[2]

James Elder and John Youl from the London Missionary Society, who visited Parramatta in March 1801, believed that Marsden 'took him [Tristan] by the Consent of his Parents, when he was very young'.[3] Marsden himself wrote about 'one of my boys … taken from his mother's breast'.[4] However, according to the Reverend Thomas Hassall, who said he had been the boy's 'school fellow & play mate', Marsden had found the infant in the bush after his mother was '<u>shot</u> by the Whites'. Hassall and Tristan both attended the school run by the missionary Reverend John Pascoe Crook at Parramatta.[5]

In a letter to his employer Sir Joseph Banks, botanist George Caley said Tristan was 'of the inland extraction'. Caley said Tristan suffered from a 'scald head … which is very common with many of them'.[6] Tristan's scalp had probably been burnt in a campfire.

Samuel Marsden planned to celebrate marriages and baptise settlers and convicts on Norfolk Island. They left Sydney Cove on 21 June 1795 aboard the 170-ton armed snow *Fancy*, commanded by Captain Edgar Dell, with a cargo of Indian rice and dholl (*dhal*) for the settlement.[7] Tristan's presence from 2 July to 1 August 1795 was recorded in the *Norfolk Island Victualling Book*, kept by Philip Gidley King, in which he is described, under the heading *Free People*, as a 'New Hollander. From whence — Port Jackson. Whither — Port Jackson'.[8]

Philip Gidley King , Norfolk Island — Lieut Governor, *Victualling Book*, 1792–1796 , *'2 July 1795 Tristan Maumby. New Hollander D. Aug 1ˢᵗ 1795'*, A 1958 / CY 3467, Mitchell Library, Sydney.

King entered the boy's name as 'Tristan Maumby', while Thomas Hassall wrote his name as 'Mambe'.[9] Moumbi, according to linguist RH Mathews (1901), meant 'quail'.[10] This was probably the totem name he adopted. After an absence of 11 weeks, the *Fancy* returned to Sydney on 3 September 1795. She made the passage to Norfolk Island in six days, but on the return voyage, heavy gales kept the ship out to sea for one month. On 28 August, strong winds almost drove the *Fancy* ashore on the south head of Broken Bay, north of Sydney.[11]

In the following years Tristan was taught to read and write and was trained as a servant in the Marsden household. In a letter dated 1 May 1796, Elizabeth Marsden told her friend Mary Stokes in London:

> I have also a little Native Boy, who takes up part of my attention — He is about six years old — and now begins to read English and wait at Table — and I hope at some future period he may be an useful member of Society — He has no Inclination to go among the natives, and has quite forgot their manners.[12]

'My native boy, whom I had now for more than four years improves much; he is become [of] use in the family; can speak the English language very well; and has begun to read', Samuel Marsden told his patron, the anti-slavery campaigner William Wilberforce, three years later.[13] Tristan was then nine years old.

Elder and Youl were impressed when they met 'Samuel Christian' (Tristan) at Parramatta in 1801. They said Tristan, then aged 11, had learned to speak English fluently, could read well and was beginning to write, but 'sometimes he runs to the Bush for the purpose of seeing his parents, as he says, but he cannot converse with them, being ignorant of his Mother Tongue'.[14]

At the age of 17, Tristan joined the Reverend Samuel Marsden, his wife and family on the storeship HMS *Buffalo* on their voyage to England. Philip Gidley King, the returning governor of New South Wales, his wife Anna Josepha and their children were also passengers. The ship left the wharf at Sydney Cove at 2.30 pm on Tuesday 10 February 1807 and was saluted by HMS *Porpoise* as she passed.[15]

Mrs Anna Josepha King kept a journal of the voyage, recording the frequent spells of illness suffered by Governor King and Samuel Marsden. Plagued with rats that ate the passengers' provisions, *Buffalo* crossed the southern Pacific Ocean, passing the Penantipodes Islands on Sunday 7 March and surviving a fireball, heavy seas, strong winds and the loss of her topmast. 'We made Cape Horn nine weeks from Port Jackson — supposed to be a very fine passage', Mrs King observed. Her journal ends on 24 May as the ship arrived at the entrance to the harbour of Rio de Janeiro. She does not mention Tristan.[16]

Governor King had arranged a pardon for his convict secretary James Hardy Vaux, a self-confessed swindler and thief, who complained: 'I was employed from morning till night in copying and arranging Captain King's papers, of which he had several large trunks full'. Vaux's duties on the ship included tutoring King's daughter, Marsden's two children, and Tristan, 'a native boy about fourteen, who had been brought up in the family of Mr. Marsden'. Vaux continued:

> This youth had received the rudiments of a good education … He could read and write tolerably well … but unhappily during our stay at Rio de Janeiro he absconded from the house of his protectors, in consequence of some chastisement for misconduct, and notwithstanding every exertion was used, he could not be recovered before the ship's departure.[17]

After an argument, Tristan ran away from the house in which the Marsdens were staying in Rio de Janeiro. Thomas Hassall, who married the Marsdens' daughter Ann, said that while Tristan was on board HMS *Buffalo* he had been 'thrown in the way of temptation and got drunk for which he was punished — At Rio de Janeiro he robbed his Master of a considerable sum of Money & ran off'.[18] The ship left Rio without Tristan on 12 August 1807 and finally reached England on 8 November 1807.

Writing from Hull, a distressed Elizabeth Marsden broke the news about Tristan in a letter to Rowland Hassall dated 9 January 1808.

> Poor Tristan ran away at Rio three weeks before we sailed and we could never hear of him … we had a great deal of trouble with him … Spirits was [*sic*] so cheap — that he was constantly tipsy — and his Master punished him and he went off … I am greatly afraid he will never do any good for himself.[19]

Marsden's insistence in training him for domestic duties might have helped Tristan avoid slavery, poverty or imprisonment. He would not have looked out of place in Rio de Janeiro. Writing to Sir Joseph Banks in 1809, George Caley said: 'The native boy that Mr. Marsden took with him to England … has lost all his native customs and may be ranked as a European, excepting in his features'.[20]

Samuel Marsden spent several days in Rio de Janeiro on his return voyage from England on the convict transport ship *Ann*. He wrote to John Stokes from Rio on 1 December 1809, saying he had found two 'Hives of Bees' that he intended to take to Sydney. He made no reference to Tristan or to any attempt to search for him.[21]

In Rio Janeiro, looking towards the Entrance, 1787, William Bradley (c. 1787–1833), Watercolour
From William Bradley, *A Voyage to new South Wales*, 1802+, ML Safe 1/14, Mitchell Library, Sydney.

John Piper (1773–1851) first arrived in Sydney as an ensign in the New South Wales Corps on the convict transport ship *Pitt* in 1792. Samuel Marsden, his wife Elizabeth and Tristan were all on friendly terms with the charismatic young officer. 'Tristan begs me to say he feels himself highly offended that you have never once mentioned his name [in letters]', Elizabeth Marsden wrote from Parramatta in July 1804 to Piper, then commandant at Norfolk Island.[22] On 15 August 1804, Elizabeth wrote again to Piper, confiding her deep grief over the death of her son John, who had been scalded in her kitchen one year earlier.[23]

Piper was promoted to captain in 1806 while on Norfolk Island. In September 1811 he resigned and sailed for London. In May 1813, he was appointed Naval Officer at Port Jackson and embarked on the male convict transport ship *General Hewitt*, which left Portsmouth on 26 August 1813. Built in Calcutta in 1811, *General Hewitt* was a large, three-masted East India Company vessel, 157 feet (47.8 metres) long, with 14 guns and a capacity of 973 tons. She carried 300 prisoners, a detachment of 70 soldiers of the 46th (South Devon) Regiment, a crew of 104 men and 15 women and five children who were free passengers.

It was a nightmare voyage for the convicts, who were chained in irons below deck for weeks at a time when the ship was in port. Dysentery soon broke out and 12 prisoners had died by the time they reached Madeira. When the convict quarters were being fumigated three weeks before reaching Rio, a squall drenched the bedding airing on the deck and it was thrown overboard, leaving each prisoner with only one blanket for the rest of the voyage.[24] On 17 November 1813, *General Hewitt* reached Rio de Janeiro, where she stayed for 15 days. The convicts, most of them sick and half starved, were locked below decks.

When the ship reached Port Jackson, 30 convicts had died of dysentery and four of typhus. 'The Troops are healthy, but the convicts on board the General Hewitt have been and are very sickly', wrote Governor Lachlan Macquarie.[25] Among the survivors were two men who would make their mark on the colony, Joseph Lycett, 'Portrait and miniature painter, aged 35', and Francis Greenway, reprieved from a death sentence for forgery, who would become Australia's first architect.

'A few years after a Gentleman to whom he was known found him [Tristan] and brought him back to N.S. Wales in a … miserable condition', wrote Thomas Hassall. The Reverend JB Marsden (no relation to Samuel Marsden), in *Life and Work of Samuel Marsden* (1913), confirmed that this gentleman was Captain John Piper, who recognised Tristan when he went ashore at Rio and took him home aboard the *General Hewitt*, which anchored in Port Jackson on 7 February 1814. In stating that 'The boy ran away from Mr. Marsden, when returning from England in 1810', JB Marsden misrepresented Tristan's actions.[26] This was not the case, because Tristan ran away in 1807 at Rio while the Marsden family was on the way to England.

Thomas Hassall was horrified by a 'sight frightful to behold' when he visited his old school friend at the General Hospital in Sydney, where he had been taken on arrival. Tristan was desperately ill, with bulging eyes and sweat pouring from his head and neck. He cried out: 'God be merciful to me a vile miserable sinner'. It is likely that Tristan had contracted dysentery or another disease on the ship from Rio de Janeiro. He died the following day at the age of 24 and was buried in the Old Church Yard (site of Sydney Town Hall).[27]

8 Gnung-a Gnung-a in North America and Hawaii

In the last decade of the eighteenth century an Australian Aboriginal man crossed the vast Pacific Ocean to North America and returned to Sydney. From the deck of an English storeship he glimpsed many strange places, visiting Norfolk Island, Hawaii, Nootka Sound (now Vancouver, Canada) and the Spanish colonies of Santa Barbara and San Diego on the Californian coast.

The man was Gnung-a Gnung-a Murremurgan, whose wife Warreeweer was the younger sister of the Wangal leader Woollarawarre Bennelong, at that time being feted in London society. The distance Gnung-a Gnung-a traversed was some 16 000 miles as the crow flies, but much further in a sailing ship driven by unpredictable winds.

The Hawaiian King Kamehameha was so impressed by the good-natured, handsome Gnung-a Gnung-a that he wanted to buy him, offering in exchange canoes, weapons and curiosities, but Gnung-a Gnung-a was anxious to return to Warreeweer and his people in New South Wales.

On the first day he ventured into the English settlement at Sydney Cove in November 1790, Gnung-a

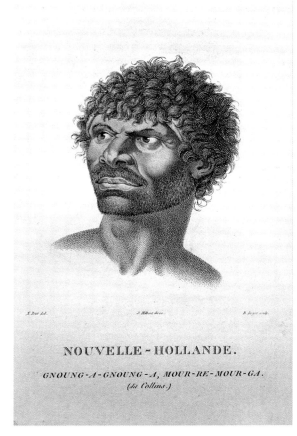

NOUVELLE - HOLLANDE.

GNOUNG-A-GNOUNG-A, MOUR-RE-MOUR-GA.
(dit Collins.)

Nouvelle Hollande — Gnoung-a gnoung-a, mour-re-mour-ga (dit Collins)
Barthelmy Roger (1767–1841) after Nicolas-Martin Petit (1777–1804)
Engraving
Plate 21, *Atlas*, François Péron, *Voyage de découvertes aux terres Australes* … Paris 1811, Mitchell Library, Sydney

Gnung-a adopted the name 'Collins' from Acting Judge Advocate David Collins, who often mentions him in *An Account of the English Colony in New South Wales*, published in London in 1789. In the language spoken by the Eora, *damuna* meant 'exchange' and *damoly* or *tamooly* described the act of exchanging a name with a friend. The person with whom you exchanged your name became your *damelian* or namesake.[1] 'This interchange of names we found is a constant symbol of friendship among them', observed Captain Watkin Tench.[2]

The stargazing William Dawes, a marine lieutenant, engineer, explorer, linguist and astronomer, recorded *Anganángan* and *Angan-angan* in 1790 in the first small notebook he used to record words and phrases from the Indigenous Language.[3] His name might be derived from the word for the bone worn through the septum of the nose by initiated men, given by Collins as *gnah-noong*.

Gnung-a Gnung-a was the principal corpse-bearer when his friend Ballooderry (Leatherjacket Fish), a Burramattagal (from the Parramatta River clan west of Sydney), was buried in Governor Phillip's garden near Bennelong Point, close by the shore of Sydney Cove, on 17 December 1791. In a cross-cultural funeral organised by Bennelong, Ballooderry was wrapped in his English jacket and a blanket and laid in his bark canoe with a spear, pronged fishing spear, *womera* (spear-thrower) and his initiation waistband. Bennelong highly approved of the performance of the marine drummers, who beat a tattoo as Ballooderry was interred.[4] Gnung-a Gnung-a also dug and cleared the site for the funeral pyre of Bennelong's wife Barangaroo, who was cremated after her death that year.[5]

It was the idea of Major Francis Grose, acting governor of New South Wales after the departure of Arthur Phillip in 1792, to embark 'a native of this country' on His Majesty's storeship *Daedalus* 'for the purpose of acquiring our language', wrote David Collins. 'He was a man of more gentle disposition than most of his associates; and from the confidence he placed in us, very readily undertook the voyage, although he left behind him a young wife (a sister of Bennillong, who accompanied Governor Phillip) of whom he always appeared extremely fond.'[6]

The 350-ton brig *Daedalus* was ordered to resupply provisions for the expedition to the north-west coast of North America commanded by Captain George Vancouver (1757–1798) in the Royal Navy ships HMS *Discovery* and HMS *Chatham*. Vancouver, a former midshipman with the famous navigator Captain James Cook on his second and third voyages, had been instructed to complete Cook's survey of the west coast of North America. He was also to investigate the North American fur trade, based on the exploitation of beavers (*Castor Canadensis*) and sea otters (*Enhydra lutris*).[7]

The 337-ton sloop *Discovery* and the 131-ton armed tender *Chatham*, both smaller vessels than *Daedalus*, sailed from Falmouth in Cornwall on 1 April 1791 via Teneriffe, Cape Town and the Indian Ocean to south-western Australia, where Vancouver named and explored King George III Sound (now Albany,

H.M.S. *Daedalus,* John Bayly after Lt Evans, Aquatint, hand-coloured, PAD 6003, National Maritime Museum, Greenwich.

Western Australia). The two ships coasted Van Diemen's Land and New Zealand and entered the Pacific Ocean, stopping at Tahiti and Hawaii. Vancouver began his meticulous survey of the Pacific coast of North America, which he named 'New Albion', by circumnavigating and exploring the large island that now bears his name.

On 29 August 1792, Captain Vancouver appointed James Hanson, a lieutenant aboard HMS *Chatham,* to command *Daedalus,* after learning that the previous commander Richard Hergest had been killed in Hawaii. Returning from North America to Port Jackson, Hanson stopped at the North Island of New Zealand, where he abducted two Maoris, Tuki and Huri, who were to be taken to Norfolk Island in the hope that they could demonstrate how to process flax. The storeship reached Sydney on 19 April 1793 and unloaded a cargo that included 70 hogs brought from Tahiti.

HMS *Daedalus,* with Gnung-a Gnung-a Murremurgan on board, sailed out of Port Jackson on 1 July 1793, passing west of the Society Islands (French Polynesia) and anchored in Owhyee (Hawaii) on 1 September 1793. The ship left Hawaii one week later 'after procuring some refreshments among those islands'.

The *Daedalus* reached Nootka Sound at dusk on 8 October 1793, but missed a rendezvous with Vancouver's ships, which had already embarked for Monterey. 'She anchored in Friendly Cove the next morning; and having obtained a supply of wood, water, and other necessaries, Mr. Hanson sailed from thence on the 13th October; agreeably to the directions I had left there for his future proceedings', wrote Vancouver in *A Voyage of Discovery to the North Pacific Ocean, and Round the World* (London 1801). Cook and his men, including Vancouver, had landed at Yuquot (Friendly Cove) in March 1778, becoming the first Europeans to encounter the Nootka Indians, who bartered bear, wolf and fox skins and dense fur pelts of the sea otter for iron knives, nails and buttons. Despite the cold climate, these people used canoes to fish for salmon and other fish. They wore fur cloaks and conical hats of woven straw and lived in long timber houses containing carved totem poles.

On 17 October 1793, *Chatham* and *Discovery* anchored in the harbour of San Francisco opposite the fortified Presidio. After a cool reception by the Spanish authorities, Vancouver decided to leave and to continue his survey of the North American coast. On 21 October 1793, *Daedalus* met the expedition ships at sea outside San Francisco Bay and sailed south, reaching Monterey on 1 November.

From the ship, Gnung-a Gnung-a sighted the Spanish settlements and missions of Alta California at Monterey, Santa Barbara and San Diego. At Santa Barbara, Chumash Indians in their sea-going timber plank *tomols* (canoes), decorated with shells, paddled out to trade fish and ornaments with the ships' crews for spoons, beads and scissors. The Chumash had first seen three Spanish sailing ships in 1542. Some of Vancouver's men went ashore for wood and water at Santa Barbara from 10 to 18 November 1793. While there, George Hewett, surgeon's mate aboard *Discovery*, obtained artefacts for his ethnographic collection, now in the British Museum, London.[8]

The English ships entered San Diego Bay on 27 November 1793, where the Spanish commander welcomed Hanson and Peter Puget when they went ashore. On 9 December 1793 the three vessels left San Diego, sailing west across the Pacific to Hawaii. They reached Hilo Bay on the east coast of Hawaii on 8 January 1794, where King Kamehameha warmly greeted Vancouver.

On Tuesday, 14 January 1794, Vancouver's ships moved to a safer anchorage in Kealakekua Bay, where Kamehameha joined them. 'Found at anchor here the Lady Washington, American trader, the ship surrounded with the Natives', midshipman Spelman Swaine wrote in his log, now in the Public Record Office, London. The *Lady Washington* was the first American ship to establish a Pacific trade in black pearls and sandalwood. The following day, Swaine noted 'a great many canoes alongside trading with hogs and vegetables'. On Thursday 16 January, *Chatham* loaded spirits from *Daedalus*.[9]

Hawaiian nobles were traditionally buried in the cliffs surrounding the mile-long volcanic coral bay at Kealakekua. William Bligh had been Master of HMS *Resolution* and George Vancouver Master of HMS *Discovery* when James Cook's third expedition entered Kealakekua Bay in January 1779. They were greeted by 1500 canoes carrying 9000 Hawaiians, with hundreds more on surfboards and, as Cook wrote in the last words of his journal, more hundreds 'swimming about the Ships like shoals of fish'.[10] It was at Kavarua Point in the bay that Cook was clubbed by a high priest and then killed by an angry mob of Hawaiians on 14 February 1779.[11]

A View of Karakakooa, in Owyhee, c. 1773–1784, [Kealakukua Bay, Hawaii] , John Webber (1752–1793) Watercolour, From *Watercolours illustrating Captain Cook's last voyage*, DL PXX 2, f39, Dixson Library, Sydney.

Gnung-a Gnung-a got on well with everyone on *Daedalus* and Hanson was pleased by his readiness to do whatever was asked. During one month in Hawaii, he often went ashore with his shipmates. 'Wherever he went he readily adopted the manners of those around him', Hanson later told Collins, who remarked, with ironic humour, that 'when at Owhyee, having discovered that favours from the females were to be procured at the easy exchange for a looking-glass, a nail, or a knife, he was not backward in presenting his little offering, and was as well received as any of the white people in the ship. It was noticed too that he always displayed some taste in selecting the object of his attentions.'[12]

Gnung-a Gnung-a must have admired the young Hawaiian men in Kealakekua Bay riding the waves on their long timber surfboards. Lieutenant James King of HMS *Discovery* said 20 or 30 young men might spend half a day in the water lying 'flat upon an oval piece of plank about their Size and breadth' catching breakers that sent them inshore 'with a most astonishing Velocity'.[13] John Webber included a detail showing one surfboard rider among the canoes in his watercolour *A View of Karakakooa, in Owyhee*. If he were tempted to try, Gnung-a Gnung-a would have been the first Australian surfboard rider.

After transferring provisions to the survey ships, *Daedalus* was ready to sail with dispatches, copies of Vancouver's survey and the first breadfruit (*Artocarpus incisa*) plants to be introduced to Norfolk Island. The storeship left Hawaii on 8 February 1794 and anchored in Sydney Cove at 4 o'clock on the afternoon of 3 April 1794. Hanson said that although 'Collins' had not learned a great deal of English, he 'seemed to comprehend a great deal more than he could find words to express'.

Following negotiations with Vancouver, King Kamehameha formally ceded Hawaii to Great Britain on 25 February 1794, shortly after *Daedalus* had left the island.

Home in Sydney Town, Gnung-a Gnung-a found that his wife Warreeweer, who was pregnant when he left for North America, was living with 'a very fine young fellow' called Wyatt. She had recently given birth to a little girl, who died not long afterwards. Warreeweer and Wyatt joined the Eora crowding around Gnung-a Gnung-a, who was dressed in English clothes. The two men 'eyed each other with indignant sullenness, while the poor wife … appeared terrified, as if not knowing which to cling to as her protector, but expecting that she should be the sufferer', wrote Collins. A few days later Gnung-a Gnung-a fought and wounded Wyatt and 'his wife became the prize of the victor'.[14]

During a ritual revenge combat in December 1795, Pemulwuy, a *koradgee* (clever man or shaman) from the Georges River Bidjigal near Botany Bay, launched a spear at Gnung-a Gnung-a that remained fixed in his back. His friends took him into the settlement to ask the English surgeons for help, but they could not extract the spear and thought he was unlikely to recover. Gnung-a Gnung-a, however, soon left the hospital and walked about for several weeks with the spear protruding from his back. 'At last', wrote Collins in a footnote, 'we heard that his wife, or one of his male friends, had fixed their teeth in the wood and drawn it out after which he recovered, and was able again to go into the field. His wife War-re-weer showed by an uncommon attention her great attachment to him.'

Before this unexpected recovery, David Collins wrote a brief appreciation of his namesake:

> He was much esteemed by every white man who knew him, as well on account of his personal bravery, of which we had witnessed many distinguishing proofs, as on account of a gentleness of manners which strongly marked his disposition, and shaded off the harsher lines that his uncivilised life now and then forced into the fore-ground.[15]

'Collins' the explorer

Gnung-a Gnung-a's part in the early exploration of New South Wales has not been appreciated, because most previous historians though 'Collins' must be a convict. Historian John Cobley was aware of this fact in 1986. On 24 January 1798, two young men, John Price and John Wilson, left to explore the inland area south-west of Sydney 'with a small party which included the native Collins' (Gnung-a Gnung-a).[16] Price was a servant of Governor John Hunter and sailed from England with Bennelong on HMS *Reliance*, and Wilson was a runaway convict who had lived with Aborigines at the Hawkesbury River and spoke their language. They called Wilson *Bun-boee*, ('jumped-up dead man') considering him to be a reincarnated Aborigine.

The party set out from Mt Hunter, 5 miles south of Camden, and tramped through the Bargo Brush, close to Mittagong, where they encountered a Gundungurra family. Price's journal for 28 January 1798 mentions, an Aboriginal person 'which we had with us', probably Gnung-a Gnung-a:

> We ran and caught one of them, a girl, thinking to learn something from them, but her language was so different from that one that we had with us that we could not understand her … the next morning we gave her a tomahawk and sent her to the rest of the natives who were covered with large skins, which reached down to their heels.

The explorers' shoes were worn through by the time they reached the Wollondilly River. After 10 days they returned to Prospect with the first specimen of the native 'pheasant' or superb lyrebird (*Menura superba*), shot by Wilson on 26 January 1798.[17] Wilson's party gave the first description of the koala (*Phascolarctos* species) — 'an animal which the natives call a cullawine, which much resembles the sloths in America' — and the 'whom-batt' or wombat (*Vombatus* spp.), which was said to resemble the English badger.[18]

With Wilson as their guide, Price, 'Collins' and Henry Hacking, former quartermaster of HMS *Sirius*, set out on a second expedition on 9 March 1798 to search for the cattle missing since the landing of the First Fleet at Bennelong Point in 1788 and to locate some salt deposits seen on their first journey. After finding two thick veins of salt near the intersection of the Nepean and Bargo Rivers, Hacking left to return to Sydney on 14 March, leaving Wilson in charge.[19] Travelling through the Cowpastures (Camden), the party fell in with a large herd of wild cattle with calves, counting 178 animals. They passed Picton Lakes and climbed Mt Jellore. On Wednesday 28 March, Price wrote: 'We saw Hundreds of Kangaroos, one of them was shot by Collins …'

They climbed Mt Towrang, overlooking the Goulburn Plains near the present city of Goulburn, and returned to Prospect on 3 April 1798.[20] Governor John Hunter sent Price's journal of these two expeditions to Sir Joseph Banks in London and they were first published in 1895 in the *Historical Records of New South Wales*.

While in Sydney with a scientific expedition commanded by Nicholas Baudin in 1802, the young French artist Nicolas-Martin Petit met Gnung-a Gnung-a and sketched a striking portrait that he captioned 'Gnoung-a gnoung-a, mour-re-mour-ga (dit Collins)'.[21]

In January 1809, the body of Gnung-a Gnung-a Murremurgan, called Collins, who twice crossed the Pacific Ocean, was found behind the Dry Store, site of the present Macquarie Park in Bridge Street, Sydney. The *Sydney Gazette* lamented his death:

> The deceased was to us well known, for his lameness, occasioned by the contraction of the sinews of his right ham: he was not less remarkable however for the docility of his temper, and the high estimation in which he was universally held among the native tribes.

Gnung-a Gnung-a's own children, others he had adopted, and his brother Old Phillip, faced a ritual ordeal, or, in the words of the *Gazette*, were forced to 'submit to an unjust peril which barbarous custom imposes on the male relatives of the deceased, whether by consanguinity or adoption'.[22]

9 Worogan and Yeranabie on *Lady Nelson*

Yeranabie and Worogan, both from Eora clans in coastal Sydney, went to sea with Lieutenant James Grant in 1801 aboard the 60-ton sloop *Lady Nelson*. During an 11-week voyage they visited Jervis Bay, 170 kilometres south of Sydney, then Westernport and Churchill Island in Port Phillip Bay, Victoria. This is the only known instance of Aboriginal voyagers who were husband and wife.

Worogan, whose totem name meant 'Crow', might have been a sister or half-sister of Bennelong, the Wangal leader.[1] In his second language notebook (1791), William Dawes included 'Wárrgan' (Worogan) with Bennelong's known sisters Wariwéar (Warreweer) and Karangarang (Carangarang).[2] Master's mate Daniel Southwell, stationed at South Head, named Worgin (Worogan) and Wa-re-wai (Warreweer) as 'Two young females in Camp' (the Sydney Cove settlement).[3]

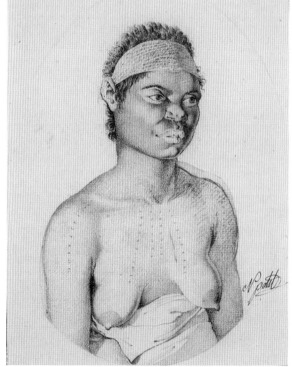

Yeranabie was the son of Maugoran, a leader of the Burramattagal (Parramatta clan) and the brother of Boorong and Ballooderry.[4] He was also called Yeranabe or Yeranibe Goruey, having exchanged names with Caruey or Carraway (White Cockatoo), a Cadigal.[5] Yeranabie was 'commonly called Palmer' by the English colonists, probably after Commissary John Palmer of Woolloomooloo.[6]

Nouvelle-Hollande – Toulgra (mere), 1802
[Worogan]
Nicolas-Martin Petit (1777–1804)
Pencil, charcoal and ink
20032.1, Muséum d'Histoire Naturelle, Le Havre, France

Detail from Petit's caption.

Worogan was the mother of Toulgra Bulldog, who in 1805 unwillingly boarded HMS *Buffalo* when he was transported to Norfolk Island on the orders of Governor Philip Gidley King. After the voyage in *Lady Nelson*, the young French artist Nicolas-Martin Petit sketched a portrait of Worogan at Port Jackson in 1802. In a pencilled caption on his original work, now in the Museum d'Histoire Naturelle at Le Havre, France, Petit wrote 'TOULGRA (mère)', indicating that she was Bulldog's mother.[7]

James Grant said Yeranabie 'comprehended and spoke English tolerably well', while Worogan … 'spoke English. She had always lived in the neighbourhood of Sydney.' Both were given European clothes when they boarded the ship in Sydney, but 'when the weather proved warm', wrote Grant, 'the woman threw aside her gown and petticoat, and preferred appearing in the state of nature, or slightly covered with a blanket'.

The *Lady Nelson* left Sydney on 8 March 1801 in company with the sloop *Bee*, on which artist John Lewin was a passenger. The *Bee* proved unseaworthy and was forced to return to port. Also on the *Lady Nelson* were George Caley, a botanist employed by Sir Joseph Banks, surveyor Ensign Francis Barrallier and four armed marines.

In the account in his journal, reproduced in *Historical Records of New South Wales (HRNSW)*, Grant spells the name as Yeranabie, but in Grant's *Narrative of a Voyage in H.M. Lady Nelson*, printed in London in 1803, his editors preferred 'Euranabie'. Both sources have been used in this account.

The *Lady Nelson* entered Jervis Bay on 10 March 1801 and anchored for three days in the southern cove. Grant and Barrallier went ashore, where they netted many fish, some of which they gave to the local Aborigines, who at first seemed friendly.

Grant wrote in his journal:

> Great numbers of the natives now came round us in their canoes; some we allowed to come on board. They seem a harmless, inoffensive people, but much more robust than those about Sydney. They all wish to get their beards cut off. They did not thoroughly understand Yeranabie, the native I have on board. Mr Baraillier [*sic*] and I went on shore with the boat, armed, in order to catch some fish and see how they would receive us, taking Yeranabie with us, who, when he got on shore, showed evident marks of fear, although one of them, an elderly man, made him a present of a waddee [club]. On my enquiring into the cause of his alarm, he told me they would kill and eat him; I therefore sent him on board in the boat directly.

On 12 March Barrallier and Caley walked 'about eight miles inland' with Grant. Barrallier came across an Aboriginal fire site littered with skeletal remains, including a human skull and vertebrae. 'I brought the human bones on board with me … I called Yeranabie and shewing him the scull [skull] part and desired him to ask if it was part of a white man, and if they had eat him.' The ship *Sydney Cove* had been wrecked on Preservation Island in Bass Strait in 1797 and Aborigines were reported to have killed two of the crew near Jervis Bay.

One of the Jervis Bay men told Yeranabie and a soldier 'who understood the Sydney dialect' that the bones belonged to a white man who had come in a small boat or canoe from the south 'where the ship *tumble down*, the expression he made use of for being wrecked'. Grant continued: 'I later interrogated Worogan, the wife of Yeranabe, who spoke English, on this point … from her I learned that the Bush Natives (who appear to be a different tribe of people from those who live by the sea-side) sometimes did eat human flesh'. Worogan gave Grant a practical demonstration to show how the 'cannibals' killed their victims, making him stretch out on the ship's deck and pretending to strike him on the neck with a *waddie* (waddy).

Grant surveyed Bowens Island at the mouth of Jervis Bay, which he named Ann's Island, unaware that Lieutenant Bowen in the convict transport turned whaler *Atlantic* had named it in August 1791. The sloop left Jervis Bay on 13 March 1801, meeting the ship *Britannia* near Point Hicks ('bound for the whale fishery') and passed Wilsons Promontory on 20 March. On 23 March they sailed into Western Port (Westernport), where the ship anchored for 40 days. Grant gave the name Seal Islands to the rocky islands 'covered with seals' and elephant seals.

While searching for a freshwater stream at the head of the harbour, seen by Surgeon George Bass, Grant found and named Churchills Island, where he decided to plant a garden. The following day Barrallier and First Mate John Murray went ashore to survey part of the harbour, while Caley 'set out on his botanical searches'. Grant wrote:

> Part of my object was to make discovery of the natives, but herein I was disappointed, as not the least traces were discoverable that any had been here. I had chosen for my companion in this research my Sydney native, whom I found in many respects very useful, especially when penetrating a thicket, as he usually went first and cleared a passage for me to follow him. Though always barefooted, and sometimes naked, he had by practice acquired a facility of passing through the thick underwood, and could effect his passage in much less time than any of us …

Grant and Yeranabie traced a saltwater creek in which several large stingrays swam. On 27 March they explored the shell-covered sandy beach at the entrance to Westernport. 'I was still attended by my faithful Yeranabie', wrote Grant. They spotted a large school of Australian salmon, a fish Grant thought was 'excellent eating'. To Grant's dismay, Yeranabie suddenly disappeared, but quickly returned from the bush with a small stick. 'Asking me for my knife, he presently sharpened one end to a point, and then stripping himself, he leaped from one point of the rock to another until he met with an opportunity of striking a fish, which he did, the stick penetrating quite through it; and in this state he came and presented it to me … Though I pressed him to take the fish several times, he as constantly refused it, but accepted of some tobacco, which he was exceedingly fond of smoking.'

The Lady Nelson — brig 6 Guns ... c. 1820s, After *View of Lady Nelson on the Thames*, Artist unknown, Oil Original: ML 86, Mitchell Library, Sydney.

Worogan found that she was pregnant about this time, which surprised Grant, who thought she might be seasick or suffering from scurvy. 'With this idea', he wrote, 'I prescribed air and exercise on shore, and obliged her to accompany her husband and me, which I was not always able to do without great difficulty'. Worogan declared her intention of 'making away with her offspring; and the reason she gave for it was, that she did not like the trouble of nursing'. Grant believed she had aborted or killed the child at birth, because he saw her in Sydney several times afterwards 'when she was without a child, and to every appearance not in a state of pregnancy'.

On 29 March, Grant sent Murray and Barrallier to survey the entrance of Port Phillip, where they anchored in calm water off a sandy beach. A sudden sea swell hit the boat, which was washed up on the beach while the crew were thrown into the sea. Yeranabie, who was with the boat party, was the first to gain the shore and the others followed.

Returning to Churchills Island, Grant found his sailors had cleared the ground for a garden, the first ever planted in what is now the state of Victoria. He sowed a variety of exotic seeds including wheat, maize, peas, potatoes, rice, hemp, some coffee berries, stones and kernels of several fruits and pippins of an apple variety he named 'Lady Elizabeth Percy's Apple'. With the felled trees they raised a blockhouse 24 × 12 feet, the first European-style building in Victoria.

The *Lady Nelson* left Western Port on 29 April 1801 and rounded Wilsons Promontory, sailing up the east coast through adverse winds and 'a succession of bad weather', which forced the sloop into Botany Bay for 24 hours. George Caley left the ship there and 'made the best of his way' to Parramatta, probably accompanied by Worogan and Yeranabie. The ship reached Port Jackson on 24 May 1801.[8]

Caley was disappointed with the specimens he collected during the voyage. In a letter written on 25 August 1801, he told Sir Joseph Banks: 'I went [on] a voyage to Bass's Straits in the Lady Nelson, but I found scarcely any thing different from what I had seen before. But had I met with many things, I could not have preserved them as I had not convenience and the weather was altogether bad.'[9]

Worogan was named as 'Calee' in a print engraved in London in 1803 from Petit's original, in the possession of Surgeon James Thomson. She might have adopted this name from George Caley during the voyage of the *Lady Nelson*.

Yeranabie faced a ritual punishment at Parramatta in December 1804 for deserting his wife while she was ill, 'her eyelids nearly closed by grief and famine'.[10]

10 Bungaree: sailing with Matthew Flinders

Boongarie or Bungaree (c. 1775–1830) is the best-known Aboriginal voyager. Because the others on board were British, Bungaree became the first Australian to circumnavigate the continent when he accompanied naval lieutenant Matthew Flinders on HMS *Investigator* in 1801–3.

Flinders, like Governor Arthur Phillip, understood that Aboriginal diplomacy and skills were essential in exploration, a fact that later European explorers like Burke and Wills ignored at the cost of their lives.

After his epic voyage, Flinders produced the first complete chart of the continent, which he labelled 'Australia or Terra Australis'. Bungaree himself was one of the first individuals to be described as an Australian.

Governor John Hunter said Bungaree came from 'the northside of Broken Bay', an inlet near the mouth of the Hawkesbury River.[1] Bungaree's great patron, Governor Lachlan Macquarie, was ambivalent about this. In 1815, Macquarie presented Bungaree with a gorget inscribed Bungaree 'Chief of the Broken Bay Tribe',[2] but in 1822 he described Bungaree as chief of the 'Pitt Water Tribe'.[3] Pittwater, home of the Garigal or Karakal, runs south from the Hawkesbury River.

'Bongary' or Bungaree's first known voyage was on HMS *Reliance*, when he sailed on 29 May 1798 from Sydney Cove to Norfolk Island with Nanbarry and Wingal, from Broken Bay or Port Stephens. It was during this 60-day round trip that Matthew Flinders first met and came to respect Bungaree. Because of adverse winds, *Reliance* took 27 days on the return leg from Norfolk Island (arriving on 25 July), compared to the usual 10-day passage. The muster shows that the three Aboriginal men were discharged from the ship on 27 July 1798.

Bungaree might have previously visited Sydney on board one of the foreign sealing or whaling vessels, like the whaler *William and Ann*, which put into Broken Bay for wood and water in 1791.[4]

Wingal or Wingle lived to a ripe old age. Wingle received government-issue blankets as a Port Stephens man in Sydney in 1850.[5] In the 1850s, Philip Cohen, with two Worimi men from Port Stephens, north of Sydney, met Wingal and Terrigal Bob from the Broken Bay clan, who were camped at Curl Curl, one of Sydney's

Detail of Bungaree's gorget, 1820, Pavel Nikolaevich Mikhailov (1786–1840), Pencil and watercolour R29213/210, Russian State Museum , St Petersburg, Image courtesy of Longueville Publications.

northern beaches.[6] 'Old Wingle' was among those who waited in the crowd to shake hands with William Charles Wentworth when he returned to Sydney from England on the P & O mail steamer MV *Benares* in April 1861.[7] James Jervis (1967) said 'Old Wingle' and his wife Kitty camped on a knoll above Double Bay (now Ascham School) with 'Bondi Charley'. They sometimes gave demonstrations of boomerang throwing in return for copper coins.[8] Wingle died of consumption at Botany in 1868.[9]

In 1799, Mathew Flinders took Bungaree with him on the sloop *Norfolk* on a survey voyage to Hervey Bay, adjoining Fraser Island, north of Brisbane. Writing in 1814, Flinders said he was accompanied by his brother Samuel and 'Bongaree, a native, whose good disposition and open and manly conduct had attracted my esteem'.[10] Bungaree was Flinders's constant companion during six weeks of

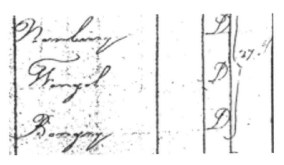

Nanbarry D}
Wingal　D}27.[6/]
Bongary　D}
*Port Jackson for a Passage to Norfolk Island,
29 May 1798*
HMS *Reliance*, Ship's Muster, Monthly Book
Adm. 36/13398, PRO Reel 7008: 166, 185,
Public Record Office, London

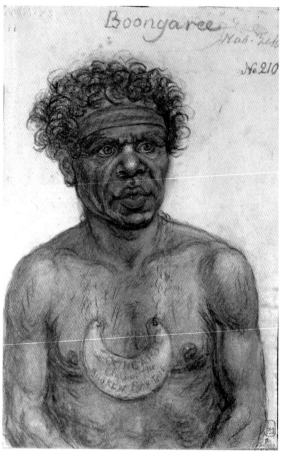

Boongaree, 1820
Pavel Mikhailov (1786–1840)
Pencil and sanguine
R29212/210, Russian State Museum, St Petersburg
Image courtesy of Longueville Publications

exploration, in which the 25-year-old naval lieutenant came to value his friendship and rely on his skill as a go-between with the coastal Aborigines.

The tiny 25-ton longboat *Norfolk*, in which Flinders and Surgeon George Bass had rounded Van Diemen's Land, was built and decked with timber from Norfolk pines at Norfolk Island and rigged as a sloop. *Norfolk* took on provisions and sailed north from Port Jackson on 8 July 1799, sighting the coast next morning just north of Port Stephens. On 11 July, Flinders and Bungaree landed and explored Shoal Bay, where they examined well-built circular Aboriginal huts, but did not see their owners.

Three days later, Flinders moored the sloop offshore in Cook's Glass House Bay. After breakfast on 16 July, he steered the ship's boat to a sandy headland, taking Bungaree, who jumped ashore to greet waiting Aborigines 'naked, and as unarmed as they themselves appeared'. Bungaree exchanged the yarn band he wore around his waist for a fillet (narrow band) of kangaroo hair. The English sailors kept their muskets at the ready in case of trouble, but the Aborigines seemed shy. Flinders, who was wearing a splendid new cabbage-tree hat, joined Bungaree. He put down his musket and gave one of the Aborigines a woollen cap. When Flinders made signs that he wanted the man's net bag, he asked for the hat in return. 'This hat was made of the white filaments of the cabbage-tree and seemed to excite the attention and wishes of the whole party.'

Flinders would not give up his hat. The Aboriginal man threw the cap on the bank behind him and moved towards Flinders and Bungaree, who slowly retreated to the boat. Another man tried to knock off Flinders' hat with a long stick and then threw a length of firewood. The incident was treated as a joke, but things became more serious when another man threw a spear over the boat. Faced with this 'impudent and unprovoked attack', Flinders loaded his musket, but the flint was wet and it twice misfired. The gun went off at the third attempt and a sailor also fired at the Aborigines, who had never before seen or heard a firearm. They fell flat on their faces in terror and then ran into the bush. One man was wounded and Bungaree reported that another had his arm broken by the second shot from the boat.

Fifteen years later in *Terra Australis*, Flinders explained this 'unfortunate occurrence' in a few brief words, with no mention of the cabbage-tree hat. 'There was a party of natives on the point, and our communication was at first friendly, but after receiving presents they made an attack, and one of them was wounded by their fire.' Flinders gave the name Point Skirmish (now Skirmish Point) to the lower end of Bribie Island where this brief clash took place. Close by today is a small resort town called Boongaree. Flinders and his men spent several days exploring Moreton Bay, but missed the entrance to the Brisbane River.

Although he usually preferred to sleep on deck, Bungaree stowed his kitbag below. While a prisoner on the Île de France (Mauritius), Flinders recalled the affection between Bungaree and Trim, a plump black cat with white markings, who could scamper up the rigging to the topmast faster than any sailor. Trim was born in 1797 on HMS *Reliance* between Cape Town and Port Jackson. Flinders wrote:

> If he [Trim] had occasion to drink, he mewed to Boongaree and leaped up to the water cask; if to eat, he called him down below and went straight to his kid [kit], where there was generally a remnant of black swan. In short, Boongaree was his great resource, and his kindness was repaid with caresses.[11]

On 31 July 1799, *Norfolk* beat out of Pumicestone Passage with the tide. The ship reached Hervey Bay in two days, Wide Bay on 1 August and Sandy Cape the following day. *Norfolk* cleared Break Sea Spit to the north of Fraser Island on 8 August and turned south for Port Jackson, arriving on 20 August 1799.[12]

Voyage of HMS *Investigator*

In 1800, Matthew Flinders, then aged 27, was appointed commander of HMS *Investigator*, with orders to survey the 'unknown coast' of New Holland. Formerly called *Xenophon*, the ship was a sloop rigged as a barque, built for the English coastal trade. The 334-ton vessel was converted at the Chatham dockyards and sailed from Spithead on 18 July 1801. Under the copper sheathing, rot was creeping through the timbers, which began to leak in the English Channel. Sir Joseph Banks, President of the Royal Society, had selected a team of distinguished 'scientific gentlemen' to take part in the expedition. They were Robert Brown (naturalist), Ferdinand Bauer (natural history painter), William Westall (landscape and figure painter), John Crossley (astronomer, who left the ship at the Cape of Good Hope), Peter Good (gardener) and John Allen (miner).

Cape Leeuwin, on the west coast of the continent, was sighted on 6 December 1801. *Investigator* anchored in King George Sound (Albany) two days later and from 5 January 1802 sailed east along the Great Australian Bight, unexpectedly meeting the French explorer Captain Nicolas Baudin in the ship *Géographe* at Encounter Bay, within sight of Kangaroo Island.[13] After a voyage of nine months and nine days, *Investigator* entered Port Jackson and moored off Bennelong Point on 9 May 1802. During 12 weeks in port, the ship was painted, the masts were re-rigged and the seams caulked inside and out.

On 10 May, Flinders sent a formal request to Governor Philip Gidley King, asking to enlist two 'natives of this country' as supernumeraries. He wrote in *Terra Australis*:

> I had before experienced much advantage from the presence of a native of Port Jackson, in bringing about a friendly intercourse with the inhabitants of other parts of the coast; and on representing this to the governor, he authorised me to receive two on board. Bongaree, the worthy and brave fellow who had sailed with me on the Norfolk, now volunteered again; the other was Nanbaree, a good-natured lad, of whom colonel Collins has made mention of in his Account of New South Wales.[14]

Bungaree and Nanbarry joined nine seamen and five convicts who replaced a boat crew lost at Spencer Gulf and two men discharged at Port Jackson. Trim, the ship's cat, was again on board, turning grey, but 'fat and frisky' as Flinders told his wife Ann.[15]

Lieutenant John Murray now commanded *Lady Nelson* and her first mate was Henry Hacking. The two ships left Port Jackson on 22 July 1802. On Friday 30 July, *Investigator* got across the dangerous sandbar at Breaksea Spit and anchored at Sandy Cape, at the northern tip of Great Sandy Island (Fraser Island) on Hervey Bay, to allow Robert Brown to collect plants on shore.

Next morning *Lady Nelson* anchored close to shore and armed boats were sent out to protect the landing parties, with Bungaree in one boat and Nanbarry in the other. Brown's party walked along the shore, while Murray's men cut wood for fuel. Flinders, with six people, 'including my native friend Bongaree', went towards Sandy Cape. He later described how Bungaree, despite his ignorance of the local language, managed to establish peaceful relations with Aboriginal warriors who were waving tree branches and gesturing to the whites to return to the ship:

> Bungaree stripped off his clothes and laid aside his spear, as inducements for them to wait for him; but finding they did not understand his language, the poor fellow, in the simplicity of his heart, addressed them in broken English, hoping to succeed better. At length they suffered him to come

up, and by degrees our whole party joined; and after receiving some presents, twenty of them returned with us to the boats, and were feasted upon the blubber of two porpoises, which had been brought on shore purposely for them.[16]

The Aborigines relished the porpoise blubber, which they ate raw 'with satisfaction & an eager Appetite; the Capn gave them red caps, Tommy hawks &c. in order to create Friendship with them', wrote Samuel Smith, a 30-year-old ordinary seaman who kept a journal.[17] 'On our joining the Captns party we found many of the natives along with them', wrote Robert Brown. 'I learned that they had intercourse with them soon after we left them … brought about by Bongare the Port Jackson native who boldly went up to a considerable party of them arm'd with spears.'[18] The Fraser Island Aborigines had never before seen a womera or spear-thrower. 'One of them being invited to imitate Bongaree, who lanced a spear with it very dexterously, and to a great distance, he, in the most awkward manner, threw both woomerah and spear together', wrote Flinders.[19]

Nanbarry sometimes went ashore with Brown, who recorded two eventful visits in his journal. While climbing a hill near Port Curtis (Gladstone) on 5 August 1802, Brown's party was 'saluted with a shower of stones' thrown by Aborigines.

> We ascended the hill & the natives retird in about a quarter of an hour some of the party among them Nanberry the native of Port Jackson having straggled a little from the rest were attacked by the natives & obligd to retreat. The attack was made with a war woop and a discharge of stones.

The attackers 'scampered off' when Brown discharged his pocket pistol and others fired their muskets.[20]

Flinders and his men spent a week exploring Shoalwater Bay (near Rockhampton), where they met some Aborigines armed with heavy spears, who were also astonished to see Bungaree launch a spear with a womera. On 30 August 1802, Brown took part in a naming ceremony with the Shoalwater Bay people. 'They introduced each other to us & the introduction seem[ed] … almost a harangue probably on the merits of the person introduced', he wrote. 'They expressd Admiration at Nanbury's Dexterity with the spear, but were terrified at the report of a musket wch we fird loaded with ball on purpose to shew them the effect of fire arms', wrote Brown. Only one Aborigine had the courage to examine the musket, which he did 'with evident symptoms of fear'.[21]

Flinders began to search for openings to break out of the dangerous reefs and enclosing islands of the Great Barrier Reef. When a promising exit appeared near the Cumberland Islands, he ordered *Lady Nelson* to return to Sydney. Nanbarry was not to be among the circumnavigators. On 18 October, 'Nanbarre, one of the two natives, having expressed a wish to go back to Port Jackson, was sent to the *Lady Nelson* in the morning'.[22]

The *Investigator* reached Groote Eylandt in Torres Strait on 5 January 1803 and spent two weeks circling the island and collecting new plants. A gallery of Aboriginal rock paintings was discovered in caves and shelters on nearby Chasm Island. William Westall copied some of the paintings, which Flinders described: 'In the caverns we found some specimens of native art, in drawings of people, turtles, kangaroos, and a hand. The porpoises were about two feet long and had had some trouble bestowed on them. They were done with something like red paint upon the whitish ground of the rock, and variegated with some scratches of black.'[23] Dr Frederick David McCarthy of the Australian Museum, Sydney, recorded some 900 Aboriginal rock paintings at 27 sites at Chasm Island in 1948.[24]

On 21 January at Morgan's Island in Blue Mud Bay, north-west of Groote Eylandt, a master's mate was speared four times when he reached out to take a spear from one man while talking to a group of Aborigines. A boat crew opened fire, killing one man. Flinders was upset by the incident and sent a boat to recover the body. William Westall made a sketch of the dead man and handed the body to Surgeon Hugh Bell. 'He was dissected and his head put in spirits', noted Peter Good.[25]

On 3 February 1803, in a deep inlet further north named Caledon Bay, Bungaree went ashore in a whaleboat with Lieutenant Robert Fowler and Surgeon Bell to search for fresh water. They spoke to 12 Aboriginal men on the beach, wrote Robert Brown, and 'by means of Bongaree the Native of Port Jackson soon came to a friendly intercourse with the Natives'. Anthropologist Donald Thomson found that a similar traditional protocol persisted more than 130 years later, when he encountered a group of Aboriginal people camped at Blue Mud Bay in July 1934.

Thomson wrote:

> This was the critical moment of meeting with the Aborigines. There was no loud exchange of greetings, no shouting, not a word was spoken at first, for the etiquette to be observed at these times is an important business and on one's behaviour at such times Aborigines are apt to base their permanent attitude.
>
> To those accustomed to regarding the Australian Aborigines as disorganised people it must come as a surprise to learn that custom, etiquette, good manners, and good taste, much as we know them are nowhere more important. An ill-mannered person, a man who does not know how to behave himself, is regarded contemptuously by these people …[26]

In the next few days, Brown was able to compile a vocabulary of some 50 words of the Caledon Bay language. On 4 February 1803, Flinders went ashore at Point Alexander in Caledon Bay. 'I landed with the botanical gentlemen; the natives running from their night residences to meet us.' They all 'expressed much joy, especially at seeing Boongaree, our good natured Indian from Port Jackson'. However, some Aborigines who followed the botanist's party stole a hatchet and a musket. Next day, an Aborigine named Yehangeree ran off with a wooding axe.

Flinders resolved to put a stop to the 'thieving'. Two Aboriginal men who brought fruit to the tents next day were captured and the older man released, while Woga (Woogah), a boy about 14 years old, was taken aboard *Investigator* as hostage for the axe. Woga begged to be released, 'promising, with tears in his eyes, to bring back the axe. He was given some clothing and presents and 'took to his heels with all his might'.

At dawn on 10 February 1802, *Investigator* left Caledon Bay, steering to the north-west corner of Arnhem Land. A week later, the survey of the Gulf of Carpentaria was complete. Rounding Cape Arnhem on 17 February, Flinders discovered 'six vessels covered over like hulks, as if laid up for a bad season'. Samuel Flinders took an armed boat to investigate and found they were 'Malay' prows (*proas*) from Macassar (today's South Sulawesi), fishing for trepang (*bêche-de-mer* or sea slug), which was cured and sold to Chinese traders in Timor. Trepang, prized by the Chinese as an aphrodisiac, was dried in the sun and then smoked over charcoal fires. Flinders met the elderly chief Pobasso who said the boats were part of a fleet of 60 owned by the Rajah of Buni. With the aid of a pocket compass he had made six or seven similar voyages over a period of 26 years.

On his first visit to Broken Bay in March 1788, Captain Arthur Phillip observed that fish was the chief food of the people there. 'The shark, I believe they never eat', he added.[27] Flinders, in *Terra Australis*, mentioned this taboo in a story that says more about Bungaree's manners and his friendship with Flinders than about his prowess at fishing. At daylight on 25 February in the English Company Island, Flinders was taking bearing from a low point to the south-west while Bungaree speared a few fish:

Bongaree was busily employed preparing his fish, when my bearings were concluded. The natives of Port Jackson have a prejudice against all fish of the ray kind [stingrays] as well as against sharks; and whilst they devour with eager avidity the blubber of a whale or porpoise, a piece of skate would excite disgust. Our good natured Indian had been ridiculed by the sailors for this unaccountable whim, but he had not been cured; and it so happened, that the fish he had speared this morning were three small rays and a mullet. This last, being the most delicate, he presented to Mr Westall and me, so soon as it was cooked; and then went to saunter by the water side, whilst the boats' crew should cook and eat the rays, although, having had nothing since the morning before, it may be supposed he did not want appetite. I noticed this in silence till the whole were prepared, and then had him called up to take his portion of the mullet; but it was with much difficulty that his modesty and forbearance could be overcome, for these qualities, so seldom expressed in a savage, formed leading features in the character of my humble friend. But there was one of the sailors also, who preferred hunger to ray-eating! It might be supposed he had an eye to the mullet; but this was not the case. He had been seven or eight years with me, mostly in New South Wales, had learned many of the native habits, and even imbued this ridiculous notion respecting rays and sharks; though he could not allege, as Bungaree did, that 'they might be very good for white men, but would kill him'. The mullet accordingly underwent a further division; and Mr Westall and myself, having no prejudice against rays, made up our proportion of this scanty repast from one of them.[28]

Many of the crew were suffering from scurvy or dysentery and his own feet were ulcerated, so on 6 March 1803, Flinders steered *Investigator* for the Dutch colony at Coupang (Kupang) on Timor. The ship anchored there on 31 March and remained for one week, leaving on 8 April.

HMS *Investigator* returned to Sydney by the west coast, stopping only at Middle Island in the Recherche Archipelago. Six seamen died during the next two months and many on board were ill when the ship moored in Port Jackson on 9 June 1803. Four more men died at Garden Island, including Peter Good, the Scottish gardener. Bungaree and the rest of the crew were discharged and HMS *Investigator* was condemned as unseaworthy and moored alongside the hulk of HMS *Supply*.

In January 1815 Governor Lachlan Macquarie reserved land and erected huts at Georges Head for Bungaree and his people to 'Settle and Cultivate'. They were given a fishing boat, clothing, seeds and farming implements. In November that year, Mrs Elizabeth Macquarie gave Bungaree a sow and pigs, a pair of Muscovy ducks and outfits for his wife and daughter. Bungaree's farm was soon abandoned.

Bungaree's first wife Matora probably took her name from *mut-tau-ra*, meaning 'small snapper' in the language of the Hunter River-Lake Macquarie area, where it is likely she was born.[29] His second wife Caroo or Cora Gooseberry (Queen Gooseberry), the daughter of Moorooboora, was a Sydney identity until her death in 1852.[30]

The spurious names 'Onion, Boatman, Broomstick, Askabout and Pincher', ascribed to Bungaree's wives in a 'biographic memoir' titled 'Bungaree, King of the Blacks', published in Charles Dickens's London journal *All the Year Round* (21 May 1859) were concocted by fiction writer John Lang (1816–1864). Like the anonymous author, Lang left Australia in 1838 to study law at Cambridge University in England. Lang's 'poetic licence' allows Bungaree to imitate New South Wales governors Sir Richard Bourke and Sir George Gipps, who did not take office until after Bungaree's death in 1830.[31]

Bungaree's boats

Governor Lachlan Macquarie saw his first Aboriginal Australian on the day he arrived from England aboard HMS *Dromedary*. According to Ensign Alexander Huey of the 73rd (Highland) Regiment, there was an Aboriginal man on the pilot boat that guided the ship through the Heads at 9 o'clock on 28 December 1809.[32]

As part of his plans to 'civilise' the friendly Aborigines, Macquarie in 1815 gave an old whaleboat to Boongaree or Bungaree, whose Broken Bay clan he established on a farm at Georges Head, near Middle Head. The boat was intended for fishing, which, said the *Sydney Gazette*, 'always furnished the principal source of their subsistence'.[33] Bungaree also used his fishing boat, rowed by two of his wives, to board foreign ships to drink the captain's health in brandy, rum or beer.

The Russian navigator Captain Fabian von Bellingshausen, whose ships *Mirnyy* and *Vostok* were anchored at Kirribilli Point in 1820, often met Bungaree, whose people were camped nearby. According to Bellingshausen:

> Boongaree and his family have a boat, given by the government; and other New Hollanders have likewise been given boats by inhabitants of Sydney on the condition that they surrender part of their daily catch of fish. They go out in these boats every day, fish at the mouth of the Bay, and then hasten back to the town to surrender the due portion of the catch; the remainder they exchange for drink or tobacco.[34]

As Sydney was a port town it was customary, observed the Russian expedition's astronomer Ivan Mikhaylovich Simonov, to give the title 'captain' to every skipper of a merchant or naval ship, whatever its size:

> As a result, captain is a pretty common title in Sydney Town. Well: Boongaree had noted this fact and on one occasion brought a fellow New Hollander to Captain Bellingshausen, recommending him to him as Captain Bellau. This he did because Bellau had his own, insignificant boat. Highly amusing it was to see these two ugly natives, both in dirty rags, shuffling now on one foot, now on the other and bowing deeply; amusing too, to see one proudly introducing the other as Captain Bellau! Both were served with a glass of rum. And the ceremonial introductions ended forthwith —for the rum had been their sole object.[35]

No Aboriginal man named Bellau can be traced in the historical record. It is probable that Simonov misinterpreted Bungaree's Aboriginal English introduction of Captain 'Fellow', which to the Russian might have sounded like Bellau.[36]

With great optimism, in 1822 Governor Macquarie built new huts at Georges Head for Bungaree and his people. On Monday 11 February 1822, one day before his departure for England, Governor Macquarie and his wife Elizabeth went by barge to Georges Head to say goodbye to Bungaree. Macquarie introduced Bungaree to the new governor, Sir Thomas Brisbane, who, Macquarie wrote, 'has, also, at my request promised to give Boongarie for himself and his Tribe a Fishing Boat with a Nett'.[37]

The Reverend John Dunmore Lang, walking by the Parramatta River with his brother George, Commissary at Parramatta, 'one beautiful evening' in 1824, met 'Bungary chief of the Sydney tribe of black natives … pulling down the river, in a boat which he had received as a present from the Governor with his two jins [gins] or wives'. They stopped to talk, and 'the good natured chief immediately desired his two jins to rest their oars'.[38] Bungaree was probably bound for the annual Native Conference or feast at Parramatta, first instituted by Macquarie in 1814.

It was a different story in January 1828, when Bungaree and Jemmy Charcoal or Nunberri 'of the tribe Bullie' (Bulli, near Wollongong), set out 'with a considerable number of their family of both sexes' for the Parramatta feast, in what *The Australian* newspaper called their 'fishing yacht'.[39] Two hundred Aborigines attended, but, as

Roger Oldfield reported in the *South-Asian Register*, 'Bungaree was not there, but remained with several others in Sydney'.[40] *The Australian* picked up the story again in its issue for 4 January:

> But few strangers visited the place of festivity. Bungaree was not there, nor his tribe: that venerable chief having made away [sold] his fishing boat (it is suspected to purchase some extract stronger than that derived from the suction of a sugar bag) a day or so before, had no suitable conveyance, and not feeling disposed to undertake the journey by land to Parramatta on foot, enjoyed his *otiom cum dignitate* [dignified leisure], the better part of Wednesday and Wednesday night, reclining by his fire upon the grassy upland bordering on Bennelong Point.[41]

Bungaree soon recovered his boat, which continued to be a familiar sight around Sydney Harbour. 'In this they frequently make excursions and row into the open sea', wrote Oldfield, 'employing themselves in catching fish, which they cook over a fire that is carried in the boat, and as they often catch more than they want, the surplus is brought to town for barter. A sailor's life would suit these blacks more than any other, except a gentleman's.' [42]

On 29 June 1829, Hyacinthe de Bougainville, who had spent three months in Sydney with the Baudin expedition in 1802, returned as commander of the scientific expedition vessels *Thétis* and *Espérance*. Hardly a day passed without Bungaree coming aboard 'to drink our health with a few glasses of French brandy which he loved so much', wrote de Bougainville. 'On more than one occasion, we marvelled at the skill he displayed in manoeuvring his boat in spite of his drunken state. On his sail were written in large letters the words King Bungaree.'[43]

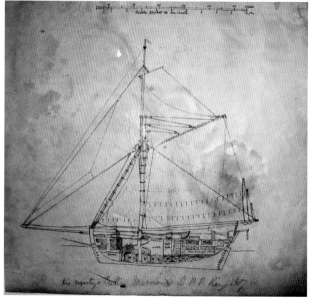

His Majesty's Cutter Mermaid, 1817
Philip Parker King (1791–1856)
Etching
Original PXC 767, No. 85,
Mitchell Library, Sydney

With Philip Parker King on the cutter *Mermaid*

In 1817, 14 years after sailing on HMS *Investigator* with Matthew Flinders, Bungaree volunteered to go to sea again with naval explorer Phillip Parker King, son of Governor Philip Gidley King, who had been born on Norfolk Island.

King, aged 26, had orders to chart the coastline of western and northern Australia missed by Flinders when he was forced to cut and run for Timor in the leaky *Investigator*. King was instructed to search for any river mouths 'likely to lead to an interior navigation into this great continent'.

Mermaid was a strong, snub-nosed cutter of 83 tons capacity, built in India of Bengal teak. Phillip King, a talented amateur artist, made many sketches of the little cutter, coastal scenery and incidents during the survey voyage of the Australian coastline. Some of these images were engraved in his *Narrative of a Survey of the Intertropical and Western Coasts of Australia*, published in London in 1827. King wrote:

> I accepted the proffered services of Boongaree, a Port Jackson native who had formerly accompanied Captain Flinders in the Investigator, and also on a previous occasion in the Norfolk schooner. This man is well known in the colony as the chief of the Broken Bay tribe; he was about forty-five years of age, of a sharp, intelligent, and unassuming disposition, and promised to be of much service to us in our intercourse with the natives.44

Sir Joseph Banks, who had sent Allan Cunningham to New South Wales in 1816 to collect plants for Kew Gardens, arranged for the botanist to join the expedition. Included in the crew, wrote Cunningham, was 'Bongaree, a chief of natives of a tribe of Broken Bay … who was taken on this voyage at his own particular request'.45

The cutter, carrying water for 12 weeks and provisions for nine months, left Port Jackson on 22 December 1817. Four days later, after being battered by a gale on Christmas Day, *Mermaid* put in to Twofold Bay for shelter and minor repairs. Bungaree resumed his role as intermediary between the Indigenous People and the English. One defiant warrior stood at the edge of the rocks at Red Point at the entrance to the bay, holding a spear and waving a weapon 'most ferociously' over his head. Bungaree replied in his 'Port Jackson language', but neither man understood the other. The ship moored in Snug Cove in the northern part of the bay, where King went ashore with Master's mate John Septimus Roe and Cunningham. 'Boongaree also accompanied us,' wrote King, 'clothed in a new dress, which was provided for him, of which he was not a little proud, and for some time kept it very clean.'46 That evening, after hauling the fishing seine net on the beach without success, the ship's party was about to leave when they spotted 'three or four natives' peeping above the long grass 70 or 80 yards up the hill, watching their movements. They walked towards the Aborigines, who suddenly ran up the hill to hide among thick trees.

> Boongaree called to them in vain; and it was not until they had reached some distance that they

answered his call in loud shrill voices. After some time in parley, in which Boongaree was spokesman on our part, sometimes in his own language, and at others in broken English, which he always resorted to when his own failed in being understood, they withdrew altogether, and we neither heard nor saw any more of them.

When they passed Red Point as the cutter left the bay the next morning (27 December 1817), 20 or 30 Aborigines came to the cliff top 'shouting and hallooing and making violent gestures' while the women and children hid among the trees and bushes. At the same time, another group of Aborigines unconcernedly cooked fish near the beach where two canoes were hauled up on the rocks.[47]

Mermaid rounded Cape Howe into Bass Strait and coasted the Great Australian Bight to King George Sound, anchoring for 11 days in Oyster Harbour in January 1818. During the voyage, Bungaree proved his skill as a fisherman and often led the crew to fresh water. 'Bungaree speared a great many fish with his fiz-gig; one that he struck with the boat hook on the shoals at the entrance of the Eastern River weighed twenty-two pounds and a half, and was three feet and a half long', wrote King.[48] Bungaree constantly went ashore in the ship's boats with the explorers, sometimes helping them to collect shells. Called on to parley with local Aborigines, he would remove his clothes. At the Intercourse Islands, King wrote: 'Bongaree was of course the object of their greatest attention: the fashion in which his body was scarred was the subject of particular remarks; and when he pointed at the sea, to shew them whence he came, they set up a shout of admiration and surprise'.[49]

According to Cunningham, Captain King named Mullet Bay on North Goulburn Island 'in consequence of the immense shoals of that fish which were seen near the shores, and of which Boongaree speared several with his fiz-gig'.[50] King mentioned Bungaree less frequently in his journal as the voyage progressed, saying he did not consider him 'an active seaman'. After a day gathering botanical specimens in an area of sand and mangroves at Port Hurd on Bathurst Island on Tuesday 26 May, Cunningham wrote:

> During the whole of this day's excursion I was accompanied by our worthy native chief, Bongaree, of whose little attentions to me and others when on these excursions I have been perhaps too remiss in making mention, to the enhancement of the character of this enterprising Australian.[51]

Finding his water casks leaking and provisions running low on 31 May, King decided to put in to Timor for supplies. On 4 June 1818, *Mermaid* anchored at Coupang. The French explorer Jules Dumont d'Urville many years later recalled a droll anecdote about Bungaree, who went ashore at Timor and demanded the change he had not been given from a glass of gin on his previous visit 15 years before when he had to quickly rejoin *Investigator* as the ship set sail.[52]

From Timor, *Mermaid* returned to Port Jackson via the west and south coasts,

Bungaree. A native of New South Wales, 1826, Augustus Earle (1793–1838), Oil, NK 118, nla.an–2256865, National Library of Australia, Canberra.

dropping anchor in Sydney Cove on 29 July 1818. The ship did not sail around the continent, so Bungaree did not circumnavigate Australia a second time.

The portrait of Bungaree painted in oils by the travelling artist Augustus Earle (1793–1838) is a well-known image now in the National Portrait Gallery, Canberra. It shows Bungaree standing on a high point of The Rocks overlooking Fort Macquarie on Bennelong Point at the entrance to Sydney Cove. Earle's painting portrays Bungaree in typical pose, his right arm raised, holding out his black cocked hat decorated with gold ribbon to greet a stranger. He wears a splendid scarlet jacket, with brass button and gold lace. On his chest, hanging from a metal chain around his neck shines his brass gorget or breastplate, shaped like a crescent, presented to him in 1815 by his patron Governor Lachlan Macquarie.

There is an air of genuine nobility in the expression and bearing of Bungaree in Earle's study, one of the earliest oil paintings of an Australian Aborigine. However, as Geoffrey Dutton perceptively remarked in *White on Black* (1974), Bungaree 'had only to look down at his bare feet to know where he stood'.[53] To Aboriginal people, conversely, Bungaree's red jacket represented a symbol of power, which they equated with the red-coated marines and their muskets from the first days of English settlement and copied for ceremonial body painting. The scene dominated by Bungaree's figure shows three British warships, the 74-gun HMS *Warspite*, HMS *Fly* and HMS *Volage*, from the Royal Navy China Squadron, commanded by Commodore Sir James Brisbane, which anchored in Sydney Cove on 17 October 1826.[54] A fourth vessel, under full sail off Bennelong Point, resembles the French corvette *Astrolabe*, under frigate captain Jules Dumont d'Urville, which reached Sydney on 2 December 1826.[55]

At this stage of his life, Bungaree relied on ships visiting Port Jackson to provide European comforts like brandy, rum and Cooper's ale, tobacco, rope and old clothing. The Reverend John McGarvie, a Presbyterian minister and naturalist, first glimpsed Bungaree when his ship *Greenock* came into port on 21 May 1826:

> Having come to anchor we saw a boat coming alongside with Bungarie chief of the Broken Bay Natives. He had 2 or 3 Gins [women] with him who remained in the boat. He got a glass of brandy, and retired after making most profitable revenewes. He is a Drunken bare legged & barefoot Savage having a brass plate on his breast intimating that he is chief of the tribe.[56]

In the decade before his death, Bungaree became a familiar figure around Sydney Town, delighting crowds in the streets by mimicking a succession of governors who had been his patrons. He survived in colonial society by adopting the elaborate manners of the Georgian period. Dressed in cast-off European uniforms and jackets and wearing his gorget or brass breastplate engraved with the words 'Bungaree, Chief of the Broken Bay Tribe 1815', he would doff his cocked hat and bow deeply to welcome the captains of ships visiting Port Jackson. This was part of the protocol demanded of an Aboriginal elder who was the undisputed leading man in the Sydney area.

Bungaree died at Garden Island in November 1830 and was buried in a wooden coffin at Rose Bay.

A few months after his death, Bungaree's image could be seen on the painted signboard hanging outside the King Bungaree public house in Clarence Street, Sydney. 'A great number of black natives have congregated around the spot since its exhibition, who point with significant gestures at their old leader', the *Sydney Gazette* reported.[57] These Aborigines were following the traditional taboo against naming the dead. Samuel Lyons auctioned the hotel in 1832.

11 Daniel Moowattin in Regency London

In 1805 a 14-year-old Aboriginal youth named Daniel sailed to Norfolk Island and Van Diemen's Land. Five years later, Dan or Daniel Moowattin (c. 1791–1816) became the third Indigenous Australian known to visit England after Bennelong and Yemmerrawanne.

Daniel lived in London for one year, where he dressed 'in the pink of fashion', was inoculated against smallpox, smoked a pipe, frequented London pubs and Chelsea coffee houses and endured a bitterly cold winter, in which the Thames filled with blocks of ice.

As a boy, Daniel, born in Parramatta, west of Sydney, became a guide and helper for the botanist George Caley (1770–1829), who came to Australian in 1800 to collect plants and specimens for Sir Joseph Banks.

His name appears on colonial maps, but there are no known portraits of Daniel Moowattin, or of his mentor George Caley.

In 1807, while searching for a koala requested by Sir Joseph Banks, Daniel 'heard a noise like the surf beating on the beach' and came across a waterfall, which Caley named 'The Cataract of Car`rung-Gurring; on the river Moowat`tin'. This was the present Appin Falls on the Cataract River. There is a good case for the original name to be restored: Caley told Banks that he had named the river 'to commemorate the memory of the native to whom I am indebted for the discovery of the cataract'.[1] Matthew Flinders shows 'Moowattin Creek' and the 'Cataract of Carrung-gurring' in the atlas of *A Voyage to Terra Australis*, published in London in 1814. Charles Grimes also used these names in his *Topographical map of New South Wales* (1806).[2]

As a consequence of his association with George Caley, Daniel was to have an extraordinary, though short, life. He accompanied Caley as a bush guide, interpreter, bird, plant and leaf-getter, servant and companion on botanising excursions around Sydney and in the Blue Mountain foothills and lived for some years in Caley's cottage on the Crescent, close to Old Government House in what is now Parramatta Park.

Norfolk Island and Van Diemen's Land
Daniel sailed to Norfolk Island and Van Diemen's Land in 1805 as a passenger on HMS *Buffalo*.[3] He reached Norfolk Island on 5 September and joined Caley, who

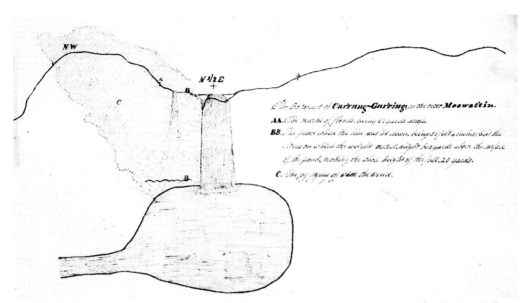

The Cataract of Car'rung-Gurring; on the river Moowat`tin, 1807, [Appin Falls], George Caley (1770–1829) Pen and ink, Natural History Museum, London.

Moowattin Creek and the *Cataract of Carrung-gurring,* Detail from 'East Coast, 1 January 1814', *Chart of Terra Australis* Plate VIII, *Atlas,* From Matthew Flinders, *A Voyage to Terra Australis*, London 1814, Mitchell Library, Sydney.

had left Port Jackson on the trading ship *Sydney*, owned by Robert Campbell.[4] They collected plant specimens together on the island while *Sydney* was taking on board settlers, their stock, and provisions for Hobart Town. Daniel's stay at Norfolk Island is corroborated by Caley's plant notes, in which he mentions *Coroy'ba* (possibly *Eucalyptus maculata*), a tree that 'grows to an immense height and may be said to be the tallest in the Forest, though not the thickest. Dan says it is taller than the pines at Norfolk Island & I myself am of the same opinion'.[5] The ship's muster shows that Daniel was discharged from *Buffalo* at the Derwent River (Hobart Town) on 15 November 1805. *Sydney*, with Caley on board, left Norfolk Island on 2 November 1805, but was delayed by strong winds and finally anchored in the Derwent on 29 November 1805.[6]

'I have been on a voyage to Norfolk Island and the River Derwent', Caley informed Sir Joseph Banks in a letter written in April 1806 after his return to Parramatta. On 5 December 1805, Caley and Daniel together climbed Mount Wellington, near Hobart, which Caley described as 'Table Hills, or Snowy Mountain, but which I shall hereafter call Skiddaw' (after the peak in the English Lakes District). They spent an uncomfortable night, warmed only by a small fire, in 'showers of mizzling rain and sleet', as Caley told Banks:

> Never did I feel such piercing cold since I left England. My fingers were so benum[b]ed that I could not hold a pen; but though I was shivering with cold I was greatly animated by the questions and conversation of an inland, or bush, native of Port Jackson, which came with me and who never had felt such a keen piercing air before.

On the mountain, Daniel tracked and caught a 'porcupine ant eater' (echidna) and a 'whombat' (wombat). The echidna got away at Slopen Island in Frederick Henry Bay, where Caley collected plants ashore from 21 to 27 December 1805. The wombat wriggled out of its collar and escaped after his return to Parramatta. 'It was becoming very tame and fed remarkably well on dry grass when on board ship … What was most singular, I could not make the dog hunt it … In the course of about two hours I got about half a dozen natives, and they could but trace [it] only a short way', wrote Caley. On 28 December the ship sailed for Adventure Bay in Bass Strait and left there on 31 December. On 8 January 1806, Caley and Daniel spent the day ashore in the Kent Group islands.[7] The *Sydney* anchored again in Port Jackson on 23 January 1806.[8]

After 1806, Caley began to refer to Daniel in his letters as 'Moowat'tin' or 'Moowattin', the name he then adopted, which suggests that the boy, then aged about 15, had taken a new name after being initiated.

According to the Reverend Samuel Marsden (1765–1838), an Aboriginal orphan born in Parramatta was given the English name Daniel. Marsden, the son of a

Yorkshire blacksmith, came to Parramatta in 1794 as an assistant chaplain to the colony of New South Wales and was chaplain from 1800 to 1818. Marsden made three separate statements about Daniel's origins. In 1816, under oath in a court of law, Marsden said he had known him for 'nearly twenty years'. He had been reared at Parramatta from infancy, Marsden testified, 'first in the family of Richard Partridge, and afterwards with Mr. Caley, botanist …' [9] Ten years later, in a report to Anglican Archdeacon Thomas Hobbes Scott on the *Aborigines of New South Wales*, Marsden spoke of a 'Native belonging to Parramatta, whom I knew from a boy, his English name was Daniel, he was a very fine youth…'[10] Marsden described Daniel, in a letter to French navigator Jules Dumont d'Urville in 1826 as a native 'of the Parramatta tribe' (*à la tribu de Parramatta*).[11]

In 1812, Daniel Moowattin was said to be 21 years of age, which would make 1791 his probable year of birth.[12] He had been adopted as an infant by Richard Partridge, a convict then aged about 31, who was appointed a watchman in Parramatta in 1791. On 3 November 1793, Richard Partridge, the son of Mary Greenwood and Richard Partridge senior was baptised at Parramatta.[13] Mary Greenwood had been a London servant and prostitute, who was sentenced to death at the Old Bailey in 1785 for stealing, but was reprieved and sentenced to transportation for seven years.[14]

Partridge gained a conditional pardon on 27 September 1794 and in September 1796 was granted 60 acres of land at the Northern Boundary Farms by Governor John Hunter.[15] A small creek ran through the property, which was bounded by the present Felton and Jenkins Roads, Carlingford, the site of James Ruse High School and an electricity sub-station.

During the 1790s Richard Partridge was the government flogger and executioner at Parramatta. From 1791, he was frequently described as 'Richard Partridge alias Rice'.[16] There is no doubt that Partridge/Rice was a brutalised product of the English convict system, a habitual criminal turned informer, flogger and finally executioner. It was said that 'Rice acted … in the two fold capacity of gaoler and the finisher of the law'.[17] Directed by Marsden, Partridge took part in the cruel punishment at Toongabbie on 6 October 1800 of Maurice Fitzgerald (or Fitzgarrel) and Paddy Galvin, described by Joseph Holt:

There was two floggers—Richard Rice and Jon Jonson, the Hangman from Sidney. Rice was a left handed man and Jonson was Right handed so they stood at each side and I never saw two trashers [threshers] in a barn move their stroakes more handeyer [handier] than those two men killers did … the flesh and skin flew in my face as they shooke off the cats.

Galvin received 300 lashes of the vicious cat o' nine tails without a whimper. 'You could see his backbone between his shoulder blades,' recalled Holt, 'they put him in the cart and sent him to hospital'.[18] 'He [Galvin] would have died on the spot before he would tell a single sentence', wrote Marsden, who ordered this 'severe punishment' in an attempt to extract information about a conspiracy allegedly planned by Irish convicts.[19] Marsden was told that the rebels had added the name of 'Richard Rice the executioner … to the death list'.[20] Jon Jonson or John Johnson was an alias of the Danish gambler, convict and explorer Jorgen Jorgensen.

George Caley, the son of a horse dealer, was born at Craven, Yorkshire. He taught himself how to recognise plants from books one hard winter and how to collect them from nature the following spring. In 1795, at the age of 25, he sent some specimens to Sir Joseph Banks, seeking employment with a botanist. Banks arranged for Caley to gain experience as a gardener's labourer in Chelsea Gardens, where he worked for two years with botanist William Curtis and was allowed to use his library.

In November 1798, Banks offered to employ Caley to collect plants and seeds in New South Wales. After many delays, Caley sailed from Portsmouth on 1 November 1799 on the *Speedy*, a 313-ton whaler owned by Samuel Enderby & Co., hired to transport female convicts to New South Wales. Also on board were the colony's new governor, Philip Gidley King and his wife Anna Josepha. After a passage of five months via Cape Town, *Speedy* arrived in Port Jackson on 15 April 1800 in company with HMS *Buffalo*.[21]

By May 1800, Caley had been put on the rations and settled in a small weatherboard cottage at Parramatta, where he had the use of Governor King's house to dry and prepare his specimens.[22] He began a relationship with Mrs Wise, the widow of Edward Wise, a weaver who had been swept overboard from *Speedy* during the voyage out.[23]

In a letter to Banks in October 1800, Caley said he planned to give 'bread to the different natives — as I find I can gain their affections, and get information from them'.[24] While Caley was aboard the brig *Lady Nelson* at Westernport and Port Phillip Bay in 1801, Aborigines at Parramatta had killed one settler, wounded others and plundered some houses. Caley told Banks in August that year:

I believe the Governor [P.G. King] gave strict orders to shoot them, and the military went in quest of them several times, but were not able to meet with them; however these bush natives have not returned into the camp ever since … Let them behave indifferently to other people, it will not do for me to fall out with them. I have every reason to believe that the whites have been the greatest aggressors on the whole. At other places in the colony the natives adjoining frequent the inhabitants. I mean to keep a bush native constant soon, as they can trace anything so well in the woods, and can climb trees with such ease, whereby they will be very useful to me and [I] shall gain a better knowledge of them.[25]

Caley might have chosen Daniel at first because of his long arms and ability to climb trees (a trait often attributed to the inland Aboriginal people by early observers) to obtain plant and bird specimens. For several years Caley relied on his assistance and knowledge of plants and places for his natural history research. Specimens of leaves, gumnuts and flowers of eucalyptus species gathered around Sydney more than 200 years ago, labelled by Caley as 'Got by Dan', survive in the National Herbarium at the Royal Botanic Gardens of New South Wales.

Daniel's sharp intelligence and understanding of English and Aboriginal dialects soon made him equally valuable as an informant. He told Caley the Aboriginal names and uses of trees, plants, birds and animals and gave him information about Aboriginal customs.

Two other Aboriginal men also collected for Caley. In January 1808, Narrang Jack (Little Jack), from the Nepean River near Penrith, obtained a specimen of *Wong'nary*, which botanist Joseph Maiden thought was *Eucalyptus haemastoma*. Caley wrote in his notes: 'I have only seen a few trees of this kind. At first I took it to be the White Gum. I am indebted to the natives in pointing out the distinction.'[26] Another man, Cadingera, collected *Burrar'gro*, believed to be a natural hybrid between grey ironbark (*E. siderophloia*) and grey box (*E. hemiphloia*).[27]

On his journeys with Moowattin and other Aborigines, George Caley developed a

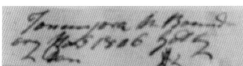

Tonugora St. Boundary Nov 1806 Got by Dan, Photo: Keith Vincent Smith 1999, Specimen identified as *E. panicula* X *E. siderophloia,* National Herbarium, Royal Botanic Gardens of New South Wales, Sydney.

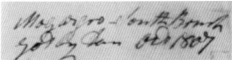

Mogargro — South Brush Got by Dan Oct 1807, Photo: Keith Vincent Smith 1999, Specimen identified as *E. beyeri* by Joseph Maiden, National Herbarium, Royal Botanic Gardens of New South Wales, Sydney.

sympathetic understanding of their way of life that was deeper than most of his contemporaries. In 1808, Caley was dismayed when he was told that Moowattin had been speared and killed. 'I have since heard that he is not dead, which has a little recovered my spirits,' he wrote to Banks, 'else I should have been unable to have written these few lines'. He continued:

> The native I have been speaking of is the most civilized, of any that I know who may still be called a savage and the best interpreter of the more inland natives' language of any that I have met with … I can place that confidence in him which I cannot in any other — all except him are afraid to go beyond the limits of the space which they inhabit with me (or indeed with any other) and I know this one would stand by me until I fell, if attacked by strangers. This man is Moowattin, I hope he will recover — I should much like to bring him to England. By shewing him the different Museums we should get a better knowledge of the animals of this part …

Caley wrote further that, although the Aborigines, by going naked, 'render them the most wretched objects to Europeans of any, yet … I can single our several who have by far better mental faculties than hundreds of the lower orders in England. Moowattin in a great measure has been bred [raised] with me.'[28]

'It was after Caley's close friendship with Moowat'tin had been established that Caley appeared to take an interest in eucalypts, since the native could collect the blossoms and fruits hitherto unattainable', wrote Joan Webb in *George Caley, 19th Century Naturalist* (1995). Sir Joseph Maiden, Director of the Royal Botanic Gardens, Sydney, located 50 specimens of eucalypts collected by Caley in the herbarium at Vienna. Webb further comments: 'These specimens, together with Caley eucalypts now in the Natural History Museum, London, tell a story of keen observation, extensive use of the natives, and an astute deduction concerning hybridisation of the ironbarks'.[29]

In a letter to Banks in February 1809, Caley said Moowattin had recovered from a severe wound caused by a spear thrust through his thigh and into his stomach, causing copious bleeding. He elaborated his reasons for seeking to bring the boy with him to England and listed the virtues of a 'native guide', which must have reflected the services Moowattin provided. 'And if there were a ship going on a voyage of discovery I should strongly recommend such a native to the Naturalist. There would be no danger of the Collectors getting lost or bewildered, which is too oftentimes the case, for the Native would trace back their footsteps.' Such a native could warn against any danger from local natives, track different animals 'unnoticed by a European' and readily obtain many new birds. 'Natives in general are excellent marksmen and quicker sighted than our people.'

> The specimens of the different trees might be procured which would otherwise have been missed or left for want of a climber. It is in this department where a native may be made most useful.[30]

Daniel in London

The frigate *HMS Hindostan*, commanded by Captain John Pasco, left Sydney on 12 May 1810 in company with HMS *Dromedary* and HMS *Porpoise*. Those on board included the deposed Governor William Bligh, George Caley, Daniel Moowattin and George Suttor, a gardener and nurseryman from Chelsea who had been sent to New South Wales by Sir Joseph Banks. Caley also took his pet parrot Jack and the vast natural history collection he had accumulated over 10 years.[31]

On 25 July, the frigate touched at Rio, which Daniel probably visited with Caley, who went for a 'ramble' with Suttor and Dr Martin Mason, one of several witnesses returning to England to give evidence for Bligh, who had been deposed as governor by the New South Wales Corps in 1808.[32]

The *Hindostan* anchored at Spithead on 25 October 1810 and sailed up the Thames to dock at Woolwich. Caley was well received by Banks at his house in Soho Square. He took lodgings near Chelsea Common, close to Battersea Bridge, probably in the same house as Mrs Wise and her daughter Sally, who had returned to England earlier (about 1806). Daniel, however, was refused permission to go ashore until a written guarantee could be given for his orderly conduct. After the tedious and terrifying ocean voyage of six months, he was confined aboard the ship through the cold dark months of November and December. His Majesty's government wished to discourage the practice of bringing natives from the South Seas to England 'as answering no purpose whatever'.[33] Soon after Bennelong returned to Sydney in September 1795, Governor John Hunter had notified Judge Advocate David Collins that King George III had 'expressed his desire that not another native should be brought home from New South Wales'.[34]

Sir Joseph Banks finally gave a guarantee for Moowattin's 'orderly conduct' early in January 1811. Although Banks thought Caley had shown poor judgment in bringing Daniel to England, he supported him at his personal expense.[35] Banks asked George Suttor to take care of Dan until an opportunity came to send him back to Sydney. 'The whole experience', wrote Australian anthropologist and historian Isabel McBryde, 'must have been devastating for Moowat'tin, and saddening for Caley'.[36]

At this time, George Caley began a personal diary, headed *Remarks on the weather &c.*, which he was to keep until 1817. These memoirs, now in the Natural History Museum in South Kensington (London), record many dull, cold days with 'mizzling rain' and 'frosty mornings' during 1811, when England was struck by a freezing winter. If he had suffered from cold winds and rain at the top of Mount Wellington in 1806, Daniel would certainly have felt a chilly blast while in London.

Caley's largely unpunctuated journal provides many insights into the experience of a 'civilised' Aboriginal man, transplanted from his life in colonial Australia to

Regency London.[37] On Thursday 3 January 1811, Caley went to Chelsea in the morning. 'Snow fell', he wrote in his weather diary. 'This night Mr Suttor brought Dan to me he having fetched him from the ship at Woolwich.'[38]

Once ashore, Daniel, a healthy, good-looking and bright young man, must have cut a fine figure. Samuel Marsden thought that, because Caley was employed by Sir Joseph Banks, Daniel was 'introduced into the first society in London'.[39] This might have been the case, but, as far as can be ascertained his presence in London was not noticed by the newspapers of the day. Compared to the way Omai the Tahitian had been lionised and Bennelong and Yemmerrawanne welcomed in high society, Daniel was hardly noticed. The vogue for exotic visitors from the South Seas had long passed and a black face was no novelty in London. African sailors, freed slaves, servants and runaways crowded the back streets behind the church of St Martins in the Field and were known as 'St. Giles Blackbirds'.

Daniel boarded at Chelsea and went regularly to a coffee house where he 'smoked his pipe of an evening, and drew much company who were desirous of seeing a native of this Colony', or so the *Sydney Gazette* recorded on his return in 1812. His excellent pronunciation of the English language was 'generally admired' by those he met. The *Gazette* report said that Daniel's clothes, provided by Banks, were of good quality and tailored in 'the very pink of fashion', that is, in the style affected by the Prince Regent and his friend George 'Beau' Brummell:

> Mr. Moowattye was to all intents and purposes a black beau. He was proud of his finery … and affected to deport himself with all the distance and gravity assumed by a pauper rising unexpectedly to fortune.[40]

Daniel would have dressed in breeches, ruffled shirts and waistcoats. He was given a silk pocket-handkerchief and a neckerchief.[41]

He soon became homesick. One morning, Lieutenant William Lawson of the New South Wales Corps met 'Dan a Black native' on the Horse Guard's Parade in St James's Park. 'I asked him how he liked the fine things in England his answer was: "I am anxious to return to my own Country, I find more pleasure under a Gum tree sitting with my tribe than I do here".'[42]

On 4 January 1811, Caley took Daniel to meet his patron Sir Joseph Banks at Soho and 'from thence to have him inoculated'. Afterwards they went to Covent Garden, a busy fruit and vegetable market by day and the haunt of theatregoers and prostitutes by night. They went several times to the Vaccine Pock Institute at No. 5 Golden Square (Westminster), established by Dr George Pearson (1751–1828) in 1799, to inoculate Daniel against smallpox. No doubt both Caley and Banks were aware of the smallpox epidemic that had killed half the Aboriginal people living around Port Jackson in 1789. Caley took Daniel with him on visits to old friends and colleagues, to the Customs House (where some of Caley's specimens were being held) and, sometimes, to see Banks.

It snowed on Wednesday 9 January and the following day, Caley 'went to Mr. Brown's, and took Dan with me'. Caley had hunted plants in the bush at North Rocks and other areas around Sydney with the surgeon, botanist and scientist Robert Brown (1773–1858), who sailed aboard *HMS Investigator* with Matthew Flinders and Bungaree. Brown supervised Banks's vast collection of plants, books, manuscripts and drawings, occupying an office in Banks's Soho Square house with a separate entrance in Dean Street.

On Saturday 12 January, 'a fair morning that turned out wet', Caley took Dan (as he called him in his journal) to the Customs House and then across London Bridge to the Borough and back over Blackfriars Bridge. The young man from colonial Parramatta must have marvelled at the city of London, but more so at the incredible sight of the ice-clogged Thames. 'The river was frozen up so far as to stop the navigation between London Bridge and Blackfriars', Caley wrote. 'The surface of the water was entirely covered with broken pieces of ice which were drifting upwards with the tide.' Logs and timber spars bobbed amid the ice. That Sunday 'Dan went out with Mr. Suttor'. On Monday, 'a dull day with mizzling rain at times', Daniel went with Suttor to see William Bligh, who was living with his family at 3 Durham Place, Lambeth.

So Dan's life went on in London. One day, Dr Pearson exhibited him to his medical students to demonstrate that the marks of his smallpox inoculation were more visible than those of his European patients.

On 2 February, a Saturday, Sir Joseph Banks 'questioned Dan about the Cola (koala) while Caley and Moowattin sorted specimens at Soho Square. While Caley was in a grocery shop at the upper end of Piccadilly, 'Moowattin left me and afterwards got lost'. Caley returned to Soho Square, but Daniel was not there. Not long afterwards, Banks's footman brought in Daniel 'reeling drunk'. He had gone to a shop, asked for directions and found the way to Sir Joseph's from a map drawn by the shopkeeper. 'Sir Joseph['s] servant', wrote Caley, 'said he had a deal of trouble in getting him along'.

'Dan went out with Mr. Suttor' while Caley compared eucalypt specimens and dined with the naturalist and ornithologist Aylmer Bourke Lambert and seedsman James Dickson the following Wednesday. Judging by later events, George Suttor led Daniel astray on this outing. On Friday 8 February, 'a dribbling rainy day', Daniel had an encounter with the landlady of a public house called the Running Horse at Piccadilly that might have cast a shadow over his future life. Caley wrote:

Dan gave me the slip in returning — some woman having told him to call on his return where he had been with Mr. Suttor — As far as I can judge it was the Landlady at the running horse public house in Piccadilly.

The father-and-son relationship between Caley and Daniel began to cool as the youth gained a taste for alcoholic liquor and the company of women in public houses. Caley himself began to frequent the Red House, an Elizabethan brick tavern adjoining swampy Battersea Fields, and sometimes took Dan there in the evening.

Returning to his lodgings in the rain after visiting Banks on Monday 11 February, Caley was shocked to meet Daniel, who was drunk and abusive. This time, Dan had gone far enough to provoke Caley's rare but fiery anger. 'As soon as we got home I could not then bear it which made me to use my fist as a retaliation', Caley wrote. He hit Daniel with such force that he broke his own thumb. In his journal, Caley railed at the obstinacy of 'Mowwattin ... as I never before observed in any of his color'. Caley felt betrayed. 'I am now well rewarded for my favors, particularly those shewn in New South Wales', he scrawled, his broken thumb so painful that he could not hold the pen properly.

On Monday 18 February, George Caley and William Anderson visited Lee and Kennedy's Vineyard Nursery at Hammersmith. Anderson was gardener to James Vere at Kensington Gore. Afterwards Caley went to Holland House in Kensington on a novel mission to obtain 'a piece of wood for a Bummaring [boomerang]—saw a Black Swan there', he noted. Banks might have asked Daniel to make a boomerang. There was ice on the ponds as Caley walked to Kew Gardens on the frosty Wednesday morning of 20 February. He heard crows calling and noted that they made a different sound from those at 'Botany Bay ... their voices was not so strong and clear, being more gruff and hoarse'. Caley recalled the occasion in his notes on Australian birds, published 15 years later in the *Transactions of the Linnean Society:*

> In Mr. Caley's MSS. are the following remarks. 'This bird is gregarious and not to be met with at all times. Its native name is Wa'gan. [Raven; *Corcus coronoides*] — Moowattin, a native follower of mine, tells me that it makes its nest like the Ca'ruck [Australian magpie; *Gymnorhina tibicen*], but that he never met with more than one nest, which was in a Coray'bo tree at the Devil's Back [near Cecil Park], about 4 miles from Prospect Hill ... I have observed that the croak of this bird is not so hoarse as that of *C. corone*. This was also remarked by the same native when with me in this country (England) on hearing a Crow one morning near Fulham.'[43]

Fulham lay on the way from Chelsea to Kew Gardens. The next day Caley went to the Customs House again — 'Dan went with me'— and Caley spent the evening at the Red House.

Caley first went to see William Bullock's Museum of natural history in Piccadilly with George Suttor on Tuesday 5 March 1811. 'Did not think it well arranged as what had been spoken of — His New Holland birds but few in number,' he wrote. Bullock's museum was packed with curious specimens, including two stuffed koalas and an echidna from New Holland.[44] Three years had passed since Caley first told Sir Joseph Banks that he wished to bring Daniel to England to show him 'the Different Museums'.

On 12 March 1811, George Caley called on Dr Martin Mason 'with a Skull' (probably an Aboriginal skull) and then met Suttor at the Red Lion public house in Pall Mall. Daniel's name does not occur in Caley's diary again until Sunday 17 March and it can be assumed that he was in the care of George Suttor, who was staying in Chelsea with his wife's family. That foggy morning Caley went to Kew Gardens with Aiton, Mason and some others — 'Took Dan with me', he wrote.

Caley was busy unpacking and organising his New South Wales botanical specimens. One day he went to Soho Square 'to pack up my cases' and on another day he 'packed up the insects' before going to Dickson's shop. Daniel's bad behaviour and Caley's resentment came to a head on Thursday 28 March, which Caley began with a visit to the Old Botanic Gardens at Brompton, where he had once worked as a gardener. Daniel suffered as a consequence; Caley wrote:

Dan this afternoon went out unknown to me and did not return by bed time — heard him knocking at the gate at about ¼ before 3 at a guess — but was determined I would not get up to let him in — found him lying at the gate seemingly suffering much from the cold.

Next morning, Caley braved the 'cold raw air' and went to Paddington with his cases. 'Dan the preceding night I learned had lost his handkerchief & a silk pocket one.' Caley also discovered that Daniel had been out drinking with Sir Joseph Banks's servant, but seemed to take a more lenient view of his transgressions. Daniel knew that Caley was due to leave London for Manchester, after which he would be left with Suttor.

On Sunday, 30 March, Caley took Daniel to 'Mr. Haworth's purposely to shew him the New Hollander'. Adrian Hardy Haworth (1767–1833), who lived in Little Chelsea, was a naturalist whose interests included botany (cactus and other succulent plants), entomology (he collected 40 000 insects) and butterflies (he was the author of *Lepidoptera Britannica*).[45]

On 1 April Caley booked two inside seats on a coach for Dorking for Mrs Wise and her daughter Sally. He spent the evening at the Red House, but wrote in his diary: 'Dan stopped out all night'. The next day he wrote: 'The account Dan gave me of himself was that he had been drunk'. Caley took 'my Mrs' to town 'to see her safe off in the coach to Dorking'. He visited Bullock's Museum again and met Suttor in St Martin's Lane, near Trafalgar Square.

A droll trio could be seen walking through the streets of London on the fine, warm morning of Thursday 4 April 1811, the day of Caley's departure for his native Yorkshire. Caley first saw Sir Joseph Banks at Soho Square and then went to the canal office in Paddington accompanied by George Suttor and Dan, who carried Jack the cockatoo, caged in a hamper 'which he pecked all to pieces'. Jack was troublesome on the journey, but was very quiet when released. Caley's boat was delayed, so they went to a public house, 'I think the [R]unning [H]orse', which must have brought back some memories for Daniel, but exasperated Caley. 'Could not get any thing to eat or drink there except some bread and cheese — cannot cook us any thing not even make us tea', he wrote. They got some tea afterwards at the Red Lion in Pall Mall. 'Took leave of Mr. Suttor and Dan about 8 o'clock', wrote Caley. He travelled by canal boat and horseback to Manchester and did not see Daniel again until 21 June.

On Wednesday 24 April 1811, Caley received a letter from the Judge Advocate General summoning him to attend the trial of Major George Johnston of the New South Wales Corps at Chelsea Hospital as a material witness. Johnston was charged with mutiny for deposing Governor William Bligh in the so-called 'Rum Rebellion' in Sydney on 26 January 1808. Returning to London on 4 May, Caley went to Chelsea and later called on Robert Brown. On Sunday 5 May, Caley saw Governor Bligh, who gave him a card to the Judge Advocate in respect of the summons he had received.

Caley and Suttor both attended the trial at Chelsea Hospital on Monday 6 May 1811. However, Caley wrote: 'the Court Martial broke off until tomorrow owing to some of the members not being well enough to attend — went to town with Mr. Suttor'. Caley was present at every sitting of the court martial, from 6 May to 5 June 1811, but was not called upon to give evidence. He spent the latter part of each day in botanical pursuits, sometimes visiting Chelsea Gardens, the Sloane Botanic Gardens or Kensington Gore. He stayed at the Fox and Hounds, a small inn near Sloane Gardens, until 14 May, going to the Red House or Covent Garden at night.

Matthew Flinders and Daniel Moowattin might have met each other about this time. On Sunday 12 May Flinders wrote in his private journal: 'Walked out in the evening. At 9, went to Sir Joseph Banks, where I met the two Daniels.' One Daniel was Banks's colleague, the botanist Daniel Solander and it is not impossible that the other might have been Daniel Moowattin.[46] On Monday 27 May 1811, George Caley called on Robert Brown, who took him to see Flinders, then living in rented rooms at No. 7 Nassau Street, London. In his private journal, Flinders wrote: 'Mr. Brown called in the evening, with Mr. Cayley [*sic*], in order to my consulting him about the parts at the back of Port Jackson …' [47] This is the chart included in the atlas of *A Voyage to Terra Australis*, published shortly before Flinders's death in June 1814.[48] Neither Caley nor Flinders mentioned Moowattin in their journals that day.

It was said after his return to New South Wales in May 1812 that, while in London, Daniel Moowattin 'attended every show he heard of, and generally appeared more surprised at the number of people assembled in a crowd than at any other circumstance'.[49] He could not have missed the spectacular military review on Wimbledon Common on 10 June 1811. 'The inhabitants of every quarter of London were in motion … immense multitudes were seen proceeding on foot at so early an hour as three o'clock towards the scene of the review', the *Times* reported.

The Prince of Wales, who had been declared Prince Regent on 5 February 1811, took the salute of some 20 000 troops in front of a crowd of 200 000 people.[50] Britain was celebrating the victory of the Duke of Wellington at Almeida that forced the French army under General André Massena to retreat from Portugal into Spain. At Chelsea Gardens that evening Caley saw 'a deal of people volunteers &c returning from the review'. He grumbled in his diary about a second military review as he walked to Kew on 23 June. 'Thought I would have been blinded with dust between home & Fulham from the running of carriages & horses', he remarked, 'there being a review on Wimbledon Common. Heard the fanfare when going through Putney.' That day Caley, with Suttor, went to Kew by way of Putney and, for the first time in months, he wrote, 'Dan along with us'. They botanised at Hammersmith the next day.

According to an anonymous contributor to *Chambers's Edinburgh Journal* (1832) 'Moo-wat-tin spoke English so well as to excite surprise at the power with which he would use the monosyllables'. The English ladies he met were pleased by his manners and politeness. 'He ate and drank very moderately, preferring sherry to any other wine, of which he never took more than three glasses.' One evening he sang a song whose meaning he translated into English as 'first we take fish, next take kangaroo, then take wife'. Moowattin was surprised by the size of London. He 'thought there were too many houses, trees were much wanted; could not imagine how all the people got food; thought the weather was *sower cold*. Clouds too near the ground; horses fine, the men strong, the women beautiful …'[51]

In August, George Caley began to make his farewells before moving permanently to live near Manchester. He called on Robert Brown on Friday 16 August and the following day saw Governor Bligh and the artist Ferdinand Bauer, but felt very drowsy, having caught a cold. On Sunday 18 August, Caley went to Spring Grove, Sir Joseph Banks's country villa near Hounslow, Middlesex, but was 'not above 5 hours absent'. Later that day, Caley gave Suttor a note from Banks 'concerning Dan having a paper provided to return' [to New South Wales]. Two days before, Banks had written a letter from Soho Square, probably to Under Secretary Sir Robert Peel:

> Allow me to request that a passage may be provided in the vessels now fitting out for New South Wales to carry out a native of that country called Dan, who was brought home several months ago by an injudicious person who had been for some years employed by me as a collector in that country. I have maintained him since his arrival, and do not wish to subject Government to any charge on his account, but only his passage home.[52]

On Monday 19 August, Caley went to town, where he called on Robert Brown. 'Dan there', he wrote in his diary.[53] This was possibly the final meeting between the botanist and his 'native follower'. It was the last time that Daniel was mentioned in Caley's diary and surviving letters. At some time during his stay in London, perhaps on this occasion, Robert Brown gave Moowattin a fowling piece, a light gun used for shooting birds, probably to obtain specimens from New South Wales. When the time came to leave London and return to Australia, Daniel 'appeared to feel mental agony at separation', making the rounds of his London friends and uttering, 'Never forget, never forget'.[54]

'A black Gentleman'

In October 1811, Daniel Moowattin and George Suttor boarded the convict vessel *Mary* at Portsmouth. The ship eventually weighed anchor on Wednesday 20 November 1811. 'We had a very fine passage out in the *Mary of London*, a hired transport, though it was long and tedious', Suttor recalled in his *Memoirs* (1859). 'We left the Mother Bank under convoy of the sloop of war the *Kangaroo*, with several other ships. We put into Rio Janeiro, where we touched on our passage home; the Royal family of Portugal was at Rio when we arrived and the place was very gay and full of business.'[55]

Going ashore at Rio in January 1812, Daniel haughtily informed an officer who overhauled his boat that he was 'a black Gentleman, sent out as a Botanist to New South Wales'. Robert Lowe, an emigrant settler on his way to Port Jackson on the same ship with his wife and two children, was impressed with Dan. He considered him to be 'a sensible man; very intelligent, and so much pleased with the manners and customs of Europeans, that he had frequently during the passage avowed a determination to conform to them entirely after his arrival'.[56]

Suttor wrote in his *Memoirs*:

> Sometime in January 1812 we departed from Rio and had a long tedious passage to Sydney, where we arrived on the 12 of May 1812, having been absent just two years ... It was about nine in the evening when I reached Baulkham Hills, I was accompanied by Dan the native (Moowattie,) who had been taken to England by my dear friend, Mr. George Caley.[57]

After all the delays and frustrations, George Suttor was overjoyed to be reunited with his family at his farm 'Chelsea House'. He brought with him a collection of date, palm and olive plants to establish in the colony. Home at last in his own Country, Daniel Moowattin was restless and unhappy. He must have realised, bitterly, that in New South Wales he was far from being the object of curiosity he had been in London. At Parramatta he was no longer a 'gentleman', but simply a 'black native' and a member of a race openly despised by the majority of European settlers.

Within two weeks of landing, Moowattin had sold, for seven shillings and sixpence, the fowling piece given to him by Robert Brown, which, said the *Sydney Gazette*, he had 'pledged the gentleman who gave it to him to keep *for ever and ever*'.

He shed his fine London clothes and ran into the bush, just as Bennelong had done after his return from London in 1795. Nearly five months later, George Suttor sent a letter to Sir Joseph Banks with this news:

> The Native which your humanity fed and clothed in England returned in health to his native country. The polished manners and comfortable living of Englishmen made but a slight impression on his mind and a few days after landing he left my house which I wished him to have made his home, made away with all his clothes &c fowling piece which Mr. Brown had given him for some Peach Cyder and returned to his countrymen and Native life.[58]

Though impressed by the crowds, Daniel was not overawed by London. When asked how he liked the fine shops and houses, he replied that they were all very good, but 'not equal to the woods in his own country'.[59] In the bush Daniel felt free. In one statement, made in 1816, Samuel Marsden said he had met Daniel Moowattin after his return from England 'naked in the woods, at a considerable distance from the settlements'.[60] In another version, on 2 December 1826, Marsden wrote:

> … the first time I saw him after his arrival he was sitting, naked, upon the stump of a tree in the woods … to the North of Parramatta. I expressed my astonishment at seeing him in that state, and asked him why he had cast off his clothes and taken to the Bush again. He replied "Me like the Bush best." [61]

Jules Dumont d'Urville's translation into French of a letter from Marsden, sent on 12 December 1826, said the spot where Marsden met Daniel was eight miles from Parramatta and gave Dan's reply as 'because he loved the woods the most'.[62]

Trial and execution

In 1816, 'Daniel Mow-watty or Mowwatting' was working as a labourer on the 100-acre farm of James Bellamy at Pennant Hills, a few miles from Parramatta. On 28 September 1816, the *Sydney Gazette* reported, in a supplement, on the trial of 'Daniel Mowatting', who was charged with the rape of Hannah Russell, the daughter of a settler, in the vicinity of Parramatta. A second Aboriginal man named Bioorah was charged with being present as an accessory to the offence, but the Judge Advocate ordered that he had no case to answer, and he was discharged.[63]

On Monday 7 October 1816, the Court of Criminal Jurisdiction passed the sentence on 'Daniel Mow-watty, for a rape — *Death*'.[64]

Daniel Moowattin was just 25 years old when he was convicted and sentenced to death. It was 10 years since he had climbed an ironbark tree at North Rocks to gather gum leaves and five years since he last walked through the streets of London and visited Kew Gardens with George Caley. He had been convicted and sentenced largely on the opinion of Gregory Blaxland and the Reverend Samuel Marsden, who testified that he knew the difference between good and evil.[65] He was the first Aborigine to be officially hanged in Australia.

Governor Lachlan Macquarie, who was devoted to his sickly wife Elizabeth and delicate son Lachlan and who bestowed his patronage on 'friendly' Aborigines like Bungaree and Bidgee Bidgee, could find no sympathy in his heart for a black man who had raped a white girl. On Friday 1 November 1816, he recorded, dryly, the last moments of the life of Daniel Moowattin:

> This morning were executed, agreeably to their respective sentences, the three Criminals under Sentence of Death — namely — Thomas Collins and Hugh McLair — for High way Robbery — and Daniel Mowwatting (a Black Native of this Colony) — for Rape and Robbery on a young Female White Woman a Native of this Colony. — The three Malefactors confessed their Crimes and all died Penitent.[66]

Before being taken to the gallows, Daniel, who had consistently denied the charges against him, is said to have confessed his crime to Samuel Marsden 'and repented of it'. The hangman placed a noose made of hempen rope around his neck and launched Daniel into eternity. Sydney people passing by were accustomed to see the bodies of hanged men, sometimes four at one time, swinging at the end of a rope at the public gallows next to the stone jail at the corner of George and Essex Streets at The Rocks, which was called Hangman's Hill. That day an Aboriginal face was seen among them for the first time, though not for the last. So ended the short, tragic life of Daniel Moowattin.

12 *Bowen Bungaree at Moreton Bay and San Francisco*

boin [Bowen Bungaree]
Pavel Mikhailov (1786–1840)
Pencil and sanguine on brown paper
R29207/205, Russian State Museum,
St Petersburg
Image Courtesy of Longueville Publications

Bowen Bungaree is unknown in Queensland history, but in 1823, with John Oxley on HM cutter *Mermaid*, he took part in the exploration of Moreton Bay. While there, Oxley found and named the Brisbane River and recommended the establishment of a settlement, while Bowen made the first known drawing on paper by an Indigenous Australian.

Bowen (Boin) was the eldest son of King Bungaree and his first wife Matora, whose totem name, *muttaura*, recorded by the Reverend Lancelot Threlkeld, meant 'small snapper' in the language of the Hunter River and Lake Macquarie, where it is likely she was born.[1] Like his famous father, Bowen (c. 1802–1853) led an adventurous life and mixed easily with the colonial hierarchy of New South Wales. A skilled fisherman and boatman, he became a sailor, interpreter, guide, go-between and a tracker of bushrangers and escaped convicts.

Bowen Bungaree and five other Broken Bay Aborigines sailed from Sydney to San Francisco at the start of the California gold rush in 1849. He is said to be the only one who came back.

In 1820 Pavel Mikhailov, an artist with the Russian scientific expedition led by Captain Fabian von Bellingshausen, sketched watercolour portraits of 'boin' (Bowen), then aged about 18, his father Boongaree (Bungaree), his mother Madora (Matora), brother Toubi (Toby) and other members of Bungaree's family who were camped at Kirribilli on the north shore of Port Jackson. These images are now in the collection of the State Russian Museum in St Petersburg.[2]

Sir Thomas Brisbane, who in 1822 succeeded Lachlan Macquarie as Governor of New South Wales, was instructed by the Home Office in London to establish a remote convict settlement for 'the worst type of felons'. In 1823, at the age of 21, Bowen Bungaree joined Surveyor General John Oxley (c. 1785–1828) on the 83-ton colonial cutter *Mermaid* to explore the Pacific Ocean coast north of Port Macquarie. Also on board were Lieutenant Robert Stirling of the Buffs, John Fitzgerald Uniacke, the Irish-born Sheriff and Provost Marshal of New South Wales, and Charles Penson, the ship's master.

The *Mermaid* left Sydney about noon on Tuesday 21 October 1823, but did not pass through the Port Jackson Heads until midnight the following day. 'Early on the morning of the 25th we came to anchor off Port Macquarie, distant north from Sydney 175 miles', wrote Uniacke. 'This place had been settled about two years before.' Oxley and his party dined with the commander Francis Allman and were afterwards 'highly amused by a dance among the natives' on the beach. Uniacke was impressed by the physique of the local Aborigines, 'many of them being upwards of six feet high'. Some Aboriginal men at Port Macquarie received rations from the store and 'in return perform some of the duties of constable, in a more efficient manner than any European could', Uniacke wrote.[3]

On Monday 27 October 1823 *Mermaid* took shelter in the lee of Cook Island, off Fingal Head, near the estuary of the Tweed River (named by Oxley) and close to the present New South Wales–Queensland border. Oxley and Uniacke landed on the island, where they found a piece of slate and a case of mathematical instruments — probably from an unidentified shipwreck.

Uniacke continued:

Mr. Oxley then ascended the hill, while I walked towards the S.E. [south-east] of the island, accompanied by a native black of the name of Bowen, whom we had brought from Sydney … on approaching a small reef … I observed, to my great satisfaction, upwards of a dozen large turtles lying asleep on a small beach: I instantly despatched Bowen for assistance, and on Mr. Penson, the master's coming up, we were fortunate enough to secure seven, some of which were very large, two of them weighing above four cwt [hundredweight].[4]

After surveying Port Curtis (now Gladstone, Queensland), Grant steered south again, anchoring in Moreton Bay on 29 November 1823 at the entrance to the Pumicestone River (now Pumicestone Passage) off Skirmish Point on Bribie Island.

'Scarcely was the anchor let go', wrote Uniacke, 'when we perceived a number of natives ... and on looking at them with the glass from the mast-head, I observed one who appeared much larger than the rest, and of a lighter colour, being a light copper, while the others were black ... when opposite the vessel the man hailed us in English'. The man, Thomas Pamphlet, was 'perfectly naked and covered all over with white and red paint'. Pamphlet, John Finnegan and Richard Parsons were timber-getters who had lived with the Aborigines on Bribie Island since their open boat had been wrecked on Moreton Island the previous April. They had been blown off course between Sydney and Five Islands (Illawarra), south of Sydney, and mistakenly sailed far to the north.[5]

John Oxley 'endeavoured to make the Natives through Bowen (our Sydney native who understood something of what they said) & Pamphlet our desire to see the other two white men'. They found Finnegan the next day and confirmed Pamphlet's story about 'a large river' that fell into the south end of Moreton Bay. The castaways were the first Europeans to see the river, which Matthew Flinders had missed in 1799. Guided by Finnegan, Oxley's party entered the river in two boats on 2 December 1823 and named it the Brisbane River in honour of Governor Brisbane. The explorers returned to the *Mermaid* on 5 December 1823.

Bowen's knowledge of the local language probably came from his father Bungaree, who sailed on the tiny sloop Norfolk with Matthew Flinders and was involved in the brief clash with Aboriginal men on 16 July 1799 that gave Skirmish Point its name. Flinders thought that 'Bungaree could not understand their language', but he was a quick learner and probably passed some of his knowledge to his son. In 1817 the elder Bungaree had also sailed on Mermaid, a snub-nosed cutter of 83 tons, then commanded by Philip Parker King in a survey of the north Australian coast.[6]

Sometime during his stay in Moreton Bay, John Oxley gave Bowen Bungaree a pencil, which he used to sketch the figure of an Aboriginal woman in the surveyor's *Field Book*. What seems at first glance to be a simple stick figure is stylistically similar to much larger human shapes outlined in Aboriginal rock engravings

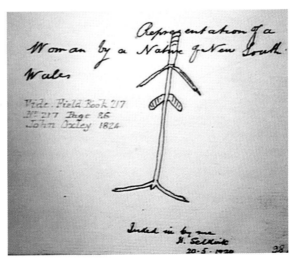

Representation of a Woman by a Native of New South Wales, 1823
Bowen Bungaree
Pencil sketch, inked in by Henry Selkirk, 1920
John Oxley, *Field Book 217,* Port Jackson to Port Curtis, October–November 1823,
CGS13889, SZ87:86,
State Records New South Wales, Sydney

throughout the Sydney area. Bowen's sketch, with extracts from Oxley's Field Book, was first printed in August 1920 in an article by RH Cambage and Henry Selkirk in *Proceedings of the Royal Society of New South Wales*, Sydney. Selkirk, then Under-Secretary for Lands in New South Wales, inked over the pencil outline so it could be more easily reproduced.[7] There are no records of other drawings by Bowen.

While Oxley was exploring, Bowen accompanied Uniacke, who spent his time shooting birds and observing the Indigenous people. When some Aborigines stole an axe from sailors cutting timber, Bowen went to their camp in the jolly boat with Uniacke and Penrose. Several men came to meet them and promised to show them where the axe was hidden, but dropped off one-by-one as they walked, until only an old man remained. He finally ran into the bush, but returned the axe the next day. After this, Uniacke allowed the Aborigines to visit the cutter and 'from this time forward not a single day passed, on which we had not ten or twelve of them on board at a time'. The ship's cats and goats astonished the Moreton Bay Aborigines. 'They were continually caressing the cats, and holding them up for the admiration of their companions on shore', wrote Uniacke.[8]

Bowen Bungaree was trusted to carry a rifle and roamed the Pittwater area at the mouth of the Hawkesbury River, north of Sydney, tracking escaped convicts and bushrangers. Writing in the *Sydney Mail* (1861), journalist Charles de Boose quoted John Farrell of Newport, who said that in about 1829 Bowen had shot and killed a bushranger named Casey. Bowen had been given a rifle by the Governor and was 'very proud of this and took it with him everywhere', said Farrell. Like his father, who usually dressed in a military jacket and cocked hat, Bowen wore European clothing, especially a dress coat with a swallow tail, but he preferred his hair 'knotted up behind, and three feathers stuck in it'.[9]

After a long illness, King Bungaree died in Sydney in 1830. He was succeeded, said the *Sydney Gazette*, 'by a fine well-made athletic youth ... well drest, and ornamented with the brass plate worn by his predecessor'.[10] In November 1831, 'Young Bungaree' was 'floored by a waddie' (waddy or club) at the conclusion of a ritual revenge combat at Woolloomooloo.[11]

Bowen and his wife Maria (Man Naney or Maria Jonza, sometimes called 'Queen Maria') usually lived in the Sydney area. They had two children, baptised as Mark and Theela at St Mary's Catholic Church in Sydney.[12] In 1834, when they collected government-issue blankets, 'Member's of Bowen's tribe' were listed as Maria, Jane, Bob, Yama, Tobin (Toby, Bowen's brother) and Dinah or Diana, the fair-haired daughter of one of Bungaree's wives and a European.[13]

In December 1834 nearly Aboriginal 100 men, women and children were camped on the eastern shore of Port Jackson in rock shelters at Camp Cove, near South Head, in the former territory of the Cadigal.

Bowen, with his brother Toby and brother-in-law Salamander, Bogy and others, owned two fishing boats and sold their catch to the crews of ships moored in Sydney Cove. They were sometimes hired to row European fishermen about Port Jackson. One such sportsman was William Proctor, from Newcastle-on-Tyne, a passenger on the ship *John Craig*. Proctor wrote:

> … Salamander in which elegant name our black companion rejoiced, ran up into the bush and presently brought three more recruits Toby, Bogy, and Bowen who seating themselves, soon pulled us off to what they considered a good place to get yellow tail, which were to be used as bait to the larger [fish], and being supplied with hooks and lines they fished along with us, and by their broken English and odd expressions which they pick up from the sailors in the harbour, they amused us very much …

'As soon as they have caught a boat load or two [of fish], they bring it up to town & will sell it for either money or rum', wrote Proctor. The going rate was half a bottle of diluted rum in exchange for a bucket full of fish, while the excess catch went to fishmongers at the King's Wharf, who hawked their wares in the streets from wheelbarrows. Bowen and his friends also guided kangaroo shooters, taking leftover fish and game or a bottle of rum in payment.[14]

In 1837 'a black-fellow named Bowen' led officials from the Broken Bay Customs Station at Barrenjoey in Pittwater, north of Sydney, to illegal liquor stills and gave information on the whereabouts of prisoners who had escaped from Goat Island in Sydney Harbour. On 11 April 1837, Bowen reported that the wanted men were on an island near Mooney Mooney Creek on the Hawkesbury River.[15] 'Bohun' (Bowen) was rewarded with a second-hand boat for leading Chief Inspector of Distilleries Robert Cassels to an illegal distillery at McCarrs Creek, near Church Point, Pittwater, in March 1845. John Howard from the customs station at Barrenjoey said Bowen was a good fisherman and a boat would allow him to 'get a living for himself & family consisting of two daughters and a son'.[16]

Aboriginal with rifle, c. 1834
[Probably Bowen Bungaree]
Unknown artist
Pencil
A74, Mitchell Library, Sydney

A pencil portrait in Sydney's Mitchell Library, titled *Aboriginal man with rifle*, shows a man with similar features and expression to Mikhailov's 1820 portrait of 'Boin'. Despite the passage of more than 20 years, he resembles Bowen Bungaree, who carried a rifle and liked to wear a white shirt and trousers.

Writing in 1923, JC Waterman, an overseer at the Sydney Domain, recalled that, in 1846, 'Bungaree's [i.e. Bowen's] party comprised eight men, women and children' including King Bungaree's widow Cora Gooseberry and her relation Ricketty Dick. 'They gave exhibitions of boomerang throwing in Hyde Park and roamed about Sydney by day, camping at night near the Centipede Rock in the Domain.'17

A voyage to San Francisco

In 1849 Bowen Bungaree and five other Broken Bay men sailed to San Francisco aboard the 119-ton brig *William Hill* bound for the California goldfields. Bowen was the only one of the Aboriginal men to return.

According to historian Maybanke Anderson in *The Story of Pittwater* (1920):

> … BLACK BOWEN. He was one of six Pittwater aboriginals who were taken to California by Mr. Richard Hill [who] took the blackfellows with him because they were used to boating, and could be employed to row the boats which were needed to carry the crowds who were flocking to the Eldorado. Black Bowen was the only one of the six who returned. The others all died far from their native home. Black Bowen always spoke with scorn of 'that country!! No wood for fire, but plenty cold wind, and plenty, plenty water. No good for me! No good for blackfellow!'18

William Phillips built the 119-ton brig *William Hill* at the Clarence River, New South Wales, for the Sydney merchant Edward Smith Hill in 1847.19 Under Captain John McDonald, the ship left Sydney on 20 January with a cargo of spirits and general goods for sale and docked in San Francisco on 25 April 1849. Edward Smith Hill and William Hill, who sailed as passengers, left San Francisco on 23 May 1849, returning via Tahiti (4 July) on the same ship (Master: William Orr), which reached Sydney on 18 August 1849. This was the first of two voyages that the *William Hill* made to California that year.

ES Hill and William Hill persuaded their relative Richard Hill to sell his house and butcher shop at 211 Pitt Street, Sydney, to go with them on the next voyage to the 'Gold Country'.20 All three members of the Hill family left Sydney aboard the William Hill on 24 October 1849 on this second voyage. In his journal, Richard Binnie, a passenger, mentions Dick or Stock-keeper, Cranky, Billy and Callaghan (Calagan) as Aboriginal members of the crew. Binnie made no reference to Bowen Bungaree. According to the *Sydney Morning Herald*, the 'Sydney tribe: 'Gooseberry … Bowen … Billy Warrall' were in Sydney to pick up government-issue blankets on

Friday 24 May 1850.[21] The *William Hill* arrived in Sydney after the second voyage on 8 June 1850.[22]

It follows that Bowen Bungaree must have been on the first voyage to San Francisco, and not with Richard Hill, as Anderson claimed. He therefore became the second Aboriginal sailor to visit Tahiti, following Tom Chaseland, who had already been to French Polynesia three times. The brig sailed from San Francisco on 23 May and moored off Papeete, west of Matavai Bay, on 23 June. While in port, the ship loaded 14 casks of sperm oil and 45 casks of coconut oil. What Bowen saw and experienced would have mirrored the description by British trader Edward Lucett on the *Samuel Robinson* one year earlier:

> Passing through the passage in the reef, we came to anchor off the town, with its white beach, cocoa palms waving, huts and houses peeping out from the orange groves … Native canoes were allowed alongside during the day, while natives, male and female, swarmed over the ship, trading with the officers and crew, but when night fell they were ordered off.[23]

The *William Hill* left Papeete for Sydney on 24 July 1849. 'She brings from California about 1200 ounces of gold dust,' noted the *Sydney Morning Herald*.[24] The Sydney correspondent of the *Maitland Mercury* was 'informed, on good authority' that this consignment fetched £3.9.0 per ounce.[25]

Bowen Bungaree died in Sydney in 1853 at the reputed age of 56. His death was registered at St Lawrence's Presbyterian Church and his occupation was given as 'fisherman'.[26] John Farrell told De Boos that Bowen was ambushed and shot dead near Pittwater by bushrangers while sitting at a campfire. 'The news was brought to me by some blacks who found his dead body by the side of the fire, and who, from the tracks around, knew that four armed whites had been there.' Farrell said he would have taken vengeance 'for I looked upon Bowen almost as a brother, and I would have had blood for blood'.[27]

The *Mermaid*, re-rigged as a schooner for use as a colonial vessel, ran aground and sank on a reef in June 1829. Archaeologists from the National Maritime Museum located the wreck on Flora reef, south-east of Cairns, Queensland, in January 2009.

13 Sealers

Visiting Sydney in 1802, the French naturalist François Péron painted a rosy picture of the international maritime character of the bustling seaport: there were ships loading coal for India and the Cape of Good Hope, convict transports leaving for China, whalers bound for New Zealand, sealers for Bass Strait, salt pork traders for the South Seas and a gun-runner taking arms to South America.[1]

Sealing would provide the first opportunities for trade and commerce in colonial Australia, employing small ships and local crews in the hunt for marine animals

Nouvelle-Hollande: Île King, L'Éléphand-marin ou phoque à trompe, Vue de la Baie des Éléphants, 1807 [Elephant seals in Sea Elephant Bay, King Island], Victor Pilliment (1767–1814) after Charles-Alexandre Lesueur (1778–1846), Engraving, Plate 32, Atlas, François Péron, *Voyage de découvertes aux terres Australes*, 2nd edition, Paris 1824, Mitchell Library, Sydney.

and their lucrative products. When the merchant ship *Sydney Cove* from Calcutta was wrecked on Preservation Island in Bass Strait in February 1797, the returning survivors reported seeing large numbers of fur seals.[2]

By 1805 a few young Aboriginal men from the Sydney area had been on sealing voyages. Ships' musters and other records show they were split into two main groups, those from Botany Bay and further south of Sydney, and those from the Hawkesbury River, 35 kilometres to the north-west. 'Several of their ['native'] youth are at this time employed in the various sealing gangs in the Straits upon lay', the *Sydney Gazette* reported on 17 March 1805.[3]

Sealers were paid on the lay system, which meant they received a small share of the revenue — from 1/100th to 1/150th — or nothing if the ship failed to bring home any seal oil or skins. Sometimes sealing gangs were paid in spirits, as shipowner Robert Campbell admitted when he complained to Governor Philip Gidley King that he was not able to import sufficient spirits to pay for their labour.[4] Willamannan (William Minam) from Port Hacking, south of Sydney, told George Augustus Robinson in June 1832 that he had spent five years sealing on islands in Bass Strait, 'during which time I could not get any money, but was supplied occasionally with Spirits in lieu thereof … the greater part of the time we lived on kangaroo … we were quite destitute of clothing'.[5]

In *The Present Picture of New South Wales* (London 1811), David Dickinson Mann mentioned Bidgy Bidgy (Bidgee Bidgee), Bundell, Bull Dog and Bloody Jack as Aboriginal men who had 'made themselves extremely useful on board colonial vessels employed in the fishing and

NOUVELLE - HOLLANDE : N° Galles du Sud.

BEDGI - BEDGI Jeune homme de la Tribu des Gwea-Sud.

Nouvelle-Hollande: Nelle. Galles du Sud
Bedgi-Bedgi, jeune homme de la tribu des Gwea-gal
[Bidgee Bidgee]
Barthelmy Roger (1767–1841) after Nicolas-Martin Petit (1777–1804)
Hand-coloured engraving
From François Péron, *Voyage de découvertes aux terres Australes*, Paris 1811
Plate 22, F980/P Atlas,
Mitchell Library, Sydney

sealing trade, for which they are in regular receipt of wages'. Mann, an emancipated convict and sometime clerk to Governor King, was referring to the period before he left New South Wales in March 1809. He commented on the life led by Aboriginal mariners: 'They strive, by every means in their power, to make themselves appear like the sailors with whom they associate, by copying their customs, and imitating their manners; such as swearing, using a great quantity of tobacco, drinking grog, and other similar habits'.[6]

In February 1798 Governor John Hunter sent naval Lieutenant Matthew Flinders in the colonial sloop *Francis* to the wreck of the *Sydney Cove*. Flinders surveyed the Furneaux and Kent islands and vividly described the terror of the fur seals on Cape Barren Island (Truwana) as the ship's sailors clubbed them to death.[7] Flinders reached Sydney on 9 March 1798 and rejoined Surgeon George Bass, recently returned after an epic journey of 1200 miles from Sydney to Wilson's Promontory and Western Port (Victoria) in a 28-foot long open whaleboat crewed by six men. In December 1798, Bass and Flinders sailed through Bass Strait in the *Norfolk*, a 25-ton sloop, proving Tasmania was an island. This discovery would lead to the colonisation of Van Diemen's Land.

Large-scale hunting of seals began in the northern hemisphere during the eighteenth century. Fur pelts, used for leather shoes, hats and warm clothing, found a ready market in Europe and China. Seal oil was clear, odourless and did not have the rancid smell of whale or fish oil. It was used in foodstuffs and to soften the fibres of manufactured cloth. Seal oil burned in household lamps with a bright pure flame and little smoke or smell, and was cheap, as one-sixth of a pint would run an ordinary wick for 12 hours.[8]

Sealers led a hard and dangerous life. Gangs were landed in remote and lonely places where they were often left for months without food or supplies. It was a grisly trade, in which defenceless animals were herded together, clubbed to death and skinned. Their skins were preserved by salting and stored in timber casks.

The most valuable pelts were taken from the Australian fur seal (*Artocephalus pusillus*), which has underfur and long hair that is shed and renewed each summer. Colonies of fur seals inhabited the islands and bred on isolated rocks and ledges in Bass Strait. The large-headed adult males, with muscular necks and chests, weigh from 220 to 360 kilograms. Fur seals, which feed mainly on *cephalopods* (squid, octopus and cuttlefish), were not considered good eating.

The Australian sea lion or hair seal (*Neophoca cinerea*), covered with long, coarse hair, has no under-fur, but yielded oil and edible blubber. This solitary large, black spotted sea leopard feeds on penguins and seabirds and was mainly taken for its blubber.

The huge southern elephant seal (*Mirounga leonina*), largest of all seals, are mainly found in Antarctic waters. The carless males might reach 4 to 5 metres in length and weigh up to 3500 kilograms. They were named for their great bulk and the grotesque elephant-like proboscis of the males. The smaller females, 2 to 3 metres long and weighing 500 kilograms can dive to a depth of 1600 metres. Elephant seals, larger and slower than fur seals, were clubbed and speared and stripped of their blubber. Seal blubber was cut into pieces and rendered in large metal cauldrons called try pots. Oil was allowed to cool and run into casks called tuns.

The French discovery vessel *Géographe*, commanded by Captain Nicolas Baudin, left Port Jackson with the 30-ton schooner *Casuarina* for 'Île King' (King Island) on 17 November 1802. The French naturalist François Péron spent two weeks ashore in Sea Elephant Bay, where a gang of English sealers had been living for one year, killing, skinning and boiling down the fat blubber of the huge animals for oil. 'The whole of the bay, when we landed, was covered with sea elephants,' wrote Péron. He continued:

> The English have invaded these hide-outs which have so long protected them. They have everywhere organised massacres which cannot fail soon to cause a real and irreparable lessening of the numbers of these animals.[9]

Péron's prediction was realised within three years, when wholesale slaughter had brought about the extinction of elephant seals on King Island.

14 Boatswain Maroot in the sub-Antarctic

Boatswain Maroot, born at Cooks River on the north shore of Botany Bay about 1796, sailed on several sealing and whaling expeditions and was one of the first visitors to the remote islands of the sub-Antarctic.

His father, the elder Maroot, recalled the ships of the First Fleet coming into Botany Bay in January 1788. Boatswain passed on his father's account in evidence to a Legislative Council *Select Committee on the Condition of the Aborigines* in Sydney in 1845.[1] 'They thought they was [*sic*] the devil when they saw them landed first, they

Movat and Salmanda, 1820, [Boatswain Maroot and Salamander], Pavel Mikhailov (1786–1840), Pencil and sanguine on brown paper, R29209/207, Russian State Museum, St Petersburg, Image courtesy of Longueville Publications.

did not know what to make of them. When they saw them going up the masts they thought they was opossums', he said. According to George Thornton, who became Protector of Aborigines in New South Wales in 1881, Boatswain's father Maroot was chief of the Botany clan and his mother was Grang Grang (Carangarang).[2]

In April 1788, Lieutenant William Bradley of HMS *Sirius* saw Aborigines 'in great numbers along the north shore of the upper part' of Botany Bay with 'many Women & Children amongst them'.[3] Marine Lieutenant Watkin Tench described a 'village' on the north-west arm of Botany Bay 'with more than a dozen houses [gunyahs or bark huts], and perhaps five times that number of people; being the most considerable establishment that we are acquainted with in the country'.[4] The huts occupied by this clan of about 60 people were near the outlet of the Cooks River. This was the heartland of the Kameygal (Spear Clan), included in a list of 'Tribes' in the semi-official *Governors' Vocabulary*, a manuscript wordlist compiled in 1791 and now held in the School of Oriental and African Studies at the University of London. *Ka-may* is given as the placename for Botany Bay in the same document, while *-gal* describes a clan or extended family.[5]

Although his father was a 'chief' and he often fought in ritual revenge battles in the streets of Sydney and was twice wounded, Boatswain Maroot admitted that he had little knowledge of Aboriginal spiritual matters and had not lost a tooth, in other words, he had never been initiated.[6]

On 11 July 1810, Captain Frederick Hasselburgh (Hassleborough or Hasslebourg), on a sealing voyage on the brig *Perseverance*, found a large island, 800 nautical miles (1500 kilometres) south-east of Tasmania, in the sub-Antarctic ocean, which he named for Governor Lachlan Macquarie of New South Wales. Macquarie Island lies midway between Tasmania and Antarctica. This southernmost Australian possession is about 34 kilometres long and three kilometres wide. In January that year Hasselburgh had sighted a volcanic island of steep cliffs and deep fiords some 700 kilometres south of New Zealand. He named it Campbell Island, after Robert Campbell of Sydney, who owned *Perseverance*, built at Port Jackson in 1805.

The American brig *Aurora* from New York put into Sydney Cove on 29 December 1810, bringing the news that Captain Hasselburgh and three others had drowned on 4 November 1810, when their boat overturned in Providence Harbour on Campbell Island. Owen Smith, captain of *Aurora*, disclosed the locations of both Campbell and Macquarie Islands, which were published in the *Sydney Gazette*.

Boatswain's first recorded ocean voyage was on a sealing vessel that, he claimed, abandoned him for two years on the remote and desolate Macquarie Island. The ship, belonging to Kable and Underwood, was the second *Sydney Cove*, which left Port Jackson in July 1809 on an extended voyage, dropping sealing gangs on the New Zealand coast and whaleboats and whaling gangs at Norfolk Island.[7] On 10 November 1810, the *Sydney Gazette* reported that the *Sydney Cove* had left

Garden Cove, Macquarie Island, 1820, Ivan Pavlovitch Fridrits, after Pavel Mikhailov (1786–1840), Lithograph
From *Atlas k puteshestviiu Kapitane Bellingsgauzena* … St Petersburg, 1831, F980/3A1, , Mitchell Library, Sydney.

Norfolk Island with only 50 barrels of whale oil and 'proceeded to the relief of her gangs in Foveaux Straits' at the tip of the South Island of New Zealand.

Months after their food rations ran out, Maroot and two European sealers stowed away on the 150-ton brig *Concord*, which reached Sydney on Friday 4 October 1811. The ship's master, Captain Garbut, had been sent to re-supply work gangs stationed on Macquarie Island. Garbut said the sealers there were in 'a deplorable condition for the want of food and other necessaries'.[8]

There were no land-dwelling animals to hunt on Macquarie Island and Boatswain was forced to live on seals, salty penguins and mutton-birds. It was cold and windy and high cliffs made fishing difficult. Joseph Barsden, a 15-year-old English seaman on the brig *Trial*, owned by Sydney ex-convict merchant Simeon Lord, visited Macquarie Island in December 1813 and remarked that although it was the 'higt [height] of summer in the southern regions we began to feel the air get extremely cold … on our approach to the land we discovered the hills covered with snow'. According to Barsden, sealers on the island made their fires by saturating brushwood with seal oil 'which is poured on to make it ignite and this is done without much expence [*sic*] it being produced from Seal and Sea Elephant, which are very plentiful on the rocks surrounding the island'. As there was no safe anchorage, 'the vessel is compelled to lye off and on, all the time the gangs are on shore', said Barsden. The *Trial* took a gang of sealers from Macquarie Island that had been there for 18 months

— 'this took us twenty-one days to accomplish … our vessel was blown off the island three days at a time'.[9]

Eight days after his return to Sydney, 'Merute' (Maroot) addressed a petition to Governor Lachlan Macquarie claiming a breach of verbal contract. The governor referred the petition to the Bench of Magistrates.

The following Petition to his Excellency the Governor, presented by one Merute a Native of this Territory was referred to this Court and ordered to be read.

"Sir, My name is Merute an Inhabitant and Native of this Country. I agreed verbally for plenty of money and Clothes and can obtain nothing. Is this an Encouragement to us?

Two years in the employ of Mr. Ja⁵. Underwood at Macquarie Island and did double duty to a White man —."

Sydney, October 9th 1811

Mr. Underwood, being called in reply says that he knows nothing of the man — that he never was in his employ, nor has ever appealed to him. But he believed he was left at Macquarie Island more than two years ago — in the Sydney Cove of which Messrs. Ball and Banks are owners & Captain MacLaren master — that he understands that Petitioner stowed away there in the Concord and came up in that vessel about ten days ago. The Sydney Cove again sailed from this Port about a fortnight ago for Macquarie Island with Supplies intending to fill there with Skins & oil & to return to this Port — she must return here for want of provisions.

Merute says that he and two Europeans left the Island for want of Provisions.

Mr. Underwood says that he is Agent for the Ship but that the owners are Bankrupt — that he has not the account of Slops furnished to Petitioner —

The petitioner says he has had some Slops.

[3] Mr. Underwood now consents to give Petitioner ten Pounds half to be paid in money & half in Goods — on Condition of Petitioner giving him a discharge of all claims upon the Ship —

To this the Petitioner now consents — & the Court are of opinion that the same is reasonable. —

[Signed]
Ellis Bent
Alexander Riley
William Broughton
Simeon Lord[10]

After losing an anchor, *Sydney Cove* returned to Port Jackson 'from the seal and sperm fishery' on Friday 12 April 1811, with 40 casks of whale oil and 'a favourable report of skins procured by her people at Macquarie Island'.[11]

It is unlikely that Boatswain Maroot was stranded on Macquarie Island for as long as two years because its location was not officially known before July 1810. Whatever the length of time, Macquarie Island, lying in 62° S latitude, with its icy winds and a mean temperature of 4° Centigrade, was a cruel climate for an Aboriginal man from Botany Bay.

After his return to Sydney, Boatswain Maroot went to live at the home of David Allan and his family. In evidence given in 1845 before the Select Committee, 'Mahroot, alias the Boatswain' was asked:

When did you first learn to speak English?
When I first joined the English, I left my father and mother and went to live with the English.

With whom did you live?
With Commissary Allen [*sic*].[12]

David Allan (1780–1852) first came to Sydney on the ship *Fortune* in June 1813 and was Deputy Commissary General from 1813 to 1819. His property covered most of the present Sydney suburb of Woolloomooloo.

We know that Boatswain Maroot was a handsome man from the watercolour portrait of Movat (Mowat or Maroot) with Salmanda (Salamander), painted in 1820 by the Russian artist Pavel Mikhailov (1786–1840) at Kirribilli, on the north shore of Port Jackson. Did Mikhailov realise that he was meeting one of the first people — certainly the first Australian Aborigine — to set foot on Macquarie Island? It is one of the ironies of history that, in late November 1820, Mikhailov sailed with the Russian Antarctic expedition led by Captain Fabian von Bellingshausen, where he drew the first known illustration of the island.

Boatswain Maroot told the Legislative Council committee in 1845 that he had gone to sea on five or six whaling expeditions, which, he complained, was 'dirty work, and hard work':

How much did you earn when you went whaling?
Twenty pounds or thirty pounds a voyage.

What did you do with that money when you came back?
I went along with the sailors and we threw it away all together.

By Dr. Lang: *In the public houses?*
Yes, and then go for more again as soon as ever that was all out.

By the Chairman: *Could not other black fellows go to whaling if they liked?*
Yes.

Why do they not like [it]?
Because it is dirty work, and hard work, and they do not fancy it at all.[13]

Boatswain admitted 'drinking up' his cheque in public houses with the rest of the whalers. Three of his voyages can be traced to the years 1822–3 on board the 156-

Balkabra [Bulgabra] *Chief of Botany flanked by Biddy Salamander and Gooseberry, wife of King Bungaree,* Charles Rodius (1802–1860), Watercolour, PXA 615/6, , Mitchell Library, Sydney.

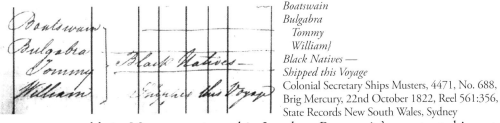

Boatswain
Bulgabra
 Tommy
 William}
Black Natives —
Shipped this Voyage
Colonial Secretary Ships Musters, 4471, No. 688, Brig Mercury, 22nd October 1822, Reel 561:356, State Records New South Wales, Sydney

ton two-masted brig *Mercury*, registered in London. Boatswain's constant shipmate was Bulgabra or Bolgobrough, brother of 'William' (Willamannan, later William Manen or Menan).

On 8 February 1822, a *Claims and Demands* notice appeared in the *Sydney Gazette*: 'BOATSWAIN, a black native, of the Brig Mercury, leaving the Colony in said Vessel, requests Claims to be presented'. Included in the ship's muster on 19 February 1822 were Boatswain, Bulgabraa (Bolgobrough), Jem (Creek Jemmy or Nurragingy) and Tommy (Tamara), described as 'Black Natives inserted in Ship at an 1/160th share'.

The *Sydney Gazette* of 11 October 1822 reported: 'On Friday last arrived, from the sperm whale fishery, the brig Mercury, Captain John Edwards. She left this port on the 22nd of February, and has procured 30 tons of oil. In a heavy gale, on the Saturday previous, her main-tops mast was carried away.'[14]

Boatswain, Tommy, Bulgabra and his brother William (Willamannan), mustered as 'Black Natives—Shipped this Voyage', sailed aboard *Mercury* for the whale fishery on 22 October 1822 and were away for nearly six months. This is the first record of Aboriginal brothers as shipmates. 'Bulgabra' and Boatswain, listed as 'Seamen', sailed again with Captain Edwards aboard *Mercury*, which left Sydney for the Bay of Islands and the New Zealand sperm whale fishery on 6 August 1823. The ship's muster stated that Boatswain Maroot had been discharged in December 1822 after a voyage aboard the ship *Midas* and was marked 'Saw discharge'.[15] The 420-ton *Midas*, built at Hull, England, had previously visited Mauritius.

Home from the sea, the enterprising Boatswain Maroot settled down once more in Kameygal country. He built two slab timber huts on the north shore of Botany Bay and used his boat to make a living as a fisherman. By sheer persistence in lobbying Governor Sir Richard Bourke, Boatswain succeeded in obtaining official acknowledgement of his land rights. A *Governor's Minute*, marked 'Immediate', written in fading sepia ink, was initialled by Bourke on 17 April 1832. It requested the Surveyor-General to allocate land to:

> Boatswain Maroot, an aboriginal Native, [who] has called at the office repeatedly respecting some Land at Botany, promised to him, as he says, by the Governor, and on which he has two Huts. He has been referred to this office as well as that of the Surveyor General several times, for an answer to his application or rather for an order to take possession … It is very desirable from every motive of Justice Humanity and Policy to fix these poor people in some certain line of life according to the structure of ~~European~~ [deleted] civilized society and the smallest indication even in one solitary instance of a desire on the part of a Native to assume industrious habits a Trade or Calling ought to be carefully encouraged.

The governor stipulated that the grant was a lease and suggested there was no need to give 'this poor Native' a written document, 'as care will be taken that he is not disturbed, and he would probably lose the document'.[16] An undated survey map by draughtsman Thomas Balcombe shows Boatswain Maroot's 10-acre lease, situated on the swampy Botany Bay shoreline close to Bumborah Point, just below 'Bunnerong House', belonging to John Brown and land marked 'Crain's' [John Crane], close to Bunnerong Creek.[17] Much of the area was covered by water at high tide. The Indigenous placename Bumborah referred to a *bombora* or swell of water caused by submerged rocks, while *bunnerong* meant 'blood'.

The Bunnerong Power Station was built in 1929 on Brown's property and has since been demolished. It is difficult to locate the site of Maroot's lease because reclamation of the coastal swamps and lagoons and large-scale earth moving to extend Sydney airport and Port Botany container terminal has altered the area beyond recognition. A huge sand dune was flattened when the electric powerhouse was built at Bunnerong and sand was dumped on the foreshore to create a park and golf course.

About the same time as his land grant was ratified by Governor Bourke, Maroot met the Swiss missionary Reverend Johann Handt, who described him as 'a civilized man, and by profession a sailor'. Maroot told Handt there were only four left of the 'Botany Bay Tribe'. Handt said Maroot had forgotten much of his own language. 'I did not see him since that time', wrote Handt on 23 April 1832, 'and suppose therefore that he has gone to sea again'.[18]

At one time, 'a good while ago', Boatswain said he had made £4 to £6 per week by fishing, which he spent on clothes, meat, flour and sugar. He grew cabbages and pumpkins until cows knocked down the garden fence. Boatswain built more huts, but by 1845, he 'hardly got four shillings a week, from rentals'. Boatswain told the Select Committee that as a child his tribe numbered 400 people, and confirmed that only he and three women remained of those who had been born at Botany and spoke their language. Boatswain said he had no brothers, but 'three sisters by another father and the same mother'.[19]

'He is very fond of the Bay, very intelligent, and has a ten-acre piece of ground and some "white-fellow" tenants', wrote Joseph Phipps Townsend. Boatswain said that when his wife died, he buried her 'like a lady' … all put in coffin, English fashion. Poor gin mine tumble down [died] … I feel lump in throat when I talk about her; but, — I buried her all genteel, Mitter'.[20]

On a visit to Botany Bay, Police Inspector and amateur anthropologist William Augustus Miles (1796–1851) found 'about eight haggard beings, the wretched remnants of this race, emaciated by drunkenness, and at times by hunger'. Miles recorded Boatswain's moving lament for his clan:

> This last of his tribe is much attached to the scenes of his younger days. His name is Maoroo [Boatswain]. He is the son of the former chief, and feels much his own desolate condition. I was walking on the bright sands of Botany soon after sunrise, when he suddenly appeared from the skirting thickets, and coming up to me (for we were not new acquaintances) — "This is all my country," said he, making a large sweep with his extended arm. "Nice country: my father chief long time ago; now I chief. Water all pretty — sun make it light. When I little fellow, plenty black fellow, plenty gin, plenty piccaninny, great corroboree, plenty fight! Eh! All gone now," and, pointing his fore finger to the earth, "All gone! only *me* left to walk about".[21]

When blankets, bread and beef were distributed to the 'remnant of the Sydney Aborigines' on the Queen's Birthday, 24 May 1849, Boatswain gave a speech 'at some length; in his native language' and proposed a toast in *bull* (watered-down rum) to Queen Victoria and the Governor.[22]

In the last years of his life, Boatswain Maroot continued to live in Kameygal country, putting up his *gunyah* (bark shelter) in the grounds of the Sir Joseph Banks Hotel at Botany, where he died on 31 January 1850. The *Sydney Morning Herald* mourned the loss of Boatswain 'whose intelligence and superior manners, coupled with the fact of his being the last of the Botany Bay tribe, rendered him a favourite with all who knew him, and especially with his white countrymen'.[23]

'Certainly not a Botany Bay aborigine is now living', wrote Richard Hill in *Notes on the Aborigines of New South Wales* (1892). Hill meant that nobody remained from the original Kameygal and Gweagal clans.

Pigeon, Potter and Jack

'Pigeon, Potter, and Jack', well-known in Sydney, joined the rush to the sub-Antarctic in the 30-man crew of the 130-ton brig *Mary and Sally*, which left Port Jackson on 12 April 1811, seeking sealskins and oil at 'the Islands of Macquarie and Campbell'.[24] When strong winds prevented the ship from landing sealers at Macquarie Island, Captain Charles Feen dropped some men at Campbell Island. After successfully landing a gang at Macquarie Island, the *Mary and Sally* was again blown offshore and returned empty on 29 November 1811 to refit in Port Jackson, but afterwards brought back 11 000 sealskins and 70 tons of oil.[25]

'Young Pigeon', described in 1806 as a 'boy', fought as an ally of Potter and Blewit (also called Ploge), two brothers from the Gweagal (Fire Clan) from the south shore of Botany Bay, in ritual revenge battles in Sydney Town. Probably for that reason he was regarded as a Botany Bay man. Thirty years later, when they both worked for John Batman in Van Diemen's Land, Pigeon was identified as the brother of Maccah or Lewis Macher, chief of the Killimbagong at the Shoalhaven River.

Pigeon was sealing at King George Sound at the south-western corner of Australia in 1827 (See Chapter 4). According to George Augustus Robinson, Pigeon also spent some time on the Bass Strait islands with sealers and had picked up some of their language.[26] Robinson said Pigeon's Aboriginal name was Weymorr, while Batman called him Warroba.[27]

In April 1806, Potter and another 'Sydney native' guided and assisted four starving survivors of the 28-ton colonial vessel *George*, wrecked north of Twofold Bay, who had set out to walk to Sydney from Jervis Bay along the coast, subsisting on shellfish.[28] 'Jack' on the *Mary and Sally* might have been Jack Richmond from the Hawkesbury River or Jacky Stuart or Stewart from the Shoalhaven.

Bolgobrough's clan

Bolgobrough's brother, the adventurous Willamannan, also called William and William Minam or Manen, went on several sealing and whaling voyages. His portrait,

William Minam
Walamata – Port Aitken – Koonemetta, 1843
Artist unknown
Engraving
PXA74,
Mitchell Library, Sydney

by an unknown artist, shows a well-built man wearing European 'slop' clothing, who has lost his right arm. Surgeons Robertson, Neilson and Stuart amputated the arm of 'William Annam' at the Colonial Hospital in Sydney in June 1838. A writer in the weekly journal *The Colonist* noted that William had 'so far recovered since his operation as to be able to call on Surgeon Neilson and thank him for his kind and assiduous attendance on him during his suffering and confinement'.[29]

Apart from statements by Boatswain Maroot, it is unusual to find a first-person life story (however brief) of an Aboriginal man. After being taken off a small island near Kangaroo Island in 1832 by the 55-ton schooner *Henry*, owned by Jonathan Griffiths, 'William' gave a brief autobiography to George Augustus Robinson:

> I am a Native of New Holland near to Botany Bay (called Port Egan) Native Name Bugerygoory alias William—Name of the Tribe "Koonametta" Chiefs Name "Boolgobra" in 1827 — I was young when I left my Tribe, I am now about 25 years old. I had been employed in a Whaling Ship, on my return I joined the blacks, after some time I joined a Sealing vessel out of Sydney and remained sealing about 5 Years, during which time I could not get any money, but was supplied occasionally with Spirits in lieu thereof — At the expiration of the first twelvemonth I wished to return but had not the means, the vessel never having returned —The greater part of the time we lived on Kangaroo — In March 1832 we were taken off Saddle Island near to Kangaroo Island by a vessel from Launceston belonging to Mr. Griffiths we were quite destitute of Clothing — There were three White Men & one New Zealander beside myself — the latter named Thomas — the Whitemen named — Bill Dutton, Tom Stack, a native of Sydney — and Hugh Scott also a native of Sydney.[30]

Port Egan or Aitken was the early name of Port Hacking (Deeban or Jibboon), where Gunnamatta Bay adjoins the beach suburb of Cronulla. Based on William's statement, his brother Bolgobrough (Bulkabra or Boolgobra) was clan head of the

Koonemetta or Gunamatta of Port Hacking. The artist's caption of the portrait of William Minam: 'Walamata — Port Aitken — Koonematta', suggests that the territory of the Gunamatta stretched north along the coast from Wallamulla ('Walamata') and across Port Hacking to include Gunamatta Bay.

John Connell, whose property covered the shoreline of Gunamatta Bay and Burraneer Bay, sent an undated request to Captain William Dumaresq, aide to Governor Sir Ralph Darling:

> The Bearer Bolgobrough is Chief of Botany Bay. Williamanann is his Brother and Generally Reside at the South Side of Botany bay, They & their tribe are Come to Sydney for his Excellency General Darling's Benevolent Donation of Blankets &c. for the Ensuing Winter — I know them for Many Years.[31]

This might have been written in 1829, when 'Bolgobrough Chief of Botany Bay' received blankets for three men, two women and one child in Sydney.[32] In 1834, the members of Bolgobrough's 'tribe', then in Sydney, were listed as Maria (his wife), 'Nanga (old), Mary, Johnny and Bobby'.[33]

The *Henry* berthed at Launceston on 26 November 1833.[34] William's familiarity with the schooner's master 'Bill' Dutton suggests that he had been working for William Pelham Dutton (1804–1878), the Sydney-born sealer and whaler who became the first European to settle in Victoria when he built a house at Portland Bay in 1829. Dutton had been whaling in the *Henry* at Kangaroo Island during 1832 and in March 1833 established the first whale fishery at Portland Bay.

15 Whalers

Year after year, for countless thousands of years, pods of Humpback whales have migrated from the southern oceans in winter, following the eastern coastline of Australia to warmer northern waters. In spring the whales return southwards with their calves to spend the summer feeding on krill in the icy Antarctic.

Whenever a whale was stranded or washed up on shore, Aboriginal people quickly gathered to feast on the rich blubber. 'A Whale, cast on shore, is quite a feast, and messengers are dispatched to all neighbouring tribes, who assemble and feast upon the monster of the deep so long as the treat lasts', wrote the Lake Macquarie (NSW) missionary Reverend Lancelot Threlkeld.[1] 'Bands would travel great distances to share a feast of whale meat, and to enjoy the social contact. The meat was usually cut from the dead animal with sharpened shell tools, commonly a valve of the Sydney cockle *Anadara trapezia*.'[2]

Governor Arthur Phillip first witnessed Aborigines feasting on a beached whale during an expedition to Botany Bay in August 1788. 'All that were seen at this time had large pieces of it, which appeared to have been laid upon the fire only long enough to scorch the outside', Phillip observed.[3]

In *Aboriginal carvings of Port Jackson and Broken Bay* (1899), surveyor William Dugald Campbell described the engraving of a whale in Botany Bay on 'a high part of the low rocky point at La Perouse', close to Bare Island and the La Perouse monument in Botany Bay:

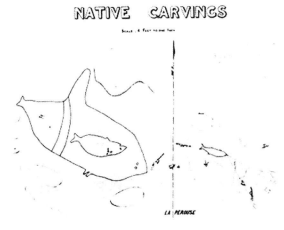

There are only two figures upon this rock, a fine carving of a whale thirty-eight feet long, and its calf fifteen feet long. The whale has a double transverse line behind a large fin, and there are two teats. In the

Native Carvings, Whale, La Perouse, c. 1891
WD Campbell after unknown Aboriginal artist
Pencil drawing
PXD223, No. 5,
Mitchell Library, Sydney

middle of the whale the calf is cut, occupying the highest portion of the rock … The Writer came upon the whale in the year 1891, when searching this part of the coast for carvings, and when questioning the blacks at the native encampment near by he was informed by an old black woman that this was a "Boora" whale.[4]

The engraving still exists at La Perouse.

A figure of a sperm whale carved on the rock face at Kirribilli on the north shore of Sydney Harbour, opposite Bennelong Point, was removed by quarrying in the mid nineteenth century.[5]

From time to time whales came into the harbour of Port Jackson, as they sometimes do today.[6] 'Whales in the early days of the colony were numerous enough, and I have on three occasions seen whales driven up high and dry on the beach at Bondi and also on Coogee Beach', Obed West recalled (1882).[7]

Hunting Leviathan

Whales are the largest marine mammals of the order *Cetacea*, which includes dolphins and porpoises. In *Paradise Lost* (1674), the English poet John Milton described these giants as the 'Sea-beast *Leviathan* which God of all his works created hugest that swim th' Ocean stream.'[8]

Ship owners despatched vessels to hunt and kill whales for their oil, which was used to make candles and soap and to fuel lamps. Whalebone corset supports and umbrella ribs were made from flexible baleen. Whalers spent their idle hours carving whale teeth and jawbones with designs of ships and other subjects, an art or craft known as scrimshaw.

Baleen whales: The *Mysticeti* or baleen whales (*Balaenopteridae*), are toothless, having plates in their mouths, symmetrical skulls and two blowholes. Baleen whales feed by sieving plankton or krill from seawater through these plates, in the upper jaw, which are not bone, but a protein substance similar to human fingernails.

This group includes blue or sulphur-bottomed whales (*Balaenoptera musculus*), the largest whales, weigh up to 150 tonnes and measure 30 metres in length.

Southern Right whales (*Eubalaeana australis*) are black and may reach 18 metres in length.

Humpback whales (*Megapetera novaeangliae*) range from 11 to 18 metres in length and have long, ragged-edged flippers, characteristic humped backs, and a spout blowing 2.5 to 3 metres high. They have a black head and back with a white throat and underside. Humpbacks usually sink when dead, so they were the last choice of colonial whalers. Humpbacks are known today for their songs that might continue for three to four hours.

Toothed whales: A second group, the *Odontoceti* or toothed whales, have an asymmetrical skull and a single blowhole and feed on fish and squid.

Sperm whales (*Physter Macrocephalus*), with distinctive boxy heads, are the largest of the toothed whales, with males growing to 18 metres in length and females to half that size. This species was most sought by colonial whalers for their oil, which was odourless and so could be used in lamps, and for their sweet, musky ambergris, once used to fix perfumes. Spermaceti, a liquid wax from inside the whale's head, was used as a lubricant and to make smokeless candles. Albino or white whales, like the famous Moby Dick, are sometimes sighted. These whales travel in groups.

Hopes for a whale fishery

'We have now … Hopes that a Whale Fishery will be established', wrote Judge Advocate David Collins in a letter to his brother George in England in November 1791.[9] Whaling in Australian waters got off to a false start that year, when five of the convict transport ships of the Third Fleet landed their stores and human cargo in Sydney and then went to sea to hunt for whales.

On Saturday 9 July 1791 the transport *Mary Ann*, bringing 240 female convicts sailed into Port Jackson. This was the first arrival of an expected convoy of transports carrying more than 1800 convicts. 'The master's name was Munro; and his ship, after fulfilling her engagement with government, was bound on the southern fishery,' wrote Watkin Tench, one of a boat party that rowed six miles out to sea to meet the ship.[10] Sergeant James Scott noted in his diary that a whale was spotted between the Heads at Port Jackson on 14 July 1791.

The *Atlantic* came into Sydney Cove at midday on Saturday 20 August 1791 with 202 male convicts and a detachment of troops from the New South Wales Corps. *Salamander* arrived the following day, bringing 160 male convicts and twelve soldiers, with stores and provisions.

The convict fleet must have astonished the Aboriginal men, women and children who stopped at Governor Phillip's house, overlooking the cove, on 23 August on their way to attend a corroboree at Botany Bay. Some of them had 'come in' to the settlement for the first time. Phillip gave them bread and metal fish hooks.[11] The next day 20 Eora returning from the Botany Bay ceremonies called at the governor's house on their way to the 'lower part of the harbour'. Some stayed in Sydney overnight.[12]

On Sunday 28 August, the 370-ton *William and Ann* brought in 180 male convicts, some soldiers and provisions. Enderby & Co. owned the ship, but the master was a North American, Captain Eber Bunker (1762–1836), born in Plymouth, Massachusetts, who later settled at Bunker Hill, in Sydney's maritime Rocks area. The storeship HMS *Gorgon*, commanded by Captain John Parker, arrived on 21 September with Major Francis Grose and a detachment of the New South Wales Corps.

While they usually found their totems in emblems of the natural world, the English sailing ships awed and fascinated the Eora. One of them, who afterwards sailed in the crew of whaling and sealing ships, took his name from the whaler William and Ann. Governor John Hunter said the name had been 'corrupted by their pronunciation to Wil-lam-an-an which he adopted from a ship of the same name that arrived here in the year 1791'.13 Willamannan's name was further corrupted by the English settlers and was later recorded variously as William, William Manen, Menan, Munnen and Minam. About this time another Aboriginal man adopted his name from the *Salamander* whaler.

The whaler *Britannia*, owned by Enderby & Co. and commanded by Captain Thomas Melville, came into Port Jackson on 14 October 1791 with 129 male convicts, stores and provisions. 'In her passage between Van Diemen's Land and Port Jackson, the master reported, that he had seen a large shoal of spermaceti whales', wrote Watkin Tench. 'I saw more whales, at one time, around my ship, than in the whole of six years, which I have fished on the coast of Brazil', Melville told Tench.[14]

When the huge three-decked, 527 ton transport *Admiral Barrington* reached Sydney Cove two days later, 'great numbers' of people flocked down to the ship to ask after relatives and friends in England. Among them, said an anonymous letter writer, were 'some few black natives out of idle curiosity'.[15]

The whaling fleet lost little time before going to sea. After a voyage to Norfolk Island, *Mary Ann* and *Matilda* sailed from Sydney on 24 October, *Britannia* and *William and Ann* the following day, and *Salamander* on 1 November, after a visit to Norfolk Island. On 26 October, *Britannia* and *William and Ann* sighted sperm

Departure of the whaler Britannia from Sydney Cove, 1796, Thomas Whitcombe (1763–1824), Oil, Nla.pic-an2253068, , National Library of Australia, Canberra.

whales. They harpooned and killed seven whales, but because of strong winds and turbulent seas, only two whales could be towed back to the ships. *William and Ann* returned to Sydney for repairs in December 1791 and then put in to Broken Bay, while *Salamander* dropped anchor in Port Stephens. On his return, Captain Melville told Tench that he had seen many thousands of whales and that the 'oil and *head matter*' of the one whale he had killed was of 'an extraordinary fine quality'.[16] Within a few weeks the whalers left the New South Wales coast and headed for their usual hunting grounds off Peru, though the 460-ton *Matilda* was wrecked near Tahiti.

Enderby & Co. again sent *Britannia* to Sydney with 94 female convicts in 1798 under the command of Robert Turnbull.[17] The ship then sailed on a long whaling voyage off Australia, returning in 14 months with 160 tuns of sperm oil.

In 1799 the 330-ton *Speedy*, an Enderby whaler commanded by George Quested, was chartered to transport 50 female convicts to Sydney. Also on board was Philip Gidley King, due to replace Captain John Hunter as governor of New South Wales. King was keen to establish Sydney as a whaling port and privately supported Enderby & Co., in which he held an interest. As a result he was criticised and reprimanded for challenging the East India Company's long-standing monopoly on trade in Asia and the Pacific. His biographers and descendants, Jonathan and John King (1981) wrote:

> In an effort to stimulate local whaling activities the governor teamed up with the Enderby family's whaling company and put some of his own money in the venture, helping it to succeed wherever possible. He had known the Enderby brothers, Charles, George, and Samuel, for many years and had borrowed a small sum of money from the family in 1794.[18]

On his return voyage to England on *Speedy*, Quested complained about the bad weather and rough seas, but advised Samuel Enderby (through King) that he had 'got 4 Whales … I think there is a great deal of Oil to be got, if not a full cargo with persevering … '[19] 'The whale-fishing on this coast and off New Zealand may now be pronounced established', King told Sir Joseph Banks on 5 June 1802. 'A full whaler (Harrington, Captain Campbell) takes these letters Home, another is almost ready to follow, and four more are filling with very good success.'[20]

When *Speedy* docked at Paul's Wharf, London, after a voyage of nearly two years, Samuel Enderby advised Sir Joseph Banks:

> Mes^rs Enderbys present their most respectful Compliments to Sir Joseph Banks and take the liberty of acquainting him that their Ship Speedy, Geo^c. Quested, Master is arrived from Port Jackson with 179 Tuns Sperma Ceti Oil—The Master says he has a Black Swan, a Native's Head in Spirits and a number of other things for Sir Joseph Banks —[21]

The 'Native's Head in Spirits' was that of the Aboriginal resistance leader Pemulwuy.

16 Hawkesbury River sailors

The first European settlers took up land at the Hawkesbury River near the Green Hills (Windsor) in 1794. Boats and small sailing vessels soon became essential for transporting farm crops to Sydney from the river farms. For many years it was illegal to build boats or ships in New South Wales because of frequent attempts by convicts to seize them to escape. Ship building began on the Hawkesbury when these restrictions were eased early in the nineteenth century.

Some of these ship builders, among them Andrew Thompson, Jonathan Griffiths and John Grono, recruited Aboriginal men from the Hawkesbury River to join their crews. James Bath, an Aboriginal orphan, became a skilled bird shooter and an

A View of the Hawkesbury, and the Blue Mountains New South Wales, c. 1818, Walter Preston (1777–?) after John William Lewin (1770–1819), Engraving, Original PXD 373/1, Mitchell Library, Sydney.

expert 'in the work of a small Hawkesbury vessel'. The circumstance of his short life and 'adoption' by a series of 'guardians' was recounted in the *Sydney Gazette* after his death from dysentery at the age of 15 on 29 November 1804:

> When an infant he was rescued from barbarism by the event of his parents' death, both being shot while they were engaged in plundering and laying waste the then infant settlement at Toongabbee [Toongabbie]. When the pillagers were driven off the infant was found, and companionably adopted as a foundling by George Bath, a prisoner. The little creature received the name of *James Bath*.

The first Aboriginal attacks against the 'New Grounds' convict farm at Toongabbie, just north of Parramatta, took place in 1792. When George Bath left New South Wales, James was looked after by David Greville, who in turn left him in the care of John Sparrow, a watchmaker and manager of the playhouse that opened in Sydney on 16 January 1796. For five years, from the age of 10 until his death, James Bath worked and lived with William Miller (Millar) who had been charged but acquitted in 1797 with the gunshot killing of another young Aboriginal voyager named Tom Rowley. Miller regularly brought fresh fruit and vegetables from the Hawkesbury to the Hospital Wharf on the western side of Sydney Cove. According to the newspaper's obituary, James Bath displayed all the desirable virtues expected from an Aboriginal youth brought up by benevolent colonists. He spoke only English, took pride in his clean clothing, was 'docile, grateful, and even affable' and considered the word *Native* 'the most illiberal and severe reproach that could be uttered'.[1]

Jack at Jervis Bay

In 1805 'a Sydney native' called Jack sailed as a servant to Captain Demaria, master of the sloop *Nancy*, on a sealing voyage to Bass Strait. Andrew Thompson, a former convict and constable, had built the 40-ton vessel on the Hawkesbury River at Green Hills (Windsor) in 1803.[2] The following year, Thompson sold *Nancy* to the emancipated convicts Henry Kable and James Underwood.

Returning to Sydney in April 1805 with a cargo of 3187 sealskins, *Nancy* was wrecked in a gale near Nowra on the south coast of New South Wales. One seaman was drowned and the ship's cargo was lost in the surf or carried off by Aborigines.

While the others were hostile, one Aboriginal man agreed to guide the survivors to Jervis Bay, where they set out to walk to Sydney. Taking the only axe, Jack left the ship's crew the day after the wreck and 'went over to his kindred'. The captain, mate and crew, hungry and exhausted, reached Sydney on 1 May 1805 after an 11-day walk.[3] Captain Demaria suspected that Jack had stolen his clothing, but all was forgiven when Jack returned to Sydney four days later carrying the captain's clothes 'safe and in the condition he brought them from the wreck'.[4]

Jervis Bay — on the East Coast of N. S. Wales, Robert Marsh Westmacott (1801–1870), Watercolour, *Drawings of Sydney and New South Wales,* DL PX53/21, Dixson Library, Sydney.

Colebee, Jack Richmond and Tom Chaseland

'Jack … Age 25', listed as a 'Black', was included in the muster of the 57-ton brig *Endeavour,* which left Sydney on 27 April 1817, 'bound for Bass's Strait & Kangaroo Island'.[5] He is likely to have been Jack Richmond, who, in 1819, joined two other Aboriginal men from the Hawkesbury River in the crew that sailed the two-masted 85-ton brig *Glory* to Sydney on her maiden voyage on 27 September 1819. The ship was built and launched by Jonathan Griffiths, the owner and master, at his farm at Richmond Hill.

Three Aboriginal men were listed in the ship's muster, taken in Broken Bay on 29 October 1819:

> 16. Coalbee   Native Black
> 17. Tom   Do. Do.
>   from the Branch
> 18. Jack Richmond   Do.[6]

In 1814, 'Coleby from Richmond' had joined William Cox's gang building the first road across the previously impassable Blue Mountains, to the west of Sydney.[7] Cox (1764–1837) became the Paymaster of the New South Wales Corps after his arrival in Sydney in January 1811. He settled at 'Clarendon' (now Clarendon Park), Windsor. Coalbee, Coleby or Colebee's sister Maria was briefly married to Bennelong's son

Dickey, who had been christened Thomas Walker Coke. The *Hobart Town Gazette* said she had 'some considerable time previous been maternally treated in the family of Mrs Hassall of Parramatta'.[8] According to the Reverend Rowland Hassall, Maria was named after Anne Maria Macarthur, daughter of Governor PG King and his wife Anna Josepha.[9] Dickey died on 6 January 1823.[10] On 26 January 1824 Dickey's widow, Maria 'Cook' (i.e. Coke), married convict carpenter Robert Lock at St John's church, Parramatta.[11]

'Coalbee', Tom and Jack Richmond remained on board the *Glory*, bound for 'Port Dalrymple and the Coasts of N. S. Wales'. After calling at Port Dalrymple in Van Diemen's Land, the brig set out on a sealing expedition to Bass Strait and, judging by the cargo brought back, also to Kangaroo Island. *Glory* put in at George Town on 13 November 1819 with 520 sealskins, 650 kangaroo skins and 263 gallons of spirits. *Glory* next sailed on a sealing voyage on 9 December 1819.[12]

It is probable that William Cox adopted and brought up John or Jack Richmond at Richmond on the Hawkesbury River and gave him the name of that township. John Richmond, seeking land at Pitt Town, was included in 1816 in a list of *Settlers who are to have Lands located and marked out for them*.[13] If he is the same man described by Surgeon Joseph Arnold, which seems likely, John Richmond had previously asked Governor Lachlan Macquarie for land and was already farming in 1815. Arnold wrote:

> Another native applied to the governor for a grant of Land, he had been brought up by an English settler, and had not learned the native language; he now lives on his farm and cultivates it properly.[14]

John Richmond, residing at 'Hawkesbury' and described as 'A Black native of the Colony' is No. 187 in a *List of new Settlers: Names of Free Settlers and other Free persons allowed to become Settlers, who are to receive Grants of Land in 1816*. On the recommendation of 'Mr. Cox' he received 30 acres at Pitt Town.[15]

In 1817, 'Jack … Age 25', listed as a 'Black', was included in the muster of the 57-ton brig *Endeavour*, 'bound for Bass's Strait & Kangaroo Island'. This was another voyage for Jack Richmond, whose shipmates included 'Tamarine … Sydney Black age 20'. Tamarine (also called Tommy Tamara or Tomaine) was from Botany Bay. The ship, commanded by Thomas Hamant, left Sydney on 27 April 1817.[16]

Tom from the Branch (Macdonald River), described in the ship's muster as 'Thos Chaseland — free by birth in N. S. Wales … age 23', signed on for another sealing voyage in *Glory*, which left Port Jackson on 3 October 1820.[17] *Glory* returned to Sydney 13 January 1822 'from a sealing voyage of fifteen months and last from Port Dalrymple'.[18] Tom Chaseland was to become a famous whale harpooner after settling in the South Island of New Zealand.

Captain seeks a boat

Captain or Black Captain probably adopted his English name after his voyages with the Hawkesbury River settler and shipbuilder Captain John Grono (1767–1847), who had known him from childhood. His Aboriginal names were variously recorded as Corriangee, Karingy, Kurringy and Kurrigan, as well as an alias, Carbone or Cobbon Jack. At first he rebelled against the settlers establishing farms on the Hawkesbury. In 1805 Corriangee was among 'Mountain natives … accused by their own tribes' of being 'the principal murderers' in the 'recent horrible enormities' following the spearing of two of John Macarthur's stockmen at Camden.[19] In March 1816, Dr Charles Throsby told Governor Macquarie that Curriangii, alias Cobbon Jack, was an 'elderly native belonging to the Richmond District'.[20] On 20 July 1816, Governor Lachlan Macquarie outlawed 'Carbone Jack (alias Kurringy)' and nine other Aboriginal men 'well known to be the principal and most violent instigators of the Late Murders'. He offered a reward of £10 to bring in the outlaws or proof of their having been killed or destroyed within three months.[21]

Karingy Jack 'came in' peacefully and received blankets at the Native Conference at Parramatta in December 1816.[22] After this reconciliation, Captain became a sailor and a shepherd and was made chief of the Caddie or Cattai 'tribe' at Pitt Town on the Hawkesbury River by Governor Macquarie.

Captain went on two separate sealing voyages lasting a total of two years on Grono's brig *Elizabeth* and once rescued a drowning man in New Zealand. The ship's maiden voyage on 8 December 1821 was a big event at the Hawkesbury. On 15 December 1821 the *Sydney Gazette* reported:

> Friday week was launched at Mr. Grono's farm [now Canning Reach], on the river Hawkesbury, a very fine brig (130 tons), which was named the Elizabeth, with the usual ceremonies, amidst the shouts of a numerous and respectable concourse of people, assembled from Windsor and the adjoining districts. The Elizabeth is the first brig, of her tonnage, that has been launched into the River Hawkesbury, and from what we are informed, she reflects great credit on the persevering sacrifices of the owner.[23]

In November 1822 'the new brig Elizabeth, Captain Grono, sailed on a sealing voyage, which is calculated to take up the next 20 months'.[24] The ship's muster reveals the destination as New Zealand, with a crew including Grono's son-in-law William Wiseman and two Maoris, Saroriagh and Aroriagh, but Captain is not noted.[25]

In 1831 John Grono submitted a petition to the Governor of New South Wales, Sir George Gipps, to supply a boat to 'Captain, Native Chief of the Caddie Tribe'. Grono stated that 'the late Governor Macquarie made [Captain] a Chief of the Caddie Tribe' and that he had been on two voyages at sea in the brig *Elizabeth* … 'for the purpose of obtaining Seal skins.' Since then the inhabitants of Pitt Town had chiefly employed him. Grono, who also called Captain 'King of the Caddie Tribe', continued:

> Petitioner had been known to me from his childhood and I have always considered him to be honest & rather more industrious than the generality of his fellow Country men. He labours hard during the harvest, and I have known him in times past to act as a Shepherd. He was at sea three years in my employ during which time he conducted himself with propriety and submission and in one instance at New Zealand when a white man was washed from the rocks by a surf and twelve Europeans standing by afraid or unable to render any assistance to the drowning Man, Petitioner at the risk of his own life plunged into the sea and rescued him from a watery grave.

Petitioners Thomas Arndell (1752–1821) of 'Caddie' and William Hall of Pitt Town said they had known Captain for 20 years and found him an honest and a worthy man. Mr M McDonald said that at one time 'Black Captain' had charge of a flock of sheep — 'he was considered our best and carefulest shepherd. I believe him to be honest and industrious …'[26]

According to Darug tradition, ancestors of the present Locke family buried Captain on his clan territory.[27]

17 Tom Chaseland: whaling in New Zealand

Thomas, Tom, or Tommy Chaseland (c. 1797–1865), the son of an Aboriginal woman and an ex-convict settler at the Hawkesbury River, north of Sydney, seems to have spent more of his adventurous life at sea than on land.

He was a tall, powerful man and a strong swimmer and rower. His eyesight was so keen that he could spot a whale at sea long before it could be seen through a ship's telescope. He was one of the first settlers in New Zealand, where he was regarded as the best whale harpooner in the South Island. There was also a dark side to Tom Chaseland, who took part in brutal massacres against the Maoris in retribution for their attacks.

According to ships' muster lists and 'Claims and Demands' notices in colonial newspapers, Chaseland shipped out of Port Jackson on dozens of voyages: to Bass

The North Cape, New Zealand and Sperm Whale Fishery, W Read after Joel Samuel Polack (1807–1882), Engraving, Frontispiece from JS Polack, *New Zealand Being a Narrative of Travels and Adventures*, vol. 1, Richard Bentley, 1838, Mitchell Library, Sydney.

Strait, Van Diemen's Land, Kangaroo Island, Macquarie Island, Calcutta, Fiji, the Marquesas, Tahiti, the Friendly Isles (Tonga) and New Zealand, working as a sailor, sealer, second mate, whaleboat steerer, interpreter of the Maori language, headsman of bay whaling gangs and as a pilot for map-makers.

There are many tales of Chaseland's exploits and lucky escapes from danger. After the shipwreck of the brig *Glory* in 1827, Chaseland steered an open whaleboat through stormy seas from the Chatham Islands (Rekohu), some 800 kilometres east of the South Island of New Zealand, to Moeraki in Otago. In 1831 the schooner *Industry*, commanded by William Wiseman, son of Solomon Wiseman, ran aground on Stewart Island (Rakiura), just south of Bluff, at the tip of the South Island. Wiseman, ten sailors and six Maori women were drowned, but Chaseland and another seaman survived.

His first wife Puna (born about 1810) was the sister of Taiaroa, a powerful Maori rangatira or chief of the Ngai Tahu or Otakou (Otago) tribe. In 1850 after Puna's death, Chaseland married Pakawhatu or Margaret Antoni, daughter of a Maori woman and a Portuguese sailor.

Searching for the Aboriginal Tom Chaseland in ships' muster lists and 'Claims and Demands' notices in colonial newspapers is complicated because there were three Thomas Chaselands or Chaselings in the family. One was his father, Thomas Chaseling or Chaseland (c. 1769–1847), a convicted criminal transported to New South Wales and an early settler at Wilberforce on the Hawkesbury River. Then there was his half-brother, Thomas Chaseland, born at Cattai about 1807 to Thomas Chaseling Senior and Margaret Mahon or McMahon, who also went to sea.[1] This Thomas and four other children were baptised on 29 November 1812, the same day that their parents were married at St Matthew's Church, Windsor.

Our subject, born about 1797, was the son of Thomas Chaseland Senior and an unknown Aboriginal woman, probably from the Hawkesbury-MacDonald River (Darkinjung) language group. A sister or half-sister, Mary or Maria, was born about 1791 to Chaseling Senior and an Aboriginal mother, probably the same woman.[2]

To further complicate matters there was another Aboriginal Tommy at Botany Bay, as well as one or more Maori, Tahitian and Marquesan 'Tommys', listed in contemporary ships' musters. Lorraine Russell (2008), archaeologist Nigel Prickett (2008) and Pamela Goesch (2009) have researched and written about Tom Chaseland and also could not be sure which of the two Chaseland half-brothers were on particular voyages unless he was listed as being Aboriginal.[3]

CLAIMS AND DEMANDS.

THE following Persons being about to depart the Colony, request all Persons having Claims or Demands against them to present the same to themselves for Payment:

In the Schooner Endeavour—Mr. Theodore Walker, Thomas Watson, Charles Griffin, John Fitzgerald, Joe an Otaheitan, and Tommy, a native boy.

Claims and Demands, Sydney Gazette, 21 December 1811.

Thomas Dowse, an ex-convict clerk to the Sydney Harbour Master, who settled in Brisbane, left an unpublished memoir titled *Tom Chaseland or the adventures of a Colonial half caste: a tale of old times*. Dowse, who knew Tom Chaseland, said his mother was a 'black princess', named Gumeereewah, who was a daughter of Bennelong. However, Bennelong's only known daughter Dilboong died as an infant. Dowse's story is obviously a work of fiction.[4]

'Tommy, a native boy', no more than 14 years of age, left Port Jackson in December 1811 aboard the 31-ton schooner *Endeavour*, taking missionaries Charles Wilson and John Davies to Tahiti. This was probably his first of many voyages. Henry Kable and James Underwood were the owners of *Endeavour*, built in Sydney in 1801. The crew of six also included 'Joe an Otahetian' (Tahitian).[5] The ship returned to Sydney from Tahiti on 24 February 1812 with a cargo of 17, 920 pounds of pork.[6]

Kable and Underwood's *Endeavour* of Sydney and Mary Reibey's ship *Mercury* were both wrecked in a gale on the same day at the Shoalhaven River on 13 March 1813.[7] 'Tommy' and four Tahitians, sailed again for Tahiti on 23 May 1813, this time aboard the 58-ton brig, also named *Endeavour*, built at Norfolk Island and owned by Isaac Nichols.[8] In October 1813, Nichols, who had a storehouse and shipyard at The Rocks, advertised 'about Twenty Tons of fine salted Pork' in exchange for 'good wool in the fleece'.[9]

Tommy, now about 18 years old, was first identified as 'Thos Chaceland (native)', when he joined the crew of Underwood's 248-ton brig *Campbell Macquarie,* master Captain Richard Siddins, which left Sydney on 11 July 1815, bound for Calcutta via Torres Strait.[10]

In 1816, 'Thomas Chaseling, son of a settler at Windsor by a native woman', sailed on the 103-ton brig *Jupiter*, Captain William Bunster, taking convict prisoners to Van Diemen's Land, leaving Sydney on 6 August and arriving in Hobart Town on 23 August 1816.[11] On 5 August 1817, 'Thos Chaseling', again identified as the son of an Aboriginal woman, sailed from Sydney, bound for Hobart on *Jupiter*.[12] The brig was forced to put back to Sydney from Twofold Bay after a convict on board was struck by lightning, which also burnt the topgallant mast. *Jupiter* again left Sydney for Hobart after repairs on 12 August 1817 in company with the government brig *Elizabeth Henrietta*.[13]

The muster of the 210-ton vessel *Frederick*, which left Sydney on 7 August 1817, bound for the Derwent and Calcutta, included as a passenger, 'Thos. Chaseland …

6 Thos Chaseling: Son of a Settler at Windsor by a Native Woman —
Colonial Secretary Ships Muster of the Brig *Jupiter of Calcutta* … 'Set Off 5th August 1817'
No. 23/115 1817,
State Records New South Wales, Sydney

Birth in NS Wales'.[14] As the Aboriginal Tom Chaseland was already on the crew of the *Jupiter*, bound for Hobart, this must be his brother Thomas, now aged 10. In December 1817, the *Sydney Gazette* reported 'Mr. and Mrs. Scully leaving the Colony on the Ship Frederick; also their servant, Thomas Chaseland'. This is probably also the younger Thomas Chaseland on the ship's next voyage.

After the voyage on *Jupiter*, Chaseland joined the ship-rigged 185-ton *King George*, which in 1818 sailed to the Marquesas Islands (now French Polynesia) for pork and sandalwood.[15]

Thomas Chaseland was aboard the brig *Governor Macquarie* on 10 August 1819, which had a stated destination of New Zealand and Tahiti.[16] The 136-ton vessel had been built in Sydney in 1811 by William and James Jenkins and was sold at auction to Mary Reibey in May 1819 for £750.00. *Governor Macquarie* left Sydney on 4 September 1819, but did not visit the Pacific islands. Instead, the brig sailed to Port Dalrymple. 'Chaseland' was among those 'leaving the Colony in the Brig Governor Macquarie' in a Claims and Demands notice in the *Hobart Town Gazette* on 2 October 1819.[17] Four days later *Governor Macquarie* sailed for Sydney from Hobart via Port Dalrymple, after landing a gang of sealers at Kangaroo Island.[18]

On 29 October 1819, 'Tom from the Branch' joined Coalbee (Colebee) and Jack Richmond, Aboriginal men from the Hawkesbury River, aboard the 85-ton brig *Glory*, then moored in Broken Bay, but bound for the Bass Strait sealing grounds.[19] The two-masted brig was built and launched at Richmond Hill by her owner and master Jonathan Griffiths. 'The Branch', often called 'First Branch', was the Macdonald River, a tributary of the Hawkesbury.[20]

'Thos. Chaseland — free by birth in N.S. Wales' signed on *Glory* again in October 1820. According to maritime historian JS Cumpston (1970), Chaseland was then aged 23. *Glory* returned to Sydney on 13 January 1822 'from a sealing voyage of fifteen months and last from Port Dalrymple'.[21] In March 1822, Chaseland sailed to the Île de France (Mauritius) aboard the 430-ton ship *Midas*.[22]

Mission to Tonga

'Thos Chaseland — Seaman — Born in Colony' was among the crew of the ship *St Michael*, which left Sydney Cove on 11 June 1822, taking the Wesleyan Missionary Reverend Walter Lawry to Tongatabu in the Friendly Isles (now Tonga) in the Pacific Ocean.[23] 'Captain Beveridge, who had frequently touched at Tonga, had made a favourable report on the disposition of the natives,' according to the Reverend Samuel Leigh. Lawry volunteered to go and Leigh obtained the consent of the Wesleyan Mission in London for 'another attempt being made for commencing this mission'.[24]

Beveridge and Lawry had jointly purchased the 170-ton *St Michael*, built in

Calcutta for £1100. The vessel, once owned by the trader Peter Dillon, was employed in a dual role: to resupply the Tongatabu mission and to trade in the South Sea Islands. 'We are now under sail … bound for New Zealand and Tonga', Lawry wrote in his journal on 18 June 1822.[25] *St Michael* sailed into the Bay of Islands on the North Island of New Zealand on 13 July 1822. Lawry held a service on the ship the following Sunday. The ship's officers and crew attended another service on shore that afternoon, but this did not stop the officers trading firearms and powder to the Maoris that day for pigs and potatoes, as Lawry noted.[26]

St Michael arrived at Tongatabu Island on 16 August 1822 and left for Sydney in November.[27] Lawry took on board two Tongan chiefs, Tattha (Tahtah) and Footacava, to be held as hostages to deter attacks by their relatives. In Sydney on 7 February 1823, said the Reverend Ralph Mansfield, the two Tongans 'exhibited some curious specimens of their dancing and singing'.[28] 'Tahtah and Footahcavah, the two natives of Tonga, have returned in the St. Michael. Those two fine men have gone home laden with presents from some of the most distinguished persons in the colony,' the *Sydney Gazette* reported on 23 April 1823.[29]

Tom 'Chaisland', newly promoted to Second Mate, sailed again on *St Michael* for New Zealand and Tonga, taking home the two chiefs. Returning from Tonga, *St Michael* again stopped at the Bay of Islands. While there, Leigh used the ship to look for a site to establish a permanent Methodist mission, first visiting Maoris at Whangarei, 170 kilometres north of Wellington. *St Michael* ran aground on rocks in the harbour and was in danger of sinking, but the crew manned the capstan and managed to work the ship into deeper water. The Maoris were exultant when it looked like the ship would be lost, believing that, like a stranded whale, it would then be their property, as Leigh wrote:

> When the natives first saw the 'St. Michael' upon the rocks, and observed that the captain and crew could not get her off, they assembled upon the shore, and vociferated 'Te Tani'wa', the 'god of the sea is killing your ship: she is dying, the ship is ours, Te Tani'wa has sent her to us.' According to their maritime laws or customs, the 'St. Michael' had become the property of their chief, being stranded upon his territory. They would have boarded and taken possession of her, but having no canoes, they could not reach her in sufficient numbers to overpower the crew.

Lawry remained below during the drama, but came on deck to offer prayers for their deliverance when the ship began to move.[30] In 1796, Maoris had captured a yawl belonging to the French Captain Jean-Francois-Marie de Surville of the 650-ton *St Jean Baptiste* when it was washed up at Tokerau Beach (north of Wellington). Surville set the village alight in retribution.[31]

St Michael sailed from the Bay of Islands on 3 October 1823 and reached Sydney on 7 November 1823.

Thomas 'Chaceland' was in the crew of the Dutch schooner *Alligator* in December 1823, but the ship was involved in a dispute and did not sail.

In January 1824 Thomas 'Chaceland' enlisted on the colonial schooner *Sally* sealing in Bass Strait and later on the 125-ton burden brig *Nereus*, commanded by Captain Thomas Swindells, which anchored at Hobart on 14 May 1824 'from the sealing Islands'.[32]

Settling in Murihiku

Later Tom Chaseland was chiefly engaged in sealing, whaling and transport and survey voyages around southern Otago, that part of the South Island of New Zealand the Maoris called Murihiku, meaning 'the tail end of the land'. Detailing events for 1823 in his history of the South Island of New Zealand, *Murihiku* (1909), Robert McNab (1864–1917) wrote: 'On the lists of those sent away we notice the names of Thomas Chaseland and James Spencer, on board the *St Michael* and John Guard, on board the *Wellington*. These are names of men who afterwards became prominent in New Zealand history.'[33]

Sealers were accustomed to a life of hardship and brutality. They spent days covered in blood and blubber, clubbing and skinning seals and sea elephants. They sometimes faced attacks by hostile Aborigines and Maoris. In one incident in May 1826, Chaseland and John Boultbee, an English sealer on the barque *Elizabeth*, killed to save their lives when Maoris attacked their gang. In the fight, at North Head (now Arnott Point) on the west coast of the South Island, the boatsteerer William Perkins and another sealer were killed. Boultbee, 'swearing and raving', defended himself by swinging a 15-foot long oar, 'screaming most diabolically'. In his memoir, *Journal of a Rambler*, Boultbee recounted the bloody revenge the sealers took next day against a nearby village inhabited by refugees from fighting at Banks Peninsula:

> The sealers, among whom was the famous Chaseland, pulled into the shore fronting the kaika [village] and in revenge shot some of the natives from the boats. They then landed and slaughtered all who did not escape into the bush. When Chaseland was aroused he became a frenzied fiend. Among his other acts he seized a child Ramirikiri, whose father and mother had been killed, and dashed her head on a rock and left her for dead. After the sealers had done all the mischief they could they left and the surviving natives crept out of the bush and returned to their desolate homes. They found the little girl living and revived her …[34]

According to the New Zealand linguist and anthropologist J Herries Beattie, as an old woman, Ramirikiri (who died at Colac Bay near Bluff in about 1900) said the massacre took place at the village of Okahau in Jackson Bay, where the Maori warriors had returned after their attack.[35] A sketch map (now in the National Maritime Museum, Greenwich) compiled from Chaseland's information locates several places where conflicts had taken place between Maoris and sealers during the 1820s, including Okahau. 'Chaseland's map indicated that thirty Maoris were killed [at Okahau]', wrote June Starke, who edited Boultbee's manuscript.[36]

Dr Edward Shortland, Official 'Protector of Aborigines' (Maoris) in New Zealand, who met Tom Chaseland in 1843, characterised him as both 'hero and villain'. Chaseland was the boatsteerer of the schooner *Scotia*, which Shortland boarded at Waikouaiti to visit other whaling stations in the south. In his early life, wrote Shortland, Chaseland 'had been cast away on the Chatham Islands, and had made the voyage thence to New Zealand in an open sealing boat, steering the whole way himself, till he and his companions landed at Moeraki [North Otago]'.[37]

Thomas Dunbavin (1931) said Chaseland 'steered a whaleboat from the Chatham Islands to Otago across 500 miles of stormy seas'.[38] Maori informants in Southland passed on an oral tradition that associated Chaseland and his first wife Puna with this feat. 'Her husband and she went to the Chathams and were wrecked', Daniel Ellison told Herries Beattie. 'They built a boat and put sufficient food on it and came back here. She was a great tohunga and pulled one of her hairs, said a karakia [powerful prayer, chant or incantation], and put it in the sea, so they had a safe passage and landed at Moeraki.' The Maori word *tohunga*, usually applied to men, meant a priest or gifted person.[39] Mrs Walscott (Ema Karetai) told Herries Beattie: 'Puna sat chanting in the bow of his boat from Chatham Island Karakia-ing to keep the storm down'.[40]

Rhys Richards (1982) linked Chaseland's voyage with another epic open boat journey from the Chatham Islands to the North Island of New Zealand in 1827. The brig *Glory* ran aground off Pitt Island in the Chathams on 15 January that year while on a sealing voyage, but no lives were lost. Captain Thomas Swindells and five others set out for the mainland of New Zealand through heavy seas on 11 May 1827 in a longboat fitted with sails. They reached the Bay of Islands just as Captain Worth in the *Samuel* was leaving for Sydney. Swindells returned to the wreck and arrived in Sydney on 11 May 1827 with '1800 prime sealskins, 3 tons of pork, 1 ton of flax and part of the wreck of the *Glory*'.[41]

Chaseland had sailed on *Glory* in 1819–20 and in 1824 was a crewman on the *Nereus*, commanded by Captain Swindells.

The first issue of the *Sydney Herald*, published on 18 April 1831, included two articles about the Hawkesbury River shipbuilder John Grono (1767–1848). The first concerned the building of his ship the *Governor Bourke*; the second reported the loss of Grono's brig *Industry*, wrecked in 'a dreadful gale of wind' at Easy Harbour, Stewart Island, on 28 February 1831. 'Ten men and six native women were drowned. W. Wiseman, the master, also, met a watery grave', the new journal reported.[42] Tom Chaseland, his wife Puna and George Moss, a Maori from Ruapuke, were the only survivors of the shipwreck. Stewart Island (Rakiura) and Ruapuke Island are both in Foveaux Strait, not far from Bluff at the southern tip of the South Island of New Zealand. According to Robert McNab in *Old Whaling Days* (1913), the *Industry* was lying at Codfish Island, north-west of Stewart Island, when the gale came up and on Chaseland's advice was steered to shelter in Easy Harbour.[43]

One story told by Basil Howard in *Rakiura* (1940), tells of Chaseland's struggle to save Puna. 'It was she, however, who at last dragged the insensible Chaseland to safety on the rocks', wrote Howard. 'This episode was made the subject of a Maori song, which is now lost.'[44] The schooner *Caroline* landed the survivors in Sydney on 6 April 1831.[45]

Grono had built the 87-ton two-masted *Industry* at Pitt Town on the Hawkesbury River. William Wiseman, the son of Wisemans Ferry innkeeper Solomon Wiseman (1777–1838), had married John Grono's daughter Matilda.[46] William Wiseman 'a remarkably active, good-looking young man … has left a very young widow,' said the *Herald*.[47] In New Zealand, William Wiseman had been living with a Maori woman named Rugig. They had two daughters, Sophia Petty and Mary Ann Petty, who were brought to New South Wales and baptised at St Alban's Church of England, Lower Hawkesbury, on 30 September 1832.[48] After a long illness, Sophia died at the age of 13 in 1840.[49]

News of the *Industry* disaster was brought to Sydney by the schooner *Samuel*, which arrived in Port Jackson on 28 March 1831 with a cargo of 500 sealskins, and the *Prince of Denmark*, loaded with 15 tons of flax.

Tom Chaseland told Dr Shortland about another lucky escape when he leapt from a boat to a rock ledge in pursuit of seals just as the boat overturned. The other sealers drowned and he was left alone on the ledge until the next day when another boat crew came in search of their lost companions.[50]

In another incident, Tommy 'Chasland', sensing danger as he harpooned a whale off Otago, jumped overboard just before the whale struck the boat and sliced it in two. Three of the crew were never seen again. Chaseland, Sam Perkins and another man clung to the overturned boat as a thick fog closed around them. While Chaseland was swimming ashore for help, a boat picked up the two frozen men, almost unconscious from cold. 'Some hours after the boats returned, having failed to find their lost chief, and towards dark, a figure was seen moving on the beach. The spyglass revealed Chasland wholly devoid of clothing coming towards the station after his exhausting swim of some six miles', said the *Otago Witness*.[51]

Taiaroa and Johnny Jones

In his frequent voyages in New Zealand waters, Tom Chaseland became involved with two powerful figures, one a Maori and one a Pakeha (white person). The first was Te Matenga Taiaroa (1783–1863), a famous chief of the Ngai Tahu or Otakou

(Otago) tribe who was the brother of Chaseland's wife Puna. Koroko, the father of Taiaroa and Puna, had been killed in 1817 when the sealer Captain James Kelly sacked Otakou.[52]

In 1823 Chaseland acted as an interpreter at the Clutha River in Central Otago for Edward Meurant, who later became a government interpreter. There was ample time at sea to learn the language from Maori shipmates.[53]

The second influential person was John or Johnny Jones (1808–1869), born in Sydney, who owned several whaling ships and bay whaling stations in New Zealand. In 1834 Jones set up a whaling station on Taieri Island at the mouth of the Mataura River (now the town of Fortrose), named Toetoes (Totoi's or Toi-tois) after a Maori chief. Chaseland and James Brown were the headsmen of a gang of 20.[54] It was at Taieri that Chaseland and his gang killed 11 whales in 17 days. Dr Shortland, who visited the station (then abandoned) with Chaseland in 1843, said that while this was regarded as 'the greatest feat of the kind ever recorded in the country', all the whale oil was lost, because, 'by the strangest neglect, no casks had been sent to the station'.[55]

When John Jones's 148-ton barque *Magnet* left Sydney on 9 December 1837 bound for New Zealand, 'T. Chaseland and wife' were listed as passengers.[56]

Edwin Palmer, a whaler from Sydney, met Tom Chaseland, who was then headsman on a sealing station in Foveaux Strait belonging to Campbell & Co. of Sydney, about 1835.[57] On 16 May 1838, John Jones appeared in a trial before Mr Justice Burton in the Supreme Court, Sydney, in which Palmer, Jones's former partner in a whaling station at Preservation Bay, New Zealand, was indicted for killing Charles Denahan, aged about 18, by beating him with a rope. Evidence was presented that Denahan and a Maori boy were in charge of a boat that was smashed in heavy surf at Preservation Bay and that Palmer had beaten Denahan so badly that he died on 4 July 1837. James Davidson, a carpenter, swore that in the middle of June 1837 he was lying in bed when he heard Denahan crying out, 'Don't beat me

Whaleboat showing position of crew, Artist unknown, Watercolour and pencil, A-032-025, Alexander Turnbull Library, Wellington, New Zealand.

Mr. Palmer, and I'll work for a year to pay for the boat'. The whipping continued. Davidson further stated that Palmer said Denahan was shamming. He continued: 'Palmer used to say to me that Chaseling the chief headsman, had told him that if the boy died he [Palmer] would be blamed for it, but he said he did not care a d—n, there was no law in New Zealand even if he had killed him, but the beating he had given him would not kill him'. Palmer was arraigned for manslaughter and Mr Justice Burton left the case to the jury, which brought in a verdict of 'Not Guilty'.

John Howard, who was also at Preservation Bay, gave a deposition before the Magistrates but was not present when the trial took place. Howard stated in his affidavit that 'the boy [Denahan] had been previously beaten by a man named Chaseline', but he had not noticed anything wrong with Denahan before Palmer came in.[58]

John Jones continued to employ Palmer after his acquittal. Palmer established the Tautuku whaling station in 1840 and settled at Bluff.

In 1838 Captain James Bruce purchased land extending from the Waikouaiti river mouth to Matananka Heads and 10 miles inland on behalf of Johnny Jones. The price paid, stated in the deed of conveyance drawn up in Sydney on 7 June 1839, was one tierce of tobacco and 10 dozen cotton shirts.[59] Jones confirmed this purchase in evidence before the Legislative Council Committee in Sydney on 6 July 1840:

> A Chief, who was in Sydney last year, sold me a quantity of land, full twenty miles square, for which I gave him property to the amount of £500. He understood English thoroughly and the transaction was regularly drawn up by a lawyer in Sydney, and duly executed and signed by the chief. I am satisfied with the Title, as I know him to be the acknowledged chief of a large district.[60]

The chief was Honi Tuhawaiki (d. 1844), paramount leader of the Ngai Tahu, who with Karaiti (Jacky White) and Taiaroa, was taken to Sydney to ratify the agreement. Tuhawaiki, called 'Bloody Jack' by the sealers and whalers, sailed to Sydney with Captain Bruce aboard *Magnet* on 4 October 1838. Jones's land purchases in 1839 led to the first permanent European settlement in the South Island of New Zealand. On 12 March 1840, *Magnet* left Sydney with the first group sent to Otago by Johnny Jones to settle at Waikouaiti. Captain Bruce's passengers included the returning 'Chiefs (5) New Zealand' who landed at Ruapuke Island.[61]

At Jones's request the Wesleyan Mission Board in Sydney in 1841 sent the Reverend James Watkin to Waikouaiti, where Jones provided the funds for a church and mission house. On 14 August 1843, Watkin officiated at the formal marriage of 'Thomas Chaseling to Puna' at Waikouaiti. At the same ceremony, Puna was baptised and took the name Meri (Mary).[62] Witnesses at the wedding were given as Hannah Watkin, the minister's wife, and Joseph Crocombe, the settlement's doctor.[63]

John Jones revived the Taieri whaling station in 1844, when an agreement was concluded between Stephen Smith, Thomas Jones (John Jones's brother) and

Thomas Chaseland for the purchase of whale oil and bone at Waikouaiti.[64] Frederick Tuckett, the New Zealand Company surveyor, left Nelson on 31 March 1844 on the ship *Deborah*, coasting south to Moeraki on 18 April, then visiting Waikouaiti and Otago Harbour, which he chose as the site for 'New Edinburgh' (Otago). Tuckett met Chaseland at the Taieri station:

> Mr. Chaseland received us with hospitality, his wife a sister of Tiroa [Taiaroa] is one of the few Maori women that I have seen capable of being a helpmate to a civilised man, and they keep a very comfortable fireside, not the less so from the bleak barrenness which surrounds their dwellings. Nowhere perhaps do twenty Englishmen reside on a spot so comfortable as this naked, inaccessible isle.[65]

The Reverend John Christie described the method of taking whales used at Jones's Waikouaiti bay whaling station. Six whaleboats, each with six rowers and a harpooner, put out to sea, two steering north and two south, with two others in the middle:

> When the whales were caught they were floated into the river mouth to the beach at the try-works, where they were cut up and the blubber boiled, and the oil put into casks for exportation. If a whale happened to be taken, and the hands too few to bring it to shore, a harpoon surmounted with a flag was stuck on the floating carcase till assistance was secured.

On shore the whale blubber was rendered into oil in a try pot, a heavy iron boiler kept in a large timber shed. Maoris were often included in the whaling parties in return for portions of whale, which they carried away for cooking and eating. 'The number of whales taken in a season would be from fifteen to twenty', wrote Christie. The best year's yield was 627 tons, but this was exceptional. 'In the last season of whaling there were only seventy tons.'[66]

Tom Chaseland's father, Thomas Chaseling [*sic*], died at the Hawkesbury at the age of 78 in 1847.[67] His descendants in Australia have continued to use that form of spelling the family name.

A document now in the Hocken Library, Dunedin, dated 1847, records a land grant by Taiaroa to 'Thomas Chaseland and Mary Puna' and an associated memorial to the Governor of New Zealand.[68] Tommy 'Chasland' is next recorded in 1848 working at Jones's whaling station at Tautuku Peninsula, a rugged headland north of Taieri.

Chaseland's wife Puna died in 1849, but the circumstances and details are unclear. Thomas Kennard, who lived near the Maori village at Waikouaiti, remembered that a woman named Puna died of influenza there when he was a boy aged seven in 1848. 'I remember the name distinctly, but I do not think it was the wife of Chaseland, as she was a young woman', Kennard recalled in his nineties. Kennard had other memories of Puna Chaseland:

I can remember seeing Tommy Chaseland's wife ironing a white shirt as well as any white woman. Tommy was a bit of a dandy in dress when he had the chance, and as a small boy I particularly admired his snowy-white trousers.[69]

On 15 August 1850, Tom Chaseland was married for the second time to Pakawhatu (born 1835), also known as Margaret Anthony (Antoni or Antonio). The German Lutheran missionary Reverend Johann Wohlers (1811–1885) conducted the ceremony at Ruapuke Island. Pakawhatu was the daughter of Joseph Antoni, a Portuguese sealer and whaler, and a Maori woman, Esther Leah Pura, born in 1820. Antonio came to New Zealand on the ship *Favourite* in 1847 and settled at Codfish Island, west of Stewart Island.[70]

Thomas and Margaret Chaseland had six children, all born on Stewart Island:

1. Maria, born 5 June 1852; christened 16 December 1856 at Ruapuke Island
2. Thomas, born 9 January 1854; christened 16 December 1856 at Ruapuke
3. John, born 26 June 1856
4. Caroline, born 27 October 1861; christened 13 October 1861 at Ruapuke
5. William Henry, born 5 March 1865
6. Margaret, born 6 April 1866[71]

Some descendants have the family names of Newton and Edwards. Caroline Chaseland, who married William Newton on 16 November 1876 at Ruapuke, died on 15 November 1887. Maria Chasland (Chaseland) married John Edwards. One son, William Edwards, died from typhoid at Bluff on 10 March 1898 while another, Thomas Chasland Edwards, died at the age of 41 on 20 November 1918.[72]

Charting Murihiku

After his years as a sealer and whaler in New Zealand waters, Tom Chaseland had an intimate knowledge of the rugged coastline of Murihiku. Dr Shortland was impressed when Chaseland pointed out a submerged rock that threatened shipping in Foveaux Strait. 'As Chaseland knew every part of the west coast, as well as this, I endeavoured to get him to draw an outline of it, with the aid of the chart which I had with me. This he was quite unable to do. He carried his map, he said, in his head, but it was useless to any one save himself.'[73]

In February 1851 Captain John Lort Stokes, in charge of a British Navy survey of New Zealand, engaged Tom Chaseland to pilot the 100-horsepower wooden side-paddle steamship HMS *Acheron* (Captain FJ Evans, master) around the Muruhiku coast as far as Dusky Sound. Half a century later, Archibald Fullerton, who had been a young sailor on board the 760 ton ship, recalled that Captain Stokes 'had the utmost confidence' in Tommy 'Chaslands'.[74] Leaving Wellington, the *Acheron* picked up Chaseland's brother-in-law Taiaroa and Walter Mantell, the New Zealand Company surveyor, at Akaroa on the Banks Peninsula.

Stokes's clerk George Hansard, keeper of the ship's log, described Taiaroa candidly as 'an old cannibal'.[75] In the log, obtained by Dr Thomas Hocken from Stokes's daughter, Hansard wrote:

> On board the *Amazon* is an Australian half-caste named Chaseland gifted with such extraordinary powers of vision that once, when stationed on the lookout, he gave notice of a whale being in sight although the master after reconnoitring with his glass declared he could see nothing — Chaseland however still persisted in his statement adding it was a dead fish with a harpoon stuck upright in his back with several fathoms of line attached — on pulling in the direction pointed out — the whale was found under the exact circumstances he had describe — they say he sees land when fully 30 miles from it. He is engaged as a pilot during the *Acheron's* western cruise …[76]

Stokes added Chaseland's name to the map in the *New Zealand Pilot* (1859):

> Chaseland's Mistake, South Otago, 101 miles south of Dunedin. Chaseland's Mistake is a rather remarkable black cleft cliff; it is nearly 11 miles from Long Point, and has a high rock standing off the shore a mile to the NE of it.[77]

James Wybrow gave the most likely reason (of many) for this placename. He said Chaseland was coming home one night with some Maoris in his boat 'when they saw a large cave full of seals, and it being dark they left the killing of them till the morning'. Next day the seals were gone 'and that', said Wybrow, 'was Chasland's mistake'.[78]

The southern Maoris identified Chaseland with the mutton-bird, calling him Tami or Tame (Tommy) Titerene. Titi is the Maori name for the sooty shearwater (*Puffinus griseus*), a gull-like Pacific seabird with grey or brown plumage. Young birds were caught in great numbers from the breeding grounds on the islands in Foveaux Strait every summer and salted or preserved in fat and packed into bags made from kelp. Mrs Te Au told Herries Beattie that 'Mrs. Mark Joss at the Bluff is the only descendant of Tami Titereni or Chaseland. She is a grand-daughter.' Daniel Ellison said: 'Womens Island for the titi at Rakiura [Stewart Island] belonged to Tuhawaiki-Parapara, who conveyed it to Puna, the wife of Chaseland or Tame Titerene [sic] and she became boss of the island'.[79] Tuhawaiki was the paramount chief of Ruapuke and the surrounding islands. Womens Island is in the northeast chain of the Titi or Mutton-bird Island group, betweens Stewart and Ruapuke Islands.

According to his daughter, Mrs Maria Edwards (born 1852), Tommy Chaseland or Chasland died on her seventeenth birthday, 5 June 1869, at Stewart Island, where he was buried.[80]

Moa flesh and bones

In 1849, Tom Chaseland, the Australian Aboriginal whaler and seafarer, made a surprising contribution to New Zealand natural science. Walking at low tide along the sandbar that joins the headland of Island Point to the mainland near the Waikouaiti River, he stumbled on some strange bones, which he at first thought were human. Chaseland had discovered two fossilised leg bones of the large flightless bird called the moa, which had been hunted and eaten to extinction by Maoris about 600 years ago.

These bones were of great interest to Walter Mantell, whose father, the English scientist Gideon Algernon Mantell, had achieved fame in the 1820s by unearthing a large tooth from a giant herbivorous reptile, the iguanodon, a dinosaur. Walter Mantell sent the moa specimens to his father, who acknowledged Chaseland's discovery of 'these splendid, unique fossils' in an address to the Geological Society of London in February 1850.

In life, Mantell's moa (*Dinornis novae zealandiae*), as it came to be known, would have weighed about 30 kilograms. 'This pair of perfect feet, my son observes, were discovered standing erect and about a yard apart,' Gideon Mantell told his London audience. 'Upon the retiring of the tide they were, fortunately, espied by "Tommy Chaseland", the best whaler in the island, who carefully dug them up. This unlucky Moa, happily for science, must have been mired in the swamp, and being unable to extricate himself … perished on the spot', the elder Mantell concluded.[81]

Tom 'Chasseland' and Edward Meurant, a sealer, settler and later government interpreter, had encountered traces of the elusive moa as early as 1823. The Reverend Richard Taylor revealed this in *Te Ika a Maui, or New Zealand and its Inhabitants*, published in London in 1855. Meurant told Taylor that in the latter end of 1823, at the mouth of the Clutha River he had actually seen a moa bone with flesh:

He saw a Moa bone which reached four inches above his hip from the ground, and as thick as his knee, with flesh and sinews upon it. The flesh looked like beef … Thomas Chaseland, the man who interpreted for Meurant, was well acquainted with the Maori language. He also saw the flesh, and, at first, they thought it was human.[82]

EPILOGUE

Tribal Warrior

Going to sea was one of the few ways that Indigenous people could earn a living and become independent in the early days of Sydney. They were highly valued as sealers and whalers in the first lucrative export industries of Australia's colonial economy.

Although some Aboriginal voyagers ended their lives tragically, by drowning, drink, mortal wounds received in payback battles and even execution, others became leaders of their people and several were officially created 'chiefs' and given fishing boats, land grants and metal gorgets.

Today, Aboriginal people continue as mariners, with many serving in the Australian Navy, as they did in World War II.

Flying the Aboriginal flag, the 15.4-metre-long gaff-rigged ketch *Tribal Warrior* set out from Gomora (Darling Harbour) in Sydney on 30 August 2001, passing under the bridge near Kameagáng (Pyrmont) and through the heads of Sydney Harbour into the open sea.

The timber-hulled former pearling lugger, more than 100 years old, carried a frequently changing crew of seven Aboriginal men, ranging from 17 to 45 years of age. In a voyage lasting 648 days, they carried a message of 'goodwill, achievement and reconciliation' to 120 Aboriginal communities scattered along the continent's 36,000 kilometre coastline. This was the first circumnavigation of Australia in a sea-going vessel crewed only by Indigenous Australians.

The *Tribal Warrior* is used to teach sailing and navigation skills to young Aboriginal men by the Tribal Warrior Association, based at The Block in the Sydney suburb of Redfern. In 1999 the first four students gained their Master Class 5 qualifications.

GLOSSARY

Barque	A three-masted sailing ship, square-rigged at foremast and mainmast and fore-and-aft rigged on the mizzen mast.
Beam	Width of a vessel at the widest part.
Boat	A small open craft (without decking) propelled by oars.
Boatsteerer	Function of a harpooner after harpooning a whale.
Boom	Spar running along the bottom edge of a sail.
Bow	Forward part of a vessel.
Brig	Two-masted, square-rigged sailing ship
Burden ('Burthen')	The carrying capacity of a ship expressed in tons.
Capstan	A rotating drum manned by deck hands to handle ropes and cables.
Claims and Demands	Notice in newspaper to collect outstanding debts from mariners leaving port.
Cutter	A fast vessel with a single mast carrying a gaff mainsail, topsail, headsails and a square topsail.
Fore	Forward or front of a vessel.
Fore-and-aft	Sails hung from stem to stern along the length of a ship.
Foremast	First mast from the ship's bow (front).
Frigate	Fully rigged navy warship armed with 16 to 24 guns.
Gaff	A spar holding a four sided fore-and-aft sail.
Harpoon	Spear or lance with a barbed head used to kill whales.
Jib	Triangular sail set before the mast.
Keel	The timber spine of a ship, running the length of its bottom.
Knot	A unit of speed at sea = one nautical mile per hour.
Log book	Record of navigation, ship's speed and daily distance.
Longboat	A ship's largest boat.
Mainmast	The second mast behind the bow; ship's biggest mast.
Mainsail	A ship's biggest sail.
Mizzen	Third or after mast of a three-masted ship.

Muster	Record of details of a ship's company.
Nautical mile	Measure of distance at sea = 1853 metres.
Schooner	A small fore-and-aft rigged vessel with a foremast and mainmast rigged like a yacht
Ship-rigged	A ship with three masts rigged with square sails on all except the lowest sail on the mizzen mast.
Sloop	A fore-and-aft rigged vessel, with its mainsail set behind the mast, like the *Lady Nelson.*
Snow	A ship with two square-rigged masts like a brig, with an extra mast carrying a small triangular sail.
Square-rigger	A ship in which the sails are suspended horizontally.
Storeship	A supply ship, carrying naval stores or armaments.
Supernumerary	Passenger not included in the crew.
Tonnage	Burden or carrying capacity of a ship.
Topsail	Sail above the lowest sail on a square-rigger.
Whaleboat	A long, narrow, open rowboat, light and fast, pointed at each end with a front platform for the harpooner.

BIBLIOGRAPHY

Abbreviations and reference works

ADB — *Australian Dictionary of Biography,* 1896 to date, Melbourne: Melbourne University Press.

BDM — NSW Registry of Births, Deaths and Marriages, Sydney.

BL — British Library, London.

BT — *Bonwick Transcripts,* Mitchell Library, Sydney.

CS — Colonial Secretary, Sydney.

DL — Dixson Library, State Library of New South Wales, Sydney.

HRA — *Historical Records of Australia, 1914—1922, Series 1,* Canberra: Library of the Commonwealth Parliament.

HRNSW — *Historical Records of New South Wales, 1892—1901,* 7 vols, Sydney: Government Printer.

HTG — *Hobart Town Gazette.*

JRAHS — *Journal of the Royal Australian Historical Society, Journal and Proceedings*, Sydney, vol. 1, 1906 to date.

ML — Mitchell Library, State Library of New South Wales, Sydney.

MUP — Melbourne University Press, Carlton, Victoria.

NHM — Natural History Museum, South Kensington, London.

NLA — National Library of Australia, Canberra.

NMM — National Maritime Museum, Greenwich, London.

OUP — Oxford University Press, Oxford.

PRO — Public Record Office, London.

SLNSW — State Library of New South Wales, Sydney.

SRNSW — State Records, NSW, Sydney.

SG — *Sydney Gazette,* 1804—1834, Sydney.

SH — *Sydney Herald,* Sydney.

SMH — *Sydney Morning Herald,* Sydney.

SOAS — School of Oriental and African Studies, University of London, London.

TBP — Treasury Board Papers, PRO, London.

Manuscripts in the Mitchell and Dixson Libraries, State Library of New South Wales, Sydney

Anon. [GW Evans], 25 March–13 April 1812, *Journal of an exploration overland from Jervis Bay to Mr. Broughton's …* C709.

Arnold, Dr J, Journals 27 August 1810–17 December 1813, C720.

Banks, J, Banks Papers, A83.

Barsden, JH, c. 1836. *Volume containing autobiographical accounts of events 1799–1816*, 7279.

Binnie, R, 1849–50. *Diary*, 29 October 1849–18 August 1850, 7326.

Collins, D, *Correspondence 1775–1810*, 700.

Flinders, M,1799. *A Journal in the Norfolk Sloop, 8 July–12 August 1799*, C2112.

[Grono, J] No date. 'Petition to Sir George Gipps Knight Captain General Governor and Commander in Chief of the Territory of New South Wales from John Grono and Others,' *Papers relating to Aboriginal Australians*, Add. 81, DL.

Handt, Rev. JS, 1855. BP Box 54.

Hassall, Rev. T, No date. *Memorandum*, Hassall Family Correspondence, 1793–c. 1900, A/677.

Holt, J, *Life*, A2024.

Huey, A, 1809. *Journal*, 28–31 December 1809, Typescript B1514.

King, PG, *Norfolk Island – Lieut. Governor, Victualling Book, 1792–1796*, A 1958.

King, PG, *Letter Book 1797–1806*, A2015, Safe 1/51.

King, PG, 1790. *Journal, 1786–1790*, C115.

Lesson, RP, 1824. *Voyage de la Coquille. Journal du manuscript … partie du voyage de la Coquille. Rèdige par Lesson*. Holograph copy, B1297.

Macarthur, WC, 1880. *A few Memoranda Respecting the Aboriginal Natives*, A4360.

Macquarie, L, *Memorandum*, Document 134, DL.

Macquarie, L, 1820. *Journal of a tour to the… country some time since discovered by Chas. Throsby Esqr. —in Octr & Novr 1820*, A782.

Macquarie, L, *Memorandum and Related Papers*, A772.

Macquarie, L, *Diary*, A773, A778.

Macquarie, L, *Journals*, A774.

McGarvie, Rev. J, *Diary 1825–1828*, A1332.

Marsden, E, *Marsden Family, Letters to Mrs. Stokes, 1794–1824*, 719.

Norfolk Island, *Annual Return of Inhabitants at the 6 Aug 1812*, CS 4/1170, COD 274, SRNSW.

Oxley, J, 1823. *Field Book*, 'Port Jackson to Port Curtis, October–November 1823', C257.

Proctor, W, 1834. *A Landsman's Log, being a Journal of my Voyage to Sydney in New South Wales … On board the "John Craig"*, B1126.

Robinson, GA, *Papers*, 1818–1924, A7022–A7092.

Smith, S, 1802. *Journal* of Samuel Smith, ZC222.

Sorell, W, Despatches to Governor Macquarie, A1351.

Suttor, G, *Memoirs of George Suttor, F. L. S. 1774–1859*, Typescript A3072.

Other manuscript sources

Anon., [1791] [Phillip, A, and Collins, D,] *Vocabulary of the language of N.S. Wales in the neighbourhood of Sydney (Native and English, but not alphabetical* [)], MS.41645 (c), London: School of Oriental and African Studies [SOAS], University of London. Referred to in this work as 'Governors' Vocabulary' [GV].

Bennelong 1796. Letter to Mr. Phillips, 29 August 1796, MS 4005, NK4048, NLA.

Berry, A, 1838. 'Recollections of the Aborigines', *May 1838*, Supreme Court, Misc. Correspondence Relating to Aborigines, No. 83, SRNSW.

Brown, R, 1802. *Journal*, 31 July 1802, MS B3V:ff 258–259, Botanical Library, NHM. Transcribed by KV Smith, London 1992.

Caley, G, *Remarks on the weather &c.*, Botanical Library, NMH. Transcribed by KV Smith, London 1992.

Carter, BB, *Journal on Ann and Hope 1798–1799*, Rhode Island Historical Society, New England Microfilming Project, Providence, Rhode Island.

Colonial Secretary, *Return of Aboriginal Natives* [Blanket Lists], SRNSW, Sydney, various dates.

Dawes, W, 1790a. *Grammatical forms of the language of N.S. Wales, in the neighbourhood of Sydney by — Dawes, in the year 1790*, MS 4165 (a), William Marsden Collection, London: SOAS, University of London. [Referred to here as 'Dawes a'].

Dawes, W, 1790b [1791]. *Vocabulary of the language of N.S. Wales in the neighbourhood of Sydney. Native and English, by — Dawes*, MS 4165(b), London: SOAS, ['Dawes b'].

Flinders, M, 1809. *A Biographical Tribute to the Memory of Trim*, Isle de France, *Flinders Papers*, MS 60/017/FLI/11A, NMM.

Fulton, Rev. H, 1805. *Aboriginal Vocabulary collected on Norfolk Island*, Norfolk Island MS, C of E, Bap. Marr. Bur. Register, SZ 1022 RG, vol. 4, 2, St. Phillip, Sydney, BMD 1787 to 1809, Norfolk Island 1792 to 1806, SRNSW.

Harman, K, 2008, *Aboriginal convicts: race, law, and transportation in Colonial New South Wales*, PhD Thesis, University of Tasmania, Hobart.

Kohen, JL, Knight, A and Smith, KV, 1999. *Uninvited Guests: An Aboriginal perspective on Government House and Parramatta Park*, Sydney: Report prepared for the National Trust.

Lawson, W, 1838. 'Mr. Lawson's account of the Aborigines of New South Wales', *Supreme Court Correspondence relating to Aborigines*, 5/1161, Document No. 83, SRNSW.

Macarthur, W, *Memorandum*, Supreme Court Miscellaneous cases relating to Aborigines 1824–40, COD/294B, SRNSW.

Murray, J, 1802. *Remarks on Lady Nelson*, Master's Log, Monday, 18 and 20 October 1802, Reel 1624, PRO London.

Paine, D, 1795. 'Vocabulary of part of the Language of New South Wales', *Manuscript kept in a Voyage to Port Jackson … by Danl. Paine*, MS JOD 172, NMM. Transcribed by KV Smith, Appendix E, *Eora Clans* 2004.

Thomson, GM, *Papers*, 0438/084, Hocken Library, Dunedin.

Smith, KV, 2004. *Eora Clans: A history of indigenous social organisation in coastal Sydney, 1770–1890*, MA thesis, Department of Indigenous Studies, SCMP, Macquarie University, Sydney.

Smith, KV, 2008. *Mari Nawi* ('Big Canoes')*: Aboriginal voyagers in Australia's maritime history, 1788–1855*, PhD thesis submitted 15 August 2008, Warawara, Department of Indigenous Studies, SCMP, Macquarie University, Sydney.

Southwell, D, 'A List of Words', *Southwell Papers 1787–1793*, Original MS 16,383:ff.147–9, BL [AJCP Reel M1538, ML].

Steele, JM, 2005. *The Aboriginal Language of Sydney*, MA Thesis, Warawara, Department of Indigenous Studies, SCMP, Macquarie University, Sydney.

Thornton, G, *Papers*, 'NSW Aboriginal', MS 3270, NLA.

Tuckett, F, *Diary*, MSS Letters of Frederick Tuckett, 1841–91, Hocken Library, Dunedin.

Wallis, J, 1816. *Journal*, CS in letters, 4/1735, Reel 2161, SRNSW.

Watkin, Rev. J, No date. *Waikouaiti Register of Baptisms, Burials, and Marriages*, Waikouaiti: Waikouaiti Library, New Zealand.

West, J, 1852. *The History of Tasmania*, Launceston.

Printed works to 1850

Angas, GF, 1846. *Savage Life and Scenes in Australia and New Zealand*, 2 vols, London: Smith,

Elder & Co.

Anon., 1797. *The spirit of the public journals for 1797, London: Printed for R. Phillips.*

Anon., 1789. *An authentic and interesting narrative of the late expedition to Botany Bay, as performed by Commodore Phillips, and The Fleet of the seven transport ships under his command … with particular descriptions of Jackfon's Bay and Lord Howe's Island …* London: Printed by W. Bailey.

Atkinson, J, 1826. An Account of the State of Agriculture & Grazing in New South Wales, London: J Cross.

Backhouse, J, 1843. *A Narrative of a Visit to the Australian Colonies*, London: Hamilton, Adams & Co.

Bond, G, 1809. *A Brief Account of the Colony of Port Jackson in New South Wales, Its Native Inhabitants, Productions, &c. &c.* London, 5th edn.

Bougainville, M Le Baron de, 1837. *Journal de la navigation autour du Globe de la Frégate La Thétis et de la corvette L'Espérance …* Paris: Arthur Bertrand.

Bradley, W, [1786–92] 1969. *A Voyage to New South Wales: The Journal of Lieutenant William Bradley RN of HMS Sirius, 1786–1792.* Facs. Reprint, Sydney: Trustees of the Public Library of NSW.

Collins, D, 1798. *An Account of the English Colony in New South Wales …* vol. I, London: T Caddell Jnr and W Davies, in The Strand. Facs. edition, Sydney: AH & AW Reed, 1975.

Collins, D, [1802] 1975. *An Account of the English Colony in New South Wales …* vol. II, London: T Cadell Jun. and W Davies. Reprinted edition, Sydney: AH & AW Reed, 1975. [Referred to here as 'Hunter in Collins II'].

Cunningham, PM, 1827. *Two Years in New South Wales*, 2 vols, London: Henry Colburn.

Dumont d'Urville, J,1830. *Voyage de la Corvette l'Astrolabe …* 14 vols, 2 Atlases, Paris: J Tartu; Rosenman, H (trans.) 1987. *Two Voyages to the South Seas …* Melbourne: MUP.

Field, B, (ed.), 1825. *Geographical Memoirs of New South Wales*, London: John Murray.

Flinders, M, 1814. *A Voyage to Terra Australis*, 2 vols, London: W Nichol.

Grant, J, 1803. *The Narrative of a Voyage of Discovery, Performed in His Majesty's Vessel The Lady Nelson …* London: T Edgerton Military Library, Whitehall.

King, PP, 1826. *Narrative of a Survey of the Intertropical and Western Coasts of Australia …* 2 vols, London: John Murray.

Mahroot [Boatswain Maroot], 1845. *Testimony by Mahroot alias the Boatswain …* Minutes of evidence taken before the Select Committee on the Aborigines, 8 September 1845, Sydney: Government Printer, MDQ 328.9106/4: 943–47, ML.

Mann, DD, 1811. *The Present Picture of New South Wales*, London: John Booth.

Mantell, GA, 1850. 'Notice of the remains of the Dinornis and other Birds, and Fossils and Rock Specimens recently collected by Mr Walter Mantell in the Middle Island [South Island]', London: PGSL, February 1850.

Marsden, JB, [1838] 1913. *Life and Work of Samuel Marsden*, Christchurch: Whitcombe and Tombs.

Marsden, W, 1834.'On the Polynesian or East Insular Languages', *Miscellaneous Works of William Marsden*, London: Parbury, Allen.

Parker, M, 1795. *A Voyage Round the World in the Gorgon Man of War …* Captain John Parker, London.

Peron, F, 1807. *Voyage de découvertes aux terres australes …* vol. 1, Paris: Chez Arthur Bertrand.

Peron, F, 1809. *A Voyage of Discovery to the Southern Hemisphere performed by the order of the Emperor Napoleon …* Translated from the French, London: Printed for Richard   Phillips.

Phillip, A, 1789. *The Voyage of Governor Phillip to Botany Bay*, London: Stockdale.

Shortland, E, 1851. *The Southern Districts of New Zealand*, London: Longman, Brown.

Strachan, A, 1853. *Remarkable incidents in the life of the Rev. Samuel Leigh*, London: Hamilton Adams & Co.

Suttor, G, 1855. M*emoirs Historical and Scientific of the Right Honourable Sir Joseph Banks …* Parramatta: E Mason.

Tench, W, 1789. *A Narrative of the Expedition to Botany Bay …* London: J Debrett.

Tench, W, 1793. *A complete account of the settlement at Port Jackson, in New South Wales, including an accurate description of the colony; of the natives; and of its natural productions …* London: G Nicol and J Sewell.

Threlkeld, Rev. LE, 1834. *An Australian Grammar … of the language as spoken by the Aborigines, in the vicinity of Hunter's River, Lake Macquarie, &c.*, Sydney.

Turnbull, J, 1805. A *Voyage Round the World in the Years 1800, 1801, 1802, 1803, and 1804*, (2 vols). London: Richard Phillips.

Tyerman, Rev. D and Bennett, G, 1841. *Voyages and Travels round the World*, London Missionary Society, London: John Snow.

Vancouver, G, [1798] 1801. *A Voyage of Discovery to the North Pacific Ocean, and Round the World …* London: John Stockdale.

Vaux, JH, 1827. *Memoirs of James Hardy Vaux, written by himself*, B. F. [Barron Field] (ed.), 2nd edn, London: CH Reynall.

White, J, 1790. *Journal of a Voyage to New South Wales …* London: J. Debrett, 1790.

Worgan, G, 1978. *Journal of a First Fleet Surgeon*, Sydney: Library Council of New South Wales.

Printed works after 1850

[Banks, J], JC Beaglehole (ed.), 1963. *The Endeavour Journal of Joseph Banks, 1768–1771*, 2 vols. Sydney: Angus & Robertson.

Barratt, G, 1981. T*he Russians at Port Jackson, 1814–1822*, Canberra: Australian Institute of Aboriginal Studies.

Bateson, C, 1963. *Gold Fleet for California, Forty Niners from Australia and New Zealand*, Sydney: Ure Smith.

Bateson, C, 1972. *Australian Shipwrecks*, Vol. 1, 1622–1850, Artarmon.

Begg, C, and Begg, NC, 1979. *The World of John Boultbee, including an Account of Sealing in Australia and New Zealand*, Christchurch: Whitcoulls.

Beattie, JH, 1911. *Pioneer Recollections, Second series, dealing chiefly with the early days of the Mataura Valley*, Gore: Gore Publishing Co.

Beattie, JH, 1912. 'Traditions and Legends', Part X1, *Journal of the Polynesian Society*, Wellington.

Beattie, JH, 1939. *The First White Boy Born in Otago: Story of T. B. Kennard*, Dunedin: AH & AW Reed.

Bonnemans, J, Forsyth, E and Smith, B, 1998. *Baudin in Australian Waters*, Melbourne: OUP.

Bowden, KM, 1952. *George Bass 1771–1803*, MUP.

Brodsky, I, 1973. *Bennelong Profile*, Broadway, Sydney: University Co-operative Bookshop.

Brook, J and Kohen, J 1991. *The Parramatta Native Institution and the Black Town*, Kensington: New South Wales University Press.

Campbell, WD, 1899. 'Aboriginal Carvings of Port Jackson and Broken Bay, *Memoirs of the Geological Survey, New South Wales*, Sydney: Department of Mines and Agriculture.

Chambers, N, (ed.), 2000. *The Letters of Sir Joseph Banks. A Selection, 1768–1820*, NMH.

Chapman, D, 1981. *1788, The People of the First Fleet*, North Ryde.

Christie, Rev. C, 1929. *Waikouaiti*, 2nd edn, Christchurch.

Clark, M, 1979. *A History of Australia*, vol. I, Melbourne: MUP.

Cobley, J, *Sydney Cove, 1788 (1962), 1789*–1790 (1963), *1791–1792* (1965), Sydney: Angus & Robertson.

Cumpston, JS, 1970. *Kangaroo Island 1800–1836*, Canberra: Roebuck Society.

Cumpston, JS,1973. *First Visitors to Bass Strait*, Canberra: Roebuck Society.

Cumpston, JS, 1977. *Shipping Arrivals and Departures Sydney, 1788–1825.* Canberra: Roebuck Society.

Cumpston, JS, 1977b. *Shipping Arrivals and Departures Sydney, 1826–1840.* Canberra: Roebuck Society Publication No. 23.

Currey, JEB, 1966. *George Caley: Reflections on the Colony of New South Wales*, Melbourne: Lansdowne Press.

Currey, J, 2000. *David Collins: A Colonial Life*, Carlton: MUP.

Dunbabin, T, 1931. *Sailing the World's Edge*, London: Jonathan Cape.

Dutton, G, 1974. *White on Black: The Australian Aborigine Portrayed in Art*, South Melbourne: Macmillan.

[Easty, J], 1965. *Memorandum of the transaction of a voyage from England to Botany Bay, 1787–1793*: A First Fleet journal by John Easty, Sydney: Trustees of the Public Library of New South Wales.

Elder JR, 1912. *Letters and Journals of Samuel Marsden*, Dunedin.

Ellis, MH, 1955. *John Macarthur*, Sydney: Angus & Robertson.

Fulton, Rev. H. [1805]. 'Obtained by the Rev. H. Fullow [Fulton] in 1801 A.D. [*sic*] from Aboriginals in Norfolk Island', 'Linguistics', *Australian Anthropological Journal*, vol. I, No. 2, 12 September 1896.

Goesch, P, 2009. *Thomas Chaseland and the next generation*, Sydney: Brynwood House.

Hall-Jones, J, 1976. *Bluff Harbour*, Bluff: Southland Harbour Board.

[Holt, J], 1988. O'Shaughnessy, P (ed.). *A Rum Story: The adventures of Joseph Holt*, Kenthurst: Kangaroo Press.

Hordern, M, 1997. *King of the Australian Coast: the work of Phillip Parker King in the 'Mermaid' and 'Bathurst' 1817–1822.* Melbourne: The Miegunyah Press.

Howitt, AW, 1904. *The Native Tribes of South-east Australia*, London: Macmillan.

Hunter, C, (ed.), 1997. The 1827 Newcastle Notebook and Letters of Lieutenant William S Coke HM 39th Regiment, Raymond Terrace: Hunter House Publications.

Jennings, G, (ed.), 1991. *My holiday and other early travels from Manly to Palm Beach 1861.* Newport Beach: Aramo Pt. Ltd.

Jervis, J, 1963. *The Cradle City of Australia*, Sydney: Council of the City of Parramatta.

Jervis, J, 1967. *History of Woollahra*, Sydney: Municipal Council of Woollahra.

King, J and King, J, 1981. *Philip Gidley King, A Biography of the Third Governor of New South Wales*, North Ryde: Methuen & Co.

Kohen, JL, 1993. *The Darug and their Neighbours*: Blacktown: Darug Link/Blacktown and District Historical Society.

Kohen, JL, 2006. *Daruganora: Darug Country– The place and the people*, Blacktown: Darug Tribal Aboriginal Corporation.

Knight, RB and Frost, A, (eds.), 1983. *The Journal of Daniel Paine, 1794–1797*, Sydney: Library of Australian History.

Levy, M, 1947. *Wallumetta: A History of Ryde and Its District, 1792 to 1945*, Ryde: Ryde Municipal Council.

McBryde, I, 1989. *Guests of the Governor. Aboriginal Residents of the First Government House*, Sydney: Friends of the First Government House.

McNab, R, 1909. *Murihiku: A History of the South Island of New Zealand and the Islands Adjacent and Lying in the South from 1642 to 1835*, Invercargill: William Smith.

McNab, R, 1913. *The Old Whaling Days: A history of Southern New Zealand from 1830 to 1840*, Christchurch: Whitcombe & Tombs.

Marryat, F, 1855. *Mountains and Molehills*, London.

Micco, HM, 1971. *King Island and the Sealing Trade*, Canberra: Roebuck Books.

Milius, PB, [1802] 1987. *Journal*, 'Sejour de Milius au Port Jackson 25 avril–22 juillet 1802, in *Récit du voyage aux terres australes / par Pierre Bernard Milius* … transcription du texte original par Jacqueline Bonnemains, Pascal Haugel, Le Havre.

Monaghan, J, 1966. Australians and the Gold Rush: California and Down Under 1845–1854, Berkeley, University of California Press.

Mulvaney, DJ and White, P, 1987. *Australians to 1788*, Sydney: Fairfax, Syme & Weldon.

[Nagle, J,] No date. JC Dann (ed.), The Nagle Journal: A Diary of the Life of Jacob Nagle, Sailor. From the Year 1775 to 1841, New York: Weidenfield & Nicolson.

Nautsch, S, 1978. *The Cruise of the Acheron: Her Majesty's Steam Vessel on Survey in New Zealand Waters 1845–51*, Wellington: Nestegg Books.

Nicholson, IH, 1983. *Shipping Arrivals and Departures Tasmania, 1803–1833.* Canberra: Roebuck Society.

Norman, L, 1938. *Pioneer Shipping in Tasmania*, Hobart.

Olssen, E, 1984. *History of Otago*, Dunedin: John McIndoe.

Parry, N, 2005. 'Musquito (c.1780–1825', ADB, Supplementary Volume, Carlton: MUP, 2005.

Peterson, N, (ed.), 2003. *Donald Thomson in Arnhem Land*, Carlton, Victoria: Miegunyah Press.

Prickett, N, 2008. 'Trans-Tasman stories: Australian Aborigines in New Zealand sealing and shore whaling', *Terra Australis*, No. 29, ANU Canberra.

Reynolds, H, 1990. *With the White People*, Ringwood: Penguin Books Australia.

Richards, R, 1982. *Whaling and Sealing at the Chatham Islands*, Canberra: Roebuck Books.

Richards, R, (ed.), 1996a. *Jorgen Jorgensen's Observations on Pacific Trade; and Sealing and Whaling in Australia and New Zealand Waters Before 1805*, Wellington: Paremata Press.

Richards, R, 1996b. *The Foveaux Sealing Yarns of Yankee Jack* … Dunedin North: Otago Heritage Books.

[Robinson, GA], Plomley, N (ed.) 1966. *Friendly Mission: the Tasmanian journals and papers of George Augustus Robinson 1829–1834*, Hobart: Tasmanian Historical Research Association.

Ross, V, 1981. *A Hawkesbury Story*, Sydney: Library of Australian History.

Rusden, GW, 1874. *Curiosities of Colonisation*, London.

Russell, L, 2008. *"A New Holland half-caste': sealer and whaler Tommy Chaseland," History Australia*, vol. 5, No. 1.

Sadleir, R, 1883. *The Aborigines of Australia*, Sydney: Thomas Richards, Government Printer.

Salmond, A, 1997. *Two Worlds: First meetings between Maori and Europeans 1642–1722*, Auckland: Viking.

Scott, J, 1963. *Remarks on a Passage to Botany Bay, 1787–1792* … Sydney: Trustees of the Public Library of New South Wales.

Shortland, E, 1881. *Maori Religious Mythology*, London: Longman.

Smith, KV, 1992. *King Bungaree: A Sydney Aborigine meets the great South Pacific Explorers, 1799–1830*, Kenthurst: Kangaroo Press.

Smith, KV, 2001. *Bennelong: The coming-in of the Eora, Sydney Cove, 1788–1792*, Roseville: Kangaroo Press.

Smith, KV, 2005. *Wallumedegal: An Aboriginal History of Ryde,* Ryde: City of Ryde.

Smith, KV and Bourke, A, 2006. *Eora: Mapping Aboriginal Sydney 1770–1850*, June–August 2006, Sydney: SLNSW.

Smith, KV, 2010. 'Bennelong among his people'. *Aboriginal History*, vol. 33, Aboriginal Studies Press, Canberra.

Stacey, AW, 1981. *A Basic History of Ryde 1792–1980*, 3rd edition, Ryde Historical Society.

Starke, J, (ed.) 1986. *Journal of a Rambler, The Journal of John Boultbee*, Auckland: OUP.

Steven, M, 1965. *Merchant Campbell 1769–1846: A study in colonial trade,* Melbourne: MUP.

Stokes, Captain JL,1859. *The New Zealand Pilot*, 2nd ed., London.

[Suttor, G], G Mackaness (ed.) 1948. Memoirs *of George Suttor*, Sydney.

Thornton, G and Hill, R, 1892. *Notes on the Aborigines of New South Wales …* Sydney: Charles Potter, Government Printer.

[Threlkeld, Rev. LE], Gunson, N, (ed.) 1974. *Australian Reminiscences & Papers of LE Threlkeld, Missionary to the Aborigines*, 2 vols, 1824–1859, Canberra, AIAS.

Troy, J, 1991.'The Sydney Language Notebooks and Responses to Language Contact in Early Colonial Sydney', *Australian Journal of Linguistics*, vol. 12, 1991:140–70.

Webb, J, 1995. *George Caley 19th Century Naturalist*, Chipping Norton: Surrey Beatty & Sons.

West, J, 1852. *The History of Tasmania*, vol. II, Section III.

[West, O,] 1988. E.W. Marriott, *Memoirs of Obed West*, Sydney.

Willey, K, [1979] 1985. *When the Sky Fell Down: The Destruction of the Tribes of the Sydney Region 1788–1850s*, Sydney: William Collins.

Wiltshire, JG, [1976] 1994. *Captain William Pelham Dutton, First Settler at Portland Bay, Victoria … W Davis & Sons.*

Windshuttle, K, 2002. *The Fabrication of Australian History*, vol. 1, Van Diemen's Land 1803–1847, Sydney: Macleay Press.

ENDNOTES

Chapter 1: Highways in the Stream

1   John White, *Journal of a Voyage to New South Wales* … London 1790:191.
2   'Saltwater/*adjective* 1. of, or relating to saltwater; 2. Inhabiting salt water; 3. *Aboriginal English* of or relating to an Aborigine who lives on the coast, as opposed to one living inland', *The Macquarie Dictionary*, Third edn, Macquarie University, Sydney, 1998:1880.
3   Tench, 1793:18.
4   '*Goomun - - -* The Fir Tree' – PG King 1790:400; *Governors' Vocabulary* (GV) 1791:20.17.
5   William Bradley, *A Voyage to New South Wales; The Journal of Lieutenant William Bradley RN of HMS Sirius 1786–1792*, Facsimile edition, Sydney: Trustees of the Public Library of New South Wales, 1969:129.
6   John Hunter, *An Historical Journal of Transactions at Port Jackson and Norfolk Island* … London, John Stockdale, 1793:63.
7   Bradley, 1969:68–9.
8   John Gardiner, *Account of the Voyage of HMS Gorgon*, MS 1 1–120, 1791:67, DL.
9   Bradley, 1969:188.
10 David Collins, *An Account of the English Colony in New South Wales* … 'Language', Appendix X11, London, [1798] 1975:510.
11 Surgeon George Worgan, *Journal of a First Fleet Surgeon*, Library Council of New South Wales, Sydney, 1978: 37–8.
12 Collins, 1975: 461; Bradley 1969:131.
13 Bradley, 1969:131.
14 Henry Waterhouse to his father William Waterhouse, 11 July 1788, MS 262/52, ML.
15 'Na-ro-wang, A paddle.' — PG King in John Hunter 1793:410.4; 'Gnar.awang   A Paddle' — David Blackburn, *List of native names, with English equivalents*, 19 March 1791, Safe 1/20, ML.
16 Waterhouse, op. cit.
17 Tench, 1793:187.
18 White, 1790: 200.
19 Collins, 1975:461.
20 Ronald Lampert and JVS Megaw in P Stanbury (ed.), *10 000 Years of Sydney Life*, Sydney 1979.
21 Collins, 1975:461.
22 Bradley, 1969:69.
23 Tench, 1793:195.
24 Phillip, to Lord Sydney, 28 September 1788, *HRNSW II*:191–2.
25 Hunter, 1793:133–4.
26 Bradley, 1969:164.
27 Collins, 1975:499–502.
28 Tench, 1793:187.
29 Watkin Tench, *A Narrative of the Expedition to Botany Bay* … J Debrett, London, 1789:93–4.
30 Collins, 1975:148.
31 Mary Ann Parker, *A Voyage Round the World in the Gorgon Man of War* … Captain John Parker, London, 1795: 102.
32 Mary Anne Reid, *Asiatic Journal*, Sydney, 1819–20.
33 George Suttor quoted in G Mackaness (ed.), Memoirs *of George Suttor*, Sydney, 1948:40.
34 John Turnbull, *A Voyage Round the World* … Blackfriars, vol. 3, 1805:232.
35 Mrs Edward Cox [Jane Maria Brooks], *Reminiscences* 1877, transcribed by Andrew Houison, Parramatta, c. 1912:10, Original MS B391, ML.
36 Glynn Barratt, *The Russians at Port Jackson, 1814–1822*, Canberra: AIATSIS, 1981:25.
37 Obed West, in EW Marriott, *Memoirs of Obed West*, Sydney, 1988:34.
38 Worgan, 1978:16.
39 Anon., *An authentic and interesting narrative of the late expedition to Botany Bay, as performed by Commodore Phillips, and The Fleet of the seven transport ships under his command … with particular descriptions of Jackfon's Bay and Lord Howe's Island*

… Printed by W Bailey, 1789:28.

40 Anon., *An authentic and interesting narrative* … London, 1789:11.

41 Cora Gooseberry to GF Angas, in *Savage Life and Scenes in Australia and New Zealand*, Smith, Elder & Co., London, vol. 2, 1846:197–8.

42 'Mahroot' [Boatswain Maroot], 'Report from the Select Committee on the Condition of the Aborigines', *Votes and Proceedings*, New South Wales Legislative Council, Sydney, 1845.

43 William Dawes, Vocabulary of the language of N.S. Wales in the neighbourhood of Sydney. Native and English, by — Dawes, MS 4165(b), London: School of Oriental and African Studies, University of London, London, b. 1791:33.4.

44 David Blackburn to his sister Margaret, 12 July 1788, MSS 6937/1/12 ML.

45 David Blackburn to his sister Margaret, 17 March 1791, Norfolk Record Office, Reel 133/3.

46 Cruwee to Obed. *West, Sydney Morning Herald (SMH)*, 1882, in Edward West Marriott (ed.), *Memoirs of Obed West*, Sydney, 1988:42–3.

47 David Collins, *An Account of the English Colony in New South Wales,* T Cadell Jun. and W Davies, in *The Strand*, London, [1798] 1975:507.

48 Tench, 1793:9–15.

49 Hunter, 1793:133.

50 Bradley, 1969:185.

51 CP Boullanger, quoted in Louis P Rivière, 'Un périple en Nouvelle-Hollande au debut du X1X^c siecle', *Comptes-rendus mensuels des séances de l'Académie des Sciences coloniales*, 13, 1953:580.

52 Reverend Daniel Tyerman and George Bennett, *Voyages and Travels round the World*, London Missionary Society, John Snow, London, 1841 (1831): 189.

Chapter 2: A Passage to Norfolk Island

1   Captain William Hill, Sydney Cove, Port Jackson, 26 July 1790, to Jonathan Wathen, Bond Court, Walbrook, London, Reel 3 201/5 (2), Public Record Office (PRO) London.

2   Tench, 1793:107.

3   Bradley, 22 March 1791, 1968:245.

4   HMS *Supply*, Ship's Muster, Reel 7006:365, PRO London.

5   Tench, 1793:107.

6   Philip Gidley King, *Journal*, Norfolk Island, 4 March 1788, Safe 1/16, ML.

7   Collins 1975:147.

8   *SG,* 27 September 1822; 6 February 1823.

9   Patyegarang to William Dawes. 'Piyidyinina white-mana ngyinari Pandalna, Pundunga } A white man | beat us three — we three | Pandal, Poondah (& myself understood)' — Dawes b. 1791:35.9 … 'obtained 27 Nov^t by Patyegarang … speaking to me' — Dawes b. 1791:35.16.

10 Tench, 1793:139; Collins, 1975:156.

11 Henry Lidgbird Ball, *A Voyage to England from Port Jackson*, Chapter XXIV in Hunter 1793:568 et seq.

12 *British Journal*, 21 April 1792, BP Box 58:501, ML.

13 Collins, 1975:288; 310; 317; 385–6.

14 WN Chapman to his mother, 17 October 1791, Chapman Papers, A197, ML.

15 PG King to Sir Joseph Banks, 25 October 1791, Banks Papers, A 78, ML.

16 Collins, 1975:152.

17 Rev. Richard Johnson to Henry Fricker, Port Jackson, 4 October 1791, Safe 1/121, ML.

18 Collins 1975:191.

19 Hunter in Collins II, 1975:39; Collins 1975:350, 395–6.

20 Court of Criminal Jurisdiction, Minutes of Proceedings, 6 October 1797, Reel 2391, 1797:353, SRNSW.

21 Tench, 1793:17.

22 HMS *Reliance*, Ship's Muster — ADM 36/13398, Reel 7008:166, April and May 1798, PRO London; Hunter in Collins II, 1802:82.

23 Hunter in Collins II, 1975:204.

24 Mann, 1811:47.

25 'In the Brothers … Two Natives', Claims and Demands, SG, 5 December 1812.

26 James Kelly, *Log of the Brothers 1812–13*, bound with *Log of Mary and Sally*, C6028, Crowther Collection, Public Library of Tasmania, Hobart.

27 *SG,* 5 June 1813, 2.

28 *SG,* 9 December 1815, 2a.

Chapter 3: Bennelong's voyages

1   See Keith Vincent Smith, *Bennelong* (2001) for Bennelong's life story before his departure for London in February 1792.

2   Phillip to Banks, 3 December 1791, Banks Papers, A81:34–44, ML.

3   Collins, 1975:211.

4   Collins, 1975:256–7.

5   'Englánd-a … In England' – *'Kuribín, Wa dyin tarungál?* Where's his Wife? P & W [Patyegarang and Warreeweer] *Englánda - - -* In England', Dawes b. 1791:32.12.
6   John Easty, *Memorandum of the transaction of a voyage from England to Botany Bay, 1787–1793* (Sydney 1965), 19 May 1792 and other dates cited for the voyage of HMS *Atlantic.*
7   Treasury Board Papers (TBP), PRO, London.
8   TBP, 1793: 382.
9   *Times,* London, 22 May 1793, 2d.
10 *Times,* 25 May 1793, 2c.
11 Isadore Brodsky, *Bennelong Profile*, Broadway, University Co-operative Bookshop, Sydney, 1973: 64. See also Keith Vincent Smith, 'Bennelong ambassador of the Eora', *Australia Heritage* No. 2, Brighton (Victoria), 2006:79.
12 J Turnbull, A *Voyage Round the World in the Years 1800, 1801, 1802, 1803, and 1804* (2 vols). Richard Phillips, London, 1805, vol. I:74–5.
13 *The London Packet,* 2 June 1793.
14 Diary or Woodfall's Register, London, 22 June 1793.
15 Brodsky, 1973:66.
16 *Morning Post,* London, 10 June 1793.
17 *True Briton,* London, 2 July 1793.
18 Phillip to Dundas, 23 July 1793, *HRNSW II*:59–60.
19 TBP, 1793:377.
20 TBP, 1793:373.
21 Elizabeth Burton, *The Georgians at Home, 1714–1830*, London: Longmans, 1967:306.
22 *Morning Post,* London, 1 August 1793.
23 TBP, 1793:373.
24 TBP, 1793:377.
25 *London Observer,* 29 September 1793; *Morning Post,* 1 October 1793.
26 TBP, 1793:373A.
27 TBP, 1793:356.
28 TBP, 1794:355.
29 TBP, 1794:319.
30 TBP, 1793–4:350.
31 *The Oracle and Public Advertiser,* London, 19 April 1794, BT Box 59: 114, ML; See *Bennelong* 2001:53.
32 *The World*, London, 17 April 1794.
33 *Sun,* London, 17 April 1794.
34 Governor Hunter Dr to W Waterhouse … TBP. 1794: 34, PRO, London, T1/733.
35 Fothergill was a patron of the young Scots artist Sydney Parkinson, employed by Joseph Banks on HMS *Endeavour,* which anchored at Botany Bay in 1770. In 1794 Fothergill reissued *Parkinson's Journal of a Voyage to the South Seas,* London, 1793.
36 Bennelong to Mr Phillips, 29 August 1796, MS 4005, NK4048, NLA.
37 Waterhouse to Lord Sydney, 20 August 1797 in *The first map of Port Jackson* … R & L Waterhouse, Sydney, 2000.
38 *London Chronicle,* 27 May, *Morning Chronicle,* 28 May and *Morning Post,* 29 May 1794.
39 *London Packet,* 16 July 1794, 1a.
40 TBP, 1794: unnumbered.
41 Hunter to John King, 5 August 1794, CO202/Pt.11: 77–8, PRO London.
42 TBP, 1794:343.
43 TBP, 1794:342.
44 Hunter to John King, 25–6 January 1795, CO201/12:3 PRO London; *HRNSW III*:745.
45 MH Ellis, *John Macarthur*, Angus & Robertson, Sydney, 1955:73.
46 KM Bowden, *George Bass 1771–1803*, Oxford University Press, Melbourne, 1952:27–8.
47 [William Marsden] 'On the Polynesian or East Insular Languages', *Miscellaneous Works of William Marsden*, Parbury, Allen, London, 1834:111–2.
48 [Daniel Paine] *Manuscript kept in a Voyage to Port Jackson New South Wales … by Daniel Paine*, MS JOD 172, NMM. Transcribed by Keith Vincent Smith, Appendix E, *Eora Clans* 2004.
49 Sarah Bass to George Bass, 22 July 1797, *Sarah Bass Papers*, 1797–1803, CY Reel 3970, ML.
50 Captain's Log, HMS *Reliance*, PRO 5736.
51 RB Knight and Alan Frost (eds), *The Journal of Daniel Paine, 1794–1797*, Library of Australian History, Sydney, 1983:8.
52 Collins, 1975:358.
53 Collins, 1973:367–8.
54 Lieutenant John Shortland to Thomas Townshend, October 1795, Townshend Papers, MSQ 522: 67, DL.
55 Henry Waterhouse to William Waterhouse, October 1795, Bass and Waterhouse Papers, DTC 9: 252–2, BL; FM4/63, ML.
56 Waterhouse to Arthur Phillip, 24 October 1795, Series 37.28: 178, PRO London.
57 Collins, 1975:362.

58 Mary Johnson to Henry Fricker, 21 December 1795, ZML MSS 6722, ML.

59 Collins, 1975:390.

60 Hunter in Collins II, 1975:61.

61 PG King, Norfolk Island *Victualling Book*, 1792–1796, 3–8 April 1796, ML.

62 Collins, 1975:389, 393.

63 Hunter in Collins II, 1975:5.

64 MF Péron, *A Voyage of Discovery to the Southern Hemisphere performed by the order of the Emperor Napoleon* … Translated from the French. Printed for Richard Phillips, London, 1809:280.

65 J. Bonnemains et al (eds), Plate 20041.2, *Baudin in Australian Waters. The Artwork of the French Voyage of Discovery to the Southern Lands 1800-1804*, Oxford University Press, Melbourne, 1988.

66 See Keith Vincent Smith, *King Bungaree*, Kangaroo Press, Sydney, 1992.

67 Jacqueline Bonnemanains and Pascal Hauguel, (eds), 'Sejour de Milius au Port Jackson 25 avril-22 juillet 1802', *Recit de voyage aux Terres Australes par Pierre Bernard Milius* … Société Havrais D'Etudes diverse Muséum D'Histoire Naturelle du Havre, Le Havre 2000:49.

68 See Péron, Table 11 (Chapter 5).

69 Holt in O'Shaunessy, 1988:68–72.

70 George Howe, 'Chronology of local occurrences', *New South Wales Pocket Almanac*, Sydney, 1806: 60.

71 *SG,* 13 January 1805, 2c–3a.

72 *SG,* 17 March 1805 3a–b; 31 March 1805, 3a.

73 *SG,* 7 April 1805, 3a.

74 WP Crook to J Hardcastle, Parramatta, 5 May 1805, BT Box 49:141, ML.

75 *SG,* 14 July 1805, 2a.

76 *SG,* 22 December 1805, 2a–b.

77 *SG,* 9 January 1813, 2a.

78 Old Philip to Joseph Arnold, *Journal*, 18 July 1815:401. In 1815 Philip and his wife settled with Bungaree at Georges Head in Port Jackson.

79 William Lawson, 'Mr Lawson's account of the Aborigines of New South Wales', *Supreme Court Correspondence relating to Aborigines*, 5/1161, Document No. 83, 1838:554–5, SRNSW.

80 'Atticus', *SG,* 29 March 1817, 1c–2b.

81 Richard Sadleir, *The Aborigines of Australia*, Thomas Richards, Government Printer, Sydney, 1883:25.

82 *The Australian Encyclopaedia*, The Grolier Society of Australia, 4th edn, Sydney, 1983.

83 CPN Wilton (ed.), *Australian Quarterly Journal of Theology, Literature, and Science*, Sydney, 1828:137.

84 Dumont d'Urville 1826, quoted in Helen Rosenman (ed.), *Two Voyages to the South Seas* … MUP, Melbourne, 19

85 *SG, 6 February 1823.*

86 *Caledonian Mercury*, Edinburgh, 26 May 1814.

Chapter 4: Indigenous pioneers

1. See Keith Vincent Smith, *King Bungaree* (1992) and *Bennelong* (2001) passim.

2. Henry Reynolds, *With the White People*, Penguin Books Australia, Ringwood, 1990:2–3.

3. James Grant, *The Narrative of a Voyage of Discovery, Performed in His Majesty's Vessel The Lady Nelson* … T Edgerton Military Library, London, 1803:149.

4. James Grant to PG King, 16 December 1800, *HRA III:* 60–2.

5. Grant, 1803:150–5.

6. Dr John Harris to PG King, 25 June 1801, *King Family Papers*, vol. 8, Further Papers, 1775–1806, MS A1980–2, ML.

7. Hunter in Collins II, 1975:239.

8. *SG,* 11 March 1804, 1–3; *SG* 18 March 1804, 2a–b.

9. *SG,* 25 March, 1a.

10. *SG,* 29 April 1804, 4 b–c.

11. PG King to Lieutenant CFN Menzies, King's Town, Newcastle, *HRA V:* 413–4.

12. Menzies to King, *HRA V:* 415–6.

13. *SG,* 9 September 1804, 2–3.

14. Menzies to King, 5 October 1804, *HRA V:* 420.

15. Menzies to King, 17 October 1804, *HRA V:* 423.

16. *SG,* 23 December 1804, 2–3.

17. Collins, 1975:145.

18. *News Chronicle*, London, July–December 1809: 385–90; 477–81; Ernest Scott, *The Life of Captain Matthew Flinders, R.N.*, Angus & Robertson, Sydney, 1914:256–9.

19. John Currey, *David Collins: A Colonial Life*, MUP, Carlton, 2000:199.

20. Currey 2000:202. The bay was named for John Sullivan, permanent undersecretary at the Colonial Office in London.

21. GA Robinson to CJ La Trobe, 22 November 1839, *HRV, vol. IIB*, Melbourne, 1983:606.

22. Currey, 2000: 209, 343.

23. *SG,* 4 December 1804, 3b.

24. *SG,* 15 January 1804, 4b.
25. James Bonwick, *Discovery and Settlement of Port Phillip*, Victorian History Series, Red Rooster Press, North Melbourne, [1856] 1999:10.
26. William Buckley quoted in John Morgan, *The Life and Adventures of William Buckley*, Hobart, 1852:14.
27. *HRA II, vol. I,* 1921:108
28. Wooraddy to GA Robinson, *Journal*, 16 January 1831 in Plomley 1966:316.
29. Samuel Smith, *Journal*, 20 July 1802, MSS ZC222: 21–2, ML.
30. Mann, 1811:33–4. For Pemulwuy, see also Keith Vincent Smith, 'Solved: Australia's oldest murder mystery', *SMH* 1 November 2003 and JL Kohen, 'Pemulwuy', *ADB*, Supplementary Volume, MUP, Carlton, 2005:318–9.
31. *SG,* 27 May 1804, 2 a–b.
32. *SG,* 10 June 1804, 3c.
33. *SG,* 22 July 1804, 3b–c.
34. *SG,* 6 November 1808, 2a.
35. Alexander Berry, 'Recollections of the Aborigines', May 1838, Supreme Court, Misc. Correspondence Relating to Aborigines, No. 83, SRNSW.
36. Peter Cunningham, *Two Years in New South Wales*, London [1827] 1966:189.
37. Rev. Lancelot Threlkeld, 'Memoranda Extracted from Twenty Four Years of Missionary Engagements in the South Sea Islands and Australia', in *Supreme Court of New South Wales Memoranda*, COD 554, CGS 13705: 48, 164, SRNSW.
38. CS Ship's Muster No. 43/145, 1817:51, SRNSW.
39. *Magill, Corroboree dance*, c.1819–20, Richard Browne (1776–1824), ML.
40. Rev. Lancelot Threlkeld, London Missionary Society Report, in Niel Gunson (ed.), *Australian Reminiscences & Papers of L. E. Threlkeld, Missionary to the Aborigines, 1824–1859*, vol. 2, 1974:206.
41. *Desmond, a N.S. Wales Chief painted for a Rarob* [Corroboree], 1826, Augustus Earle (1793–1838), nla.pic–an2820718, NLA.
42. Hunter, 1997:79.
43. Cynthia Hunter, (ed.). *The 1827 Newcastle Notebook and Letters of Lieutenant William S. Coke H.M. 39th Regiment*, Hunter House Publications, Raymond Terrace, 1997:58–75; 94–6.
44. *SG,* 12 January 1830.
45. Surveyor Felton Matthews saw the *Sophia Jane* at Newcastle on 19 June 1831 and went on board on 29 June: Felton Mathews, *Journal*, NLA, Canberra.
46. Rev. Lancelot Threlkeld (John Fraser ed.), *An Australian Language* … Charles Potter, Govt. Printer, Sydney, 1892:88.
47. James Backhouse, *A Narrative of a Visit to the Australian Colonies*, London, 1843:379–80.
48. CS, Return of Aboriginal Natives, Sydney 1836, SRNSW.
49. Rev. Lancelot Threlkeld, *Report of Mission*, 31 December 1839, ML; *Register of Coroner's Inquests*, 1834–1859, 4/611–13, AO Reel 2921, SRNSW.
50. Iaen McLachlan, *Place of Banishment*, Hale & Iremonger, Sydney, 1988:99.
51. *Daily Examiner*, Grafton, 24 February 1923:2.
52. *SG* 19 February 1829 2f. Further reports may be seen on the Macquarie Law website: http://www.law.mq.edu.au/scnsw/Cases1829-30/html/r_v_ballard_or_barrett__1829.htm
53. Biriban, alias M'Gill, to Reverend Lancelot Threlkeld, 2 March 1829, in Gunson 1974:104–5.
54. *Australian,* 16 June 1829, 3c.
55. Henry Smyth, Commandant's Office, Port Macquarie, to 'Captain Robert Barratt', 25April 1830, SRNSW.
56. Macdonald to Governor Richard Bourke, enclosed in a letter to Viscount Howick in London, 11 September 1832, *HRA I, vol. 16*:449.
57. Jules Dumont d'Urville, *Voyage de la Corvette l'Astrolabe* … Paris 1830–35:102–3.
58. WC Ferguson, 'Mokaré's Domain', *Australians to 1788*, Fairfax, Syme & Weldon, Sydney, 1987:121–145.
59. 'Clergy and Schools Corp Proceedings of Ctee No 1', 4/292:175–6, SRNSW, quoted in J Brook and JL Kohen, *The Parramatta Native Institution and the Black Town*, New South Wales University Press, Kensington, 1991:212.
60. This account is based on the 'Journal of Major Lockyer', *HRA III*, VI, 1923:460–470.

Chapter 5: Musquito and Bulldog

1 Richard Atkins, 'Opinion on the Treatment to be Adopted Towards the Natives', 20 July 1805, *HRA 1*, vol. V:502.
2 Kristyn Evelyn Harman, *Aboriginal Convicts: Race, Law, and Transportation in Colonial New South Wales*, PHD thesis, University of Tasmania, Hobart, May 2008:ix.
3 Samuel Marsden to Archdeacon Scott, ' Report on the Aborigines of N.S.W., 2 December 1826', in Niel Gunson (ed.), *Australian Reminiscences and Papers of L.E. Threlkeld, Missionary to the Aborigines, 1824–1859*, vol. 2, Canberra, AIAS, 1974:348; *SG* 15 February 1831.
4 NJB Plomley, *Friendly Mission*, Tasmanian Historical Research Association, Hobart, 1966: 445, note 106.
5 Macquarie, *Journal*, Tuesday 5 November, 1816, A774, ML.
6 *SG,* 21 April 1805; In1816 Governor Macquarie made Branch Jack 'Chief of the Hawkesbury Upper Branch' of Aborigines.
7 SG, 28 April 1805.

8   *SG,* 29 April 1805, 1a.

9   *SG,* 19 May 1805, 2c–3a.

10   *SG,* 30 June 1805, 2a.

11   *SG,* 7 July 1805, 2b.

12   *SG,* 4 August 1805, 2b.

13   *SG,* 7 July 1805, 2b.

14   *SG,* 7 July 1805, 2a. The girl was possibly Mary or Maria Chaseland, daughter of Thomas Chaseland and an Aboriginal
    woman, born about 1791 (see Chapter 15).

15   *SG,* 15 September 1805, 2a.

16   PG King to Lord Camden, Sydney, 20 July 1805, *HRNSW,* vol. V:658.

17   *SG,* 11 August 1805, 2a.

18   Keith Willey, *When the Sky Fell Down: The Destruction of the Tribes of the Sydney Region 1788–1850s,* William Collins,
    Sydney [1979] 1985:180.

19   Collins 1975:339. Note: Grassby & Hill (1998:91) wrongly attribute this crime to the settlers, stating: 'Some of the
    English exacted petty revenge by seizing a young woman of Pemulwuy's family, raping and torturing her.'

20   *SG,* 25 August 1805, 1b.

21   Hunter in Collins II, [1802] 1975:149.

22   *SG,* 1 December 1805, 2a.

23   PG King to Lord Castlereagh, 27 July 1806, *HRA V:*753.

24   King to Bligh, King Papers, 1808 ML, quoted in AGL Shaw, 'King, P.G', ADB, vol. 2, MUP, 1967:5–61.

25   Norfolk Island Annual Return of Inhabitants at the 6 Aug 1812, CS 4/1170, COD 274, SRNSW.

26   Naomi Parry, 'Musquito (c. 1780–1825), *ADB,* Supplementary Volume, MUP. 2005:299.

27   Harman, 2008:1.

28   Benjamin Bowen Carter, Log of the Ann and Hope, 23 October 1798:85, Rhode Island Historical Society, Providence,
    Rhode Island.

29   *SG,* 16 October 1803, 2a.

30   *SG,* 12 January 1806, 1c.

31   *SG,* 19 January 1806.

32   *Alexander Monro, Elements of the anatomy of the human body in its sound state … Edinburgh 1825:23.*

33   Rhys Jones, 'Images of Natural Man', Chapter 6 in Bernard Smith et. al. (eds), *Baudin in Australian Waters, The Artwork
    of the French Voyage of Discovery to the Southern Lands 1800–1804,* Oxford University Press, Melbourne, 1988:63.

34   *Nouvelle Hollande — Toulgra (mère),* No. 20032, Nicolas-Martin Petit, Museum d'Histoire Naturelle, Le Havre, France.

35   'Benelàng – Warwéar – Karangarang – Wárrgan – Munáguri', William Dawes b. 1791:9.4.

36   CSO 1/177; 4306:219–223, Archives Office of Tasmania.

37   Keith Windschuttle in *The Fabrication of Aboriginal History,* vol. 1, Van Diemen's Land 1803–1847, Macleay Press,
    Sydney, 2002:66, wrongly states that Musquito 'had been sent down [from Sydney] by the government in 1813 to help
    track bushrangers'.

38   'Philip, Jemmy, and Scotchman, Natives', Claims and Demands, *In the Brig Active, SG,* 1 May 1813.

39   *Joseph Henry Barsden, Volume containing autobiographical account of events 1799–1816, compiled c. 1836, MS
    7279, ML.*

40   *SG,* 15 Jan 1809, 2a.

41   Colonial Secretary to Lieutenant Governor Davey, 17 August 1814, CS Reel 6004; 4/3493:25, SRNSW.

42   Ian H Nicholson (ed.), *Shipping Arrivals and Departures Tasmania,* vol. 1, 1803–1833, Roebuck, Canberra, 1983:36.

43   Philip to Dr Joseph Arnold, *Journal,* 18 July 1815, MS C720: 401, ML.

44   Sorrel to Macquarie, Hobart Town, 12 October 1817, *HRA II,* vol. II: 284.

45   *SG,* 31 January 1818, 2b.

46   *HTG,* 14 February 1818, 2a.

47   *HTG,* 21 March 1818, 2a.

48   *HTG,* 18 April 1818.

49   See PP King, *Narrative of a Survey …* London, 1826: 232.

50   Sworn oath by John McGill, Hobart Town, 19 September 1818, Present: Rev. R Knopwood, Reprinted in *A Bloodthirsty
    Banditti of Wretches,* Sullivan Cove, Adelaide, 1985.

51   William Sorell, *Despatches to Governor Macquarie,* 18 November 1818, MS A 1351, CY Reel 1096:91, ML.

52   John West, *The History of Tasmania,* vol. II, Section III, Launceston, 1852:12.

53   Rev. William Horton, Letter to the Wesleyan Missionary Society, Hobart Town, Van Diemen's Land, 3 June 1823, BT
    Box 52:1269–74, ML.

54   *HTG,* 29 October, 1824.

55   West, 1852:14.

56   *HTG,* 25 February 1825; *SG,* 17 March 1825.

57   Henry Melville, *The History of the Island of Van Diemen's Land From the Year 1824 to 1835 Inclusive,* Smith & Elder,
    London, 1835:35–40.

Chapter 6: Dual: sentenced and reprieved

1 Hamilton Hume, Letter to the *Sydney Monitor*, 26 November 1826; JP McGuane, 'Appin's Pride', Centenary of Campbelltown 1920–21, Campbelltown.
2 Rev. W Ross, Preface in *Hamilton Hume, A Brief Statement of Facts*, 2nd edn, Yass, 1872:18.
3 April 1816, Governor Lachlan Macquarie, CS Reel 6065, 4/1798:44, SRNSW.
4 Ibid.
5 'Doo-ull - - - the spear by which Yer-ren-iby was wounded' — GV 1791: 14.17; 'Doo-ull - - - A short spear' — David Collins 1975:509.
6 *SG* 9, 16, 21 March 1816. GT Palmer was the brother of Commissary John Palmer.
7 Macquarie to Bathurst, 8 March 1816, *HRA IX:* 54.
8 Charles Throsby to D'Arcy Wentworth, 5 April 1816, Wentworth Papers, A752/CY699:183–6, ML.
9 Lachlan Macquarie, *List of Names of Black and White Guides employed with Capts Shaw* [Schaw] *& Wallis*, Reel 6065; 4/1798:45, SRNSW.
10 Macquarie to Bathurst, 8 June 1816, *HRA IX:* 139–40.
11 Macquarie, *Journal*, 10 April 1816.
12 Captain James Wallis, *Journal*, 17 April 1816, Colonial Secretary in letters, 4/1735 Reel 2161:52–60, *SRNSW.*
13 CS Reel 6045, 41/1735:60–2, SRNSW.
14 Wallis, 1816:52-60.
15 Information from the Repatriation Program Director, National Museum of Australia, Friday 4 June 2002. The remains of both men have since been returned to the Aboriginal community.
16 Richard Sadleir RN, Master of the Male Orphan School, Liverpool, *Report to the Committee on the Aboriginal Question,* Friday, 21 September 1833, Votes and Proceedings No. 29, Legislative Council of New South Wales.
17 Review of *Illustrations of Phrenology, Edinburgh Monthly Review*, January 1821:106.
18 William Byrne, *Old Times*, Sydney, May 1903:105.
19 *SG,* 11 May 1816, 2c.
20 Lachlan Macquarie, *Journal*, Tuesday 4 June 1816, MS A773:21, ML.
21 Government Public Notice and Order, Reel 6038; SZ759:232–5, SRNSW.
22 Macquarie to Major Stewart, 31 July 1816, *HRA III:*171.
23 Macquarie, *Journal*, 5 August 1816; Reel 6006; 4/3499:188 SRNSW.
24 Secretary Campbell to Lt. Governor Sorell, 1 December 1818, CS Reel 6006; 4/3499:188, SRNSW.
25 Lieut-Governor Sorrel to Colonial Secretary Campbell, 2 January 1819, *HRA III:*375.
26 *SG,* 28 August 1818.
27 Campbell to Cimetiere, Sydney, 30 January 1819, Reel 6006; 4/3499:296, SRNSW.
28 William Macarthur, *Memorandum*, Supreme Court Miscellaneous cases relating to Aborigines 1824–40, COD/294B, SRNSW.
29 *HRA, vol. X:* 182–3; *SG,* 31 May 1819.
30 Charles Throsby to Governor Lachlan Macquarie, 25 April 1819, CS Reel 6034 4/3500:76, SRNSW.
31 Lachlan Macquarie, *Journal of a tour to the… country some time since discovered by Chas. Throsby Esqr. —in Octr & Novr 1820,* 23 October 1820, MSS A782, ML.
32 Thomas Mitchell, *Stonequarry* [Picton], c. 1828, Mitchell Papers, MS A295–3:425, ML.
33 Throsby to Macquarie, 11 May 1819, CS Reel 6034; 4/3500:89, SRNSW; *SG,* 5 June 1819, 1b.
34 *The Times,* London, 1 November 1819:2.
35 William Macarthur, *Memorandum*.
36 *SG,* 11 June 1822, 3a.
37 James Atkinson, *An Account of the State of Agriculture & Grazing in New South Wales*, London: J. Cross, 1826:137–8.
38 Dumont d'Urville, translated in Helen Rosenman, *Two Voyages to the South Seas …* MUP, Melbourne, 1987:85–90.
39 *The Australian*, Sydney, 19 January 1826.
40 Colonial Secretary, Return of Aboriginal Natives, 1833, SRNSW 4/1735.
41 William Macarthur, *Memorandum*.
42 'Tribes — Norongeragàl' — GV 1791: 45.7; Richard Hill, *SMH* 1892.

Chapter 7: Tristran: a runaway in Rio

1 JR Elder, (ed.), *Letters and Journals of Samuel Marsden*, Dunedin, 1912:36.
2 Robert Hughes, *The Fatal Shore*, Pan Books, London, 1988:187.
3 James Elder and John Youl, *Journal*, 5 March 1801, Rio to Pt. Jackson, 1800–01, London Missionary Society, South Seas Journals, No. 9.
4 Reverend Samuel Marsden to Commissioner JT Bigge, 26 January 1821, BT Box 26:5923, ML.
5 Reverend Thomas Hassall, *Memorandum* (no date), Hassall family — Correspondence 1793 — c. 1900, A/1677: 84, 87–8, ML. See Appendix. This was the school run by the Reverend William Pascoe Crook (1775–1846) at Parramatta.
6 George Caley to Sir Joseph Banks, 16 February 1809, DTC, vol.17:253–6, Department of Botany Library, NHM, London.
7 Collins, 1975:351.

8 PG King, *Norfolk Island* — Lieut. Governor: *Victualling Book*, 1792–1796, 2 July–1 August 1795, A 1958/ CY 3467, ML.
9 Thomas Hassall, *Memorandum*, n.d.
10 RH Mathews, *Dharruk words*. Printed leaflet in RH Mathews Papers, MS 8006/3/5 1901:157, NLA.
11 Collins, 1975:358.
12 Elizabeth Marsden to Mrs Mary Stokes, Parramatta, 7 May 1796. Letter No. 5, *Marsden Family, Letters to Mrs. Stokes, 1794–1824*, MSS 719, ML.
13 Samuel Marsden to William Wilberforce, Parramatta 1799, BT Box 49:77, ML.
14 James Elder and John Youl, 1801.
15 *SG*, 15 February 1807, 2a.
16 Anna Josepha King, Journal on HMS Buffalo, *King Family Papers*, MSS 1973X, ML.
17 JH Vaux, *Memoirs of James Hardy Vaux, written by himself*, BF [Judge Barron Field] (ed.), 2nd edn, CH Reynall, London, 1827:151–2.
18 Thomas Hassall, *Memorandum*.
19 Elizabeth Marsden to Rowland Hassall, Hull, Jan 9th 1808, *Hassall Correspondence*, A 859:174, ML.
20 Caley to Banks, 1809.
21 Samuel Marsden to John Stokes, *On Board the Ann*, Rio, Decr. 1, 1809, MSS A1992, vol. 1: 83, ML.
22 Elizabeth Marsden to John Piper, Parramatta, 17 July 1804. *Piper Papers*, p. 42, ML.
23 Elizabeth Marsden to John Piper, 15 August 1804, *Piper Papers*, vol. 3:423, C244: 6–7, ML.
24 *Proceedings of the Medical Court of Enquiry, holden at Sydney in New South Wales*, 16th of March, 1814 … to enquire into the causes of the very great mortality among the Convicts on board the Transport "General Hewitt" during the Passage from England to New South Wales … Conducted by William Redfern, Asst Surgeon, *HRA* VIII:245 et seq.
25 Lachlan Macquarie to Undersecretary Goulburn, Sydney, N.S. Wales 7th Feby 1814, *HRA* VIII, 1813–1815:138.
26 JB Marsden, *Life and Work of Samuel Marsden*, Whitcombe and Tombs, Christchurch, [1838] 1913:63.
27 Thomas Hassall, *Memorandum*.

Chapter 8: Gnung-a Gnung-a in North America and Hawaii

1 Collins, 1975:250–1.
2 Tench, 1793:36.
3 William Dawes, *Grammatical forms of the language of N.S.Wales, in the neighbourhood of Sydney (Native and English, but not alphabetical, by — Dawes, in the year 1790*, MS 4165 (a):6.16; 42.1, Marsden Collection, School of Oriental and African Studies, London.
4 Smith, 2001:124–6.
5 Smith, 2001:136.
6 Collins, [1798] 1975:250–1.
7 This and following references to Captain George Vancouver and the survey expedition of North America by HMS *Chatham* and HMS *Discovery* are from George Vancouver, *A voyage of discovery to the North Pacific Ocean, and Round the World* … John Stockdale, London, [1798] 1801:296–364.
8 Charles H. Read, 'An Account of a Collection of Ethnographic Specimens found during Vancouver's voyage in the Pacific Ocean 1790–1755', *Journal of the Anthropological Institute of Great Britain and Ireland*, vol. 21, London, 1892:99 et seq.
9 Log book kept by Spelman Swaine, Master's Mate on HMS *Discovery*, 1793, Reel 1556, PRO London.
10 James Cook, Journals vol. III:400–1, quoted in JC Beaglehole, *The Life of Captain James Cook*, Hakluyt Society, London, 1974:649.
11 Beaglehole, 1974:670–2.
12 Collins, 1975:301–2.
13 James King, 1779, in James Cook, Journals III, quoted by JC Beaglehole (ed.), in *The Journals of Captain James Cook* … Hakluyt Society, London, vol. 3, 1967:268.
14 Collins, 1975:303, 305.
15 Collins, 1975:371–2.
16 John Cobley, *Sydney Cove 1795-1800*, Angus & Robertson, Sydney, 1986:205.
17 Hunter in Collins II, 1975:61–4.
18 HRNSW, Appendix C, vol. 111:820–828; *HRA vol. II*:134.
19 Hunter in Collins II, 1975:214.
20 John Price, 2nd *Journey*, 9 March–2 April 1798, John Hunter to Sir Joseph Banks, 21 August 1801, Banks Papers, Series 38.21, ML.
21 Plate XXI, François Péron, Atlas, *Voyage de découvertes aux terres Australes* … Paris 1811.
22 *SG,* 15 January 1809, 2a.

Chapter 9: Worogan and Yernabie on *Lady Nelson*

1 'Wau-gan - - - Crow' — Collins, 1975:512.
2 'Benelàng . Warwéar . Karangarang . Wárrgan . Munáguri', William Dawes, b. 1791:9.4.
3 Daniel Southwell, 'A List of Words …' 1791, *Southwell Papers* 1787–1793, Original MS 16,383:ff.147–9, British

Library, London; AJCP Reel M1538, ML; *HRNSW II*:697.

4 William Dawes, a 1790:3.
5 'Gare-a-way - - - White Cockatoo' — Collins 1975:512; 'Gar-ra-way - - - White Cockatoo' — GV 1791:24.5.
6 *SG,* 10 December 1804.
7 Nouvelle-Hollande — Toulgra (mère) [Worogan], 1802, Nicolas-Martin Petit (1777–1804),
   20032.1, Muséum d'Histoire Naturelle, Le Havre, France.
8 James Grant, *Remarks &c., on board His Majesty's armed surveying vessel, Lady Nelson, on a voyage to explore Basses Straits,*
   1801, HRNSW 1V, Sydney 1896:477–479; *The Narrative of a Voyage of Discovery, performed in His Majesty's Vessel, The*
   Lady Nelson, of sixty tons burthen, with sliding keels … By James Grant, Lieutenant in the Royal Navy, London: Printed for
   T Egerton, Military Library, Whitehall, 1803:99–148.
9 George Caley to Sir Joseph Banks, 25 August 1801, Banks Papers, Series 18.032, ML.
10 *SG,* 16 December 1804, 4c; 23 December 1804, 3a.

Chapter 10: Bungaree: sailing with Mastthew Flinders
1 Hunter in Collins II, 1975:162.
2 *SG,* 4 February 1815, 1b.
3 Macquarie, *Journal,* 11 February 1822.
4 Tench 1793:209.
5 *SMH,* 27 May 1850.
6 Philip Cohen, Letter to the Editor, SMH, 27 May 1890.
7 *SMH,* 19 April 1861.
8 James Jervis, *History of Woollahra,* Woollahra, 1967:44.
9 *SMH,* 18 July 1868.
10 Matthew Flinders, *A Voyage to Terra Australis,* W Nicol, London, 1814:cxciv.
11 Matthew Flinders, *A Biographical Tribute to the Memory of Trim,* Isle de France, 1809,
   Flinders Papers, MS 60/017/FLI/11A, NMM, Greenwich.
12 Narrative based on Matthew Flinders, *A Journal in the Norfolk Sloop, 8 July–12 August 1799,* MS C2112, ML; also
   draws on Hunter in Collins II, 1975:161–180.
13 Flinders, 1814:188–90.
14 Flinders, 1814:235.
15 Flinders, Correspondence 1925:46–9.
16 Flinders, vol. 2, 1814:10.
17 Samuel Smith, *Journal,* 30 July 1802, MS ZC222, ML.
18 Robert Brown, *Journal,* 31 July 1802, Botany Library, NHM. Transcribed by Keith Vincent Smith, London 1992.
19 Flinders, vol. 2, 1814:11.
20 Brown, *Journal,* 5 August 1802.
21 Brown, *Journal,* 30 August 1802.
22 Flinders, vol. 2, 1814:97.
23 Flinders, vol. 2, 1814:188–9.
24 FD McCarthy, 'The Cave Paintings of Groote Eylandt and Chasm Island: American-Australian Scientific Expedition to
   Arnhem Land,' *Records of the Australian Museum,* 1960:297–414.
25 Phyllis I Edwards (ed.), *The Journal of Peter Good,* Bulletin of the British Museum (Natural History), London,
   1981:112.
26 Nicolas Peterson (ed.), *Donald Thomson in Arnhem Land,* Miegunyah Press, Carlton, revised edition 2003:60.
27 Arthur Phillip to Lord Sydney, 28 September 1788, *HRNSW II*:192.
28 Flinders, vol. 2, 1814:238–9.
29 'Mut-tau-ra   The small snapper', L. E. Threlkeld, An Australian Grammar … of the language, as spoken by the
   Aborigines, in the vicinity of Hunter's River, Lake Macquarie, &c. New South Wales, Sydney 1834:86.
30 Keith Vincent Smith, 'Gooseberry, Cora (c. 1777–1852)', *Australian Dictionary of Biography,* Supplementary Volume,
   MUP, 2005:148.
31 This information, based on recent research, replaces the section 'Dickens as Myth-Maker?' in Keith Vincent Smith, *King*
   Bungaree, 1992:155 et seq. Lang was named by 'M' in the SMH 17 July 1880:7, though the writer wrongly recalled that
   the subject of the article was Bennelong's brother-in-law Harry.
32 Alexander Huey, *Journal,* 28–31 December 1809, Typescript B1514, ML.
33 *SG,* 4 February 1815.
34 Barratt, 1981:36.
35 Barratt, 1981:50.
36 An interpretation first suggested by Irene Smith on 19 July 2007.
37 Lachlan Macquarie, *Journal* 1818–1822, 11 February 1822, MS A774: 258–60, ML.
38 JD Lang, *An Historical and Statistical Account of New South Wales … 2* vols, Cochrane and McCrone, London,
   1838:263.
39 *The Australian,* Sydney, 2 January 1828.

40   Roger Oldfield (ed.), *South-Asian Register*, Sydney, vol. 3, 1828:278.

41   *The Australian*, 4 January 1828, 3.

42   Oldfield, vol. 2, 1828:104.

43   M Le Baron de Bougainville, *Journal de la navigation autour du Globe de la Frégate La Thétis et de la corvette L'Espérance … Arthur Bertrand, Paris*, 1837:485–7.

44   Philip Parker King, *Narrative of a Survey of the Intertropical and Western Coasts of Australia,* John Murray, London, 1827:2.

45   Ida Lee, *Early Explorers in Australia*, Methuen, London, 1925:310.

46   King, 1827:4.

47   King, 1827:5–6.

48   King, 1827:15–16.

49   King, 1827:45, 47.

50   Lee, 1925:360.

51   Lee, 1925:391.

52   D'Urville, 1824:294.

53   Geoffrey Dutton, *White on Black: The Australian Aborigine Portrayed in Art*, Macmillan, South Melbourne, 1974:29.

54   *SG*, 21 October 1826, 2a.

55   *SG*, 6 December 1826, 2a.

56   Rev. John McGarvie, *Diary 1825–1828*, 21 May 1826, MS A1332, ML.

57   *SG*, 16 July 1831.

Chapter 11: Daniel Moowattin in Regency London

1   George Caley to Sir Joseph Banks, 25 September 1807, Banks Papers, A83, vol. 20:281, ML.

2   Charles Grimes, *Map of New South Wales* 1803 (with 1806 additions), HRNSW, vol. 6: opp.410.

3   HMS Buffalo, Ship's Muster Book 1805, ADM 36, Reel 7018 36/17313: 91, PRO London.

4   Ship News, SG, 6 October 1805, 1c.

5   Joan Webb, *George Caley 19th Century Naturalist*, Surrey Beatty & Sons, Chipping Norton, NSW, 1995:55. See Appendix D, 'Caley's Eucalypts', 1995:175.

6   *SG*, 1 December 1805, 2a.

7   Caley to Banks, 9 April 1806, *HRNSW VI*:65–68.

8   *SG*, 2 February 1806, 1c.

9   Supplement to *SG*, 28 September 1816:1–2.

10   Marsden to Scott, 2 December 1826. London Missionary Society, Australian Letters. Quoted in Niel Gunson (ed.), *Australian Reminiscences & Papers of L. E. Threlkeld Missionary to the Aborigines, 1824–1859*, Canberra, 1974:348.

11   Marsden to Dumont d'Urville, 12 December 1826,*Voyage de la Corvette L'Astrolabe … Paris*, vol. 1, 1830:523.

12   *SG*, 23 May 1812, 3c.

13   Cobley 1793–5:113; V1793322 1A/1793, Registrar General, Births, Sydney.

14   Don Chapman, 1788, *The People of the First Fleet*, North Ryde, 1981:103.

15   Cobley, 1793–5:187; Collins, 1975:327.

16   For example, in Cobley, 1791–2:95, 217.

17   *The Australian*, 25 November 1834:2 ff. See Hunter in Collins II, 1975:145–6; 151; 271–2.

18   Joseph Holt, *Life*, MS A2024:294–5, ML. See O'Shaughnessy, Peter (ed.), *Joseph Holt, A Rum Story*, Sydney, 1988.

19   Marsden to King, Parramatta, 30 September 1800, *HRA II*:639.

20   Marsden to King, 27 March 1802, quoted in GW Rusden, Curiosities *of Colonisation*, London, 1874. Original document no longer available.

21   George Howe, *New South Wales Pocket Almanack and Colonial Remembrancer*, Sydney, 1806:34.

22   King to Banks, 3 May 1800, *HRNSW IV*:82.

23   King to Banks, 28 September 1800, *HRNSW IV*:205–6.

24   Caley to Banks, 12 October 1800, *HRNSW IV*:248.

25   Caley to Banks, 25 August 1801, *HRNSW IV*:513–4.

26   Webb, 1995: 55:176.

27   Webb, 1995: 58:175.

28   Caley to Banks, 3 November 1808, Banks Papers A83, vol. 20:287–9.

29   Webb, 1995:55.

30   Caley to Banks, 16 February 1809, DTC c. 17:253–8, NHM London.

31   *SG*, 12 May 1810, 2a.

32   George Suttor, *Memoirs of George Suttor, F. L. S. 1774–1859*, Typescript MS A3072:78-9, ML.

33   *SG*, 23 May 1812 3c. The informant was probably George Suttor.

34   *HRA,* vol. III:238.

35   Banks to unnamed recipient, *HRNSW VII*:578.

36   Isabel McBryde, *Guests of the Governor*, Sydney 1983: 30–1.

37   The extracts from Caley's manuscript *Remarks on the weather &c.*, that follow were obtained by Keith Vincent Smith in

1992 at the Botanical Library, Natural History Museum, London. Relevant dates are quoted. See 'George Caley and Daniel Moowattin' in JL Kohen, A Knight and KV Smith, *Uninvited Guests*, Report prepared for the National Trust, Sydney 1999:44–60.

38   Caley Remarks, 3 January 1811.

39   Marsden to Dumont d'Urville, op. cit.

40   *SG*, 23 May 1812, 3c.

41   Caley Remarks, 29 March 1811.

42   William Lawson, 'Mr. Lawson's account of the Aborigines of New South Wales', Supreme Court Correspondence relating to Aborigines, 5/1161, Item No. 82, 1838:554–5, SRNSW.

43   NA Vigors and TA Horsfield, 'A description of the Australian Birds in the Collections of the Linnean Society', Transactions of the Linnean Society, vol. XV, London: 1826: 262.

44   DD Mann, 1811:49–50.

45   *Gentlemen's Magazine*, October 1833:377–8.

46   Matthew Flinders, Private Journal, 1803–1814, 12 May 1811, MS S1/48, ML.

47   Flinders, Private Journal, 27 May 1811.

48   Matthew Flinders, *A Voyage to Terra Australis*, W. Nichol, London, 1814: 478–496; ADB 1966:390–1.

49   *SG*, 23 May 1812, 3.

50   *Times*, 11 June 1811.

51   Anon., *Chamber's Edinburgh Journal*, 1832:199-200; reprinted in *Atkinson's Casket*, London, vol. 10, 1835:570-1.

52   *HRNSW, VII:* 578.

53   Caley Remarks, 19 August 1811 (final quotation).

54   Chamber's, Ibid.

55   Suttor, *Memoirs* 1858:87.

56   *SG,* 28 September 1816.

57   Suttor, *Memoirs*, 1858:87.

58   Suttor to Banks, 12 November 1812, Banks Papers 323–4.

59   *SG*, 23 May 1812.

60   *SG,* 26 September 1816.

61   Marsden in Gunson, 1974:348.

62   Dumont d'Urville, 1830:523.

63   Supplement to *SG*, 23 September 1816. On 25 March 1993 Joan Webb (personal comment), author of *George Caley 19th Century Naturalist* (1995), first informed me of the trial of Daniel Moowattin.

64   Supplement to *SG*, 12 October 1816, 2a.

65   Supplement to *SG*, 23 September 1816. See Macquarie Law website, viewed 20 January 2010: http://www.law.mq.edu.au/scnsw/html/R%20v%20Mow-watty,%201816.htm

66   Lachlan Macquarie, Diary, Friday, 1 November 1816, MS A773, ML.

Chapter 12: Bowen Bungaree at Moreton Bay and San Francisco

1   Mut-tau-ra - - - The small snapper' — Reverend LE Threlkeld*, An Australian Grammar … of the language, as spoken by the Aborigines, in the vicinity of Hunter's River, Lake Macquarie, &c. New South Wales*, Sydney 1834:86.

2   See 'The Russians at Kirribilli' in Keith Vincent Smith, *King Bungaree*, Kangaroo Press, Kenthurst, 1992:103–115.

3   John Uniacke, 'Narrative of Mr. Oxley's expedition to survey Port Curtis and Moreton Bay with a view to form a convict establishment there' in Barron Field (ed.), *Geographical Memoirs of New South Wales*, London, 1825:29–32.

4   Uniacke, 1825:36–7.

5   Uniacke, 1825:54–5.

6   Smith, 1992: 31–34.

7   Royal Society Papers, 9/37, DL, Sydney.

8   Uniacke, 1825:62–5.

9   Guy Jennings (compiler), *My Holiday and other early travels from Manly to Palm Beach 1861*, Newport Beach: Aramo Pty. Ltd, 1991. Reprinted from the *Sydney Mail*, 22 June 1861 and successive Saturdays.

10   *SG*, 23 December 1820:3.

11   *SH*, 14 November 1831, 4a.

12   Registrar General, Sydney 'Aboriginal – Theela – Father Bowen – Mother Maria' – Births, V18301399 128/1830; 'Aboriginal Mark – Father Bowen Bungaree – Mother Maria' – Births, 125/1832.

13   Colonial Secretary, *Return of Aboriginal Natives* (Blanket Lists), 1834, SRNSW.

14   William Proctor, *Journal on the John Craig*, 21 December 1834: 118–122, MSS B1126, ML.

15   *SH*, 17 April 1837.

16   Ian Jacobs, *A history of the Aboriginal clans of Sydney's northern beaches*, Brookvale, 2003:144–7; Reel 4/2723 SRNSW; *SMH*, 8 March; 17 April, 19 August 1845.

17   JC Waterman, *JRAHS*, vol. VIII, 1923:259.

18   Maybanke Anderson, 'The Story of Pittwater', *JRAHS*, vol. VI, Part 1V, 1920.

19   Charles Bateson, *Gold Fleet for California, Forty Niners from Australia and New Zealand*, Ure Smith, Sydney, 1963:40.
20   *SMH*, 28 August 1849; Bateson 1963:99.
21   'Distribution of Blankets to the Aborigines', *SMH,* 27 May 1850.
22   *SMH,* 10 June 1850.
23   'A Merchant' [Edward Lucett] *Rovings in the Pacific, from 1837 to 1849; with a glance at California* … vol. 1, London: Longman, 1851:72.
24   *SMH,* 20 August 1849.
25   *Maitland Mercury,* 25 August 1849.
26   Registrar General, Sydney, *Deaths*, 1853721 139/1853, 106/1853.
27   De Boos in Jennings, 1991:55.

Chapter 13: Sealers
1   François Péron, *Naval Chronicle*, London, July–December 1809.
2   Hunter in Collins II, 1975:32.
3   *SG,* 17 March 1805 4a.
4   *HRA,* vol. 1, 5:131.
5   'William' (Willamannan) to GA Robinson, in *G.A. Robinson Papers*, 22 June 1832, vol. 35, MS A7056/CY Reel 1470: 205, ML.
6   Mann, 1811:47.
7   *Narrative of an expedition to Furneaux's Islands on the coast of New South Wales in the Port Jackson colonial schooner Francis by Matthew Flinders, 2nd Lieutenant of H.M.S. Reliance, March 1798* — Manuscript copy made in May 1877 by W Flinders Petrie, on presenting the original to the Melbourne Public Library.
8   Margaret Steven, *Merchant Campbell 1769–1846: A study in colonial trade,* OUP, 1965:106.
9   Péron, *Naval Chronicle*, London, 1809.

Chapter 14: Boatswain Maroot in the sub-Antarctic
1   *SG,* 13 January 1805 3a; SG 12 January 1806 1c; Mahroot, alias the Boatswain [Boatswain Maroot], 'Report from the Select Committee on the Condition of the Aborigines', *Votes and Proceedings*, New South Wales Legislative Council, Sydney, 1845.
2   George Thornton Papers, 'NSW Aboriginal', MS 3270, National Library of Australia [NLA], Canberra.
3   William Bradley (21 February 1788), *A Voyage to New South Wales* … (Facsimile) Trustees of the Public Library of NSW and Ure Smith, Sydney, 1968:85.
4   Tench, 1789:97.
5   *Governors' Vocabulary,* 1791:45.12.
6   Evidence of Mahroot [Maroot], 1845.
7   *SG,* 23 July 1809, 2a.
8   *SG,* 5 October 1811, 2c.
9   Joseph Henry Barsden, *Volume containing autobiographical accounts of events 1799–1816, completed c. 1836*, ML MSS 7279, CY 4345A, ML.
10   Minutes and Proceedings, Bench of Magistrates, County of Cumberland, Colonial Secretary Papers, Reel 658; SZ773, SRNSW.
11   *SG,* 13 April 1811, 2a.
12   Evidence of Mahroot, 1845.
13   Evidence of Mahroot, 1845.
14   SG, Friday 11 October 1822, 2a.
15   CS Ship's Musters, 1 August 1823, 4/4773, COD/419 SRNSW.
16   CS Governor's Minutes 1832 Ledger, Minute No. 1836, 17 April 1832, 4/996, SRNSW.
17   Thomas Balcombe, Draughtsman, *Sketch shewing the situation of Huts in the Parish of Botany belonging to Boatswain Maroot*, Surveyor General, Sketch Books, vol. 1, Botany, Folio 76, SRNSW.
18   Rev. JS Handt, Bonwick Transcripts, BT Box 54:1855, ML.
19   Evidence of Mahroot, 1845.
20   Joseph Phipps Townsend, *Rambles and Observations in New South Wales*, London, 1849:120.
21   W. Augustus Miles JP, Commissioner of Police, Sydney … 'How did the natives become acquainted with demigods and daemonogy …?' *Journal of Ethnological Society of London*, vol. III, 1854:4.
22   *SMH*, 26 May 1849:2.
23   *SMH,* February 2 February1850:5.
24   *SG,*16 March, 23 March 1811, 13 April 1811.
25   *SG,* 30 November 1811.
26   Batman to Anstey, 13 October 1829, CSO1/320/7578, Tasmanian State Archives, Hobart.
27   GA Robinson Papers, 22 June 1832, vol. 4, MS A7025:206, ML.
28   *SG,* 18 May 1806.
29   *Sydney Herald, /* June 1838; *The Colonist,* 6 June 1838.

30 William (Willamannan) to GA Robinson, 22 June 1832.
31 John Connell, Pitt Street, Sydney, to Captain Dumaresq, 30 April (no year), MS A84, CY Reel 3583, ff.146–151, ML.
32 CS, 'Return of Aboriginal Natives', 8 April 1829, 4/2045, SRNSW.
33 CS, 'List of Blankets given in the Sydney district', Special bundles 1833–35, Reel 3706, SRNSW.
34 Jean M Nunn, *This Southern land: A social history of Kangaroo Island 1800–1890*, Hawthorndene (SA): Investigator Press, 1989:45.

Chapter 15: Whalers
1 Rev. LE Threlkeld, c. 1825, quoted in Gunson 1974:55.
2 JL Kohen and Ronald Lampert, 'Hunters and Fishers in the Sydney Region', Chapter 18 in *Australians to 1788*, DJ Mulvaney and J. Peter White (eds.), Fairfax, Syme & Weldon, Sydney, 1987:355; 357.
3 Phillip, 1970:75.
4 WD Campbell, *Aboriginal Carvings of Port Jackson and Broken Bay*, Memoirs of the Geological Survey, New South Wales, Department of Mines and Agriculture, Sydney, 1899:6.
5 Samuel Bennett, *The History of Australian Discovery and Colonisation*, Sydney 1865:279.
6 For example, in 1999 a female southern right whale swam around Sydney Harbour for 21 days; in July 2002, three southern right whales came almost to Bennelong Point; in 2005 two humpbacks came into Manly Cove and in May 2008, four humpbacks spent an hour frolicking near Little Manly.
7 Obed West, *SMH* 1822, in Marriott 1988:40.
8 John Milton, *Paradise Lost*, London 1674:199–200.
9 David Collins to his brother George, 25 November 1791, Correspondence 1775-1810, MSS 700, ML.
10 Tench, 1793:134.
11 Hunter, 1793:542–3.
12 Hunter, 1793:544.
13 Hunter in Collins II, 1802:41.
14 Tench, 1793:209.
15 Anon. in Cobley, 1965:126.
16 Tench, 1793:209.
17 Hunter in Collins II, 1975:86–7.
18 Jonathan King and John King, *Philip Gidley King, A Biography of the Third Governor of New South Wales*, North Ryde: Methuen & Co., 1981:96.
19 George Quested to PG King, 25 September 1800, MS A322: 595, ML.
20 PG King to Sir Joseph Banks, 5 June 1802, Banks' Papers, Series 39.068, ML.
21 Samuel Enderby, Paul's Wharf, to Sir Joseph Banks, 24 November 1802, Banks Papers, Series 23.19, ML.

Chapter 16: The Hawkesbury River sailors
1 *SG*, 2 December 1804, 2b–c.
2 *SG*, 23 October 1803, 3a.
3 *SG*, 5 May 1805, 2a–b.
4 *SG*, 12 May 1805, 4a.
5 CS Ships' Musters, 27 April 1817, 4/4771 COD/420, No. 11/103: 16, SRNSW.
6 CS Ships' Musters, 29 October 1819, 4/4771, No 49/232: 187, SRNSW.
7 William Cox, *Journal*, 27 August 1814, Memoirs of Joseph Cox 1901: 63.
8 HTG, 15 March 1823.
9 Rowland Hassall, BT Box 49, ML.
10 Registrar-General NSW, Death, V1823, 5654 2B and V 1823, 1349, 148.
11 Registrar-General NSW, Marriage, V1824 3276, 3B/1824.
12 HRA, 3.3.722.
13 CS Land Grants 1816, No. 11, Fiche 3266; 9/2652:26, SRNSW.
14 Joseph Arnold, *Journal*, Sydney, 19 June–13 July 1815, MS C720, ML.
15 CS Land Grants 1816, No. 187, Fiche 3266:26, SRNSW.
16 CS Ship's Musters, 27 April 1817, 4/4771 COD/420, No. 11/103:16, SRNSW.
17 CS Ships' Musters, 3 October 1820, 4/4771 R561, No. 53/296, COD 420, SRNSW.
18 JS Cumpston, *Kangaroo Island 1800–1836*, Roebuck Society, Canberra, 1974:54.
19 *SG*, 5 May 1804, 4b–c.
20 Charles Throsby to Governor Lachlan Macquarie, 24 March 1816, Reel 6065; 4/1798: 49, SRNSW.
21 Lachlan Macquarie, *Proclamation*, Macquarie to Bathurst, *HRA IX*:362-4.
22 Lachlan Macquarie, Journal, 22 December 1816, DL.
23 *SG*, 15 December 1821, 4a.
24 *SG*, 22 November 1822.
25 CS Ships Musters, 24 October 1822, COD/419; 4/4773:360, SRNSW.
26 Petition to Sir George Gipps Knight Captain General Governor and Commander in Chief of the Territory of New

South Wales from John Grono and others, *Papers relating to Aboriginal Australians*, DL MS Add.81:71–73, DL.

27 JL Kohen, *Daruganora: Darug Country — The place and the people*, Blacktown: Darug Tribal Aboriginal Corporation, 2006:25.

Chapter 17: Tom Chaseland: whaling in New Zealand

1 Valerie Ross, *A Hawkesbury Story*, Library of Australian History, Sydney, 1981:130–1.
2 Pamela Goesch, *Thomas Chaseland and the next generation*, Brynwood House, Sydney, 2009.
3 See Bibliography.
4 Thomas Dowse, *Tom Chaseland or the adventures of a Colonial half-caste: a tale of old times*, MS OM79–68/20, John Oxley Library, State Library of Queensland, Brisbane.
5 *SG,* 21 December 1811 1c. There was another *Endeavour*, an 85-ton brig.
6 HE Maude, *Of Islands and Men: Studies in Pacific History*, OUP, Melbourne, 1968:228.
7 *SG,* 20 March 1813, 2a.
8 *SG,* 29 May 1813.
9 *SG,* 23 October 1813.
10 *SG,* 20 May 1815 2c; *SG,* 15 July 1815, 2a. An earlier ship with the same name was wrecked on Macquarie Island.
11 CS Ship's Musters 1816–21, COD 420, 6 August 1816, SRNSW; *HTG,* 4 January 1817, 1a.
12 CS Ships' Musters 1816–21, No. 23/115:31, 3 August 1817, SRNSW.
13 L Norman, *Pioneer Shipping in Tasmania*, Hobart, 1938:618.
14 CS Ship's Musters 1816–21, No. 21/141:69, 5 August 1817, SRNSW.
15 CS Ship's Musters 1816–21, COD 420 SRNSW; *HTG,* 14 February 1818.
16 Claims and Demands, SG 7 August 1819.
17 *HTG,* 2 October 1819, 2c.
18 *HTG,* 19 October 1819, 1b.
19 CS Ship's Musters 1816–21, No. 49/232:187, SRNSW.
20 CS Ship's Musters, 29 October 1819, 4/4771, No 49/232: 187, SRNSW.
21 Cumpston, 1970:34.
22 *SG,* 15 February 1822.
23 CS Ship's Musters Reel 561, No. 39, 1822, SRNSW; SG, 21 June 1822, 2a.
24 Rev. Alexander Strachan, *Remarkable incidents in the life of the Rev. Samuel Leigh*, Hamilton, Adams & Co., London, 1853:136.
25 SG Claughton, Lawry, Walter (1793–1859), ADB, vol. 2, MUP, 1967:95–6.
26 Strachan, 1853:137.
27 Sarah S Farmer, *Tonga and the Friendly Isles*, Hamilton, Adams & Co, London, 1855:154.
28 Rev. Ralph Mansfield, letter, 9 August 1824.
29 *SG,* 24 April 1823, 2.
30 Strachan, 1853:141.
31 Anne Salmond, *Two Worlds: First meetings between Maori and Europeans 1642–1722*, Viking, Auckland, 1997:209.
32 *SG,* 1 January 1824; HTG, 14 May 1824.
33 McNab, 1909:262.
34 John Boultbee, 'Journal of a Rambler', c. 1835 in A. Charles Begg and Neil C. Begg, *The World of John Boultbee including an Account of Sealing in Australia and New Zealand*, Whitcoulls, Christchurch, 1979:145.
35 J Herries Beattie, 'Traditions and Legends', Part X1. *Journal of the Polynesian Society*, 1912:219.
36 June Starke (ed.), *Journal of a Rambler, The Journal of John Boultbee*, Oxford University Press, Auckland, 1986:xlvi.
37 Edward Shortland, *The Southern Districts of New Zealand*, Longman, Brown, London, 1851:153.
38 Thomas Dunbavin, *Sailing the World's Edge*, Jonathan Cape, London, 1931:141.
39 'Tohunga, a person skilled in karakia, also skilled in any craft' — Edward Shortland, *Maori Religious Mythology*, Longman, London, 1881 (Appendix).
40 J Herries Beattie quoted in Rhys Richards, *Whaling and Sealing at the Chatham Islands*, Roebuck Books, Canberra, 1982:36. Raniera Taheke Ellison, also known as Daniel Ellison (1839–1920) was a whaler and the son of a European father and a Taranaki Maori mother.
41 Richards, 1982:36.
42 *Sydney Herald* (*SH*), vol. 1, No. 1, 18 April 1831, 4a.
43 Robert McNab, *The Old Whaling Days: A history of Southern New Zealand from 1830 to 1840*, Whitcombe & Tombs, Christchurch, 1913:85–6.
44 Basil Howard, *Rakiura: A history of Stewart Island*, AH & AW Reed, Dunedin, 1940:85.
45 *SG,* 31 March 1831; SG, 9 April 1831.
46 NSW BDM, Marriages, V1829 222 162A.
47 *SH*, 18 April 1831 4a.
48 *Commercial Journa*l, 14 March 1840; Robert McNab, Murihiku: *A History of the South Island of New Zealand and the Islands Adjacent and Lying to the South, from 1642 to 1835*, William Smith, Invercargill, 1907:399; Mutch Index, ML.
49 SMH, 2 December 1840.

50 Shortland 1851:154.
51 Otago Witness, 22 December 1898:20b.
52 Eric Olssen, *History of Otago,* John McIndoe, Dunedin, 1984:6.
53 Rev. Richard Taylor, *Te Ika a Maui, or New Zealand and its Inhabitants*, Wertheim and Macintosh, London, 1855:238.
54 Olssen, 1984:81–83.
55 Shortland, 1851:145.
56 McNab, 1913:186.
57 Edwin Palmer to Dr TM Hocken, quoted by John Hall-Jones in *Bluff Harbour*, Southland Harbour Board, Bluff, 1976:22.
58 *SH*, 17 May 1838; Supreme Court Sydney, Wednesday 16 May, before Mr. Justice Burton and a civil jury. Based on the text in McNab, *The Old Whaling Days*, 1913:205 et seq.
59 Rev. Charles Christie, *Waikouaiti*, 2nd ed., Christchurch 1929: 67–9. A tierce was a unit of volume, equivalent to 42 gallons or 139 litres. The word was derived from the Latin *tertius*, meaning one-third.
60 John Jones, Evidence to the Legislative Council Committee, Sydney, 6 July 1840. Quoted in McNab, *Murihiku* 1907:278.
61 *Commercial Journal*, Sydney, 14 March 1840.
62 Jane Thomson, Biographical note on *Hakena*, Internet website of the Hocken Library, University of Otago, Dunedin, 2007.
63 Rev. James Watkin, Waikouaiti Register of Baptisms, Burials, Marriages. Transcribed by C.D. Dean, Waikouaiti Library, New Zealand.
64 GK Thomson Papers, MS–0438/084, Hocken Library, Dunedin.
65 Frederick Tuckett, Diary, MSS Letters of Frederick Tuckett, 1841–91:215, Hocken Library, Dunedin.
66 Christie, 1929:64.
67 Registrar General, New South Wales: Deaths, V184779 32B/1847 Chaseling Thomas Age 78. Thomas Chaseling senior's gravestone in Wilberforce Cemetery states his age as 76 years.
68 Thomson Papers, MS–0438/097, Hocken Library, Dunedin.
69 Thomas Baker Kennard to Herries Beattie in *The First White Boy Born in Otago: Story of T.B. Kennard*, AH & AW Reed, Dunedin, 1939:48–9.
70 Bishop George Selwyn, visiting Ruapuke Island on 7 February 1844, noted 'Joseph Antonio, 1826, wife Esther Pura, children, 2 girls'; cited in Rhys Richards, *The Foveaux Sealing Yarns of Yankee Jack* …, Otago Heritage Books, Dundein North, 1996:102–3.
71 Birth and christening information, supplied by the Lutheran Church to the International Genealogical Index, Southwest Pacific.
72 Bluff area deaths and burials, Maori and European families. Transcribed by Colin Printz, Internet Website, 14 September 2009: http://freepages.genealogy.rootsweb.ancestry.com/~babznz/bluff.html
73 Shortland, 1851:150–1.
74 *Otago Witness*, Golden Jubilee Issue, 18 March 1908:55.
75 Sheila Nautsch, *The Cruise of the Acheron: Her Majesty's Steam Vessel on Survey in New Zealand Waters 1845–51*, Nestegg Books [1978] 1998:84, 86.
76 HMS *Acheron*, log, quoted in Howard 1940:392.
77 Captain John Lort Stokes, *The New Zealand Pilot*, London, 2nd ed. 1859.
78 James Wybrow, Senior, in Beattie, *Pioneer Recollection*, 1911:92.
79 Beattie in Richards, 1982:36.
80 Wybrow in Beattie, 1911:136.
81 GA Mantell, 'Notice of the remains of the Dinornis and other Birds, and Fossils and Rock–Specimens recently collected by Mr. Walter Mantell in the Middle Island [South Island]', *Proceedings of the Geological Society*, London, 27 February, 1850:336–7.
82 Taylor, 1855:238.

INDEX

ABORIGINAL AUSTRALIANS
Canoe culture and connection with sailing ships

PEOPLE

PLACES

SHIPS

CompuServe ID Inf

Write your CompuServe User ID here, so

_____

Don't write down your password here! Keep it somewhere safe!

WinCIM Icons

 Bring up your list of favorite places to visit on CompuServe.

 Search the online CompuServe directory for any topic you like.

 Bring up the Services window.

 GO directly anywhere on CompuServe.

 Get current stock prices.

 Check out the weather forecast.

 Search through your WinCIM In-Basket.

 See what you're waiting to send in the Out-Basket.

 Rummage through your categorized Filing Cabinet.

 Flip through your WinCIM Address Book.

 Log off CompuServe and exit WinCIM.

 Log off CompuServe.

 Look at waiting mail messages.

 Get some help.

 Print the current window directly to your printer.

 Save the current window into a file on your computer.

 Leave the extended services area.

tear here

que

Free CompuServe Support Forums

Here are some important forums you'll want to keep handy. They're the official CompuServe support forums, where you can get all your CompuServe questions answered, and they're free. The GO word is in parentheses.

New Members Forum (NEWMEMBER)   Everyone should stop by here to meet other CompuServe neophytes.

The Practice Forum (PRACTICE)   Test out most of the CompuServe features you'll find in all the forums.

CompuServe Help Forum (HELPFORUM)   Get all your general CompuServe questions answered here.

WinCIM Support Forum (WCIMSUP)   Where to go when WinCIM starts acting up.

CompuServeCD Forum (CCDSUP)   Talk about CompuServe's bi-monthly multimedia CD-ROM with support people and other subscribers.

CompuServe Windows Navigator Support (WCSNAVSUP)   Get some help on CSNav to automate your CompuServe connections here.

CompuServe Costs

Monthly Fees:	$9.95
Extended Fees:	$4.80/hour (Extended fees have a + by them)
Premium Charges:	Pay by the service—be careful, they add up quickly. (Premium fees have a **$** by them)
Clubs:	You get three hours of Internet time with your CompuServe membership, but if you find yourself using the Internet more than 9 hours a month, you can save money by joining the Internet Club. For $15 a month, you get 20 hours of Internet time (additional time is $1.95/hour). **GO INTERNET**.
	To join the CompuServe CB Simulator Club, **GO CBCL UB** and get CB hours for bargain basement prices.

Important Member GO Words and Information

GO PHONES to find a local access number on CompuServe.

GO PASSWORD to change your online password. Don't forget to change your password in WinCIM as well.

GO BILL to review your current and past charges.

GO RATES to get the most current pricing plan information.

GO WINCIM to download the latest version of WinCIM.

GO CANCEL to cancel your CompuServe membership.

Call CompuServe Customer Service at 1-800-848-8990 or (614) 457-8650 for help with the following:
- ➤ A forgotten password.
- ➤ WinCIM problems.
- ➤ Local access phone numbers.

Call Membership Sales at 1-800-848-8199 for help with the following:
- ➤ First time logon questions.
- ➤ Free CompuServe membership kits.
- ➤ More membership information.

The COMPLETE IDIOT'S GUIDE TO CompuServe

by Andy Shafran

que

Macmillan Computer Publishing
201 W. 103rd Street, Indianapolis, IN 46290

To Elizabeth Muska, who taught me when to take a break (if only she could teach herself).

©1995 Que Corporation

International Standard Book Number: 1-56761-607-0
Library of Congress Catalog Card Number: 94-73565

97 96 95   8 7 6 5 4 3 2 1

Interpretation of the printing code: the rightmost number of the first series of numbers is the year of the book's printing; the rightmost number of the second series of numbers is the number of the book's printing. For example, a printing code of 95-1 shows that the first printing of the book occurred in 1995.

Printed in the United States of America

Publisher
Roland Elgey

Vice President and Publisher
Marie Butler-Knight

Editorial Services Director
Elizabeth Keaffaber

Publishing Manager
Barry Pruett

Managing Editor
Michael Cunningham

Development Editor
Faithe Wempen

Senior Editor
Michelle Shaw

Copy Editors
Audra Gable
Howard Peirce

Cartoonist
Judd Winick

Cover Designer
Scott Cook

Designer
Kim Scott

Indexer
Rebecca Mayfield

Production Team
*Amy Cornwell, Anne Dickerson, Maxine Dillingham, Chad Dressler,
Amy Durocher, DiMonique Ford, John Hulse, Beth Lewis,
Paula Lowell, Kim Mitchell, Kaylene Riemen, Kris Simmons,
Scott Tullis, Jody York*

*Special thanks to Christopher Denny for ensuring
the technical accuracy of this book.*

Contents at a Glance

Introduction

Everybody's talking about "going online." It seems like everyone who's anyone has a computer, a modem, and an account on CompuServe. Millions of people are exploring the Information Superhighway daily and using CompuServe as their vehicle.

I can't exactly remember when I went online. It was probably a couple of years ago, right after I bought my first brand-new computer. I had just spent thousands of dollars on the latest technology, and I was ready to revolutionize my life. So, I took the new computer home, spent a couple of days trying to set it up, and then I was ready to go. After watching *War Games*, I knew that the fate of the entire world could be in the hands of me and my new computer (I played chess all the time to practice for this situation).

Back then, the only people who owned computers were scientists and computer geeks. You found the same people in the online world as well—online services were a way for people around the world to talk techie with other computer people around the world. CompuServe was much smaller back then. It was an information service for those who truly loved computers and could translate binary-to-English in their heads.

 **Binary** For those who aren't computer geeks, binary is a code of 1s and 0s that forms a computer's native language. Each number or letter is made up of an eight-digit code of 1s and 0s. It's nearly impossible for people to decipher.

Nowadays, things are much different. Almost everyone has a computer on his or her desktop. Still, most people don't fully understand the range of amazing feats a computer can perform. You've probably heard about all the fun things you can do with your computer and modem. If you're interested in learning about what CompuServe can do for you, you made a good choice in buying this book.

I remember my first time on CompuServe, and although I'm no idiot, I had some trouble understanding what was going on. I've written this book so you can have an easier time with it. Terms such as *online, log in,* and *chat* may seem like a foreign language to you now, but once you've had a little experience and some guidance, they'll start to show up in your everyday vocabulary.

Right now, you just want someone who will explain things to you in a way that 99 percent of the human population can understand. Stop your searching—you've found exactly what you've been looking for. This is *The Complete Idiot's Guide to CompuServe*. I've devoted this entire book to answering everything about CompuServe you really want, and need, to know. The first time I figured out this whole CompuServe thing, I was pretty excited, and I want you to experience that same enthusiasm. There really is a bunch of neat stuff on there.

How Can I Help You?

What can you do, armed with this book? Just about anything that CompuServe offers. This book gives you the basic survival skills to navigate CompuServe without breaking your bank account. You'll learn:

> ➤ How to become a CompuServe member, including what computer equipment you must have and complete directions for installing the software (included with this book) that lets you join.

> ➤ What types of stuff you'll find online and what services are available. Things such as forums, mail, news, entertainment, and reference information are on your plate, and I'll show you the proper way to devour them.

> ➤ How much you'll pay for all these wonderful opportunities. It's not cheap, but I don't think it's that bad a deal either.

All the software you need comes with this book. You'll find the most up-to-date version of the CompuServe Information Manager (CIM) for Windows, WinCIM, inside the back flap of this book. That means this book is all you need to become a CompuServe member. I'd say that's pretty convenient.

How to Use This Book

I don't expect you to read this entire book straight through. In fact, I'd be really surprised if you did. Instead, you'll probably want to use it to familiarize yourself with CompuServe. You can read the first few chapters, and then flip around through the book (no fair jumping to Chapter 22, "Games Galore," first). I've set up the book so you can jump from chapter to chapter and learn exactly what you want to know. Feel free to use the index and Table of Contents to lead you straight to the really interesting stuff on CompuServe, and skip the stuff you don't really want to know about.

But keep this book around, and look through it when you need to. I won't tell anyone if you decide to read it straight through, and you're bound to learn all sorts of neat tricks for using CompuServe.

Throughout this book, you'll find a lot of special tidbits of CompuServe-related information. Such as:

Don't Skip These Special bits of extra information, conveniently pulled out into boxes for easy reading. These extra bits give you all sorts of additional information about the subject you're learning. You'll find shortcuts, definitions of new words, or amusing anecdotes about my own experiences with CompuServe, so I'm sure you'll want to read them all.

Extra Info for Aspiring Techno-Nerds
If you're one of those people who wants to know all the techie little background details and special features, look for these boxes along the way.

Acknowledgments

There are a lot of people whom I would like to thank for helping me make this book possible. It may seem easy to write a Complete Idiot's Guide, but believe me, it was quite a chore.

Most importantly, I would like to thank Elizabeth Muska. She's been by my side throughout this entire project. Without her late-night cajoling, and strong personal opinion, I probably would have gone batty writing this book and going to school at the same time.

Of course, I would like to thank the team over at Que. Seta Frantz and Barry Pruett have been top-notch (even when I forgot the meaning of the word "deadline"), and are a real pleasure to work with. Without them, this book would have been just a twinkle in my eyes, and would never have seen the light of day.

Contents

Part 1
Getting Started

Out of all the neat and exciting things you can do with a computer and modem, CompuServe is one of the best. If you're brand new to the world of information services, you're probably ready to tear into CompuServe and see what you can find online. These first seven chapters will get you up and running and prepared for the really fun stuff to come later.

ON YER' MARK...

Chapter 1

The Least You Need to Know

In This Chapter

I know you're ready to dive into CompuServe and see what it really means to be online. There's a lot of information in this book, and I thought it would help if I tried to pick out some of the most important things you should know about CompuServe.

Everything listed here is discussed in depth later in the book; I just wanted to shed some light on what you need to know about using CompuServe. So unless you have other plans, let's get this show on the road. Here's what you can expect from CompuServe.

Expect to Become a Member

CompuServe is members-only, but it's very easy to become a member. Setting up your computer and modem is the hard part. If you've got a credit card and a pulse, CompuServe welcomes you to the world of online information. Using the software that comes with this book, you'll be up and running in no time. Chapters 3 and 4 take you through the software installation and sign-up process so you know what to expect when you call CompuServe for the first time.

Expect to Pay for Everything on CompuServe

This is a really important lesson that'll be hammered home throughout this entire book. Nothing on CompuServe is free. At the very least, you'll spend $9.95 a month for a standard, basic account. Realistically, you'll spend more than that. While you won't have to get a second mortgage to use CompuServe (probably), you can expect to spend more than $9.95 every month because most of the really good stuff is beyond Basic Services. You'll pay an extra $4.80 an hour to read messages about your hobbies and pick up a magazine or two online. Chapter 6 gives you all the information you need to know about how things are priced on CompuServe and how you can keep track of your bill.

Send E-Mail to Anyone You Want

Almost everyone I know has an e-mail account of some sort. Whether they're my friends on CompuServe or old buddies who have Internet e-mail addresses, I can talk to them as often as I want. I can't afford to pay AT&T to call them on the phone, but sending them CompuServe e-mail is a great deal. I get 90 e-mail messages free every month, and I only pay about a dime for each one above 90. Read Chapters 8 and 9 to learn about all the cool e-mail things you can do on CompuServe.

Hang Out with People from Around the World

CompuServe has about three million members just like you worldwide. Tons of people around the United States, Europe, and Australia are all online with you at the same time. You don't know whether you're talking to someone from Germany or your neighbor across the street (the language difference might clue you in). Use CompuServe conferences and the CB Simulator to make new friends and get to know them before meeting in person—if ever. I've actually seen several marriages come about this way.

Forget Your Newspaper

No longer do you need to worry about the morning paper accidentally dipping into your cup of coffee. With CompuServe, the newspaper is quickly going the way of the ditto machine. Almost every newswire around the world has a direct feed in CompuServe, and you can fulfill your current events cravings easier and faster online. Of course you don't get newsprint smeared all over your hands, but some things in life we just have to do without. Everything from the AP wire to weekly magazines makes its way to CompuServe, so be sure to stop by Part 3 of this book, "The CompuServe Newsstand," where I spend lots of time talking about news.

Have Fun

If having all this knowledge at your fingertips is beginning to hurt your head, don't worry—just take a look at Part 4 of this book, "Entertainment and Games." There are several chapters that talk about nothing but fun. With all the neat games, movie clips, and Hollywood gossip, you'll be able to relax in no time. Be careful that you don't become addicted to the games. Since you can play against other CompuServe users, every time you play you're in for a new treat. Heed this warning: once you start playing, it'll be hard to stop (unless you join Gamers Anonymous).

Become More Powerful

CompuServe won't build any major muscle groups, but if information equals power, CompuServe must make a lot of people very powerful. There's more information online than in most libraries. I know I talked about all the news a few moments ago, but news is just a small part of the information you'll find on CompuServe. Don't be afraid to search through the CompuServe warehouse of information about any topic under the sun. Chapter 24 talks about many of the different kinds of information you'll find online.

Surf the Net

CompuServe has everything you always wanted out of the Internet, but it's much easier to use. The hottest buzzword nowadays is *Internet*. Wherever you go, you find references to the "Information Superhighway." Look no further than CompuServe. You've got everything the Internet has to offer right at your fingertips. Stuff like FTP, Telnet, Usenet, World Wide Web, and e-mail are all a part of daily life with CompuServe. Their slogan is "Internet Made Easy," and I've yet to find an easier on-ramp to the information super-highway than CompuServe.

Safeguard Your Checkbook

Did I mention that you'll spend lots of money using CompuServe? I won't harp on this too much more, but keep an eye on your wallet when you're using CompuServe. For important money-saving tricks and techniques, check out Chapters 26 and 27 and learn how to use CompuServe Navigator and the CompuServeCD.

Find Your Own Corner

There's room for you on CompuServe, guaranteed. Not only is CompuServe a very weird-shaped building (with three million corners), but there are plenty of people with similar interests online. For every hobby, profession, and personal interest you have, you'll find a CompuServe message base that's just right for you. CompuServe is a booming metropolis with different shops and buildings on every street corner. It'll take forever for you to explore it completely.

Chapter 2

What Is CompuServe?

What Is CompuServe?

Think of the biggest library you've ever seen, and then imagine the largest mall in the world (which, of course, is that oversized supermall in the middle of Minnesota). Mix those two together and toss in your local community center. Add a newspaper or two and *Sports Illustrated*, and then sprinkle lightly with computer geeks. Voilà! You have the complete recipe for CompuServe—and no, I'm not exaggerating.

I like to think of CompuServe as a booming metropolis. Close to three million people use CompuServe for everything from shopping to romantic correspondence (Rush Limbaugh even met his wife through CompuServe). Whether you're a Trekkie or a stamp collector, there's a special place online for you (far away from Limbaugh, I hope). You can stop by a broker's office and cringe at the latest stock market quotes, or send a letter instantaneously to anyone across the world. After work, you can even head to a local "pub" where you can meet all sorts of people with similar interests. As in any other large city, there are plenty of things to see and do on CompuServe, and it would take forever to explore every little nook and cranny.

The only major difference between CompuServe and a real city is the type of people you'll meet. Because CompuServe is an exclusive club, you'll only meet CompuServe members. CompuServe's one membership requirement is money—but you don't have to be independently wealthy to join. Anyone who has a few bucks a month (and, of course, a computer) can become a CompuServe member.

I'll be your tour guide through the CompuServe city. As we go, I'll tell you which restaurants to eat in and where to shop, and I'll show you some of the trendiest night-spots. And since you're paying to use CompuServe, I'll give you tips on how to get more bang for your buck and cut costs with coupons and discounts.

In the Beginning

Take a seat and listen while I spin a little yarn. I'm going to tell you the story about when CompuServe was just a baby computer service, not the massive juggernaut that it is today.

Way back in 1969, in Columbus, Ohio, an insurance company decided they had too much money lying around, and they wanted to buy lots of computers to perform all sorts of data processing-type work (just think how expensive those computers were back then). So they created a subsidiary called CompuServe Network Incorporated. CompuServe Network hummed along in its own little world until it became an independent company in 1975. This little company provided online information to big companies around the world (the only people who could afford computers).

In 1980, H&R Block bought CompuServe because they wanted to create an online service for everybody with personal computers. They started out with a whopping 4,000 members. Like most companies, CompuServe thrived through the Reaganomic years, adding thousands upon thousands of new members every year. By the time it was 20 years old, CompuServe had bought its biggest competitor and had half a million users. The rest is history.

Today CompuServe includes nearly three million members, and that number greatly increases every month.

How Does It Work?

CompuServe is called an *online service*. "What the heck is that?" you might ask. "Some riveting religious experience?" No, an online service is a source of information. Using your computer, a modem, and your phone line, you can dial into CompuServe and get almost any kind of information you might need. You can access newspaper and magazine articles, talk with other people interested in classic automobiles, send mail to a buddy back home, or find out who played that little black-haired kid with the baseball cap on "The Little Rascals." CompuServe lays a world of information at your feet.

You can only access the information CompuServe holds when you're online or connected with your *modem*. But when you are online, the possibilities are endless. You can experience anything within the CompuServe city from your personal computer at home or at work.

Although you tie up your phone line when you use CompuServe, don't worry about your long-distance bill skyrocketing. There's a local CompuServe phone number in nearly every major city (and most minor cities) across the U.S., and there are thousands more around the world. Every local phone number connects you to the main CompuServe computers located in the "Heart of it All," Columbus, Ohio, so you don't have to support Ma Bell single-handedly. Unless you live in a very, very, very remote part of the country, there is probably a local CompuServe number for you to call. If not, there will be one soon.

A **modem** is a piece of equipment that enables your computer to call other computers using regular phone lines. The modem converts digital information (computer language) into analog information (phone language) and vice versa. Modems come in two varieties: internal, which you plug into an open slot inside your computer, and external, which you connect to the outside of your computer by a cable.

CompuServe makes it easy for you to log on with *CIM (CompuServe Information Manager)*. Back in the old days, connecting to CompuServe was a pain in the neck. You had to know all this incredibly detailed information about your computer and modem (parity, duplex, the list goes on and on) just to log on. Fortunately, in this modern day and age, you've got CIM to take care of all the details for you. And because CIM primarily uses the Mac or Windows interface, you can control it all with a mouse. You can explore the millions of CompuServe nooks with no problem, and you might even find some crannies, as well. See Chapter 3 for instructions on installing CIM on your machine.

Why You Should Be Online

Nowadays, it seems that everyone who's anyone is getting hooked up online. Almost every magazine, business, and organization is represented electronically, and even President Clinton has an e-mail account. And if Newt Gingrich has his way, everything Congress does will soon be available to those of us who take the plunge and jump online.

You can't afford to be left in the dust. Think how bad you'll feel if Congress makes it online before you do. As a general rule, the government is usually about 20 years behind the rest of the public. (That's why I don't worry about my loans. If the government doesn't have to, why should I?)

Why am I online? Because it really helps me keep in touch with the outside world. I like to stay up with current events, and for me, CompuServe is the easiest way to do that. I can send e-mail to my friends and get a response in a few moments (think how much Federal Express would charge for that!), and I can talk to computer companies directly if I have a problem; almost all of them have accounts on CompuServe.

Why Join CompuServe?

There is a handful of other online services out there, and you may have heard of them. They run around with cute names such as PRODIGY, GEnie, Delphi, and America Online. Honestly, they can't compare with CompuServe. CompuServe has been around for well over 25 years and is the biggest, best, and cheapest service available.

In addition, I'm sure you've had the phrase "Information Superhighway" pounded into your skull a million times. Well, when you sign up with CompuServe, you're tossed right in the middle of the road. You get all the benefits of the Internet with your CompuServe membership.

As I've already stated, CompuServe tries to make it as easy as possible to get online. Most of the people on CompuServe are very friendly, and there are tons of CompuServe employees who can help you out if you get into a jam. (On the other hand, if you get lost on the Internet, you're more likely to become roadkill than to find a good Samaritan.) Unfortunately, CompuServe is so big that you probably need a road map to figure out where you're going. Consider this book your friendly atlas to everything you want to do on CompuServe.

The **Internet** is a loosely organized network of computers all around the world. Through the Internet, approximately 20 million users (most of whom have nearly no idea how to use the Internet) can communicate with each other. But that's another book; pick up *The Complete Idiot's Guide to the Internet* if you're interested.

Some Neat Things You Can Do

When you visit New York City, there are a lot of neighborhoods you can wander through. With Chinatown, Little Italy, Central Park, and Wall Street, you can engage in a variety of activities—and you certainly have an excellent chance of being mugged. Just like New York City, CompuServe consists of several different subdivisions. The only differences are that on CompuServe, these sub-divisions are things you can do, and you're less likely to be mugged.

Downtown CompuServe

CompuServe is basically pure information. I log onto CompuServe every day to read the Associated Press newswire and a whole host of other things. Popular magazines such as *Fortune*, *U.S. News & World Report*, *People*, and *Sports Illustrated* all come out on CompuServe weekly. There's also an entire library of reference information online. In addition to the traditional mundane resources (encyclopedias and dictionaries), there's financial information on thousands of companies and a magazine article database that contains the complete articles from thousands of magazines.

But that's not even the best part. There are nearly 1,000 discussion forums that cover almost every topic imaginable, from fly fishing and stamp collecting to home repair and human sexuality. You name it, and CompuServe's got it. Included in the 1,000 forums are nearly 500 computer-related message forums. Almost every major software company has its own discussion forum for its software products. You'll find stalwarts such as Apple, Lotus, IBM, and Microsoft mixed in with hundreds of other companies (even the publisher of this book: Macmillan Computer Publishing). If you need computer help or just want to talk about a hobby, you'll find a forum for you.

Constant Communications

I wouldn't be doing CompuServe justice if I didn't mention the endless ways in which you can meet and talk to other people. Of course, there's e-mail—that wonder of modern technology that beats your U.S. postal carrier any day of the week. With e-mail, you can send a letter to millions of people connected to CompuServe and the Internet around the world, and it will get to them within minutes or hours.

Sometimes you just want to relax and hang out. If so, check out the CB channels on CompuServe. Just like a trucker, you can pick your own handle and start chatting. There are well over a hundred topics to choose from (most of them adult orientated), and people chat in there all day and all night.

After Hours

For some strange reason, America is obsessed with Hollywood. I don't know if it's because of the grandeur of the silver screen or simple jealousy of the salaries, but we suck up movie reviews, Hollywood gossip, and entertainment information better than all the Hoover vacuums combined.

If entertainment is what you want, CompuServe will satiate even your wildest fantasies. You can find movie reviews, movie clips, and movie star pictures in an entire section of CompuServe centered around the entertainment industry.

And of course, there are lots of games. Trivia, role-playing, military, and board games are all available for a price on CompuServe.

Personal Servants

We all wish we could afford our own travel agent, stock broker, or weather forecaster, but most of us can't. Only people like Ross Perot and Bill Gates can afford to own their own financial institutions; the rest of us have to scour around to get that info.

If you hate going to the travel agency and planning a trip with someone who looks (and acts) like a shark, use CompuServe, instead. There are a couple of online travel systems that let you plan a trip from start to finish—without budging from your seat.

Do you ever wonder if your local weather forecasters predict the weather using a Ouija board? Why bother to watch the news? I often find the farmer's almanac more believable than the local forecast. With CompuServe, however, you can get the current and forecasted weather for any major city around the world—psychic free.

And since the stock market seems to vary with the weather, it makes sense to have an online broker, too, doesn't it? I use CompuServe to keep track of my personal portfolio of stocks (one share in IBM that my grandparents gave me when I was four years old). You can get up-to-the-minute stock prices and information for any stock, bond, or mutual fund.

Leave CompuServe on the Subway

The hottest word in the computer industry today is the Internet. Everyone is worried about getting hooked up to the Internet or sending e-mail over the Internet. Internet *this* and Internet *that*—that seems to be all I read about. Realizing that everyone wants to use the Internet, CompuServe enables you to do pretty much anything related to the Internet that you want.

For example, using CompuServe, you can take advantage of such resources as newsgroups, FTP, Telnet, e-mail, Internet forums, and World Wide Web. I realize none of these things mean much to you now, but it won't be long before you'll be dropping those terms as often and easily as you say your own name.

Pay to Play

There's no such thing as a free lunch: everything you do on CompuServe costs money. Although you pay a monthly fee (around $10) that is automatically charged to your credit card up front, there are approximately 100 cool things included with this monthly charge. Sports, news, weather, travel, and financial information are all available at no extra cost. However, the vast majority of information resources you'll seek on CompuServe cost extra. You pay around $5 an hour to browse through any of the thousand or so discussion bases or to transfer a new file to your computer.

If you're careful and don't waste time, CompuServe can be quite a bargain. There's almost nowhere else in the world you can get so much information in one sitting. But if you're not careful, you'll quickly learn why CompuServe's nickname is Compu$erve. In the past, I've racked up hundreds of dollars worth of bills (when I was a CompuServe addict; I'm better now, thanks for asking). Since I know you're not rich, I'll spend a lot of time talking about costs and how you can avoid or at least minimize them.

CompuServe Quiz

So you're ready to tear into CompuServe (or you're completely confused with what the heck an information service really is). To test you, I've prepared this short quiz. Don't worry, you won't be graded.

1. What is CompuServe?

    a) A large Norwegian bird that mates only once a century.

    b) A little, friendly robot whose goal in life is to serve you complimentary drinks (like the servers in Las Vegas).

    c) A huge vat of information that you can tap into with your computer and modem.

2. How expensive is CompuServe?

    a) Cut up your credit cards now.

    b) You'll quickly learn what loan amortization means.

    c) Only $10 a month plus lots of extra nit-picky charges.

In case you guessed wrong, both answers were c. I just wanted to make sure you could tell the difference between a Norwegian bird and CompuServe. Such information comes in handy occasionally.

The Least You Need to Know

Now that you've finished this chapter, you're probably ready to start checking out all the cool things I mentioned. But keep in mind the following CompuServe facts:

➤ All you need is a computer, modem, and credit card to jump onto CompuServe.

➤ CompuServe is the biggest and best information service available.

➤ You're on the Information Superhighway because with CompuServe, you have direct access to the Internet.

Chapter 3

Installing CompuServe

In This Chapter

➤ Do you have the right equipment?

➤ Installing CompuServe Information Manager

At this point, you're probably shaking with anticipation, you're so anxious to log on to CompuServe. Maybe you're eager to send e-mail to your cousin in Budapest or to check out the daily soap opera summaries.

But first things first. Before you can go off exploring, you have to make sure you have the right equipment to use CompuServe, and you have to set up and install the software correctly.

The Right Equipment

Before you can start using CompuServe, you need to make sure you have the right equipment. Here's a handy checklist for what you need:

➤ Computer

➤ Modem

➤ Telephone line

➤ Electricity (or a pet gerbil that can run in its exercise wheel *really* fast)

➤ CompuServe membership kit (or this book)

➤ Credit card (preferably yours)

A Word About Computers

You can access CompuServe from nearly any computer made in the past 20 years. That means you can even pull out your rusty old Commodore 64 and talk to people in Germany about your favorite strudel recipes. However, I give one word of caution: just because these old computers *can* work with CompuServe doesn't mean that you *should* use them.

WinCIM Short for Windows CompuServe Information Manager; software specifically designed by CompuServe to make it easier to access all the types of online information. Besides WinCIM, you can also get DOSCIM, MACCIM, or OS2CIM for other operating environments (DOS, Macintosh, and OS/2 respectively). With WinCIM, you have all the software necessary to connect to CompuServe. No additional communications software is required.

I recommend you use an IBM compatible (running DOS, Windows, or OS/2) or a Macintosh because CompuServe makes special software for those computers. Using that special software (CompuServe Information Manager or CIM), you can access everything in CompuServe in an organized and graphical way.

Throughout this book, I use WinCIM, CompuServe's software for IBM compatible computers running Windows. The other versions (for DOS, Mac, and OS/2) work in much the same way the Windows version does. I strongly recommend that you use CIM to access CompuServe. It not only will save you a lot of time and money, but also a lot of hassle. I'll tell you all about CIM in a moment.

For the benefit of those who can't—or don't want to—use a version of CIM, I'll also briefly explain how to log on to CompuServe "plain" (that is, without special software) in Chapter 4. But take my word, you'll probably regret it.

A Word About Modems

A modem is one of the important ingredients in this entire process. It doesn't really matter if you have the newest model computer. The speed and ease with which you communicate with CompuServe depends mostly on the speed and capability of your modem.

What is a modem? It's a device that converts computer data to audio signals that can be sent across phone lines, and then converts them back to computer data at the other end. Through a modem, your computer can talk with CompuServe's computer, so that CompuServe's computer can transmit information onto your screen.

There are lots of brands and types of modems you can get. The brand name is not all that important, but the speed is crucial. Since you pay for each minute you are connected, a faster modem lets you get more information more quickly so you don't have to be on CompuServe as long. And since CompuServe charges you the same amount whether you log on with a fast modem or a slow one, you are much better off using a fast modem.

I recommend that you buy a 14,400 bps modem. They're cheap and pretty much the standard nowadays. For more information on modems, look for *The Complete Idiot's Guide to Modems and Online Services*, by Sherry Kinkoph.

Unfortunately, CompuServe doesn't support 14,400 baud modem access all over the world. In some places, you can connect with only 9600 baud, and in others, only 2400. In general, if you live in a big city, 14,400 access is available (28,800 access is almost ready as well). Small towns and places with sparse populations will most likely have only 2400 or 9600 baud access.

> **bps** Short for bits per second; a measure of how many bits of data are transferred. Each letter on the keyboard represents approximately one byte (8 bits). Graphics and images can easily comprise several hundred thousand bits per picture.

Regardless of the fastest service you can get, I recommend that you buy a 14,400 baud modem anyway. Why? There are three reasons.

➤ A 14,400 baud modem is only $20–30 more expensive than a slower modem. You may have other uses for your modem than CompuServe, and the additional investment is worth it.

➤ A 14,400 modem can access any slower modem (2400 or 9600, for example) if necessary, but a 2400 baud modem can't access a faster modem.

➤ CompuServe is slowly upgrading its 2400 and 9600 baud modems to 14,400 (and faster). Sooner or later, you will have local 14,400 baud access.

A Word About Membership Kits

Sorry Amiga Users I called CompuServe and asked if they had or were planning a CIM for the Amiga. After the customer service representative stopped laughing, he told me they recommend using a Mac or IBM to access CompuServe because they encourage using CIM to log on.

You may think you're ready to call into CompuServe just because you have a computer and a modem—but you're not quite ready yet. You need to get what CompuServe calls a membership kit. This membership kit includes all the necessary information for signing up with CompuServe. They'll assign you a user number, give you a password, and provide you with a list of all the CompuServe phone numbers. And, most importantly, nearly all membership kits come with a version of CIM. As I mentioned above, there are several versions of CIM, and it's available for both the Macintosh and IBM compatible.

Fortunately for you (if you're a Windows user, that is), this book comes with everything you need to connect with CompuServe, including WinCIM. Although you won't get everything that comes with a full-fledged membership kit, all the essentials are included. However, there are two reasons you may want to get the full membership kit.

1. If you want all the CompuServe manuals that I mentioned above, and/or

2. You're not a Windows user, and you want CIM for your computer.

There are two ways to go about getting the full membership kit.

➤ **The expensive, immediate-gratification way:** Go to your favorite computer store and buy one. Mine cost $25.99 and included one month of usage, $25 worth of credit, and CIM (they have kits for Windows, Macintosh, DOS, and OS/2).

➤ **The thrifty way, for patient people:** Call 1-800-848-8199. After maneuvering through the automated phone system, you can have CompuServe mail you a membership kit for free. That's right, absolutely FREE. Amazingly, it also includes one month of usage, $25 worth of credit, and CIM. The only drawback is that you have to wait 7–10 days to get it in the mail. (I only had to wait three days.)

I was really annoyed when I found out I had wasted $26 for the exact same kit I could have gotten free if I had called first. Since it's free, I suppose it doesn't hurt to have CompuServe send you a kit in the mail. But don't buy one—unless of course you have money to burn.

Installing WinCIM

Installing WinCIM is a relatively painless process. Here's a step-by-step guide to installing WinCIM on your personal computer. CompuServe likes to change the installation process every few months, so my steps may not match your installation exactly, but I'm sure they'll be close. Let's go!

For Mac, DOS, or OS/2... In this book, I've assumed that you are running Windows. If you use a Macintosh or a personal computer that uses only DOS or OS/2, you'd better use one of the two methods I described previously to get a membership kit for your machine.

1. Turn on your machine and start Microsoft Windows.

2. Insert the disk from the back of this book (labeled WinCIM, Version 1.4) into your disk drive.

3. Open the **File** menu and choose **Run**. The Run dialog box appears, as shown below. Type **a:\setup** (substitute the drive letter of your disk drive for *a* if necessary), and click on **OK** to begin the installation process.

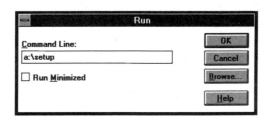

Run the Setup command from your WinCIM disks.

4. After a few moments, the WinCIM installation screen appears, asking where on your hard drive to install WinCIM (see the figure on the next page). CompuServe recommends the default directory unless you have a really, really good reason and know exactly what you're doing. If you're not sure, just click on **OK**, and WinCIM is installed in the C:\CSERVE subdirectory.

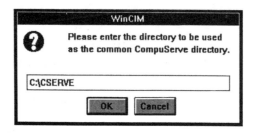

Unless you're a Windows guru, just hit OK to move on.

Did you see the Pause and Exit icons in the bottom-right corner of the Installation screen? You can click on them anytime during this installation process if you need to.

5. Next, WinCIM wants to know if you want to install the sounds that come with it. You might as well choose Yes, because you can turn them off anytime in the future. I thought they were pretty neat at first, but they got on my nerves after a while.

6. Now CompuServe wants to know if you're already a member. Since you probably aren't, click on **Yes** to install the sign-up files necessary to join CompuServe.

7. A few moments later, CompuServe finishes installing WinCIM. However, you now need to sign up for your new CompuServe membership. Click on **Yes** to sign up now. If you prefer to sign up later, click on **No** now. You can sign up later by double-clicking on the **Membership Sign Up** icon.

8. If you clicked Yes to sign up now, the Installation process starts the CIM Signup program. Open the **Signup** menu and choose **Sign Up** (see figure below).

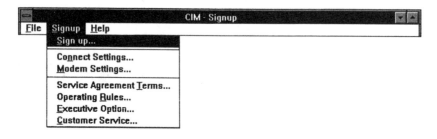

Click on Sign up to become a member now.

9. Next, you see the Signup - Billing/Country dialog box, as shown below. This is where you enter the billing information. You'll find the agreement number and serial number for your membership on the card included with the disk at the back of this book. Type those numbers in their respective boxes. Then select the country you are calling from and indicate whether this account is for business or personal use (different billing options are available for business use).

10. The last choice you have to make here is for a payment method. As you can see, you can choose to have CompuServe automatically charge any of multiple credit cards, ranging from AMEX to VISA. At the bottom of the list is Direct Debit. This means that CompuServe will take your charges directly from your checking account. Some people like this, and others don't. I like to be billed on my VISA instead of paying automatically from my bank account. If you want to pay by direct debit, you'll need your checking account number (found on the bottom of your checks).

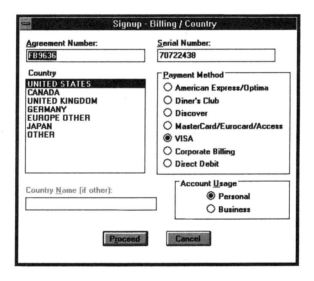

Paying by credit card is the easiest choice for me.

11. Now it's time to get personal. In the CIM - Signup dialog box (see the figure on the next page), type in your name, address, and phone numbers, pressing **Tab** to move between fields. Then type in your credit card or direct debit information. (That's not my real number, so don't even try.)

12. Select or deselect the check boxes of the four options described here. By default, they're all selected, but you may not want them all. Make your choices and click on **Proceed**.

Membership Options	Description
CompuServe Magazine	Sets up a subscription to the monthly CompuServe magazine. It's free, and it's pretty nice; you want to keep this one.
Member Directory	Controls whether you are listed in the CompuServe's equivalent to the telephone White Pages. Other CompuServe members can look up your name to see if you are online. Unless you are a celebrity, you probably want this too.
Promotional Mail	Puts you on a mailing list to receive information about special CompuServe deals and opportunities.
External Mailings	Enables CompuServe to sell your name and address to other companies so you hear about their special deals and opportunities. (I don't mind this because getting mail makes me feel important. But you might.)

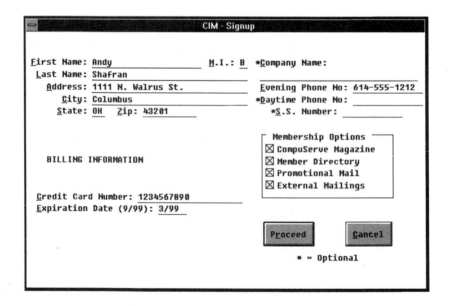

Give CompuServe all your personal information.

13. Do you want to be part of the Executive Service Option? Some services online are available only to those who have this option. However, this option is now free with all CompuServe memberships (as of February 1995), so just click on **Yes** and move on. Sooner or later, CompuServe won't even ask you this question.

14. The next dialog box gives you CompuServe's legal spiel. Basically, these terms outline what you can and cannot do online. I'd read them over, but there are no hidden clauses that make you lose your first-born child or anything like that. Click on the **Rules** button to see explicit rules. You can print them if you want, but I'd just click on **Proceed** and move on.

15. Unless you live *way* out in the middle of nowhere, you probably have a touch-tone phone. Click on **Touch Tone** and click on **Proceed**.

16. The next dialog box (see the figure below) requires you to know something about your computer setup. Modems connect to computers by way of communications ports located at the back of your computer. If you know for sure which port your modem is connected to, click on the corresponding button and click on **OK**. If not, click on **Auto-Detect** and click on **OK**.

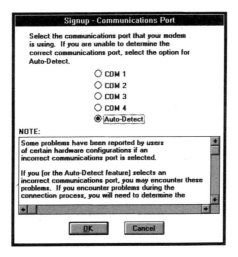

If you're clueless, try Auto-Detect.

17. The next step is my favorite part. CompuServe calls up a 1-800 number with your modem and registers you as a member. All the personal information is sent to CompuServe, and your membership info is sent back. You'll see the Welcome! screen, as shown on the following page.

18. Once all that information is sent to CompuServe, you must agree to be charged monthly for CompuServe use. You'll pay $9.95 a month (which is subject to change) to do close to a hundred different cool things, and you'll pay extra for everything else. Again, you can print the rules (this time they might be more useful). If you don't agree with these pricing terms, click on **Cancel**.

19. Eventually, you'll be asked to type **AGREE** in the box in the bottom left-hand corner. Do it, and then click on **Proceed**.

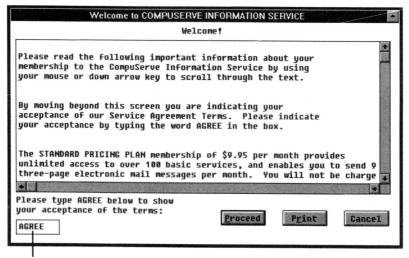

Type AGREE here.

More rules and regulations to wade through.

20. After you agree to the pricing terms, CompuServe shows you your user ID, default password, and local access numbers (see the figure on the next page). Write these down and store them somewhere safe! CompuServe automatically conveys all this user information to WinCIM so you don't have to type it. However, you want to

Check out Chapter 7 for a way to get up to $15 additional usage credit.

have a copy of this information just in case you need it. This password is temporary, a new one will be mailed to you by U.S. mail in a week or so.

Oh, by the way, notice the $15.00 usage credit? That's pretty nice of CompuServe, don't you think? Once you've written everything down, click on **Proceed** to go on.

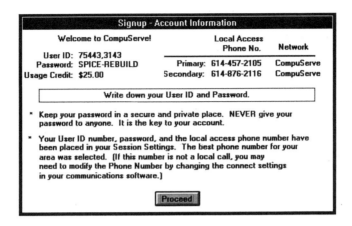

This was my default Signup info. Don't worry, I changed the password.

21. In the next dialog box (shown below), you confirm that you've seen your user ID and password. Type them into the appropriate boxes and click on the **Finished** button. When CompuServe tells you that you've typed everything correctly, click on **OK** to continue.

Confirm your ID and password by entering them here.

22. Hooray, you're done! CompuServe displays some more information for you about your local access number, with instructions for choosing a new one if necessary. Click on **Print** to print the information for future use, and then click on **Done**.

When you're finished, you'll see a program group in Windows (shown below) that contains the CompuServe icon (which you'll click on the next time you want to use CompuServe) and an icon for Membership Sign Up (which is what you just went through).

You'll click here when you're ready to log on to CompuServe.

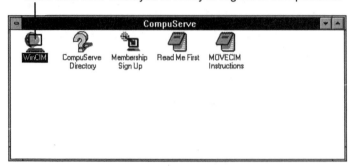

CompuServe Windows icons and stuff.

In a week or so, you'll get your permanent password in the mail. Until then, you won't be able to use some of the expensive features of CompuServe. But that's okay—you probably didn't want to use them anyway.

If you have any problems with this process, call CompuServe's Membership Support Office at 1-800-848-8199. They're really friendly and will help you out quite a bit.

The Least You Need to Know

➤ All you need to log on to CompuServe is a computer, a modem, and this book.

➤ If you're running Windows, this book has all the software you'll need. If not, you can get a free membership kit for the Mac, DOS, or OS/2 by calling CompuServe directly.

➤ Installing WinCIM is pretty easy, but be careful of how you choose to pay your bill and the options you select.

Chapter 4

Your First Sign-On

In This Chapter

➤ Getting around in WinCIM

➤ Logging on without CIM

➤ Using the Interneet to access CompuServe

➤ Logging off CompuServe (when it's time to get on with your life)

You just spent most of the previous chapter installing CIM on your computer. Now it's time to start using it.

Most people use WinCIM (or MacCIM, or OS2CIM, or DOSCIM) to log on to CompuServe, rather than logging in "plain." But if you aren't running a CIM of any type, don't despair. There's hope for you, as well. You can pretty much log on to CompuServe with any computer made, as long as you've got a modem and your own communications software. You can even log on through the Internet.

If you use CIM, you don't need to worry about the second half of the chapter—just focus on the CIM part.

Your First Login: Drumroll Please

If you've installed CIM (see Chapter 3), you're ready to roll. If not, go back there and do the installation first.

To begin with, make sure you have your used ID and password handy. During the WinCIM installation and signup process, every new user on CompuServe is assigned an ID. Remember? I made a big deal about writing it down back in Chapter 3. This ID consists of two sets of numbers separated by a comma. Your ID looks something like this:

75443,3143 (that's mine)

You'll want to keep track of your CompuServe ID—it's very important. You use your ID for logging on and as your mailing address for receiving electronic mail. Along with your ID, you'll also get a password assigned to you. Your password will look something like:

star*ship

Limbaugh!Stern

Of course, you can change the password to almost anything you want (CompuServe has a few general rules about passwords). Make sure you store your ID and password in a safe place, where nobody else can find them. See Chapter 6 for more information on your password.

No 8s or 9s?

Did you notice that your CompuServe ID has no 8s or 9s in it? That's because CompuServe uses *octal* numbers when assigning user IDs. Octal numbers run from 0 to 7. (If you had "the new math" in high school, you might remember something about base-10 arithmetic, base-12 arithmetic, and so on. Octal numbering is the same thing as base-8 arithmetic.) In the octal world, the number 11 translates into the familiar decimal (base-10) number 9. CompuServe uses octal numbers because, way back when CompuServe started, their systems were octal-based.

Your First Time On

Once WinCIM is installed, you're ready to go. Since the installation process takes you through most of the administrative overhead like getting your credit card, registering your address and personal info, and selling your soul to the devil, there's nothing holding you back. Think of buying a new car. First you go to the dealership and pick out the 1979 Chevette of your choice. Then you have to sit down and fill out three reams of papers. But once you're done, you can just drive the car right off the lot.

It's a Local Call By the way, the installation also automatically figures out which local telephone number CompuServe should call.

From your Windows Program Manager, double-click on the **CompuServe** program group to open it. Then double-click on the **WinCIM** icon from the CompuServe program group to start your WinCIM's engine (see figure below).

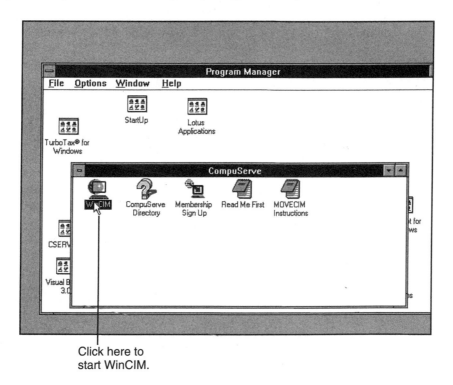

Click here to start WinCIM.

Click on the WinCIM icon to get going!

The first time you start WinCIM, you'll see the default Connect to CompuServe box. This box comes up automatically every time you start WinCIM unless you deselect the **Show at Startup** check box.

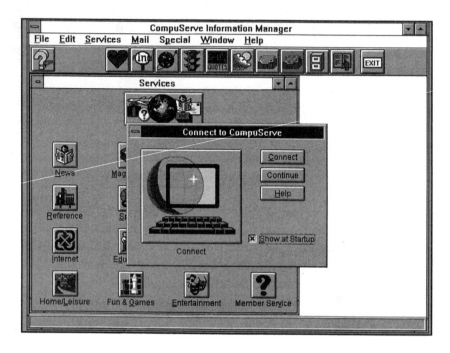

Unless you're legally blind (and even then, I'd wonder), you can't miss the default Connect icon.

I got rid of this initial Connect to CompuServe dialog box immediately. Let me tell you why. This is your basic WinCIM screen. See the 17 icons in the Window labeled Services? Clicking on any one of these icons automatically calls CompuServe up and logs you on. Similarly, many menu commands you select from the menu bar will log you on to CompuServe, as well.

Not only does CompuServe log you on, it also shows you a window of available CompuServe services in the category you've clicked. Click on the **Entertainment** icon. Observe how WinCIM automatically dials, connects, and logs on. This is why I like WinCIM. It is the ultimate tool for a lazy bum like myself. So you don't need the Connect to CompuServe box.

Taking a Look at the WinCIM Screen

Now that you know how to start WinCIM, check out the figure below to see what all the different parts of the window do. I'll describe how to use WinCIM in more detail in Chapter 5, "Getting Around in CompuServe."

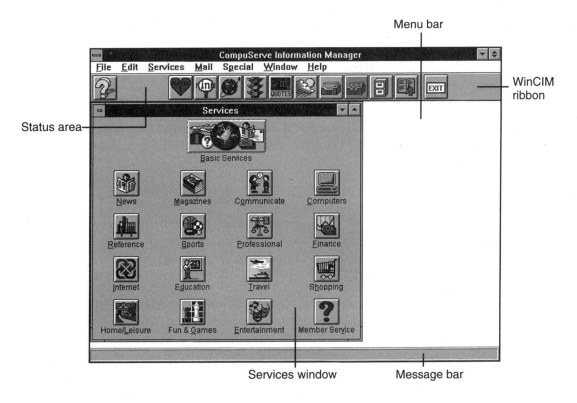

You should get to be familiar with the basic WinCIM screen.

Part	Function
Menu bar	Use the menu bar to access all the WinCIM commands.
Status area	When you're logged on, use the status area to see how long you've been connected.
Ribbon	Click on an icon on the ribbon to quickly execute a command or jump to a feature.
Message bar	Look here for messages about e-mail and extended services.
Services window	Click on an icon to see one of CompuServe's 17 service areas.

Glutton for Punishment: Logging On Without a CIM

This is the only chapter in which I'll ever mention using CompuServe without CIM. It's difficult, and not many people do it. But just in case you're in a position where you have to connect this way, I thought I should mention it.

There are several reasons why you might want to connect to CompuServe without a CIM program. Maybe you have a really old computer that doesn't accept DOS, Windows, OS/2, or Mac software. Or maybe you bought a specialized computer (for instance, a Sun workstation) which doesn't have a special version of CIM made for it. Or maybe you just hate graphical interfaces. Whatever.

Almost any computer ever made can connect with CompuServe. Whether you use an Apple II, Commodore 64, or Kaypro (with the 8-inch disk drives), if you've got a modem, a credit card, and a basic communications (modem-dialing) program for your computer, you're set.

Instead of the pretty CIM interface, everything appears as text, in plain old black-and-white. There are no icons to click on, and your mouse won't work, but all the information is still the same. You can still read the news, get the weather forecast, and participate in discussions about the merits of vegetarianism.

What You Need to Connect

I can give you only a sketchy outline of how to log on to CompuServe this way, since everyone's communications program, modem, and computer are different. But in general, here's what you need:

➤ A computer system

➤ A modem

➤ Communications software (installed and working with your computer and modem)

➤ A basic knowledge of how to use your computer

➤ A CompuServe membership kit, or at least a user ID and password

You can use practically any communications software in the world, as long it works with your computer and modem. I've used Procomm, Qmodem, and a handful of various communications programs, and they all work just fine.

The best way to get info about using CompuServe without CIM is to call the following number: 1-800-848-8199. The CompuServe representative will probably suggest that you buy a new computer, but try to convince him or her to send you a membership kit anyway.

Occasionally, you might find membership kits without CIM included in computer stores, but that's becoming less common everyday. Your best bet is to call the 800 number and get a free kit. Besides, if you're using a 10-year-old computer, waiting another week or so won't hurt you.

Connecting the Non-CIM Way

Once you get your membership kit, you'll probably want to rush right home and try it out. Rest assured, complete directions for logging on to CompuServe for the first time are included in the membership kit.

Just like with WinCIM, CompuServe sends you a membership kit with an ID and a temporary password. This membership kit does not come with your own communications software (WinCIM). You'll need your own software package to get your computer and modem to work together and call CompuServe.

Once you have your membership kit and communications software, follow the instructions in the kit for how to log on. It goes something like this:

1. Have your communication software dial the telephone number specified in the startup kit.

2. When you connect, answer all the questions it poses by typing your answers into the computer.

3. At one point, you'll be given a local access number, which is the number to dial the next time you want to connect. (It'll save on your long-distance bill.) Write it down.

4. Later, you'll be given a user ID and temporary password, if one wasn't included in your membership kit. Write these down, too. About two weeks later, you'll receive a permanent password in the mail.

CompuServe estimates over 80 percent of its members use CIM, so they don't spend an overwhelming amount of time worrying about non-CIM access. If you get stuck, give them a call on the 800 number, but don't expect the parting of the Red Sea when you call.

The figure below shows a sample screen from a non-CIM CompuServe connection.

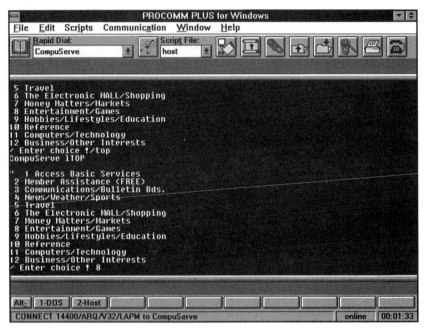

With just text, CompuServe can be pretty dull.

Connecting Through the Internet

If you're already hooked into the Internet, you'll be pleased to know that you can access CompuServe by Telnet. If you have no clue what I'm talking about (like most of us), don't worry.

But if you know how to use the Internet and want to access CompuServe through the real Information Superhighway, enter the following command after you've logged into your Internet account.

TELNET COMPUSERVE.COM

Then at the Host Name: prompt, type

CISAGREE

CISAGREE is a shortcut to log on quickly. Type CIS for the long way.

Then you'll be asked for the modem speed of your Internet connection. Type **14400** (or whatever speed you connect at) and press **Enter**. After that, you'll be asked for your CompuServe ID. Type it, and press **Enter**.

Finally, you'll be asked for your User ID password (see figure below). When you type, you'll notice that the characters don't appear on-screen. That's so your friends peering over your shoulder don't borrow your CompuServe account and take it for a spin (on your credit card).

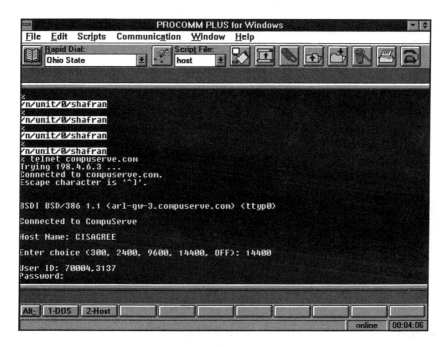

A successful Telnet logon is just my User ID password away.

That's it—now you're on. Remember, you pay for CompuServe whether you access with WinCIM, generic communications software, or the Internet. I like using the Internet to log on to CompuServe occasionally, but it's all text-based. I like the graphical interface much better, so I usually just stick with WinCIM.

35

Logging Off CompuServe

Eventually, you'll want to log off CompuServe and get on with your regular life. Of course, you've probably maxed out your credit card finding new things on CompuServe, but that's the price you've got to pay for technology.

If you're like me, and you hate long and tearful goodbyes, then just pull down **File** from the menu bar and choose **Exit**. WinCIM will disconnect you, and return you to your regularly scheduled program.

Sometimes you might want to log off CompuServe, but not leave WinCIM. In that case, pull down **File** from the menu bar and choose **Disconnect**.

Since I'm lazy, I just use the WinCIM icons on the ribbon to disconnect and exit WinCIM (see figure below). I bet you can't guess which icon exits WinCIM. I'll give you a hint: it says EXIT.

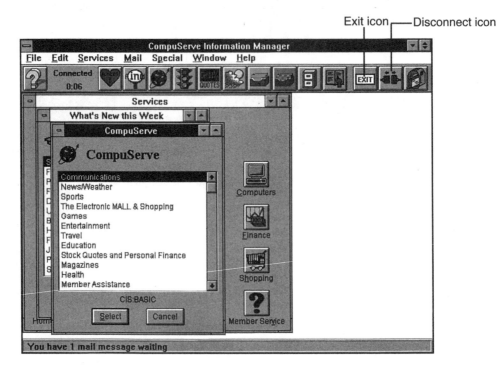

How to leave WinCIM or log off CompuServe.

The Least You Need to Know

Welcome to the electronic world of CompuServe. In this chapter, you learned how to log on to CompuServe from CIM, from a regular communications program, and from the Internet. In the interest of saving you money, I also taught you how to log off.

Remember these things:

Logging Off Without a CIM
If you're not using CIM to access CompuServe, there's no neat icon you can click, but the textual command is pretty easy to remember. Just type **/BYE** at any CompuServe prompt and press **Enter**, and you'll be disconnected.

➤ Your CompuServe ID is your own personal, unique ID number that also doubles as your mailing address.

➤ Wherever you live, there's bound to be a local access number for CompuServe. Call 1-800-848-8199 to find out what it is.

➤ WinCIM has several icons that you can click on to make it easier to accomplish common tasks (such as accessing the weather, stocks, and logging off).

➤ To log on to CompuServe through the Internet, you should be familiar with the Telnet command.

➤ Connecting to CompuServe without CIM isn't too difficult if you know the ins and outs of your modem and communications package—but it's not quite as pretty.

G'WAN PAST THE MODEMS, OVER PAST THE CD ROMS, AND UP THE HARD DRIVES A PIECE. YOU CAN'T MISS IT...

Chapter 5

Getting Around in CompuServe

In This Chapter

➤ Issuing basic CIM and CompuServe commands

➤ Moving among CompuServe's services

➤ Searching CompuServe for information on a specific topic

➤ Getting the latest version of the CIM software

I'd *like* to tell you that CompuServe developed the CompuServe Information Manager (CIM) to make the service easier to use. It would be nice to think CompuServe decided to invest millions of dollars in this product just to make our lives a little bit easier, wouldn't it?

But in fact, CompuServe didn't have such altruistic motives. It was simply a business thing. CompuServe's two major competitors (PRODIGY and America Online) had developed their own customized Windows software, and they were leaving CompuServe in the dust. So CompuServe got busy and developed CompuServe Information Manager—CIM for short—for the Macintosh, DOS, Windows, and now OS/2.

Today, almost everyone who uses CompuServe uses CompuServe Information Manager. In fact, CompuServe even discourages new users from accessing CompuServe by using any other communications software. When I called them pretending to be "Jim the

Focus on WinCIM Since Windows CIM (aka WinCIM) is the most popular of the variations, we'll focus mostly on it, but the other versions work basically the same way.

Amiga user," their customer service rep actually recommended that I buy a new computer to use CompuServe. Amazing.

CIM is pretty easy to use, no matter which version you're working with. Whether you're familiar with Windows or another environment, CIM should be a snap. However, because of the way CompuServe works, there are some interesting quirks that need extra explanation. That's what this chapter is about.

Finding Your Way Around

Have you ever tried giving a friend directions to your house over the phone? There are lots of ways you can send them. The shortcut (the way you travel yourself) winds through a maze of one-way streets with no street signs. The easy way takes twice as long, but it's completely idiot-proof.

Using WinCIM to go from place to place in CompuServe is like that: there are several ways to move around. I'll start you out with the most generic way (the "easy route"), and then I'll teach you the shortcuts.

Cruising the Services Window

In my opinion, the best part of WinCIM is the Services window. The Services window contains a number of icons that help you quickly find what you want (see figure below).

CompuServe's main categories.

Me, I'm a news buff, so I want to look at the News options first. Click on the **News** icon, and you'll see the News window. Remember, if you're not logged on when you select one of the Services icons, WinCIM automatically calls and connects you to CompuServe.

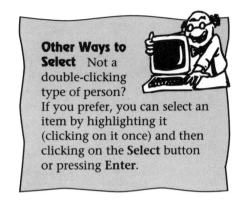

Other Ways to Select Not a double-clicking type of person? If you prefer, you can select an item by highlighting it (clicking on it once) and then clicking on the **Select** button or pressing **Enter**.

In the News window (see figure below), you have a whole bunch of news-ish items to choose from. If you see one you're interested in, all you have to do is double-click on it to select it. If you're not in the mood to pursue any news items right now, press **Esc** or click the **Cancel** button to close the News window.

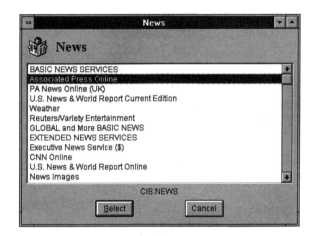

The News window pops up when you click on the News icon.

I like to wander through the various groups of services (but I generally stay away from finances and shopping since I don't make enough money to invest or shop). Through the Services window, you can access practically everything CompuServe has to offer. But if you're in a hurry, wandering around can become tiresome. For example, let's say you're looking for Joyce Jillson's astrology column, one of the syndicated columns CompuServe has online. To go through the Services window, you would have to click on the News icon and wade through several other windows to get there. Stepping through the Services icons will make you feel like you're on a ladder—climbing slowly one rung at a time.

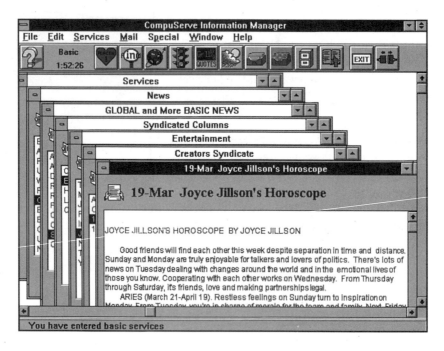

You're here, but look at all the windows you had to open.

Finding Joyce Jillson's Column

In case you're interested in that last reference, here's how you would actually go about finding Joyce Jillson's column by wading through all those menus.

Click on the **News** icon in the Services window and double-click on **GLOBAL and More BASIC NEWS**. Double-click on **Syndicated Columns** and double-click on **Entertainment**. Then double-click on **Joyce Jillson's Horoscope** to see your weekly psyche with the stars, and *another* window comes up. Finally, you can pick which week's horoscope you want to read and double-click on the column you want to read.

Now that I've been using CompuServe for a while, though, I find that I seldom use the Services window. Instead, I like to use GO words to move directly to my destination.

GOing from Here to There

Don't you hate navigating through those annoying automated phone systems? You know, the ones where you push 1 for customer help, 2 for complaints, or 3 for death threats? Sometimes it seems like you have to make hundreds of selections to get where you want to go, and even if you call the same place time and time again, you still have to go through the entire system.

You'll probably feel the same boredom and frustration when you access CompuServe through the icons in the Services window. You may know exactly where you're going, but you have to navigate through a maze of six or seven windows to get there. Well, the people at CompuServe took that into consideration. And although they didn't create CIM simply because it would make your life easier, they did include one feature that does just that: *GO words*.

Nearly every single service on CompuServe has a unique identifying name. This name, usually referred to as a GO word, enables you to jump from one point in CompuServe to another instantaneously (or at least as instantaneously as your modem will let you). Whether you're reading e-mail or browsing through a discussion, you can always just GO somewhere else.

The Origin of GO

GO words were originally thought up when CompuServe was a text-based system. Since no one had even heard of a mouse, much less Windows, GO words made it easy for CompuServe users to jump from one part of the information system to another without getting lost.

To use GO, click on the **Go** icon on the WinCIM ribbon (the one that looks like a traffic light). When you do, the Go dialog box pops up (shown below), asking you for the unique word of the service to which you want to go. Type the special GO word and click **OK**. For instance, if you want Joyce Jillson's column (sorry to be harping on that, but I'm an astrology buff), start out with the GO word "columns." The Syndicated Columns screen will appear, as shown on the next page.

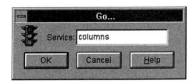

Jump directly to the list of columns.

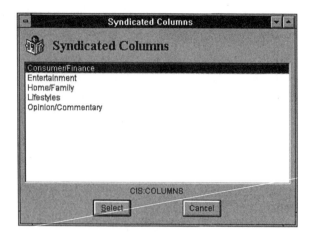

The GO word appears right above the Select and Cancel buttons.

What's the GO Word?

See the text right above the Select and Cancel buttons in the Syndicated Columns Window? That's the GO word for that window. Write down important GO words as you wander through CompuServe so you can get back to that location any time.

One really cool thing about GO words is that they work even when you're not logged on. Let's say you have WinCIM open but you're not connected to CompuServe. If you click on the GO icon and type a GO word, CompuServe automatically calls and logs you on and then immediately jumps to the service you requested.

In essence, you never really have to use the Connect dialog box that I mentioned in Chapter 4 (the one you access with the really BIG icon). Every time you open WinCIM, you can either click on one of the icons in the Services window or use one of the GO words you've memorized. Then zoom! You're off to the service.

A Few of My Favorite Places

If your memory is half as bad as mine, I'm sure you forget unimportant things like GO words all the time. Sure GO words make it easier to find your way around CompuServe, but they can also be confusing and difficult to remember—especially if you don't use them all the time.

Lucky for you (and me!), you can keep a list of your favorite places to visit in CompuServe. In the Favorite Places window, you can easily mark a particular forum or column (like Daily Soap Opera Summaries) for future reference.

To open the Favorite Places window, pull down the **Services** menu and select **Favorite Places** or click on the **Favorite Places** icon (the one with a heart on it) on the WinCIM ribbon. The Favorite Places dialog box appears with a number of places already listed (see figure below).

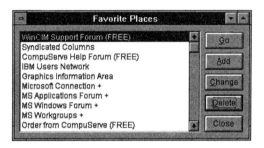

By default, the Favorite Places dialog box already lists several common CompuServe locations.

To go to one of the places, just double-click on it. You're whisked to the place you've selected, and the Favorite Places dialog box disappears. You can even open your list of Favorite Places when you're not logged on. As soon as you select a place from the list, CompuServe dials the number, logs you on, and jumps you to the chosen place.

Another Way to Go Instead of double-clicking on a favorite place, you can single-click on it and click the **Go** button.

Although CIM comes with several preselected favorite places, you can change them if they're not *your* favorites. And, of course, the real benefit of keeping track of your favorite places is that you can add your own to the list. That way you won't have to write down GO words or remember the cumbersome path you have to take to maneuver through the CompuServe Services windows.

To add an item to your Favorite Places list, first travel through "normal" channels (the Services window or the GO word) to that service. Then click on the **Favorite Places** icon on the WinCIM ribbon. Click on the **Add** button in the Favorite Places dialog box, and another dialog box pops up with the name of the service you just travelled to already filled in (see the following figure).

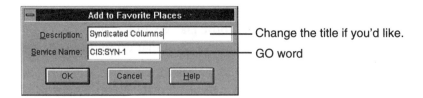

Change the title if you'd like.

GO word

It's psychic! CompuServe fills in the Add to Favorite Places boxes automatically.

You can change the title to be anything you like (I just left mine Syndicated Columns). The GO word should already be filled in correctly. Click on the **OK** button, and this is added to your list of Favorite Places (see figure below).

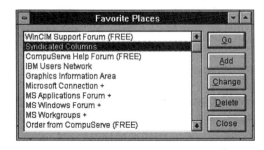

Syndicated Columns is right there in my list!

GO Word Variations Some services have more than one GO word. For example, to get to Syndicated Columns you can use the GO word CIS:SYN-1, but CIS:COLUMNS also works. And what's CIS:, you may be wondering? Well, *CIS* stands for *CompuServe Information Service*, the full name of CompuServe. In most cases, you can leave out the CIS: part of the GO word, and it won't make any difference.

Strictly speaking, you don't have to travel to a service before you add it to your Favorite Places list. Just open the Favorite Places list at any time, click on **Add**, and delete whatever appears in the blanks, if anything. Then type the correct description in the Description box and the correct GO word in the Service Name box. Click on **OK**, and you're done.

As you add your own favorite places to the list, you'll probably want to delete some of the default ones that you never use. To do so, open the Favorite Places dialog box, click on the entry you want to delete, and click the **Delete** button. CompuServe asks you to verify the deletion in order to make sure you're not accidentally deleting a valuable entry.

Of all the ways to access the different pieces and parts of CompuServe, I use the Favorite Places box the most. It's easy to manage my personal list of favorites, and I don't have to remember GO words.

What's the Best Way to Get Around?

Since there are so many ways to access the same information through WinCIM, I let the following three rules guide me:

➤ If I am just browsing around looking for neat things to do, I use the icons in the Services window. I don't care how many steps it takes because I'm just exploring.

➤ If I hear about a specific service that I want to try out immediately, I use the GO word. That way I don't have to hassle with finding it through the hierarchy of CompuServe Services.

➤ If I think I'll visit the sample place over and over, I add it to my list of favorite places. I don't have to worry about remembering the GO word or finding my way back again—I can just get there with a couple of mouse clicks.

Sleuthing for Subjects

Since there are thousands of things to do on CompuServe, sometimes it's hard to find a specific topic just by browsing. For this reason, one of WinCIM's best features is that it enables you to search all of the services CompuServe offers for a specific topic.

Let's say you're interested in comic books. You used to read *Superman* as a kid, and you wanted to find other comic book fans like yourself. If you start browsing through the icons in the Services window, you might not even know where to start. Comic books could conceivably be found under Entertainment, Fun & Games, or Home/Leisure. It's possible that you might find a comic book dealer in the Shopping area, and there's even a case to be made for placing comic books in the Education category (all right, so I'm stretching a little bit). Regardless, you could spend a lot of time (and money) just looking to see if CompuServe even has a special place online for comic book fans.

Never fear, loyal comic book fanatics! If there is such a place, you can find it with the Find command. With Find, you enter a subject, and CompuServe comes back with a listing of every-thing that pertains to that topic.

Search Adventures
Every time I try to find a topic, I get interesting surprises. One time I was searching for "Fish" (for no reason whatsoever), and I found out that CompuServe has a newswire service that collects articles about pets. Pets!!!

To use WinCIM's Find command, open the **Services** menu and choose **Find** or click on the **Find** icon (which looks like a magnifying glass over the word "Find") on the WinCIM ribbon. The Find dialog box appears (as shown below), in which you type the topic about which you're looking for information.

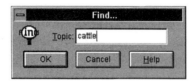

Enter the topic you're searching for in the Find dialog box.

This time, let's see if CompuServe has anything for people interested in cattle. Type **Cattle** to see if CompuServe has any information that's of the bovine nature. Then click the **OK** button. CompuServe searches through its database and displays all the subjects related to cattle in a Search Results dialog box, as shown below.

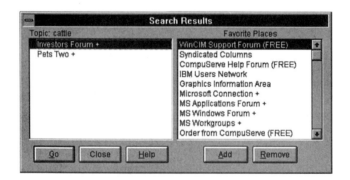

I knew investors were called "bulls," but this is ridiculous.

The left side of the window shows the results of your search. Conveniently, the Search Results window also contains your Favorite Places list, so you can put the results of your search directly into your list of favorite places to visit if you want to. To add a topic from the Search Results to your Favorite Places list, just click on it to select it and then click on the **Add** button. A check mark appears to the left of the topic in the Search Results list to indicate that you've added it to your Favorite Places list (see the following figure).

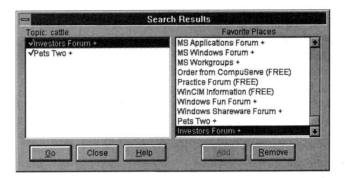

I added the two entries on the left to my list of favorite places.

I use Find all the time. As you can tell, sometimes it doesn't give you the best results, but it's usually pretty comprehensive. After searching for Cattle, however, we know that CompuServe isn't the source of choice for bovine information.

Help, WinCIM, Help!

I have a confession to make. No matter what program I am using, I never use the built-in Help. Instead, I just complain to my friends about how the stupid program doesn't work, or I just forget about the entire situation completely.

Therefore, you'll find that this is a classic case of "do as I say, not as I do." Just because I'm stubborn doesn't mean that you have to be. WinCIM has just about the best Help system I have ever seen in my life. It actually answers the questions I have. You really should use it.

Let's take a simple example. If you want to follow along, make sure you're looking at your plain old WinCIM screen with just the Services window open. Are you ready? Okay, press F1 on the keyboard or click on the **Help** icon (the big yellow question mark) on the WinCIM ribbon.

The WinCIM Help screen pops up, displaying a smaller version of the Services window. Now move your mouse over the icons in the Help window. See how the mouse changes from a pointer to a hand? If you click when the mouse looks like a hand, the built-in Help feature gives you more information on a subject. For example, click on **News,** and you'll see a description box with lots of helpful information about CompuServe's News area (see the following figure).

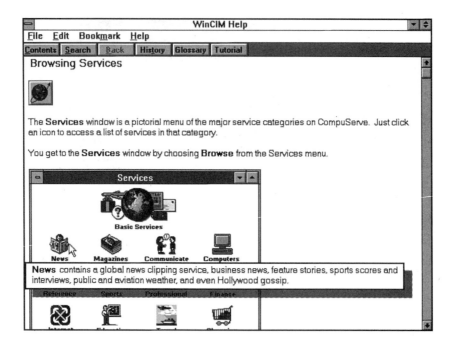

WinCIM gives information about CompuServe's News area.

Notice how you can click on every icon? I think that's downright cool. And you'll find that in almost every screen and dialog box you come across in WinCIM, you can just push F1 to figure out exactly what each icon or button does.

To get out of Help, open the **File** menu and choose **Exit**. You'll be returned to your regular WinCIM screen, where you can apply your new knowledge.

Don't Neglect Your Connection!

One of my worst vices is my impatience. I hate sitting around idly, waiting for something to happen. CompuServe is the same way. If you're logged on but don't send a command for 15 minutes, CompuServe sends you a reminder that you're neglecting it.

Sometimes it's pretty annoying when WinCIM lets you know you haven't done anything for 15 minutes. No matter what you're doing in Windows, WinCIM yanks you back for a moment to make sure you want to stay logged on (see the following figure).

```
┌─────────────────────────────────┐
│ ▬            Warning            │
├─────────────────────────────────┤
│   You have been idle for too long!  │
│                                 │
│        CompuServe will be       │
│         Disconnecting in        │
│           49 Seconds            │
│                                 │
│  ┌──────────────┐ ┌───────────┐ │
│  │Stay Connected│ │ Disconnect│ │
│  └──────────────┘ └───────────┘ │
└─────────────────────────────────┘
```

Even WinCIM gets lonely after 15 minutes.

If you've simply forgotten that you're logged on, this handy reminder is useful (especially if you were in a discussion forum that costs $4.80 an hour). If that's the case, click on the **Disconnect** button in the Warning dialog box. You're logged off CompuServe immediately.

On the other hand, if you meant to ignore CompuServe because you were doing something else in Windows, click on the **Stay Connected** button. You won't be bothered by WinCIM for another 15 minutes.

Updating Your CIM

As is true of any other software product, new versions of CIM are released all the time. As I'm writing this book, the current version of CIM is 1.4, but I'm sure a new version will have been released by the time you read this. Don't worry, though. Once you're a CompuServe member, upgrading is simple and doesn't cost you anything. You can *download* new versions of CIM whenever you want.

Download To use your modem to copy a file from a computer far away. When you download from CompuServe, you ask CompuServe to send a file to your computer where you can store it.

Here's a quick overview of how to get the newest version of CIM. On CompuServe, use the GO word **WINCIM**, **MACCIM**, **OS2CIM**, or **DOSCIM**, depending on which version of CIM you are running. The CompuServe Information Manager dialog box appears, as shown in the following figure.

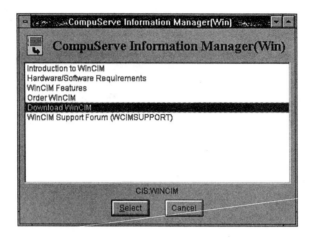

Here's my WinCIM window.

From here, select **Download WinCIM**. You'll enter another window that guides you through the download process. Eventually, you'll transfer one file from CompuServe to your personal computer. Then you'll get to install the new version of WinCIM onto your computer. Don't worry; CompuServe guides you through this entire process because they want you to have the latest and greatest version of CIM possible.

The Least You Need to Know

In this chapter, you became close friends with WinCIM. I showed you how to find your way around CompuServe and how to use a few neat features that help you keep track of its services. I'll talk a lot more about WinCIM and how to use it in various situations (such as sending a letter to Santa Claus) in future chapters.

➤ You can wander aimlessly through CompuServe by clicking on the icons in the Services window.

➤ Every service has a secret GO word to make it easy to access.

➤ You can search CompuServe for just about any topic imaginable to find information you need.

➤ WinCIM Help is neat and can really help you out when you're confused.

➤ You can get the latest version of the software by using the GO word WINCIM, DOSCIM, MACCIM, or OS2CIM (whichever's appropriate).

Chapter 6

Routine Maintenance: Prices, Passwords, and Phone Numbers

In This Chapter

➤ Which pricing plan is right for you

➤ Pretending you're from the IRS and auditing your bill

➤ How to keep your password secret

➤ Finding a new local access number

Once you know the WinCIM basics, you may feel empowered—but hold on to your hat for just a minute. Just as there are things you need to do to maintain your car, there are some basic things you need to do to maintain CompuServe. Although I don't have to know how to change my oil or flush the radiator (someone else can do that), I do have to know how to change a flat tire, pay my car insurance, and make my monthly car payment. There are similar maintenance facts you should know about CompuServe. Follow along and learn some basic CompuServe tips that everyone should know.

How CompuServe Services Are Priced

The best way to keep your costs down while using CompuServe is to understand how you are billed for the various services you use and to minimize the amount of unnecessary time you spend in the extra-cost areas. What's an extra-cost area? Well, it depends on your pricing plan.

There are two types of billing/pricing plans available on CompuServe; they are creatively titled "standard" and "alternative." The vast majority of CompuServe users have the standard pricing plan, so I'll tell you about it first.

The standard plan is pretty straightforward. It's easy to understand and not too expensive for most of us. I suppose if you're like Al Gore and spend every waking moment on the Information Superhighway, even the standard plan will get expensive. But fortunately (or unfortunately), not many of us are like Al Gore.

The Basic Services

Under the standard plan, you pay $9.95 a month for unlimited access to the Basic Services, which covers approximately 100 areas online. These include such areas as e-mail (up to a certain point), news, and the encyclopedia (where you can find out that lemmings are small, furry creatures that fall off cliffs). CompuServe likes to call these 100 services "free," but I know that clever marketing ploy won't trick you. Don't overlook the fact that you're paying well over a hundred bucks a year for these "free" basic services. (Personally, my definition of free is just a little bit different.)

Here's a quick list of some of the best basic services included with your monthly fee:

AP news

U.S. News & World Report online

National Weather Service reports

Regular stock quotes

CIM support

Eaasy Sabre travel reservation service

Online dictionary and encyclopedia

Roger Ebert's movie reviews

Several online games

The electronic malle

Subscription to CompuServe's monthly magazine

E-mail (you can send 90 3-page e-mail messages a month)

3 hours of exploring the Internet

There's Always a Charge Even if you don't log on to Compu-Serve during a given month, you'll still be charged the $9.95 monthly fee. "Wait a second," you might say. "I didn't even use CompuServe during the entire month!" Too bad. You pay $9.95 whether you log on every day or never. So don't just stop using CompuServe and forget about it (which isn't likely, anyway).

I think CompuServe's Basic Services are a great deal. I check the news and my e-mail daily. If you're not an information-hungry lunatic, you can probably get by with just the 100 or so basic services. But what's included in the basic services isn't even the tip of the iceberg of what's available online. To get the full picture, you have to delve into the extended and premium services, too (which are still a part of the standard pricing plan).

Extra Cost 1: Extended Services

Nearly 1,000 message *forums* ranging from computer-related topics to personal hobby topics are available online, and almost every one of them costs extra to access. Message forums are the heart of the information on CompuServe. That's where CompuServe makes most of its money (and where you can spend nearly all of yours). In addition to message forums, the extended services include a real-time CB system that enables you to chat simultaneously with hundreds of people.

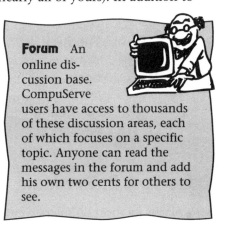

Forum An online discussion base. CompuServe users have access to thousands of these discussion areas, each of which focuses on a specific topic. Anyone can read the messages in the forum and add his own two cents for others to see.

Each extended service has a plus sign (+) after its name. To see an example, in WinCIM's Services window, click on the **Magazine** icon. (If you aren't logged on, CompuServe automatically logs you on.) The Sports dialog box appears, listing all the sports areas you can access online. As you can see in the figure below, *Sports Illustrated* magazine online is an extended service.

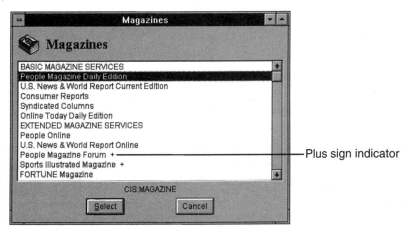

See what extended services are available online.

Anytime you access an extended service, you will be charged an extra $4.80 per hour. For example, if you choose to read *Sports Illustrated* online, you'll pay $4.80 an hour to read the magazine. (This isn't exactly a bargain; you can pick it up at the newsstand for $2.95 and spend as much time reading it as you want.) All extended services cost $4.80 per hour extra, so be careful to watch for those plus signs (they are all clearly marked).

Current Rates

Although the current Compu-Serve rate for extended services is $4.80 an hour as of today, that could change by the time you read this book. Use **GO RATES** to get the most current pricing information.

The Internet Club

Today, everyone is interested in exploring the Internet; luckily, CompuServe includes three hours of time on the Internet in your monthly $9.95. If you're an Internet freak, however, you'll want to check out CompuServe's special Internet pricing plan. **GO INTERNET** for more information.

Extra Cost 2: Premium Services

Access for most online reference material sources is priced differently from that of the basic and extended services. CompuServe includes all sorts of reference databases for topics ranging from AIDS to recent legal decisions. But instead of pricing them per hour of use, CompuServe charges you per article you read. Services charged this way are the premium services.

Anything labeled with a dollar sign ($) is a premium service and is priced a certain amount for each article you read. This means you pay by the article. Each premium service charges a different amount, but they're usually clearly labeled. For example, check out the Magazine Database Plus reference library (**GO MAGDB**), shown in the following figure. This is a big database that includes complete magazine articles from tons of magazines from the past nine years. Using Magazine Database Plus, you can find and read online magazine articles about any topic imaginable. Be careful, though. Each magazine article you read costs $1.50. So if you searched the magazine database for Reaganomics and read all the articles that came up, you'd probably be charged something near our national debt.

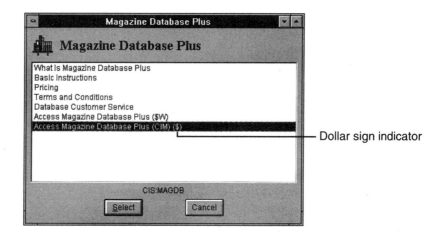

Premium services cost a bundle, but their information is top-notch.

Miscellaneous Money-Eaters

Almost everything you'll encounter on Compu-Serve falls into the basic, extended, and premium services categories. But there are a few other ways to spend your hard-earned money. One excellent example is the CompuServe Mall. The Mall comprises approximately 100 stores in which you can buy everything from Levi's to bug repellent.

When you shop in these stores, you see items and buy online, but you'll usually pay a premium for the convenience. I'll talk more about the Mall later on, but I just wanted you to identify it as a consumer of your hard-earned cash.

It's Not Cheap!
Remember that most of this information is available in your local library, but you'd have to get dressed and go there to get it. If I need something quickly or can't find it elsewhere, I'll use a premium service. But I can't afford pre-mium services on a regular basis.

The Alternative Pricing Plan

In addition to the standard pricing plan (which I described earlier), CompuServe has another plan called the alternative pricing plan. Although most people go with the standard plan (that's why it's called "standard"), this plan might just be a good deal for someone out there. So let me explain how it works.

Under the alternative plan, you pay $2.50 a month for administrative charges, and after that nearly everything you do costs extra. You pay up to $22.80 an hour when you're logged on (whether you are reading mail or sifting through a forum), and each e-mail message costs about a dime on top of that.

There are only a handful of services that don't cost extra; they are very clearly labeled "FREE." To see an example of this, click on the **Communicate** icon in the WinCIM Services window. The Communicate screen will appear, as shown below. It doesn't cost extra to access the areas that are labeled FREE, but there aren't many.

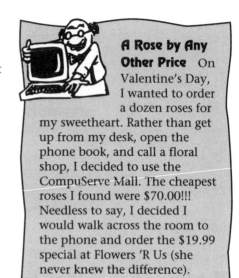

A Rose by Any Other Price On Valentine's Day, I wanted to order a dozen roses for my sweetheart. Rather than get up from my desk, open the phone book, and call a floral shop, I decided to use the CompuServe Mail. The cheapest roses I found were $70.00!!! Needless to say, I decided I would walk across the room to the phone and order the $19.99 special at Flowers 'R Us (she never knew the difference).

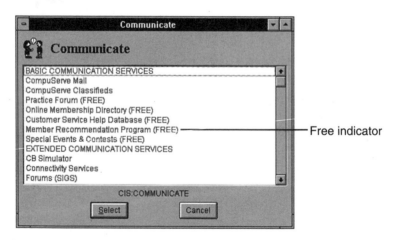

Add up all the FREE stuff, and you don't have much.

Some alternative, huh? To be quite honest, I really don't understand why there is an alternative pricing plan—or who in their right mind would use it. The only scenario in which I foresee it being useful is if you needed to stop using CompuServe for several months, but you didn't want to cancel your account. Suppose, for example, that you were going to the Arctic Circle for a year but didn't want to lose your CompuServe User ID. You could switch to the alternative pricing plan and pay only $2.50 a month instead of $9.95 a month. Then you could change back to standard pricing when you returned and started using CompuServe regularly again.

Unless you know what you're doing, don't switch to the alternative pricing plan. Chances are, you'll just end up messing up your bill and paying more money than you should have.

Switching Pricing Plans

By default, your new CompuServe account is set up with the standard pricing plan. Avoid the alternative pricing plan like the plague: it's bad news. However, if you absolutely have to switch from one pricing plan to the other, use **GO CHOICES** from WinCIM. The CompuServe Pricing Plans dialog box appears, as shown below.

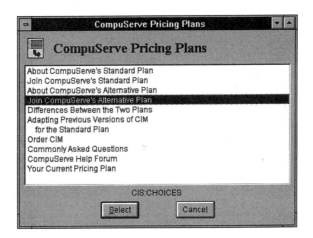

Swap pricing plans here.

To change to the alternative plan (the Arctic Circle is calling), double-click on **Join CompuServe's Alternative Plan**. An information window labeled CONVERSION appears. Now don't get me wrong, CompuServe doesn't care what religious faith you are; they just want to make it easy for you to switch between pricing plans. After you've read the conversion info, click on **Proceed** to continue. The next dialog box that appears asks you to type **AGREE** if you want to join the alternative service or **EXIT** if you don't. Type **AGREE** and click **OK** to join the alternative pricing plan (or click on **Cancel** if you regain your senses—or cancel your trip).

If you want to switch back to the standard pricing plan, **GO CHOICES** and choose **Join CompuServe's Standard Plan**. You'll have to go through the same rigmarole (click **Proceed** in the CONVERSION window and type **AGREE** and click **OK** in the resulting dialog box).

Settling Your Bill

No, I'm not referring to the President; he's busy gnashing his teeth with Congress, and only Hillary has to settle him. I'm talking about your monthly bill from CompuServe. Even though CompuServe is a benevolent company, you'll probably want to understand how their billing policies work.

Unless you're a business, there are two ways CompuServe likes to bill. Either they automatically withdraw your monthly charges from your checking account, or they bill the credit card of your choice (make sure it's yours, or you might get into some hot water).

When you sign up with CompuServe, you select a default billing method. Most people have CompuServe automatically bill their credit card (that's what I did). Personally, I don't like the idea of someone else automatically withdrawing some random amount of cash from my checking account every month. It's not that I don't trust CompuServe, I just want to see the billing every month on my credit card statement. That way if I notice a $600 charge, I know to be a little suspicious. Besides, I have to pay my credit card every month anyway, so it's not like I'm paying a separate bill if I charge CompuServe to my VISA.

Checking Your Balance

Some people like to track everything they do that costs them money and itemize those expenses all along the way. Others, like me, never care how much something costs unless we happen to notice an exceptionally high charge. I suppose I should check my VISA statement every month, but if I even look through the itemized bill, I pat myself on the back.

If you want to get a crystal clear view of your CompuServe bill, use **GO CHARGES**, and the Review Your Charges dialog box appears, as shown below. In this window, you can check out how much you currently owe CompuServe, see whether you're within the allotted number of "free" e-mail messages (about 90 a month), or even get a complete session-by-session history of everything you've done on CompuServe for the past 12 weeks. You can also check out the status of any CompuServe *Clubs* and monthly charges you accrue.

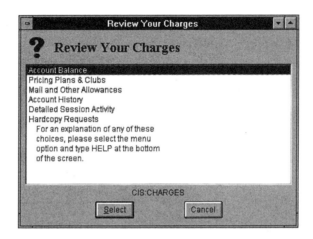

I wonder if Bill Gates tracks himself here.

Double-click on **Account Balance** to see how much you currently owe. You'll see a screen like the one shown on the following page with a comprehensive breakdown of charges, purchases, credits, and so on. CompuServe updates these numbers on a weekly basis, so depending on the day of the week, your most current account information may or may not be available.

A **club** is like a frequent flyer card for some part of Compu-Serve. For example, if you chat on the CompuServe CB system a lot (it costs $4.80 an hour because it's an extended service), you can join CupCake's CB club and get a big discount on your hourly CB fee. Of course, joining a club costs money, as well.

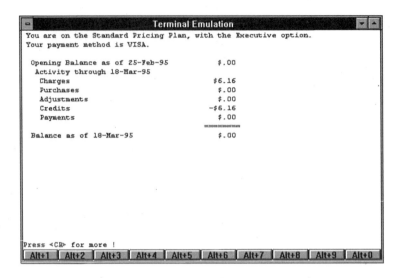

My monthly balance is pretty low so far; not bad for a slow week.

Press the **Enter** key to see the next page of your account history. Once you've seen your entire balance, CompuServe takes you back to the Review Your Charges window.

See Your History

Some people like to know exactly how and where they've spent their money. That's why CompuServe offers a detailed account history. You can scan through your CompuServe bill one week at a time to see where you spent your money. To do so, in the Review Your Charges dialog box, double-click on **Detailed Session Activity**. CompuServe displays a week-by-week list and the total amount you spent that week (see the following figure).

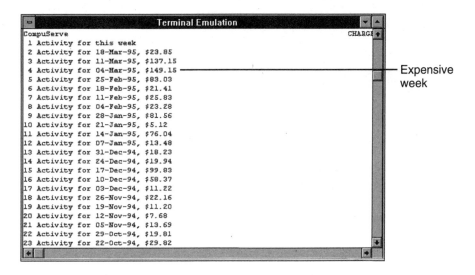

```
─                          Terminal Emulation                    ▼ ▲
CompuServe                                                   CHARG ↑
  1 Activity for this week
  2 Activity for 18-Mar-95, $23.85
  3 Activity for 11-Mar-95, $137.15
  4 Activity for 04-Mar-95, $149.15 ──────────────────────── Expensive
  5 Activity for 25-Feb-95, $83.03                               week
  6 Activity for 18-Feb-95, $21.41
  7 Activity for 11-Feb-95, $25.83
  8 Activity for 04-Feb-95, $23.28
  9 Activity for 28-Jan-95, $81.56
 10 Activity for 21-Jan-95, $5.12
 11 Activity for 14-Jan-95, $76.04
 12 Activity for 07-Jan-95, $13.48
 13 Activity for 31-Dec-94, $18.23
 14 Activity for 24-Dec-94, $19.94
 15 Activity for 17-Dec-94, $99.83
 16 Activity for 10-Dec-94, $58.37
 17 Activity for 03-Dec-94, $11.22
 18 Activity for 26-Nov-94, $22.16
 19 Activity for 19-Nov-94, $11.20
 20 Activity for 12-Nov-94, $7.68
 21 Activity for 05-Nov-94, $13.69
 22 Activity for 29-Oct-94, $19.81
 23 Activity for 22-Oct-94, $29.82                               ▼
← █                                                              →
```

Check out the week of 04-Mar-95! Wow, was that expensive.

If you want to look at a week's charges in more detail, type that week's number at the CompuServe prompt and press **Enter**. CompuServe comes back with a day-by-day summary of charges (see the following figure). You can tell the difference between basic and extended services as well as other monthly charges such as your membership fee.

Mouse Tip

Sometimes CompuServe uses terminal emulation to show information. When it uses terminal emulation, there is no pretty window available in which you can use your mouse to select options. However, you *can* use your mouse in the account history screen. Instead of typing 4 and pressing Enter, double-click on the week number you want to see. Works like a charm.

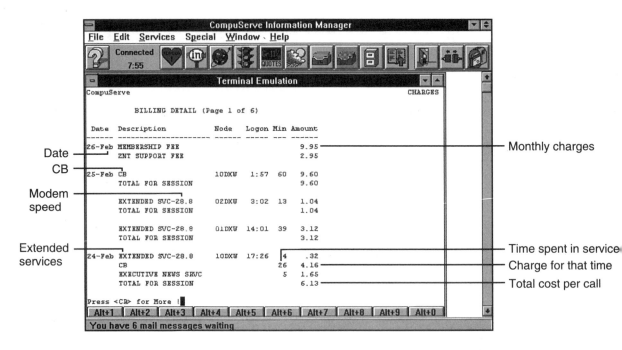

I forgot about those charges...

Press the **Enter** key to scroll through all your charges. When you're done, press **Enter** again to return to the Review Your Charges window.

Checking Your Mail Charges

If you send a lot of mail and want to make sure you're within your "free" monthly limit, double-click on **Mail and Other Allowances** in the Review Your Charges window. CompuServe shows you how much mail you can send per month ($9.00 worth), how much you have sent so far, and how much you can still send within your monthly mail allowance (see the following figure).

Parents Take Note If you want to make sure no one else is using your account without your knowledge (like your kids), keep your own record of when you log on and for how long, and then compare it to the complete account history CompuServe displays. You might make some interesting discoveries.

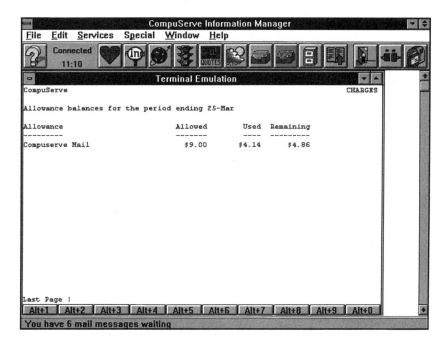

I'm not even close to my limit, so why worry?

When you're done, press the **Enter** key to return to the Review Your Charges dialog box.

Frankly, I don't send much mail, so I'm not concerned enough to check regularly. But if you want to, you'll find that it's pretty easy to stay updated.

And the Password Is...

Take a look at your keychain. You've got a key for your house, car, office, gym, and who knows what else. You probably even have some keys that don't fit any lock you know of. You can think of your CompuServe password as your very own key to the big CompuServe house.

Your password is very important because that's how CompuServe identifies you when you call. If someone else knew your password, he or she could call CompuServe and rack up all sorts of bills that you would have to pay (and be able to read through your e-mail—Yikes!).

For your own CompuServe safety, follow this list of password guidelines:

➤ Never tell anyone else your password. You might trust him with your password, but he might tell someone else. CompuServe isn't *that* expensive. If someone else needs to use it, tell him to get his own account (call 1-800-848-8199 for a free membership kit).

➤ Change your password regularly. If you change your password regularly, even if someone figures it out, they won't have it for long.

➤ Don't use common words or personal phrases. Nicknames, spouses names, and children's names, though easy to remember, make terrible passwords.

➤ Report any problems (like a $3,000 bill) to CompuServe immediately.

If you follow these guidelines, you should have no problem with your password. I change mine about every six months or whenever I think about it. I have so many passwords between work, my ATM card, and home, I confuse them all the time—but I somehow manage.

Changing Your Password

Changing your password on CompuServe is really easy. Just **GO PASSWORD**, and CompuServe displays the Change Password screen, as shown on the next page.

Type in your current password and press **Enter**. (Note that when you type your password, it doesn't appear on-screen, just in case someone is looking over your shoulder.) Type your new password and press **Enter**. CompuServe asks you to retype your new password to make sure you didn't enter a typo. Type the new password and press **Enter** again.

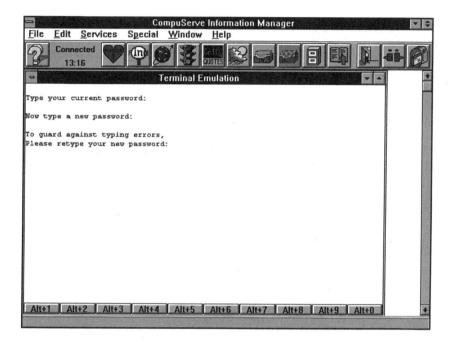

I've typed my new password twice, and I'm all set.

CompuServe has two rules regarding passwords:

➤ The password must be between 8 and 24 characters long (so "poppins" and "supercalifragilisticexpealidocious" won't work).

➤ The password must have at least one of the following characters in it:

" ! " # $ % & ' ( ) * + , – . / : ; < = > ? @ [\ ] ^ "

In case you were wondering, my password is "sara/toga." It's short, easy for me to remember, and hard for someone else to figure out. (Don't bother trying it, though; before this book hits the shelves, I'll have changed it to something really obscure.)

Passwords in WinCIM

Since you're probably using CIM, it's likely that your password is stored so CIM can automatically log you on. If it is, you don't have to type your password every time you log on to CompuServe. This is handy, but you'll have to remember that when you change your password online, you also need to change it within CIM.

When you change a lock on your house, you have to make sure everyone who had a key before has the new key, or they won't be able to get in (unless that was why you changed the locks in the first place). Likewise, if you change your CompuServe password online and you don't change it in CIM, CIM won't be able to get in anymore.

To change your password in WinCIM, pull down the **Special** menu and choose **Session Settings**. Your Setup Session Settings dialog box appears, as shown in the following figure.

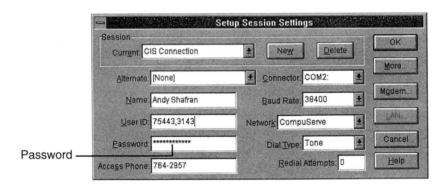

Password ——

Your password is stored here.

Click on the **Password** box or press **Tab** several times until the Password box is highlighted. Press **Delete** to erase your old password, and then type your new one. The ***** characters appear in the box as you type your password so others can't see what it is. When you're done, click **OK**, and your password is changed.

All the experts say that you should not write down your password. I disagree. Since it is stored in WinCIM, I usually let WinCIM log me on, and I don't enter the password myself. Therefore, if I don't write my password down, I can't remember it six months later when I want to change it.

However, if you write down your password, you need to be very careful. When I write down my password, I leave out the special characters and store it in a safe place. For example, I would write down "saratoga." Then in six months, I only have to remember that my special character was a front slash (/) that was in the middle of the word—instead of having to remember the whole password.

Remember, too, that with your password stored in WinCIM, anyone who has access to your computer can log onto CompuServe automatically, without knowing your password. That could be a problem if you share computers.

Forget Your Password?

Even the best of us forget our password on occasion. I do all the time. If you forget yours, all you have to do is call 1-800-848-8990 (or 614-457-8650) and sheepishly tell the customer service rep your story. The customer service representative will reset your password for you.

I like to make up these grandiose stories about how I was kidnapped, had my brain erased, and lost my password, because I feel dumb telling them I just plain forgot. Actually, I get annoyed with CompuServe because they tell me not to write down my password, but then they make me feel like an idiot for forgetting it.

Password Tip If you don't want to store your password in WinCIM, open the **Special** menu and choose **Session Settings**. In the Setup Session Settings dialog box, delete your old password and click on **OK** (don't enter the new one). Every time you log onto CompuServe, you'll be prompted to type in your password.

Finding a New Local CompuServe Number

There are local CompuServe phone numbers all over the world. Chances are, wherever you go, you'll be able to make a local call to access CompuServe. That's one of the reasons CompuServe is so popular for people who go on trips. They can take their laptops (doesn't everyone have one?) and call CompuServe from the beaches of Florida. I know it sounds like an AT&T commercial, but you really can if you want to. Of course, who'd *want* to is another question entirely.

Whether you're visiting someone, working during a business trip, or actually moving, there will come a time when you'll need to find a local access phone number in another city.

Getting the Phone Numbers

There are lots of ways to get local access phone numbers, but I'm only going to show you the two easiest.

➤ On your telephone, call 1-800-848-8990 (or 614-457-8650). CompuServe has an automated phone system through which you can find local access numbers without even talking to a human being. Just follow the instructions and have a pen and paper handy.

➤ If you're online, **GO PHONES**. You'll see the Telephone Access Numbers screen, as shown below. Every local access number is listed online, and you can easily find the one you want. The only problem is that you'll have to go through about five windows to find the local access number you want.

1-800 Access If you do a lot of traveling or live where there is no local access number, try using Compu-Serve's 1-800 line. 1-800-848-4480 is the 1200/2400 baud line, and 1-800-331-7166 is the 9600/14400 line. But be warned: this special service costs an extra six bucks an hour for connection. So use it sparingly.

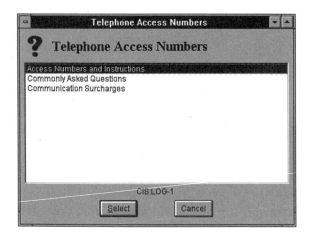

Start here to find a local access number.

Updating WinCIM's Phone Number

Changing your local access number in WinCIM is as easy as changing your password. Pull down the **Special** menu and choose **Session Settings**. The Setup Session Settings dialog box appears, as shown in the following figure. Remember it? You just used it to change your password in the previous section.

70

This time, click on the **Phone** box or press the **Tab** key to highlight it. Press **Delete**, and then type in the new phone number. Then click on **OK**. The next time you dial CompuServe, you'll use the new number.

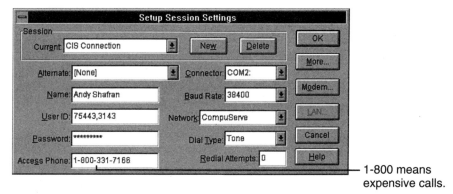

1-800 means expensive calls.

I feel rich, so I'll use the 800 line.

The Least You Need to Know

Everything in this chapter is basic CompuServe information that every new user needs to know. You'll probably never change your password and don't even care about your pricing plan, but it's important that you know all about them. So hang in there. You made it through this chapter, and we're just about ready to get to some of the fun stuff on CompuServe.

➤ Forget the alternative pricing plan and stick with the good old standard plan.

➤ Your password is sacred. **GO PASSWORD** and change it often—and don't forget to change it in WinCIM.

➤ Extended services may be nice, but they cost an extra $4.80 an hour. Use them wisely.

➤ Premium services are big bucks: you pay for the convenience.

➤ You can **GO CHARGES** to see your complete list of charges anytime you want.

➤ Take CompuServe to the beach, your new home, or wherever you go. Just find out what the local access number is.

71

Chapter 7

Becoming a Good CompuServe Citizen

In This Chapter

➤ Get $15 by barely lifting a finger

➤ Make Miss Manners proud with CompuServe etiquette tips

➤ Learn the law of the land

➤ Quit this CompuServe thing for good

There are nearly 3 million people using CompuServe, and every one of them had to start somewhere. Most of them weren't lucky enough to have this book, so consider yourself privileged.

I spent the previous chapter telling you a lot of basic administrative info about CompuServe. Now I am going to go over a few things that will help you fit into the CompuServe world. You'll want to read through this chapter to learn about the rules of the land and learn what kind of stuff you do and do not want to do on CompuServe.

You can actually earn back most of the cost of this book by following the suggestions I make in this chapter. What a bargain!

CompuServe's New Member Welcome Center

When you drive into a state park for the first time, you almost always stop in the welcome center. Usually you want to pick up some park maps, sign up for a tour, or most likely, go to the bathroom (if it was a long trip). The welcome center gets boring after a little while, and you won't stop there as often in the future, but you know it's there if you need it.

Although there aren't any online rest rooms, CompuServe has its own welcome center. You can find tips for using CompuServe, lists of fun stuff to do, and even $15 of extra CompuServe credit. It's free, and worth stopping by on one of your first few visits to CompuServe.

To drop by the CompuServe welcome center, click on the **Member Services** icon in the Services window. From there, double-click on **New Member Welcome Center** (GO MEMBER). You'll see the screen shown below.

Not quite like the Grand Canyon Welcome Center, but it does the job.

Free $10 Credit

Here's how you can get back almost the entire cost of this book in just a few minutes. In the welcome center you can earn $10 of CompuServe credit by taking the CompuServe IQ test. The test consists of 15 true-or-false questions. If you get at least 10 of them right, you get $5 credit, but if you get all 15 correct, you get $10 credit. This credit goes towards the charges you accrue while looking through CompuServe's extended services (the ones that cost $4.80 an hour). You can take the quiz only once (too bad), and it has to be within your first three months as a CompuServe member. It almost sounds like a scam, but it's just CompuServe's way of saying hello.

Don't worry about pulling an all-nighter for this quiz. I'll let you copy off my paper, just don't get caught. You'll have the right answers, so you're guaranteed to get all the questions right. I know, I know, this is academic misconduct, but some of the questions are tricky, and it'd be a shame to lose $10.

From the New Member Welcome Center, double-click on **Test Your CompuServe I.Q** to bring up the Alert dialog box. This dialog box just reminds you of the rules of the CompuServe Quiz.

Click on the **Proceed** button. CompuServe asks you if you're ready to take the quiz now. Type **Y** and then click on the **OK** button. You'll see the screen shown below.

The first question is really easy. Read it through, click on **True** or **False**, and then click on the **OK** button. CompuServe will tell you whether you're right or wrong.

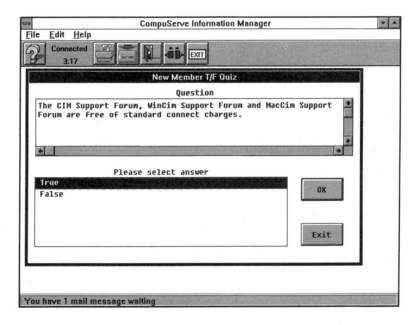

This is the first question (here's a hint: True).

Here are the next 14 questions, and the correct answers:

2. Zagat's Restaurant Guide is online for 10 cities. (False)

3. Consumer Reports Complete Drug Reference is part of Basic Services. (True)

4. If you recommend a friend who joins CompuServe, both you and your friend will receive a $15 connect-time credit as a "thank-you." (False)

5. CompuServe has a Disabilities Forum, a Cancer Forum, and a Diabetes Forum. (True)

6. Microsoft, Adobe, Borland, Corel, and Novell all offer online support forums. (True)

7. The Electronic Mall has 32 stores. (False. Merely 32 stores isn't enough—there's at least 100.)

8. It is possible to send a message to a member of Congress online. (True)

9. Basic Quotes and Fundwatch Online are both part of Basic Services. (True)

10. Special Events and Contests is updated once a month. (False)

11. Dun and Bradstreet offers three searchable directories of business information online: one for the U.S., one for Canada, and one for International. (True)

12. CompuServe has a Florida Forum, a U.K. Forum, a California Forum, a Japan Forum, and an Arkansas Forum. (False)

13. It is possible to send electronic mail over CompuServe to an Internet address, an MCI address, or an AT&T Easylink address. (True)

14. It is possible to view color weather maps of North America, the United Kingdom, Continental Europe, the Pacific Rim, and Australia/New Zealand online. (True)

15. CompuServe is the information service you won't outgrow, no matter how hard you try. (True—but if I eat enough brownies, I can outgrow anything.)

Once you've finished the last question, consider yourself $10 richer, or at least $10 no poorer. Click on the **Proceed** button on the Congratulations window to go back to the welcome center.

Make Another $5 with the New Member Survey

Surveys Pay
The new member survey is how CompuServe figures out what kind of new information to make available. Last year, they asked all their new members how many of them owned CD-ROM drives. A vast majority of members said they did, so CompuServe started producing its own bimonthly CD-ROM. I'm actually impressed by how much CompuServe pays attention to these surveys.

The free stuff isn't quite done coming your way. You can earn yourself another $5 of CompuServe credit by filling out the New Member Survey. CompuServe asks you all sorts of questions about how much you like them and how they can improve, as well as personal profile information. Their questions aren't *that* personal, but they do want to know your gender, salary class, how much you use CompuServe, and what you had for breakfast. You know, the regular stuff.

From the New Member Welcome Center, click on **Take the New Member Survey**. CompuServe brings up a window making sure you want to continue and take the survey. Click on **Proceed** to continue. You'll see the screen shown on the next page.

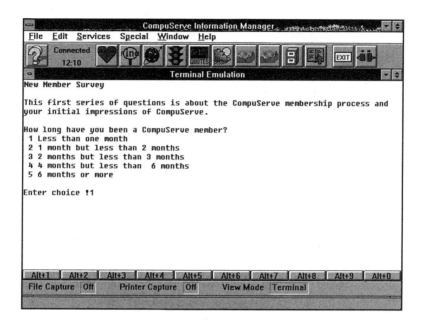

Here's the first question, and they don't get any harder than this.

In the next window, you're thanked profusely by CompuServe, and they explain that they are bribing you with $5 to get this information from you. Press the **Enter** key (or double-click anywhere on the screen) to start the survey.

I didn't count how many questions there were, but the questions seemed to go on forever. Fortunately, there is no right or wrong answer to these questions, and you'll get the $5 automatically. As each question comes up, type your answer and press the Enter key.

You'll get to the end of the survey in about five minutes or so. I actually made sure that my answers were correct, but some people have filled out the survey by typing **1** as the answer to every question (to get through the survey more quickly). I'd recommend taking the time to answer each one individually.

The Rest of the Welcome Center

I showed you the welcome center so you could get $15 of free CompuServe credit. There are a few other things to do at the welcome center, but not too much on the "must-see" list.

You can read a welcome letter from the CEO of CompuServe, learn about CIM (which you already know), and find out about some neat things on CompuServe. Double-click on **CompuServe Service Highlights**. A new window comes up that lets you browse through the major services (see figure on the following page). This is the equivalent to using the icons in the Services window to browse around.

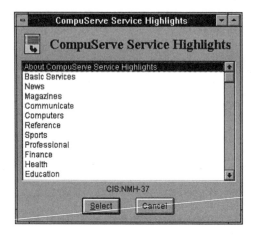

Browse through the highlights if you have time.

Just like in a park, you probably won't stop by the welcome center again (unless you need to use the rest room) after your first trip. But wasn't it worth the trip?

Citizenship 101: Online Etiquette

Remember third grade, when Mrs. Smith lectured about minding your Ps and Qs? You also learned another really important lesson way back then: the Golden Rule. No, I'm not talking about Bill Gates' golden rule. (He who has the gold makes the rules.) I'm referring to *"Do unto others as you would have others do unto you."*

Netiquette
Netiquette came about through the Internet (aka *the Net*). It's a general list of common-sense rules for handling yourself in the electronic world.

This simple rule should guide your manners online. On the phone, it's hard for people to see your facial expression—you've got to rely a lot more on your tone of voice to get your point across. On CompuServe, all you've got is typed text. If you send sarcastic messages to friends, they might not understand what you meant.

This is where etiquette comes in. Etiquette offers guidelines for how to deal with everyday situations. There are general etiquette practices for answering a phone, eating dinner, even dropping your firearm in public (say "excuse me"). On CompuServe, common etiquette practices are called *netiquette*.

Here's a standard list of common netiquette practices that you should follow on CompuServe. Think of them as general guidelines for how to behave.

Do be considerate of others. Other people have opinions, participate in conversations, and even occasionally make mistakes, so be understanding and tolerant.

Do respond to your e-mail often. Since electronic mail is delivered immediately, it is really annoying to wait a week to hear back from someone via CompuServe.

Do read over your messages before sending them. You can avoid typos and most grammatical errors if you actually read what you type. But don't worry, there are no grammar police on CompuServe.

Do realize that every CompuServe user has feelings. Don't think that you are the only one out of 3 million CompuServe users that can be offended.

Don't cuss. People don't need to see four-letter words like that. It's a waste of time.

DON'T TYPE IN ALL CAPS. IT'S THE EQUIVALENT OF SHOUTING.

Sometimes, people include **smileys** in their messages to show they are joking. It's the equivalent of saying, "Just kidding." Smileys come in all sorts of shapes and sizes, but generally look like :) or some variation. (Turn your head 90 degrees to the left if you don't see the smiley face).

Don't assume people understand your sarcasm. Without your voice or facial expressions, you could really tick someone off when you were just trying to be funny.

Don't be racist or sexist. Give me a break; that stuff can go out with the trash.

Citizenship 102: Following the Rules

Everywhere you go, you'll find different rules and regulations. Whether you travel to another state, or even a foreign country, you're expected to abide by those rules and laws (does Michael Fay come to mind?). CompuServe is no different. Think of CompuServe as a foreign electronic community. You still need a VISA to get in, and the CompuServe community has rules that everyone is expected to follow.

Don't confuse etiquette with rules. Following general etiquette guidelines will help you make friends with other users. You don't have to follow all the etiquette suggestions. On the other hand, following the rules is required.

There aren't many rules, and no one usually has a problem with them, but you should be aware that they exist. I don't want to sound too much like a CompuServe cop, so I'll only talk about them briefly.

Copyright Laws

Everybody knows about copyright laws. If Tom Clancy writes a new book, you can't type it on your computer and publish it under your name. That's against the law. Similarly, you can't put your copy machine into overdrive and sell photocopies of the book either.

Copying software works the same way. If you buy a word processing program in the store, it's against the law to give a copy of it to everyone under the sun (even one person) unless it's shareware.

CompuServe is very particular about this rule. There are thousands of computer programs available for download. You can find tax software, graphics, and games galore, but they're all shareware. You won't find copywritten software available on CompuServe without the author's consent. You can get in trouble if you upload copyrighted software. You'd also get in trouble if you keyed in Tom Clancy's book and uploaded the complete text as well (why you'd want to is beyond me).

Shareware Software

Shareware software is available to be distributed and shared by as many people as possible. This software is free to test drive, but you need to buy it if you use it after the test period. Usually the authors of shareware programs include their addresses so you can send them money if you like the program. Please don't steal a shareware program. Not only is it illegal and unkind, but if the people who write the shareware programs don't get any money for them, they won't be able to afford to keep writing them. That means we (the users) would miss out on a lot of great programs.

Pornography

The age-old battle over pornography has carried on into the computer world. A common buzzword nowadays is *cybersex*. Cybersex is anything that relates to sex and uses a computer. Whether you are reading messages, looking at pictures, or talking with someone else via computer, cybersex is one of the hottest commodities around.

There are very strict laws covering the issue of sex. That's why a ten-year old boy can't buy a *Playboy* magazine. You'll find lots of adult-themed discussions, files, and pictures all over CompuServe, and it is usually extremely popular. I'm not a pornography expert, so I won't pretend to tell you about all the laws, but be aware that there is potentially offensive material on CompuServe—especially if you have kids using your account.

Internet Rules

Here's where the laws get a little funny. Since the Internet is a worldwide network, there is no single set of rules that everybody abides by. What's illegal in the United States may be legal somewhere else, and vice versa.

There are no boundaries on the Internet, no borders to cross. It's just as easy to talk to someone in India as it is to chat with a buddy in Sacramento. The U.S. can't prosecute someone in a foreign country for copyright violations if that country doesn't have copyright laws. As a result, you may find copyrighted or pornographic material on the Internet as well.

Instead of laws, there is a general set of Internet guidelines that most people tend to follow. Throughout this book, in each chapter that talks about the Internet, I'll give you more etiquette suggestions.

Pornography Laws The laws regarding sex and the online world are still being shaped. Very few cases have gone to trial, and precedents are still being made all the time. In one recent case, a computer bulletin board operator in Memphis, Tennessee was arrested for providing access to adult material to people under the age of 18. I'm sure the CompuServe lawyers are carefully watching the outcome of that case.

Canceling Your CompuServe Membership

Maybe CompuServe just isn't for you. All this information is nice and all, but it's too overwhelming. Maybe you're spending too much money. I regularly have high monthly bills. Of course I use CompuServe all the time, and consider it money well spent. Or maybe you like CompuServe, but don't need to keep your account while you visit the Arctic Circle for a year.

Whatever the reason, you won't get any hassle—it's guilt-free. All you have to do is **GO MEMBER** with WinCIM from anywhere on CompuServe. Canceling your membership is a membership option.

From there, select **Cancel Your Membership** from the list of options, and CompuServe will ask you a big "Are you sure?" Remember that if you want to keep your account, but you won't be using it for several months, the alternative pricing plan costs only $2.50 a month to keep your User ID intact.

Click on the **Proceed** button if you're sure this is the end of the road with you and CompuServe. You'll have to wade through another window that makes you select **Cancel Your Membership** again (see figure on the following page).

Choose Cancel again.

After you've selected **Cancel** again, here's your last chance. CompuServe asks you once and for all if you *really* want to cancel your membership. Type **Y** and press **Enter** if so.

I am always very surprised to hear of CompuServe cancellations. I know that it costs $120 a year minimum, but I'm a die-hard CompuServe user. There is so much available online that there's literally something for everyone. Make sure you explore CompuServe for at least a month or so before you cancel. But don't hesitate if you feel like you aren't getting your money's worth.

The Least You Need to Know

It's easy to get along with everyone else on CompuServe. You're all there to get lots of information and communicate. Take heed of the etiquette rules and don't break any laws. Everyone's a new user at least once, so don't worry if you make a mistake or two.

➤ Get $15 of bonus CompuServe credit if you drop by the New Member Welcome Center.

➤ Since CompuServe is a community, make sure you practice netiquette—etiquette in cyberspace—at all times.

➤ **GO MEMBER** to cancel your CompuServe membership at any time.

Part 2
Mail and Forums: The CompuServe Essentials

Electronic mail, or e-mail, as it's called, is the most popular feature of CompuServe. Chapters 8 and 9 teach you how to create mail, receive it, and file it away for future use or abuse.

And then there are forums, where you're likely to find just about anything. Chapters 10–14 teach you how to use them to your best advantage.

Chapter 8

Cheaper Than a Stamp: E-Mail

In This Chapter

➤ Sending electronic mail through CompuServe

➤ Getting your CompuServe Mail

➤ Using WinCIM's Address Book

Unless it's a bill, we all love to get mail. Although we're always hoping for a postcard from a friend vacationing in Cancun, a refund from the IRS (never happens), or a month-late birthday card from Grandma, even junk mail and catalogs are better than nothing. However, regardless of what's in the mail, sending and receiving mail is vital to nearly everyone's lifestyle.

Realizing this, CompuServe created its own mail service that is cheaper and faster than the U.S. Postal Service (and has few problems with disgruntled workers). You're probably familiar with electronic mail, or e-mail. Maybe your company uses it for correspondence—or so everyone can keep up on the office gossip. To use e-mail, you simply type your message into a computer and send it to someone else who has an e-mail account. The recipient can then either read the message on-screen or print it out, send you a reply, and/or store the message for future use. With e-mail, you don't have to worry about finding the right size envelope, coming up with a stamp, or (yuck) licking the envelope shut.

Probably the biggest advantage to using e-mail is its fast delivery time. Once you send a message, your recipient will be able to read it within minutes. No more waiting two weeks for a crumpled letter to get to New York. Even e-mail sent to other countries arrives in moments.

A Bird's Eye View of CompuServe Mail

Sending a letter via CompuServe mail follows the same principles as sending a letter via the USPS (U.S. Postal Service). You look up your buddy's address in your address book, write the letter, put the letter in your mailbox, and raise the mailbox flag. Periodically (every couple of minutes), the CompuServe mail carrier picks up the mail message from you and determines (from the address you provided) where the message is supposed to go. The mail is then delivered, and it only takes a few moments because CompuServe knows where to find the recipient's mailbox. The next time the recipient logs on to CompuServe, he is told that he has new mail.

Just as you can send traditional forms of mail anywhere in the world, you can send e-mail to almost any computer *network* around the world as well. All you have to know is

Network A bunch of computers that are linked to each other so the people using the various computers can communicate with each other easily. For example, CompuServe and the Internet are both networks.

the correct address of the person you're trying to reach. For example, let's say you want to send a letter to a friend who has an e-mail account on the Internet. When the CompuServe mail carrier picks up the mail and looks at the address, he recognizes that you are trying to send a message to the Internet and drops it off in a special mailbox for messages going to the Internet. This concept is the same as if you were sending mail to Australia: your mail carrier picks up the mail and routes it so that sooner or later it is placed on an airplane destined for the land down under (unfortunately that may take several weeks).

Once your mail is dropped off to the Internet, it appears in the recipient's mailbox in a flash. You can send mail to millions of users on dozens of worldwide e-mail networks including the following:

Internet	Telex
Postal messages (USPS)	Fax messages
ATTMail X.400	EasyLink (Western Union)
SprintMail	MCIMail (all the long distance companies seem to have their own)

Advantis (IBM) X.400	BT Messaging Service X.400
Infonet X.400	Unisource Business Networks Ltd. X.400
NIFTY-Serve X.400 (Japan)	Deutsche Bundepost X.400 (Germany)

Does It Cost an Arm and a Leg?

Actually, no. CompuServe mail is a pretty good bargain. As part of your $9.95 monthly fee, you get $9.00 worth of mail privileges. Specifically, CompuServe charges you $.10 for the first 7500 *characters* (approximately three pages) in a message, and $.02 for every 7500 characters above that within the same message (which adds new meaning to "putting in your two cents worth"). So based on those rates, you're allowed to send 90 three-page letters every month at no cost. That's a lot of mail. I've never even come close to sending 90 e-mail messages a month—that's three a day.

Sending CompuServe e-mail is quicker then sending a Fedex package and cheaper than calling someone long distance. If you use e-mail on a regular basis, it could really take a bite out of your phone bill—and you could get by with licking fewer stamps.

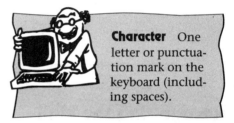

Character One letter or punctuation mark on the keyboard (including spaces).

One String Attached

Unfortunately, e-mail is not quite *that* straightforward. You do incur other charges using electronic mail, particularly when you send mail to the Internet. For example, when someone on the Internet sends you mail, you have to pay the $.10 for the first 7500 characters and $.02 for subsequent 7500 characters for every message you read. These charges are also counted in your $9 monthly allowance, so be careful

Here's an e-mail success story for you. In my friend's family, the grandparents talked to everybody at least twice a month. With seven children and many grandchildren (ranging from infant to college age), the grandparents were spending a boatload on phone calls. Last year for Christmas, they got CompuServe membership kits for everyone (all seven of their children and five of the grandchildren). Now they all talk more often over e-mail, and they spend a fraction of what they used to. It sounds corny, but everyone is using e-mail nowadays.

Not only is CompuServe e-mail cheaper than long distance calls, it's cheaper than regular mail and is delivered immediately. Use this handy little chart to compare CompuServe and USPS mail rates. As you can see, CompuServe mail is cheaper—but the U.S. Postal Service does offer expanded flexibility for sending important food items across state lines.

Mail Item	CompuServe	U.S. Mail
One page letter to a friend in Boise	$.10	$.32
Three page letter to Parma, Ohio	$.10	$.32
24 page love letter to Ft. Lauderdale	$.26	$.54
A pop-tart sent to North Carolina	(not possible)	$.82 (Yes, it works—send it in the foil and mark "Please hand stamp" to amuse the postal workers.)

Recognizing the Mail

Everyone knows what mail looks like: it's small and white and comes in a rectangular envelope, right? Nope, not CompuServe Mail. Your CompuServe e-mail looks like just a line of typed characters (because that's what it is). As you'll see in a later figure, for each message, you see the subject (which describes the contents of the message) and the name of the person who sent the message to you.

One of the first things you'll want to know is how to tell when you've got mail in your mailbox. Every time you log on using WinCIM, CompuServe displays a message at the bottom of the screen informing you how much mail is waiting for you. When you have mail waiting, an extra icon (the Get New Mail icon) appears on the WinCIM ribbon (see the following figure).

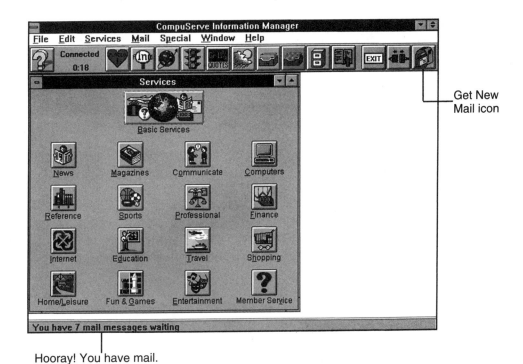

Get New
Mail icon

Hooray! You have mail.

Keep one eye on the message area of your WinCIM screen to see if you've got mail.

Opening Your Mail

When you log on and CompuServe tells you that you've got some mail waiting, you're
going to want to open it, right? The easiest way to do that is to click on the **Get New
Mail** icon on the WinCIM ribbon, which appears if you have mail waiting when you log
on. Alternatively, you could open the **Mail** menu and choose **Get New Mail** as soon as
you start WinCIM. Either way, you'll be connected to CompuServe, and your mailbox
will open automatically (**GO MAIL**).

You've now opened your mailbox, and there's a list of all the mail messages waiting for you (see the following figure). If you want to read one of the messages, just select it (click on the message) and click on the **Get** button.

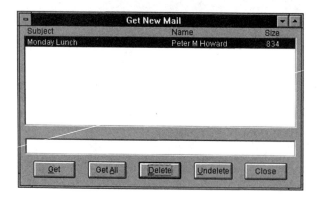

I've only got one mail message waiting for me right now.

When you select some messages, you'll notice that an additional note is displayed in the Mail dialog box (see the following figure). For example, if your mail is coming from the Internet, you'll see a note that tells you how much you'll be charged for reading it. Fortunately, though, you are charged only for the Internet mail you actually read (not all that you receive). So if the messages from the Internet have descriptive subjects, you can use them to tell which messages you want to read, which will help you cut down your e-mail costs. Other notes you might see here include a High Priority note, which informs you the e-mail is important, and a Sender Notified note, which generates an automatic message that's sent back to the e-mail sender when you've read the message. (No, you are not charged for the automatic message that's sent back—the recipient is.)

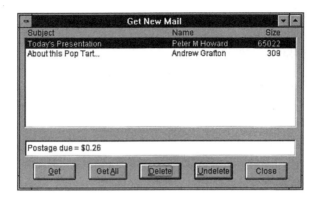

It will cost me only 26 cents to read this message.

Reading the Mail

Select the mail message you want to read and click on the **Get** button. Another window opens, and you can read the entire message (see figure below). You'll be able to see who the message is from, when he sent it, and a list of all the people who received this e-mail message. Make sure you scroll through the entire message so you don't miss any important details at the bottom.

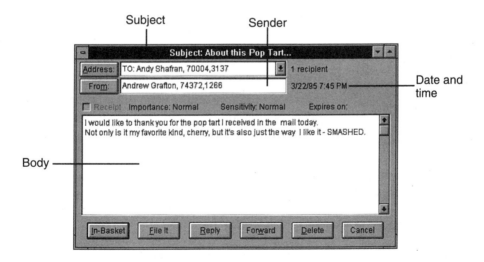

Here's a regular e-mail message.

Remember that the e-mail message remains on CompuServe until you remove it. Suppose, for example, that you walk down your driveway to the mailbox (if you live in an apartment, just imagine). Even if you open and read your mail standing right there, you probably don't want to put the mail back in your mailbox because you'll just have to deal with it tomorrow. So you bring it inside.

Filing Your Mail

Once you've read the entire message, you have several options available. Six buttons line the bottom of the mail window. Once you've read your mail, click on the appropriate button, as described here.

In-Basket	Moves the message from your online CompuServe mailbox to your personal computer. This is like bringing the mail into the house from the street and piling it on the table. Sure you can open it up outside, but once you've brought it in, you can pull it out of the pile and reread it anytime you want.
File It	Stores your mail message in your personal message filing cabinet. The filing cabinet is similar to the in-basket, except that in the filing cabinet, you can sort and organize the messages. (This is discussed in depth later.)
Reply	Enables you to create a note to send back to the sender.
Forward	Enables you to send the current e-mail message to someone else. (If you get a joke from a friend, you can forward it to someone else without having to retype the entire message.)
Delete	Erases the message you were reading. Gone, vamoose, zapped.
Cancel	Takes you back to your list of e-mail messages. Your mail will be waiting for you next time you log on.

Your best bet is to put most of your mail in the in-basket so you can go through your messages anytime you want. Personally, I also use my filing cabinet a lot because I can categorize where each mail message goes. If I need to look for "Jokes" in the future, I'll know exactly where to find them.

Should I Store My E-Mail Locally?

A lot of CompuServe users don't delete their mail or store it on their personal computers once they've read their messages. They either hit Cancel when they're done reading, or they just delete the really useless messages. I've seen people who have 20–30 messages waiting for them online each time they log on, and they've already read each one! I suggest that you save your messages to the filing cabinet.

There are two disadvantages to keeping everything online. First, you've got to actually dial up CompuServe to read any of your messages. This is a real pain if you just want to reread a particular message quickly. Second, messages that you do not access remain online for a period of only 30 days. If you get some important mail from a friend, you may decide not to write back immediately but to keep the message online. If you don't get around to rereading the message for a month (you see it every time you log on, but keep procrastinating), it is purged automatically.

Taking a Peek at the In Basket

Your e-mail is automatically sent to the In Basket if you click the In-Basket button while reading a message. As you've probably figured out, reading your mail is pretty easy; however, keeping track of it can be confusing if you are not familiar with how CompuServe and WinCIM work.

I used to click the Get All button all the time, thinking I was deleting my mail—until I realized what I was actually doing. By the time I checked my In Basket, I had more than 300 pieces of old mail that I didn't care about. Every time you click the Get All button (instead of Get) while looking at the list of e-mail in your mailbox, the mail is placed in the In Basket just as it would be if you had clicked In-Basket.

Basically, the In Basket acts the same as the online mailbox except that you don't need to be logged on to read from it. You can read any mail in your In Basket by opening the **Mail** menu and choosing **In-Basket** or by clicking on the **In-Basket** icon on the icon bar. You will see a list of all the mail stored on your machine (see figure below). You can read and reread each mail message to your heart's desire, or you can reply, delete, forward, or file the message at any time, just as you can from the online mailbox.

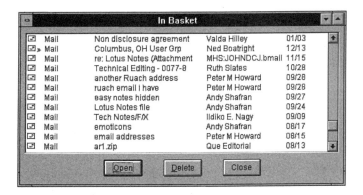

Your In Basket can be useful for looking through the same messages again and again or tracking conversations in the future.

93

Opening Your Filing Cabinet

If you like order and neatness, you'll probably prefer using the filing cabinet to using the In Basket. I don't like to store my messages in the In Basket because all of the messages get jumbled, making it hard to find important e-mail in the future. I use the built-in WinCIM filing cabinet most of the time.

When you're reading e-mail and you want to store a message in your filing cabinet, click on the **File It** button. You'll see a list of the folders in your filing cabinet (see figure below). Each folder can hold all sorts of messages, from e-mail messages to messages from a CompuServe Forum. This is just like having a big metal filing cabinet with pull-out drawers and manila folders. In your real filing cabinet, you can put clipped newspaper articles, printouts, and notes that are related in the same folder. That way they're all organized for future reference. WinCIM's filing cabinet works much the same way.

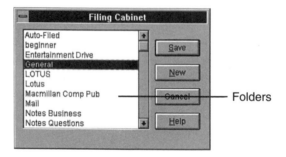

Your drawerless WinCIM filing cabinet.

Select the folder in which you want to store your e-mail and click on the **Save** button. Your e-mail message is downloaded and saved into the folder you've selected. You can create a new folder by clicking on the **New** button instead and typing the folder's name in the dialog box that appears (see figure below).

Useless Pop Tart-related mail will be saved here.

Anytime you are in WinCIM, you can open the **Mail** menu and choose **Filing Cabinet** to read the messages stored in the folders in your cabinet.

Responding to Mail

Sending a response to mail you've gotten is just about the easiest thing you can do. All you have to do is click the **Reply** button while you're reading the mail and WinCIM takes care of the rest. A response window comes up automatically (see figure below), addressed to the sender of the message you're responding to, and WinCIM even fills in a default Subject. Of course, feel free to change the subject (if a different shoe fits) by clicking in the subject area and typing over the existing text.

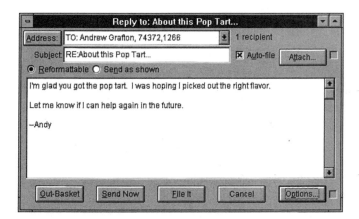

Your Own Audit Trail
By default, CompuServe saves a copy of every piece of e-mail and every message you send in the Auto-Filed folder in your filing cabinet. So if you send lots of secret e-mail that you don't want traced to you, make sure you delete it from here.

When you finish typing your message, you simply click the **Send** button, and CompuServe carries it off. If you're replying to a message that you are reading online, the reply is sent immediately. If you're responding to a message from your In Basket, CompuServe logs on and sends the reply automatically (it still goes out pretty quickly).

A sample reply that uses the same subject as the original message.

Mail from Scratch

By now you're pretty good at handling CompuServe Mail. You can read, save, and even respond to stuff delivered to your own mailbox. The next step is to create new mail from scratch.

What's Included? Any e-mail or online message you read will contain the name and, more importantly, the ID number of the person who created the message.

Honestly, this is almost as easy as responding to someone else's message. The only difference is that you have to indicate to whom you're going to send your mail. Remember your CompuServe ID (you know, the one that looks something like 70004,3137)? Well that's also your personal mailing address. When you send mail to someone, you address it to her specific ID, not her name. So addressing mail to Elizabeth Muska won't work; you'll have to find out her personal CompuServe ID.

I Know the Address

Once you've got the address of the person you want to write to, open the **Mail** menu and choose **Create New Mail**. The Recipients List dialog box appears, showing the WinCIM address book on the left and the Recipients list on the right (see figure below). In the WinCIM address book, you can store people's e-mail addresses permanently. The Recipients list shows who you are sending your message to.

If this is the first time you've sent e-mail to this person, follow these steps to address a message to him.

1. Type the recipient's name (**Barney Rubble**) in the **Name** box, press **Tab** or click in the **Address** box, and type the address (**77777,7776**).

2. Click on the **Add** button. Barney Rubble's name and address appear in the Recipients list to show he will be a recipient of your upcoming message.

I Don't Want Him in My Address Book If you don't want to add your recipient(s) to your address book, simply click OK in the Recipient List dialog box to access a window where you can create your message.

If you want to send a copy of the same message to several people, type all of their names and addresses and click the **Add** button after each one. All of these recipients' names appear in the Recipients list on the right side of the dialog box.

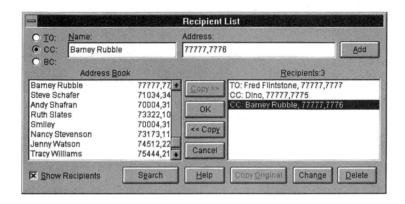

Send the same e-mail message to a bunch of people by listing multiple recipients.

When you're finished adding people to the list of recipients, you'll probably want to add those recipients to your address book. To do so, select a name and click **<<Copy**. The Add to Address Book dialog box appears, as shown below. In the Comments area, you can type a note about that person, if you like, so you remember who he is.

In the Comments field, I type information that will help me remember who the person is and what he does.

You can use and reuse addresses you put in your address book. It's like an online Rolodex. If you want to check out your address book in the future, open the **Mail** menu and choose **Address Book**. The Address Book dialog box appears, as shown below, listing everyone in your address book. From here you can add to and delete from your address book, as well as change a person's personal information.

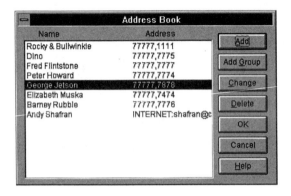

My address book feels like a big cartoon.

Use and Reuse

If you've sent mail to someone before and he's already in your address book, you can skip all the baloney in the previous section. You don't have to type his name and address again, just scroll through the address book window instead. When you find the right recipient, click on **Copy>>** to copy his name and address from the Address Book list to the Recipients list.

You've got to use the address book to create mail; it's the only way to address a letter. When you're done and the recipients' names and addresses appear in the Recipients list, click the **OK** button, and you're returned to the Create Mail window.

Sending the Letter

Now that your e-mail is addressed, type the subject of the letter and the actual letter (this is the easy part). Remember, it costs the same ($.10) to send a one-word e-mail message or a three-page message. So if you've got a lot to say, don't be afraid to say (er, type) it.

When your message is complete, click on **Send Now**, and off goes the message (see the following figure). If you aren't currently logged on, CompuServe dials itself up and sends the e-mail automatically.

Here's a letter of paramount (or maybe Warner Brothers) importance that I want to send immediately.

Bulk Mail

If you have lots of messages to send, you might want to get each one ready and then send them all at once. You do this by putting your completed messages in your Out Basket. Using the Out Basket lets you compose all your letters while you're not connected to CompuServe. This prevents you from tying up your phone line while creating the e-mail and lets you type at your own pace.

When you finish creating a message, instead of choosing Send Now, click on the **Out-Basket** button. Putting your e-mail in the CompuServe Out Basket is like stacking up your bills at home. When you've written, addressed, and licked shut every one, you drop them all off at the Post Office.

Once you've put every letter in the Out Basket and they're all ready to go, choose **Mail Out-Basket**. You'll see a list of all your addressed messages. Click **Send All**, and watch WinCIM log on and put them in the CompuServe mailbox.

The Least You Need to Know

Everyone uses CompuServe mail because it's cheap and easy. Make sure that you check your mail often and regularly so you don't miss any important messages. (It's too bad you still have to use snail mail to send birthday cards, thank you notes, and bills.)

➤ The average cost of a CompuServe letter is only a dime, and you have a nine dollar monthly allowance.

➤ Read, sort, and reply to your mail offline by storing the messages on your own computer. This cuts down on your online time (and how often your friends get a busy signal when they try to call).

➤ The address book lets you keep track of all the people to whom you send e-mail.

Chapter 9

More on Mail

In This Chapter

➤ Sending and receiving Internet mail

➤ Mailing files to other CompuServe users

➤ Sending special stuff, like a Valentine's day CUPIDgram.

In the previous chapter, I showed you the ropes of using CompuServe e-mail. You learned how to use CompuServe to send, receive, and file all your messages, and how e-mail stacked up with the U.S. Postal Service. In this chapter, you're going to learn about some other things you can do with CompuServe e-mail.

You can send e-mail to non-CompuServe people all over the world, including people on the ubiquitous Internet. Seeing how everyone who's anyone has read up on the information superhighway (I have to apologize for using that phrase; it's been used entirely too much), you'd better keep up with the Internauts.

You can even send e-mail to Santa Claus and Congress. I like to categorize them both in the same boat, since they're both useless. You're more likely to get grief than games from your little Congressional elves.

Internetional Mail

Lots of other people around the world besides CompuServe users have access to e-mail. Sooner or later you're going to want to send mail to some of your friends who have e-mail accounts provided by MCI, AT&T, and of course, the Internet. There are over a dozen different mail systems by which you can send and receive e-mail directly from CompuServe. There are well over 20 million users on the Internet alone that are just waiting for you to send them some mail (I know I'm waiting with bated breath to get some e-mail from you).

All you need is their address. No, not "1459 Wydown St., Columbus, OH," but their electronic address. Remember how you sent mail to other CompuServe users? You addressed the e-mail to their CompuServe ID. Sending mail to non-CompuServe users is almost exactly the same.

No Responsibility

When you send a letter from your house in Cleveland to a friend in China, U.S. postal workers have no way of knowing whether the Chinese address is correct. They just see the "China" on your envelope, and send it over on the next plane. The Chinese postal workers then have to interpret your address. If the address is wrong, the letter will be returned to the U.S., and eventually makes it back to Cleveland. e-mail works the same way. CompuServe has no way of knowing whether your e-mail address is correct when you send mail to a foreign network. They provide examples, and will help you if asked, but you've got to get the right address on your own.

Use a Mail Prefix!

Once you've gotten the recipient's e-mail address, you're all set. All e-mail addresses for non-CompuServe users have two parts: the prefix and the address. To understand the prefix, think about how the post office sends mail to other countries.

When you drop a letter off in the mailbox, the first thing the U.S. Postal Service checks (after they crumple the envelope) is whether you are sending international mail. If they see a "Canada" or "Tanzania" on your letter, they don't even bother reading further. The mail is sent to the corresponding country. Postal workers in that country now have the responsibility to actually deliver your mail according to the address you used.

Prefixes work just the same way. When CompuServe picks up your mail, it sorts the outgoing e-mail messages into various piles according to prefixes. Then those messages are sent to the other e-mail system, where the message is sent to the address you've typed.

Sending Internet Mail

Unless you live in a shoe, you've heard of the Internet and how millions of people all over the world have access to it. Well, pat yourself on the back—when you signed up to CompuServe, you've increased that number by one. There are lots of neat Internet things you can do on CompuServe, but the most important is e-mail.

Besides regular CompuServe users, most of the e-mail you send will probably go back and forth between the Internet. You should know how to send it—in case someone says "Hey, drop me some e-mail sometime," at the next wild party you go to.

The first step is to get the other guy's Internet address. Every Internet address looks something like this:

shafran@cis.ohio-state.edu

This translates as: "Send mail to the user named SHAFRAN (that's me) who is located in the CIS department of Ohio State, which is an educational institution." Every Internet address must have a person's name, the @ sign (pronounced "at"), and what's called a *path* to find them. You don't need to understand the path of the Internet address, but I thought it'd be helpful to understand how it works in this example.

Once you get the Internet address of the person you want to send some e-mail to, all you need is the special Internet prefix and you're set. The prefix is **INTERNET:** (pretty tricky, huh?).

Compose the e-mail message just like you did in Chapter 8. Choose **Mail**, **Create Mail** from the WinCIM menu bar. WinCIM brings up the Recipient List window. Since I'm probably not in your WinCIM address book yet, you'll have to add my information. Type the recipient's name (Andy Shafran); then make sure you put the prefix and the Internet address (separated by a colon) in the Address box, like this:

INTERNET:shafran@cis.ohio-state.edu

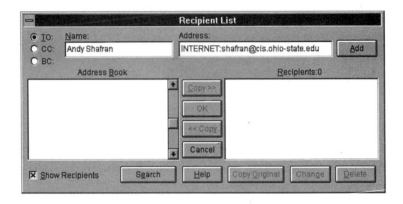

I know I'll regret giving out my e-mail address in this book.

Click on the **Add** button to add the e-mail address to the Recipient's List window, and click on the **OK** button. Type your message just like a regular e-mail message (don't forget the subject), and click on the **Send Now** message. Your e-mail is now delivered to the Internet through CompuServe.

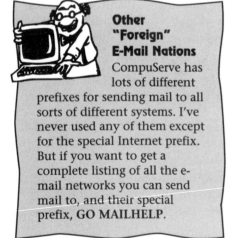

Other "Foreign" E-Mail Nations
CompuServe has lots of different prefixes for sending mail to all sorts of different systems. I've never used any of them except for the special Internet prefix. But if you want to get a complete listing of all the e-mail networks you can send mail to, and their special prefix, **GO MAILHELP.**

Don't forget that it costs money to send and receive mail from the Internet. Every time you send out a message, you're likely to receive one (as a response) as well. Of course, as long as you stay within your $9.00 monthly limit, you won't pay anything extra. To send or read a message from the Internet, you'll pay 15 cents for the first 7500 characters in the message, and 5 cents for each subsequent 2500 characters. It's an okay value, except that you have to pay to read the Internet messages, as well.

Actually, it doesn't cost money to receive mail from the Internet, only to read the messages. When you get your new CompuServe mail, Internet messages are labeled "Postage Due," and you pay for the postage from your $9.00 credit when you read the message. If you delete it before reading, there's no charge to you. Since you can see the subject line of a message before reading it, you have some control over what messages you'll be charged for.

Giving Out Your Address

Of course, Internet dwellers can send you some e-mail as well. You can now brag about your Internet e-mail address, put it on stationery, resumes, or even business cards.

Let's say your CompuServe ID is 75443,3143. That means that your Internet address is:

75443.3143@compuserve.com

The comma in your User ID changes into a period, and you slap the "@compuserve.com" onto the end of it. That's the Internet path to CompuServe. It's that simple, and anyone on the Internet can send you e-mail.

Receiving Internet Mail

There's one more step you have to take before you can receive Internet mail. Since all mail sent from the Internet to your CompuServe ID is postage due, you've got to tell the CompuServe postmaster that you want to accept those messages delivered to your mailbox. You won't actually be charged until you read your Internet e-mail, but by default, the CompuServe postmaster won't deliver postage-due mail to your mailbox.

To accept postage-due messages, **GO ASCIIMAIL**. CompuServe accesses your mailbox without using WinCIM's graphical interface. Press the **Enter** key to open your mailbox and at the prompt and type:

SET RECEIVE YES

"Please CompuServe postmaster, deliver postage due messages."

Press the **Enter** key, and CompuServe thinks about your command for a second. Press the **Enter** key again to leave ASCIIMAIL.

CompuServe does this to protect new users from getting lots and lots of Internet messages if they don't want them. You'll only have to change this setting once.

Sending Files via E-Mail

Nowadays, almost every business has a fax machine. With a fax, you can send several pages of information to people all around the world. Faxes work just like copy machines, only over a telephone. So if every company has a fax machine, why do companies like Federal Express and UPS exist? Why can't you just fax everything across the world instead of mailing it?

The answer is that not everything can be faxed, of course. If you are the Montgomery Inn in Cincinnati, OH, and Bob Hope orders a few slabs of ribs delivered to his house in California (which he does often), faxing him the ribs just doesn't score so well on the Hope-o-meter. That's where Priority Overnight service from FedEx comes in.

Furnishing Files
Lots of publishing companies use CompuServe to send files back and forth between the author and the publisher. For example, when an author finishes writing a chapter of a book, he can send it to the editor via CompuServe. There's no extra wait like there is with Federal Express; it's just there. Authors really love the extra day for deadlines. Personally, I never miss my deadlines—just ask my editors. [Editor's note: Yeah, right.]

Sending e-mail on CompuServe is quite common and very useful, but just like sending a fax, e-mail has its limitations. You could e-mail Bob Hope a textual description of the ribs, "hot, steamy, and covered with barbeque sauce," but not a computer graphic depicting the steaming ribs.

Knowing how important it is to be able to send computer graphics of ribs to Bob Hope, CompuServe lets you e-mail files to other CompuServe users in addition to regular e-mail messages. Rib computer graphics aren't the only type of file you can send. Everything from compressed files and word processor files to games and useful programs can be mailed to another CompuServe user.

Just like e-mail, the files are delivered immediately, and you can download them onto your local computer.

Just Send It

Sending files over CompuServe uses the same procedure as sending regular e-mail. Pull down **Mail** from the WinCIM menu bar, and choose **Send File**. WinCIM brings up the recipient list window so you can choose who's going to receive your file. Type the recipients or choose them from your WinCIM address book.

Make sure you select only other CompuServe users. Sending a file to a foreign networks like the Internet is a more involved process that requires special software for the sender and recipient. Only other CompuServe users can send and receive files with each other.

CompuServe lets you send files of all types. By default, you're sending a binary file. This will work for all files you send. If you are sending a text file or graphic, you can be more specific by clicking on **File type**.

Pick the recipient(s) and click on the **OK** button. WinCIM will bring up the Send File Message box. All you have to do is type a subject for your message and figure out which file to send.

Since files are just like regular e-mail except with a file instead of a message, type a subject in the Subject box. It's always nice to put useful information in the subject that identifies the file in this particular e-mail message. I've labeled mine "Barbeque ribs slowly cooking over a fire (file)."

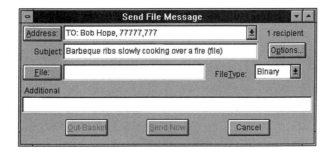

Sending a picture doesn't quite hit the same spot as the real thing.

After typing the subject, click on the **File** button to bring up a Windows dialog box. Use your mouse to scroll through your hard drive until you find the file you want to send. Select the file with your mouse and click on the **OK** button.

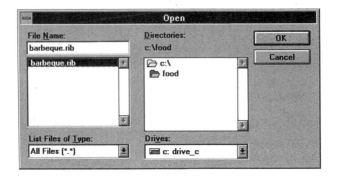

I store my ribs in my C:\FOOD directory.

Once you've selected the file to send, click on the **Send Now** button. WinCIM dials up CompuServe, logs you on, and sends your file.

Sending a file over e-mail costs the same as a regular message. The first 7500 characters costs 10 cents, and each additional 7500 characters costs two cents. So if my barbeque ribs picture is 28,000 characters large, it would cost me 16 cents to send it over CompuServe mail. Since I have a $9.00 monthly mail allowance, I'm not too worried about it.

Scrunch Your Files Since you pay by the size of the file, it is common to use a compression program to scrunch your file. A common program like PKZIP can compress some files by as much as 90 percent, which can add up to quite a savings if you send a lot of files. I'll show you how to download PKZIP in Chapter 11.

If the file you send is larger than 7500 characters, CompuServe reminds you that it will cost more than 10 cents by bringing up a window and telling you how much you're going to be charged. It's only 16 cents to send this file, but some big files can cost several dollars or more.

Just click on **OK**, and CompuServe starts sending the file. The next time my friend checks out his CompuServe mail, he'll have a picture of his favorite ribs waiting for him.

Receiving a File

Unless you're a prisoner in jail, you can receive a file at all hours of the day or night. Of course someone has to send one to you first. Choose mail from the WinCIM menu bar, and choose **Get New Mail** to bring up a listing of new messages (or maybe files) sent to you. You can't really tell whether or not any of your waiting messages is a file until you select the message to read. That's why it's helpful to put a useful subject line on files when you send them.

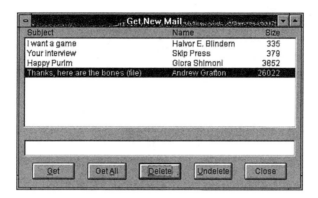

Here are my waiting messages. I know there's a file lurking in here somewhere.

You've got to highlight and **Get** a message just like you would normally read it to know if it's really a file. I'm sure the rib message is a file because of the subject. Let's **Get** it and see what the e-mail looks like.

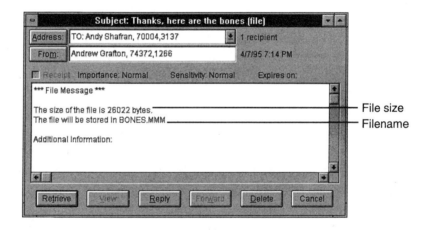

Getting a file sent over CompuServe mail.

The e-mail message tells you basic information about the file that was sent to you. You know how big the file is and what the file name should be. To download it to your personal machine, click on the Retrieve button. WinCIM brings up a window that lets you choose where to store the file on your personal machine. I usually click the **OK** button and store my files into the WinCIM default download directory.

Once you click on the **OK** button, you'll immediately start downloading the file. It's the same process as uploading, only backwards.

Cool E-Mail Things

Watch Your Speed Sending and receiving files really makes a difference with a faster modem. With a 2400 baud modem, sending a picture of a full rack of ribs could take around 25 minutes. If I use a 14,400 baud modem, it takes only four minutes. Since you pay based on file size, it's your time wasting if you use a slow modem.

There are a lot of other neat and useful things you can do with CompuServe mail. Everyone sends and receive regular e-mail, and a lot of people communicate with denizens of the Internet. Not a lot of people use the special mail services I'm about to describe, but they're worth reading about.

My favorite special mail service is sending a letter to Santa. It saves me a trip to the local mall in December, and all the strange looks when I sit on his lap. All the special mail services cost above and beyond your monthly $9.00 allowance, so use them sparingly. Here's a quick rundown of the special mail services you can use, their cost, and their rating on the usefulness scale. If you need more information about any of these special services, **GO MAILHELP** online.

Faxes

You can send a CompuServe e-mail message via fax to anyone's fax machine around the world. This is really useful when the boss says to you, "Hey, fax me those numbers." Of course, not everyone has a fax, and if you don't, you're sweating bullets trying to figure out how to fax your information.

Remember talking about Internet mail? You had to use the special Internet prefix to address your e-mail (**INTERNET:**). Sending a fax is similar, except that you use the prefix **FAX:** instead. To send a fax to (513) 555-1212, you would address your e-mail like this:

FAX:15135551212

Then you can type your message like normal and send it off. CompuServe will take care of the fax for you. It costs 75 cents for the first 7500 characters and 25 cents for each additional 7500 characters.

When you send off your e-mail, CompuServe asks you for the specific recipient's name.

Faxing through CompuServe isn't too bad. You get a cover sheet, all your pages are numbered, and you get five retries if the fax number is busy. You can't send graphics, files, or ribs through CompuServe's faxing service though, so be wary of those limitations.

U.S. Mail

I don't understand why, but you can send a letter through the U.S. Postal Service directly from CompuServe mail. I like to think of e-mail as a significant step above the standard postal system, and I'm not sure why anyone would want to type up an e-mail message, and have it sent via pony express. But you can.

Unfortunately, you can't create a U.S. Mail message from WinCIM, so you've got to **GO ASCIIMAIL**. From the text menu system, type **2** and press **Enter** to compose a new e-mail message. Type each line of your message until you're done and type /**EXIT** on the last line.

Here's my boring message. What a waste of money!

Then CompuServe prompts you for the address of the e-mail message. Instead of typing a User ID, type:

POSTAL

CompuServe then asks for the actual Postal address of the person you are sending this mail to and the return address. Once you are finished with the addresses, you can enter a subject for your message, and then you are done. A CompuServe laser prints your complete message, folds it neatly, puts it into an envelope, and drops it in the nearest mailbox. For this convenience, you're charged $1.50 for the first page, and $.20 for each additional page after that. International mail costs a bit more.

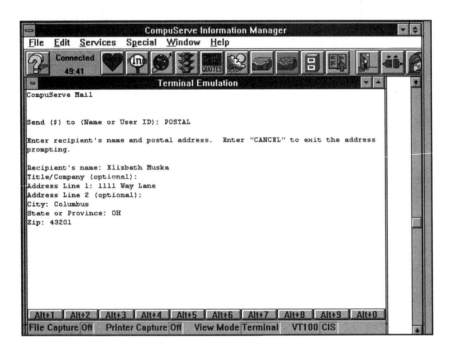

Send postal mail to anyone across the world, or in my case, town.

Give a Gram

Periodically throughout the year, you can send special e-mail messages called *grams*. Grams are special e-mail services that CompuServe likes to charge an arm and a leg for to capitalize on a special holiday or event. They may be expensive, but they're cute, and fun to explore. For example, on Valentine's day, you can send a CUPIDgram. Either through the U.S. Postal Service or CompuServe e-mail, you can send a special love message. It's only $2.00 a shot, and each CUPIDgram has Love emblazoned all over it. I got one last year and thought it was really cute, but kinda corny (aka *stupid*). Of course, it was the thought that counted.

In the Christmas shopping season (July through December), you can also send SANTAgrams. These letters to Santa are just what the doctor ordered when you don't want to handwrite your entire list of toys. I suppose it was only a matter of time before Santa caught up to the nineties.

Any time of the year, you can send a personalized CONGRESSgram to the Prez, Vice Prez, or any member of Congress. For $1.00, CompuServe will print and mail (via the US Postal Service) your typed message lambasting our country's leaders. I sent a letter to the president, and actually received a response (6 months later). I doubt Bill actually reads my mail, but it makes me feel better.

Like I said before, most grams are seasonal. **GO GRAMS** from WinCIM to find out what sorts of grams you can do now. They're becoming more popular every day, so I wouldn't be surprised if more unique grams were on the way.

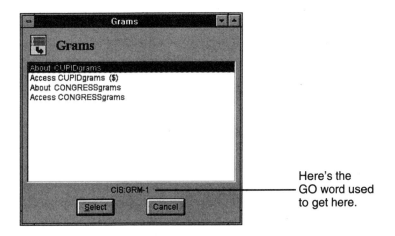

Here's the GO word used to get here.

Cupid and Congress, not an ideal match. I'll wait for Santa.

The Least You Need to Know

Besides the regular sending and receiving mail stuff, there are all sorts of neat things you can do with CompuServe mail. CompuServe is very flexible, and finds new ways for you to spend your money all the time.

➤ **GO ASCIIMAIL** to set up your account to receive Internet messages.

➤ Send e-mail to any Internet user around the world through your CompuServe account.

➤ Files are sent just like regular e-mail. They make it really easy to share files with other CompuServe users immediately.

➤ Send personal grams to help you get into the holiday spirit; send CUPIDgrams on Valentine's day, and SANTAgrams at Christmas.

Chapter 10

An Intro to Forums

In This Chapter

➤ What is a forum?

➤ A look at what forums have to offer

➤ How much does it cost?

➤ Joining a forum

➤ Searching for forums that match your interests and hobbies

In school, there were all sorts of clubs you could belong to if you wanted. Some people joined the computer club, others enjoyed public speaking. There were clubs for practically any interest: if you were a vegetarian, liked fishing, or were actively religious, you could find other people just like yourself to hang out with (unless you're a born-again vegetarian fisherman—then you might have trouble).

Just like a college campus, CompuServe makes room for everybody and their various interests. When I say everybody, I mean *everybody*. You'll find a forum for nearly every computer company, hobby, and interest imaginable. Need help with Excel? Stop by the Microsoft forums. Want the recipe for brisket? Visit the Cooks Forum. Looking for Nancy Reagan? Hop over to the Astrology Forum.

What's a Forum, and Why Would I Want to Use One?

So what exactly is a forum? A forum is a special niche in CompuServe dedicated to one particular interest. Forums are the heart of CompuServe, and I'll guarantee that there's at least one where you'll feel at home. Later in this chapter, I'll explain how to find the forums you're interested in.

Each forum has three sections to it: Messaging, Files, and Conferences. These three sections let users discuss whatever interests them, exchange knowledge or files, or just shoot the bull.

Reading and Writing Messages

Theoretically, the main purpose of a CompuServe forum is to enable people to read and leave messages for other people in the forum. To that end, each forum has several different message sections organized by topic. For example, in the UFO Encounters Forum there are different message sections for UFO Abductions, Ghosts, Skeptics, and JFK, to name a few. (No, *The X-Files* does not yet have its own forum. Thanks for asking; check out **GO TVZONE** to find other X-philes.)

Forum Equals SIG In CompuServe lingo, forums are sometimes called *special interest groups* (SIGs, rhymes with "pigs"), especially when we're talking about personal interest forums (that is, forums not sponsored by a company). Nobody except CompuServe people actually refers to forums as SIGs, but you might hear the term once in a while.

I like to think of messaging as a big bulletin board where people can leave different messages. Anyone who meanders by the bulletin board can read the messages on it, and if they like, can tack up their own response. Soon, if a lot of people walk by the bulletin board, you've got a lot of messages and a bunch of thumbtacks.

Downloading and Uploading Files

There are lots of files found in each forum as well, and not just dreary old files, but the good stuff, too. You'll find text files, pictures, and even programs that will run on your computer. In the UFO Encounters Forum, there's a whole set of text files that contain CompuServe users' experiences with UFOs, and a nifty Windows program that lets you keep track of the articles in the Weekly World News gossip rag (it's all true, I swear).

There are hundreds of thousands of files scattered throughout the CompuServe forums. You can download and run these files to your machine at home. I find a new Windows utility, game, or psychic experience almost daily.

No matter what type of computer you use, there are some useful files available for you. Windows and Macintosh are the most popular by far, but you'll find a lot of files for OS/2, Amiga, Atari, as well as such obscure systems like CP/M, Kaypro, and Timex-Sinclair (not the watch, but an actual computer built way back when I was a wee babe). See Chapter 12 for everything you want to know about files in forums.

Conferencing: Stopping By for a Chat

The third major part of forums are conferences. When you are exploring a forum, you can have conversations with other CompuServe users. These conversations consist of chatting in *real time* with one or more CompuServe users. Conferencing is like running into a friend while you're tacking up your own note on the bulletin board.

Real time is just another phrase for "It's happening right now." While e-mail involves sending messages to be read later, real-time chatting is having a live conversation.

You can have a conference with one other person, or with big groups of people at the same time. While you're sitting in your underwear in New York, you can be typing back and forth to someone else basking in Cancun. You can see what other people are typing and take part in all sorts of conversations. It's like hanging out in your local coffeeshop. You can talk about anything that comes to mind and get to know strange and colorful people.

Conferences vary from forum to forum, but usually relate to the general forum topic. You won't find a conference on child rearing in the Fish Forum, unless you're talking about baby guppies.

You can have impromptu conferences with any CompuServe users in a forum at any time, by simply inviting them to chat. Forums sometimes sponsor more structured conferences at specific dates and times, and usually provide a leader or moderator to keep the discussion on-track. Some forums even hold big conferences with celebrities in a forum. I've seen conferences with Jon Stewart, Rush Limbaugh, Aerosmith, and even computer book authors (like yours truly!).

Strange but True... One conference I try to stay away from is in the New Age Forum. There are regular conferences with a guy and the spirit that channels through him. My own channeled spirit would get jealous if I spoke to another spirit.

How Much Does It Cost?

Almost every forum costs $4.80 an hour to use. There are only a handful of forums included free with your $9.95 monthly charge. Except for the Missing Children Forum, most of the freebies are CompuServe support forums for CIM and new CompuServe members. You can tell whether a forum costs extra to explore if it has a + in its name, such as the Showbiz+ Forum.

Playing around in forums can really add up. Even if you use CompuServe twice a week for an hour or two, you could rack up a $50-60 monthly bill in no time. During my first month using CompuServe, I spent so much time exploring forums, I had a $250 bill. I hate to spend so much time talking about CompuServe's cost, but it's your hard-earned dollars you're spending.

Who's Running This Place?

On every forum in CompuServe, there is at least one System Operator (SysOp), the person in charge of everyday life on the forum. It's the SysOp's paid job to read every message and look at every file on the forum.

SysOp The SysOp also enforces standard CompuServe rules regarding profanity, harassment, and copyrighted files. If you get mad and create a message using a lot of four-letter words, the SysOp will probably drop you a message asking you to cool off. The SysOp is a moderator (Jimmy Carter would make a great SysOp) and wants the majority of people on the forum to be happy.

Some busy forums may have several different SysOps running the place. In the Lotus forums, there are several SysOps employed to make sure everyone's questions are answered. In other forums, like the Comic Book Forum, SysOps are there to make sure conversation stays on track. If you start talking about how to rebuild your 1968 Camaro's engine, the Comic Book SysOp is likely to ask you to move your discussion into the Automobile Forum (**GO CARS**).

I've never met a SysOp that wasn't extremely kind and courteous. Since CompuServe pays SysOps to monitor forums, they make sure SysOps are knowledgeable and treat CompuServe users well. In fact, every SysOp I've sent messages to or conferenced with has been friendly and helpful.

SysOping Pays Off SysOps are paid depending on how much use their forum gets. Being a SysOp can really pay off if you run a really busy forum. The SysOp of the Microsoft forums makes six figures for keeping track of several different Microsoft forums.

The Great Forum Hunt

When I showed you how to use WinCIM, I spent some time explaining how to get yourself around CompuServe. I told you how to use your favorite places and GO words, and how to find new things online that interest you. Now it's time to practice what I've preached.

Every forum has its own unique GO word which lets you jump there directly. So if you pull down the **Services** menu and select **Go**, WinCIM brings up a GO dialog box. You can type the unique GO word to any forum and CompuServe takes you there immediately.

From now on, for every forum and service I talk about, I'll list the GO word in parentheses so you can take a look at what I'm talking about, even the ones I make fun of.

What's Available?

There are lots of different types of forums online, and sometimes the GO word is not obvious. That's why you need a basic understanding of how the forum system is constructed, so you can find what you want.

For the most part, all forums can be organized into three main categories: computer, personal, and professional.

Run with the Wolves The publishers of this book even have their own forum online. Try **GO MACMILLAN** and you'll be able to hang out with authors and other people who build these books.

Some computer forums are sponsored by computer hardware and software companies. Most of them provide actual support for their products, so you don't have to call them on the telephone. For example, both Microsoft (**GO MICROSOFT**) and Lotus (**GO LOTUS**) offer full technical support on their entire suite of products. With millions of users online, I almost always find something useful when I go to the Windows Forum (**GO MSWIN**). Big computer companies like IBM, Compaq, and Apple all have their own online areas as well. Other computer forums focus on games, utilities, or other computer hobbyists.

Want a Listing?
For a complete list of all the software forums available on CompuServe, **GO SOFTWARE**. For hardware forums, **GO HARDWARE** instead.

Professional forums include those that are business related. There's a Computer Consultant Forum (**GO CONSUL**), a Lawyer Forum (**GO LAWSIG**), even a Crime Enforcement Forum (**GO TWCRIM**).

The rest of the forums fall under the personal category. You can debate Bill Clinton's merits in the Republican and Democrat Forums (**GO REPUBLICAN**, **GO DEMOCRAT**), talk about the latest Hollywood news in the Entertainment Forum (**GO EFORUM**), or discuss your spiritual beliefs in the religion forum (**GO RELIGION**).

There are also a whole bunch of free CompuServe support forums where CompuServe employees hang out and answer any question under the sun. Here's a list of most of them along with their GO words. These are completely free, so I'd recommend going there first to get the hang of working with forums. (There are files and messages, but conferencing is disabled.)

FORUM	GO WORD
New Members Forum	NEWMEMBER
The Practice Forum	PRACTICE
CompuServe Help Forum	HELPFORUM
WinCIM Support Forum	WCIMSUP
MacCIM Support Forum	MCIMSUP
OS/2CIM Support Forum	OCIMSUP
DOSCIM Support Forum	DCIMSUP
CompuServeCD Forum	CCDSUP
CompuServe Windows Navigator Support	WCSNAVSUP
CompuServe Macintosh Navigator Support	MNAVSUPPO

A good way to browse through available forums is to **GO FORUMS**. A window showing all the available forum categories pops up. When I'm bored, I like to browse through the online listing of forums organized by category.

Finding Forums to Fit Your Fancy

Of course, the problem with using GO words to visit different forums is that you might not *know* the GO word for the forum. You might not even be sure that the forum exists!

One method of looking (not the best method) is to try a GO word at random. Maybe you're looking for aquarium talk, or you want to know if I have any eights. Try **GO FISH**. Didn't work did it?

Luckily, there are better ways to search. One is to use the WinCIM Find command, and the other is to browse through the WinCIM icons until you hit the jackpot. Which is better? For me, it depends on the mood I'm in when I'm looking for a new forum. Remember in Chapter 5 when I showed you how to get around CompuServe with WinCIM?

Sometimes Find doesn't find what you want. Let's say you collect Hard Rock Cafe buttons. If you try using the WinCIM Find command looking for **Hard Rock Cafe**, you'll find nothing. Try looking for **buttons**. Again, nothing. You know there are tons of people out there who collect Hard Rock Cafe buttons, but no luck finding the right forum.

Let's try to find a forum for Hard Rock Cafe button collectors. I'll start with **GO FORUMS**. This brings up a list of the 12 main categories of forums.

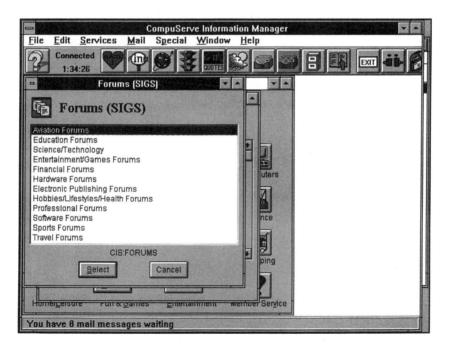

Hmm, I wonder where button collectors would be?

Every forum available online falls into one of these twelve categories. Since I'm looking for fellow button collectors, I'm going to select **Hobbies/Lifestyles/Health Forums** to see what I can find. Another window pops up and lets me choose an even more specific category of forums.

I'll choose **Hobbies** from the subsequent window. Aha, a list of hobby related forums comes up! I bet I can find other Hard Rock Cafe button aficionados in the **Collectibles Forum**, so that's where I'm headed. I double-click on **Collectibles Forum**. Since it's my first time here, a dialog box pops up asking me if I want to join the forum. (I'll cover joining forums in the next section.)

As you can see, finding the right forum isn't always straightforward. If the Find command doesn't work, use **GO FORUMS** to search through general forum categories.

To Join or Not to Join...

The first time you go to a forum, CompuServe shows you the welcome information for that forum. Usually, this welcome info is a mundane description of the kinds of information you can find in that particular forum. For instance, the welcome information for the Comic Book Forum (**GO COMICS**) basically says, "This forum is devoted to the massive industry that sprang up to take advantage of your childhood memories of superheros and comic books."

Finding All the Forums at Once If you want to get a list of all the forums on CompuServe, use the WinCIM Find command (**Services**, **Find**) and search for the word **Forum**. A window listing all of the hundreds of forums comes back which you can scroll through. They're listed in alphabetical order, and it may take several minutes to get down to the Zs.

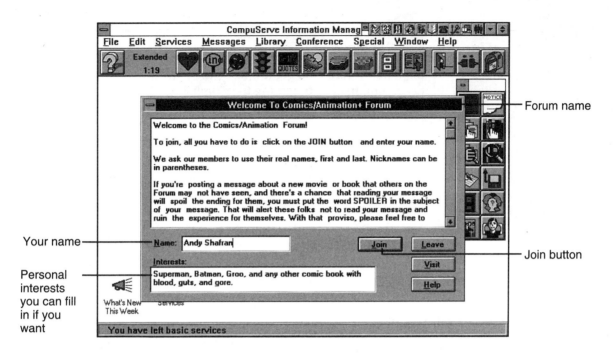

Here's the welcome screen for the Comic Book Forum.

On your first time there, you also get the option to join or visit the forum. Visiting a forum is pretty much pointless. You get limited privileges and don't get to fully explore a new forum. Joining a forum costs nothing extra and only takes a single mouse click.

Make sure your name is correct in the **Name** box. I usually ignore the Interests box because I don't feel like typing my personal interests for joining each forum (I'd say only five percent of people actually do). In fact, this is the only time I've filled any interests in (just for this example). When you're ready, click on the **Join** button to enter the forum.

Once you click on the **Join** button, you're now a member of the forum. Congrats! You'll probably join a hundred different forums or so through your CompuServe career (I've joined 361 so far). Nowadays, whenever I go to a new forum, I don't even read the welcome screen. I just immediately click on the Join button.

Clark Kent or Superman?

When you join a new forum, you get to specify the name by which you're known on that forum. Instead of joining the Comic Book Forum as "Andy Shafran," I could type Superman, Wolverine, or She-ra in the Name box. My user ID stays the same, but the name people will know me by in the forum will be whatever I choose. You can pick a different alias for almost every different forum.

The down side to pretending to be someone else is that most forums require you to join with your real full name. I wouldn't be allowed to participate if I joined a Microsoft forum as Superman (or Bill Gates). Your best bet is to just use your real name and not worry about picking a different name. I never join a forum under an alias. Most forums tell you whether or not you must use your real name to join. If in doubt, use your real name.

Some forums have their own logos. These logos are usually in the form of small graphics that are downloaded to your computer as soon as you join the forum. You only have to download the logo on your first visit. The logo appears in the background of WinCIM every time you go into that forum. It's just a nice personalized touch for joining new forums.

Since the Comic Book Forum has its own logo, you'll download it automatically when you join. It's not much to look at (they rarely are), but it makes CompuServe a little bit nicer.

Once the logo has finished downloading (usually no more than a minute or two, depending on the speed of your modem), you're a full-fledged member of the forum. Whenever you come back to this forum in the future, CompuServe will recognize that you've been here before, and you won't have to join or download the logo again.

It's like applying for membership at one of those wholesale warehouse clubs. The first time

Friendly Forums Some forums automatically send welcome e-mail to new members who join. This e-mail is just a way to entice you to come back and visit the forum more often. The Telecommunications forum (**GO TELECOM**) is like this. I was wandering through and joining forums left and right and randomly joined the telecommunications forum. The next time I logged on, I had e-mail from the person in charge of the forum thanking me for joining and welcoming me back. It was great to feel loved, and reading e-mail is free, so I didn't mind.

you go in, you have to get your picture taken and you get a membership card. After that, all you have to do is show your card and you're in without any hassle.

I'm now a card-carrying member of the Comic Book Forum. Hooray. Maybe I can figure out how to sell my old collection of GI Joe comics before it turns into a pile of dust.

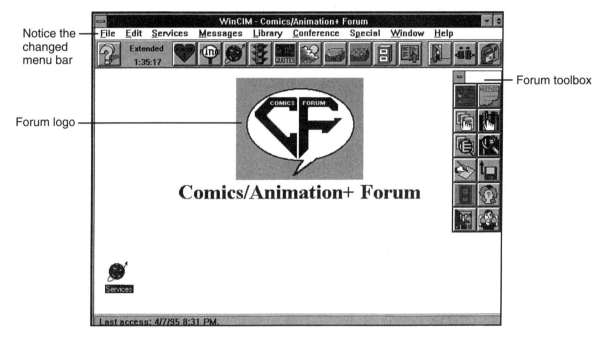

Notice the changed menu bar

Forum logo

Forum toolbox

Here's what a forum looks like in WinCIM.

Here's what your WinCIM screen looks like when you go into any forum. You'll use only a few of the icons in the Forum Toolbox regularly, but I'll talk about them in the next couple of chapters.

The Least You Need to Know

Forums are the meat of most of the information on CompuServe. You can find a forum on almost any topic and talk with people around the world who share your interests. Read the next two chapters to learn more about using all the neat features forums have to offer.

➤ Each forum has bulletin boards of messages, buckets of files, and live conversation.

➤ Forums are where most people spend most of their time (and money) on CompuServe. There are hundreds of forums around, and at least one of them is bound to be right for you.

➤ Don't bother visiting a forum; you might as well join.

➤ Use **GO FORUMS** to browse through CompuServe's categories of forums if you want to get a complete picture of what's available.

➤ Most forums cost $4.80 an hour to explore, so don't waste your time poking your nose into every forum you find.

➤ Be creative when looking for forums on a specific topic. Finding button collectors in the Collectibles Forum makes sense, but you have to think of looking there.

Fun with Forums 1: Messages and Conferences

Now you basically know what forums are about. It's time to jump feet first into them and have some fun. I'm sure you'll spend a lot of time in forums because you can talk to people all around the world.

So now you need to learn how to communicate with other CompuServe users on a forum. In the previous chapter, I introduced you to CompuServe forums; I hope the meeting was amicable. In this chapter, I'll show you how to exchange forum messages and conference with other people just like yourself. So grab your box of thumbtacks and let's learn how to trade messages with the 3 million CompuServites exploring forums as well.

All About Forum Messages

Forums are usually based on one general topic of interest, such as dinosaurs, politics, or sailing. Then within each forum, there are several different sections that are related to the general topic. These sections help break up the general topic into specific categories of conversation.

It's not as confusing as it sounds. For example, I love baseball. I couldn't memorize more useless trivia about batting averages and fly balls if I wanted to. I'd really like to talk to other baseball fanatics like myself and argue with other fans about how the Cincinnati Reds would have gone to the World Series had there not been a strike.

There's no forum specifically dedicated to baseball, but there is a Sports Forum (**GO FANS**) for armchair slugs like myself. Within the Sports Forum, there is a specific message section where all baseball-related messages can be found. Within this message section, I can always find a plethora of baseball-related topics. Brutish football fans stay away— you've got your own message section to play with in the Sports Forum.

Topics A topic is a group of messages about the same subject. For example, if Don M. leaves a message about the baseball strike, then Nolan R. tosses in his two cents, both of those messages fall under the same message topic. Other CompuServe users can leave follow-up messages about the baseball strike to continue the message topic.

In each message section, messages are organized by topics. The topic name, along with the number of messages in that topic of conversation, is listed when you look at the list of sections. Each message subject is listed, and you can read the topics you want depending on the subject.

For the remainder of this chapter, I'm going to hang out in the Sports Forum and show you how to read and send messages there. All forums work the same, though, so I won't get upset if you decide to hang out in the Tennis Forum instead of talking baseball with me. (Can you believe that? Tennis has its own forum: **GO TENNIS**.)

Choosing a Message Section

Once you're in a forum (see Chapter 10), check out the messages sections. To do so, click the **Browse Message Sections** icon, or open the **Message** menu and select **Browse**. A window pops up and lists all the message sections in the forum (see the figure on the following page).

Each forum has between 5 and 22 message sections. You can scroll through the list of sections with the scroll bars. When you're done admiring all the section names, double-click on the one you want. A window containing all the message topics appears (see figure at bottom of next page).

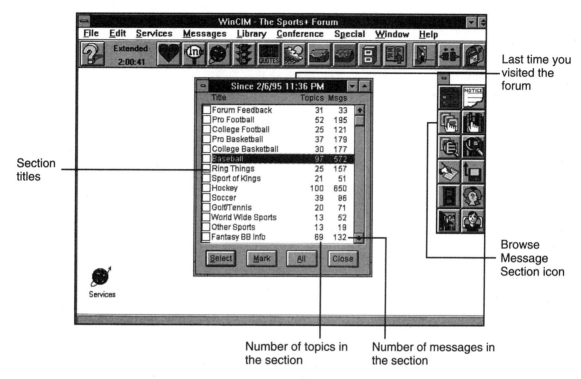

Section titles — Number of topics in the section — Number of messages in the section — Last time you visited the forum — Browse Message Section icon

Football, basketball, baseball, hockey...wait a second, where's the squash message section?

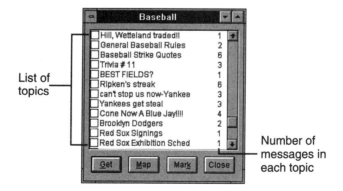

List of topics — Number of messages in each topic

Aha! That's where all the double-headers went.

Reading Messages

To read the messages, just double-click on one of the topics. A screen like this appears.

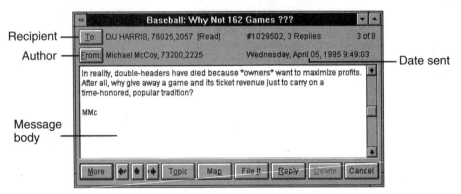

Here's a message that interests me.

There are a lot of buttons at the bottom of the message window that you use to read messages. Here's what each one does:

More   Shows the next screenful of the message. If you're at the end of a message, **More** brings up the next message in the topic. If you're at the end of a topic, **More** brings up the next topic. If you're at the last message in the last topic in the section, **More** is unavailable.

Left Arrow   Brings up the previous message in the topic you're reading.

Up Arrow   Brings up the message that this message is a reply to.

Right Arrow   Brings you to the next message in your current message topic.

Topic   Brings you to the first message of the next topic.

Map   Shows a genealogy map of the first message in that topic, and all the responses in a graphical format. Personally, I've never liked using this feature.

File It   Downloads the message you're reading and saves it in your WinCIM Filing Cabinet along with your e-mail and other messages.

Reply   Opens a window where you can respond to the message, with a message on the forum or through e-mail.

Delete   Erases the message you're reading. You can only delete a message you created yourself, although you will probably find messages by other people you'd like to wipe out.

Cancel   Closes the message window.

Personally, I read the first message in a topic that sounds interesting, then I keep clicking on the **More** button. Since the **More** button brings up each message in its entirety, then goes on to the next message in the topic, I can read an entire topic of messages by using only one button. I never use the Arrow buttons, but I occasionally file a message if it's really interesting.

Finding Messages Addressed to You

You never want to miss a message that's addressed to you specifically. Maybe someone is answering your question about the World Series, or asking you a different question. Whatever the reason, out of all the messages in a forum, you want to ensure that you'll get to read the ones specifically addressed to you. If you have messages waiting to be read, CompuServe sends you a note at the bottom of the WinCIM screen whenever you enter the forum.

Scrolling Messages Messages only stay on a forum for so long (each forum is different). So you might miss some messages if you don't check the forum regularly. What if you visit a forum once and never come back? Any messages addressed to you (private or public) that you don't read by the time it scrolls off the forum are automatically sent to you via e-mail. It's like a backup message service so you don't miss personal messages.

You can read through the message sections and topics, but it's often hard to find the specific message addressed to you. An easier way is to select **Get Waiting** from the **Messages** menu, or click the **Get Waiting Messages** icon. A window displaying the messages available pops up, and you can read the messages just like you were browsing through a section.

Forum Messages Aren't Like E-Mail!

I want to make sure you understand the differences between sending messages through forums and sending e-mail. I talked about e-mail in Chapters 8 and 9.

Sending forum messages is related to e-mail, but it's different in some major ways:

➤ E-mail is private; forum messages aren't. When you send e-mail to a friend in California, he's the only one who can read your message. In forums, messages can be read by anyone who joins that forum.

➤ E-mail is free to read; forum messages aren't. No matter how much e-mail you receive, you're covered with your $9.95 monthly fee (unless it's Internet mail). You can read and re-read the same e-mail message as many times as you want. Since most forums cost $4.80 an hour, reading forum messages can add up quickly.

➤ E-mail access is worldwide; forum access is limited to CompuServe users. You can send e-mail to people all across the world. Whether they're on the Internet, have MCIMail, or work at IBM, you can reach out and touch them. With forums, only CompuServe members can read the messages you post.

➤ Mail waits for you; forums don't. If I send e-mail to my grandma in Atlanta, the e-mail gets delivered to her mailbox and waits for her to read it. On the other hand, if I post a message to my grandma on the Motorcycle Forum, the message will scroll off the forum after a certain time (although it will be e-mailed to her eventually). She has to check the Motorcycle Forum regularly to see if there are any messages waiting for her there.

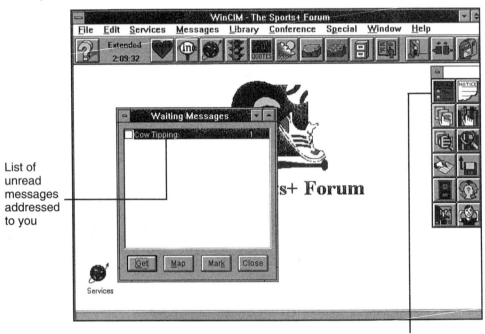

List of unread messages addressed to you

Get Waiting Messages icon

I've got some important Cow Tipping messages addressed to me. Can't afford to miss them.

Saving Time (and Money!) in Forums

I know I'm not made out of money, and you're probably not either (actually, you're about 80 percent water). It'd be nice if I could afford an unlimited monthly CompuServe bill. I could spend all my spare hours checking out a different forum every night. But

132

reality sets in, and I discover that I can't afford to pay $4.80 an hour for my entertainment. I'd say reality set in when I got my first $250 bill and my family had to call 911 to scoop me off of the floor.

If you're not careful, you can spend a *lot* of money in forums. It's very addicting to go to interesting forums and read all sorts of neat topics. Not only do I argue about baseball on the Sports Forum, but I probably hang out in 15 others on a regular basis.

My secret is to log onto CompuServe, download forum messages onto my personal computer (into my WinCIM Filing Cabinet), and then log off. I can read through the messages I've downloaded at my leisure after I've logged off, without worrying about an hourly bill.

I can download hundreds of messages in the time it takes to read just a handful online, so it saves a lot of time connected to CompuServe.

There's More Help If You Want

Easy message downloading is not one of WinCIM's major strengths. WinCIM is great for browsing through forums and exploring most of CompuServe.

There are several other computer programs that are more geared for downloading forum messages for you. They will automatically log on to CompuServe, download the messages you want and log off. The most popular ones are OZCIS, TAPCIS, and CompuServe Navigator. I'll talk a little bit about Navigator in Chapter 26.

Downloading Your Messages

I already showed how to store a single message in your Filing Cabinet. All you do is click the **File It** button when you're reading the message.

What if you want to download an entire message topic? You could have a topic with 30 messages in it, and you certainly don't want to download each message individually. (What a pain in the neck.)

Instead, you want to **Mark** the entire message topic. When you are browsing through the list of topics in a forum section, click on the check box to the left of the topic name. An × appears in the checkbox next to the topic. You can mark as many topics as you want.

× marks the spot for topics to be downloaded.

To download all the messages about this topic, select **Retrieve Marked** from the **Messages** menu to bring up the Retrieve Marked Messages dialog box.

Click on the **Get All** button to download the topics listed. CompuServe puts them in your WinCIM Filing Cabinet automatically, in a folder with the same name as the forum. After I download these messages, I've got a new folder in my filing cabinet labeled **The Sports Forum**. I can log off of CompuServe and read the messages in my filing cabinet one at a time.

Downloading Entire Sections

Sometimes I don't want to even spend the time going through all the topics in a message section and figuring out which ones I want to download. Since it's much faster to download lots of messages than read a few, I like to download entire message sections in one fell swoop.

Yes, You Can Have It All! If you want to download every message (since your last visit) from a forum, click on the **All** button instead of marking each section individually. CompuServe marks every section with new messages.

All you have to do differently is mark the sections you want to download instead of the topics. Select the section name with your mouse, and click on the **Mark** button to mark an entire section for download.

Just follow through with the **Messages**, **Retrieve Marked** command, and you download entire message sections to your WinCIM Filing Cabinet.

I don't usually download entire message sections with WinCIM, because sorting through them all using the Filing Cabinet is a pain, but I know plenty of people who do, and for some demented reason, they love it.

Searching for Specific Forum Messages

In the Sports Forum, if you want to find messages about baseball, it's pretty obvious which message section you'd choose (I'll help you out, it's **Baseball**). Although if you were looking for messages about Deion Sanders, you'd have just as much luck looking in the Pro Football section as well, since Deion is confused about which sport he likes to play better.

If you're unsure which section your person, place, or thing of interest falls into, use the Search feature which enables you to search through messages in a forum. You can look for a particular word, subject, or message number, and you can find messages to or from a specific person.

Click on the **Search for Messages Matching** icon from the forum toolbox. On the left, you can select the message sections you want to search through, and on the right, you decide what you're searching for.

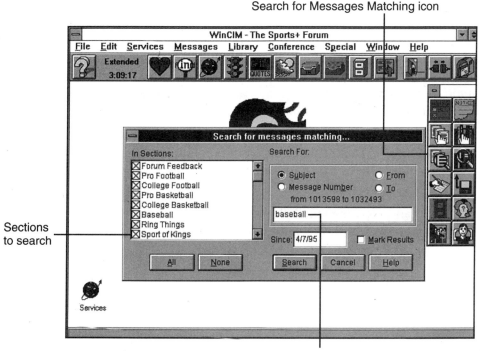

I'm looking for baseball messages (of course).

When you're ready, click on the **Search** button and WinCIM brings you back a list of messages that fit your search critieria.

Posting Forum Messages

I don't know about you, but I get tired of passively reading other people's opinions. I want to put some of my own messages onto the forum. I'm sick of these idiots spreading false rumors about the Durham Bulls, my favorite minor-league team, on the Sports Forum, and I need to clear the air a little.

Creating messages is a lot like e-mail: you've got to figure out to whom you're sending the message, type up the subject and the message, and send it off. Just like e-mail, you can create messages offline (and use the Out-Basket) or while you're connected to CompuServe.

Responding Publicly to a Message

You'll most likely spend most of your time responding to messages left by other people. That's how conversation gets going.

I'm still in the Sports Forum, but you can respond to messages in any forum on CompuServe. Start reading through messages until you find one you want to add your own opinion to. While you're reading the message, click on the **Reply** button, and CompuServe brings up a Reply to Forum Message dialog box.

Your message is automatically addressed to the person you're replying to, and the subject is filled in for you. Don't change the **Subject** box if you want the reply to follow the same message topic. That's why topics are listed by subject when you read messages.

All you have to do is type your reply and click on the **Send** button. CompuServe will post your message and everyone and their mother (and father) will be able to read it. Or, if you prefer, click on the **Out Basket** button to save the message for posting later.

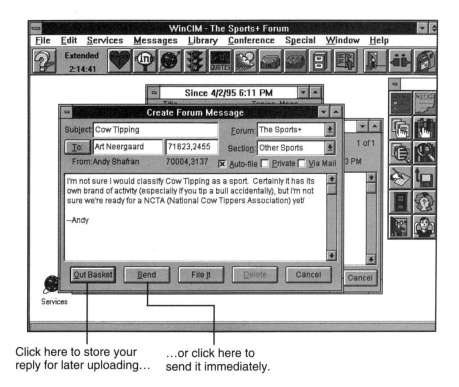

Click here to store your
reply for later uploading…

…or click here to
send it immediately.

It's time for a serious reply.

Responding by Private Message or E-Mail

Sometimes you don't want to send a public message that can be read by everyone. Maybe
you're trying to make a business contact, or maybe you're talking about something very
personal (like cow tipping). In that case, you may want to send a private forum message
or even e-mail instead. Although most forums support private messages, some do not.
You can ask the forum SysOp, or if your message is top secret, use e-mail.

See the **Private** checkbox on the reply screen? If you click on the checkbox, then
only the person you're sending this message to can read it. Other people on the forum
won't even know it exists. The next time she checks the forum, she'll be notified that
messages are waiting for her (specifically addressed to her), and she can then read your
personal message.

You could also check the **Via Mail** checkbox instead. Then your message becomes a
regular e-mail message sent to the recipient's personal mailbox. This is nice because the
recipient doesn't have to check the forum again to read her messages. I always send **Via
Mail** if it's an important message.

Creating a Brand-New Message

Eventually, you'll want to create your own messages from scratch. Maybe you have your own question about cow tipping or another topic that isn't currently being discussed. Whatever the reason, creating new forum messages is almost as easy as responding to existing ones.

Click on the **Create Forum Message** icon, or choose **Create Message** from the **Message** menu, and you'll see a blank message screen, ready to fill in.

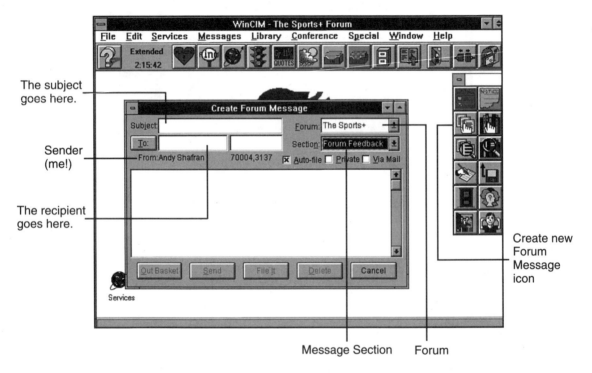

A blank forum message.

Type the subject of your message (up to 25 characters) in the **Subject** box. Then you've got to figure out who you're addressing the message to. There are four different addresses you can use to send your forum messages to:

ALL   Means that you're not talking to anyone in particular, and welcome all responses. You may get put in an institution if you do this in the real world, but on CompuServe, sending messages to no one in particular is encouraged.

SYSOP   Directs the message to the SysOp of the forum. This is useful for asking specific questions about the forum you're in.

*SYSOP   Sends a private message to the SysOp to talk about private things such as potentially embarrassing questions and problems with other forum members.

User Name, User ID   If you want to leave a message for a certain user, address the message to their ID specifically. Other people will be able to read it, too, though.

When you send a message to ALL, SYSOP, or *SYSOP, you only need to fill in the first address box in your forum message (directly to the right of the **TO** button). However, if you want to send a message to a specific user, you've got to include both the name *and* the User ID. That's because everyone is just a number to CompuServe: it doesn't recognize people by just their names.

The last addressing step is to figure out which section to post your message to. You can put your message in any section on the forum, but be sensible. You wouldn't post a question about sumo wrestling in the baseball section. Click the down arrow next to the **Section** box, and a list of sections drops down. Click on the one you want. Then type your message and click on the **Send** button. Your message will zip up to the forum and everyone can read, respond, and tear it up.

Posting to Someone You Know   If you want to send a message to someone in your WinCIM Address Book, click on the TO: button. You can select a recipient who is listed in your address book.

Save Money by Composing Messages Offline!

WinCIM also lets you create new forum messages when you aren't logged onto CompuServe. That way you won't have to pay hourly charges while you're typing your message. You can create forum messages from the main screen that appears when you start WinCIM.

If this idea floats your boat, select **Create Forum Message** from the **Mail** menu. The only difference between composing a message offline and in a forum is that you have to tell WinCIM which forum to post the message to.

Click on the down arrow next to **Forum:**, and you'll see a list of every forum you've joined. Click on the forum you want to post your message to. Don't forget to choose the right section as well. Then address and type your message like normal. Click on the **Send** button when you're finished and CompuServe will call and log to that forum for you and send the message.

Talk, Talk, Talk: Forum Conferencing

There's No Free Lunch Don't forget, you pay $4.80 an hour while in a forum, and you can't chat in the free CompuServe Support Forums because they disable conferences and conversations.

Everybody likes to talk. That's why we all have phones, gossip at the water cooler, and call radio talk shows. Sending messages back and forth to each other is fine, but we all need some live conversation every now and then.

Built into almost every forum is the ability to carry on real-time conversations with anyone else that happens to be in that forum at the same time. You could be half a world apart from someone, but you can carry on a conversation as if he were sitting right there in your living room.

You can have a personal one-on-one chat with a friend, talk in private to a group of people, or throw your hat into public conversations that anyone can take part in.

Talking Tête à Tête (That's French for Head-to-Head)

The easiest way to have a conversation with someone online is to talk to them one-on-one. You can strike up a conversation with anyone who's in the same forum with you. These types of conversations are private, just like a telephone call. Only the two of you can see the stuff you type.

First, you've got to see which other CompuServe members are in the forum with you. Click on the **Who's Here** icon and you'll get a complete list of the other CompuServites in that forum.

Profile   Shows the personal interests of the person highlighted. Most people don't bother with them, so this is pretty useless.

Talk   Requests a conversation with the selected person.

Freeze   Freezes your list of Who's Here so that new people aren't added to the list.

Cancel   Closes the window.

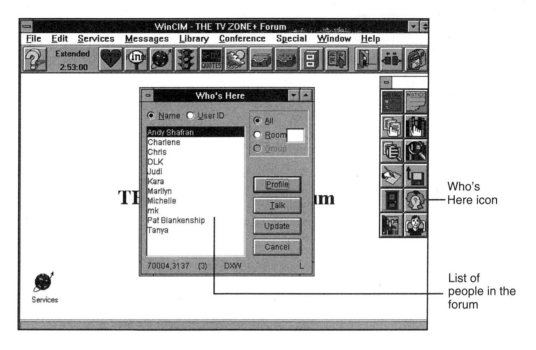

Here's a list of who's here in this forum with me.

To talk to someone else, click on the person's name, and click on the **Talk** button. A new window comes up.

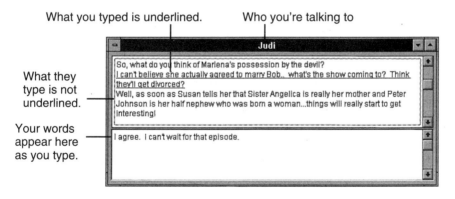

A one-on-one conversation.

If you want to completely ignore someone, click on the **Ignore** icon from the toolbox. Select the people you want to ignore and click **OK**. They can't request a conversation with you when you ignore them.

You send one line of conversation back and forth at a time. Type your message, and press the **Enter** key to send it. You can type as much as you want.

After sending my first line, a window pops up on Judi's WinCIM, who types back to me.

To stop talking one-on-one, press the **Escape** key, or double-click the **Control Menu** box of the window.

Who should you talk to? Well, it depends on how desperate you are for conversation. As a general rule, I don't talk to complete strangers. I'll meet them in a public conference room (read on), or exchange some messages with them first. I consider people who just talk to me out of the blue a pain in the neck. If I wanted to talk, I'd be in a conference.

The Next Best Thing to Long-Distance

One popular use of Talk is for two CompuServe members who live far away from each other to chat online. Since you pay only $4.80 an hour, talking is cheaper than a phone call. You can make plans with friends to be in the same forum at the same time if you want to talk to them.

Private Conference Groups

You can also have private conversations with more than one person at a time. Ma Bell calls this three-way calling. On CompuServe, it's more like three-way, four-way, five-way...basically, you can have a private conversation with many people at once. It's pretty much the same process as talking to another user, except that you get to pick and choose who you want to chat with.

Click on the **Invite** icon. A window comes up that lists the people in the forum. This window is a lot like the **Who's Here** window, except that each person has a checkbox to the left of their name. Click on the checkbox next to someone's name if you want to invite them into a private conversation. Then click on the **Invite** icon.

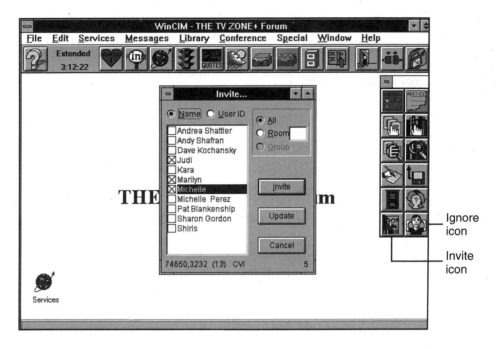

I'm inviting a couple of good friends to chat with me.

Everyone who you've selected gets invited to have a group conversation with you. They get to click on **Yes** or **No** and decide whether or not they want to talk to you. In general, if you want to ask a complete stranger to talk to you, you should invite them instead of just talking to them. That gives them the option of turning your invitation down without feeling harassed.

Once your invitations go out, a Group Conversation window appears. Everyone who accepts your invitation automatically joins the group conversation (the same window appears on their end as well). This is really the same concept as talking, except that since more than two people can be involved in the conversation, your name is listed along with every comment you type.

Just like talking one-on-one, your messages aren't sent until you press the **Enter** key.

These private conversations are a lot like talking one-on-one. No one else can take part if they aren't invited. So feel free to talk about CIA operations, corporate espionage, and the secret formula to Coca-Cola without eavesdroppers.

Joining a Public Conference

I Can't Click on the Enter Room Icon! The Enter Room icon is highlighted only when other users are already having a conference in one of the rooms. This means that if no one in the entire forum is in a conference room, **Enter Room** is shaded and not clickable. This is basically CompuServe's way of telling you that no one is talking right now. Don't despair, you can still enter a conference room (you'll be lonely unless someone else joins you). Choose **Conference** from the menu bar and then choose **Enter Room**.

Last but certainly not least, forums also have their own areas where you can engage in a public conference. This is like walking into a coffee shop and seeing some friends you recognize. They're just chatting, so you sit down and join them.

Most forums have several different conference rooms, each with its own specific topic. For example, in the Issues Forum, there are seven different conference rooms. To see a list of the available rooms, click on the **Enter Room** icon in the Forum Toolbox. A window comes up listing all of the Conference Rooms. None of them have comfy chairs or hardwood tables, but it's better than nothing.

At any point, you can see who's in which conference room, so if you see a friend hanging out in the soap opera chat room, you can join them there (see the following figure).

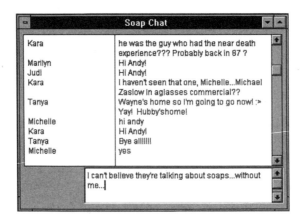

Here's a stimulating conversation about my favorite soap.

The biggest difference between conferences and talking is that conferences aren't private. Anyone can join or eavesdrop on a conversation in a public conference room. However, if you are just talking, you might not want people to join in and shout their opinions.

To join a conference, double-click on the room you want to join. A window that looks suspiciously like the Group Conversation window pops up. You can type messages and talk to people just like a private group conversation. The only difference is that System messages don't appear as they do in private chats.

If you aren't sure that you want to join a conference room, but just want to peek in and see what people are talking about, click once on the room and then click the **Listen** button. A window comes up that lets you see all the messages in the conversation, but you can't type your own two-cents worth. You've got to join the room to do that.

The Least You Need to Know

In this chapter, you learned how to communicate with the millions of CompuServe users that use forums. You should feel comfortable sending messages about cow tipping and chatting with people online about Rush Limbaugh.

➤ Pick and choose which message topics you want to read. Messages are organized by topic in any of the thousand forums online.

➤ Spout your own opinion in a forum by clicking on the **Create Message** icon.

➤ Address a message to *SYSOP if you have a private question for the forum's big cheese.

➤ Save time and money by composing forum messages offline. You can also mark messages from other people to retrieve, so you can read them offline when you're not connected and paying CompuServe.

➤ You can have a deep, meaningful, and private conversation with any other CompuServe user one-on-one or with multiple people at one time.

➤ I'm not done explaining everything forums have to offer. The next chapter covers everything to do with files and forums.

Chapter 12

Fun with
Forums 2: Files

In This Chapter

➤ Browse forum library sections

➤ Download interesting files

➤ Search forums for files on one specific topic

➤ Upload your own files to share with the CompuServe public

On CompuServe, you can find files in all shapes and sizes. From a pretty picture of Aruba at night to a transcript of a supposed alien encounter, you can find all sorts of interesting, unique, and even useful files on CompuServe. For example, I recently found a program that keeps track of my lucky lottery numbers. I'm sure I'll hit the jackpot soon, but until then, I'm stuck writing books (sigh).

When all is said and done, there are probably about 500,000 different files to be found on CompuServe. Big files, little files, red files, blue files, neat files, and useless files are all available for you to download. Just about every forum has its own section where you'll find related files. For example, in the travel forum (**GO TRAVSIG**), you can find files that list cheap apartments in London, a map of Paris, and day-by-day vacation itinerary planners.

In this chapter, you'll discover how to find the files you want and transfer them to your own computer.

What Kinds of Files?

In general, most files on CompuServe can fall into one of the following three categories:

Text   A bunch of typed text saved together.

Graphic   Images ranging from a thoroughbred horse to a beautiful beach.

Binary   Everything else. Programs, compressed files, or other neat stuff that's not text or graphics.

You'll find games, pictures, and all sorts of neat files in the forums you'll explore. For example, Microsoft offers updates to some of its programs in the Microsoft forums, and Lotus has tons of 1-2-3 macros free to anyone who wanders in.

Where the Files Are...

Virus Free
One of the main jobs of SysOps online is to check out each and every file in their forum. They run a virus checker on all the files. That makes CompuServe one of the safest places around to get files. I can't guarantee that every file is virus free, but I've never heard of anyone finding a computer virus anywhere on CompuServe.

Finding files is the same no matter which forum you're using, so let's go to one of my favorite forums, the Outdoors Forum (**GO OUTDOORS**), and take a look at what kinds of files are available there.

Just like with messages (see Chapter 11), there are several different sections (libraries) of files within each forum. Each section contains files about a specific topic that's related to the forum. You can see what file sections are in the forum by clicking the **Browse Library** icon, or by selecting **Browse** from the **Library** menu. A list of available library sections comes up (see the first figure on the next page).

Checking Out a Library Section

To see the list of files in a library section, double-click on the name of the section. A list of all the files in that library section comes up, dated in chronological order with the most recent files at the top. I just finished watching *A River Runs Through It*, and I have an insatiable urge to find files with a fishing theme. So my first stop is going to be the Fishing section. The bottom figure on the next page shows the list of fish topics I got.

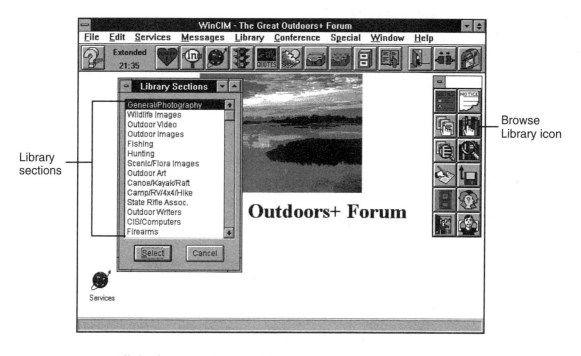

All the fun categories an outdoorsy person would love.

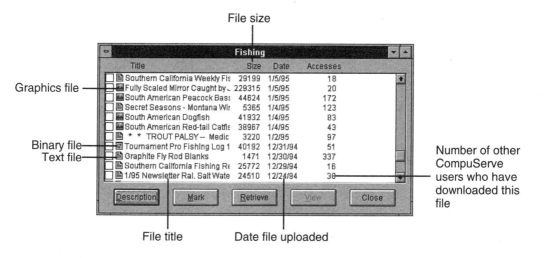

Look at all these fishy files.

From this list, you can learn the size of the file (which is directly proportional to the amount of time it will take for you to download it), the date it was uploaded, and the number of times it's been downloaded by other people.

Each file also has a little graphic by it (to the left of its title). That graphic tells you what kind of file it is (graphic, text, or binary). I'll explain why CompuServe breaks files down into these three categories in just a moment.

Reading a File's Description

You can scroll through the list of files available in that specific library section, looking for something that interests you. Since the files are listed chronologically, the newest files are always at the top. Make sure you scroll through the list. Just because a file isn't brand-spanking-new doesn't mean it won't interest you.

Once you see a file that looks neat, double-click on it to see more information about it. Every file has a description, called an *abstract*. That abstract, along with other important information about that file, comes up when you double-click the title, or highlight the file by clicking once with your mouse and then click the **Description** button. The following figure shows the abstract for FlyTech, a shareware program that teaches you how to tie flies.

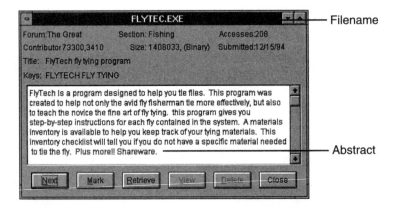

Filename

Abstract

No fisherman could live without this vital program.

Once you've read the abstract, you can decide whether or not you want to download that file onto your computer. If you don't, click on the **Close** button, and you'll continue to browse through the files in that section. If you do, read on—downloading is next.

Retrieving a File

Honestly, downloading a file is easier than deciding which one to download. I spend most of my time searching through libraries upon libraries of files looking for ones that actually interest me. Once I find one, downloading it is simple.

When you find a file to download, click on the **Retrieve** button. You can choose **Retrieve** while you are reading the abstract about a file, or just looking through the library listing—they both do the same thing. In the library listing, make sure you select the file you want to download before clicking **Retrieve**.

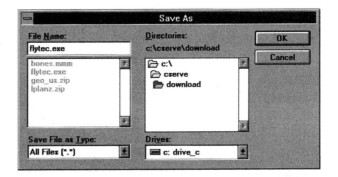

Downloading is really a piece of cake; your modem does all the work.

WinCIM asks you where on your computer you want to put the file and what you want the file to be named. Each file has a default name (the person who uploaded it set that), and it will be sent to the WinCIM section of your computer's hard drive. Unless you want to change the default settings, just click **OK**. I almost always keep the default downloading information unless I have a really good reason (for example, if a file with the same name already exists). In that case, type a new name in the **Filename** box.

Once you click **OK**, the download process begins. A window showing the status of the download comes up and gives you the estimated length of time for the download.

While you're downloading, you can also continue exploring the forum. You can chat with other users or read forum messages. Downloading occurs in the background, so you can take care of several things at one time.

Help, I Got Cut Off

Sometimes you might get disconnected from CompuServe while you're downloading a file. This isn't really a problem if the file is tiny, but it's really annoying when you lose your CompuServe connection halfway through a huge file, especially when you're paying $4.80 an hour. Fortunately, CompuServe is like a Swiss army knife: it has everything. If you go back into the forum and download the exact same file again, CompuServe doesn't miss a beat. It will pick up downloading where it got cut off.

Compressed Files

Most non-text and non-graphic files on CompuServe are compressed. A compression program is like a professional luggage stuffer. It takes lots of different files, folds them up, and packs them into one combined file, squeezing them as tight as it can. You can open up the file and unsqueeze everything inside of it as long as you have the decompression program.

The most popular compression program by far is called PKZIP, and it is available free to anyone who wants it. If you download a file that has the extension .ZIP, you'll need PKZIP to decompress it.

To download PKZIP, go to the Macmillan Computer Books Forum (they publish this book)—**GO MACMILLAN**. Check out the library section named "Utilities." There's always a current version of PKZIP found there.

Text and Graphics

I just described the general steps for downloading any file on CompuServe. It doesn't matter whether it's a binary, text, or graphic file; you can retrieve them all in the exact same fashion. Slowly.

If you're looking at a binary file, retrieving it is the only way to get your hands on that hot little item, but there's an easier way to check out text and graphics files. You can take a look at them directly online.

Viewing Text

Scroll through the listing of files in the Fishing library section. Click on one of the text files. See how the **View** button becomes available? (It's grayed out when a binary file is selected.) The **View** button lets you read through the text file online, one screen at a time, instead of just downloading it to your computer.

Click on **View**, and WinCIM brings up a window containing the actual text from the file. You can read the entire file by using the scroll bars on the right side of the window. When you're done, click on the **OK** button to close the window.

If you read the text file and decide you want to download it, don't bother. Instead choose **Save** from the **File** menu. You can save your current CompuServe window directly into a file (just type the filename). I only suggest viewing a text file if it is really big and you're trying to decide whether you want to download it. Even then, I only read a little bit of the file to make sure it's worthwhile to me. Since forums are expensive, you're paying $4 an hour to read it online. Normally, it makes more fiscal sense to download it and read the file when the meter is not running.

Viewing Graphics Files

You can also view graphics online. While you shouldn't always check out text files online, you're free to view graphics, because you can see graphics as you download them. With text files, you might have to read the entire thing before you can decide whether or not it will be worth your time to download. With graphics, you can only view them while they are being downloaded. After they download, you get the option of saving the graphic or not. If you don't like what you see when you're viewing the graphic, you can close the window and stop viewing the image while you're downloading. This helps you save time and money.

A large drawback to viewing graphics is that you can only do one thing at a time. If you told WinCIM to download the image, you can continue to read messages and/or chat in the forum; when viewing images, you can't.

To view a graphic, select one from the library section (the files with the little picture of the sun over the mountains next to them), and click on the View button. Immediately, a new window appears and the graphic starts downloading. Keep your eye on the bottom of the WinCIM window to follow how much of the graphic has been downloaded. Double-click the box in the top left of the image window to cancel viewing the graphic at any time.

To save your graphic as a file on your computer, choose File and then Save from the WinCIM menu. Click on OK to accept the default filename (or type your own).

Marking a File

Downloading files is pretty easy and straightforward. It takes a little bit of adjustment to figure out what's actually happening, but after that, it's no problem.

But what if there are a lot of files you want to download? Maybe you want to download all the fishy pictures that you can find on CompuServe. You don't want to have to download them one at a time—that could lead to madness.

When you go to a fast food restaurant, it doesn't make sense to get in line three times to order your hamburger, fries, and Coke separately. Instead, you give your complete order to the person at the counter. They wander off to the vast grease pits in the bowels of the restaurant and come back with your food.

On CompuServe, you can order all your files to be downloaded at once, as well. You don't have to search through a library, retrieve a file, twiddle your thumbs while your computer is downloading, then repeat the whole process again (and again). Instead, you can search through the file libraries, mark all the files you want to download, then take a nap while CompuServe retrieves them all.

To mark a file for downloading from the file listing, click on the check box next to the file. CompuServe asks you what to name the file on your computer just like it does when you click on **Retrieve**. The box to the left of the file title becomes checked to signify it is marked for downloading.

Files
with an
× are
marked.

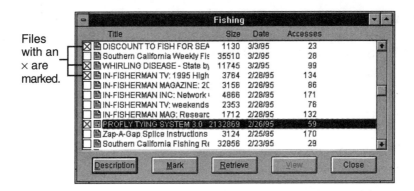

If X marks the spot, these files must hit the target.

Once you've finished marking all the files you want to download, choose **Retrieve Marked** from the **Library** menu to bring up the Retrieve Marked Files dialog box. From here, click on **Retrieve All** to download your marked files. Make sure you click on the **Disconnect when Done** checkbox if you won't be around when the download is complete. Otherwise CompuServe will remain logged on, and you'll continue to pay hourly charges.

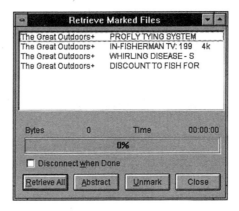

Download all the marked files at one time when you're finished exploring the forum.

I recommend always marking files you want to download instead of doing it one at a time. Even if there's only one file you want to download in the entire forum, once it's marked, you can download anytime while you're in the forum, and don't have to worry about watching CompuServe download it so you can log off.

If you leave a forum before downloading marked files, CompuServe makes sure you want to actually leave instead of downloading the files. Don't worry if you've got to run. You can come back to the forum anytime to get the files because WinCIM remembers the files and forums it marks.

File Forum Searching

One of the problems with files on CompuServe is that there are just so many of them. Since each forum has thousands of files, it would take a while to explore them for exactly the right files. What if you are in the Outdoors forum and you want to find files that talk about bears. You might want a picture of a bear, tips on hunting bears, or rules for not feeding the bears at Jellystone National Park.

What library sections would you look under? State Rifle Assoc.? Wildlife Images? Camp/RV/4x4/Hike? You can find bears in all of these library sections, but you'd have to look through every file in all those sections just to find the one or two that talk about big furry creatures that hibernate in the winter. It'd be really nice if you could just go into a forum and say, "Show me all the files about bears," and have a list of relevant files to choose from.

Well, you can. You can search all the library sections within a forum for files about a topic, from a specific user, or with a certain filename. This makes bear-hunting an easy task. Even the best bear hunters won't find a grizzly as easily as you can with CompuServe.

To search for specific files, click on the **Search Library** icon in the Forum Toolbox to bring up the Search for Files dialog box.

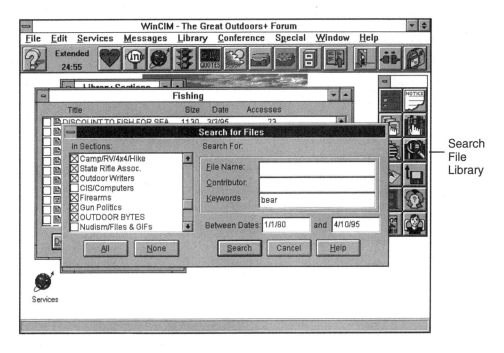

Search File Library

Searching for bears has never been easier.

On the left, you can choose which library sections to search through. Click on the library section name to mark or unmark it from the search. There's bound to be some sections that you don't need to bother searching through. For example, I'm probably not interested in any bear files that I find in the CIS/Computers and Nudism/Files and Gifs sections, so I unmarked them. If you want to look through all the sections regardless, click on the **All** button to mark the entire list.

On the right side of this dialog box you can enter your search criteria. If you know the exact filename or contributor's User ID (the person who uploaded it) you're looking for, type it in; if not, leave those two boxes blank. Then type the keyword describing the files you're looking for. You can also search for files that were uploaded between a certain range of dates. I haven't found a use for this yet. The only search criteria I ever use is **Keywords**. I almost never know the filename, User ID, or upload dates, so I don't even mess with those boxes.

When you're all ready to begin, click on the **Search** button. CompuServe goes off, thinks for a few seconds, and soon returns with a complete listing of all the files that meet your search criteria.

You can access these results just like you might browse through a regular library section. You can see the file abstracts, retrieve files one at a time, or mark them for a batch download.

Uploading a File to a Forum

If you have an interesting file, you can upload it to the CompuServe forum(s) of your choice. If you are a computer programmer and develop a neat game, you might want to upload it to the Gamers Forum. If you're a photographer and snap pictures of race cars, send a picture to the Automobiles Forum.

The only rule is that you can only upload files that you made yourself. If you buy Myst in a store, it's against the law to upload that game to a CompuServe Forum. Similarly, if you see a really interesting article in *National Geographic*, you can't type the article into a text file and upload it to the Outdoors Forum.

Every file uploaded is checked out by the SysOp of that forum. The SysOp checks to make sure you haven't broken any copyright or pornography laws and searches your files for computer viruses. Once they approve your upload, it becomes available in the library sections for others to download it.

To upload a file, click on the **Contribute** icon in the Forum Toolbox. A Library Contribute dialog box comes up. Click on the **File Name** button to choose the file you want to contribute to CompuServe's massive libraries. Choose the right **File Type** in the top left corner (default is binary), and make sure the correct **Forum** and **Library Section** you want to send the file to is selected.

Type a brief title describing the file in the **Title** box. In the **Keys** box, type all the keywords that this file may classify into. This list of words lets people find files when they're searching, so the more comprehensive the list, the better. Separate each word with a space.

In the **Description** box, type a complete description of the file. This is the abstract that other CompuServe members can read to make sure they want to download it. Make sure the Forum and Library Section are set correctly, and then click on the **OK** button.

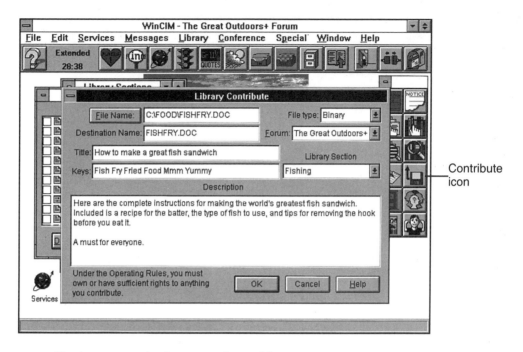

Contribute icon

Here's a great recipe I want to share with everyone.

After clicking **OK**, a window showing the uploading progress appears. You aren't charged any hourly fees for uploading files. CompuServe figures they'll make enough money when hundreds of people download them so they want to encourage uploads.

The Least You Need to Know

With hundreds of thousands of files online, you're bound to find at least one that you'll like and use. Finding the files you like is the hard part. There are so many files in forums that the useful ones often get lost with the mass plenitude of the useless ones.

➤ Browse through forum library sections to see what kinds of files are available.

➤ Mark all the files you want to download, and retrieve them all together.

➤ Graphics and text files can be viewed online instead of downloading them, kind of like a "try before you buy" philosophy.

➤ Upload your own pictures and files to share them with other CompuServe members.

Chapter 13

Searching CompuServe for Cool Stuff

In This Chapter

➤ Locating files with File Finders

➤ Using WinCIM's CompuServe Directory

➤ Browsing the complete CompuServe Index

I spent the last three chapters explaining everything about forums, including discussions of messages, conferences, files, cow tipping, fish, and Rush Limbaugh. The references to cow tipping, fish, and Rush were extremely interesting to some of you, but probably not everyone.

That's the whole point: everyone has his or her own interests. We all have our own hobbies, professions, and pedantic habits. The key to getting the most out of CompuServe is to find your own niche in the online world. In this chapter, you'll learn a few of my favorite tips for finding just the right file, forum, or service on CompuServe.

File Finder

When I first heard about the CompuServe File Finders, I scoffed. What good would an index of hundreds of thousands of files do me, someone who downloads files very rarely, and always at random? (I explore a forum and see something neat, so I grab it.)

I quickly saw the error of my ways, converted, and now I'm a true believer. File Finder is one of the most useful things I've encountered on CompuServe.

Here's how it works: Every month CompuServe collects a list of every single file from around 150 forums. They compile that list into a searchable index. You can search that index online to find files that meet your search criteria in all 150 forums. Then you can download those files directly from File Finder without even going into the forum.

It's like having a catalog of 150 forums at your fingertips. All you have to do is flip through the catalog to the right page and you've got the file. Searching through File Finder is like searching through a forum's library sections; it's that easy.

Remember my bear search from Chapter 12? I was looking in only one forum, and I found lots of files. Think of all the bears I could find if I used File Finder!

Where Do I Find File Finder?

There are actually five different File Finders available on CompuServe. Each File Finder works the same way, but each contains an index of different files. Here's a list of the different File Finders, their respective GO words, and the number of files they index.

File Finder	GO Word	Number of Files (approx.)
PC File Finder	PCFF	130,000
Graphics File Finder	GRAPHFF	45,000
Macintosh File Finder	MACFF	28,000
Atari File Finder	ATARIFF	4,000
Amiga File Finder	AMIGAFF	5,000

The PC and Graphics File Finders are the most popular by far. The PC File Finder indexes most of the hardware and software support forums sponsored by companies, games, and popular utilities that run on your PC. The Graphics File Finder indexes the graphics, photography, and art-related forums on CompuServe.

Let's Find Some Files!

Since I love honey, let's try using the Graphics File Finder to search for pictures of bears. So **GO GRAPHFF** and I'll show you how to search for files.

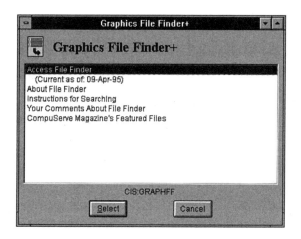

Start your file search here.

A window introducing you to the Graphics File Finder appears. Double-click on **Access File Finder** to begin your search.

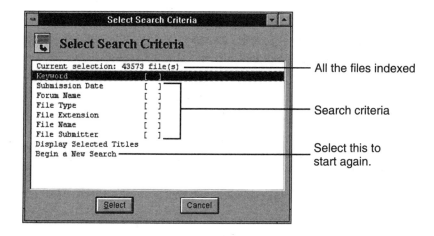

Here's your search engine for finding that special file just for you.

The first line tells you how many files your search criteria have selected. Since you haven't created any criteria yet, there are a huge number of files available because none of them have been weeded out yet. Don't worry, we'll pare down the 44,000-plus files to a reasonable number.

Search Criteria

Double-click on the **Keyword** line. A new dialog box appears that lets you type in the keyword(s) of the files you want.

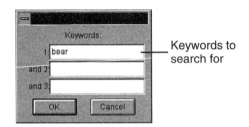

Keywords to search for

Lions and tigers and bears—that's right, I want bears!

Type one word per keyword box. For a file to match your search, it has to have a keyword that matches what you type. Since I typed **bear**, I don't have to worry about finding files that contain **bare** instead (those are different pictures). Usually I only type one keyword. The more keywords, the more restrictive your search is. I don't want to accidentally miss some important files because my search was too restrictive.

When you're done typing your keyword(s), click on the **OK** button to return to the Select Search Criteria window. Notice that the number of files currently selected (top line) has been reduced considerably. There's not a lot of bearish files.

The other criterion I'm going to use is **Submission Date**. By clicking on it, I can tell CompuServe to only select files since a certain date. I only want files from the past three years.

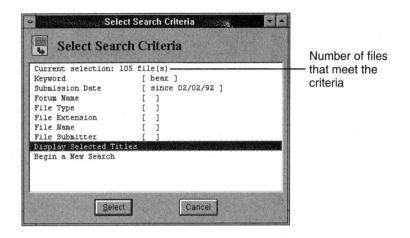

Only 105 files fit, and it's time to check them out.

There are several other search criteria available. Honestly, I don't use them. I like to use File Finder to locate files of a certain topic across lots of forums, so I like to have more general criteria. If you want to restart your search and clear all the search criteria (start with the initial 44,000 files again) click on **Begin a New Search**.

Downloading a File

Once you're finished entering your search criteria, you'll want to see the files that match what you're looking for. Double-click on **Display Selected Titles** to bring up a listing of all the file titles and the forum in which they are found.

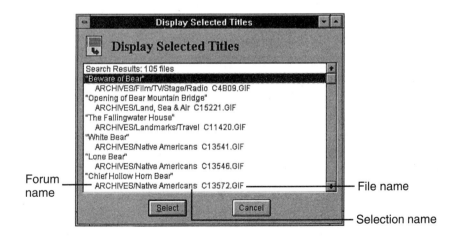

I feel like I'm in the woods with all these bears around.

Fabulous File Finder File Finder is arguably very useful, but it has an extremely annoying interface and is slow and expensive (you pay extended hourly charges just as if you were in a forum). One solution is to use the CompuServeCD. CompuServe releases a bi-monthly CD-ROM that has all the File Finder information on it. You can search for files offline and have CompuServe automatically retrieve them for you. It's *really* nice. Check out Chapter 27 for more details about the CompuServeCD.

Each file listing takes two lines. The first line is the actual file title you would see if you looked at the file in a forum, and the second line is general information on which forum and section the file is stored.

Scroll through the list of files until you find the one you're looking for. You can always write down the forum names and visit the forum directly if lots of files on your topic are saved there. For example, there seem to be a lot of *Bear* files in the Archives forum, so I may want to head there if those bears are my cup of tea.

To download a file, double-click on the title. A window giving you all the vital stats of the file comes up. To download the file, click on the **Retrieve** button. Of course, you can **View** graphics and text files online just as you can in forums.

Here's the annoying thing about how the File Finders work. Once you select and retrieve a file, all your search criteria is deleted, and you've got to start your search all over again. That means if you find six different files that you want, and you download the first file after using File Finder, you've got to step through the entire process five more times. Some people just write the forum name of their files and go directly to the forum.

The CompuServe Directory

Remember installing WinCIM? You had to answer a million questions, tell CompuServe everything about your financial sources, and sign your life away to a big brute named Luigi (Luigi, I'm just kidding, you're not a brute at all) who is CompuServe's debt collector.

Well, when WinCIM was installed, you also got an extra goody tossed in for free, the CompuServe Directory. The CompuServe Directory is a separate Microsoft Windows program that contains a complete listing of what's available online.

I bet you never even wondered what the CompuServe Directory was.

From Windows, open the CompuServe Directory by double clicking on the big question mark icon. The directory appears and you can start searching through it.

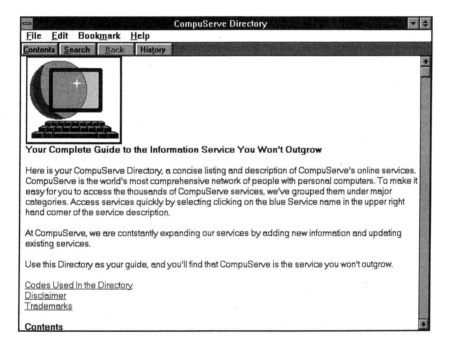

Here's the directory. It may not look like much, but it's pretty complete.

You can navigate through this directory using just your mouse. Click on underlined text to move to a new screen, and press the **Back** button to return to the previous one. Scroll through the available topics. Click on **Personal Interests and Hobbies**. Another screen appears listing lots and lots of services and forums CompuServe has for different hobbies.

Click on **Family Handyman Forum**, and another window comes up that tells you exactly what to expect in that forum.

Click on this GO word to go to that forum.

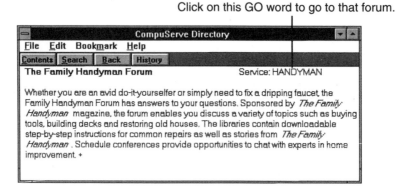

I've got to hand it to the CompuServe Directory. They make going to forums pretty easy.

You're probably saying, "Big deal, I can do the same thing through WinCIM." Not really. The CompuServe Directory gives you a pretty complete description of each forum. Searching online doesn't.

But here's the cool part of the CompuServe Directory. See the word HANDYMAN in the top right corner of the window? That's a GO word for a forum. When you place your mouse over it, your mouse cursor turns into a hand. Then, if you click on the GO word, WinCIM will be loaded, and you'll automatically GO to the forum you click on.

Getting It All: The Comprehensive Online Index

You can also get to the CompuServe Directory from the **Help** menu in WinCIM.

Every year you get a new White Pages from your phone company. The White Pages are great for finding most people, but they're never completely current. New families move to town, others leave. We just assume that the White Pages are pretty current, but not exactly up to date. If we need up-to-the-minute info, we dial 411 and pay the operator to look someone up for us.

The CompuServe Directory is never completely current either. Forums open and close on CompuServe all the time. Most of them are still around, but some of them have changed. Just like 411, there's an up-to-the-minute index of CompuServe services online as well.

GO INDEX to get to the online index. Once you enter the index you have a couple of options. You can see a complete listing of every forum and service, or you can search for a specific topic.

I'm going to try searching for something that's very near and dear to me: beer. Follow along with me, substituting your own word of interest. First, type **1** and then press **Enter** to search the index. CompuServe asks you to type the topic you want to search for and then push **Enter** again.

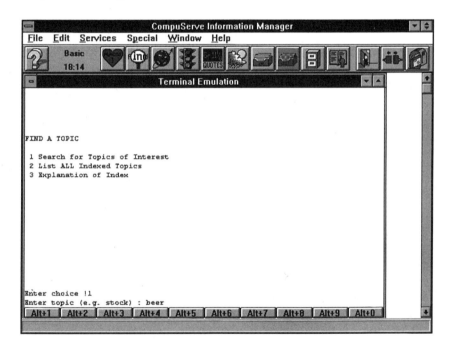

The beer hunter.

After pressing **Enter** a second time, CompuServe searches the index and brings back a list of related forums and services and their unique GO words.

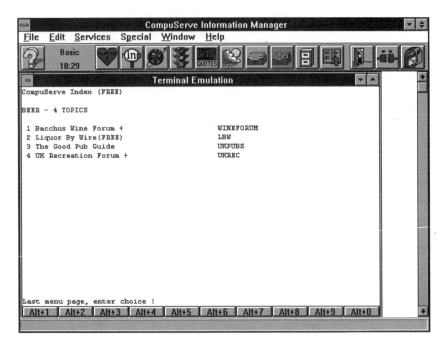

```
┌─────────────────────────────────────────────────────────────┐
│  ▭             CompuServe Information Manager          ▼ ◆   │
│  File  Edit  Services  Special  Window  Help                │
│ ┌────┬──────┬──────────────────────────────────────────────┐│
│ │ ?  │Basic │ ♥ |ⓘn| ◉ |▒| [QUOTES] ✦ ▦ ▦ ▤ ▥ |▦| |◆| ✉    ││
│ │    │18:29 │                                               ││
│ ├────┴──────┴──────────────────────────────────────────────┤│
│ │ ▭                  Terminal Emulation            ▼ ▲   ▲ ││
│ │CompuServe Index (FREE)                                  ││
│ │                                                         ││
│ │BEER - 4 TOPICS                                          ││
│ │                                                         ││
│ │ 1 Bacchus Wine Forum +            WINEFORUM             ││
│ │ 2 Liquor By Wire(FREE)            LBW                   ││
│ │ 3 The Good Pub Guide              UKPUBS                ││
│ │ 4 UK Recreation Forum +           UKREC                ││
│ │                                                         ││
│ │                                                         ││
│ │Last menu page, enter choice !                           ▼│
│ ├──────┬──────┬──────┬──────┬──────┬──────┬──────┬──────┬───┤│
│ │Alt+1 │Alt+2 │Alt+3 │Alt+4 │Alt+5 │Alt+6 │Alt+7 │Alt+8 │...││
│ └──────┴──────┴──────┴──────┴──────┴──────┴──────┴──────┴───┘│
└─────────────────────────────────────────────────────────────┘
```

That's it? No Anheuser-Busch Forum?

You can go directly to any of the services listed by typing its number, or press **Enter** to return to the previous screen.

Listing It All

Déjà Vu
Searching the Index is a lot like using the **Find** command in WinCIM, except you can't add services to your list of favorite places.

Instead of searching for a particular topic, you can list *everything* available on CompuServe. This is *the* definitive list of what to do and where to go. It's updated constantly. Back at the main index screen, instead of typing 1 to search the index, type **2**. Every service along with its GO word is listed in alphabetical order (see the following figure). You can scroll through the list by pressing **Enter**, or you can go directly to a service by typing the number. If you want to return to the first index screen, type / **MENU**.

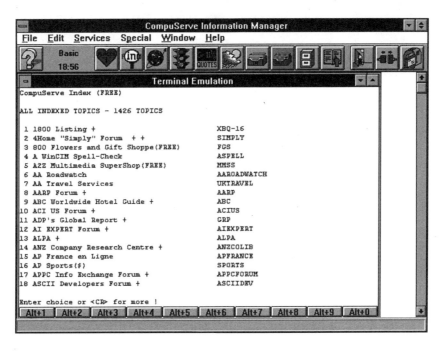

1,426 topics? Wow, there's a ton of different things to do.

The Least You Need to Know

When you drive to a new city, you're not going to remember every street name or restaurant and store you pass. You're going to whip out your AAA map and figure out how to get to your hotel.

With CompuServe, there's no need to become a complete expert. You don't need to worry about memorizing every GO word for every service in the index, or keeping track of every file in the File Finders, but it's nice to know how to get around without getting lost. That's what I talked about in this chapter: how to use the maps provided by CompuServe to get around. Otherwise, you'll probably end up in some flea market in the bad part of town.

➤ If you're looking for some files but don't know what forum to look in, use a File Finder. The PC File Finder is at **GO PCFF**.

➤ The CompuServe Directory that comes with WinCIM is a great reference for finding different things to do. It's in the CompuServe program group in Windows's Program Manager.

➤ Use the online index for the complete list of all the services and forums. To get to it, use **GO INDEX**.

171

Chapter 14

FTP: Finding Files Around the World

In This Chapter

➤ Learn what FTP is (it's not a floral delivery service) and how to use it

➤ Find out when you want to use FTP instead of File Finder

➤ Download files not available on CompuServe

I spent most of the previous two chapters talking about working with files from CompuServe—finding the ones you want and downloading them. There are so many files on CompuServe, it'd take about 43 years of downloading to get them all (Can you imagine your bill?). Surely that's enough files to keep anyone happy, right?

Well, don't decide just yet, because here comes FTP. *FTP, or File Transfer Protocol,* is Internet-speak for two computers exchanging files with one another. When you exchange files with CompuServe, it's called *downloading* (and *uploading*). With the Internet, it's called *FTP*. Why? Don't ask me—*I* didn't name it.

For years, FTP was used only by Internet geeks to send files back and forth to each other. Recently though, CompuServe announced FTP access to all of its users. It's part of their plan to make everything on the Internet available on CompuServe. Now the millions of files available on the Internet can be downloaded by you. You could download the rest of your life—even with a very speedy modem—and not even scratch the surface of what's available.

How Does This FTP Thing Work?

There are thousands of computers that make up that big nebulous network called the Internet. Each one of them has files that can be downloaded (or FTPed). Using FTP, you can pick and choose the files you want to download from any computer on the Internet.

Enunciate Your FTP

By the way, FTP is pronounced by spelling out the letters: eff-tee-pee. It's not *fttph*, like a rude noise.

If you want to sound like a real Internet traveler, you've got to know how to use FTP properly in a sentence. FTP can be used as either a noun or a verb, but not an adjective. You can impress your friends by saying "I FTPed that new game Death 'n Destruction to my computer at home," or "I'll use FTP to pick up the files later." You'll be spotted a mile away if you say "I think I'll wear my FTP jeans today." Either way, I wouldn't recommend using FTP in a pick-up line. "Download" is much more effective.

If you thought File Finder had a lot of files (500,000), wait till you check out what's available through FTP. There are literally millions upon millions of files available for downloading (of course, many of them are 15 years old or worthwhile only if you have a $25,000 computer).

Unfortunately, FTPing files isn't quite as easy as downloading them from CompuServe. Often there's no title or abstract about each file, only the filename. That makes it hard to figure out what you're downloading.

Fortunately, to help you wade through this massive amount of information, CompuServe provides you with a roadmap to many of the popular FTP Internet sites.

What's the Difference between Finding with FTP and File Finder?

I like to think of CompuServe File Finder as a well-organized library. Every bookshelf is clearly marked and there are several librarians whisking around helping you find just the right book. It's a big library, but pretty easy to find the book or magazine you want. Even the computerized card catalog system is up to date. You'd be able to find the Agatha Christie books in no time flat. At the end of the day, all the books are reshelved, and the library is tidied up.

Now imagine a library five times as big (a *huge* library). Due to Republican budget cuts, there's only one librarian at the front counter, no card catalog, and books are strewn all over the place. Try finding a mystery novel there. You'd spend days just finding the fiction section, before finding the whodunit books. And once you look in the right spot, there's no guarantee that the books are even on the bookshelf. Huge stacks of books are teetering in the middle of the floor waiting for the poor librarian to find time to put them away, and candy bar wrappers are strewn along the ground. That's FTP.

So which library would you probably spend more time in? The CompuServe library has enough books for me. There might be more quantity in the FTP library, but that doesn't mean there's better quality. The key to using the FTP library is finding all that information before you turn old and senile.

In general, I'd always check out the CompuServe File Finder first. Using FTP to find files can be very frustrating and painful unless you have divine patience. Personally, I use FTP just to browse around. If I find a neat file that I can't live without, I grab it, but I almost never venture out onto the Internet looking for a specific file.

FTP Made Easy

Now that you know *what* FTP is, let me tell you *how* to use it.

I want to give a disclaimer first, though. FTP is one the most confusing things I have ever found on CompuServe. It's difficult to use, clunky, and often unreliable. There are so many different FTP sites on the Internet that I couldn't possibly explain all the idiosyncrasies of each. CompuServe helps you get over most of that, but it's still confusing. I don't want to scare you away from FTP, I just want you to understand that it may take a little patience to get the hang of downloading files from the Internet.

That said, let's get started. You can find FTP online with **GO FTP**. A window comes up giving you lots of different FTP-related choices (see the following figure). With your monthly CompuServe membership, you get three free hours of Internet services. So spend some time exploring FTP; it's on CompuServe.

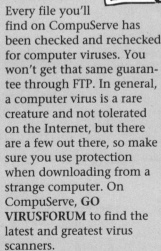

Cover Your Mouth—Virus Protection
Every file you'll find on CompuServe has been checked and rechecked for computer viruses. You won't get that same guarantee through FTP. In general, a computer virus is a rare creature and not tolerated on the Internet, but there are a few out there, so make sure you use protection when downloading from a strange computer. On CompuServe, **GO VIRUSFORUM** to find the latest and greatest virus scanners.

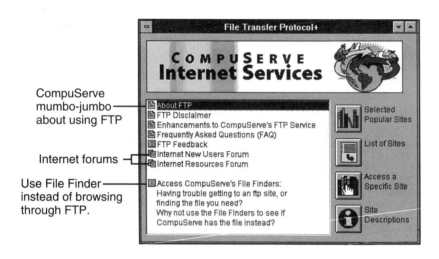

CompuServe mumbo-jumbo about using FTP

Internet forums

Use File Finder instead of browsing through FTP.

Here's the gateway to FTPing with CompuServe.

That's Not What I See!

To access CompuServe's FTP service, you need to be running WinCIM 1.3 or newer. If you installed the WinCIM from the back of this book, you're fine. If you are running an older version of WinCIM, you might want to consider upgrading (it's free). **GO WINCIM** to find the newest version online. Read Chapter 5 for more information on updating your WinCIM.

From this dialog box, you've got several options. For one thing, you can read the CompuServe official description about FTP and their legal disclaimer, "We aren't responsible if you blow your computer up." You can also jump directly to the Internet forums or send e-mail back to CompuServe employees sharing your opinion of FTP.

When you're ready to stop playing around and get busy, check out the right-hand side of the FTP window. There are four buttons you can click on. Use these buttons to access FTP. Here's a description of what each of them does:

Selected Popular Sites—Lets you access several popular FTP sites, through graphical icons.

List of Sites—A slightly larger list of popular FTP sites (no icons). These first two buttons do the same thing, except that **List of Sites** lists a couple more places you can FTP into.

Access a Specific Site—Lets you FTP to a specific Internet site that isn't in CompuServe's list of sites.

Site Descriptions—Presents a paragraph about each popular FTP Site CompuServe helps you get to.

If you're like most people, the only button you'll really use is **List of Sites**. Internet geeks who know a specific FTP address not listed by CompuServe (there are thousands, CompuServe only lists 10–20 really popular ones) can click on **Access a Specific Site**.

Connecting to FTP Sites

Click on **List of Sites** to get CompuServe's list of some popular Internet FTP sites that you can explore—for instance, big companies like Microsoft, IBM, Apple, and Sega have their own FTP sites that you can check out through this list.

My favorite FTP site listed is **Book Stacks Unlimited**. There are thousands of complete books available at that FTP site, free for the downloading. Let's go there. Double-click on it on the list, and we're off.

First, the FTP logon screen comes up, as shown in the following figure. This is the information that you need to fill in to access another computer on the Internet via FTP.

What to Expect What you'll find on each site varies. For example, you'll find hundreds of technical questions and answers at the Microsoft FTP site, while IBM has a bunch of useful things for those of us who are dedicated to Big Blue.

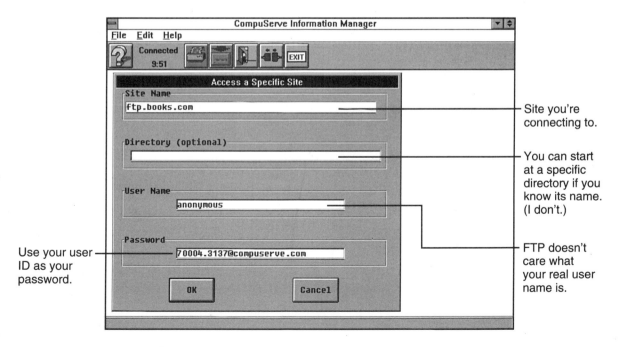

Here's my logon information to an Internet FTP site.

FTP Busy Signal
FTP sites have a specific limit as to how many users can be logged on at one time. As a result, sometimes you'll get an error that asks you to "Try back again later" when they're less busy. Other times the FTP site is just not responding to CompuServe's knock on its door. If you have trouble logging onto an FTP site, try again in a few hours; it's probably just really busy.

You probably won't need to change any of the information in this window. CompuServe fills in everything you need by default, so just click on **OK** to continue and you'll try to FTP to Book Stacks Unlimited.

A message from the Internet site appears letting you know whether or not you were able to log in to your FTP site. It's a good idea to read through this message window for important information about the FTP site.

When you're finished reading the Internet message, click on the **OK** button and you can explore the FTP site (see figure below).

Finding and Downloading Files

Here's where FTP gets a little confusing. All the files on an FTP site are stored in file directories, so you have to navigate through the right directories to find files. It's kind of like going through a maze. You can't see the ending, but can always retrace your steps if you make a wrong turn.

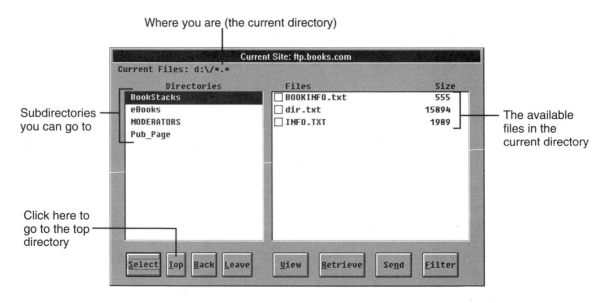

Finding your way around is no problem if you are a DOS or UNIX expert, but confusing to the rest of us.

There are two parts to your FTP screen. The left side shows what subdirectories you can switch to. Files are organized into several subdirectories to make it easier to find what you're looking for. To go into another subdirectory, double-click on the directory name.

Within each directory, there can be several more subdirectories to choose from. For example, if you go into the **eBooks** subdirectory, you have to choose from one of five more subdirectories, each of which has more directories in them as well.

If you want to move back one subdirectory, click on the **Back** button. If you want to return to the very top level of subdirectories, click **Top**.

For Your Viewing Pleasure You can also view text files from an FTP site instead of retrieving them. Click on the file's check box to mark it, and then click on **View**. Viewing often lets you see whether you want to download the entire file. You can also view GIFs instead of downloading them (just like in forums). GIFs are files that end with a .GIF.

On the right side of your screen is a list of files you can download to your personal computer. Downloading here is just like in forums. Double-click on a file to retrieve it.

Once you're finished exploring the FTP site, click on **Leave**, and you'll leave the Internet and come back safe and sound to CompuServe.

Off-the-Beaten-Path FTP Sites

Besides the several FTP sites that CompuServe gives access to, you can log on to most FTP sites around the world. From the FTP window on CompuServe, click on **Access a Specific Site** to go to a different FTP site. You'll see the dialog box shown on the next page.

Type the address of the site you want to go to in the Site Name line, and click on **OK**. (Your user name and password should already be filled in.) You'll connect in no time flat. Just as a cautionary tale though, most FTP sites aren't as friendly as Book Stacks Unlimited was. It wasn't too bad finding neat things to download there. It'll take a lot more patience and wandering through subdirectories at most FTP sites.

For a complete list of available FTP sites on the Internet, go to the Internet New Users Forum (**GO INETFORUM**) and check out the FTP library section. In the meantime, here's a list of a few neat FTP sites you might want to explore that aren't in CompuServe's list.

Internet Access
CompuServe offers a whole bunch of different Internet services. There are several Internet Forums, Telnet and World Wide Web (WWW) access, and you can even check out the USENET newsgroups (I talk about those in chapter 17). **GO INTERNET** to find a complete listing of everything Internetty you can do on CompuServe, and special prices for using the Internet services.

Site Name	FTP Address
Macmillan Publishing (that's us)	mcp.com
NASA space pictures and files	ames.arc.nasa.gov
Library of Congress	marvel.loc.gov
NCSA (home of Mosaic)	ftp.ncsa.uiuc.edu

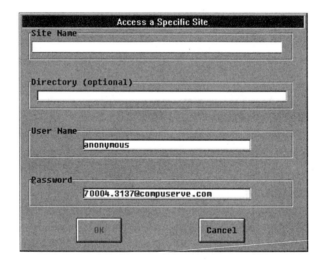

Now you have to provide the site address to which you want to FTP. Besides that, everything else works the same as before.

The Least You Need to Know

There now, FTP wasn't that bad, was it? Honestly, unless you use the Internet a lot, you probably won't want to waste your time on FTP. Almost everything that you'll ever need can be found on CompuServe. I've never been required to use FTP to download a neat utility or work on something productive. I usually waste my time downloading pictures of NASA space shuttles, or books that I'll never read anyway. While this stuff is neat, I'm not sure I'd care to spend too much money on it.

➤ FTP is like a file finder that's ten times as big as what you'll find on CompuServe. **GO FTP** to learn how to connect to different sites.

➤ FTP is the Internet's way of sending files back and forth between computers.

➤ **GO INET FORUM** to find an extensive list of FTP sites to download.

➤ CompuServe provides 10 main FTP sites to start exploring. You may never need more.

Part 3
The CompuServe Newsstand

Extra, extra, read all about it! Don't you just hate a soggy newspaper first thing in the morning, the boring weatherman spouting stats you don't understand or care to (you just want to know if you should cancel your picnic), and the late-to-arrive newsmagazine with already-old news? Well, CompuServe has the solution for you. It has more news than Dan Rather, Connie Chung, and Tom Brokaw combined. And no commercials!

Your Basic News and Weather

In This Chapter

➤ Read Associated Press news stories anytime you like

➤ Confirm your suspicions that your meteorologist makes up the forecast

➤ Find out the weather worldwide (with cool maps)

➤ Get wired with *U.S. News & World Report* online

You love to read the daily newspaper and watch the nightly news, but that's still not enough news for you. You want to be current on current affairs. For you news junkies, CompuServe provides AP newswire that you can access whenever you like. This means if you have an insatiable urge to know what's going on in Bolivia at 4:00 in the morning, you can log on to CompuServe and find out.

Perhaps you like to sit back and read a weekly news magazine to get extended coverage on current events. CompuServe brings you one of the most popular of these weeklys, *U.S. News & World Report*. With *U.S. News*, you may have to wait longer to find out what's happening in Bolivia, but you'll get an in-depth analysis.

But wait, there's more. With CompuServe, you can also get up-to-date weather forecasts and conditions from around the world. You can figure out whether it's going to rain in Seattle (hint: it always does) or snow in Canada. You can even *download* those cool weather maps that your local meteorologist always uses during the newscast. No, the clouds don't move, but the maps do show you the current weather patterns.

Eavesdropping on the Associated Press

Download
The process of bringing a file from CompuServe to your personal computer to store it for future use. You can download all sorts of files, ranging from pictures to programs that will run on your computer. See Chapter 12 for more details.

With reporters covering the world, the Associated Press (AP) is one of the nation's largest news services. Its stories range from Hollywood gossip to White House politics and appear in newspapers around the world. Within minutes of publication on the AP wire, these stories become available online at CompuServe. From there, you can pick and choose which ones you want to read.

The best part about this service is that it's included with your monthly membership fees. You can access the AP newswire as often as you want at no additional cost. CompuServe brings the news to you 24 hours a day, seven days a week (even on holidays). Just think, this means you don't have to trudge outside to pick up a newspaper that's soggy from last night's thunderstorm.

Getting the News Hot off the Presses

Using WinCIM to get to the news is easier than turning on the TV (unless you have a remote control). All you have to do is click on the **News** icon from the main WinCIM screen (**GO NEWS**). You'll see the News screen, as shown below.

You can choose from all sorts of news to read, such as *U.S. News & World Report*, Syndicated Columnists, and CNN Online. (You'll hear about these in the next couple of chapters.) For now, just click on **Associated Press Online** to jump to the news stories.

When you click on Associated Press Online, CompuServe shows you the AP copyright box. Basically, this is CompuServe's friendly reminder that everything on the AP newswire is copyrighted. You are not allowed to go start your own newspaper and use the AP stories without permission from them (which costs a lot of money). Click on **Proceed** to skip this intro. It doesn't get any more interesting after you've read it once, and it's debatable whether it's interesting the first time.

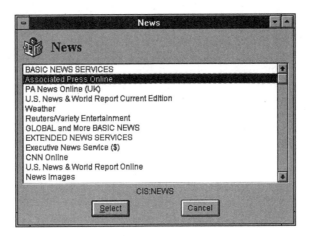

From here, you can pick all sorts of interesting news-related items.

The news stories are organized into such categories as National, World, Entertainment, Sports, Political, Business, and Science. To get a list of the latest important headlines, choose **Latest News-Updated Hourly** (see figure below). To read the news stories under a particular section, simply click on the appropriate topic name, such as **National**, and then click the **Select** button.

Shortcut!
Instead of clicking on a topic and then clicking on the Select button, simply double-click on the topic.

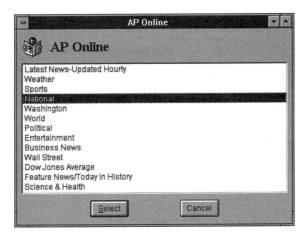

Click on the news area that has the stories you want to read.

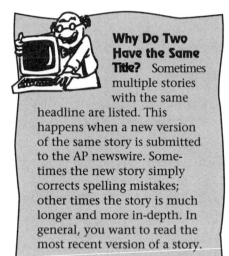

Why Do Two Have the Same Title? Sometimes multiple stories with the same headline are listed. This happens when a new version of the same story is submitted to the AP newswire. Sometimes the new story simply corrects spelling mistakes; other times the story is much longer and more in-depth. In general, you want to read the most recent version of a story.

You can pick whichever area contains stories that most interest you. Once you choose a general area, you get a list of related news stories, with the most recent ones displayed at the top of the list. Each story has a one- to two-day life on CompuServe. After that, a story is *old* news and scrolls off the list of available news articles. Make sure you read your news often enough that you don't miss any important articles.

Each news story is identified by its headline, which usually makes it easy to pick the ones you want to read (see figure below). Scroll through the list of headlines and select the story you want to read by clicking on the headline and clicking **Select** or by double-clicking the headline.

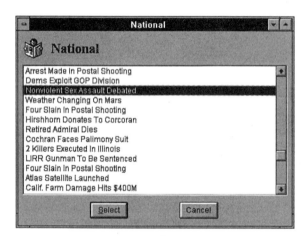

National news stories you can choose from.

If this news isn't enough, be sure to check out the next chapter. In Chapter 16, I discuss all sorts of specialty news services.

Future Reference

You can file news articles in your personal WinCIM filing cabinet just as you do e-mail and forum messages. While the news article is displayed on-screen, click the **File It** button. You'll be able to pick which filing cabinet to put the message into for future reference.

If you want to print the article, that's just as easy. Choose **File Print** from the menu bar, and the current article is sent directly to your printer. Pretty convenient, huh?

Scoping Out U.S. News & World Report

There are more news services online than just the AP wire. For example, you can peruse the latest issue of *U.S. News & World Report.* Each week, CompuServe puts out the current issue of *U.S. News* for everyone to read. Why bother subscribing when you can read it all online? In fact, you can actually check out the forthcoming edition on Sunday night while subscribers have to wait until Tuesday for it to be delivered via snail-mail (the U.S. Postal Service). What's more, there are no ads in the CompuServe edition of *U.S. News.* Yes, that's right. No more annoying subscription inserts that fall into your lap.

The stories, the pictures, and even the editorial cartoons from *U.S. News* are accessible to CompuServe members at no extra charge. It's all included with your monthly membership. Sound too good to be true? It probably is, but don't tell the folks over at CompuServe. Make sure you don't miss an issue. Back issues are expensive: you'll pay $1.50 an article to access them later from the Magazine Plus Database.

More Where That Came From If you like reading *U.S. News & World Report* online, you'll probably be happy to know that *People, Fortune,* and *Sports Illustrated* (yes, even the swimsuit edition) are also available on CompuServe. *U.S. News* is probably the best value, however, because it is included with your monthly fee, and the entire magazine is always available online. Chapter 18 covers online magazines in detail, so I'll see you there.

Where's the Glossy Paper?

If you aren't too attached to flipping pages, you'll probably find that reading *U.S. News* online is for you. It's much easier to pick and choose the stories you want to read. Personally, I always skip the boring national stories and go straight to the News You Can Use section.

You can find *U.S. News* in the same place you found the AP Wire. Click on the **News** icon from the main WinCIM screen and choose **U.S. News & World Report Current Edition (GO EUN1)**. The U.S. News welcome screen appears, as shown on the next page.

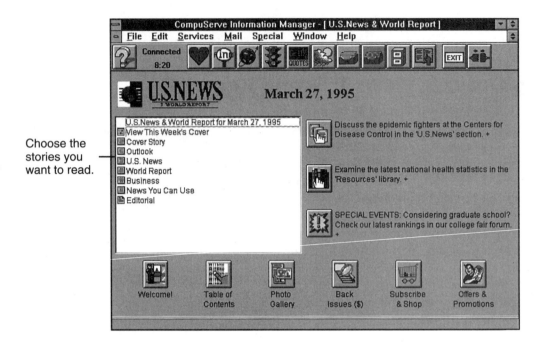

Choose the stories you want to read.

The U.S. News welcome screen.

In the U.S. News welcome screen, you'll find a list of the various sections of the magazine as well as a number of icons. There's even an icon (Subscribe and Shop) that gives you access to subscription information for *U.S. News*—in case you *really* miss those advertisements.

To read a story, click on the section you are interested in, and CompuServe displays a list of headlines of all the stories available in that section. Then you can read each story individually. Just as you did in the AP news area, double-click on the story you want to read. If you want to see a list of all the stories in the entire issue, click on the **Table of Contents** button.

Picture Pages

What would a magazine be without pictures? Not much fun. All those glossy pages would be a waste. Understanding this, *U.S. News* also lets you view some of the most interesting pictures in each week's edition.

For example, every week you can look at the cover and approximately ten other images included with the magazine. Luckily, they don't scan in any advertisements.

To check out the cover, just click on **View this Week's Cover**, and CompuServe brings up the picture for you. If you want to see all the pictures for the current issue, click on the **Photo Gallery** button and pick the specific photo you want (see figure below).

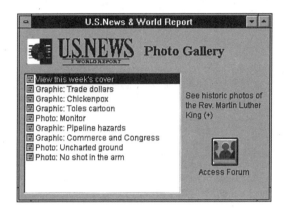

The pictures listed are available to you through U.S. News.

Venting Your Opinions

U.S. News also sponsors a forum (**GO USNFOR**) that's tied to the weekly magazine, where you can debate the latest issues. This could be your chance to prove that Limbaugh spelled backwards is Satan or to yell at some ninny about government spending. Jump to the forum by clicking on the top right button on the U.S. News welcome screen.

The editorial staff of *U.S. News* hangs out in this forum. Sometimes they even print posted responses directly on CompuServe. Other than that, this is a regular CompuServe forum with several discussions about the issues brought up within the magazine.

Tomorrow It'll Be Sunny and 95—with Flurries

Personally, I have little faith in my weather forecaster. Call me crazy, but the only surefire way I know it will rain is if I've forgotten my umbrella at home. No longer! Now I can check the weather forecast and current weather while I am dry and cozy in front of my computer.

Just as you read the news online, you can check the weather anytime of the day or night. All you have to do is open the **Services** menu from the WinCIM menu bar and choose **Weather** (**GO WEATHER**) or click on the **Weather** icon on the ribbon. (It's the icon with the sun and clouds on it. Imagine that!) The Weather dialog box appears, in which you indicate the area for which you want weather information (see the figure on the next page).

By default, CompuServe assumes you want local weather readings, but you can change that. To do so, click on each text box, type the location (city, state/province, and country) of where you want to get the weather, and click **OK**. If you prefer, you can scroll through a list of available cities by clicking on the down arrow in the Weather box. (This can be extremely helpful if you don't know how to spell the name of a city or country.)

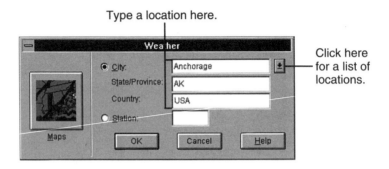

Let's see what the weather is like in Alaska.

CompuServe displays the complete National Weather Service forecast for the area you've selected (see figure below).

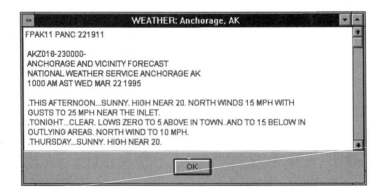

What a surprise! It's cold in Alaska.

Get the Picture?

Not only can you get the weather forecast, you can also see radar pictures showing the current weather situation for various cities, states, countries, and continents. Using the National Weather Service's pictures, you can check out precipitation and cloud cover for all the major cities in the world.

To see one of these maps, click on the **Maps** icon in the Weather dialog box. The CompuServe Weather Maps dialog box appears, as shown below. Pick which type of map you want to see: a satellite picture or temperature forecasts.

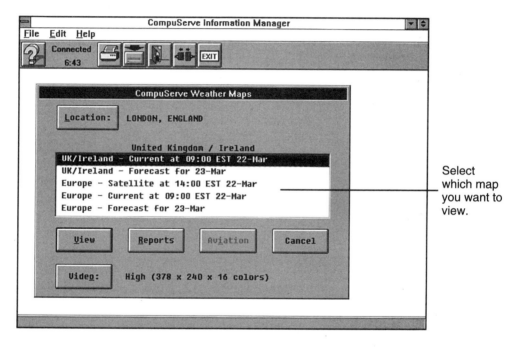

Select which map you want to view.

*Select the type of map you want to display and click **View**.*

Click on the type of map you want to display, and then click on the **View** button. CompuServe downloads the map and displays it automatically on your screen (see the figure on the following page).

Always a popular choice, the map of Europe shows cloud cover from the last pass of the weather satellite.

If you want further information, you might need to use the other buttons in this window. The Reports button gives you the short-term forecast, while the Aviation button shows you flying conditions (if available). If you click on Location, you can see maps from somewhere else, and if you click on Video, you can change the resolution of the maps you download.

The Least You Need to Know

You have only hit the tip of the iceberg when it comes to finding news on CompuServe. Don't be afraid to use CompuServe to replace your favorite news sources (newspaper, TV, coffee break).

➤ You can read online the same AP stories that your paper prints and get up-to-the-minute news. Simply click on the **News** icon, select **Basic News Services**, and click on **Associated Press Online**.

➤ *U.S. News & World Report* comes out earlier and cheaper on CompuServe—and it doesn't have any advertisements. Just click on the **News** icon and click on **U.S. News & World Report**.

➤ Getting current weather maps and forecasts is a breeze; simply click on the **Weather** button on the WinCIM ribbon.

Extra-Cost News Services

In Chapter 15, you learned how to get the latest AP news stories online from the AP newswire. However, if you're switching from the traditional newspaper to online news, you might feel like something's missing. There's a lot more to your daily newspaper than AP stories. You can't forget about the editorials, the sports coverage, or the horoscopes. They're the best parts!

With CompuServe, you can have all of the sections of a newspaper at your immediate disposal. You can read what Miss Manners has to say about how to eat a peach, or you can succumb to the cosmos and access Joyce Jillson's horoscope (everybody reads it, but nobody admits to it). If you're one of those gung-ho fans who thinks 22 hours of sports a weekend is not enough, the AP Sports Wire brings you super in-depth coverage of sporting events around the world. More thorough than the regular AP wire, the Sports Wire is a must-see for sports fanatics.

In addition to all that, there is also the Executive News Service. With this feature, CompuServe gives you access to newswires around the world. This makes it possible for you to get up-to-date worldwide information from various viewpoints (in addition to the Associated Press).

Columns: Pillars of Interest

CompuServe runs nearly twenty popular syndicated columns online. You can find the exact same columns—from Alan Dershowitz to Miss Manners—that are printed in newspapers. Most columns are available for at least a month, so you can easily catch up on Marilyn Beck's Hollywood Insight if you miss a week when you're vacationing in the French Riviera.

Syndicated columns are easy to find online. All you have to do is click on the **News** icon from WinCIM and then choose **GLOBAL and More BASIC NEWS (GO COLUMNS)**. CompuServe displays a list of newswires from other countries such as Australia, France, Germany, and the UK (see figure below).

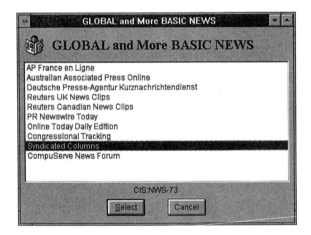

If you speak French, you might want to click on AP France en Ligne. If not, click on Syndicated Columns.

Near the bottom of the list, double-click on **Syndicated Columns**. The Syndicated Columns dialog box appears, as shown on the following page, listing the available syndicated column topics.

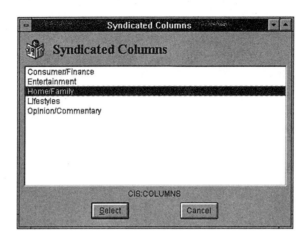

Choose the topic of syndicated columns you're interested in.

Pick the topic of columns you want to check out. As you can see, the categories aren't very detailed. Which one do you think Miss Manners' articles are hiding behind? You could arguably choose topic #2 Entertainment, topic #3 Home/Family, topic #4 Lifestyles, topic #5 Opinion/Commentary, or the $50 hidden somewhere in this book. Of course, you'd all take the $50 and run, but there's really no free money hidden. So you'd better highlight topic #2 **Home/Family** and click on **Select**. The Home/Family dialog box appears, as shown below.

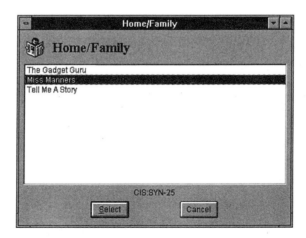

The list of columnists.

In the Home/Family dialog box, you choose the columnist you want to read. To do so, click on the columnist's name and click **Select**. To read a column, simply double-click on its name. For example, let's pick Miss Manners (my favorite) and see what topics she has written about recently. The next dialog box displays all of Miss Manners' recent articles and their publication dates, as shown below.

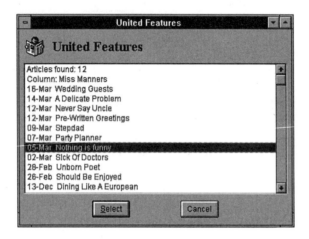

Miss Manners covers a wide range of topics.

To read a specific article, just double-click on it. Although they all look tempting, I'm going to pick the column entitled "Nothing is funny" to see if Miss Manners says etiquette requires one to laugh at jokes one does not find funny.

Wired for a Win

Smash! Pow! Ooof! Just imagine how close you can be to the sports action when you use Sports Illustrated Online's Sports Services. Maybe the "typical" sports fan can get enough sports from the Associated Press Online (Chapter 15), but not you. You don't just want the basketball, football, and baseball news; you want to know everything there is to know about sports, and you want to keep up on every sporting event around the globe. You need Sports Illustrated Online.

I know you, you're foaming at the mouth, chomping at the bit. How do you get all this sports information? Simply click on the **News** icon from WinCIM and double-click on **Sports** (or **GO SPORTSILL**). You'll be thrown right into Sports Illustrated Online (see the figure on the following page). From here, you can see the latest scores and stats, play in a fantasy sports league or two, read *Sports Illustrated* (the magazine), or take a look at the latest news on any sport you can imagine.

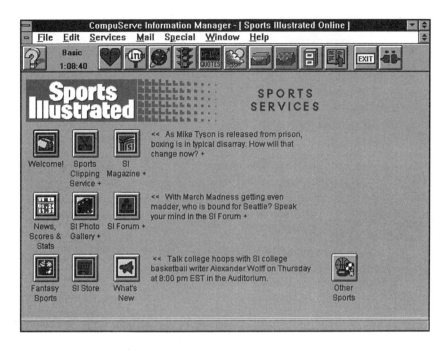

Sports Illustrated Online's opening screen.

Sports Illustrated Online's opening screen guides you through many of the sports services available on CompuServe. To read the latest news as organized by sport, click on **Sports Clipping Service**. If you play fantasy football or baseball, click on **Fantasy Sports**. Personally, I like to read the most recent issue of *Sports Illustrated* (click on **SI Magazine**) and shop in the SI paraphernalia store (click on **SI Store**).

If you're a die-hard sports fan, you'll need to see the latest and greatest sports scores and stats. To see who won the most recent Cubs game, click on **News, Scores, & Stats**. Then click on whichever sport you want to read about (see figure below).

Although it's very interesting (and addictive), don't dilly-dally around in Sports Illustrated Online. You're paying $15.00 an hour for the privilege of reading about the European golf tour or a monster truck rally.

Click on College Basketball to see who's really Number 1.

More News Services

There are a lot more news services on CompuServe than just the AP Wire. Personally, I use the AP almost every day, but sometimes I want more detailed news about a specific topic. That's where extra news services like the AP Sports Wire (that I just talked about) come in. There are a ton of special news services, and it would take an entire book to describe them all. Here's a list of the extra news services available on CompuServe, along with their GO words.

News Service	GO Word
AP France en Ligne (AP in French)	APFRANCE
Australian Associated Press	AAPONLINE
PA News (News from England)	PAO
Reuters Canadian News Clips	RTCANADA
The Business Wire	TBW
NewsGrid (worldwide news categorized)	NEWSGRID
News Source USA (articles several days old)	NEWSUSA
NewsNet (Business Newsletters)	NN

For "hot" topics, CompuServe often collects news stories from all the newswires available worldwide. So if you want to read all the stories about AIDS, you can find them all together; CompuServe collects all the stories that mentions AIDS in one spot. Such topics come and go as various issues are popular. For example, here's a list of all the topics that were available the day I wrote this chapter.

News Topic	GO Word
Cuba	CUBA
AIDS	AIDSNEWS
Apple (the computer company)	APPLENEWS
Baseball strike	BBSTRIKE
Bosnia	BOSNIA
Haiti	HAITI
Northern Ireland	NIRELAND
Outdoors	OUTNEWS
OJ Simpson	OJNEWS
Rwanda	RWANDA
Microsoft Windows	WINCLIPS

Wire Clipping with the Executive News Service

Let's say you were in the banana business, and you wanted to keep tabs on the competition. One way would be to sift through all the big newswires in the world and look for articles with the word "banana." (Don't search for "Carmen Miranda.") It might take a while, but eventually you'd pick up all the AP stories that mentioned bananas, all the financial press about banana stock, and all the international news about banana growers. Wouldn't this be useful?

To help you search many different newsfeeds, CompuServe provides the Executive News Service (ENS). Basically, you can have CompuServe search the AP, UPI, Reuters, and Washington Post newswires for a specific topic or set of topics. Because CompuServe stores all related messages together, you can easily scan through them and read the ones that interest you.

As new stories are added to the newswire, CompuServe scans each story to see if it is about a topic in which you are interested (you tell it which topics to watch for). If it is about one of your specified topics, CompuServe clips the article into a folder for you. CompuServe organizes the articles you want into folders that function like online filing cabinets. So if you were in the banana business, you could create a "banana" folder to keep track of your main business, and a separate "papaya" folder if you wanted to follow the news on other fruity topics.

Executizing Yourself

To access the Executive News Service (**GO ENS**), click on the **News** icon in the WinCIM window, and then double-click on **Executive News Service**. Or, you could open the **Services** menu and choose **Executive News**. Either way, the Executive News Service window appears with the Select Folder dialog box open, as shown below.

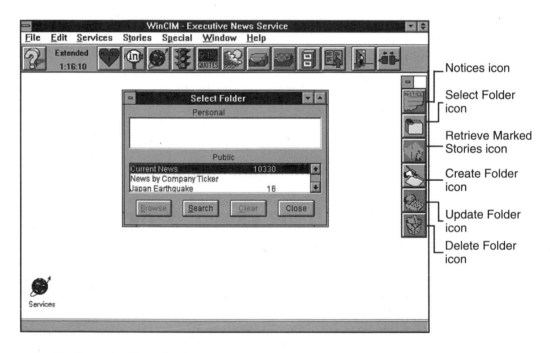

The Executive News Service screen.

Your Executive News Service screen is a little different from the normal WinCIM screen. Each time you access this screen, the Select Folder dialog box appears, in which you select a folder of articles you want to read. You can choose a personal folder you've created yourself (which contains articles that match your personal interests) or a public folder (which contains articles on more general topics). In addition, icons appear down the right side of the screen. You use these icons to create and modify the folders.

Clipping
CompuServe's means of copying a story that's of interest to you from its original source and putting it in your personal folder for that specific topic.

There are two ways to use the Executive News Service. You can search through a conglomeration of all the articles from the available newswires, or you can have CompuServe *clip* all articles that pertain to a particular topic and store them in a personal folder so you can read them later.

Checking Out All the Wires

If you want to look through the entire network of newswires, choose the public folder entitled **Current News** and click on the **Search** button. In the resulting dialog box, you tell CompuServe which newswires you want to search. If you want to search all the wires, click the **All** button. If not, click on each newswire you want to explore (the check box has an X through it when you've selected it) and click on the **Search** button again.

In a flash, CompuServe displays every story from the newswires you've selected, with the most recent articles first (see the figure on the next page). CompuServe keeps the latest 9,500 news stories available for you to search through (but who'd want to?). Scroll through the list using the scroll bar and click on any article you want to read to select it. Then click on the **Get** button to read the story, the **Preview** button to preview the first paragraph of the story, or the **Mark** button to indicate that you want to download the story to your filing cabinet.

I've found this feature to be useful only when a really hot news item hits the presses, because I can see several different viewpoints about important issues. However, because there are thousands upon thousands of stories daily, in general, it would be a mammoth task to keep track of them all. That's why I prefer to use personal folders, which I tell you about next.

Creating a Personal Folder

If you don't want to wade through every story that was written in the past week, you can have CompuServe search more than twenty-five different newswires for a specific topic. To do so, follow these steps:

Look at all those stories!

1. Click on the **Create Folder** icon on the right side of the Executive News Service window. The Create Folder dialog box appears, as shown below, asking you for some information.

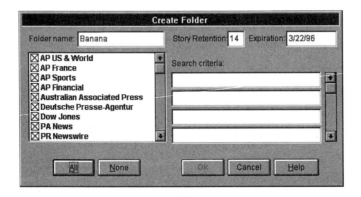

2. Enter a name for your folder in the **Folder name** text box.

3. In the list box on the left side of the screen, click on the newswires you want CompuServe to search. When you select a newswire, an X appears in the box next to its name. This tells CompuServe which newswires to search. Click on the box again to remove the X, if necessary.

4. Enter the information you are looking for in the Search criteria boxes. (If, for example, you enter "Bill" in one box and "Hillary" in the second, you'll get all the stories with the words "Bill" and "Hillary" in them.)

5. When you are finished entering your search criteria, click on **OK**.

If you want to make sure you don't miss any articles on your topic, choose all of the newswires by clicking on the **All** button.

Unfortunately, you can have only three personal folders per account, so use them wisely. If you want to delete one of your existing folders (presumably to make room for a new one), click on the **Delete Folder** icon, which looks like a trash can. A window appears listing your three folders. Click on the name of the folder you want axed and press **Delete**.

Checking Up on Your Folders

Well, now that you've created your personal folder(s), you can reap the benefits of having CompuServe automatically search newswires for you. If you created a personal folder called IBM, CompuServe would probably find lots of news stories to clip because IBM is mentioned in so many articles. Depending on how narrow your topics are, however, it might be a couple of days before CompuServe finds any pertinent news stories to clip. For example, if you created a personal folder called banana, you wouldn't have to check your folder more than every couple of weeks or so because there aren't a lot of banana stories.

CompuServe will clip and store a maximum of 500 stories in each personal folder. Make sure you check your personal folders and clean them out often so the stories don't accumulate. This can quickly become a hassle to keep up to date.

When you first access Executive News Service, CompuServe tells you how many stories it has clipped into each of your personal folders (500 means that you've maxxed out). To browse through those stories, click on your personal folder in the Select Folder window and click on the **Browse** button (see the figure on the following page).

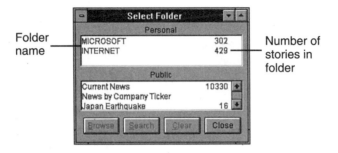

CompuServe has clipped 302 stories about Microsoft.

That's Not What I Wanted to Read About

Remember that CompuServe cannot distinguish between the various meanings of a word. For example, when you search for the word "Lotus," CompuServe clips all articles relating to the lotus flower, Lotus cars, Lotus Corporation, and any other random reference to the word "Lotus." It is up to you to decide which stories are of value.

For each story in your personal folder, you can click on the **Get** button to read the story, the **Preview** button to see the first paragraph (to determine if you want to read it), the **Mark** button to retrieve the story, or the **Delete** button to clear it from your personal folder.

Cleaning Up Your Personal Folders

Once you've looked through your personal folders and read all the stories you wanted to read, you'll want to clean out the folder so you don't find the same articles the next time you look. But don't jump the gun and just delete all the stories! First retrieve any marked stories.

Mark When you mark an article, you're telling CompuServe that you want to download that article to your WinCIM filing cabinet. Then when you're ready to download, you click on the **Retrieve Marked Stories** icon, and CompuServe downloads all marked stories and deletes them from your personal folder.

Once you've retrieved your marked stories, simply select the personal folder in the Select Folder window and click the **Clear** button. The Clear folder dialog box appears, as shown on the following page.

You can delete stories older than a certain date, or just eliminate them all.

To delete stories older than a specific date, click on the **Delete stories older than** option button and enter a date. If you prefer to wipe the entire folder clean, click on the **Clear all stories in this folder** option button. When you're ready to delete the stories, click on **OK**. CompuServe wipes out all the old articles you indicated.

The Least You Need to Know

There's a lot more to news on CompuServe than just the AP wire and *U.S. News & World Report*. You've seen just a few more places to go to find interesting information on current events.

➤ Syndicated Columns are easy to keep up with at your leisure on CompuServe.

➤ Sports Illustrated Online is as in-depth and thorough as ESPN and your local paper—but it comes with a hefty price.

➤ Clipping from 25 different newswires is a great way to find all current articles on everything from bananas to computer products.

Chapter 17

USENET: Messages from the Masses

> ## In This Chapter
> ➤ Familiarizing yourself with newsgroups
> ➤ Communicating with millions of people outside of CompuServe
> ➤ Responding to articles posted on a specific newsgroup

What would you say if I told you that there are thousands upon thousands of forum-like discussion groups available to you through CompuServe? Well, there are. They are called newsgroups, and millions of people besides CompuServe customers can read and reply to newsgroups and send messages back and forth to each other.

Newsgroups, which were created shortly after the inception of the Internet, enable people all over the world to participate in conversations with millions of other Internet users worldwide. A newsgroup is a discussion group that focuses on one general topic and is similar to a forum, except that there is no "section" of files, no Sysop (generally), and no online conferences.

Not interested in newsgroups? You should be. Newsgroups number in the thousands, and there is a newsgroup on nearly every topic imaginable, from marching bands to laser printers, and for nearly every personality imaginable, from saxophonists to Brady Bunch enthusiasts. In fact, you'll probably find hundreds of newsgroups that interest you.

What Is USENET?

USENET was originally created so professors from different universities could talk to each other in a public discussion. Since e-mail is a private conversation in which only recipients can take part, they wanted to make it easier for people to eavesdrop on their conversations. So, using the Internet, they created USENET, which consists of thousands of discussion groups to which information is posted back and forth (newsgroups).

Store and Forward

USENET uses a technique called "store and forward" that allows the different sites on the Internet to distribute news articles. When a computer on the Internet gets a news article for a newsgroup, it stores the article with the rest of the newsgroups, and then automatically sends it to the next computer in the Internet.

When newsgroups were first created, there were only very, very technical (and boring) newsgroups. Today, however, there's bound to be at least one that interests you (heck, there may be 25). With your monthly CompuServe membership, you get three free hours of Internet services. So spend some time exploring USENET.

How's It Set Up?

The USENET founders didn't want to have one big discussion base where people talked about everything. (Just think what it would be like if CompuServe had only one forum: sure there'd be a lot of cool things there, but it might get a bit confusing.) So they decided to use a naming system that would break up conversations into hundreds of different subcategories. You access the newsgroups that interest you by working your way from general to more specific.

Accessing newsgroups is similar to contacting your local phone company: you push 1 for customer service, 2 for installation, 3 for Monopoly information, and so on. Once you make a choice, you're bumped to another menu system (push 1 for billing inquiries, 2 to cancel service, 3 for equipment maintenance, and so on) until you finally work your way to a customer service person. Using this system, the phone company ensures that you are directed to someone who can deal with your problem.

Newsgroups are usually categorized into two types: USENET and Other. The USENET newsgroups are structured similarly to the phone system I just described. There is one main "number": USENET (User's Network). From there, you choose from several different newsgroup categories. Then you continue to pick subcategories until you're in the right newsgroup.

And the Category Please...

USENET consists of only seven categories and has strict rules for creating new newsgroups within those categories. The newsgroups within these categories tend to focus on cut-and-dried topics for serious and studious users. The following table describes the seven main newsgroup categories.

The Main USENET Categories

Category	Description
comp	Computer-related issues (all the computer geeks hang out in these newsgroups)
news	Technical talk about USENET itself
rec	Recreational and fun stuff
sci	High-tech scientific babble (check out **sci.physics**)
soc	Discussion pertaining to social issues
talk	Heated debates on hot topics (for example, **talk.abortion**)
misc	Topics that fit into all or none of the categories

Because USENET categories are so strict and its topics are so serious, several "Other" categories have been created to handle creative newsgroup ideas. CompuServe newsgroup categories that would fall under "Other" include:

Category	Description
alt	Everything—and I mean EVERYTHING (check out **alt.buddha.short.fat.guy** for a creative view of Buddhism)
bionet	Biological and environmental issues
compuserve	CompuServe-sponsored newsgroups about the information service (a good place to start)
k12	Discussions on issues pertaining to education

Who's the Boss Here?

The short answer is "Nobody": there is no CEO or Sysop of USENET. The long answer is "Everybody": USENET is more of a community where lots of opinions rule. To understand this concept, consider the process a person goes through to create a new newsgroup.

If you want to create a new newsgroup, you have to submit a formal proposal to a USENET committee. If the proposal meets certain requirements (if the format is okay and the proposal has 100 electronic supporters), it is put up for a full vote and every user on the Internet has the opportunity to vote on it. It takes approximately three months to get through the whole rigmarole. Although this may sound like mass chaos, it's organized mass chaos.

There are plenty of USENET experts who are available to help out new users, and most people are forgiving if someone makes a mistake (like posting the Pledge of Allegiance to **alt.anarchy**). However, the USENET has a very independent and free spirit that does not allow any one person to control it.

You may find some newsgroups that you consider blatantly offensive (**alt.atheism** or **alt.sex.stories**, for example) or others that you consider just plain boring (**sci.agriculture.beekeeping**). But remember, the prevalent attitude is that there is something for everyone. If you don't like a newsgroup, stay away from it; there's no one to complain to.

Finding USENET Online

You'll have no trouble tracking down the USENET newsgroups on CompuServe: they're hard to miss. Just click on the **GO** button from WinCIM, type **USENET**, and press **Enter**, and you'll be whisked away to the USENET service.

From the main USENET menu, you can choose from several options before you jump right into the newsgroups. There's an introduction to USENET, a disclaimer, an etiquette notice, a list of common questions, and a mechanism to send feedback to CompuServe. Most people don't read this standard information because they are too impatient. You can read it in your spare time. For now, let's jump in and get started.

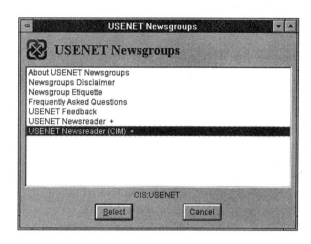

The main USENET menu shows you all the USENET stuff CompuServe has to offer.

To start reading the newsgroups, double-click on **USENET Newsreader (CIM)**. The USENET Newsgroups dialog box appears. (If you choose the USENET Newsreader option, you'll be forced to read and send articles through a boring terminal connection even if you are using WinCIM.)

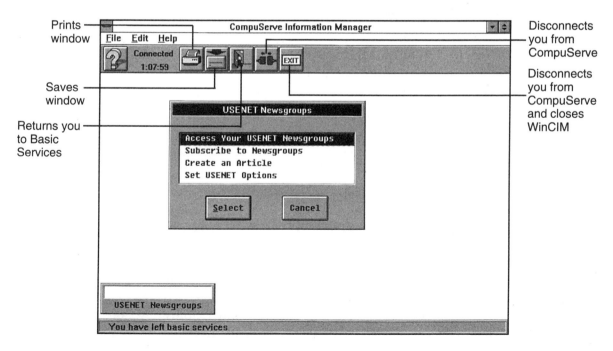

Okay, you're here—now what?

213

Note the new icons in your WinCIM ribbon. Clicking on the Print icon sends whatever you are looking at to your printer. Clicking on the Save icon saves the current window to your computer by downloading it.

Setting Your USENET Options

Signature
Several lines of text that are automatically appended to the end of each message you send onto the newsgroups.

The first thing you'll want to do is customize your newsgroup options, so double-click on **Set USENET Options**. You'll only have to do this once (unless you want to change them in the future). In the Options dialog box, you can change the name associated with your CompuServe ID, change how many messages are available at a time, or even create a signature.

```
┌──────────────────────────────────────────────────────────────┐
│                            Options                            │
├──────────────────────────────────────────────────────────────┤
│ Name: Andy Shafran                                            │
│                                                               │
│ Organization: Alpha Books (author)                            │
│                                                               │
│ Default articles for newly subscribed newsgroups: 200         │
│                                                               │
│ X Display newgroups with no articles                          │
│                                                               │
│                          Signature                            │
│ ┌──────────────────────────────────────────────────────────┐ │
│ │ --Andy Shafran                                           ▲│ │
│ │                                                           │ │
│ │                                                          ▼│ │
│ └──────────────────────────────────────────────────────────┘ │
│   ┌──────┐  ┌──────────────────┐ ┌──────────────────┐ ┌────────┐ │
│   │  OK  │  │ Set Ignore Options│ │ Get Message By Id│ │ Cancel │ │
│   └──────┘  └──────────────────┘ └──────────────────┘ └────────┘ │
└──────────────────────────────────────────────────────────────┘
```

Set your personal preferences in the Options dialog box.

Make sure you enter your name so that other people who read your message can associate your postings with your name. Otherwise, the messages you send out onto a newsgroup will only be identified by your CompuServe ID (not your name). If you fill in the organization field, other people can see who you are representing or where you work. You'll find that this information sometimes has an effect on which messages you actually read. For example, if you're looking at articles in **comp.news.lotus-notes.misc**, you'll likely pay more attention to a message from a Lotus employee.

When you subscribe to a new newsgroup, by default CompuServe shows you the 20 articles placed in that newsgroup most recently. However, you can change that number by setting a new default in the Options dialog box. Personally, I set that number to 200 because when I sign up for a new newsgroup, I like to catch up on the latest discussions. Most people find an optimum setting between 100 and 200. You can set it higher than that, but the number of messages in some newsgroups can be mind-boggling.

Creative Signatures
Some people spend months designing the perfect signature. I don't really suggest this—unless you have nothing to do for the next few months. A small signature that's to the point works just fine.

Finally, you can create your signature. Creating a signature for news articles follows the same concept as signing your e-mail. A short and sweet signature is your best bet. Try to keep it to three or four lines maximum. As you can see in the figure, my signature gets straight to the point (boring). But if it works, why knock it?

When you've finished setting all the options in the dialog box, click the **OK** button.

Subscribing to Newsgroups

Now that you've finished with the grub work, you can tell CompuServe which newsgroups you want to subscribe to. You can subscribe to as many newsgroups as you'd like, but remember that you're paying $4.80 an hour for this extended service.

When you subscribe to a newsgroup, you tell CompuServe that you want to see all messages posted to that newsgroup. Conveniently, once you've subscribed, CompuServe keeps track of the last message you've read. So the next time you access the newsgroup, CompuServe shows you only messages that have been posted since the last time you checked.

To subscribe to a newsgroup, double-click on **Subscribe to Newsgroups**, and the Subscribe to Newsgroups dialog box appears. Browse through the various hierarchies of newsgroups in the scroll box on the left side. When you see a hierarchy that interests you, click on it and press **Select**. To start off, your best bet is to choose a hierarchy of CompuServe's own newsgroups. From the list of categories, choose **CompuServe only (compuserve.*)**.

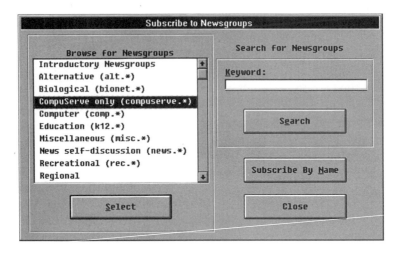

The CompuServe only hierarchy contains newsgroups available only to CompuServe members.

Then you can scan through the newsgroups in that hierarchy. When you find a newsgroup you want to subscribe to, click on its check box and click the **Subscribe** button. For example, select **compuserve.general** and click on **Subscribe**. You should always check this newsgroup for CompuServe-related messages. There usually aren't a lot of messages in it, but they are usually interesting for CompuServe members.

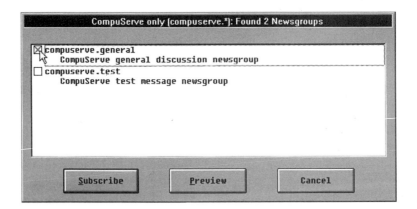

CompuServe.general is the one you want to read through.

In the future, you can search through the rest of the newsgroups to find the exact ones you want. However, remember that the clock is ticking, and it's easy to loose track of time within the USENET.

Finding the Private News

CompuServe has several thousand newsgroups available. They've taken the time and effort to collect most of the major newsgroup hierarchies to make it very easy to subscribe and follow several different newsgroups. However, there are several newsgroups to which CompuServe does have access but that are not shown in the browsing list. For example, the newsgroup **alt.sex** isn't listed, but you can subscribe to it if you know its exact name.

To access an unlisted newsgroup, in the Subscribe to Newsgroups dialog box, click on the **Subscribe By Name** button, type the exact name of the newsgroup, and click **OK**. CompuServe subscribes you to the newsgroup, and you can read messages from it like any other newsgroup.

Take a Peek If you select a newsgroup and then hit the Preview button instead of Subscribe, CompuServe gives a preview of the newsgroup by showing you the most recent messages in that newsgroup. Try this before you subscribe to a newsgroup to see if it's for you. (If you read one discussion in **comp.lang.eiffel**, you'd realize how boring it is and not waste your time subscribing to it. It's about obscure computer terminology, not Paris.)

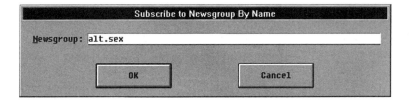

Close your eyes, kids—we're subscribing to an adults-only newsgroup.

Where Are They?

For a list of the newsgroups to which CompuServe has access but doesn't list, check out the file section of the Internet forum (**GO INETFOR**).

USENET, One Article at a Time

It's time to start reading some articles from the newsgroups you've subscribed to (finally). Choose **Access Your USENET Newsgroups** from the USENET Newsgroups window, and WinCIM shows a list of all the newsgroups to which you've subscribed.

Article A message created by a user and distributed via a newsgroup. Anyone with access to newsgroups can create his own articles.

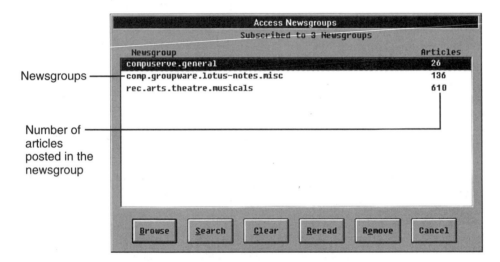

Newsgroups —

Number of articles posted in the newsgroup

Access Newsgroups	
Subscribed to 3 Newsgroups	
Newsgroup	Articles
compuserve.general	26
comp.groupware.lotus-notes.misc	136
rec.arts.theatre.musicals	610

Browse   Search   Clear   Reread   Remove   Cancel

The Access Newsgroups dialog box shows the newsgroups to which you've subscribed. Looks interesting, huh?

Select the newsgroup you want to read and click on the **Browse** button. You'll see an entire screenful of messages in a thread. As they are in a forum, groups of messages are organized by thread so you can read through an entire "conversation" at one time.

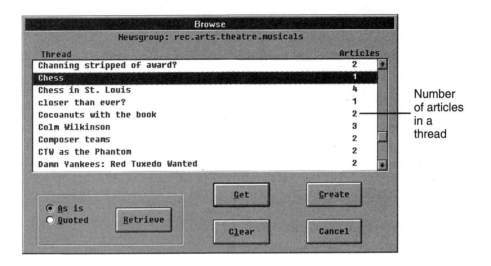

Browsing in a newsgroup.

Scroll through the available threads until you find one that looks like a winner. Select it and click on the **Get** button to read the article. You're now reading an article in a newsgroup. Use the scroll bars to read the entire article. When you've finished reading that article, you have several options. You can read the next message in the thread, jump directly to the next thread, or reply to the current message. Click the > button to move forwards or the < button to move backwards through articles and message threads.

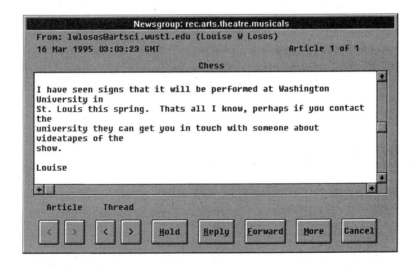

You can read through the entire thread (as you can in a forum) or reply to the message very easily.

When you've finished reading an article, you won't be able to access it again. The next time you read the newsgroup, CompuServe only shows articles that have been added since the last time you opened the newsgroup. (This works just like CompuServe forums.)

Start Spreading the News

Every now and then you'll want to create some messages of your own. You might want to send a message to **rec.sport.olympics** asking about our hopefuls in 1996 or respond to one of your peers in **sci.engr**. Whatever the reason, you can create new messages from scratch or respond over the newsgroup or via e-mail to an article.

Remember that when you send or post a message from the Internet, you are likely to receive at least a few responses via personal mail, for which there is an extra charge. You can learn from my experience. Once I posted a message to **rec.arts.theatre.musicals** asking about people's favorite shows currently playing on Broadway. I received more than 60 personal responses from Internet mail and had to pay for them. So be careful when soliciting information from people via the newsgroups—unless you have a bottomless wallet.

Responding with Your Own $0.02

When you're reading a message and you have a burning desire to add to the current topic of conversation, simply click on the **Reply** button, and the Reply to USENET Message dialog box appears.

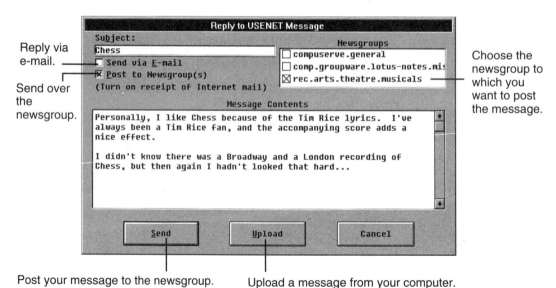

Reply via e-mail.

Send over the newsgroup.

Choose the newsgroup to which you want to post the message.

Post your message to the newsgroup. Upload a message from your computer.

Replying to a newsgroup message.

By default, CompuServe retains the subject that has been used throughout the message thread and sends the message via e-mail to the original poster. All you have to do is type your message and click on **Send**.

Don't Sign Your Name Because CompuServe automatically adds your signature to the bottom of your message, you don't need to "sign" your response.

If you want to send a response to the entire newsgroup, select the **Post to Newsgroup** check box. For the most part, I post a follow-up message to the entire newsgroup only if I think it'll be useful to multiple people. (If it weren't, I'd just send e-mail.) When you press **Send**, the message is posted to the newsgroup, and everyone around the world has access to it.

Be a Leader—Start Your Own Thread

Creating a message from scratch is pretty much the same as responding to a newsgroup message, except you have to type in a subject and designate which newsgroup you want to post the message to.

While browsing through the list of message threads, you can create a new message by clicking on the **Create** button. The Create USENET message dialog box appears. Notice that this screen looks like the reply screen, except that the subject field is blank. Fill in the subject and type your all-important message.

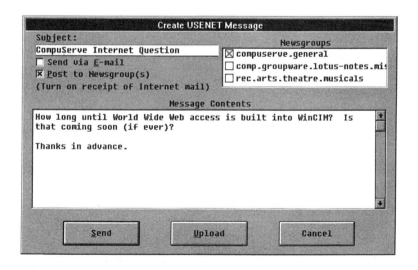

Creating a message from scratch.

When you're finished with your message, click on the check box next to the newsgroup to which you want to post the message. If you accidentally select multiple newsgroups, your message will be sent to all of them. When you're ready to post your message, click on the **Send** button, and the message is whisked away.

Can't Find Your Message?

Don't expect messages you post to newsgroups to appear there immediately. CompuServe needs a little time to process and send the message out to the entire USENET. Wait a few minutes and then read the newsgroup again. The message will probably be waiting for you (and everyone else).

The Golden Rules

Since newsgroups are accessible to more people than just CompuServe users, it is especially important to maintain good "Newsgroup Etiquette." Think of proper newsgroup etiquette in relation to how you would act at a friend's house. At your own home, you can lay down on the couch, put your feet on the coffee table, and get comfortable—it's your own place. But at a friend's house, you respect his home and property—and you don't jiggle his antique Chinese vase by kicking your Nikes up on his coffee table.

Don't forget that most of the people who read and send messages on newsgroups are not CompuServe users. Unlike forums, newsgroups don't have paid professionals that help new users, answer beginners' questions, or moderate the newsgroups. If you ask a question that is basically pointless (such as sending a message to **alt.comics.superman** asking, "Isn't Clark Kent really Superman?"), you will probably be flamed, and you'll develop a bad reputation online.

Flamed To be bombarded with messages that insult your personal demeanor.

Some newsgroups get the same questions over and over (and over) again. Therefore, many newsgroups now have a list of frequently asked questions, called FAQs. On a regular basis, FAQs and their answers are posted to the newsgroup they relate to. If you have patience, read through the next posting labeled FAQ on your favorite newsgroup. You should also look there first when you have a question to see if the answer is readily available.

As a general rule, follow standard rules of etiquette when sending messages back and forth to newsgroups. Here's a short list of things you want to keep in mind when using newsgroups from CompuServe.

➤ Hang around a newsgroup for at least a week before you send a message. Make sure you get a feel for how the discussion goes before you jump into it. Some conversations are slow organized discussions, while others more closely resemble a rodeo.

➤ Nobody wants to waste her time reading pointless messages. If you agree with a discussion, don't send your own message saying "Yes, I agree." Just nod your head and talk to yourself instead.

➤ Don't forget that millions of people read the USENET newsgroups. If you want to respond to Bob's theory of Armageddon, maybe you could send him some e-mail instead of posting it on **alt.destroy.the.earth** (no kidding; it exists!).

The Least You Need to Know

USENET newsgroups open up a whole new world out there in addition to CompuServe forums. While you get structure, rules, and a Sysop on CompuServe, you can find anarchy and mass unorganized information through the USENET. Here's a list of key things to remember.

➤ Etiquette, etiquette, etiquette. USENET readers can change from your best friend to your most hated enemy with a single obnoxious or careless message. But don't let that scare you; for the most part they are people just like you.

➤ A message sent to the USENET is sent to approximately 100,000 computers worldwide—so make sure you have something worth saying when you create a new article.

➤ The variety of available newsgroups is much greater than the variety of available CompuServe forums. But, for the most part, if there's a USENET newsgroup on a particular topic, you can find a similar discussion on CompuServe.

Reading Online Newspapers and Magazines

There seems to be something utterly romantic about newsprint. I can't decide if it's the crummy ink that rubs onto your hands and clothes, or the wet dog smell of a soggy newspaper. It's just so quaint imagining little reporters running around in brown fedoras trying to get the daily scoop.

Nowadays newspapers are a little bit different. Journalists have traded in their trenchcoats and fedoras for laptop computers and Internet accounts. Fortunately, though, they're still predictable. Instead of important news about the world, you can bet that a sensational story about a sports star on trial for killing his ex-wife will be on the front page for at least ten months straight.

Magazines are a little bit classier, but not much. Their glossy paper may be nice, but those darn subscription cards drive me batty. Let's see what kinds of newspapers and magazines CompuServe has online. Maybe we'll find a press pass or two lying around.

Online Newspapers

For newspapers, going online seems to be the rage nowadays. Almost every rinky-dink paper is available on some online service or another. Newspaper companies seem to think the future of newspapers is in the computer and modem. They just don't seem to understand that we like to read our morning paper while drinking high-octane coffee.

I don't mind reading the AP News online (see Chapter 15), but I still subscribe to my local paper, the *Columbus Dispatch*. **GO NEWSPAPERS** to see a list of all the papers available through CompuServe.

Definitely Detroit

Probably the biggest newspaper on CompuServe is the *Detroit Free Press*. Located in the armpit of the midwest, the *Free Press* has its own section online (**GO DETROIT**).

Rave to the editor, check through back issues, or see what's hot in the nation's ninth largest newspaper.

If you live anywhere in that state up north (I'm not allowed to say its name, since I'm from Ohio State), you'll want to check out the Free Press Forum. Current stories, pictures and chit-chat about the comings and goings of Detroit abound.

Fantastic Florida

Delivering to the entire state, *Florida Today* also has it's own forum on CompuServe (**GO FLATODAY**). The parent newspaper to the popular *USA Today,* you'll find lots of editorials, articles, and pictures uploaded to the forum daily. They're particularly good about covering NASA launches and the space program.

New York Newslink

New York Newslink is a must visit for anyone who lives in or near New York. News articles about the hottest issues to hit the state are uploaded daily, as well as a weekly nightlife guide to the finer parts of living in the city.

GO NEWYORK to hang out with people who don't understand the proper use of the word *pop,* and think getting mugged is a natural part of the day.

Sifting Through Other Newspapers

While there may not be a whole bunch of newspapers online, that won't stop you from finding out the latest news across the country. No one wants to miss what the Madison, Wisconsin school board voted on last night.

Besides the fancy online newspapers, you have access through CompuServe to over 60 daily newspapers that you can flip through to get the newest news from cities like Boston, Anchorage, and New Orleans. I'm talking about the Newspapers Archives (**GO NEWSARCHIVES**). Through this cool service, you can search through the full text of any of the 60 daily papers for stories that interest you.

Of course you'll pay a pretty penny for this convenience. Every story you read costs you $1.50 (five times as much as an entire issue of the *Dispatch*), but for researching, or finding the exact story you need, this is the way to do it. Fortunately, you only pay $1.50 for the articles you actually read.

Not enough news?
Compared to some of the other online services, CompuServe has relatively few newspapers available. Prodigy has made it their own personal quest to sign up as many newspapers as possible. I don't care much for reading local news online, but if you do, you might want to take a look at what Prodigy has to offer.

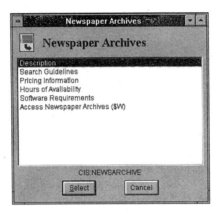

Don't waste your time reading about Newspaper Archives—start searching!

From the Newspaper Archives window, click on **Access Newspaper Archives ($W)**. (The **$W** means you pay by the story, not an hourly fee.) CompuServe brings up a disclaimer telling you all about the costs you'll accrue. You're probably used to these sorts of disclaimers by now. Just click on **Proceed** to enter the Newspaper Archives. It'll take a few moments, but CompuServe will bring up a window that lets you select the newspaper you want to search through (you can only search through one at a time).

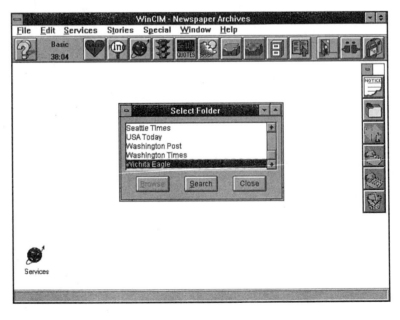

*You'll find a lot of biggies here (*Washington Post, Boston Globe*) as well as some not-so-big newspapers (like the* Witchita Eagle*).*

Select the newspaper you want to search through and click on the **Search** button. The Search for Stories dialog box appears. Select whether you want to search through the **Story Headlines, Story Lead,** or **Story Body**. Then type the word or phrase you want to search for into the **Search Terms** box. When you're ready, click on the **Search** button.

Use Some Special Search Characters

There are a few special characters you can use when searching for news stories. These characters, +, −, |, and *, help you create more efficient and useful searches.

Use + to separate two words when you want to make sure both of those words are in your story.

Use | between two words when you want to select stories with either one of your words.

Use − before a word when you want to select stories that don't have that word in it. You'll usually use this one in conjunction with + or |, as in **CALVIN–HOBBES,** which selects stories that contain the word *Calvin,* but not *Hobbes.*

Finally, use * as a wild card. If you search for **star*** you'll return stories with *star, stark,* or *starter* in them.

*I know this must drive people from Kansas nuts, but I've lost track of my
ruby slippers.*

I've just searched through all the stories in the *Wichita Eagle* that have the words *Kansas* and *Toto* in them. You can bet that I'll get back stories talking about everything from Munchkins to flying monkeys.

So far, I haven't actually spent any money in the Newspaper Archives. The only way I'm charged is if I select the checkbox to the left of the story I want to read, and click on the **Get** button. From there, I can read through the entire article and then store it in my WinCIM Filing Cabinet for future use.

Marking Your Articles

If you don't want to download the stories one at a time, you can mark several stories by clicking in their checkbox and pulling down **Stories** from the menu bar and choosing **Retrieve Marked Stories**. You'll download every marked story (at $1.50 each) directly into your WinCIM Filing Cabinet.

Retrieving News Photos

Reuters is one of the world's largest news services. They have trenchcoat-wearing reporters and photographers all over the world covering every major event and occurrence.

That's good news for you, because there's a Reuters Newspaper Pictures Forum on CompuServe that has thousands of photographs of current events from around the world. New pictures are constantly being uploaded by the folks over at Reuters. I find a new picture of a world leader (to use as a dartboard) every time I stop by. If you're a photographer or think the pictures are the best part of the paper, **GO NEWSPIC**, and you won't be disappointed.

Online Magazines

If you think newspapers are hopping into the online world in a major way, hold onto your hat. In the last year or so, almost all of the top magazines have established themselves as regulars on CompuServe, Prodigy, or America Online. You can now read the latest issue of almost any major magazine with your computer and modem. If it wasn't for the lottery, our newsstands would probably go out of business!

As far as magazines go, CompuServe has the best of the bunch. A couple of chapters ago I wrote about *US News & World Report.* That's just one of the heavy hitters online. You can find the latest issues of *Fortune, Sports Illustrated, People, Consumer Reports,* and *PC World* only on CompuServe. And those are just the major magazines. There are all sorts of technical and computer-related magazines for computer geeks.

Fortune Magazine

There's no denying that money makes the world go 'round. I'm all for peace and harmony with my neighbors and stuff, but without money, I can't even afford to have neighbors let alone think about peace.

If financial and business news interests you, **GO FORTUNE** on CompuServe. *Fortune* magazine has its own corner of CompuServe that includes its current magazine, the ever-famous Fortune 500 lists, and tips and information about personal investments.

To read the most current issue of *Fortune*, click on the icon labeled **Current Issue**, and you can read all the stories and see all the charts and pictures that are printed in the magazine.

Sports Illustrated

There's really only one sports magazine out there. Sure there's a few second-rate competitors, but *Sports Illustrated* is the king of them all. It's one of the most defining sources of sports information in the world. You can find in-depth articles, features and statistics about nearly every sport. **GO SPORTSILL** to find the magazine online.

You can check out the current issue of *SI* by clicking on the icon labeled **SI Magazine**. Stories, photos, and interviews are all available to be read.

What About Those, Ummm, Sport...Swimsuits?

Yes, the swimsuit issue is available for downloading as well. I'm not sure what swimsuits have to do with sports, but for some reason it's immensely popular with the masses. Check out *Sports Illustrated* in the first week of February every year to "read" the swimsuit issue.

You can also keep track of the latest sports news and information. Click on the icon labeled **News**, **Scores**, **& Stats** to see a breakdown of the latest games and news organized by sport.

Other Magazines Online

Fortune and *Sports Illustrated* aren't the only magazines available online—there is a whole slew of others. Some are published online in their entirety, others have their own forums. Here's a list of most of the magazines that you can find online. New ones are added all the time, so your favorite may be on its way.

Magazine	GO Word
Consumer Reports	CONSUMER
PC World	PCWORLD
People	PEOPLE
Dr. Dobb's Programming Journal	DDJ
Database Advisor	DBADVISOR
DBMS Magazine	DBMSFORUM
Lan Magazine	LANMAG
The Electronic Gamer	EGAMER
WordPerfect Magazine	WPMAG
NetGuide Magazine	NETGUIDE
Rice Krispie Treat Weekly	SNAPCRACKLEPOP (Just teasing)

Magazine Database Plus

My grandma gets more magazines than anyone I've ever met. When Ed McMahon tells her she can win a million dollars, she takes the entire set of magazine stickers and sends them back to Publisher's Clearinghouse. Every time I visit her I am amazed at the magazines I find.

What's even more amazing is that she never throws any of them away. Her entire basement is chock-full of thousands and thousands of magazines, each one meticulously read. I don't know where she puts them all. She insists that one day she'll need one, and will be glad she kept them all.

In some convoluted way, she makes sense, but in my world, I'd just use the Magazine Database Plus on CompuServe (**GO MAGDB**) if I ever needed to find an article in *Time* from five years ago. Magazine Database Plus contains every article from well over 200 publications for nearly the past ten years. Like Newspaper Archives, each article costs $1.50. You can search the MAGDB for any topic imaginable and a list of stories that contain your word will appear. From that list you can read and download the complete article.

Some people research papers with MAGDB, others are simply curious about a specific topic. Whatever the reason, besides my grandmother's basement, you won't find a more comprehensive index of magazine articles.

Find any magazine article you could imagine from the MAGDB.

Choose **Access Magazine Database Plus (CIM)** from the MAGDB window. You'll have access to search through the entire database for any word or phrase. Unfortunately, MAGDB costs you hourly extended fees as well as $1.50 a story retrieved to use.

I think MAGDB is a great value. I've used it several times for research papers when I couldn't find what I needed in the library (or grandma's basement). It cost me a bit, but for the convenience of downloading the entire article (not just an abstract), I gladly paid the price.

The Least You Need to Know

I admit it, I'm a big fan of magazines online. I think every magazine should be available on CompuServe and have it's own forum. Newspapers on the other hand are a different story. I enjoy reading the morning paper (then washing my hands), and for some reason, I've never seen any newspaper comics online. I'll be a convert as soon as I can read "Fox Trot" daily on CompuServe.

➤ Read local newspapers in New York (**GO NEWYORK**), Detroit (**GO DETROIT**), and Florida (**GOFLATODAY**) to see what's happening in your neighborhood, or someone else's neighborhood.

➤ **GO NEWSARCHIVES** to search through the complete text of 60 daily newspapers to find out what's happening around the country (and world).

➤ CompuServe has many magazines online ranging from the popular ("People") to ultra geeky ("LAN"). **GO MAGAZINE** to see a list of them all.

➤ Let your *SI* subscription run out. You can read the weekly issue and keep a much closer look at sports by reading the magazine online (**GO SPORTSILL**).

➤ Throw away all your old magazines that you've been keeping on a shelf in your closet. If you need a story bad enough, Magazine Database Plus (**GO MAGDB**) lets you search for and download in just a few seconds.

Chapter 19

Financial News You Can Use

I'm not very good with investments. I don't understand all the financial mumbo-jumbo that I see on the news (what the heck does *Dow* actually mean?) or pretend to know how to work much more than my piggy bank.

As a result, everyone likes to give me stock advice. Every week my neighbor down the street has a new hot investment tip for me. He always has some insider news about what stock's going to skyrocket. Fortunately, I tune him out when he starts to blather about his financial prowess. I suppose I gave up listening to him when he confidently told me "No savings and loan could ever fail under *any* circumstances." Maybe that's why he's still driving a 1979 Chevette.

Instead, I turn to the financial wizards on CompuServe to keep track of my financial futures. I can keep track of the daily stock market, watch over my personal financial portfolio, and save lots of time and money every year during tax time by checking out the right forums and services on CompuServe.

Checking Out the Stock Market

CompuServe makes it easy for you to periodically see how your favorite stocks are doing during a grueling day at the stock market. You don't need your own ticker-tape machine, either. Armed with WinCIM, you can see stock prices as they update periodically during the day.

Click on the **Quotes** icon from your WinCIM ribbon to bring up the Stock Quotes window (or **GO QUOTES**). You can get the current prices of any stock you want by creating your own list of ticker symbols (the abbreviations that stocks are recognized by).

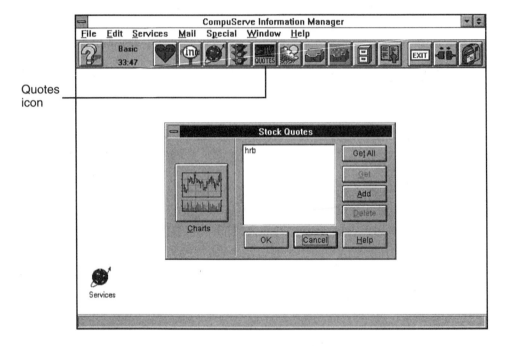

Quotes icon

You can see current stock prices at all hours during the day, night, or weekend.

By default, the stock whose ticker is named *HRB* is in your Stock Quotes dialog box. *HRB* is short for H&R Block, the massive tax company that owns CompuServe. You probably don't care too much about H&R Block and have your own set of stocks that you want to follow instead. Click on the **Add** button to add a stock to your list and WinCIM asks you for the Ticker symbol of the stock you want to track.

236

I'm going to look up that mega computer conglomerate, Microsoft, and see how the software monopoly is doing nowadays. You can type any ticker symbol you want, and then click on the **OK** button. When you return to the Stock Quotes dialog box, you'll see that your stock (in my case, **MSFT**) is now listed along with **HRB**. You can add as many ticker names as you want to keep dibs on.

You can remove ticker names just as easily. Select the one you want gone and click on the **Delete** button.

See Your Stock

Seeing your stocks is a piece of cake. Just click on the **Get All** button, and CompuServe goes off and gets the current price of your stock as well as other related information. I use the **Get All** button because it take just as long for CompuServe to grab information about five stocks as it does for one. Otherwise, click on the stocks you want to look up, and click on the **Get** button. CompuServe will return information about the ticker names that are selected.

> **Ticker Talk**
> Each stock that is traded on a public market has it's own unique ticker name for identification purposes. Before you can check on a stock, you've got to know the ticker symbol that represents that stock. You can look up any company's ticker name in the CompuServe Issue/Ticker Lookup, which is part of CompuServe's basic services. Just **GO LOOKUP** and you can search for any stock's ticker name.

Current Price

Change since the stock market opened this morning

Last time this price was updated (E.S.T.)

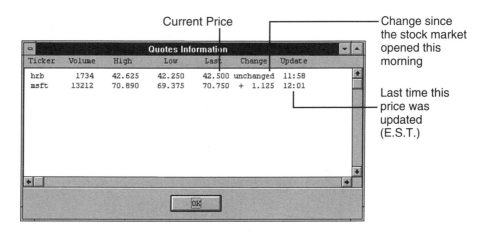

Ticker	Volume	High	Low	Last	Change	Update
hrb	1734	42.625	42.250	42.500	unchanged	11:58
msft	13212	70.890	69.375	70.750	+ 1.125	12:01

Here's the info for the stocks I'm following.

Unfortunately, you can't see up-to-the-minute stock information on CompuServe. Because of SEC government rules, CompuServe must wait 15 minutes before they can make stock prices available online. I'm not sure why, but remember that these are the same people who've created a trillion dollar deficit. It's no skin off my back—I'm not a stockbroker. I just want to keep an eye on my stock prices. I usually check my stocks in the evening anyway, long after the NYSE has shut down.

See Stock Charts

What is your favorite part about checking the weather on CompuServe? Even though I like the local weather forecasts and the ability see the weather anywhere in the world, my favorite part is the cool weather maps that I can download. All I need is a bad toupee and I feel like a real weatherman.

Neat pictures and charts are my favorite part of the checking my stocks on CompuServe. You can get a chart showing the financial history of any stock or security that you want. From the Stock Quotes dialog box, just click on the **Charts** icon (or **GO TREND**).

Next to **Issue**, type the ticker name of the stock you want to chart. Then select the periodicity (the number of periods) you want to see.

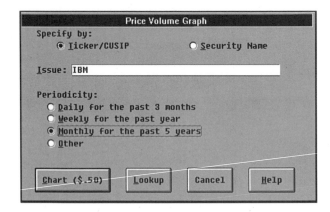

Let's take a look at Big Blue's performance over the past few years.

When you're ready, click on the **Chart ($.50)** button. You have to pay half a buck for each chart you look at, plus hourly extended service fees. Charting stock performance isn't overly economical, but it does come in handy when you're researching stock history and past trends. I just like it because it's neat.

Wow, what a roller coaster ride IBM stock has taken.

Create Your Own Portfolio

Once you start buying and selling stocks in the real world, your stockbroker creates a portfolio for you. This portfolio keeps track of the stocks you own, how much you paid for each stock, and the commission your bloodsucking stockbroker charges every time you buy or sell.

You can create an online portfolio to track your stock purchases and figure out the market performance for each stock that you own. Basically, you tell CompuServe what stocks you own, how much you paid, when you bought them, and how many shares you purchased. Then, anytime you want, you can compare that information with the current value of your stocks. This is nicer than any portfolio I've ever seen, because CompuServe actually calculates how much money you've made (or if you're like me, lost) playing the stock market.

Select **Services, Portfolio** to bring up your online stock portfolio.

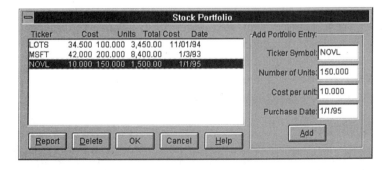

I only wish I had enough to money to really gamble like this on the stock market!

239

On the right side of the screen, enter all the information about each stock you own. Then click on the **Add** button. CompuServe adds each stock, sorted by ticker name, to the window on the left. When you've entered all your stocks, click on the **Report** button. CompuServe will get the most current information about every stock you own and create a handy report for you. My real stock portfolio is so depressing, I had to make up a fake one for this book. I can't stand seeing my report, because I'm annoyed with how much money I've lost. If only I could do it again. My vision is so clear in hindsight.

Other Juicy Financial Tidbits on CompuServe

Getting the latest stock information isn't all you can do with CompuServe. You can also look up important information on any company that has traded publicly.

Yesterday's Market News

Every day you can get a thorough and complete summary of the previous day's stock market occurrences (**GO MARKET**). You can see the biggest winners, losers, and a history of other important stock information.

Quick Company Info

For a quick summary of any company that's listed on the worldwide stock exchanged, **GO BASCOMPAN**. You can find out a company's home address, phone number, and the big cheese, as well as see basic information about the company, in general. Most listings include yearly sales and employees, in addition to a business description.

In-depth Stats on a Company

If what you want is the serious lowdown on a company, you can search through the complete set of documents every company must file with the SEC, called *disclosure reports*. These disclosure reports include all the public information companies send to their shareholders, including a detailed financial listing and major stockholders. You'll pay a lot of money though. Only the hard-nosed investor, or someone who is thinking about plopping down a lot of dough, should **GO DISCLOSURE**. You won't find a more complete description of a company than its disclosure report.

Online Stock Brokers

Online discount brokers let you buy and sell your stock 24 hours a day, and are usually cheaper than the big Wall Street houses. **GO QWK** to hang out with the folk from Quick & Reilly, the biggest stock broker on CompuServe. They'll be glad to help you invest your hard-earned savings (for a piece of the action).

For Wannabes: The Stock Market Game

Investing in the stock market is just like a fun game, except that it's usually with your own money. Nobody likes to lose their own cash, but inexplicably, we love gambling. If you've ever dreamed of playing the stock market, but didn't want to risk your own money, **GO ETGAME**.

Every month you get $100,000 cash to invest in the stock market. In the game, you can buy any stock or investment you want. You're competing against hundreds of other CompuServe gamblers to see who can build up the biggest nest egg. Each month, the winner walks away with $50.00 CompuServe usage credit.

Follow Your Funds

Maybe playing the stock market directly isn't your cup of tea. If you invest in mutual funds instead, **GO FUNDWATCH**. *Money* magazine sponsors a comprehensive database of nearly 2000 mutual funds. You can search through the listing to find a particular fund that meets your risk and investment needs. You can find out the latest information about any mutual fund you own or are thinking about purchasing. You can get all the nitty-gritty details about how well the mutual fund performs and all that financial mumbo-jumbo.

The Taxman Cometh

Every year during the month of April, some strange phenomenon comes over our country. We feel an impending sense of doom as the ides of April looms closer and closer. People scrambling to their libraries, calling up their tax lawyer buddies, and spending hours cursing at IRS forms are part of mid-April tax ritual. Don't worry, there's a light at the end of the tunnel. It's *IRS Form 2350: Application for Additional Extension of Time to File U.S. Individual Income Tax Return.*

Okay, so maybe that's not the best solution. You might as well take care of your taxes during April like 100 million other individuals around the country. Lest you forget, CompuServe is owned by one of the largest tax return companies in the world, H&R Block. It'd be rather disappointing if there was nowhere on CompuServe where you could get assistance figuring out what exemptions to take, or how many kids you can claim (does your dog count?).

Online Filing
To file electronically, you need to purchase either Intuit's TurboTax or MacInTax, or Meca's TaxCut (owned by H&R Block), both of which are available for downloading directly from CompuServe (or in any local computer store). There are explicit directions included in both TurboTax and TaxCut which explain who's allowed to file electronically, and who has to do it the hard way.

In fact you can even file your taxes online, directly through CompuServe if you'd like. Using popular PC software packages like TurboTax and TaxCut, you can send all your tax forms straight into the IRS computers. If you smell a refund coming your way, filing electronically will get that check coming your way faster than mailing in your tax return.

Check out the CompuServe Tax Connection (**GO TAXES**), which serves as an umbrella for all the income tax services available online.

From this window, you can download any IRS tax form, file electronically, grab some tax-preparation software, or go to financial forums to get some help.

I'd also recommend going to the free H&R Block area. There's always useful information about this year's new tax rules, hints, and potential pitfalls to avoid. Double-click on **H&R Block** to get there.

The Least You Need to Know

You don't have to be a stockbroker or a number cruncher to be interested in investments and taxes. I don't have much money to invest, yet I am constantly updating my portfolio and keeping track of several stock prices as they rise and fall.

➤ **GO QUOTES** to get the latest price on any stock that's publicly traded.

➤ Download a chart of your favorite stock's performance in the past weeks, months, or years.

➤ Read through all public SEC documents on a company to see if you should invest all your money in them through Disclosure.

➤ Play the stock market game for real (**GOQUK**) or virtually (**GO ETGAME**).

➤ **GO MONEY** to find all sorts of financial services and databases on CompuServe. Most of them are aimed at the professional investor, but you'll find a lot of neat tips for managing your money.

➤ CompuServe is one of the best comprehensive sources of tax return help and information. Download software to your PC and create the perfect return with a little help from **GO TAXES**.

Part 4
Entertainment and Games

Okay, we've come to the most addicting part of the book. I'm talking more addicting than chocolate and soap operas combined. Yes, it's entertainment and games. Chapters 20–23 include information on how to get to games, CBing, Hollywood updates, and even movie reviews. Good luck! If you're spending more time on CompuServe than you sleep, it's a good sign that you're addicted.

Chapter 20

A Peek at the Silver Screen

In This Chapter

➤ Talk to other moviegoers like yourself about hit films and stars

➤ Read through Roger Ebert's personal collection of movie reviews

➤ Keep up on all the latest Hollywood News and Information with Hollywood Hotline

---

I've never understood why it's called the Silver Screen. Whenever I've been to movie theaters, it looks white to me. Maybe off-white, or even ivory, but definitely not silver. But the nickname has hung around to confuse yet another generation of movie goers. Maybe that's why so many bad films (I won't mention *Dumb & Dumber*) are such box office smashes. We're all too confused to tell the difference between good movies and bad ones because we're too busy trying to figure out the actual color of the movie screen.

I don't know about you, but I love seeing movies. Even the really bad ones have a place in my fame-loving heart. That's why I'm glad CompuServe has lots of movie-related things online to keep me happy.

Don't get me wrong, I like all the important and professional stuff on CompuServe (like news, computer talk, and forums). But like everyone else I'm addicted to what's happening in that one little town in California—Hollywood. I can't read enough gossip about Kim Basinger, Tom Hanks, or Oliver Stone to satisfy my movie star cravings.

There's almost nothing I like more than going to the movie theater and buying the gallon size of pure cholesterol popcorn, and gluing my eyes to the movie screen.

Online, you can download actual movie clips, read daily Hollywood gossip (Did you hear? Allison is going to break up with Troy, and Demi and Bruce had a baby), and even read Roger Ebert's movie reviews. Buckle up, put on your sunglasses, and prepare to hang out in tinseltown.

Entertainment Drive

The first place you'll want to stop in your quest to find stardom on CompuServe is the Entertainment Drive (**GO EDRIVE**). Entertainment Drive (**EDrive**) is an online clearinghouse for television- and movie-related information. On EDrive you can download movie clips of latest flicks, talk about the latest hit TV shows, and follow the career of your favorite Hollywood star.

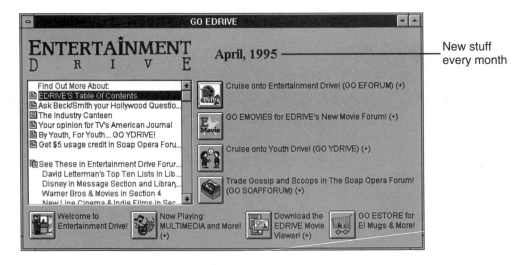

If entertainment's your game, EDrive is the place to be.

Take a look at your EDrive screen. There are lots of different options and buttons you can click on. On the left is a table of contents that usually tells you what's happening on EDrive. You can find information about conferences with movie stars, what's new in EDrive, and the latest contests to earn free CompuServe usage credit!

On the right side of your EDrive screen are several buttons that take you directly to the Entertainment Drive forums. Besides the popular EDrive, there's a Youth Drive that talks about Disney and Saturday morning cartoons, a Soap Opera Forum for those addicted to *Days of Our Lives,* and a special forum for downloading movie clips that will run on your PC at home.

Forum	GO Word
Entertainment Drive	EFORUM
Youth Drive	YDRIVE
Soap Opera Forum	SOAPFORUM
Entertainment Movie Clips	EMOVIES

Park in the EDrive

The Entertainment Drive Forum is by far one of the most popular forums online. Every time I log into it, there are tons and tons of users reading messages and downloading files. I highly recommend visiting every now and then.

In it, you'll find David Letterman's daily top 10 list (from the night before), pictures of some of your favorite actors and actresses, and there's even a file section sponsored by Playboy (I'm not allowed to tell you what you'll find in there; just make sure you're over 18 years old).

You'll even find several message sections talking about your favorite television shows. EDrive regularly hosts conferences with big-name Hollywood and television stars.

Movie Watching the Lazy Way

Besides several forums, one of the other main points of Entertainment Drive is all the different movie clips available online. In a clever form of advertising, you can download clips from several popular movies and watch them on your own PC. Hot movies such as *The Lion King* and *Interview with a Vampire* have specific movie clips available.

Cheap $1 Movies If you don't feel like paying $9.95 for the Movie Viewer, check out library section 16 in the Entertainment Forum (EDRIVE Multimedia), and you can find an older, free version of the movie viewing program. It's not the latest or greatest, but it works just fine for spying movie clips.

There are three things you'll need to watch movies on your PC (or Macintosh):

➤ **A Movie Clip.** Go to the Entertainment Movies Forum (**GO EMOVIES**) to get your grubby hands on all the movie clips I've talked about. No doubt by the time you read the book there'll be bigger and better movie clips available.

➤ **A Special Decompression Program.** The movie clips on CompuServe are stored in a special compressed format that lets both Macintosh and PC users download the same files. As a result, you can't use your standard decompression program, like PKZip or StuffIt. In the Entertainment Movies Forum, check out the library section titled **Quicktime** for the decompression program you'll need to watch the movies.

➤The Movie Viewer. Before you can watch the movies on your PC, you've also got to download the Movie Viewer. Without the Movie Viewer, you've just got this big reel of film without a projector to use. You're going to pay $9.95 for downloading the Movie Viewer (**GO VIEWER**), but you only have to download it once.

Do You Have a Bottomless Pocket?

Downloading movie clips is really neat, but make sure you realize how much it'll cost ahead of time. Most of the movie clips are quite large (10–30 minutes downloading at 14,400 baud), and you pay CompuServe's hourly extended service fee. Movies in my neck of the woods run $5.50 a person (not including the popcorn and candy). Personally, I'd rather pay a few dollars more and see the complete movie in a movie theater than download tons of movie clips. I'm sure you'll want to download at least one or two clips; just don't go hog wild.

Roger Ebert's Movie Reviews

I don't know what it is about Siskel and Ebert. For some reason Americans listen to these two movie critics more than anyone else in the biz. Their trademark thumbs up or thumbs down has become the cornerstone for movie ratings (as if a movie should only fall into a good or bad category, with no in-between).

Newsweek, the *New York Times,* and your local newspaper could all pan a movie, but if Siskel and Ebert like it, everyone else is forgotten. Movie studios plaster "Two thumbs up," "I laughed, I cried, I lost control of my body," all over an advertisement for the latest films.

En route to CompuServe, Roger Ebert ditched his movie review buddy and has his own area dedicated to movie reviews (**GO EBERT**). You can find Ebert's entire compendium of movie reviews and a whole bunch of interesting movie trivia and information for avid moviegoers.

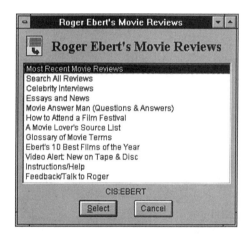

Forget your local movie reviewer; Ebert's words are as good as gold.

To check out recent movie reviews, select **Most Recent Movie Reviews** with your mouse and click on the **Select** button. A list of recent review comes up. Select the movie you want to read about to see Ebert's review.

I like to search Ebert's complete listing of movie reviews and see how he liked some of my favorite movies. Click on **Search All Reviews** and press the **Select** button. You can search for a movie review by Title, Actor/Actress's Name, or Director.

Hollywood Hotline

Roger Ebert in a Bikini Last October, CompuServe sponsored a "Cruise with Ebert" in which, for $1,000, hundreds of CompuServe members could set sail on a beautiful cruise ship aimed at the Bahamas, with special guest Roger Ebert on board. I don't think I'd pay extra to see Ebert in a swimsuit, but I heard it was a good time.

If you want to drop Roger a personal note, he hangs out in the Showbiz Forum (**GO SHOWBIZ**) a lot, or e-mail him at 76711,271.

Complementing Entertainment Drive in popularity is CompuServe's own glitzy and glamorous service, Hollywood Hotline. EDrive is a set of movie and television forums that are sponsored by businesses. Companies like Paramount, Disney, and Playboy pay big bucks to make their movie clips available for everyone to download. On the other side of the board, Hollywood Hotline gives you all the latest industry and behind the scenes gossip.

Hollywood Hotline (**GO HOLLYWOOD**) is organized by Elliot Stein, one of the biggest names in the entertainment news industry. He's been spreading Hollywood gossip, fads, and news on CompuServe since 1982, making Hollywood Hotline one of the oldest services around.

From Hollywood Hotline you can read daily news updates on what's happening in the TV and movie worlds or participate in Stein's regular online Conference with the industry's biggest stars.

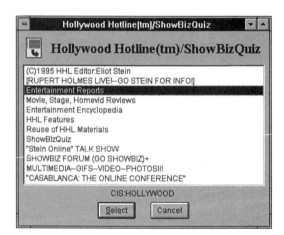

Though not quite as flashy as EDrive, I get all my gossip on the stars from Hollywood Hotline.

Here's a complete description of the different pieces and parts of Hollywood Hotline that you can select from the main window above.

Entertainment Reports   Three times a week, news from California and the entertainment industry makes it onto CompuServe. Stein finds out about everything, no matter how small. There's no better place to find out what's happening in Gary Coleman's career (remember *Different Strokes?*).

Movie, Stage, Homevid Reviews   Although not nearly as in-depth as Roger Ebert's repertoire, there are movie and video reviews available for the pickings. As a special bonus, you can also read Broadway musical reviews for all the latest shows to grace New York (the only place on CompuServe to find them).

Entertainment Encyclopedia   Find out who won best actor in 1975 (Jack Nicholson, *One Flew Over the Cuckoo's Nest*), or what famous movie stars were born on your birthday.

ShowBizQuiz   If you think you're a showbiz fan, you've got to take a ShowBizQuiz. There are almost 80 different quizzes about popular movies and television shows. There are quizzes about *Star Trek, The Wizard of Oz,* and *Leave It to Beaver,* to name a few, but no *Ishtar* quiz, yet.

Stein Online   Elliot Stein interviews Hollywood stars online and lets CompuServe members join in and ask questions. Choose this selection to find out when his next conference is.

The Rest of the Story

I told you about the three biggest and best sources of entertainment news and gossip on CompuServe. But there's a lot more where that came from. If you're hopelessly addicted to soap operas or can't watch enough TV, there's a place online for addicts just like yourself.

Here's a handy list of entertainment-related forums you might want to check out. Honestly, the EDrive Forum is probably the best, but you may find some of these interesting as well.

FORUM/SERVICE	GO WORD
Soap Opera Forum	SOAPFORUM
Daily Soap Opera Summaries (you can't miss this one)	SOAPS
Marilyn Beck and Stacy Smith's daily gossip (er, entertainment) column	BECK
Hollywood Hotline Forum	FLICKS
Showbiz Forum	SHOWBIZ
Gossip about alien visitors from Mars	MARSGOSSIP (That one's a joke.)
Archived Movies Forum	ARCFILM
TV Zone Forum	TVZONE
People magazine Daily News	PEOPLE

The Least You Need to Know

I just took you through a whirlwind tour of the biggest and brightest cinematic stuff on CompuServe. EDrive is full of the latest movies, and has several forums which let you talk to other movie-loving CompuServites. Hollywood Hotline is the cable version of EDrive. There's a lot more information for the movie and entertainment fan. Since they're included with CompuServe's basic services, I like to test my trivia knowledge with the online quizzes. Occasionally, I'll read the daily news reports.

➤ If EDrive (**GO EDRIVE**) is network TV, and Hollywood Hotline (**GO HOLLYWOOD**) is cable, I'd classify Roger Ebert as Public Broadcasting.

➤ Leave the sticky seats of the movie theater alone. Download hit movie clips from EDrive and watch from the comfort of your own PC (**EMOVIES**).

➤ Decide which movies you'll pay $5 to see and which ones you can miss by reading through Roger Ebert's up-to-date movie reviews (**GO EBERT**).

➤ Test your entertainment trivia skills with ShowBizQuiz. You're sure to learn more useless trivia about your favorite television show.

Chapter 21

Art, Music, and Literature: The Finer Things in Life

In This Chapter

➤ Keep up on the latest news about your favorite rock-and-roll artist or group with RockNet

➤ Read through thousands of album reviews on every band imaginable

➤ Talk to other book aficionados about the books you like to read

➤ Check out the Fine Art forums

Every one of us has an artistic side (believe it or not). Don't believe that bull about left-brained or right-brained people. We can all enjoy reading a good book or listening to some relaxing music every now and then. Some of us, *gasp,* even like to go to art museums to relax. Regardless of your preference or tastes, everyone can appreciate some of these finer points of life.

There are a lot of music, book, and art forums and services on CompuServe. I could spend an entire chapter telling you about all the music- and rock-related stuff alone. I won't bore you with all the details. Instead I'm going to introduce you to some of the most useful (and my favorite) places to be.

Rock On

If you enjoy reading trade magazines such as *Rolling Stone* and *Spin,* the next stop in your worldwide tour should be RockNet (**GO ROCK**). It's the definitive place to keep track of your favorite rock band or singer. You can find out when Pearl Jam's newest album is due, who's on tour with Sheryl Crow, and how many chickens Ozzy Osbourne has decapitated with his mouth lately.

This is the latest rock reporting on CompuServe.

Once you're finished exploring around with the news and information part of RockNet, make sure you jump into the RockNet forum (**GO ROCKNET**). Wild discussions rage on the hottest concert fads (lifting people on your shoulders and throwing them headfirst into a wall), what a rave is, and how to mosh.

Of course you'll find tamer discussions on traditional rock stars like U2, the Boss, and Madonna, as well as sample music clips, and a healthy trade in unauthorized bootleg tapes.

All Music, All the Time

If music is your game, you'd better check into the All-Music Guide (**GO ALLMUSIC**), one of CompuServe's basic services. It is comprised of an unbelievable collection of albums, ratings, and reviews of musicians. Any record or artist you can imagine is listed in the All-Music Guide (AMG)—there are over 160,000 entries.

I've never seen anything like it. Even the most obscure artists in my personal CD collection were listed in the All-Music Guide. Have you have heard of the Housemartins?

Whether you're into rock, jazz, classical, or country, AMG has your type of music. The following figure shows the main categories in AMG.

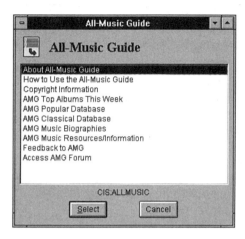

You've got a lot of different musical choices from the AMG.

Don't be afraid to explore AMG for an album. It's really a lot like using CompuServe's File Finder; I'm sure you'll get the hang of it in a few moments. Select **AMG Popular Database** and click on the **Select** button.

You can search for a particular album or a band's biography. Every band that I could think of had its own biography, which has a complete listing of every album released, and a brief description of the group.

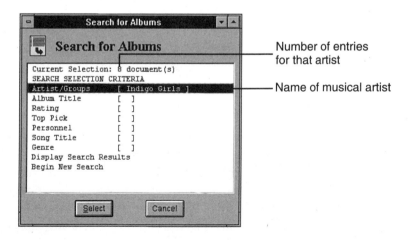

Number of entries for that artist

Name of musical artist

I'm searching for album reviews of the Indigo Girls, one of my favorite bands.

Searching for albums is just like using CompuServe's File Finders. You can search for a particular artist, album, or song. If you find an album or artist who isn't listed in the All-Music Catalog, **GO AMGFORUM** and leave a message explaining your discovery. Who knows, maybe they'll put your review in the catalog!

Club CD

I'm sure you've seen the compact disc clubs. You know, the ones where you tape a penny to a postcard and get 10 free CDs sent to your house? All you have to do is spend $765 buying five more CDs, and you're free from a life of bondage.

I used to belong to one, but it became too confusing. I would always forget to mail back the right information, and all these CDs that I didn't want were sent to me. It became such a mess that I finally signed away my first-born child, and the compact disc club left me alone for good.

 **Video Killed the Radio Star** If you're an MTV freak, or just like to see lots of music videos, then **GO ROCKVID**. For about $4 a month, a tape with 10 different videos (your choice of the music category) will be shipped out to you.

Okay, so CD clubs aren't that bad. If you are organized and keep track of all the rules and special deals, you can make out quite nicely by joining up with BMG (**GO BMG** to find BMG Music Service's area) or Columbia House (**GO FREECD** to join Columbia House), the two big CD clubs.

Both BMG and Columbia House have their own online areas. You can sign up and get your 10 free CDs sent to you within a few days. BMG even offers $5 CompuServe usage credit when you sign up. You can even tell BMG not to send you their featured monthly CD if you don't want it, through CompuServe directly. With Columbia House, you still have to put a stamp on your envelope and find a disgruntled postman.

Bunches of Books

Are you a true believer of the written word? I'm not sure if the pen is really mightier than the sword (it'd have to be an awfully large pen), but I still like to read a good book every now and then. Like half the country, I'm hooked on vampires, witches, and books about the Pope and O.J. Simpson. For some reason, I can't read enough stories about blood (O+ is my favorite).

If you like to talk about the latest books you've read, **GO LITFORUM** to jump into the Literary Forum. You can argue about what books classify as "literature," and you can meet other avid readers like yourself.

There are tons of other book-related forums on CompuServe. There's a couple for authors, one for science fiction, and even a few book publishing companies are online as well.

GO Word	Description
WRITER	Sponsored by the Literary Forum, the Writer's Forum is a place where aspiring writers can meet and chat with each other.
TWAUTHOR	Time-Warner Books has its own Author's Forum as well.
MACMILLAN	Meet computer book authors like myself, download sample chapters, and ask questions about new books.
COMICPUB	While comic books aren't the most traditional form of literature, the Comic Book Forum has sample comic books and a wide ranging discussion on publishing (and your favorite character as well).
SFMEDIA	While the SF/Fantasy Media Forum talks about all sorts of science fiction topics, SF and fantasy books are often talked about.

Project Gutenberg

Project Gutenberg is an ambitious project that wants to make books freely available in electronic format. Named after the inventor of the modern printing press, Project Gutenberg lets you download classic novels by Lewis Carroll, Jack London, Mary Shelley, and many more. Books that are in the public domain are made available to you directly through Project Gutenberg.

While reading a book on your computer can't compare to cuddling by the fireplace, they're free, and you don't have to worry about crinkling the pages. Besides, they leave more space on your bookshelf for soon-to-be classics by Danielle Steele and Tom Clancy.

GO GUTENBERG to see what books are available for downloading online. Most of the books are what's deemed as a "classic" (a classic is one of those really boring books that you had to write reports on in high school English). There are over a hundred available now, with more added every month. See the following figure for the main categories available in The Gutenberg Collection.

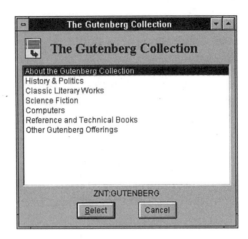

Choose one of these categories to find an interesting book to download.

Books in Print

Books in Print is a complete set of almost all the books that are currently available in print. You can search for books of a particular name, by a certain author, or about a specific subject. It's like searching through your local library's computer. You find general information and a short summary about that particular book. **GO BIP** for more information.

Ziff-Net

Project Gutenberg is part of Ziff-Net, which is an extra part of CompuServe. Ziff-Net costs $3.50 extra per month, but you get access to all sorts of publications in the Ziff Davis publishing empire. Discounts on books, weekly computer magazines (PCWeek & MACWeek), and of course, Project Gutenberg are all part of Ziff-Net.

If you don't want to join Ziff-Net, then check out Chapter 14, where I talk about FTP. You can FTP to Book Stacks Unlimited, where they have thousands of free books available for downloading.

Art in All Its Splendor

We may not agree with it all, but art is always on the cutting edge of technology. One of the first computer programs ever created let you draw and print simple text pictures (yes, they used a computer the size of a building to do that). Computer art is an up-and-coming field that lets you use such dazzling concepts as virtual reality and intense graphics as forms of expression.

CompuServe has several different forums for artists and art appreciators to spend time in. **GO FINEARTS** to talk with and about popular modern artists, discuss art history, and download full color graphics covering any topic imaginable.

The Artist Forum (**GO ARTIST**) is geared more towards starving artists, and their attempt to survive. Artists, illustrators, and one-eared geniuses hang out and talk about artistic issues here.

Virtual Reality
Virtual reality is a computer created-world in which you can interact. Without actually moving yourself, virtual reality lets you pretend you're in a different world created by a computer.

If computer-created art is more your style, **GO COMART** to download some of the weirdest images I've ever seen.

The Met

Every time I visit New York City, I go to the Metropolitan Museum of Art. Besides being the best museum in the world, it's the most fascinating place I've ever seen. I could spend days wandering through the Met.

Along the way, I became a member of the Museum, and started receiving their quarterly catalog. You can buy all sorts of pictures, posters, and art and sculpture related items directly through the catalog.

I'm not much of a catalog shopper, but I buy gifts from the Metropolitan Museum's catalog all the time. Imagine how excited I was when I found out that the Met had a catalog online. You can see a picture of everything in the catalog *before* you buy it. It's the ultimate form of electronic shopping (see the following figure).

GO MMA to see what kind of stuff the Metropolitan Museum of Art has available.

Even if you don't want to buy anything, you can at least have a free catalog sent to you, or search for the nearest Metropolitan store near you. I double-clicked on **SHOP THE METROPOLITAN MUSEUM ONLINE** to find my mom the perfect birthday gift.

I spent about half an hour browsing through all sorts of different ideas until I found the perfect gift. Usually it takes me several days to shop for the perfect birthday gift, and I was really excited to know I'd have it shipped straight to me with plenty of time to spare.

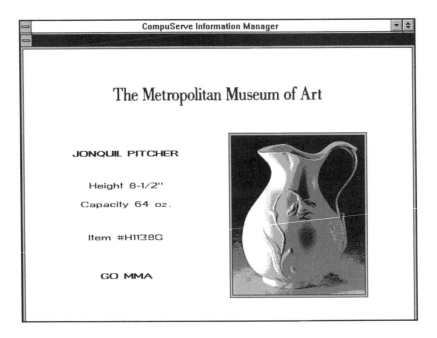

Here's the gift I bought. Think my mom will like it? She did :)

The Least You Need to Know

Art, music, and literature are important parts of the world we live in. We all need something to hang over our sofa or a good book to sit down and read. Don't be afraid to start up a conversation in the Literary Forum about your favorite author, book, or short story. I'm sure you'll find other people who have your same tastes.

➤ Make sure you keep your eyes open for new stuff on CompuServe. Last year, Aerosmith released a brand-new song only on CompuServe, and authors and artists hold conferences all the time.

➤ As in-depth and up-to-date as *Rolling Stone,* RockNet lets you track your favorite music superstars. (**GO ROCK**)

➤ Find a review of any CD you want in the All-Music Guide (**GO AMG**), then join the BMG Music Service (**GO BMG**) and have it sent to you for pennies.

➤ The Literary Forum is a hotbed of in-depth reviews and discussion about the classics and books that are popular today. Authors actually stop in themselves for a little discussion as well. (**GO LITFORUM**)

➤ The truly cultured **GO FINEARTS** to talk about art-related issues and see pictures of artists' new paintings and work.

Chapter 22

Games Galore

In This Chapter

➤ Learn how to play all the different games on CompuServe

➤ Start playing modem-to-modem games through CompuServe

➤ Find new games to download in the hottest game forums

Almost everyone I know bought their brand-new computer so it could help them to be more productive. They talked about all these neat programs that would help revolution-ize their lives. As it turns out, over half of them end up just playing games. You won't hear them admit it, but I know. When I ask them how their computer is doing, they invariably say "Great—if only I could get to level 3 in Super-Kombat-Commando-Killer," or "Do you think Solitaire is rigged so that I never win?"

These people would *love* CompuServe. There are so many different games to play that you'd never get to them all. Trivia, adventure, role-playing, head-to-head, modem-to-modem, simulations, and board games are all within a mouse click's reach. While the games you buy at the store have better graphics and sound, CompuServe games have one ultimate feature that store-bought games lack: other people.

Many CompuServe games are played simultaneously with or against other CompuServe users. This added dimension of uncertainty (you never know when Mark the Ogre is going to squash you like a bug) makes playing games online really fun.

Freebie Games

A handful of games comes free with your monthly CompuServe charge. That means you can play these games for as long as like, as often as you want without opening up a $4100 bill at the end of the month. **GO GAMES** (or click on the **Fun & Games** icon in WinCIM) to bring up a list of games to play (see the following figure).

Look at all the ways to waste time.

The free games fall into one of three categories: trivia, adventure, and other. Overall, they're pretty neat to play, and a good way to waste an hour or two, but they're just there to whet your appetite for playing the other games.

Trivia Games

These games test how much useless information you can regurgitate on a bunch of different topics. I mentioned ShowBizQuiz in Chapter 20 (**GO SBQ**), where you can test your knowledge of over 75 different entertainment- and movie-related categories.

The Grolier's Whiz Quiz (**GO WHIZ**) asks you questions directly from the *Grolier's Encyclopedia* (they're pretty hard) from your choice of 12 categories. You can play this game with four people at one time from your computer. So if you and three buddies get bored one Friday night, Grolier's is the place to be.

For all you heavy-duty scientists out there, the Science Trivia Quiz (**GO SCITRIVIA**) tests you over biology, chemistry, and physics.

Adventure Games

Adventure games are fun because you control what happens in them. You tell the computer where you'd like to go (or, if you've had a bad day, where *it* can go), what to look at, and what to do. In each of these games, your goal is to find lots of treasure, kill the bad guys (or gals), and escape alive.

Jane, Stop This Crazy Thing! For all of the adventure games, you can type **HELP** at any time to get a list of commands, or **QUIT** to leave the game.

They're all pretty much the same—text only. You type your command and CompuServe writes what happens.

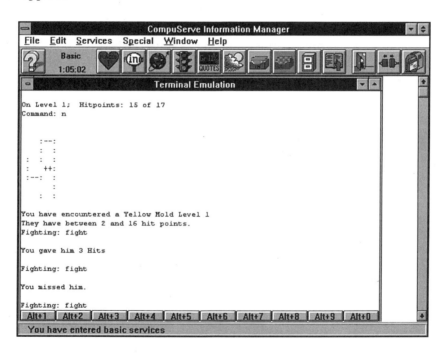

Cheer me on, I'm kicking some monster butt.

Adventure Find lots of treasure in a cave and try to live. **GO CLADVENT.**

Enhanced Adventure Find lots of treasure in a bigger cave and try to live. **GO ENADVENT.**

Castle Quest Find lots of treasure in a big castle and try to live. **GO CQUEST.**

BlackDragon Find lots of treasure in a cave, kill the Arch-Demon, and try to live. **GO BLACKDRAGON.**

Read the Instructions

Most games have a set of instructions that describe a little bit about them and provide explicit instructions for playing them. For the easy games, instructions aren't really that important. Once you start playing some of the complex simulations and role-playing games, though, the instructions alone can take an hour to read! You should look at and print (Choose **File** from the WinCIM menu bar and select **Print**) the instructions for every game you play. Believe me, it'll come in handy to have the full set of instructions sitting by your computer when you're in a life-or-death struggle with a troll.

Hangman

This may sound silly, but my favorite game on CompuServe is Hangman (**GO HANGMAN**). To me, it's just as addicting as playing Windows Solitaire. I like to sit back and guess word after word until the dawn breaks. Hopefully they'll get a graphical version soon (with sound effects).

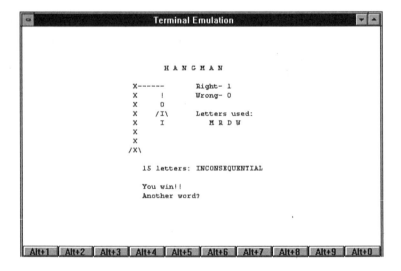

I almost got hung here. Good thing I thought of the right word.

Extended Games

Once you've gotten a chance to explore the standard games, you'll probably try at least one or two extended games, ones that you pay by the hour to play. Honestly, some of these extended games are really great, because you're playing against fellow CompuServe members at the same time. You can talk to, fight, and work with other CompuServe people who are playing the game at the same time. That's what makes these games so addicting and fun. You'll never play the exact same situation twice.

Since these games are more complicated, it's even more important that you read the instructions before playing. Otherwise, you may get so confused that the only way you can log off CompuServe is by turning your computer off (not the recommended method).

Fantasy/Role Playing Games

In these games your goal is to become an all-powerful wizard (or witch). Other CompuServe members are playing in the same game as you, so you're bound to run into other people just like you wandering around and killing things. You want to find lots of treasure and avoid being killed by monsters and other, more powerful, CompuServe members. Hang out with the other game players in the Role Playing Games Forum (**GO RPGAMES**).

MUD These types of games are particularly popular on the Internet. They're called Multi-User Dungeons (MUDs), and players from all over the world spend hundreds of hours MUDding in their eternal quest to become an all-powerful wizard.

British Legends	**GO LEGENDS**
The Island of Kesmai	**GO ISLAND**

War/Simulation

The online simulation games are the most popular games around. They are very complex, and take a while to get accustomed to, but be warned, once you start playing, you'll have trouble not going back for more. Here's a list of the multi-player games. To discuss strategy or talk to other players, **GO MPGAMES** to join the Multi Player Games Forum.

Don't Stop Here! If you like to play games against other people, but aren't impressed with the ones CompuServe has to offer, you might want to check out the Play-By-Mail Game Forum (**GO PBMGAME**). Several interactive games start all the time, with most of the action happening in mail or forum messages instead of in real time.

Sniper You're the commander of a squad of soldiers fighting in WWII. You compete with other squadron commanders to whip the enemy and earn promotions. Good luck soldier! **GO SNIPER**.

MegaWars I Conquer the universe and build starbases before the big bad wolf comes and blows your house down. **GO MEGA1**.

265

MegaWars III   The sequel's sequel to MegaWars I. **GO MEGA3.**

Air Traffic Controller   You control and direct planes flying in and out of your section of airspace. Make sure you don't send two planes to land in the same place at the same time, because you'll loose points (and hear a big *kaboom!*). **GO ATCONTROL.**

Modem-to-Modem Games

Modem-to-modem games (MTM) are regular computer games that you buy in a store. Of course, you can play these games on your computer at your leisure. But, if you have a modem, you can call anyone else in the world who has the same game, and play against them.

Battle Chess Is Just the Beginning...
Actually, you can play well over 30 popular modem-to-modem games, including Falcon, Flight Simulator, Battleship, Populous, Modem Wars, Tracon II, The Perfect General, and Wordtris through CompuServe. Not all MTM games are supported, so stop by the Modem Games Forum to find out about your favorite.

For example, one of my favorite MTM games of all time is Battle Chess. Battle Chess was a neat chess game that showed the different pieces actually killing each other. It was true gratuitous violence. Whenever I wanted, I could sit down and play a good game against the computer (I never won, but I liked seeing all the pieces kill each other). I had a friend who lived in Nashville who also had Battle Chess. Instead of playing against the computer, we could call each other up with our modems, and play against each other. It was really neat, except for how much we paid in long-distance phone bills.

If only I had known then what I know now. Instead of calling each other up long distance, we could have used CompuServe instead. There's a special modem game area of CompuServe that lets two users call in CompuServe locally, and play their MTM games that way. It's not much cheaper than a long-distance phone bill ($6 an hour), but if you play a lot, it's probably worth your money. Besides, you can meet all sorts of other people who play Battle Chess against each other as well.

GO MTMCHALLENGE to search for other CompuServe users who play MTM games. If you're brand-new to MTM games, but the concept sounds intriguing, start out in the Modem Games Forum (**GO MODEMGAMES**). You'll find lots of people willing to teach you the ropes there. You actually play in the Modem Games Lobby (**GO MTMLOBBY**), but you have to find an opponent first.

Getting Some Games for Your Own PC

If playing games online doesn't attract you, there are plenty of other ways to take care of your entertainment needs. You can download all sorts of fun games and play them on your computer. That way you don't have to worry about paying CompuServe's hourly rate to fight pixies and direct planes into mountains.

The best two places to head to are the Gamers Forum (**GO GAMERS**) and the Action Gamers Forum (**GO ACTION**). They used to be one forum until they became so popular that they split. In these two forums are all sorts of shareware games, hints, and lots of other people who like to play computer games. The Gamers Forum focuses on role-playing and adventure games, while knowing how to use an Uzi is a prerequisite for entering the Action Forum.

One Man's Trash Is Another's Treasure In each forum, there is a library section for people buying and selling used games. When I bought my CD-ROM drive, I started looking through all the games people were selling and bought several games. As a result, I never get any work done between playing games on CompuServe and my CD-ROM. I haven't seen better prices anywhere.

You can also get all sorts of recommendations about games you are thinking of buying. Before you plop out $50 in a store, post a message in one of the games forums asking for people's opinions.

Several extremely popular commercial and shareware games are available for download online. **GO HOTGAMES** to see what games you can download, and how much you'll pay for each one (some of them are free, others cost as much as $30, and you pay extended hourly rates for downloading them all).

Oh, look—I can download DOOM. That sounds like a nice peaceful game to play.

267

The Least You Need to Know

Some people like the satisfaction of trouncing on their opponent, while others just enjoy the challenge of competition. Whatever your reasoning is, set your priorities straight. Stop reading this book and start playing some games! I'm just about ready to start playing Hangman now.

➤ Always print out the instructions of every game you play online. The instructions will give you a background of the game, tell you how to play, and most importantly, tell you how to STOP playing when you're through.

➤ Play the basic games (**GO GAMES**) as often as you like because they're part of your monthly charge.

➤ Extended games like British Legends (**GO LEGENDS**) and Sniper (**GO SNIPER**) are extremely challenging and lots of fun, but can rack up quite a bill if you aren't watching the clock closely.

➤ **GO GAMERS** to find the most die-hard group of computer game players I've ever seen.

Chapter 23

Breaker, Breaker, Good Buddy: CB Chatting

In This Chapter

➤ Talk to people from around the world on CompuServe's CB Simulator

➤ See how talking in CB is more exciting than chatting in forums

➤ Learn how to join the CB Club

Way back in Chapter 11, you learned about chatting with other members in forums, and that was fairly cool. But most people don't hang out in forums to chat with other CompuServe members—they hang out there to download files and read messages. Occasionally, you'll find a conference or someone to talk to. But if chatting with other people online is what you like to do, head over to the CompuServe CB Simulator.

CompuServe's CB is 100 percent talk, 0 percent fat. Since talk is all you can do on CB, everyone is just aching for a good conversation.

No Antennae Required

Chatting in the CB Simulator is just like chatting in a forum, except there are more conference rooms. You can have a one-on-one talk, a private group conversation, or hang out in one of the public conference rooms. If you're used to talking in a forum, you'll pick up CBing in no time flat. **GO CB** to find the CB Simulator online.

The CB Simulator is designed to work just like a real-world CB, minus the truckers. While you won't see lots of messages talking about smokeys, there is a lot of regular old chit-chat. The CompuServe CB Simulator is split up into three bands, each with 36 channels (in CBspeak, a *channel* is a public conference room). That means there are 108 different conference rooms in which you can hang out.

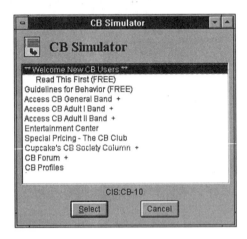

Here's the gateway into the CB Simulator.

Cybersex You've probably heard about cybersex in the newspapers or on TV. Cybersex is the exchange of sexually explicit messages through e-mail or chat. I won't get much more graphic than that, but if you hang out in the two CB adult bands, you'll run into it. If you don't approve of that sort of thing, don't use the adult bands.

Each CB band has its own general theme. The General Band is an open discussion about everything. There are conference rooms for new CBers, teens (the most popular one), college students, members speaking a foreign language, and many others. If you want to have a pleasant, general conversation with people from around the world, then hang out in the General Band.

The other two bands are geared specifically toward adults. You must be 18 to enter (parents are responsible for making sure their kids don't explore). I'd say most of the conversation is not appropriate for children.

Exploring the CB Simulator

Since this is a family-oriented book, let's go into the General Band. Double-click **Access CB General Band**. CompuServe will take you into the CB Simulator.

The first thing CompuServe asks for is your handle. Your handle is the nickname by which people will address you. You can pick anything you want as your handle. Handles work the same as they do for truckers. Nobody ever says, "John Smith, how are you doing?" on the CB. They say things like, "Shepherd calling Little Bo Peep," where Shepherd and Little Bo Peep are CB handles for real people.

I'm all smiles about the CB Simulator.

Type your handle, and click **OK**. I chose *Smiley* as my handle because I like to laugh a lot. Some people pick handles based on their mood, time of day, weather pattern, or use a different one every time they log on. After typing your handle, you're ready to get started.

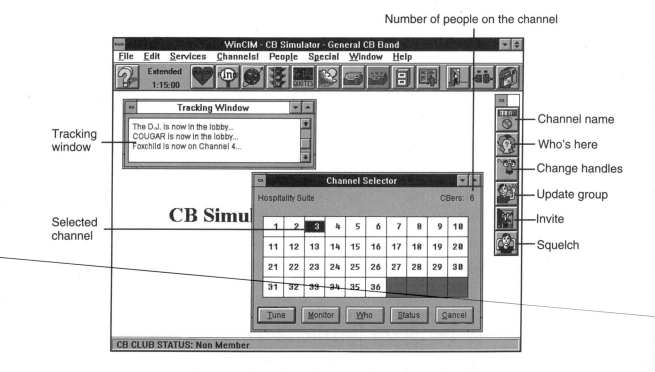

Here's what your CB screen looks like when you start off.

271

Other people won't be able to use your handle and user ID to search through CompuServe logs for your real name. Some people like to take on alternate egos when they CB and be a different person online.

Click on each channel to see its name and how many people are talking there. You can join any channel you want by double-clicking the channel number (or selecting the channel and then clicking the **Tune** button). A window for that channel opens, and you can talk just like you did in forums.

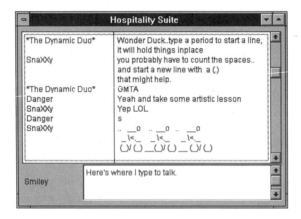

I joined Channel 1 to see what everyone was talking about.

You can tune into only one channel at a time. Remember that each channel is a public conversation. Anyone can join, listen, and talk with anyone else. Read on if you want to have a private conversation.

If you just want to eavesdrop on a channel, select the channel number and click **Monitor**. The same window as above appears, except there isn't a box for you to type in.

Once you get the hang of CB, you might want to monitor a couple of channels at once. While you can tune to only one channel at a time, you can monitor another channel. That lets you follow two different conversations.

Private Talks

You can have private conversations with other people in the CB Simulator, just like you can in forums. For a private conversation, click on the **Who's Here** button from the CB Toolbox. A window will pop up showing you all the CB users in the entire band (see the following figure). You can see all the handles that other people chose for themselves. Scroll through the list of **Who's Here**, select the person you want to chat with, and click on the **Talk** button.

Is that the real *Dynamic Duo?*

If you want to invite several people to have a private conversation, click on the **Invite** button on the CB Toolbox. You'll see the same list of CBers as the Who's Here window shows, but check boxes appear next to their names. Select the people you want to invite, and click on **Invite**, and they'll all be invited to your private conversation.

Going Clubbing

Talking on the CompuServe CB is *very* addictive. It's amazing how easy it is to spend hours and hours just talking to other users. Be careful you don't become addicted—I don't know of any CB Anonymous groups where you can get help.

If you find yourself spending a lot of time CBing, you might think about joining the CB Club. For a monthly fee, the CB Club offers you substantial savings off the $4.80 an hour you have to pay at the regular extended service rate. There are two club options.

➤ For $10 a month, you only pay $2.50 an hour to CB. It's cheaper than paying $4.80 an hour, but can still add up quickly.

➤ For $30 a month, you pay the rock-bottom price of $1 an hour. If you're addicted, and not afraid to admit it, this option probably makes the most sense to you.

I'm sure you can figure out that you only need to spend a couple hours in CB each month to make joining one of the clubs worth your while. In addition, you can reserve your CB name (get a * in front of it). This is like walking around with a big nametag that labels you as part of the exclusive CompuServe crowd. Some people are quite proud of this. I wouldn't be.

GO CBCLUB to learn more about joining one of the two clubs.

Permanently Handling the Situation

If you don't want to type your handle every time you join a CB band, then follow these steps to save your handle in WinCIM.

Select **Special**, **Preferences**, **CB Simulator**. In the box labeled **Handle** at the top of the screen (see the following figure), type your full-time handle and click on **OK**. Now every time you go CBing, CompuServe knows what your name is.

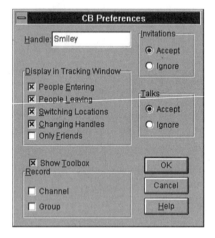

I've decided that I'll be all smiley for a while.

The Least You Need to Know

CompuServe CB is for people who like to talk. If your friends call you a motormouth, or people constantly tell you, *"shhh!"* in movie theaters, you might want to explore the CompuServe CB Simulator.

No matter what time of the day or night, there are always hundreds of people hanging out in the various CB bands (although the adult bands tend to be busier at night). So if you're lonely at home, or just like to meet new people, you're bound to meet others with your exact same interests.

➤ **GO CB** to meet lots of people who like to chat on the General and adult CB bands.

➤ The adult CB bands are not for the prudish. Frank conversations of sex are common.

➤ Nobody knows who you really are—they only know your handle.

➤ A CB Club (**GO CBCLUB**) is the economical choice if you find yourself CBing all the time.

Part 5
Other Useful
CompuServe Stuff

You're on the homestretch now to becoming a super CompuServe user! There is still so much more out there, but it's now up to you to use your sleuthing skills to track down what you're interested in. Chapters 24–28 cover a whole grab-bag of stuff that will aid you on your trip and help you save some money on the way.

YEAH, IT'S WEIRD BUT HE RETRIEVES LOST FILES LIKE NOBODY ELSE.

Chapter 24

The Reference Bookshelf

In This Chapter

➤ Search through the online *Grolier's Encyclopedia*

➤ Use CompuServe to check your spelling

➤ Leaf through White and Yellow Pages for the entire country

➤ Dig through the 800 databases accessible through IQuest

Wouldn't you like to have your own personal library at your fingertips? Research would be a snap. You could have an entire bookshelf of reference materials at your beck and call. Need to know kangaroo eating habits? Check the encyclopedia. Don't know how to treat your kid's chicken pox? Look it up in a big, heavy-duty medical book. Want to know how many leaders of France were named Louis? Flip through your almanac. (The answers: herbivores, oatmeal baths, and 18, respectively.)

The problems with owning a personal library are the cost and the space to house it. You'd have to spend several hundred dollars on the set of encyclopedias alone. Add in the rest of the stuff on your bookshelf, and you've got quite an investment just to learn about kangaroos and chicken pox. Instead of going out and buying your own set of reference books, use CompuServe.

Besides all the regular reference information, you can search tons of information on drugs, government issues, and even a complete United States phone and address directory. You're already familiar with some of the reference material you'll find online. In Chapter 18, I showed you how to search for magazine and newspaper articles, and in Chapter 19 you saw how to look up important information about publicly held companies. In this chapter, I'll show you around some of the more popular reference books on CompuServe and give you a taste of what's out there.

Standard Reference

There's a whole slew of standard reference books online waiting for you to use. You'll find such stalwarts as the encyclopedia, dictionary, almanac, and medical reference, just to name a few.

Personally, I don't even own a dictionary. Between my word processor's spell check feature and CompuServe's online dictionary, I never misspell a word (well, almost never). Here's a list of some common reference books. The best part of all these online reference books is that they're all included as part of the basic services—there's no extra charge.

Encyclopedia

Back in the old days, a set of encyclopedias was a status symbol. Every family with kids had to have the biggest set of encyclopedias for their kids to plagiarize. My family's set of encyclopedias was from 1947, and didn't even have all 50 states listed. That made it rather difficult to do "current event" book reports. Nowadays, an entire encyclopedia can fit on one CD-ROM, so the excitement of looking through moldy pages may be lost forever.

There are two encyclopedias on CompuServe, the *Grolier's Academic American* (**GO ENCYCLOPEDIA**), and the *British Hutchinson Encyclopedia* (**GO HUTCHINSON**). Both offer the complete text of the printed versions available to read online. Unfortunately, you can't download pictures or charts yet, but the encyclopedia is updated every three months. I always use the *Grolier's Encyclopedia* myself.

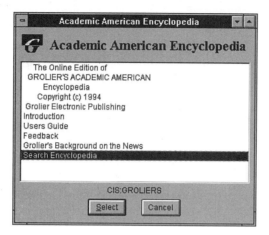

Carrying around this encyclopedia is a lot easier than the traditional 26-volume World Book.

To search through your encyclopedia, double-click **Search Encyclopedia**. WinCIM asks you for the subject you want to search for and brings back a list of results.

Here are the results for my search on the most divine food ever created.

Dictionary

Don't you hate it when you hear a word that everyone else seems to know but you? Or when you're writing a letter and can't remember if the principal is in your school, or your mortgage payment? Of course, that's when a dictionary comes in handy. If you're in need of that one special word, **GO DICTIONARY** to access the *American Heritage Dictionary.*

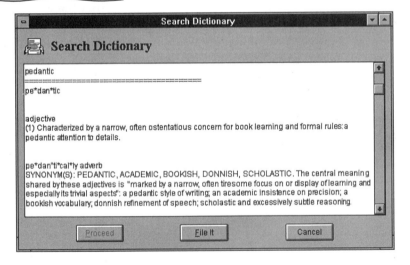

Willkommen! CompuServe also has an online dictionary that's in German. So if you *sprechen Sie Deutsch,* but don't know how to *sprechen* very well, you might want to check out the Bertelsmann Lexikon.

All you do is type the word, or part of the word you're looking up. You can then see the exact meaning and pronunciation of that word (see the following figure). If you don't know exactly how to spell a specific word, try typing only the first few letters. For example, if I didn't know how to spell *pedantic,* I could have typed **ped**, and the dictionary would have brought up a list of all words that began with those three letters. That's how I figure out how to correctly spell misspelled words all the time.

```
Search Dictionary

🖨  Search Dictionary

pedantic
=========================================
pe*dan*tic


adjective
(1) Characterized by a narrow, often ostentatious concern for book learning and formal rules: a
pedantic attention to details.


pe*dan"ti*cal*ly adverb
SYNONYM(S): PEDANTIC, ACADEMIC, BOOKISH, DONNISH, SCHOLASTIC. The central meaning
shared by these adjectives is "marked by a narrow, often tiresome focus on or display of learning and
especially its trivial aspects": a pedantic style of writing; an academic insistence on precision; a
bookish vocabulary; donnish refinement of speech; scholastic and excessively subtle reasoning.

    Proceed            File It            Cancel
```

I heard this word on Seinfeld one night, but never knew what it meant.

Almanac

Before using CompuServe, I had never used an almanac. I always seemed to slide by with encyclopedia and magazine articles whenever I needed statistics. One day I decided to see what kinds of information I could find in the *Information Please Almanac* on CompuServe (**GO GENALMANAC**).

I was amazed at the vast amount of information that I found. Every statistic and number imaginable as well as lots of handy tables and charts are all available for you to peruse online.

Besides the regular almanac, CompuServe also has the *Information Please Business Almanac* (**GO BIZALMANAC**), which has all sorts of information about businesses that you might find useful.

HealthNet

Are you feeling a little under the weather? Do you have bumps on the back of your neck? If Pepto Bismol has become your best friend, you might want to search through the HealthNet database on CompuServe. You might find some conventional wisdom for dealing with a hangover (eat a popsicle) or an immediate flag that indicates that you should see your physician immediately (your skin is melting).

GO HNT to look through the online medical reference library. I like looking through HealthNet to find out about cool diseases. Honestly though, if I'm really sick, I don't bother reading through CompuServe; I just take two aspirin and call myself in the morning.

Hypochondriacs, enjoy!
If you have a strange affinity for always getting sick, no matter how healthy your doctor says you are, you'll love the HealthNet database. You can look up any disease and create your own symptoms around it. Or, if any of your friends or relatives are hypochondriacs, sign them up to CompuServe and point them this way.

Phone Directories

If you thought your local White Pages was big, just imagine the size the CompuServe Phone*File service (**GO PHONEFILE**). Phone*File is a compilation of all the white pages nationwide that you can search through. You can use Phone*File to find addresses and phone numbers of people throughout the country.

Similar to Phone*File, Biz*File (**GO BIZFILE**) lets you search through all the business listings in the nation. You can find out Dr. Schwartz's address in New York, or how to get a hold of Microsoft in Seattle.

Searching for that special someone

Often Phone*File and Biz*File are used to locate or track down people whom you haven't seen or spoken to in a while. You can check to see if your best friend from high school is still living at home, or what the address of a forgotten relative is. If searching for long-lost people is interesting to you, try using CompuTrace (**GO TRACE**). CompuTrace lets you search through lists of 100 million living and deceased individuals to locate long-lost friends and relatives. It's expensive, though. Exploring CompuTrace costs an extra $15 an hour.

IQuest

I couldn't talk about reference information on CompuServe without mentioning IQuest. Short for *Information Quest,* IQuest is the most comprehensive source of reference information available anywhere. There are well over 800 different databases that you can search through using IQuest. You can search through books, magazines, credit information, abstracts, and many more types of databases looking for almost any information you can imagine. IQuest databases are organized in the following categories:

Art, Literature, & Entertainment

Business & Industry

Laws, Patents

Medicine

International News

State News

Philosophy, Religion

Reference

Science & Technology (the biggest category)

Social Science

Fulfilling Your Quest

GO IQUEST to find IQuest on CompuServe. You can read through a description of IQuest and the pricing information. Using IQuest is not cheap. You pay $3.00 per abstract you look at, and $18.00 to have a specific article photocopied and sent to you. And, of course you're paying $4.80 an hour on top of everything else. IQuest is certainly not a cheap service, but it's incredibly thorough and useful.

After you **GO IQUEST**, to search through the IQuest databases, double-click **Access IQuest ($W)**.

Searching IQuest

Once you enter IQuest, you can pick and choose the database or databases you want to search through. For example, if you are looking for a list of books about your religion, you probably wouldn't search through the art, literature, and entertainment databases.

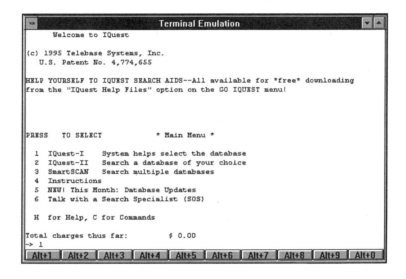

Here's the introductory IQuest Screen.

IQUEST-I guides you through a series of menus to help you find the right database to search through.

IQUEST-II lets you type the exact name of the database you want to search through (for regular IQuest users). I can never remember the name, so I always use IQUEST-I.

SmartSCAN lets you search through multiple databases at one time. Of course you'll pay an extra $5.00 per search for this extra convenient benefit.

The Least You Need to Know

Information is what CompuServe does best. Sure, you can chat with other users and play a good game or two, but first and foremost, CompuServe is an information service. Just about the only reference book missing is the *Guinness Book of World Records,* and I'm not sure whether that really falls under the reference category.

Before you go out and buy your next reference book, I'd check and see what CompuServe has online. Many of them are included with your monthly charge, and you can probably afford the others if you use them sparingly.

➤ By using the online encyclopedia (**GO ENCYCLOPEDIA**), you can afford to buy other amenities for your house.

➤ Find out how contagious chicken pox really are by searching through the HealthNet medical reference (**GO HNT**).

➤ Millions of individual and business addresses and phone numbers are publicly accessible through the Phone*File (**GO PHONEFILE**) and Biz*File (**GO BIZFILE**) databases.

➤ Even though it's absolutely comprehensive, use IQuest sparingly because it is extremely expensive. It's almost worth traveling to the library if you need to use IQuest a lot (**GO IQUEST**).

Chapter 25

Handy Travel Services

In This Chapter

➤ Learn how to use EAASY SABRE, the worldwide listing of flights, hotels, and car rentals

➤ Discover the amenities in your hotel before you get there

➤ Use Traveler's Advantage to find different vacation packages around the world

Having been on a vacation once or twice in my lifetime, I know just how much fun they can be. In college, we would pile 14 people into a Plymouth Horizon (some people had to be strapped to the roof) and set off on a roadtrip to Florida. Of course the hotel had never heard of our reservation, half our luggage got stolen, and as a result, I'm sure there's an FBI file on me (and my vacation tendencies) somewhere.

Nowadays, my vacations are a little bit more tame (12 years later). I'm pretty meticulous about getting the right hotel, eating at the best restaurants, and getting the biggest bang for my buck while I'm on vacation. Generally, I use CompuServe as a helpful travel agent. You can make actual room and flight reservations, check out hot night spots and great restaurants, and read about your vacation spot while you're on CompuServe.

If you're a traveler, this chapter is for you. I talk about the different travel and vacation services online, and give you some ideas for planning an ideal vacation. See you in Aruba!

EAASY SABRE

If you're trying to plan a vacation, EAASY SABRE is probably one of the first places you'll want to check out. With EAASY SABRE you can reserve flights, hotel rooms, and even rental cars directly through your CompuServe User ID. EAASY SABRE was created by American Airlines (get it, *EAASY SABRE?*) and has millions of flights from over 300 airlines available for reservations.

You can pretty much plan an entire trip, complete with your hotel room, in one session with EAASY SABRE. You can even put everything on your credit card. The prices listed are usually pretty good. Sometimes I get a really good price (New York to Columbus for $100, round trip); other times EAASY SABRE is more hassle than it's worth ($11,278 from Columbus to Paris, by way of Japan and Budapest—no kidding).

Membership Required Only members of the AAdvantage Club (American Airlines Frequent Flyers club) can use EAASY SABRE. Daunting as that may sound, membership is free and open to anybody. The first time you use EAASY SABRE, you'll have to fill out a quick and painless information sheet about yourself.

As an example, let's take a look at how easy it is to visit EuroDisney in Paris before it shuts down. **GO SABRECIM** to bring up the EAASY SABRE introduction. Click on **Access EAASY SABRE (CIM)** to log into the EAASY SABRE reservation system.

Once you log into EAASY SABRE, you can choose from flight, hotel, and car reservations. I make a beeline straight for **Flights and Fares** to see how much I'm going to have to borrow from the bank so I can afford to buy a ticket (see the following figure).

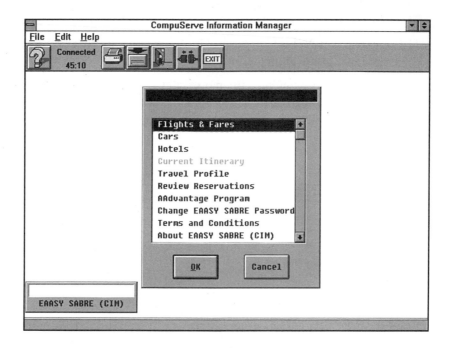

I've got some spare time on my hands; maybe I'll fly to Europe. On second thought, I'll probably just use an airline.

The Destination dialog box appears and asks me what my travel arrangements are (see the following figure). I have to type the city I'm leaving from, where I'd like to go, when I'm traveling, and the number of travelers.

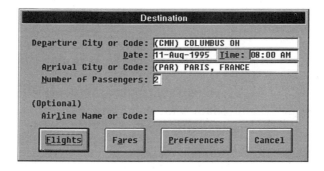

Here's where you enter your destination. I've wanted to visit the Louvre all my life.

You don't need to know the special airline abbreviation for the cities you are traveling to (for example, CMH is Columbus, Ohio). Just type in the city name and EAASY SABRE will look up the abbreviation for you.

Once you have all your basic info filled out, click on the **Flights** button. EAASY SABRE searches through its flights and brings up a list of all the ones that come close to what you were searching for (see the following figure). Sometimes this search can take a minute or two, especially during the middle of the business day, so be patient (and since CompuServe is worldwide, it's always the middle of the day somewhere).

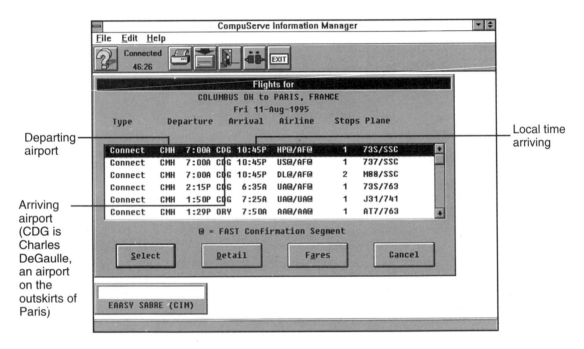

Wow, there are a lot of flights available, but what a long trip.

Needless to say, I've got a lot of different choices for flying to Europe. They all look good, but now I've got to figure out how much it'll cost. Highlight a flight and click on **Select** to see more information about it.

I don't usually use EAASY SABRE to make the actual reservations. For some reason, I still like to talk to my travel agent—she always seems to know exactly what's happening. Call me old fashioned, but I'm always wary of spending hundreds (if not thousands) of dollars online.

But I do use EAASY SABRE to research how much I can expect to pay, *before* I visit my travel agent. That helps me get a grip on what price range I'm looking at, and lets me know if my travel agent did a good job booking me.

Having a Place to Stay

Besides actually getting to your dream vacation spot, your hotel is the most important part of the trip. Since you'll be there during the night, you probably want to make sure there aren't too many live animals crawling around as soon as the lights go out.

When Making Reservations

If you decide to use EAASY SABRE to make your reservations, make sure you book a flight home as well. I know this sounds silly, but you don't want to get stuck somewhere without a ride home. Also, sometimes you can get a better price on a round-trip ticket than on two one-ways.

The most thorough hotel listing on CompuServe is the ABC Worldwide Hotel Guide (**GO ABC**). Use this big index of thousands of hotels to find the one that meets your exact needs. Whether you want a hotel that rents by the hour or one with all the amenities that you could imagine, you can find the right hotel without any problem.

You can search for hotels by country, cost, or extra special services; just work your way through the text menus.

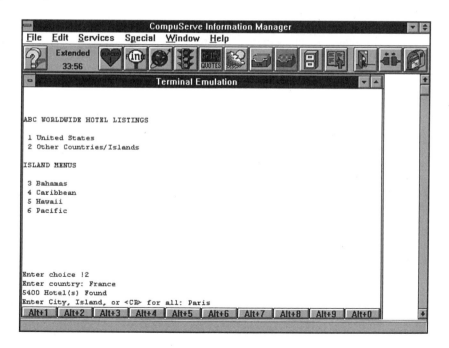

Here, I've chosen (2) Other Countries/Islands, and then entered the specific country (France). It found 5400 hotels, so I narrowed my search to Paris.

Food Would Be Nice...

Try This at Home

Most likely your city (or one near you) is listed in Zagat's Restaurant Guide. Why wait for a vacation to see what good food is around? I've lived in Columbus my entire life and was surprised by some of the restaurants I found listed.

I don't know about you, but I'm rather partial to eating when I'm on a luxurious vacation. Actually, I like to splurge on food. Normally I'll just eat a Big Mac and small fries for dinner, but when I'm on vacation, I'll get a large order of fries. I have become quite a connoisseur of french fries around the world (that's why I want to go to France).

If you're going on vacation somewhere in the United States, make sure you look at the Zagat Restaurant Guide on CompuServe before you go. Renowned for their current and complete restaurant reviews, Zagat's Guide knows of thousands of places to eat around the country. From tourist traps to hole-in-the-wall bistros, you can find any type of restaurant you want.

GO ZAGAT to find the Zagat Restaurant Guide online. You search for restaurants by criteria like city, cuisine, and price. I was very impressed with the Zagat survey. I've never been disappointed by a restaurant it said I would like.

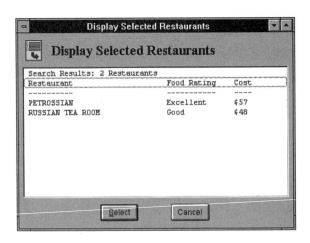

In New York City, only two restaurants specialize in caviar (fish eggs if you're uncultured), and boy, are they expensive.

Travel Forums

Besides all the neat travel services I've mentioned so far, there's at least one more place you'll want to stop by on CompuServe before setting out for EuroDisney. The Travel Forum (**GO TRAVSIG**) is a virtual font of vacation and travel knowledge.

There are message and file sections for people who like everything from cruises and casinos, planned touring trips through Europe, to rough hiking trips through Central Africa. Travel experts and professionals are always around to answer even the silliest questions about traveling ("How do you pronounce *crepe?*").

In the file libraries, there are free programs that you can download to plan your itinerary, get big discounts at special hotels, or read firsthand accounts of a fellow CompuServe member's vacation experience.

In addition to the Travel Forum, several states and countries have their own CompuServe forums, as well. You can talk to other frequent travelers, learn the ins and outs of the country (or state), and find out where to go for the hottest nightlife.

States with their own Forums	GO Words
California	CALFORUM
Florida	FLORIDA
Ohio Travel	OHIO
New York	NEWYORK

Countries with their own Forums	GO Words
Hong Kong	HKFORUM
Israel	ISRAEL
Italy	ITALFORUM
Japan	JAPAN
United Kingdom	UKFORUM

Traveler's Advantage

Once you decide where to go, make sure you stop by Traveler's Advantage (**GO TRAVAD**). Traveler's Advantage (TA) is an online travel agent that helps you get low airfares and hotel rates throughout the world. They brag about half-price hotel rooms and special travel packages.

Don't Forget to Quit If you don't quit TA within three months, you're automatically charged $49 for an entire year's membership. Make sure you cancel your TA account before those three months are up if you don't feel like spending $49.

Of course, only members of TA can take advantage of these opportunities. Normally it costs $49 a year to join TA. That's too expensive for someone like me who doesn't vacation much anyway, but you can sign up for three months for only $1. This lets you get a taste for TA to see if it's of any use to you.

Why am I pushing TA? Simple. Once I figure out what I want to do, I stop by TA and see what kind of prices they can give me. I figure it's worth $1 to see if TA can save me some money on my next trip.

The Least You Need to Know

Before a vacation, I spend countless hours making sure every detail is correct, so I'm not lost in Zimbabwe without a place to stay. I don't like to deal with a lot of hassle when I'm on a trip. There are a lot of neat things on CompuServe to help plan the perfect vacation. Don't be afraid to explore EAASY SABRE or the ABC Hotel Guide just because you work with a travel agent. If anything, it makes you more informed and confident about your travel agent's abilities to find you good deals and great times.

➤ Use American Airline's travel service EAASY SABRE to find airline flights around the world (**GO SABRECIM**).

➤ See a list of hotels that meet your requirements with the ABC Worldwide Hotel Guide (**GO ABC**).

➤ The Zagat Restaurant Guide shows you the best places to eat, whether you want to grab a steak in Chicago or suck mudbugs in New Orleans (**GO ZAGAT**).

➤ **GO TA** to explore the services of an online travel agent.

➤ You'll find fellow world travelers wandering around the Travel Forum. Don't be afraid to post a message or two before your next trip (**GO TRAVSIG**).

Chapter 26

Saving Time with CompuServe Navigator

In This Chapter

➤ Learn what CompuServe Navigator is and how it can save you cash.

➤ Create a simple script from scratch.

➤ Figure out which tasks are better suited for WinCIM and which are ideal for CompuServe Navigator.

By the time you read this chapter, you will have seen all sorts of different places to visit on CompuServe. You've seen how to read news, send e-mail, check a forum—I could go on forever. You've probably even done a bit of your own exploring as well.

There is so much information on CompuServe that you could spend hours reading messages, downloading files, or researching projects. Unfortunately, you pay out the nose for each of those hours. I used to log on once every day and read three or four forums. By the time I added up all the time I spent reading and replying to messages, I paid about $100 a month just for reading forums (not to mention CB chatting and researching).

That's when I found out about *CompuServe Navigator (CSNav)*. CSNav lets you automatically call CompuServe and download e-mail and forum messages so you can read them while you're off-line. When I started using CSNav, I drastically cut down the amount of time I actually spent online. Now, with more change jingling in my pocket, I can explore more forums and keep my bill to less than half of the original one.

What Is CompuServe Navigator?

Script A *script* is a sequence of events that explains what actions to take. You get to pick what kind of stuff you want to put in the script and in which order. Pretend you're writing a movie script, with only one character (CSNav), who can only do a limited set of actions (like Sylvester Stallone). You can pick and choose from those actions to decide what you want your script to do. All scripts come from the same set of actions but are arranged differently (kind of like Rocky I–V).

Like WinCIM, CompuServe Navigator (CSNav) is special software that lets you call and log onto CompuServe. However, that's where the similarity ends, because they function quite differently.

You use WinCIM to browse around online, read the news, or download a file. When you tell WinCIM to **GO** to a forum, poof—you're automatically there. If you want to read your mail, a single mouse click will bring you to your online mailbox instantaneously (or at least as fast as your modem will let you).

CSNav is a lot different. With CompuServe Navigator, you create a *script* that tells the program what forums to download messages from, what to do with your mail, and get other important information like Stock Quotes and Weather. CSNav logs on to CompuServe, downloads all the information you tell it you to, and then logs off immediately. There's no need for dilly-dallying around.

Once you get used to WinCIM, working with CSNav is the next logical step (unless someone else is footing the bill), so read on and figure out how to save *mucho dinero* on your CompuServe bill.

Downloading CSNav

To get to CompuServe Navigator online, **GO CSNAV** from WinCIM. You can read about the latest CSNav bells and whistles and download CSNav directly (see the following figure). Although not free, it's pretty cheap. You are charged $20 to download it, and get a $10 usage credit, making the total cost of CompuServe Navigator only $10.

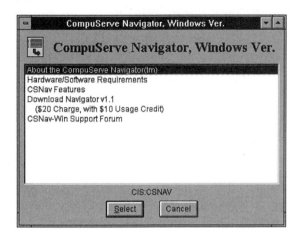

What a bargain—CSNav used to be $50, now it's only $10.

To download CSNav onto your computer, choose **Download Navigator v1.1** (there might be a new version of CompuServe Navigator out by the time you're reading this) and click on the **Select** button. Follow the instructions, and you'll soon be downloading one big executable (EXE) file (2.6 megabytes, or about 40 minutes with a 14,400 baud modem). Download the file to a separate directory and then to your regular WinCIM download directory so you can easily delete the installation file when you're done using it.

Installing CompuServe Navigator

Installing CSNav is a piece of cake. All you have to do is run the file that you just downloaded. CSNav takes care of all the hard stuff so you don't have to. From the Windows Program Manager, select **File, Run**. Then type in the name of the CSNav Installation file you downloaded.

If you saved the file into your default CompuServe download directory, your **Run** command will look something like this:

C:\CSERVE\DOWNLOAD\CNINST.EXE

Then click on the **OK** button. CompuServe will ask you one or two questions, and then install CSNav for you.

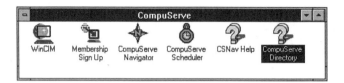

Once you've installed CompuServe Navigator, some neat new icons appear in your CompuServe program group.

Meet CompuServe Navigator

CompuServe Navigator is a pretty advanced program that takes some getting used to. Being familiar with WinCIM helps, but it'll take some practice to become an expert with CSNav.

Click on the **CompuServe Navigator** icon in the CompuServe program group to start CSNav. The following screen should appear.

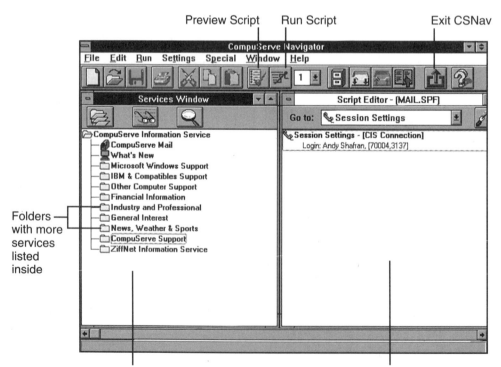

It's a lot different from WinCIM, isn't it?

Sculpting a Script

Once CompuServe Navigator is started, you'll need to create a script. This script, on the right side of the screen, tells CSNav exactly what to do when it's online. When you run the script, CSNav just reads it and performs each step listed. Like an actor who can't improvise, CSNav only reads directly from the script. Right now my script is empty because I haven't told CSNav what I want to do.

I'm sure your Shakespearean instincts will force you to create a masterpiece of a script. To add new tasks into your script, drag services from the left side of the screen to the right. For example, if I want CSNav to automatically check my mail each time it logs on, I click and hold my cursor on **CompuServe Mail** in the Services Window on the left and drag it to the **Script Editor** on the right. Then I let go of the mouse button, and *voila!*—checking CompuServe mail is now added to my script.

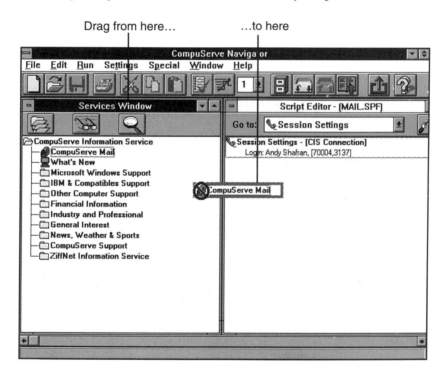

Here's an action shot of me adding CompuServe Mail to my CSNav script.

You can explore the various folders in the Services window and drag as many different services and forums as you want onto your script.

Once you've got several services listed, you have to tell CSNav what exactly you want to do with these services. In my script window below, notice how I have CompuServe Mail listed. I have got to tell CSNav what it's supposed to do with my mail, so I click on the **All Mail** check box underneath **Retrieve Mail**. This tells CSNav to automatically download all CompuServe mail directly into my Filing Cabinet every time it logs on.

Similarly, I have to tell the script what to do in each forum. I have the **Since** check box selected underneath **Retrieve Messages**, which will download all the new messages in the WinCIM forum since the last time I logged on.

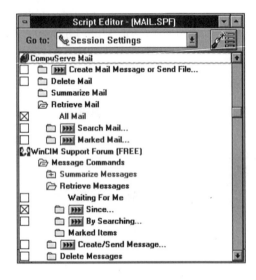

Just like with a grocery list, check off each task you want CSNav to do for you.

When you're done creating the script, click on the **Preview Script** button in the CSNav Ribbon at the top of the screen. A window comes up and shows you everything your script is set to do when you run it. Check it over carefully so you don't accidentally download 11,000 messages in the Entertainment Drive Forum by accident.

My script looks just about right.

When you're all ready to go, click on the **Run** button and watch your computer go nuts. Not missing a beat, CSNav calls CompuServe and proceeds to follow the script line by line.

Scheduling Some Automatic Action

Not only can CompuServe Navigator download your messages and mail for you, but you can schedule it to run automatically. Let's say you always get home from work at 6:00 in the evening and you want to have your forum messages and stock reports waiting for you.

Like an obedient dog who fetches your slippers, CSNav can be scheduled to run periodically at any set interval (monthly, weekly, daily, or even hourly) using the CompuServe Scheduler that comes with CSNav.

Saving Is Important
Don't forget to save your script when you've finished it. Choose **File** from the CSNav menu bar, and pull down **Save** to store your script in order to use it over and over again in the future.

To schedule CSNav, double click on the **CompuServe Scheduler** icon from your CompuServe program group (the icon looks like a stopwatch). Up comes a VCR-like console that lets you set the time you want to schedule CSNav to run. I know that 90 percent of us can't set a VCR (or else 12:00 must be a very popular time), but the Scheduler is easy enough to use.

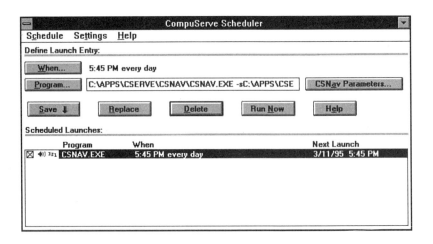

I've set the Scheduler to run CSNav at 5:45 every day.

Satisfying Schedules

You can set CompuServe Scheduler to work with any Windows application. I've seen people schedule the Windows clock to come up at midnight, reminding them to go to bed, or set their Tax software to start at 5:00pm on April 14 (plenty of time if you're only filing an extension).

Now What?

Once your script has completed, you can read and download messages or information (like the weather), create response messages and mail, or fine-tune your script a little.

I use both WinCIM and CSNav all the time. I like to use CSNav to keep track of all the forums I follow regularly. There's only a handful (Macmillan is one of them) that I spend a lot of time in, and CSNav is the most economical choice for me. I read through all the messages off-line, create responses, and upload them all in CSNav.

To be honest, I use WinCim more. I like to check the AP news, read Miss Manners, and chat in the CB Simulator, none of which can be done with the CompuServe Navigator. Except for CB chatting, I have a tendency to log on with WinCIM and browse around all the free stuff (maybe even play a game of Hangman). I'll explore forums here and there, and when I find one I like, I'll add it to my CSNav script. As a general rule, if it costs extra money, I use CSNav.

Both programs work well together and complement each other. Once you're a regular CompuServe user, you might as well take the plunge and download CompuServe Navigator. I can almost guarantee it'll cut down on your CompuServe bills, once you learn how to use it.

If you have questions or problems with CompuServe Navigator, you might want to take a look at the CSNav-Win Support Forum (**GO CSNAVSUP**). CompuServe employees monitor this free forum and will step you through getting CSNav working perfectly.

The Least You Need to Know

You're playing a game of "Beat the Clock" when you use CompuServe. You want to find interesting news, conversations, and files, all without breaking the bank. CompuServe wants you to log on all the time and spend lots of money (so they make lots of money). To play fair, CompuServe levels the playing field by providing neat software that makes it more affordable to be a member.

WinCIM is nice because it lets you create e-mail and forum messages off-line. CSNav is another great help. It takes the pain out of reading through hundreds of messages in a forum. Now you can sit back, relax, and read the messages at your own pace, instead of zooming through them online.

➤ Download CSNav for only $10 (**GO CSNAV**), and you'll save at least that much money in your first month.

➤ Navigator and WinCIM are meant to work together, so don't be afraid to try out CSNav if you are an experienced WinCIM user.

➤ Double-click on the **CompuServe Navigator from Windows** icon to start CSNav.

➤ You can create your own CSNav script in under five minutes to read your mail and forums.

➤ Schedule CompuServe Navigator to automatically run through a script whether you're at or away from your computer. Start Scheduler by double-clicking the **CompuServe Scheduler from Windows** icon.

Chapter 27

Using CompuServeCD

In This Chapter

➤ Ordering the new CompuServeCD and plowing into the CD-ROM world

➤ Reading the multimedia magazine that comes with your CD

➤ Using CompuServeCD to find files offline (that is, cheaply!)

If you thought CompuServe Navigator was great, just wait until you see what else CompuServe has got up its sleeve. CSNav pales in comparison to CompuServe's bimonthly multimedia magazine, the CompuServeCD.

There's no way around it—the CompuServeCD is genuinely cool. It's by far one of the most interesting, fun, and exciting CDs I've ever seen, and a new issue comes out every other month! The CompuServeCD is on the cutting edge with animation, video, music, and spectacular graphics making up each issue. And in this chapter, you'll learn how to grab the latest issue of CompuServeCD.

Smaller Than a Frisbee (and Sharper, Too!)

Going multimedia is the hottest trend around. Compact discs that are created especially for computers can store over 650 megabytes of sound, graphics, and video, turning your computer into a virtual entertainment center.

Multimedia
A buzzword meaning that your computer has a CD-ROM and sound card installed. With those two pieces of equipment, you can watch videos, see animation, and listen to music directly from your PC (and the games are incredible).

Last year CompuServe launched their own CD-ROM. Each issue of CompuServeCD includes an interactive multimedia magazine, the latest version of WinCIM, and the complete index of the PC and Graphics File Finders, fully searchable without logging on (you'll say "Wow" about that in a few moments).

Getting the Disc

Of course, the CompuServeCD doesn't come with your monthly membership fees. Each issue costs $5.95 (plus $1.50 S/H). That's a pretty good deal for a CD-ROM, especially with all the neat stuff CompuServe piles on it. To order the most recent issue of CompuServeCD, **GO CCD** online. You can have the latest issue sent to you, or become a regular subscriber. The latest CD will be sent to your house. Currently, a new CD comes out every other month, but in the near future CompuServe plans to make their CD on a monthly basis. So if you subscribe, you'll be paying the extra few bucks every month instead of every other month.

Get Help Now
If you have any trouble or questions about the CompuServeCD, call the special CD support line at 800-CDROM-89 (1-800-237-6689) and you'll talk to a CompuServe expert who can help you out. Online, **GO CCDSUPPORT** to get to the CompuServeCD Forum.

Before you order the CompuServeCD, make sure you have the following computer equipment (minimum), or you might as well not bother:

Windows 3.1 or higher

4MB RAM/8MB recommended

About 5 MB of space on your hard drive

640x480 monitor resolution with 256 colors

Single-speed CD-ROM drive/double-speed recommended

16-bit sound card with MIDI support recommended

External speakers recommended

Getting Started

Once you get your CompuServeCD in the mail, pop it in your CD-ROM drive. To install it from Program Manager, choose **File**, **Run** and run the program D:\SETUP.EXE (if your CD drive is D:).

CompuServe will ask you one or two questions, and then install the CompuServeCD for you. When you're all finished, you'll get several new icons added to your CompuServe folder in Windows.

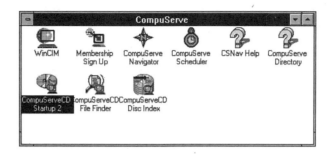

I'm getting quite a collection of icons in my CompuServe folder.

Let's See Some Multimedia

Once you've installed the CD, click on the **CompuServeCD Startup 2** icon from the CompuServe program group to enter the multimedia world of CompuServeCD.

Opens the CompuServeCD magazine

Installs the newest version of WinCIM

Searches through the CD's built-in File Finder

Here's the introductory page for the CompuServeCD. Point and click wherever you want to go.

Let's go to the magazine first; it's the neatest thing on the entire CD. Click on the magazine cover in the top-left corner of your screen and you'll bring up the multimedia CompuServeCD magazine. CompuServe calls their magazine "critically acclaimed"— which means it's either incredibly cool, or misunderstood.

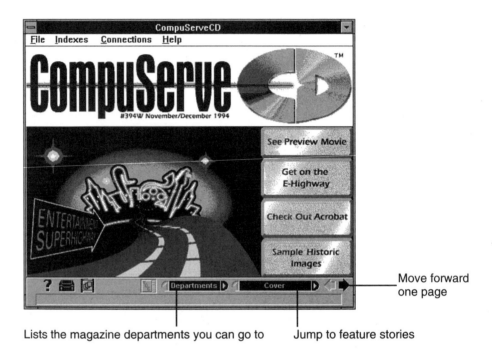

Lists the magazine departments you can go to   Jump to feature stories

Move forward one page

This issue focuses on, you guessed it, "The Entertainment Superhighway."

Each issue of the CompuServeCD magazine has a different focus. This one is all about entertainment and fun stuff, both on CompuServe and in the computer world. In general, there's always a link between the stuff you find in the magazine and what's available online. You can think of the CompuServeCD as a really great commercial for finding unique things on CompuServe.

Here are the seven departments found in each issue of CompuServeCD. Each department has its own section, graphics, and stories for you to peruse.

Department	Description
Technology and Trends	Shows the newest in graphics, demos, and over-priced computer equipment.
Arts/Entertainment	A current sampling of what's hot in the entertainment industry. You'll find movie previews, celebrity interviews, and music samples.
Home & Leisure	Stuff you like to do in your spare time.
Civilization	Geared towards those of us who like to talk about art, science, education, human relations, and world affairs.
Personal Enterprise	How to make the most out of your business and personal financial information
Member Services	Neat things on CompuServe that will make your stay a little bit more pleasurable.
Shopping	A plethora of things you can buy from the electronic mall.

You can go to each department directly by clicking on **Departments** at the bottom of the screen. You'll find video and audio samples in almost every story. Each one of these exciting demos has its own button you can click to begin.

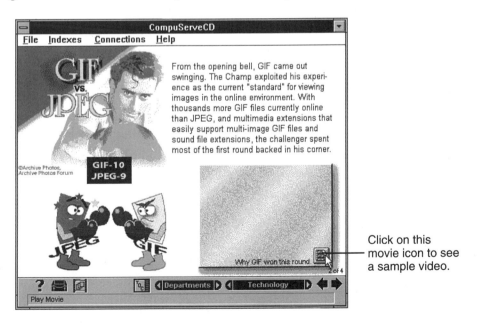

Click on this movie icon to see a sample video.

Here's an interesting story about the different kinds of graphics found on CompuServe.

File Finding Made Easy

Remember using CompuServe's different File Finders? In Chapter 13, I showed you how to search through the online File Finders to find that one perfect file. You could even download the files you wanted directly from File Finder.

Out-of-Date CDs

The one problem with the CompuServeCD File Finders is that they go out of date quickly. On CompuServe, the File Finders are updated monthly. Once you buy a CD, it'll never change, ever. That means new files may be uploaded and your CD will never know about them. The easiest way to get around this problem is to always use the newest version of the CompuServeCD.

As you recall, I had two gripes about File Finders. One was the cost. File Finder is pretty slow on CompuServe, and I'm paying $4.80 an hour to do the search (not to mention my download). My second gripe was that File Finder would reset after every file you downloaded. So, if you wanted to grab three different files, you had to go through the exact same steps *three* times (and pay for the slow-as-molasses File Finder to search all three times).

If for no other reason, you should order the CompuServeCD because the File Finder indexes come built-in. That's right, you can search through the PC and Graphics File Finders while off-line. But wait, there's more. After searching, you can mark all the files you want to download, and then have the CompuServeCD automatically download them for you. It's like a CompuServe Navigator for files! Of course you have to pay to download the files, but at least the search is free.

File Finding from CD

To use the built-in File Finder, double-click on the **CompuServeCD File Finder** icon from Windows. A much more stylish window than the online File Finder comes up.

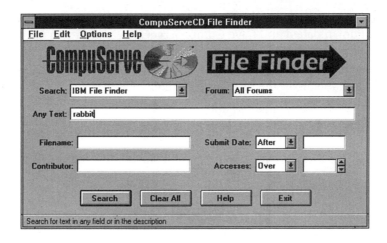

Shhhh…be vewy quiet. I'm hunting wabbits…

First, choose the File Finder you want to dig through in the **Search** box (PC or Graphics are your only two choices). Then type the word (or words) you want to search for in the **Any text:** box and click on the **Search** button.

File Finder wanders around into the bowels of your CD-ROM drive for a few moments and returns all the files that match your search criteria.

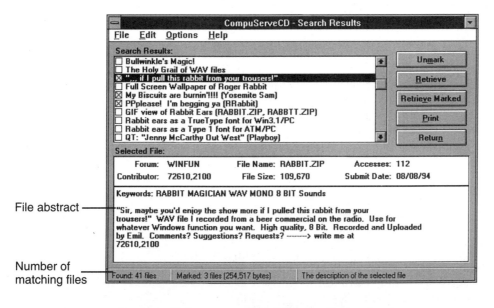

Look at all those wascally wabbits on CompuServe.

The best part about using the File Finder on CD-ROM is that you can mark all the files you want downloaded and have CompuServeCD retrieve them for you automatically. Just mark the check box next to each file (or select the file and click on the **Mark** button). When you're done file marking, click on **Retrieve Marked** and you'll log onto CompuServe and download the files immediately.

The Least You Need to Know

The CompuServeCD is a great way to waste time. So far, I've gotten all the issues and read them from cover to cover. The stories are usually pretty good, but I like the special effects and video clips best of all.

If you own a CD-ROM, order an issue of the CompuServeCD. You won't be disappointed. If you don't have a CD-ROM, catch up to the rest of us technology geeks and go multimedia.

➤ The CompuServeCD is a steal at $5.95 an issue. To order it, **GO CCD**.

➤ Each issue is organized into several departments and has lots of graphics, video clips, and music samples thrown in.

➤ Use the CompuServeCD File Finder instead of paying connect time charges to search online.

Chapter 28

My Favorite Stuff

In This Chapter

➤ The latest services CompuServe has to offer

➤ Neat places to stop on CompuServe

This is my favorite part of the whole book. Here's where I get to tell you some of the neatest and most unusual places to hang out on CompuServe (in my opinion). Some of these places are really useful, but most of them aren't. It was hard picking out my 10 favorite places on CompuServe, so I hope you like the list.

Enjoy, and remember that the meter is still running.

Absolut Museum: GO ABSOLUT

I love the creative and innovative ads for Absolut vodka. Even though I don't drink vodka, I still think the advertisements are really neat.

Absolut has a program (the Absolut Museum) that you can order for $30 that has over 200 different Absolut images from the past 20-plus years. There's also a handful of sample pictures that you can view for free online. I skip the museum and download the free pictures; they're enough for me.

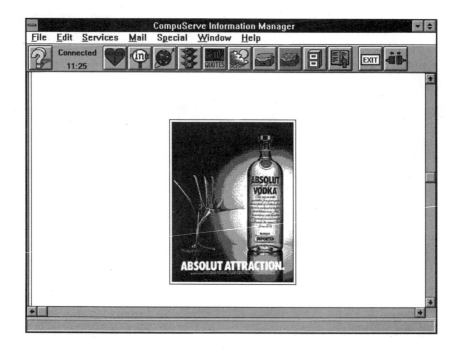

Absolut ads seem to be the craze nowadays. This is my favorite on CompuServe.

Congressional Tracking: GO BUDGET

This is the ultimate way to figure out how those boneheads in Washington really feel on the issues. The actual vote of each senator and representative on every bill dealing with governmental spending is publicly available to anyone who stops by. Find out if your Congressperson just talks the talk, or actually walks the walk. Power to the people!

World Community Forums: GO WCOMMUNITY

Using state-of-the-art software, CompuServe created the World Community Forum. The World Community Forum is available in four different languages. Each language has its own forum, but they all have the exact same messages. CompuServe translates each message into English, French, Spanish, and German so you can talk to people all across the world in your native language.

The translations aren't the best, but it's still very neat, and worth exploration.

I can forget the French I learned in high school; CompuServe translates for me.

WinCIM Spell Checker: GO ASPELL

Whenever I send e-mail or messages on CompuServe, I hate to re-read the entire message just to make sure I didn't misspell a word. As a result, most of my correspondence has all sorts of little typos in it (my friends yell at me all the time). I was in a quandary until I found the WinCIM Spell Checker.

For $19.57, you can buy an add-on WinCIM Spell Checker that will save you lots of pain. $20 may be out of your price range, but if you're like me, a lousy speller, you'll find this product a godsend.

David Letterman's Top 10 Lists: GO EFORUM

There's something about this late night talk-show host that cracks me up. Maybe it's the gap in his front teeth, or it could be the stupid pet tricks—it doesn't matter. Arguably, the best part of Dave's show is the Top 10 List he reads every night.

The following day, you can read the most recent Top 10 List in the Entertainment Drive Forum's library sections. They're always good for a laugh.

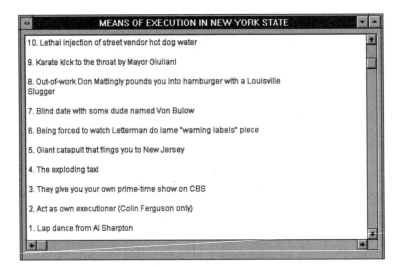

Here's one of my favorites.

CompuServe Magazine

Okay, so the CompuServe Magazine isn't actually online. Instead, it's mailed monthly to your home. I read every issue almost cover to cover. The stories are well written, and there are always interesting features about neat things to do on CompuServe.

Since every member gets a free subscription, the price is certainly right.

New Car Showroom: GO NEWCAR

If you're car hunting, make sure you stop by the New Car Showroom. You can find the complete specs on hundreds of cars, along with a nice picture of most of them. You can find out everything from gas mileage to safety features of the newest cars available.

Here's my next new car (it looks like I'll be buying used cars for a long while).

Microsoft Connection: GO MICROSOFT

Since we're all at the beck and call of Bill Gates, we might as well talk to other people who suffer from the same ailment, Windows. Ha ha, just kidding Mr. Gates, please don't throw my resume away when I apply.

Microsoft has an impressive presence online. There are lots of Windows and Windows-related forums chock-full of useful programs and helpful people.

WorldsAway: GO AWAY

WorldsAway is CB chatting to the next level. Instead of just chatting with other people online, WorldsAway lets you *see* who you are talking to, making for a fantastic visual experience. Although it won't be ready for several months, WorldsAway is causing quite a stir and looks to be one of the greatest things to hit CompuServe.

Stop by here often to keep track of the WorldsAway project.

Internet Resources Forum: GO INETRESOURCE

Through CompuServe, you have virtually unlimited Internet access. I stop by this forum to talk with other Internet travelers and to learn more about visiting different sites and trying out new technologies (like the World Wide Web). The file libraries are a great source of Internet-related information.

The Least You Need to Know

➤ Find useful utility programs to make your life easier. **GO ASPELL** for a WinCIM Spell Checker and **GO MICROSOFT** to find a neat Windows program.

➤ CompuServe is constantly adding new types of technology online. **GO WCOMMUNITY** to chat with users in four languages, and WorldsAway (**GO AWAY**) to interact with other CompuServites visually.

➤ Don't forget that CompuServe has reference information on everything. You can follow your Congressperson's vote (**GO BUDGET**), and see the car he probably just bought with that big government salary (**GO NEWCAR**), just to name a few.

Speak Like a Geek: The Complete Archive

abstract   The summary of each file in a forum.

America Online   A competing online information service that's nearly as big as CompuServe (but not nearly as cool).

article   Another name for a message within a forum.

band   The group of CB channels you choose to converse on in the CB Simulator.

baud   Roughly equal to the number of data bits transferred per second between your computer and CompuServe. Each letter on the keyboard represents approximately eight bits (one byte). Graphics and images can easily represent several hundred thousand bits for each picture.

bits   The ones and zeros that computers use to talk to each other. Each one or zero is a bit.

bytes   A collection of eight bits (you have one lion, or if many, a pride).

CB Simulator   The online chatting arena in CompuServe that lets you talk to other users in real time.

channel   The conversation in which you are participating on the CB Simulator.

chatting   Talking with another CompuServe user in real time through a forum or through the CB Simulator.

CIM   See *CompuServe Information Manager.*

club   A group on CompuServe that you can join to receive discounted services. For example, if you chat on the CompuServe CB a lot, you can join CupCake's CB club and get a big discount on your hourly CB fee. Joining a club costs money as well.

CompuServeCD   The bimonthly multimedia magazine that you can subscribe to. Each issue comes with a magazine, an updated CompuServe Directory, the complete listing for File Finder, and the latest CompuServe software.

CompuServe Information Manager (CIM)   The graphical interface for using CompuServe. CIM is made for several different systems, including OS/2, Macintosh, DOS, and Windows.

CompuServe Navigator (CSNav)   A program that automatically uploads and downloads messages for mail and forums, reducing your connect time, and subsequently, your total bill.

conferencing   Like chatting, only with lots of people at one time.

DOSCIM   See *CompuServe Information Manager.*

download   Using your modem to copy a file from CompuServe to be stored on your own computer.

E-Mail   Personal messages that you type and send to other users.

File Finder   A big index of thousands of files you can search through and find online.

flame   An abusive or impolite correspondence with another user online.

forum   An online discussion base. CompuServe users have access to hundreds of different forums, each one centered on a specific topic.

freeware   Software that is given out for free by the author. You are allowed to make as many copies of freeware as you like.

FTP   File Transfer Protocol—the method of downloading files from the Internet onto your personal computer.

GIF (Graphical Image Format)   A picture or image of something saved onto your computer. CompuServe developed GIFs.

GO word   The unique word each service has to directly access it from anywhere in CompuServe.

handle   The nickname by which people will address you. Handles often represent your personality. Use handles in the CB Simulator.

information service A big computer network that you can connect to with a computer and a modem. The information service stores lots and lots of data, all available for a price.

Internet A bunch of powerful and expensive computers that are hooked up to each other across the world. Representing nearly 20 million users, the Internet is the largest network in the world.

library Where files are stored within Forums.

log file Where you store information from your CompuServe session.

lurker Someone who reads messages but never publicly shares their own opinion.

MacCIM See *CompuServe Information Manager*.

modem A piece of computer equipment that lets your computer connect with other computers using regular phone lines.

multimedia A buzzword meaning your computer has a CD-ROM and sound card installed. With those two pieces of equipment, you can watch videos, see animation, and listen to music directly from your PC.

netiquette A general list of common sense rules for handling yourself in the electronic world.

network A bunch of computers linked together, letting lots of people easily share information with each other.

offline When your computer is not connected to a distant computer. When you're not logged on to CompuServe (or another online service), you're offline.

online When your computer is connected with a distant computer through your modem.

online service A company that provides access to current news, entertainment, shopping, and a whole lot more. You can join an online service and access it with your modem.

OS/2 CIM See *CompuServe Information Manager*.

password Your ultra-secret word that lets CompuServe know that you are really who you pretend to be.

Prodigy Another competing information service, run by IBM and Sears.

ribbon The set of icons at the top of your CIM screen.

scan Storing a drawing or photo in electronic form into a computer with a special piece of equipment that is related to a photocopier.

script   A sequence of events that explains exactly what the CompuServe Navigator should do.

shareware   Software available to be spread and shared by as many people as possible. If you use it regularly, though, you must pay a registration fee. See also *freeware*.

SIG   See *forum*.

signature   Several lines of text that are automatically appended to the end of each message you send.

SysOp   The big boss of the forum. The SysOp also enforces standard CompuServe rules regarding profanity, harassment, copyrighted files, and tries to keep the forum majority happy.

telnet   A program that lets you log onto any computer on the Internet.

threads   A group of multiple messages that are all about the same topic within a forum.

toolbox   The floating set of icons that lets you perform common and useful commands with your mouse. There are separate toolboxes for CompuServe forums and CB chatting.

upload   Making a copy of a file from your computer and sending it to CompuServe for everyone else to be able to download.

USENET   The group of newsgroups that spreads millions of messages about every topic imaginable all over the world.

User ID   Your unique number that lets you log onto CompuServe (along with your password), and also acts as your e-mail address.

virtual reality   A computer-created world in which you can interact. Without actually moving yourself, virtual reality lets you pretend you're in a different world created by a computer.

virus   A program whose goal in life is to damage your computer. Stay away from these.

WinCIM   See *CompuServe Information Manager*.

World Wide Web   The large multimedia network that spans the entire Internet.

Index

Symbols

$ (dollar sign) Premium Service indicator, 56
* (asterisk) wild card, 229
+ (plus sign)
  Extended Service indicator, 55
  Newspapers Archives searches, 229
- (dash) Newspapers Archives searches, 229
:-) smileys, 79
| (vertical bar) Newspapers Archives searches, 229
1-800 numbers, *see* phone numbers

A

AAdvantage Club, 286
ABC Worldwide Hotel Guide, 289
Absolut Museum, 311-312
abstracts (forum files), 150, 158, 317
Access Newsgroups dialog box, 218
accounts
  billing records, 62-64
  reviewing balance, 60-62
Action Gamers Forum, 267
Add to Address Book dialog box, 97
Address Book command (Mail menu), 98
Address Book dialog box, 98

addresses
  e-mail, 96-99, 102
    address book, 96-98
    prefixes, 102-103
    saving, 96-98
    wrong addresses, 102
  forum messages, 131, 138
  FTP sites, 179-180
Advantis (IBM) X.400, sending e-mail, 87
Adventure game, 263
Air Traffic Controller game, 266
airline tickets
  EAASY SABRE, 286-289
  Travel's Advantage, 292
Alert dialog box, 75
aliases (forums), 124
All-Music Guide, 254-256
almanacs, 281
alt (alternative) newsgroups, 211
alternative pricing plan, 54, 58-59
  current rates, 56
  switching to standard plan, 59-60
America Online, 10, 317
American Airlines' EAASY SABRE, 286-288
American Heritage Dictionary, 280
Amiga CIM, 18
Amiga File Finder, 162
analog information, 9

AP (Associated Press), 186-189
  AP France en Ligne, 200
  articles
    filing, 188
    headlines, 188
    printing, 189
    reading, 186-188
  Australian Associated Press, 200
  copyrights, 186
  syndicated columns, 196-198
AP France en Ligne news service, 200
Archived Movies Forum, 252
archives
  e-mail, 92-95
  Newspapers Archives, 227-228
    downloading articles, 230
    marking articles, 230
    searching, 229-230
  stock market, 240
art
  Artist Forum, 259
  Computer Art Forum, 259
  Fine Arts Forum, 259
  Metropolitan Museum of Art, 259-260
articles (news articles)
  Associated Press
    filing, 188
    headlines, 188

E

F

X-Y-Z

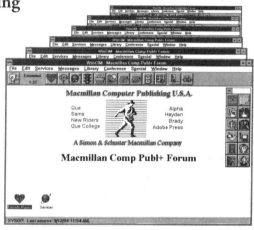

PLUG YOURSELF INTO...

THE MACMILLAN INFORMATION SUPERLIBRARY™

**Free information and vast computer resources from
the world's leading computer book publisher—online!**

FIND THE BOOKS THAT ARE RIGHT FOR YOU!

A complete online catalog, plus sample chapters and tables of contents give you an in-depth look at *all* of our books, including hard-to-find titles. It's the best way to find the books you need!

● STAY INFORMED with the latest computer industry news through our online newsletter, press releases, and customized Information SuperLibrary Reports.

● GET FAST ANSWERS to your questions about MCP books and software.

● VISIT our online bookstore for the latest information and editions!

● COMMUNICATE with our expert authors through e-mail and conferences.

● DOWNLOAD SOFTWARE from the immense MCP library:
  - Source code and files from MCP books
  - The best shareware, freeware, and demos

● DISCOVER HOT SPOTS on other parts of the Internet.

● WIN BOOKS in ongoing contests and giveaways!

TO PLUG INTO MCP: →

GOPHER: gopher.mcp.com

FTP: ftp.mcp.com

WORLD WIDE WEB: http://www.mcp.com

Also Available!

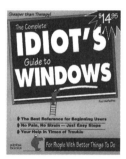